enVisionmath 2.0

SCOTT FORESMAN · ADDISON WESLEY

Volume 2 Topics 9–14

Authors

Randall I. Charles
Professor Emeritus
Department of Mathematics
San Jose State University
San Jose, California

Jennifer Bay-Williams
Professor of Mathematics
Education
College of Education and Human
Development
University of Louisville
Louisville, Kentucky

Robert Q. Berry, III
Associate Professor of
Mathematics Education
Department of Curriculum,
Instruction and Special Education
University of Virginia
Charlottesville, Virginia

Janet H. Caldwell
Professor of Mathematics
Rowan University
Glassboro, New Jersey

Zachary Champagne
Assistant in Research
Florida Center for Research in
Science, Technology, Engineering,
and Mathematics (FCR-STEM)
Jacksonville, Florida

Juanita Copley
Professor Emerita, College of
Education
University of Houston
Houston, Texas

Warren Crown
Professor Emeritus of Mathematics
Education
Graduate School of Education
Rutgers University
New Brunswick, New Jersey

Francis (Skip) Fennell
L. Stanley Bowlsbey Professor
of Education and Graduate and
Professional Studies
McDaniel College
Westminster, Maryland

Karen Karp
Professor of Mathematics
Education
Department of Early Childhood
and Human Development
University of Louisville
Louisville, Kentucky

Stuart J. Murphy
Visual Learning Specialist
Boston, Massachusetts

Jane F. Schielack
Professor of Mathematics
Associate Dean for Assessment
and Pre K–12 Education,
College of Science
Texas A&M University
College Station, Texas

Jennifer M. Suh
Associate Professor for
Mathematics Education
George Mason University
Fairfax, Virginia

Jonathan A. Wray
Mathematics Instructional
Facilitator
Howard County Public Schools
Ellicott City, Maryland

PEARSON

T 25695

Glenview, Illinois   Boston, Massachusetts   Chandler, Arizona   Hoboken, New Jersey

Mathematicians

Roger Howe
Professor of Mathematics
Yale University
New Haven, Connecticut

Gary Lippman
Professor of Mathematics and
Computer Science
California State University,
East Bay
Hayward, California

ELL Consultants

Janice R. Corona
Independent Education
Consultant
Dallas, Texas

Jim Cummins
Professor
The University of Toronto
Toronto, Canada

Common Core State Standards Reviewers

Debbie Crisco
Math Coach
Beebe Public Schools
Beebe, Arkansas

Kathleen A. Cuff
Teacher
Kings Park Central School District
Kings Park, New York

Erika Doyle
Math and Science Coordinator
Richland School District
Richland, Washington

Susan Jarvis
Math and Science Curriculum
Coordinator
Ocean Springs Schools
Ocean Springs, Mississippi

Velvet M. Simington
K–12 Mathematics Director
Winston-Salem/Forsyth
County Schools
Winston-Salem, North Carolina

ISBN-13: 978-0-328-82777-0
ISBN-10: 0-328-82777-0

PEARSON

3 4 5 6 7 8 9 10 11 V064 19 18 17 16 15

Digital

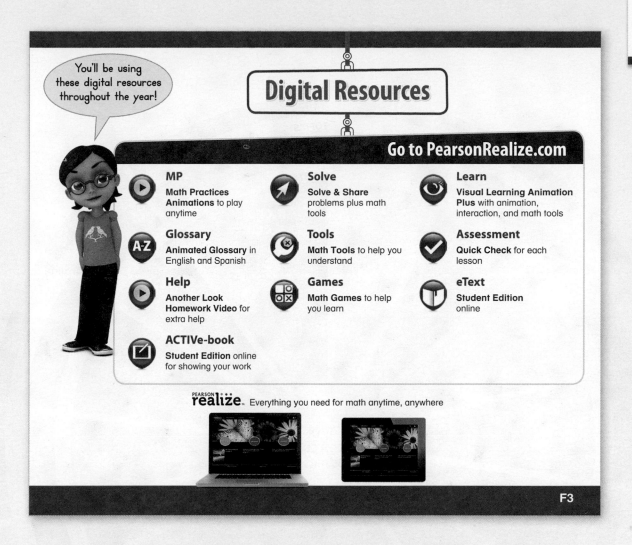

You'll be using these digital resources throughout the year!

Digital Resources

Go to PearsonRealize.com

MP
Math Practices **Animations** to play anytime

Glossary
Animated Glossary in English and Spanish

Help
Another Look Homework Video for extra help

ACTIVe-book
Student Edition online for showing your work

Solve
Solve & Share problems plus math tools

Tools
Math Tools to help you understand

Games
Math Games to help you learn

Learn
Visual Learning Animation Plus with animation, interaction, and math tools

Assessment
Quick Check for each lesson

eText
Student Edition online

realize Everything you need for math anytime, anywhere

F3

Additional Digital Resources

 eText

Teacher's Edition eText includes all pages from the Teacher's Edition plus access to printable resources and the animated glossary.

 PD

Professional Development Videos include a **Topic Overview Video** that is presented by the authors and provides important information about the topic. A **Listen and Look For Lesson Video** at the start of each lesson provides helpful information for teaching the lesson.

 Story

 Interactive Math Story at the start of each topic is available as an online story book and an animated story.

 Think

Today's Challenge for each topic is a set of 5 problems on separate screens that use the same data. They can be projected in class or assigned electronically to individuals. A Teacher's Guide with a page for each problem is available in print and online.

 Assessment

Online assessments are auto scored and include: Placement Test, Lesson Quick Check, Topic Assessments, Cumulative/Benchmark Assessments, End-of-Year Assessment, and Fluency Assessments.

All print resources are also available online as eText pages or PDF files at PearsonRealize.com.

GRADE K CONTENT OVERVIEW

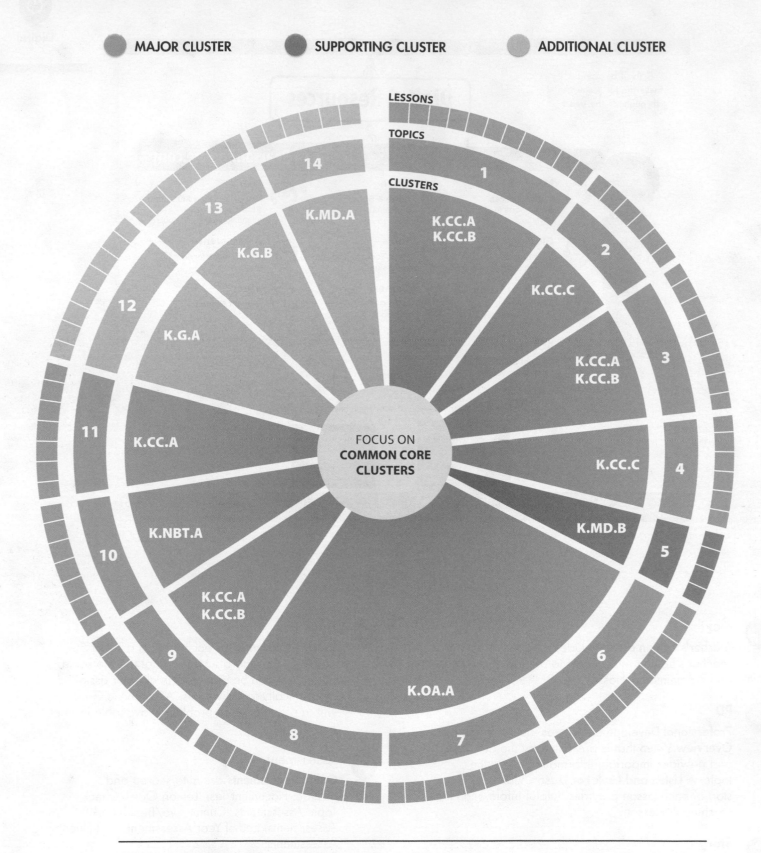

● MAJOR CLUSTER   ● SUPPORTING CLUSTER   ● ADDITIONAL CLUSTER

LESSONS

TOPICS

CLUSTERS

FOCUS ON
**COMMON CORE
CLUSTERS**

K.CC.A
K.CC.B

K.CC.C

K.CC.A
K.CC.B

K.CC.C

K.MD.B

K.OA.A

K.NBT.A

K.CC.A

K.G.A

K.G.B

K.MD.A

1
2
3
4
5
6
7
8
9
10
11
12
13
14

COMMON CORE DOMAINS

K.CC   COUNTING AND CARDINALITY

K.OA   OPERATIONS AND ALGEBRAIC THINKING

K.NBT   NUMBER AND OPERATIONS IN BASE TEN

K.MD   MEASUREMENT AND DATA

K.G   GEOMETRY

 FOCUS
COHERENCE
RIGOR

▷ Content is developed with focus, coherence, and rigor. The attention to rigor reflects the balances of conceptual understanding, procedural skill and fluency, and applications in the Common Core Standards. See each Cluster Overview and lesson.

FOCUS ON	TOPICS
MAJOR CLUSTER **K.CC.A** Know number names and the count sequence. MAJOR CLUSTER **K.CC.B** Count to tell the number of objects.	**1** Numbers 0 to 5
MAJOR CLUSTER **K.CC.C** Compare numbers.	**2** Compare Numbers 0 to 5
MAJOR CLUSTER **K.CC.A** Know number names and the count sequence. MAJOR CLUSTER **K.CC.B** Count to tell the number of objects.	**3** Numbers 6 to 10
MAJOR CLUSTER **K.CC.C** Compare numbers.	**4** Compare Numbers 0 to 10
SUPPORTING CLUSTER **K.MD.B** Classify objects and count the number of objects in each category.	**5** Classify and Count Data
MAJOR CLUSTER **K.OA.A** Understand addition as putting together and adding to, and understand subtraction as taking apart and taking from.	**6** Understand Addition **7** Understand Subtraction **8** More Addition and Subtraction
MAJOR CLUSTER **K.CC.A** Know number names and the count sequence. MAJOR CLUSTER **K.CC.B** Count to tell the number of objects.	**9** Count Numbers to 20
MAJOR CLUSTER **K.NBT.A** Work with numbers 11–19 to gain foundations for place value.	**10** Compose and Decompose Numbers 11 to 19
MAJOR CLUSTER **K.CC.A** Know number names and the count sequence.	**11** Count Numbers to 100
ADDITIONAL CLUSTER **K.G.A** Identify and describe shapes (squares, circles, triangles, rectangles, hexagons, cubes, cones, cylinders, and spheres).	**12** Identify and Describe Shapes
ADDITIONAL CLUSTER **K.G.B** Analyze, compare, create, and compose shapes.	**13** Analyze, Compare, and Create Shapes
ADDITIONAL CLUSTER **K.MD.A** Describe and compare measurable attributes.	**14** Describe and Compare Measurable Attributes

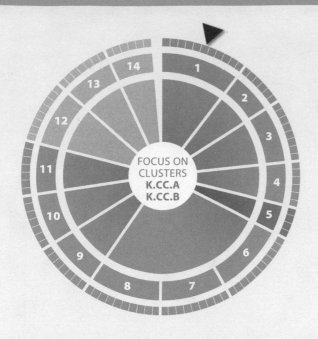

FOCUS ON
CLUSTERS
K.CC.A
K.CC.B

IN TOPIC 1, FOCUS ON

MAJOR CLUSTER K.CC.A
Know number names and the count sequence.

MAJOR CLUSTER K.CC.B
Count to tell the number of objects.

TOPIC 1 CLUSTERS OVERVIEW

You can use numbers to show the number of objects.

4

TOPIC 1
Numbers 0 to 5

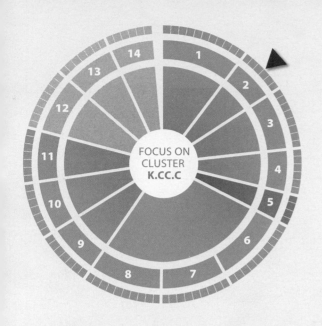

FOCUS ON
CLUSTER
K.CC.C

IN TOPIC 2, FOCUS ON
MAJOR CLUSTER K.CC.C
Compare numbers.

TOPIC 2 CLUSTER OVERVIEW

There are more tennis balls than footballs when you compare.

TOPIC 2
Compare Numbers 0 to 5

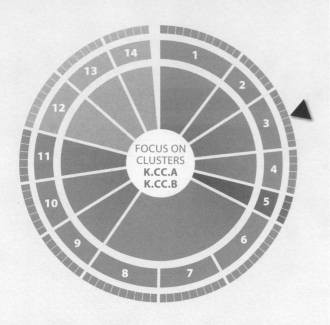

FOCUS ON
CLUSTERS
K.CC.A
K.CC.B

IN TOPIC 3, FOCUS ON

MAJOR CLUSTER K.CC.A
Know number names and the count sequence.

MAJOR CLUSTER K.CC.B
Count to tell the number of objects.

TOPIC 3 CLUSTERS OVERVIEW

You can use counters to show how many.

TOPIC 3
Numbers 6 to 10

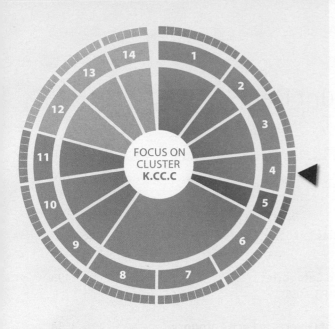

FOCUS ON CLUSTER K.CC.C

IN TOPIC 4, FOCUS ON
MAJOR CLUSTER K.CC.C
Compare numbers.

TOPIC 4 CLUSTER OVERVIEW

There is a greater number of red fish than purple fish.

TOPIC 4
Compare Numbers 0 to 10

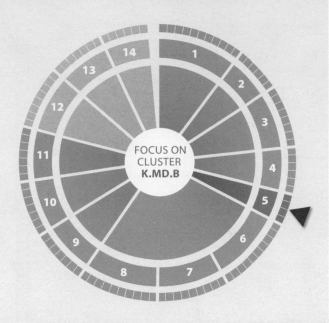

FOCUS ON
CLUSTER
K.MD.B

IN TOPIC 5, FOCUS ON

SUPPORTING CLUSTER K.MD.B
Classify objects and count the number of objects in
each category.

*Supporting Cluster K.MD.B supports Major Clusters
K.CC.B and K.CC.C. The Topic 5 problems that involve
counting objects in categories apply the work with
cardinality in Topics 1 and 3. The Topic 5 problems
that involve sorting apply the work with comparing
numbers in Topics 2 and 4.*

TOPIC 5 CLUSTER OVERVIEW

The animals are classified into
a category of animals with hair and a
category of animals without hair.

Hair   NO Hair

TOPIC 5
Classify and Count Data

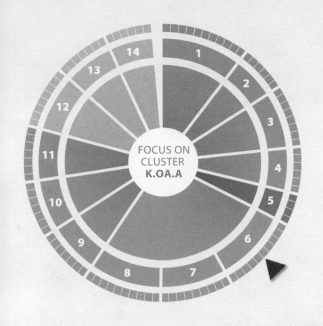

FOCUS ON CLUSTER K.OA.A

IN TOPICS 6–8, FOCUS ON

MAJOR CLUSTER K.OA.A
Understand addition as putting together and adding to, and understand subtraction as taking apart and taking from.

TOPICS 6–8 CLUSTER OVERVIEW

You can use addition to show joining groups.

TOPIC 6
Understand Addition

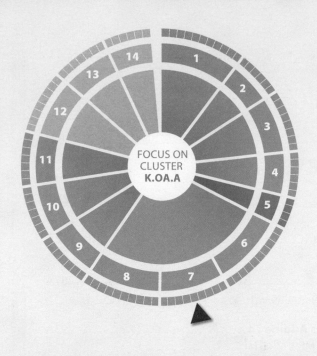

IN TOPICS 6–8, FOCUS ON

MAJOR CLUSTER K.OA.A
Understand addition as putting together and adding to, and understand subtraction as taking apart and taking from.

TOPICS 6–8 CLUSTER OVERVIEW

This shows 5 − 2 = 3.

TOPIC 7
Understand Subtraction

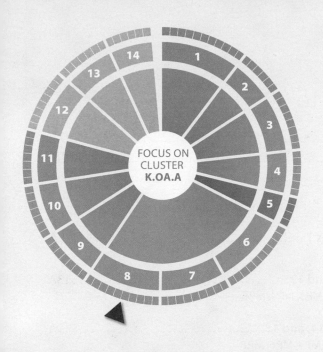

FOCUS ON CLUSTER K.OA.A

IN TOPICS 6–8, FOCUS ON

MAJOR CLUSTER K.OA.A
Understand addition as putting together and adding to, and understand subtraction as taking apart and taking from.

TOPICS 6–8 CLUSTER OVERVIEW

You can write equations to show parts of numbers.

$$8 = 2 + 6$$

TOPIC 8
More Addition and Subtraction

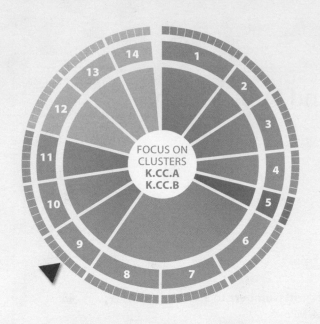

IN TOPIC 9, FOCUS ON

MAJOR CLUSTER K.CC.A
Know number names and the count sequence.

MAJOR CLUSTER K.CC.B
Count to tell the number of objects.

TOPIC 9 CLUSTERS OVERVIEW

TOPIC 9
Count Numbers to 20

You can count objects and write the number to tell how many in all.

eleven

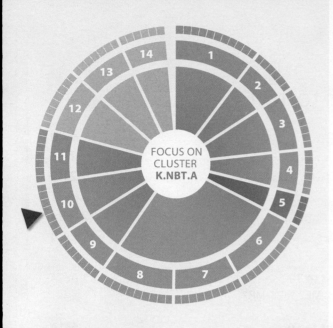

FOCUS ON
CLUSTER
K.NBT.A

IN TOPIC 10, FOCUS ON

MAJOR CLUSTER K.NBT.A
Work with numbers 11–19 to gain foundations for place value.

TOPIC 10 CLUSTER OVERVIEW

The equation tells how many cubes in all.

TOPIC 10 Compose and Decompose Numbers 11 to 19

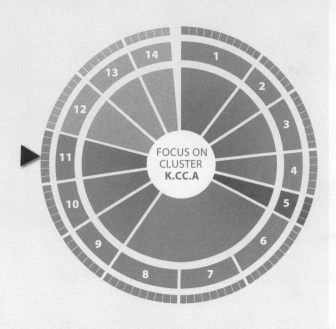

FOCUS ON
CLUSTER
K.CC.A

IN TOPIC 11, FOCUS ON

MAJOR CLUSTER K.CC.A
Know number names and the count sequence.

TOPIC 11 CLUSTER OVERVIEW

You can use part of a hundred chart to count and find patterns.

1	2	3	4	5	6	7	8	9	10
11	12	13	14	15	16	17	18	19	20
21	22	23	24	25	26	27	28	29	30

TOPIC 11
Count Numbers to 100

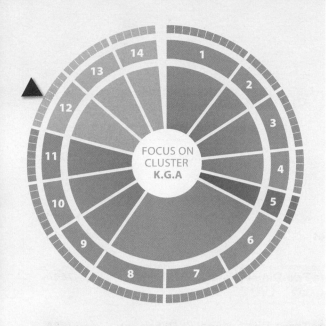

FOCUS ON CLUSTER K.G.A

IN TOPIC 12, FOCUS ON

ADDITIONAL CLUSTER K.G.A
Identify and describe shapes (squares, circles, triangles, rectangles, hexagons, cubes, cones, cylinders, and spheres).

TOPIC 12 CLUSTER OVERVIEW

There are flat and solid objects in our environment. The notebook paper and envelope are flat. The cup and tissue box are solid.

TOPIC 12
Identify and Describe Shapes

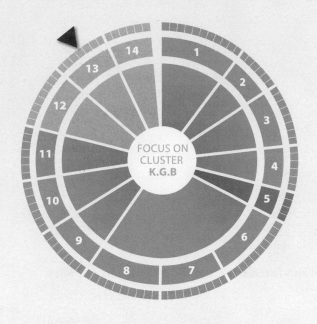

FOCUS ON
CLUSTER
K.G.B

IN TOPIC 13, FOCUS ON

ADDITIONAL CLUSTER K.G.B
Analyze, compare, create, and compose shapes.

TOPIC 13 CLUSTER OVERVIEW

The side of this cube is a square.

TOPIC 13
Analyze, Compare, and Create Shapes

FOCUS ON CLUSTER K.MD.A

IN TOPIC 14, FOCUS ON

ADDITIONAL CLUSTER K.MD.A
Describe and compare measurable attributes.

TOPIC 14 CLUSTER OVERVIEW

You can compare the sizes of different objects.

Shorter

TOPIC 14 Describe and Compare Measurable Attributes

STEP UP to Grade 1

These lessons help prepare you for Grade 1.

GRADE K COMMON CORE STANDARDS

You may wish to have students take home these six pages of Common Core Standards and share them with their families. Students can create a booklet of these pages by putting the three sheets in order and then stapling the left side of the sheets at the top, the middle, and the bottom.

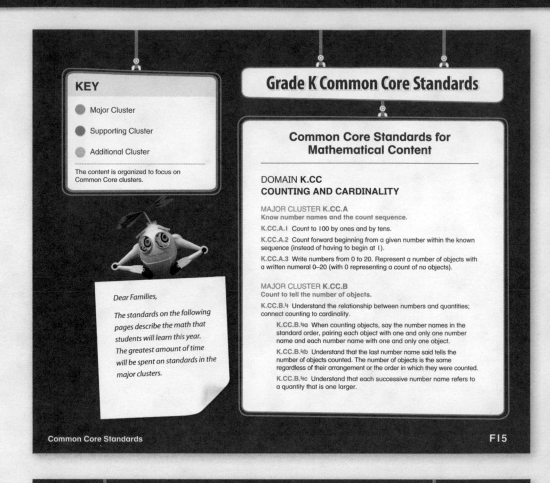

KEY

● Major Cluster

● Supporting Cluster

● Additional Cluster

The content is organized to focus on Common Core clusters.

Dear Families,

The standards on the following pages describe the math that students will learn this year. The greatest amount of time will be spent on standards in the major clusters.

Grade K Common Core Standards

Common Core Standards for Mathematical Content

DOMAIN K.CC
COUNTING AND CARDINALITY

MAJOR CLUSTER **K.CC.A**
Know number names and the count sequence.

K.CC.A.1 Count to 100 by ones and by tens.

K.CC.A.2 Count forward beginning from a given number within the known sequence (instead of having to begin at 1).

K.CC.A.3 Write numbers from 0 to 20. Represent a number of objects with a written numeral 0–20 (with 0 representing a count of no objects).

MAJOR CLUSTER **K.CC.B**
Count to tell the number of objects.

K.CC.B.4 Understand the relationship between numbers and quantities; connect counting to cardinality.

> **K.CC.B.4a** When counting objects, say the number names in the standard order, pairing each object with one and only one number name and each number name with one and only one object.

> **K.CC.B.4b** Understand that the last number name said tells the number of objects counted. The number of objects is the same regardless of their arrangement or the order in which they were counted.

> **K.CC.B.4c** Understand that each successive number name refers to a quantity that is one larger.

Common Core Standards   F15

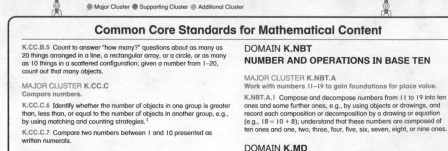

● Major Cluster ● Supporting Cluster ● Additional Cluster

Common Core Standards for Mathematical Content

K.CC.B.5 Count to answer "how many?" questions about as many as 20 things arranged in a line, a rectangular array, or a circle, or as many as 10 things in a scattered configuration; given a number from 1–20, count out that many objects.

MAJOR CLUSTER **K.CC.C**
Compare numbers.

K.CC.C.6 Identify whether the number of objects in one group is greater than, less than, or equal to the number of objects in another group, e.g., by using matching and counting strategies.[1]

K.CC.C.7 Compare two numbers between 1 and 10 presented as written numerals.

DOMAIN K.OA
OPERATIONS AND ALGEBRAIC THINKING

MAJOR CLUSTER **K.OA.A**
Understand addition as putting together and adding to, and understand subtraction as taking apart and taking from.

K.OA.A.1 Represent addition and subtraction with objects, fingers, mental images, drawings[2], sounds (e.g., claps), acting out situations, verbal explanations, expressions, or equations.

K.OA.A.2 Solve addition and subtraction word problems, and add and subtract within 10, e.g., by using objects or drawings to represent the problem.

K.OA.A.3 Decompose numbers less than or equal to 10 into pairs in more than one way, e.g., by using objects or drawings, and record each decomposition by a drawing or equation (e.g., $5 = 2 + 3$ and $5 = 4 + 1$).

K.OA.A.4 For any number from 1 to 9, find the number that makes 10 when added to the given number, e.g., by using objects or drawings, and record the answer with a drawing or equation.

K.OA.A.5 Fluently add and subtract within 5.

DOMAIN K.NBT
NUMBER AND OPERATIONS IN BASE TEN

MAJOR CLUSTER **K.NBT.A**
Work with numbers 11–19 to gain foundations for place value.

K.NBT.A.1 Compose and decompose numbers from 11 to 19 into ten ones and some further ones, e.g., by using objects or drawings, and record each composition or decomposition by a drawing or equation (e.g., $18 = 10 + 8$); understand that these numbers are composed of ten ones and one, two, three, four, five, six, seven, eight, or nine ones.

DOMAIN K.MD
MEASUREMENT AND DATA

ADDITIONAL CLUSTER **K.MD.A**
Describe and compare measurable attributes.

K.MD.A.1 Describe measurable attributes of objects, such as length or weight. Describe several measurable attributes of a single object.

K.MD.A.2 Directly compare two objects with a measurable attribute in common, to see which object has "more of"/"less of" the attribute, and describe the difference. *For example, directly compare the heights of two children and describe one child as taller/shorter.*

SUPPORTING CLUSTER **K.MD.B**
Classify objects and count the number of objects in each category.

K.MD.B.3 Classify objects into given categories; count the numbers of objects in each category and sort the categories by count.[3]

F16   © Pearson Education, Inc. K   Common Core Standards

Common Core Standards for Mathematical Content

DOMAIN **K.G**
GEOMETRY

ADDITIONAL CLUSTER K.G.A
Identify and describe shapes (squares, circles, triangles, rectangles, hexagons, cubes, cones, cylinders, and spheres).

K.G.A.1 Describe objects in the environment using names of shapes, and describe the relative positions of these objects using terms such as *above, below, beside, in front of, behind,* and *next to.*

K.G.A.2 Correctly name shapes regardless of their orientations or overall size.

K.G.A.3 Identify shapes as two-dimensional (lying in a plane, "flat") or three-dimensional ("solid").

ADDITIONAL CLUSTER K.G.B
Analyze, compare, create, and compose shapes.

K.G.B.4 Analyze and compare two- and three-dimensional shapes, in different sizes and orientations, using informal language to describe their similarities, differences, parts (e.g., number of sides and vertices/"corners") and other attributes (e.g., having sides of equal length).

K.G.B.5 Model shapes in the world by building shapes from components (e.g., sticks and clay balls) and drawing shapes.

K.G.B.6 Compose simple shapes to form larger shapes. *For example, "Can you join these two triangles with full sides touching to make a rectangle?"*

¹Include groups with up to ten objects.

²Drawings need not show details, but should show the mathematics in the problem. (This applies wherever drawings are mentioned in the Standards.)

³Limit category counts to be less than or equal to 10.

Common Core Standards for Mathematical Practice

MP.1 MAKE SENSE OF PROBLEMS AND PERSEVERE IN SOLVING THEM.

Mathematically proficient students start by explaining to themselves the meaning of a problem and looking for entry points to its solution. They analyze givens, constraints, relationships, and goals. They make conjectures about the form and meaning of the solution and plan a solution pathway rather than simply jumping into a solution attempt. They consider analogous problems, and try special cases and simpler forms of the original problem in order to gain insight into its solution. They monitor and evaluate their progress and change course if necessary. Older students might, depending on the context of the problem, transform algebraic expressions or change the viewing window on their graphing calculator to get the information they need. Mathematically proficient students can explain correspondences between equations, verbal descriptions, tables, and graphs or draw diagrams of important features and relationships, graph data, and search for regularity or trends. Younger students might rely on using concrete objects or pictures to help conceptualize and solve a problem. Mathematically proficient students check their answers to problems using a different method, and they continually ask themselves, "Does this make sense?" They can understand the approaches of others to solving complex problems and identify correspondences between different approaches.

MP.2 REASON ABSTRACTLY AND QUANTITATIVELY.

Mathematically proficient students make sense of quantities and their relationships in problem situations. They bring two complementary abilities to bear on problems involving quantitative relationships: the ability to *decontextualize*—to abstract a given situation and represent it symbolically and manipulate the representing symbols as if they have a life of their own, without necessarily attending to their referents— and the ability to *contextualize*, to pause as needed during the manipulation process in order to probe into the referents for the symbols involved. Quantitative reasoning entails habits of creating a coherent representation of the problem at hand; considering the units involved; attending to the meaning of quantities, not just how to compute them; and knowing and flexibly using different properties of operations and objects.

MP.3 CONSTRUCT VIABLE ARGUMENTS AND CRITIQUE THE REASONING OF OTHERS.

Mathematically proficient students understand and use stated assumptions, definitions, and previously established results in constructing arguments. They make conjectures and build a logical progression of statements to explore the truth of their conjectures. They are able to analyze situations by breaking them into cases, and can recognize and use counterexamples. They justify their conclusions, communicate them to others, and respond to the arguments of others. They reason inductively about data, making plausible arguments that take into account the context from which the data arose. Mathematically proficient students are also able to compare the effectiveness of two plausible arguments, distinguish correct logic or reasoning from that which is flawed, and—if there is a flaw in an argument—explain what it is. Elementary students can construct arguments using concrete referents such as objects, drawings, diagrams, and actions. Such arguments can make sense and be correct, even though they are not generalized or made formal until later grades. Later, students learn to determine domains to which an argument applies. Students at all grades can listen or read the arguments of others, decide whether they make sense, and ask useful questions to clarify or improve the arguments.

MP.4 MODEL WITH MATHEMATICS.

Mathematically proficient students can apply the mathematics they know to solve problems arising in everyday life, society, and the workplace. In early grades, this might be as simple as writing an addition equation to describe a situation. In middle grades, a student might apply proportional reasoning to plan a school event or analyze a problem in the community. By high school, a student might use geometry to solve a design problem or use a function to describe how one quantity of interest depends on another. Mathematically proficient students who can apply what they know are comfortable making assumptions and approximations to simplify a complicated situation, realizing that these may need revision later. They are able to identify important quantities in a practical situation and map their relationships using such tools as diagrams, two-way tables, graphs, flowcharts and formulas. They can analyze those relationships mathematically to draw conclusions. They routinely interpret their mathematical results in the context of the situation and reflect on whether the results make sense, possibly improving the model if it has not served its purpose.

Common Core Standards for Mathematical Practice

MP.5 USE APPROPRIATE TOOLS STRATEGICALLY.

Mathematically proficient students consider the available tools when solving a mathematical problem. These tools might include pencil and paper, concrete models, a ruler, a protractor, a calculator, a spreadsheet, a computer algebra system, a statistical package, or dynamic geometry software. Proficient students are sufficiently familiar with tools appropriate for their grade or course to make sound decisions about when each of these tools might be helpful, recognizing both the insight to be gained and their limitations. For example, mathematically proficient high school students analyze graphs of functions and solutions generated using a graphing calculator. They detect possible errors by strategically using estimation and other mathematical knowledge. When making mathematical models, they know that technology can enable them to visualize the results of varying assumptions, explore consequences, and compare predictions with data. Mathematically proficient students at various grade levels are able to identify relevant external mathematical resources, such as digital content located on a website, and use them to pose or solve problems. They are able to use technological tools to explore and deepen their understanding of concepts.

MP.6 ATTEND TO PRECISION.

Mathematically proficient students try to communicate precisely to others. They try to use clear definitions in discussion with others and in their own reasoning. They state the meaning of the symbols they choose, including using the equal sign consistently and appropriately. They are careful about specifying units of measure, and labeling axes to clarify the correspondence with quantities in a problem. They calculate accurately and efficiently, express numerical answers with a degree of precision appropriate for the problem context. In the elementary grades, students give carefully formulated explanations to each other. By the time they reach high school they have learned to examine claims and make explicit use of definitions.

MP.7 LOOK FOR AND MAKE USE OF STRUCTURE.

Mathematically proficient students look closely to discern a pattern or structure. Young students, for example, might notice that three and seven more is the same amount as seven and three more, or they may sort a collection of shapes according to how many sides the shapes have. Later, students will see 7×8 equals the well remembered $7 \times 5 + 7 \times 3$, in preparation for learning about the distributive property. In the expression $x^2 + 9x + 14$, older students can see the 14 as 2×7 and the 9 as $2 + 7$. They recognize the significance of an existing line in a geometric figure and can use the strategy of drawing an auxiliary line for solving problems. They also can step back for an overview and shift perspective. They can see complicated things, such as some algebraic expressions, as single objects or as being composed of several objects. For example, they can see $5 - 3(x - y)^2$ as 5 minus a positive number times a square and use that to realize that its value cannot be more than 5 for any real numbers x and y.

MP.8 LOOK FOR AND EXPRESS REGULARITY IN REPEATED REASONING.

Mathematically proficient students notice if calculations are repeated, and look both for general methods and for shortcuts. Upper elementary students might notice when dividing 25 by 11 that they are repeating the same calculations over and over again, and conclude they have a repeating decimal. By paying attention to the calculation of slope as they repeatedly check whether points are on the line through $(1, 2)$ with slope 3, middle school students might abstract the equation $(y - 2)/(x - 1) = 3$. Noticing the regularity in the way terms cancel when expanding $(x - 1)(x + 1)$, $(x - 1)(x^2 + x + 1)$, and $(x - 1)(x^3 + x^2 + x + 1)$ might lead them to the general formula for the sum of a geometric series. As they work to solve a problem, mathematically proficient students maintain oversight of the process, while attending to the details. They continually evaluate the reasonableness of their intermediate results.

INTRODUCTION

INTRODUCING THE HANDBOOK

This handbook can be used at the beginning of the year and at any teachable moment. Explain to students that the handbook will help them become good math thinkers and good math problem solvers. Note that the student pages shown in this Math Practices and Problem Solving Handbook are from Volume 1 of the Student's Edition.

F21–F30A   Math Practices

F31   Problem Solving Guide

F32   Problem Solving Recording Sheet

INTRODUCING THE MATH PRACTICES

Use pages F21–F30A to introduce students to the Mathematical Practices. Math Practices are the habits of mind, processes, and dispositions that enable a learner to understand mathematics and to use or do mathematics with understanding. Encourage students to refer back to these pages any time during the year, either in the Student's Edition or the eText.

The Thinking Habits, shown in the clouds on pages F23–F30, help students to engage the various math practices. These Thinking Habits are also shown in the Math Practices and Problem Solving lessons within the topics.

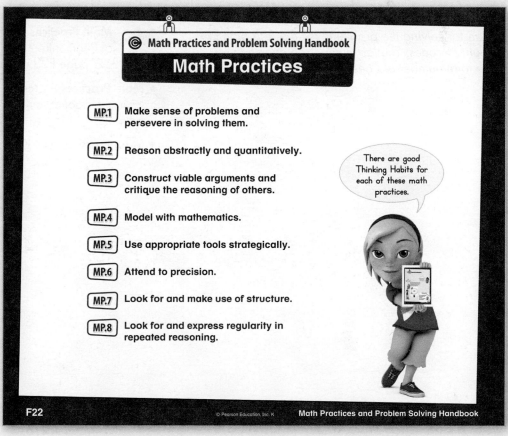

1. Develop MP.1

What MP.1 Means

Discuss what Marta is saying on top of page F23. The key elements of MP.1 are understanding the meaning of a problem, making a plan to solve it, and to not give up when you get stuck.

Sample Use of MP.1

Have students review the problem statement and how Jackson made sense of the problem. Discuss answers to these questions.

• *How did Jackson plan to solve the problem?* [He made a plan to count the bees.]

• *How does Jackson know what the total number of bees will be?* [He said the last number he counted would be the total number of bees.]

• *What else could Jackson do to check that his answer is right?* [Sample answer: He could use counters to cover the bees and then count the counters.]

Thinking Habits for MP.1

• *Which of the Thinking Habits questions were helpful to Jackson?* [Sample answer: *What's my plan for solving the problem? He made a plan to count the bees. The last number he counted was the total number of bees.*]

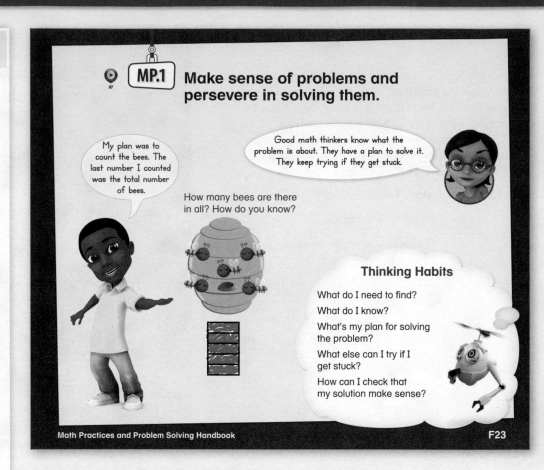

MP.1 **Make sense of problems and persevere in solving them.**

My plan was to count the bees. The last number I counted was the total number of bees.

Good math thinkers know what the problem is about. They have a plan to solve it. They keep trying if they get stuck.

How many bees are there in all? How do you know?

Thinking Habits

What do I need to find?

What do I know?

What's my plan for solving the problem?

What else can I try if I get stuck?

How can I check that my solution make sense?

Math Practices and Problem Solving Handbook · F23

Other Resources for Developing MP.1 include the following:

• **Math Practices Animations** An animation for each math practice is available at PearsonRealize.com. You might want to play the MP.1 animation as you use page F23 and at other times throughout the year as needed.

• **Math Practices Posters** A poster for each math practice is available to display in your classroom. You might want to display the MP.1 poster after playing the MP.1 animation.

• **Math Practices and Problem Solving Lessons** Lesson 13-4 focuses on MP.1.

2. Connect MP.1

Connect MP.1 to Content

To see the many places MP.1 is connected to content standards within lessons, look for "MP.1" in red type.

Also see "Connecting Math Practices to Content Standards" in the Teacher's Edition, pages 1F, 85F, 135F, 199F, 245F, 281F, 507F, 563F, 621F, 675F, 745F, and 799F.

Below is a problem from Topic 13 where students apply MP.1 by making sense of attributes of shapes to identify the correct shape. Students may choose a plan to eliminate shapes after they hear each clue, for example.

I am a solid figure. I can stack and slide.
I have 6 flat surfaces. What shape am I?

Connect MP.1 to Other Math Practices

Deep understanding of mathematics, as well as success with problem solving, calls for engaging a combination of math practices. MP.1 is an overarching practice that strongly connects to all other mathematical practices. The following examples illustrate connections between MP.1 and other math practices.

- **MP.2 Reasoning** When students make sense of problems and persevere in solving them, they often reason about how quantities are related and use math symbols to represent the problem situation.

- **MP.6 Be Precise** As students make sense of problems, they need to be precise in their work. Do they understand definitions of math words and symbols? Are they using definitions correctly in their answers? MP.1 and MP.6 often work together.

3. Assess MP.1

MP.1 Behaviors

Listen and look for the following behaviors to monitor students' ongoing development of proficiency with MP.1.

✓ Gives a good explanation of the problem.

✓ Thinks about a plan before jumping into the solution.

✓ Thinks of similar problems, tries special cases, or uses a simpler form of the problem.

✓ Organizes data or uses representations to help make sense of the problem, if needed.

✓ Identifies likely strategies for solving the problem.

✓ Pauses when solving problems to make sure that the work being done makes sense.

✓ Makes sure the answer makes sense before stopping work.

✓ Does not give up when stuck.

✓ Looks for ways to get past being stuck.

✓ Tries alternative ways to solve the problem when stuck.

Use the list of MP.1 behaviors above and the following rubric to evaluate a student's overall proficiency with MP.1.

Math Practices Proficiency Rubric	
4	**Exemplary** The student exhibits all of the behaviors.
3	**Proficient** The student exhibits most of the behaviors.
2	**Emerging** The student exhibits about half of the behaviors.
1	**Needs Improvement** The student exhibits less than half of the behaviors.

1. Develop MP.2

What MP.2 Means

Discuss what Jada is saying on top of page F24. The key element of MP.2 is reasoning about what the numbers and words in problems mean and how numbers in a problem relate to each other.

Sample Use of MP.2

Have students review the problem statement and how Daniel thinks about the quantities or numbers of objects in the problem. Discuss answers to these questions.

- *What do the numbers in the problem stand for?* [The number 4 stands for the number of frogs and the number of dragonflies.]

- *What is the same and different about the number of frogs and dragonflies in the problem?* [There are 4 frogs and 4 dragonflies in the problem, so the number is the same. How Daniel shows the number 4 with dragonflies is different than how the number 4 is shown with frogs.]

- *Can you show 4 objects in different ways and still use the number 4 to describe the objects?* [Yes, you can show numbers in different ways and not change the number.]

Thinking Habits for MP.2

- *Which of the Thinking Habits questions were helpful to Daniel? Explain.* [Sample answer: The first three questions were useful to thinking about the numbers and pictures in the problem and how they relate.]

Other Resources for Developing MP.2 include the following:

- **Math Practices Animations** An animation for each math practice is available at PearsonRealize.com. You might want to play the MP.2 animation as you use page F24 and at other times throughout the year as needed.

- **Math Practices Posters** A poster for each math practice is available to display in your classroom. You might want to display the MP.2 poster after playing the MP.2 animation.

- **Math Practices and Problem Solving Lessons** Lessons 8-3 and 9-7 focus on MP.2.

2. Connect MP.2

Connect MP.2 to Content

To see the many places MP.2 is connected to content standards within lessons, look for "MP.2" in red type.

Also see "Connecting Math Practices to Content Standards" in the Teacher's Edition, pages 1F, 85F, 135F, 199F, 245F, 281F, 507F, 563F, 621F, 675F, 745F, and 799F.

Below is a problem from Topic 8 where students will apply MP.2 in two ways. The have to reason about quantities to solve the problem. They also have to connect this equation to a real-world context.

Carlos's teacher wrote this equation on the chalkboard: $4 + \boxed{} = 5$. Can you tell a story for that equation?

Connect MP.2 to Other Math Practices

Deep understanding of mathematics, as well as success with problem solving, calls for engaging a combination of math practices. The following examples illustrate connections between MP.2 and other math practices.

- **MP.3 Construct Arguments** As students construct arguments, they often have to explain how quantities in problems are related as well as explain how their drawing, equation, or other solution method represents the problem.

- **MP.4 Model with Math** When students reason about quantities, they apply the math they know to represent the situation mathematically. Students may use objects, drawings, equations, or other methods to represent how quantities relate in order to solve a problem.

3. Assess MP.2

MP.2 Behaviors

Listen and look for the following behaviors to monitor students' ongoing development of proficiency with MP.2.

✓ Identifies and understands the quantities in the problem.

✓ Shows and explains how quantities are related (e.g., bar diagram.)

✓ Translates real-world contexts correctly to numbers, expressions, equations, or concrete or pictorial representations.

✓ Connects numbers, expressions, equations, or concrete or pictorial representations back to real-world contexts.

Use the list of MP.2 behaviors above and the following rubric to evaluate a student's overall proficiency with MP.2.

Math Practices Proficiency Rubric	
4	**Exemplary** The student exhibits all of the behaviors.
3	**Proficient** The student exhibits most of the behaviors.
2	**Emerging** The student exhibits about half of the behaviors.
1	**Needs Improvement** The student exhibits less than half of the behaviors.

MP.3 CONSTRUCT VIABLE ARGUMENTS AND CRITIQUE THE REASONING OF OTHERS

1. Develop MP.3

What MP.3 Means

Discuss what Daniel is saying on top of page F25. The key elements of MP.3 are to critically analyze the mathematics of others and to develop clear and accurate mathematical arguments to explain and justify solutions.

Sample Use of MP.3

Have students review the problem statement and Marta's explanation. Discuss answers to these questions.

- *How does Marta use a picture and words to explain her answer?* [She counts the stars and counters and then explains that both boxes have 3 things.]

- *Is Marta's explanation clear and complete? Explain.* [Sample answer: Yes, she uses words and numbers to explain her reasoning and provides an example.]

Thinking Habits for MP.3

- *Which of the Thinking Habits questions were helpful to Marta? Explain.* [Sample answer: The first three questions about using math, numbers, and having a clear explanation were helpful in helping explain how the second box was like the first box.]

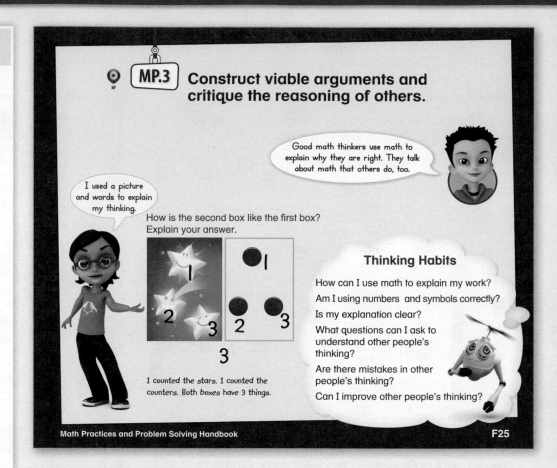

Other Resources for Developing MP.3 include the following:

- **Math Practices Animations** An animation for each math practice is available at PearsonRealize.com. You might want to play the MP.3 animation as you use page F25 and at other times throughout the year as needed.

- **Math Practices Posters** A poster for each math practice is available to display in your classroom. You might want to display the MP.3 poster after playing the MP.3 animation.

- **Math Practices and Problem Solving Lessons** Lessons 1-11 and 5-4 focus on MP.3.

2. Connect MP.3

Connect MP.3 to Content

To see the many places MP.3 is connected to content standards within lessons, look for "MP.3" in red type.

Also see "Connecting Math Practices to Content Standards" in the Teacher's Edition, pages 1F, 85F, 135F, 199F, 245F, 281F, 507F, 563F, 621F, 675F, 745F, and 799F.

Below is a problem from Topic 5 where students apply MP.3 by critiquing the reasoning of Carlos. They support their answer (or argument) by using numbers, pictures, or stated words.

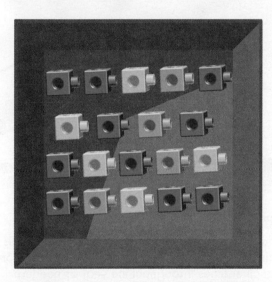

Carlos says that the number of blue cubes is equal to the number of cubes that are NOT blue. Does his answer make sense? Use numbers, pictures, or words to explain your answer.

Connect MP.3 to Other Math Practices

Deep understanding of mathematics, as well as success with problem solving, calls for engaging a combination of math practices. The following examples illustrate connections between MP.3 and other math practices.

- **MP.2 Reasoning** Students make sense of how quantities are related in order to construct viable arguments or analyze a mathematical statement for accuracy. They use logical reasoning and identify reasoning that is flawed.

- **MP.6 Be Precise** Students use clear and precise mathematical language when constructing arguments to justify their reasoning or the reasoning of others. They use numbers and symbols correctly and calculate accurately.

3. Assess MP.3

MP.3 Behaviors

Listen and look for the following behaviors to monitor students' ongoing development of proficiency with MP.3.

✓ Provides complete and clear explanations of one's thinking and work.

✓ Decides if other students' explanations make sense; clarifies or improves other students' arguments.

✓ Uses counterexamples when appropriate.

✓ Asks questions to understand other people's thinking.

✓ Identifies mistakes in other people's thinking.

✓ Provides suggestions for improving other people's thinking.

Use the list of MP.3 behaviors above and the following rubric to evaluate a student's overall proficiency with MP.3.

Math Practices Proficiency Rubric	
4	**Exemplary** The student exhibits all of the behaviors.
3	**Proficient** The student exhibits most of the behaviors.
2	**Emerging** The student exhibits about half of the behaviors.
1	**Needs Improvement** The student exhibits less than half of the behaviors.

MP.4 MODEL WITH MATHEMATICS

1. Develop MP.4

What MP.4 Means

Discuss what Marta is saying on top of page F26. The key elements of MP.4 are identifying and applying previously learned concepts to show and solve problems.

Sample Use of MP.4

Have students review the problem statement, Alex's plan, and Alex's work. Discuss answers to this question.

- *How does Alex's drawing represent the problem?* [It shows two colored boxes to show the number of worms Peeps found.]

Thinking Habits for MP.4

- *Which of the Thinking Habits questions were helpful to Alex? Explain.* [Sample answer: Alex used a drawing to show the problem, so the second question was helpful.]

- *Alex knows how to count. So, how did knowing how to count help him find the answer?* [Sample answer: Alex had to count the number of worms. He had to color that many boxes and then count the colored boxes to check his work.]

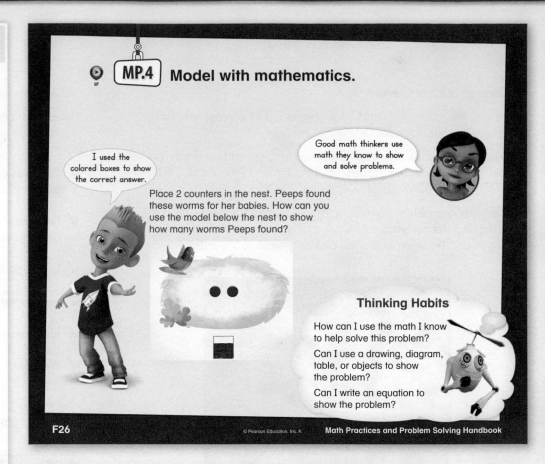

MP.4 Model with mathematics.

I used the colored boxes to show the correct answer.

Good math thinkers use math they know to show and solve problems.

Place 2 counters in the nest. Peeps found these worms for her babies. How can you use the model below the nest to show how many worms Peeps found?

Thinking Habits

How can I use the math I know to help solve this problem?

Can I use a drawing, diagram, table, or objects to show the problem?

Can I write an equation to show the problem?

F26   © Pearson Education, Inc. K   Math Practices and Problem Solving Handbook

Other Resources for Developing MP.4 include the following:

- **Math Practices Animations** An animation for each math practice is available at PearsonRealize.com. You might want to play the MP.4 animation as you use page F26 and at other times throughout the year as needed.

- **Math Practices Posters** A poster for each math practice is available to display in your classroom. You might want to display the MP.4 poster after playing the MP.4 animation.

- **Math Practices and Problem Solving Lessons** Lessons 2-6 and 6-10 focus on MP.4.

2. Connect MP.4

Connect MP.4 to Content

To see the many places MP.4 is connected to content standards within lessons, look for "MP.4" in red type.

Also see "Connecting Math Practices to Content Standards" in the Teacher's Edition, pages 1F, 85F, 135F, 199F, 245F, 281F, 507F, 563F, 621F, 675F, 745F, and 799F.

Below is a problem from Topic 6 where students apply MP.4 by using a drawing and an addition equation to solve a problem.

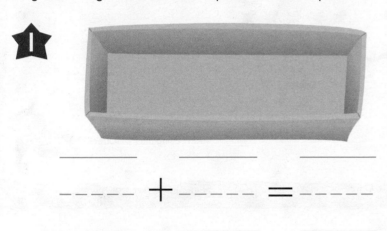

There are 4 balls in the box. Paolo puts 1 more ball in the box. How many balls are there in all?

Connect MP.4 to Other Math Practices

Deep understanding of mathematics, as well as success with problem solving, calls for engaging a combination of math practices. The following examples illustrate connections between MP.4 and other math practices.

- **MP.2 Reasoning** When students model with math, they apply the math they have learned to a new problem. Oftentimes how they represent their solution will show their reasoning. Make sure to ask students to explain their thinking in the drawings or equations they use to represent and solve problems.

- **MP.5 Use Appropriate Tools Strategically** When students model with math, various tools help them represent the math they know to solve a problem. Students can use tools such as blocks, counters, paper and pencil, technology tools, and more to make a mathematical representation or model.

3. Assess MP.4

MP.4 Behaviors

Listen and look for the following behaviors to monitor students' ongoing development of proficiency with MP.4.

✓ Identifies the correct prior knowledge that needs to be applied to solve a problem.

✓ Identifies the hidden question(s) in multiple-step problems.

✓ Uses numbers, symbols, and words to solve problems.

✓ Identifies the operation(s) needed to solve a problem.

✓ Uses estimation as appropriate.

Use the list of MP.4 behaviors above and the following rubric to evaluate a student's overall proficiency with MP.4.

Math Practices Proficiency Rubric	
4	**Exemplary** The student exhibits all of the behaviors.
3	**Proficient** The student exhibits most of the behaviors.
2	**Emerging** The student exhibits about half of the behaviors.
1	**Needs Improvement** The student exhibits less than half of the behaviors.

MP.5 USE APPROPRIATE TOOLS STRATEGICALLY

1. Develop MP.5

What MP.5 Means

Discuss what Carlos is saying on top of page F27. The key element of MP.5 is picking the right tool to solve a problem and using the tool the correct way.

Sample Use of MP.5

Have students review the problem statement and the tool Jada used to solve the problem. Discuss answers to these questions.

- *What tools could Jada use to solve the problem?* [counters, connecting cubes, or other objects]

- *What tool did Jada choose?* [counters]

- *Did Jada use the counters the correct way to help count the number of leaves?* [Sample answer: Yes, Jada used one counter for each leaf. She could then count the counters to find the number of leaves.]

Thinking Habits for MP.5

- *Which of the Thinking Habits questions were helpful to Jada? Explain.* [Sample answer: Which tools can I use? and Am I using the tool correctly? By using counters correctly, Jada found there are 5 leaves in all.]

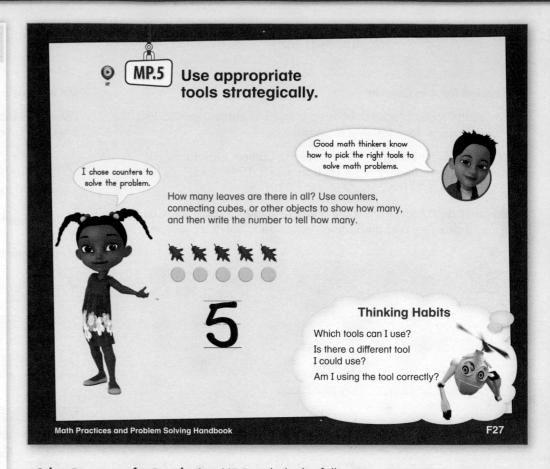

Other Resources for Developing MP.5 include the following:

- **Math Practices Animations** An animation for each math practice is available at PearsonRealize.com. You might want to play the MP.5 animation as you use page F27 and at other times throughout the year as needed.

- **Math Practices Posters** A poster for each math practice is available to display in your classroom. You might want to display the MP.5 poster after playing the MP.5 animation.

- **Math Practices and Problem Solving Lessons** Lesson 7-9 focuses on MP.5.

MP

2. Connect MP.5

Connect MP.5 to Content

To see the many places MP.5 is connected to content standards within lessons, look for "MP.5" in red type.

Also see "Connecting Math Practices to Content Standards" in the Teacher's Edition, pages 1F, 85F, 135F, 199F, 245F, 281F, 507F, 563F, 621F, 675F, 745F, and 799F.

Below is a problem from Topic 7 where students apply MP.5 by deciding what tool to use to solve a problem.

Carlos collects stamps. He has 9 stamps in all. He puts 1 stamp on the cover. He puts the rest inside the book. How many stamps does Carlos put inside his stamp book?

What tool can you use to help solve the problem? Tell a partner and explain why.

Connect MP.5 to Other Math Practices

Deep understanding of mathematics as well as success with problem solving call for engaging a combination of math practices. The following examples illustrate connections between MP.5 and other math practices.

• **MP.4 Model with Math** Students can use tools such as counters, paper and pencil, technology, and more to create a mathematical representation or model that shows the solution to a problem.

• **MP.6 Be Precise** When students use a tool, they often have to think about how to attend to precision using the tool. For example, when they use counters to show the number of objects or pictures on a page, they have to make sure they align the counters to the objects precisely. If not, students may end up using too many or too few counters and get incorrect results.

3. Assess MP.5

MP.5 Behaviors

Listen and look for the following behaviors to monitor students' ongoing development of proficiency with MP.5.

✓ Identifies available tools.

✓ Thinks about correct tools to use without prompting.

✓ Uses tools correctly and accurately.

✓ Knows when to use a particular tool.

✓ Decides if the results obtained using a tool make sense.

Use the list of MP.5 behaviors above and the following rubric to evaluate a student's overall proficiency with MP.5.

Math Practices Proficiency Rubric	
4	**Exemplary** The student exhibits all of the behaviors.
3	**Proficient** The student exhibits most of the behaviors.
2	**Emerging** The student exhibits about half of the behaviors.
1	**Needs Improvement** The student exhibits less than half of the behaviors.

MP.6 ATTEND TO PRECISION

1. Develop MP.6

What MP.6 Means

Discuss what Jada is saying on top of page F28. The key element of MP.6 is students being clear and precise in their work and explanations.

Sample Use of MP.6

Have students review the problem statement and how Carlos was precise in his work. Discuss answers to these questions.

- *Carlos said he was careful when he counted. Why is it important to be careful when you count?* [Sample answer: If you don't count carefully, you could say the wrong number.]

- *Carlos also said he was careful when he colored. How does that make his answer clear?* [Sample answer: You can see that he colored two boxes for the two worms each time because his coloring was careful.]

Thinking Habits for MP.6

- *Which of the Thinking Habits questions were helpful to Carlos? Explain.* [Sample answer: Is my answer clear? Carlos was careful about his work so that his answer about the number of worms would be clear.]

Other Resources for Developing MP.6 include the following:

- **Math Practices Animations** An animation for each math practice is available at PearsonRealize.com. You might want to play the MP.6 animation as you use page F28 and at other times throughout the year as needed.

- **Math Practices Posters** A poster for each math practice is available to display in your classroom. You might want to display the MP.6 poster after playing the MP.6 animation.

- **Math Practices and Problem Solving Lessons** Lessons 12-8 and 14-6 focus on MP.6.

2. Connect MP.6

Connect MP.6 to Content

To see the many places MP.6 is connected to content standards within lessons, look for "MP.6" in red type.

Also see "Connecting Math Practices to Content Standards" in the Teacher's Edition, pages 1F, 85F, 135F, 199F, 245F, 281F, 507F, 563F, 621F, 675F, 745F, and 799F.

Below is a problem from Topic 12 where students apply MP.6 by using location and geometry words clearly and appropriately.

Have students mark an X on the object above the bed that looks like a cube. Then have them explain how they know they are correct.

Connect MP.6 to Other Math Practices

Deep understanding of mathematics as well as success with problem solving call for engaging a combination of math practices. The following examples illustrate connections between MP.6 and other math practices.

- **MP.1 Make Sense and Persevere** To make sense of problems, students often have to understand what words, numbers, and symbols mean. For example, when students try to make sense of an addition word problem, they need to know how to use the correct symbol for addition.

- **MP.4 Model with Math** When students create a mathematical representation to show the solution to a problem, they have to be precise in their work. For example when using counters to show an addition problem like $2 + 3$, they need to clearly match the number of counters to each addend to get the correct sum and to represent the problem correctly.

3. Assess MP.6

MP.6 Behaviors

Listen and look for the following behaviors to monitor students' ongoing development of proficiency with MP.6.

✓ Computes accurately.

✓ Uses symbols and definitions appropriately.

✓ Accurately uses problem-solving strategies.

✓ Specifies and uses units of measure appropriately.

✓ Decides whether an exact answer or estimate is needed.

✓ Calculates efficiently, accurately, and fluently.

✓ Communicates clearly.

Use the list of MP.6 behaviors above and the following rubric to evaluate a student's overall proficiency with MP.6.

Math Practices Proficiency Rubric	
4	**Exemplary** The student exhibits all of the behaviors.
3	**Proficient** The student exhibits most of the behaviors.
2	**Emerging** The student exhibits about half of the behaviors.
1	**Needs Improvement** The student exhibits less than half of the behaviors.

MP.7 LOOK FOR AND MAKE USE OF STRUCTURE

1. Develop MP.7

What MP.7 Means

Discuss what Jackson is saying on top of page F29. The key element of MP.7 is looking for patterns in math and ways to break problems into simpler parts.

Sample Use of MP.7

Have students review the problem statement and how Emily found a pattern to solve the problem. Discuss answers to these questions.

- *Emily sees a pattern in how the birds are arranged. What number does the bird pattern show?* [4]

- *How does Emily use counters to show she is right?* [Sample answer: She uses 4 counters to show the 4 birds.]

Thinking Habits for MP.7

- *Which of the Thinking Habits questions were helpful to Emily? Explain.* [Sample answer: She uses the Thinking Habits on patterns. She could see how the 2 and 2 square pattern shows 4 birds.]

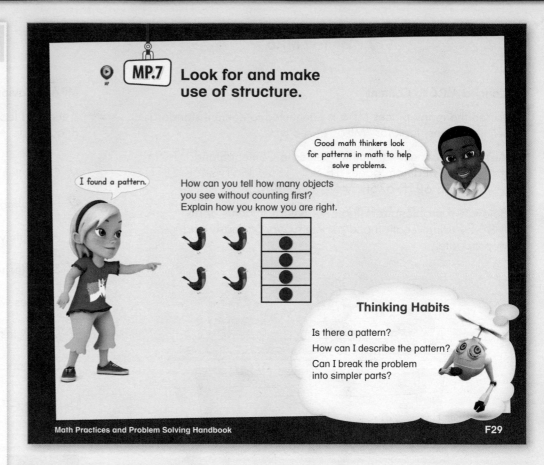

Math Practices and Problem Solving Handbook   F29

Other Resources for Developing MP.7 include the following:

- **Math Practices Animations** An animation for each math practice is available at PearsonRealize.com. You might want to play the MP.7 animation as you use page F29 and at other times throughout the year as needed.

- **Math Practices Posters** A poster for each math practice is available to display in your classroom. You might want to display the MP.7 poster after playing the MP.7 animation.

- **Math Practices and Problem Solving Lessons** Lessons 3-8, 10-7, and 11-7 focus on MP.7.

2. Connect MP.7

Connect MP.7 to Content

To see the many places MP.7 is connected to content standards within lessons, look for "MP.7" in red type.

Also see "Connecting Math Practices to Content Standards" in the Teacher's Edition, pages 1F, 85F, 135F, 199F, 245F, 281F, 507F, 563F, 621F, 675F, 745F, and 799F.

Below is a problem from Topic 11 where students apply MP.7 by looking for place value patterns in numbers to count.

41	42	43	44	45	46	47	48	49	50
51	52	53	54	55	56	57	58	59	60
61	62	63	64	65	66	67	68	69	70
71	72	73	74	75	76	77	78	79	80

Have students start at 42 and make a path to show how to count up 21 using ones and then tens. Have them circle the number where they end, and then explain how they used the number chart to find the answer.

Connect MP.7 to Other Math Practices

Deep understanding of mathematics as well as success with problem solving call for engaging a combination of math practices. The following examples illustrate connections between MP.7 and other math practices.

- **MP.1 Make Sense and Persevere** Students can use patterns at times to make sense of problems and make it simpler to solve problems. For example, students look for ways to make 5 with two numbers in Topic 1. They see the pattern of how one number goes up and one number goes down as they make sense and persevere in finding different ways to make 5.

- **MP.8 Generalize** When students find a pattern, they can sometimes use that pattern to solve similar problems. When counting by 10s, they see that the tens digit always goes up by one. They can apply this pattern if they start counting by 10s from 10 or from 40 or another tens number.

3. Assess MP.7

MP.7 Behaviors

Listen and look for the following behaviors to monitor students' ongoing development of proficiency with MP.7.

✓ Analyze and describe patterns in numbers.

✓ Analyze and describe common attributes and patterns in shapes and solids.

✓ Analyze expressions, equations, procedures, and objects to represent, describe, and work with them in different ways.

Use the list of MP.7 behaviors above and the following rubric to evaluate a student's overall proficiency with MP.7.

Math Practices Proficiency Rubric	
4	**Exemplary** The student exhibits all of the behaviors.
3	**Proficient** The student exhibits most of the behaviors.
2	**Emerging** The student exhibits about half of the behaviors.
1	**Needs Improvement** The student exhibits less than half of the behaviors.

MP.8 LOOK FOR AND EXPRESS REGULARITY IN REPEATED REASONING

1. Develop MP.8

What MP.8 Means

Discuss what Emily is saying on top of page F30. The key element of MP.8 is looking for things that repeat in a problem and looking for how to use something you learn in one problem to solve other problems.

Sample Use of MP.8

Have students review the problem statement and how Daniel found something that repeats to solve the problem. Discuss answers to this question.

• *Each new row has 1 more counter than the last row. The 1 more repeats. How does that help Daniel figure out how many counters are in the next row?* [Sample answer: The first row has 1 counter. The next row has 2 counters colored. It has 2 counters. The next row must have 3 counters colored because 3 is 1 more than 2.]

Thinking Habits for MP.8

• *Which of the Thinking Habits questions were helpful to Daniel? Explain.* [Sample answer: The question on looking for something that repeats. Knowing that each row has 1 more counter helped Daniel find the number of counters in the next row.]

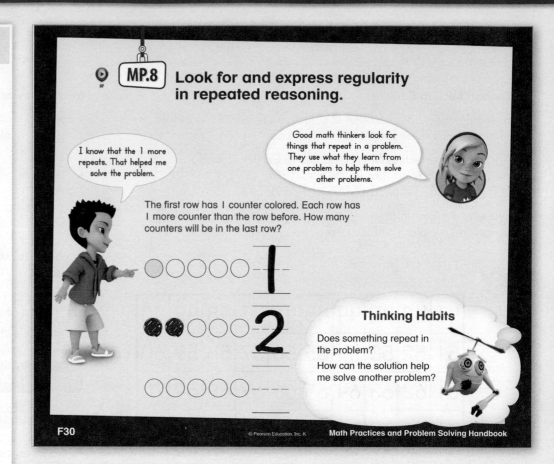

Other Resources for Developing MP.8 include the following:

• **Math Practices Animations** An animation for each math practice is available at PearsonRealize.com. You might want to play the MP.8 animation as you use page F30 and at other times throughout the year as needed.

• **Math Practices Posters** A poster for each math practice is available to display in your classroom. You might want to display the MP.8 poster after playing the MP.8 animation.

• **Math Practices and Problem Solving Lessons** Lesson 4-6 focuses on MP.8.

2. Connect MP.8

Connect MP.8 to Content

To see the many places MP.8 is connected to content standards within lessons, look for "MP.8" in red type.

Also see "Connecting Math Practices to Content Standards" in the Teacher's Edition, pages 1F, 85F, 135F, 199F, 245F, 281F, 507F, 563F, 621F, 675F, 745F, and 799F.

Below is a problem from Topic 4 where students apply MP.8 by generalizing what they know about counting and comparing numbers to solve a new type of problem.

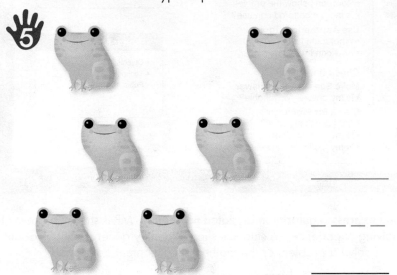

Alex sees frogs at the pond. Then he sees 1 more. How many frogs are there now? ... Have students explain their reasoning.

Connect MP.8 to Other Math Practices

Deep understanding of mathematics as well as success with problem solving call for engaging a combination of math practices. The following examples illustrate connections between MP.8 and other math practices.

- **MP.2 Reasoning** As students look for something that repeats in a problem, oftentimes they are looking at numbers. They have to look at how numbers relate to each other to see how something repeats. By seeing how things repeat in a problem, they can often find shortcuts to solving problems.

- **MP.3 Construct Arguments** Students can use what they know about one problem to solve other problems. That's MP.8. They can use what they know from other problems to construct arguments about why their answer to a new problem is correct.

3. Assess MP.8

MP.8 Behaviors

Listen and look for the following behaviors to monitor students' ongoing development of proficiency with MP.8.

✓ Notices and describes when certain calculations or steps in a procedure are repeated.

✓ Generalizes from examples or repeated observations.

✓ Recognizes and understands appropriate shortcuts.

✓ Evaluates the reasonableness of intermediate results.

Use the list of MP.8 behaviors above and the following rubric to evaluate a student's overall proficiency with MP.8.

Math Practices Proficiency Rubric	
4	**Exemplary** The student exhibits all of the behaviors.
3	**Proficient** The student exhibits most of the behaviors.
2	**Emerging** The student exhibits about half of the behaviors.
1	**Needs Improvement** The student exhibits less than half of the behaviors.

PROBLEM SOLVING GUIDE

PROBLEM SOLVING GUIDE

Background from the Authors

Mathematical Practices are involved in all aspects of mathematics learning. Because the **enVision**math**2.0** authors believe that mathematical practices have a particularly strong link to the phases of problem solving, we developed the Problem Solving Guide to help teachers infuse the phases of problem solving with the relevant mathematical practices. All eight of the mathematical practices are built into the Problem Solving Guide.

- **MP.1 Make sense of problems and persevere in solving them.** Students need to make sense of problems as well as their work and answers throughout the entire problem-solving process. MP.1 is particularly relevant when beginning to solve a problem and when checking one's work and solution.

- **MP.2 Reason abstractly and quantitatively.** MP.2 comes into play when first making sense of a problem. Students need to identify the quantities in the problem and understand how they are related.

- **MP.3 Construct viable arguments and critique the reasoning of others.** MP.3 is particularly important when solving a problem, sharing one's work, and when reviewing the work of others.

- **MP.4 Model with mathematics.** MP.4 is at the heart of problem solving. Students must identify previously learned concepts and procedures that they can bring to bear to find solutions.

- **MP.5 Use appropriate tools strategically.** MP.5 is part of every problem-solving experience. Students need to decide which tools are best for helping to understand and solve problems. They then need to apply the chosen tool or tools strategically to find solutions.

- **MP.6 Attend to precision.** MP.6 is involved in all phases of problem solving. Students need to be precise in understanding the conditions of a problem. They need to be precise in their work finding a solution, and they need to be precise in communicating their work and answer to others.

- **MP.7 Look for and make use of structure.** MP.7 is helpful in identifying a possible solution strategy for a problem. MP.7 helps students identify math they have used before that might be helpful in solving a given problem.

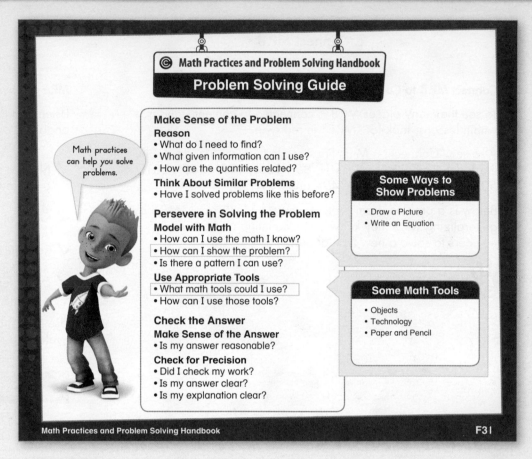

Math Practices and Problem Solving Handbook   F31

- **MP.8 Look for and express regularity in repeated reasoning.** MP.8 should be part of every problem-solving experience, as students should identify generalizations about the process used to solve a problem or the mathematical content developed.

Some Suggestions for Using the Problem Solving Guide

- For students who often struggle, use the guide to walk through solutions to problems. Doing this models the thinking students can do when they tackle problems on their own.

- For students who are stuck solving a given problem, use questions from the guide to help assess why they are stuck and help them get past being stuck.

- Reference the guide to remind students of ways they might represent problems or tools they might consider for solving a problem.

- Use the Problem Solving Guide together with the Problem Solving Recording Sheet to facilitate classroom conversations.

PROBLEM SOLVING RECORDING SHEET

PROBLEM SOLVING RECORDING SHEET

Background from the Authors

The three main phases in the Problem Solving Recording Sheet correspond to the three main phases in the Problem Solving Guide shown on the facing page. Here is some more information about these phases.

Research in mathematics education has made clear that there are certain thinking phases in the problem-solving process that students move through when solving a problem. Some people have described three phases, others four, and others more. Also, many different words have been used over the years to capture the essence of a phase. The Problem Solving Recording Sheet shown here shows three phases of problem solving. Here are those phases together with common words used over the years that you may have encountered.

- Make Sense of the Problem (Understand the Problem)

- Persevere in Solving the Problem (Plan and Solve the Problem)

- Check the Answer (Answer the Problem and Look Back)

We have learned some things about phases of problem solving.

- They are almost never followed in a linear fashion.

- They are not independent of one another.

- They do not reflect an algorithm for solving problems; following them does not guarantee correct solutions.

- They help many students approach solving problems systematically, increasing their chances of success.

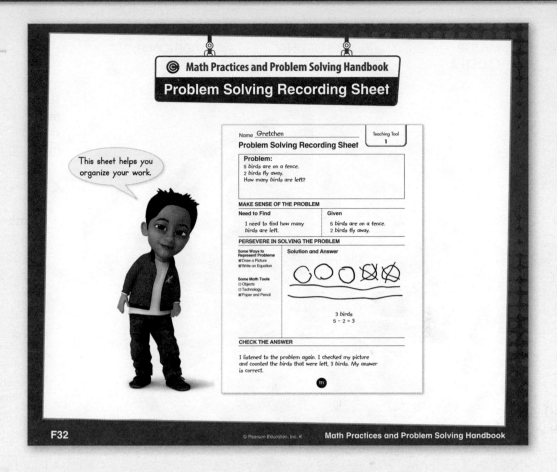

Some Suggestions for Using the Problem Solving Recording Sheet

- If some of your students have anxiety and negative beliefs about their abilities as problem solvers, use the Problem Solving Recording Sheet as a tool for helping them to solve problems.

- Use the Problem Solving Recording Sheet in class when modeling and discussing problem solutions like those in the Math Practices and Problem Solving section of the lesson.

- Have students use the Problem Solving Recording Sheet when working on problems in groups or independently.

A Caution

Be careful to not use the Problem Solving Guide or the Problem Solving Recording Sheet to lower the cognitive level of thinking and reasoning students are doing when solving a problem. If students are actively applying a strategy for solving a problem, whether correct or incorrect, do not interrupt their thinking. Allow errors to unfold and be resolved. Also, do not direct students to use a particular tool that is mentioned. Allow students to choose tools they feel are helpful. And finally, do not treat the questions like a series of closed questions which, if answered correctly by students, will guarantee the correct solution is found.

FCR FOCUS | **COHERENCE** | **RIGOR**

● **MAJOR CLUSTER**   ● **SUPPORTING CLUSTER**   ● **ADDITIONAL CLUSTER**

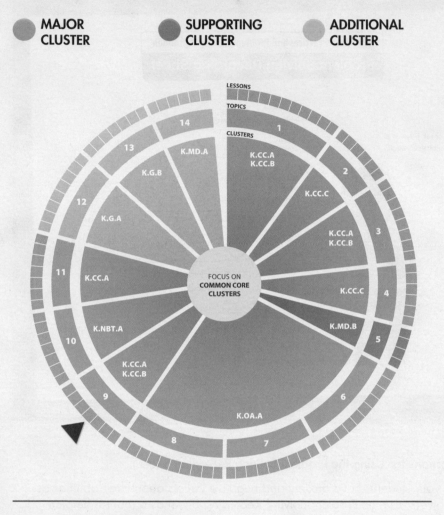

TOPIC 9   Count Numbers to 20

TOPIC 9 FOCUSES ON

© **MAJOR CLUSTER K.CC.A**
Know number names and the count sequence.

© **MAJOR CLUSTER K.CC.B**
Count to tell the number of objects.

Content Focus in **enVision**math2.0

Topic 9 continues the counting sequence with a focus on numbers 11 to 20. It highlights the principles necessary for accurate counting as well as a variety of representations including numeral writing.

COUNT QUANTITIES 11 TO 20

- **Number Sequence and the One-to-One Principle**
Throughout Topic 9, students use the correct words as they count 11 to 20 objects. As done previously with a lesser number of objects, students "tag" each object with one and only one number. It is important to note that the verbal sequence for the teen numbers 14, 16, 17, 18, and 19 follows a pattern by beginning with the ones place and then adding "teen" on the end. It can be confusing for students that the other numbers do not follow that same verbal pattern. If it did, one would say "oneteen" for 11, "twoteen" for 12, "threeteen" for 13, and "fiveteen" for 15. The written pattern, however, for the teen numbers is clear and consistent, and it should be emphasized. (K.CC.B.4a)

- **Cardinality of a Group of Objects** Each lesson in Topic 9 reinforces the important concept that when counting a group of objects, the last number name said tells how many objects are in the group. (K.CC.B.4b)

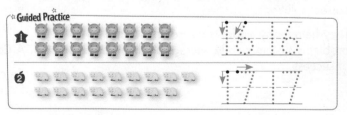

Count the piggy banks in each group, and then practice writing the number that tells how many.

PD

Content Focus in **énVision**math 2.0 (continued)

- **Draw or Count Out Quantities of Objects** Students draw
11 to 20 objects. Ten-frames help to underscore that each
successive number name refers to a quantity that is one larger.
(K.CC.B.4, K.CC.B.5)

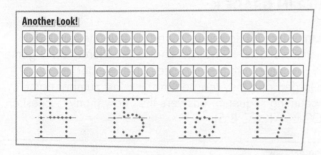

- **Visually Picture Number Quantities 11 to 20**
Throughout Topic 9, students are shown many different
arrangements of objects to reinforce that the number
of objects is the same regardless of their arrangement.
(K.CC.B.5)

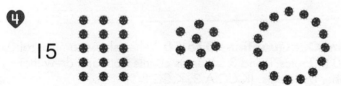

Draw a circle around the groups with 15 bugs.

NUMERALS 11 TO 20

- **Write Numerals to Tell How Many** In Lessons 9-1, 9-2,
9-3, and 9-4, students use tracing and dot prompts to read
and write numerals that represent how many objects they
counted. (K.CC.A.3)

PROBLEMS RELATED TO QUANTITIES OF 11 TO 20

- **Solve Problems Involving Counting** Throughout
Topic 9, and especially in Lessons 9-5, 9-6, and 9-7,
students solve problems involving counting and counting on.
They explain their answers using objects, pictures, and/or
numbers. (K.CC.A, K.CC.B)

Some dogs are playing in the park. 1 or 2 dogs
are resting in a doghouse. Count the dogs playing
in the park, and then draw a circle around the
numbers that tell how many dogs there could be in all.

Professional Development Videos Topic Overview Videos
and Listen and Look For Lesson Videos present additional
important information about the content of this cluster.

PD

Content Coherence in enVisionmath2.0

Students learn best when ideas are connected in a coherent curriculum. This coherence is achieved through various types of connections including connections within clusters, across clusters, across domains, and across grades.

BIG IDEAS IN GRADES K–6

Big Ideas are the conceptual underpinnings of **enVision**math**2.0** and provide conceptual cohesion of the content. Big Ideas connect Essential Understandings throughout the program.

A Big Idea that connects the work in this cluster involves the base-10 numeration system, a scheme for recording numbers using digits 0 through 9, groups of 10, and place value. In this topic, students count 11 to 20 objects by ones. These objects are often shown grouped (e.g., using ten-frames or ten-bars of connecting cubes) as 1 ten and some extra ones, or as 2 tens for 20.

For example, a ten-bar and 8 ones visually shows 18.

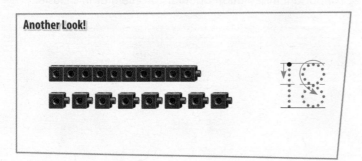

This topic serves only as an introduction to the place-value system and continues to emphasize numbers as representatives of a counting sequence.

For a complete list of Big Ideas, see pages 110–111 in the *Teacher's Edition Program Overview.*

LOOK BACK

How does Topic 9 connect to what students learned earlier?

EARLIER IN GRADE K

- **Count 1 to 10** In Topics 1 and 3, students counted quantities of 1 to 10 objects shown in different arrangements. They recognized that each successive number name is one larger, and they learned that the last number name in the counting sequence answers the "how many?" question. (K.CC.B.4, K.CC.B.5)

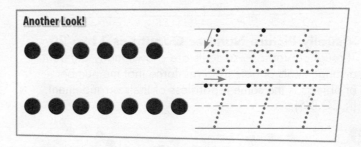

- **Count Out Quantities 0 to 10** When shown a numeral 0 to 10 in Topics 1 and 3, students counted out and drew that number of objects. (K.CC.A.3, K.CC.B.5)

- **Solve Problems Involving Counting to 10** In Topics 1 and 3, students solved problems involving counting quantities 0 to 10. (K.CC.B.4, K.CC.B.5)

- **Count Data** In Topic 5, students sorted objects into two categories and then counted the number of objects in each category. (K.MD.B.3)

TOPIC 9

How is content connected within Topic 9?

- **Organization of Concept Development** The concept development in this topic is connected from lesson to lesson. In Lessons 9-1, 9-2, 9-3, and 9-4, the numbers 11 to 20 are introduced in order, thus reinforcing the understanding students acquired previously: each successive number name refers to a quantity that is one larger. As each new number is introduced, students learn how to apply the counting sequence to different arrangements of objects and how to write the numeral to show how many. The concepts of counting and counting on connect the later lessons in the topic. Students count forward from any number to 20, count objects in two ten-frames by counting forward from 10, and solve problems that involve counting on. (K.CC.A.3, K.CC.B.4, K.CC.B.5)

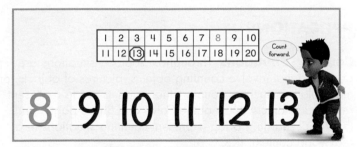

- **See Quantities as They Relate to 10** Ten-frames or sets of ten connecting cubes are used to represent the numbers 11 to 20. While other arrangements are shown, arrangements that include a group of 10 are important for understanding the base-10 system. (K.CC.A.3, K.CC.B.4, K.CC.B.5)

- **Counting Problems** Throughout Topic 9, students apply the understanding they are developing about counting to 20 to solve problems involving counting groups of real objects or pictures of objects. (K.CC.B.4, K.CC.B.5)

LOOK AHEAD

How does Topic 9 connect to what students will learn later?

LATER IN KINDERGARTEN

- **Compose and Decompose Numbers 11 to 19** In Topic 10, students will gain a foundation for place value by composing and decomposing numbers from 11 to 19 into 10 ones and some further ones. (K.NBT.A.1)

- **Extend the Counting Sequence** In Topic 11, students will extend the counting sequence and count by 1s and by 10s to 100. Students will also use number charts, including the hundred chart, to help them count on from any number and to count by 10s. (K.CC.A.1, K.CC.A.2, K.CC.B.4c)

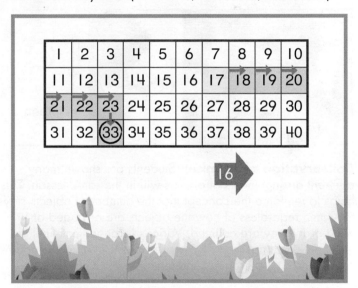

GRADE 1

- **Relate Counting to Addition** In Topics 2, 3, and 4, students will use counting on and counting back as strategies for adding and subtracting within 20. (1.OA.C.5, 1.OA.C.6)

- **Extend the Counting Sequence to 120** In Topic 7, students will count from any number less than 120 to 120, and read and write numbers to 120. (1.NBT.A)

FOCUS | COHERENCE | FCR RIGOR

Content Rigor in enVisionmath2.0

A rigorous curriculum emphasizes conceptual understanding, procedural skill and fluency, and applications.

CONCEPTUAL UNDERSTANDING

- **Connect Counting to Cardinality** Throughout Topic 9, quantities are represented visually in an effort to build mental representations of numbers. The visual representations involving ten-frames or sets of ten connecting cubes are particularly important as children begin to recognize that quantities 11 to 20 can be related to 10 (e.g., some number more than 10) and related to 20 (e.g., some number less than 20). Students label quantities with numerals or other representations and give one number in answer to a "how many?" question. (K.CC.B.4, K.CC.B.5)

- **Conservation of Number** Students are shown many different arrangements of objects within the same lesson. This helps to reinforce the concept that the number of objects stays the same regardless of how the objects are arranged or in what order they are counted. Various arrangements include different groupings (e.g., by twos), objects in a line, random arrangements, ten-frames, and ten-bars. (K.CC.B.4b)

- **Relationship Between Successive Numbers** In Topic 9, students are introduced to two or three successive numbers at a time. For example, in Lesson 9-2 students learn to count and write 13, 14, and 15 to help them understand the concepts that 15 is 1 greater than 14, and 14 is 1 greater than 13. This reinforces the general understanding that each successive number name refers to a quantity that is one greater than the number before it. (K.CC.B.4c)

PROCEDURAL SKILL AND FLUENCY

There are no standards in this cluster that call for fluency.

- **Accurately Count Quantities 11 to 20** Students count objects saying the numbers in the standard order, relate each object counted to a number in the counting sequence, keep track of objects counted, and use a numeral or other representation to tell how many objects there are. (K.CC.A, K.CC.B)

- **Accurately Count On from Any Number to 20** Topic 9 helps students develop the skill of counting on from any number. (K.CC.A.2)

APPLICATIONS

- **Counting Situations** Throughout Topic 9, situations are presented that involve counting objects, pictures of objects, or manipulatives such as counters that students use to represent real-world objects. Most of the Solve and Share pages and the Visual Learning Bridges present counting situations in a real-world context. (K.CC.B)

Jada has a collection of piggy banks. How can Carlos show the number of piggy banks Jada has? Use counters, and then draw them to show one way.

Connecting Math Practices and Content Standards in eNVisionmath 2.0

Math practices and content standards are connected within all lessons including the lessons that focus on math practices.

MATH PRACTICES WITHIN LESSONS

- **MP.1** Make sense of problems and persevere in solving them.

  Students persevere by using strategies to keep track of objects they have already counted. (e.g., p. 533, Items 3–5)

- **MP.2** Reason abstractly and quantitatively.

  Students reason when they use the number sequence to count forward from a number other than 1. (e.g., p. 538, Do You Understand?)

- **MP.3** Construct viable arguments and critique the reasoning of others.

  Students construct arguments to justify counting strategies. (e.g., p. 516, Items 7–9)

- **MP.4** Model with mathematics.

  Students use representations to model quantities greater than 10. (e.g., p. 519, Solve and Share)

- **MP.5** Use appropriate tools strategically.

  Students use tools such as counters to understand and count quantities greater than 10. (e.g., p. 531, Solve and Share)

- **MP.6** Attend to precision.

  Students consider the parameters of the problem when deciding how to use symbols and numbers correctly. (e.g., p. 540, Item 8)

- **MP.7** Look for and make use of structure.

  Students look for patterns in how groups of objects are organized. (e.g., p. 527, Items 3–7)

- **MP.8** Look for and express regularity in repeated reasoning.

  Students use repeated reasoning when they generalize about different configurations for the same number of objects. (e.g., p. 520, Visual Learning Bridge)

LESSON THAT FOCUSES ON MATH PRACTICES

- **Lesson 9-7** This lesson focuses on MP.2. Students use various types of reasoning to solve problems involving numbers to 20.

Jada knows that there are 17 bunnies at the animal sanctuary. Some are sitting in the grass. Some are hiding behind a bush. What clues can she write to have her friends guess the number of bunnies in all? Tell your friend the clues. How many bunnies can he or she see?

Revisit the information about MP.2 in these other resources:

- **Math Practices and Problem Solving Handbook** before Topic 1; includes Math Practices Proficiency Rubrics.

- **Math Practices Posters** to display in your classroom

- **Math Practices Animations,** one for each math practice, available at PearsonRealize.com.

MP

TOPIC 9 · MAJOR CLUSTERS K.CC.A AND K.CC.B

DIFFERENTIATED INSTRUCTION

 **I** Intervention   **O** On-Level   **A** Advanced

PEARSON
realize.
PearsonRealize.com

Learn   Assessment   Tools   Games

Ongoing Intervention

1 RtI **During the core lesson,** monitor progress, reteach as needed, and extend students' thinking.

Guiding Questions

• **In the Teacher's Edition** Guiding questions are used to monitor understanding during instruction.

 Online Guiding Questions Guiding questions are also in the online Visual Learning Animation Plus.

Learn

Error Intervention: If... then...

This feature in the Teacher's Edition is provided during Guided Practice. It spotlights common errors and gives suggestions for addressing them.

Reteaching

Reteaching sets are at the end of the topic in the Student's Edition. They provide additional examples, reminders, and practice. Use these sets as needed before students do the Independent Practice.

Higher Order Thinking

These problems require students to think more deeply about the rich, conceptual knowledge developed in the lesson.

Strategic Intervention

2 RtI **At the end of the lesson,** assess to identify students' strengths and needs and then provide appropriate support.

Quick Check

✓ **In the Student's Edition** Assess the lesson using 2-3 items checked in the Teacher's Edition.

 Online Quick Check You can also assess the lesson using 5 online, machine-scored items.

Assessment

Intervention Activity **I**

Teachers work with struggling students.

Reteach to Build Understanding **I**

This is a page of guided reteaching.

Technology Center **I O A**

 Digital Math Tools Activities reinforce the lesson content or previously taught content using a suite of digital math tools.

Tools

 Online Games provide practice on the lesson content or previously taught content.

Games

Homework and Practice **I O A**

Use the leveled assignment to provide differentiated homework and practice.

Additional resources to support differentiated instruction for on-level and advanced students include:

On-Level and Advanced Activity Centers **O A**

• **Center Games** are provided in on-level and advanced versions.

• **Math and Science Activity** is related to the topic science theme introduced at the start of the topic.

• **Problem-Solving Reading Mat** is used with a lesson-specific activity.

Intensive Intervention

3 RtI **As needed,** provide more instruction that is on or below grade level for students who are struggling.

Math Diagnosis and Intervention System 2.0

• **Diagnosis** Use the diagnostic tests in the system. Also, use the item analysis charts given with program assessments at the start of a grade or topic, or at the end of a topic, group of topics, or the year.

• **Intervention Lessons** These two-page lessons include guided instruction followed by practice. The system includes lessons below, on, and above grade level.

• **Teacher Support** Teacher Notes provide the support needed to conduct a short lesson. The lesson focuses on vocabulary, concept development, and practice. The Teacher's Guide contains individual and class record forms and correlations to Student's Edition lessons.

Resources for Fluency Success

• A variety of print and digital resources are provided to ensure success on Common Core fluency standards. See Steps to Fluency Success on pages 431E–431H.

THE LANGUAGE OF MATH

realize
PearsonRealize.com

Glossary   Games   Story   Story

English Language Learners

Provide ELL support through visual learning throughout the program, ELL instruction in every lesson, and additional ideas in an ELL Toolkit.

Visual Learning
The visual learning that is infused in **enVision**math**2.0** provides support for English language learners. This support includes a Visual Learning Animation Plus and a Visual Learning Bridge for each lesson.

English Language Learners Instruction
Lessons provide instruction for English language learners at Beginning, Intermediate, and Advanced levels of English proficiency.

English Language Learners Toolkit
This resource provides professional development and resources for supporting English language learners.

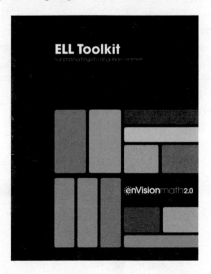

Math Vocabulary

Build math vocabulary using the vocabulary cards, vocabulary activities, vocabulary review, and glossary plus the online glossary and vocabulary game.

My Word Cards
Vocabulary cards for a topic are provided in the Student's Edition. Use the cards with students to study and learn new vocabulary words.

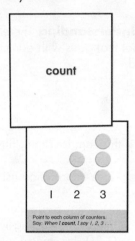

Vocabulary Activities
The Teacher's Edition provides vocabulary activities at the start of topics. These include activities for vocabulary in My Word Cards and/or activities for vocabulary in Review What You Know.

Vocabulary Review
A page of vocabulary review is provided at the end of each topic. It reviews vocabulary used in the topic.

Glossary
A glossary is provided at the back of the Student's Edition.

Animated Glossary
 An online, bilingual, animated glossary uses motion and sound to build understanding of math vocabulary.

Online Vocabulary Game
 An online vocabulary game is available in the Game Center.

Math and Reading

Connect reading and math using a data-filled reading mat for the topic with accompanying activity masters and guide. Also use topic interactive math stories.

Problem-Solving Reading Mats
There is a large, beautiful mat for each topic. At the start of the topic, help students become familiar with the mat and the vocabulary used by reading the mat aloud as students follow along. Use the Problem-Solving Reading Activity Guide for suggestions about how to use the mat.

Problem-Solving Reading Activity
At the end of some lessons, a Problem-Solving Reading Activity provides a page of math problems to solve by using the data on the mat.

Interactive Math Stories
  An interactive math story provides an introduction to each topic. The story is available as an online story book and an animated story at PearsonRealize.com as well as a color-in, take-home story in the Teacher's Resource Masters.

Lesson 9-1	Lesson 9-2	Lesson 9-3
COUNT AND WRITE 11 AND 12 pp. 513–518	**COUNT AND WRITE 13, 14, AND 15** pp. 519–524	**COUNT AND WRITE 16 AND 17** pp. 525–530
Ⓒ Content Standards **K.CC.A.3, K.CC.B.5** Mathematical Practices **MP.2, MP.3, MP.4, MP.6**	Ⓒ Content Standards **K.CC.A.3, K.CC.B.5** Mathematical Practices **MP.3, MP.4, MP.6, MP.8**	Ⓒ Content Standards **K.CC.A.3, K.CC.B.5** Mathematical Practices **MP.2, MP.4, MP.6, MP.7**
Objective Count and write the numbers 11 and 12.	**Objective** Count and write the numbers 13, 14, and 15.	**Objective** Count and write the numbers 16 and 17.
Essential Understanding There is a unique symbol that goes with each number word.	**Essential Understanding** There is a unique symbol that goes with each number word.	**Essential Understanding** There is a unique symbol that goes with each number word.
Vocabulary eleven, twelve	**Vocabulary** thirteen, fourteen, fifteen	**Vocabulary** sixteen, seventeen
ELL Listening: Seek clarification of spoken language.	**ELL Speaking:** Give information using key words.	**ELL Reading:** Use visual support to develop background knowledge.
Materials Counters (or Teaching Tool 6), Number Cards 0–10 (Teaching Tool 3), Number Cards 11–20 (Teaching Tool 4), Ten-Frame (Teaching Tool 22), clay or modeling dough, small objects	**Materials** Counters (or Teaching Tool 6), Number Cards 0–10 (Teaching Tool 3), Number Cards 11–20 (Teaching Tool 4), sheets of construction paper, cotton balls, glue	**Materials** Counters (or Teaching Tool 6), Number Cards 11–20 (Teaching Tool 4), large tray of sand, small objects such as paper clips (per student), small tray of sand, strips of paper
On-Level and Advanced Activity Centers • Center Games	**On-Level and Advanced Activity Centers** • Center Games	**On-Level and Advanced Activity Centers** • Math and Science Activity

LESSON RESOURCES

Digital

Print

- Student's Edition
- Daily Common Core Review
- Reteach to Build Understanding
- Center Games
- Math and Science Activity
- Problem-Solving Reading Mat
- Problem-Solving Reading Activity

Digital

- Listen and Look For PD Lesson Video
- Student's Edition eText
- Today's Challenge
- Solve & Share
- Visual Learning Animation Plus
- Animated Glossary
- Math Tools
- Quick Check
- Another Look Homework Video
- Math Games

Lesson 9-4

COUNT AND WRITE 18, 19, AND 20 pp. 531–536

 Content Standards **K.CC.A.3, K.CC.B.5**
Mathematical Practices **MP.1, MP.5, MP.7, MP.8**

Objective Count and write the numbers 18, 19, and 20.

Essential Understanding There is a unique symbol that goes with each number word.

Vocabulary eighteen, nineteen, twenty

ELL Speaking: Express opinions in sentences.

Materials Counters (or Teaching Tool 6), Number Cards 11–20 (Teaching Tool 4), Double Ten-Frame (Teaching Tool 23), blank books with 10 pages plus cover, rubber stamps, ink pad

On-Level and Advanced Activity Centers
• Problem-Solving Reading Mat

Lesson 9-5

COUNT FORWARD FROM ANY NUMBER TO 20 pp. 537–542

 Content Standards **K.CC.A.2, K.CC.B.4c**
Mathematical Practices **MP.2, MP.4, MP.6, MP.7**

Objective Count forward from any number to a number within 20.

Essential Understanding You use the count sequence to count from any number within 20. Numbers become greater when you count on.

Vocabulary row

ELL Listening: Use visual support to confirm understanding.

Materials Counters (or Teaching Tool 6), Double Ten-Frame (Teaching Tool 23)

On-Level and Advanced Activity Centers
• Center Games

Lesson 9-6

COUNT TO FIND HOW MANY pp. 543–548

 Content Standard **K.CC.B.5**
Mathematical Practices **MP.1, MP.5, MP.7, MP.8**

Objective Count to find how many are in a group.

Essential Understanding Counting tells how many are in a set, regardless of their arrangement or the order in which they were counted. The last number said when counting a set is the total. Counting is cumulative.

Vocabulary None

ELL Reading: Use visual support to develop vocabulary.

Materials Counters (or Teaching Tool 6), basket, connecting cubes (or Teaching Tool 8), paper

On-Level and Advanced Activity Centers
• Math and Science Activity

TOPIC RESOURCES

Digital

Print

Start of Topic
• Topic Centers
• Interactive Math Story
• Math and Science Project
• Home-School Connection
• Review What You Know
• My Word Cards

End of Topic
• Fluency Practice Activity
• Vocabulary Review
• Reteaching
• Topic Assessment
• Topic Performance Assessment

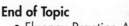

Digital

Start of Topic
• Topic Overview PD Video

End of Topic
• Math Practices Animations
• Online Topic Assessment
• ExamView® Test Generator

COUNT NUMBERS TO 20

Lesson 9-7

MATH PRACTICES AND PROBLEM SOLVING: REASONING pp. 549–554

Mathematical Practices MP.2, MP.1, MP.3, MP.4
Content Standards K.CC.A.2, K.CC.B.5

Objective Use reasoning to count and write numbers to the number 20.

Essential Understanding Good math thinkers know how to think about words and numbers to solve problems.

Vocabulary None

ELL Strategies: Use strategic learning techniques: drawings/illustrations.

Materials Counters (or Teaching Tool 6), small bag, Number Cards 0–10 (Teaching Tool 3)

On-Level and Advanced Activity Centers
- Problem-Solving Reading Mat

Notes

Movement Center

More or Fewer

Materials
Connecting cube trains of different lengths

- Give each student connecting cube trains of different lengths. Some students should have 3-cube trains, some 5, some more than 10, and some more than 15.

- Tell students that the goal is to end up with exactly 10 connecting cubes in their trains within 1 minute's time. When you say *Go!*, students must go around the room and ask others for more or fewer cubes to make their 10. "I have 6 cubes. I need more to make 10." "I can give you 1 more."

- After 1 minute, say, *Stop!* Have students explain whether they have the desired number of cubes and if they have more than 10 cubes or fewer than 10 cubes.

- Vary the game by changing the goal to 15 cubes and/or increasing the number of cubes each student is given. Have students decide how many more or fewer they need.

Art Center

Popcorn Fun

Materials
Large amount of popped corn in a bowl, construction paper, glue, crayons

- Have students take a set number of pieces of popcorn, anywhere from 11 to 20.

- Have them make a simple drawing and use the popcorn to fill in the picture.

Science Center

20 Questions

Materials
Objects from nature, such as pine cones, stones, twigs, leaves (or pictures of them); chart paper

- One student in the group should be designated as "the counter" to make tally marks on a board or sheet of paper.

- One student holds an object behind his or her back. The other students can ask up to 20 questions to find out what the hidden object is.

- "The counter" should make a tally mark for each question.

- Once the correct object is identified, students can count the tally marks together: "1, 2, 3, 4 . . . ."

- The student who arrives at the correct answer gets a turn to hide something behind his or her back.

Writing Center

Number Picture

Materials
Construction paper, crayons

- Students choose a number from 11 to 20.
- They draw a picture to illustrate that number.
- Students dictate a sentence about their picture.

When I look in the sky, I see 19 stars.

Math Center

Make It Right

Materials
Number Cards 0–20 (Teaching Tools 3 and 4)

- Shuffle the cards 0–20.
- Have partners work together to place the numerals in order on the floor.
- When they finish, have them count softly together: "0, 1, 2, 3 . . . ."

Building Center

More than 10

Materials
20 blocks

- Have students start with 10 blocks in a tower. Then have them add 2 more, 3 more, and so on. Each time, have them tell how many blocks they started with, describe what happened, and tell how many blocks they have now. For example, "I started with 10 blocks. I added 2 blocks, so now I have 12 blocks."
- Once students understand the game, have them work in pairs—one giving the directions, the other building the tower. Then have them switch roles.

PDF Story · Story

Before the Story

Picture Walk

Project the online PDF that contains a full-color version of this story. Read the title, author's name, and illustrator's name to students. *How does the title of the story help you predict what the story is about?* [It's often a big clue.] *Matt is the name of one of the characters. Can you tell what some of his favorite things are by just looking at the picture?* [Yes, it looks like one of his favorite things is toy cars.] Have students scan the other pictures and discuss them.

Activate Prior Knowledge

In this story, we will count some of Matt's favorite things, and you will meet his friend Gina and also count her favorite things. Write the numbers from 10 to 20 on the board. Count them aloud with students.

Play the animated version of the story.

DURING THE STORY

This book belongs to:
David

TOPIC 9 Story

Favorite Things

Written by Sandy Riggs
Illustrated by Holli Conger

Matt has many small cars.
Look and count.

11 cars

Topic 9 · 1

Matt shows Gina his cards.
Look and count.

14 cards

Topic 9 · 2

READ

Read the story aloud for enjoyment. Then read each page aloud and have students respond to the text. Page 1: *Does Matt have more than 10 or fewer than 10 toy cars?* [More] *How many more than 10?* [1] Page 2: *How many baseball cards does Matt have?* [14] Page 3: *How might you group the pigs to count them easily?* [Answers will vary.]

GESTURE

Have students go from page to page and count the favorite things again. Then have them use connecting cubes to show the number of cars, the number of cards, the number of pigs, and the number in each set of stickers.

COLOR

Distribute the Interactive Math Story books to students. Then have students use a blue crayon to circle a group of objects on each page to show how many more than 10 there are. Students may want to count 10 objects first and mark an X on each object as they count. On page 4, tell them to treat the stars and the birds as separate pages.

Gina likes to collect things, too.

Look and count.

18 pigs

Topic 9 ③

Gina shows Matt her stickers.

Look and count.

19 birds and **20** stars

Counting can be fun.

Topic 9 ④

fold down

Extension

Set up a display table on which students can place one or more of their favorite things. You might want to focus on one category such as favorite toys, favorite stuffed animals, or favorite puzzles. Label objects in the display for students. Have students count the number of objects. Allow time for discussion of the objects.

You may wish to have students take home their Interactive Math Story books and share what they have learned about counting numbers to 20.

WRITE

Revisit the first page of the story. Call on a volunteer to count the toy cars aloud. Then have each student write the total number of cars in the box. [11] Continue in the same manner for the remaining pages, having a volunteer count aloud and the students write the total number in each box.

SPEAK

Invite students to retell the story in their own words. Then have them share some of their favorite things with the class. Students can also bring some objects from home and talk about them.

TOPIC OPENER

COUNT NUMBERS TO 20

TOPIC ESSENTIAL QUESTION

How can numbers to 20 be counted, read, written, and pictured to tell how many?

Revisit the Topic Essential Question throughout the topic, and see a note about answering the question in the Teacher's Edition for the Topic Assessment.

MATH AND SCIENCE PROJECT STEM

The science theme for this project is **What Can We Get From Plants?** This theme will be revisited in the Math and Science Activities in Lessons 9-3 and 9-6.

Discuss with students the different ways plants help humans and animals to survive (e.g., shelter, food, water, sunlight). Ask students to name ways in which plants help to shelter humans and animals. Then ask them to name foods that are plants.

Project-Based Learning Have students work on the **Math and Science Project** over the course of several days.

EXTENSION

Using their posters, have students compare the ways plants provide food and shelter to humans and animals.

Sample Student Work for Math and Science Project

Math and Science Project: What Can We Get From Plants?
Directions Read the character speech bubbles to students. **Find Out!** Have students find out ways plants impact and change their environment. Say: *Talk to friends and relatives about what plants do for the environment. Ask them how humans and animals use things in the environment, such as plants, to meet their needs.* **Journal: Make a Poster** Have students make a poster. Ask them to draw some ways that plants can provide food and shelter for animals and humans. Finally, have students draw an orange tree with 15 oranges.

Topic 9   five hundred seven **507**

Home-School Connection

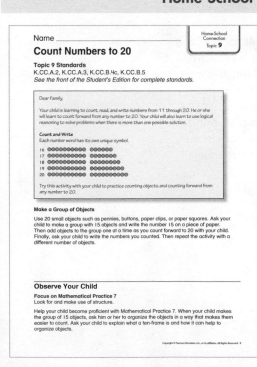

Send this page home at the start of Topic 9 to give families an overview of the content in the topic.

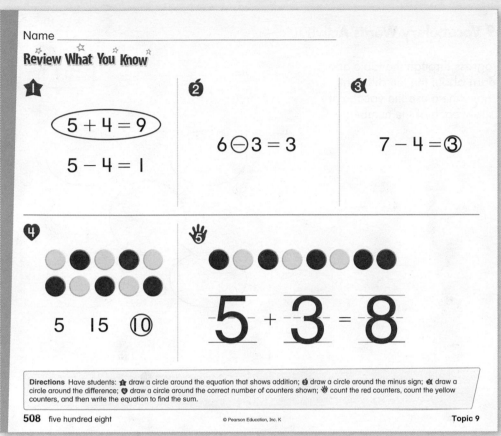

Name _____

Review What You Know

1

$$\boxed{5 + 4 = 9}$$

$$5 - 4 = 1$$

2

$$6 \ominus 3 = 3$$

3

$$7 - 4 = ③$$

4

5   15   ⑩

5

$$5 + 3 = 8$$

Directions Have students: ★ draw a circle around the equation that shows addition; ● draw a circle around the minus sign; ◆ draw a circle around the difference; ● draw a circle around the correct number of counters shown; ✋ count the red counters, count the yellow counters, and then write the equation to find the sum.

© Pearson Education, Inc. K

Topic 9

Vocabulary Review Activity

Use the Vocabulary: Picture the Word (Teaching Tool 48) as a graphic organizer to help students fully understand their meanings. Have students write one of the vocabulary review words (addition) on the line at the top of the page. Then have them draw or write the definition or an example of the word. Students can use words and pictures to complete the model. You may wish to have students work in groups to complete models for the different vocabulary review words.

Name _____

Teaching Tool
48

Word: _____

Picture:

Vocabulary: Picture the Word **48** Copyright © Pearson Education, Inc., or its affiliates. All Rights Reserved. K

Topic 9 Vocabulary Words Activity

Ways to Show a Number

Use the Vocabulary: Some Ways to Show a Number (Teaching Tool 51) graphic organizer. Make one copy of the teaching tool and write the number word *eleven* in the center circle. Draw two ten-frames in one oval and a write-on line in another. Then make copies so that every student has his or her own page. Have students draw or write a different way to show the number 11 in each of the ovals.

As you progress through the topic and students learn about the ten different numbers, have them use the vocabulary model to show each of the numbers.

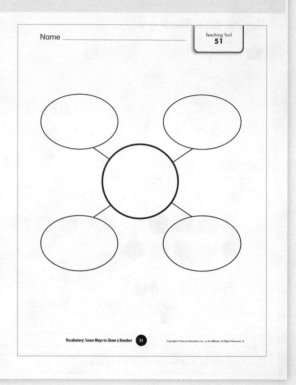

My Word Cards **Directions** Have students cut out the vocabulary cards. Read the front of the card, and then ask them to explain what the word or phrase means.

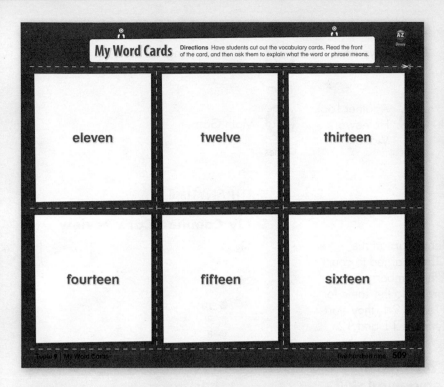

eleven

twelve

thirteen

fourteen

fifteen

sixteen

Topic 9 | My Word Cards   five hundred nine   509

My Word Cards **Directions** Review the definitions and have students study the cards. Extend learning by having students draw pictures for each word on a separate piece of paper.

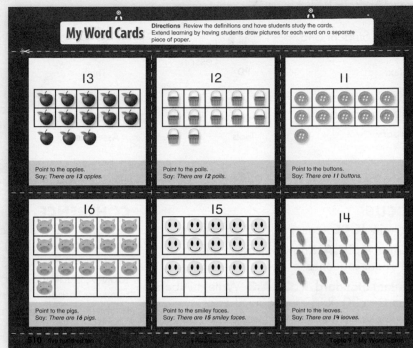

13

Point to the apples.
Say: *There are 13 apples.*

12

Point to the pails.
Say: *There are 12 pails.*

11

Point to the buttons.
Say: *There are 11 buttons.*

16

Point to the pigs.
Say: *There are 16 pigs.*

15

Point to the smiley faces.
Say: *There are 15 smiley faces.*

14

Point to the leaves.
Say: *There are 14 leaves.*

510 five hundred ten   Topic 9 | My Word Cards

My Word Cards **Directions** Have students cut out the vocabulary cards. Read the front of the card, and then ask them to explain what the word or phrase means.

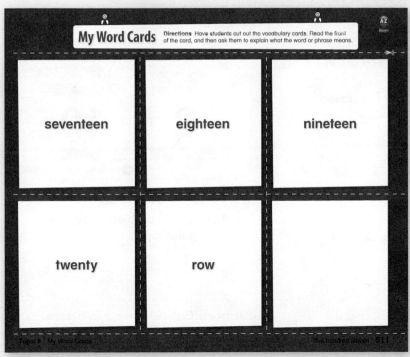

seventeen

eighteen

nineteen

twenty

row

Topic 9 | My Word Cards   five hundred eleven   511

My Word Cards **Directions** Review the definitions and have students study the cards. Extend learning by having students draw pictures for each word on a separate piece of paper.

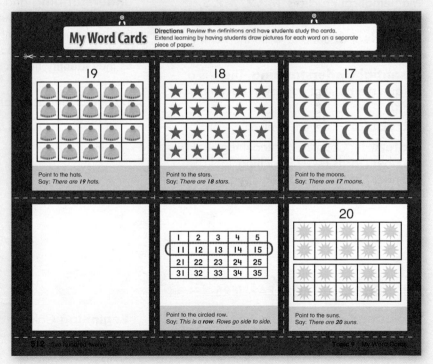

19

Point to the hats.
Say: *There are 19 hats.*

18

Point to the stars.
Say: *There are 18 stars.*

17

Point to the moons.
Say: *There are 17 moons.*

1	2	3	4	5
11	12	13	14	15
21	22	23	24	25
31	32	33	34	35

Point to the circled row.
Say: *This is a **row**. Rows go side to side.*

20

Point to the suns.
Say: *There are 20 suns.*

512 five hundred twelve   Topic 9 | My Word Cards

COUNT AND WRITE 11 AND 12

DIGITAL RESOURCES PearsonRealize.com

eText Student and Teacher eTexts

 PD Listen and Look For Lesson Video

 Think Today's Challenge

 Solve Solve and Share

Visual Learning Animation Plus **Learn**

 Glossary A-Z Animated Glossary

 Tools Math Tools

 Assessment Quick Check

 Help Another Look Homework Video

 Games Math Games

LESSON OVERVIEW 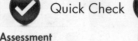 FOCUS • COHERENCE • RIGOR

FOCUS

Domain K.CC Counting and Cardinality

Cluster K.CC.A Know number names and the count sequence.

Content Standard K.CC.A.3 Write numbers from 0 to 20. Represent a number of objects with a written numeral 0–20 (with 0 representing a count of no objects). Also **K.CC.B.5**

Mathematical Practices MP.2, MP.3, MP.4, MP.6

Objective Count and write the numbers 11 and 12.

Essential Understanding There is a unique symbol that goes with each number word.

Vocabulary eleven, twelve

Materials Counters (or Teaching Tool 6), Number Cards 0–10 (Teaching Tool 3), Number Cards 11–20 (Teaching Tool 4)

COHERENCE

In Topics 1 and 3, students learned the numbers 0 through 10. They learned to count, read, and write each of the numbers. In Topic 9, students will learn to do the same for numbers through 20. In Lesson 9-1, they start to count and write the numbers 11 and 12.

RIGOR

This lesson emphasizes **conceptual understanding** and **procedural skill**. Students build upon their understanding of numbers and the count sequence. They also work on the procedural skill of counting as they identify how many objects are in a group.

 PD Watch the Listen and Look For Lesson Video.

MATH ANYTIME

Daily Common Core Review

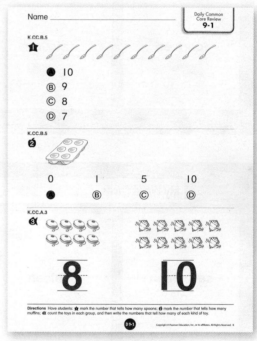

Today's Challenge

Think Use Topic 9 problems any time during this topic.

ENGLISH LANGUAGE LEARNERS

Listening Seek clarification of spoken language.

Use with the Visual Learning Bridge on Student's Edition, p. 514.

Show students 11 objects, and then ask them to listen as you count each one aloud. Have them draw the same number of objects for each number as you count (e.g., 1 truck for 1, 2 birds for 2).

Beginning Call out a number, and ask students to point to the correct number in their drawings.

Intermediate Call out a number. Ask students to point to the correct number in their drawings and write out each number next to the drawing (e.g., one for 1, etc.).

Advanced Call out a random number between 0 and 11, and ask students to draw objects to show the number. Ask them to write the numeral next to their picture.

Summarize How can you recognize the numbers that you hear?

COHERENCE: Engage learners by connecting prior knowledge to new ideas.

Students use counters to count, read, and write the number for a group of 12 objects. This prepares them for the next part of the lesson where they count, read, and write the numbers for groups of 11 and 12 objects.

10–15 min

BEFORE

1. Pose the Solve-and-Share Problem

MP.4 Model with Math In this problem, students produce multiple representations of the number 12.

Give each student 15 counters.

Say: *Carlos has a collection of toy cars. How can Carlos show the number of cars he has? Use counters, and then draw them to show one way.*

2. Build Understanding

What are you asked to show? [One way to show the number of cars Carlos has] *What do you already know about a ten-frame?* [If a ten-frame is filled, there are 10 in the group. If the ten-frame is not filled, there are less than 10 in the group.]

DURING

3. Ask Guiding Questions As Needed

What is one way to show the number of cars Carlos has? [Place 10 counters on the ten-frame and 2 counters below the ten-frame.] *Can you show the number of cars without using counters? Explain.* [Yes; I can write the number.]

AFTER

4. Share and Discuss Solutions

 Start with students' solutions. If needed, Solve project and analyze Lila's work to discuss how counting 12 counters shows there are 12 toy cars.

5. Transition to the Visual Learning Bridge

Counting tells how many are in a group.

When you count, the last number counted tells the number in the group.

Later in this lesson, you will learn how to count groups of 11 and 12 and how to write the numbers that represent those groups.

6. Extension for Early Finishers

Have students shuffle a set of number cards and then arrange them in counting order from 1–12.

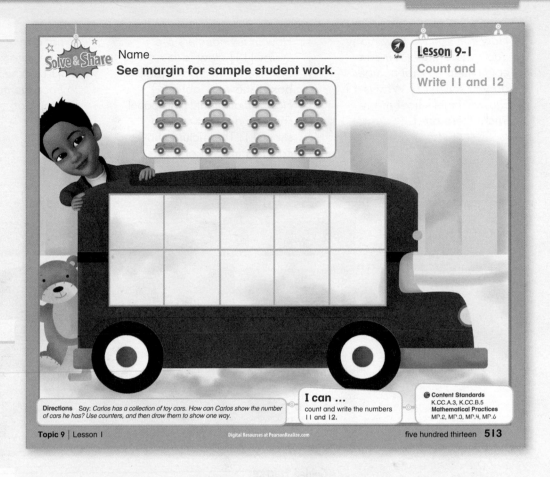

Solve & Share

Name _____

See margin for sample student work.

Lesson 9-1
Count and
Write 11 and 12

I can ...
count and write the numbers 11 and 12.

Content Standards
K.CC.A.3, K.CC.B.5
Mathematical Practices
MP.2, MP.3, MP.4, MP.6

Directions Say: Carlos has a collection of toy cars. How can Carlos show the number of cars he has? Use counters, and then draw them to show one way.

Topic 9 | Lesson 1

Digital Resources at PearsonRealize.com

five hundred thirteen **513**

Analyze Student Work

Lila's Work

Gustavo's Work

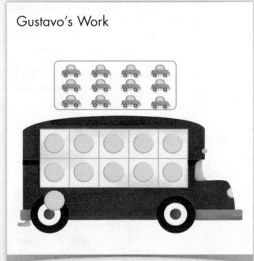

Lila correctly places 10 counters in the ten-frame and 2 counters below the ten-frame.

Gustavo correctly places 10 counters in the ten-frame but places only 1 counter below the ten-frame.

The *Visual Learning Bridge* connects students' thinking in Solve & Share to important math ideas in the lesson. Use the *Visual Learning Bridge* to make these ideas explicit. Also available as a *Visual Learning Animation Plus* at PearsonRealize.com

E L L
Visual Learning

Learn   Glossary

How can you tell how many trucks there are? [You can count them.] *What number do you see?* [11] *Why is 11 shown?* [It tells how many trucks there are.]

How many counters are there? [11] *How is this box like the first box?* [Both boxes show 11 objects.] *How is it different?* [This panel shows a different way to show 11. The picture shows counters instead of trucks.]

What do you think this number will be if you trace it? [11] *Where do you start to trace the number?* [At the first top dot]

MP.2 Reasoning *What number do you see?* [11] *Why do you think this number is in this box?* [To tell how many trucks there are in all]

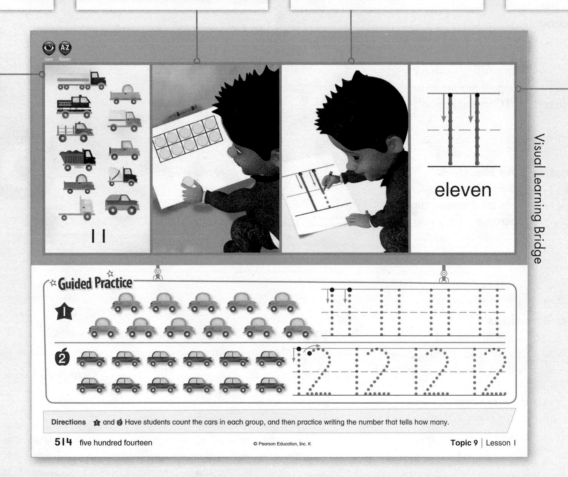

Visual Learning Bridge

Directions ★ and ✿ Have students count the cars in each group, and then practice writing the number that tells how many.

514 five hundred fourteen   © Pearson Education, Inc. K   Topic 9 | Lesson 1

Complete the *Do You Understand? Show Me!* problem before starting Guided Practice.

Do You Understand? Show Me! **MP.6 Be Precise** Show a ten-frame with 10 counters on it and 1 counter below it. *Which number card shows how many counters there are?* Have students hold up the number card for 11. Repeat with counters and the number card for 12. *Where do you start tracing the number?* [I start at the first top dot.]

Essential Question
Ask the following Essential Question: *Why does each number need its own symbol?* [Sample answer: So that there is no confusion over which number you mean.]
Remind students that writing numbers tells you how many objects are in a group and that you can use written numbers to tell how many objects are in a group.

Error Intervention: Item 2
If students have difficulty writing the number 12,
then have them practice by using a finger to trace over the numbers on their number cards or in the air.

✔ **QUICK CHECK**
Check mark indicates items for prescribing differentiation on the next page.
Items 7 and 8 are worth 1 point. Item 10 is worth up to 3 points.

20–30 min   Tools Assessment

Item 3 MP.4 Model with Math *What number should you write?* [11] *Why do you think you write this number?* [It shows that there are 11 toy cars.] *How can you represent this group of cars using a number?* [Sample answer: I counted 11 cars, so I can write the number 11 to tell how many.]

Item 5 If students have difficulty writing the number, then have them practice by tracing 12 with a finger. Students should practice writing 12 on varied surfaces. They are just beginning to write 2-digit numbers, but they have already written the numerals 1 and 2. Now they need to understand that both numbers together make the number 12.

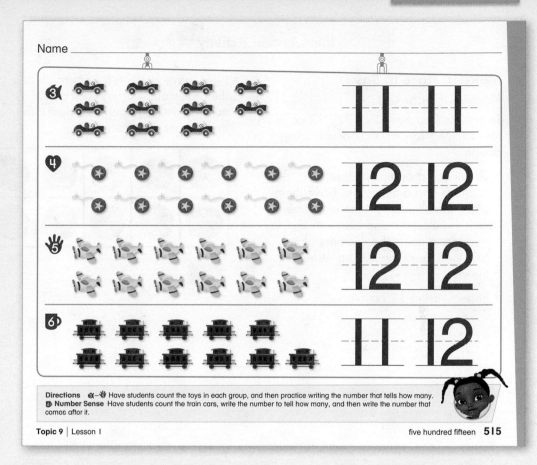

Items 7–9 MP.3 Construct Arguments *Tell how you know how many objects are in a group.* [The last number I say when I count tells how many there are.] As the numbers get larger, students will need to have an organized strategy to count the objects. The toy vehicles are in rows, so students can count them straight across.

Item 10 Remind students that there is a special symbol that stands for 11 and another that stands for 12. For this exercise, students will be drawing 11 objects and writing the number. Encourage students to find 11 objects in the classroom to draw or trace. Have them organize their drawings into rows for clearer counting.

Coherence This lesson is the first in a series that teaches students about counting and writing double-digit numbers. This prepares them for Topic 10 in which they will compose and decompose numbers 11 to 19.

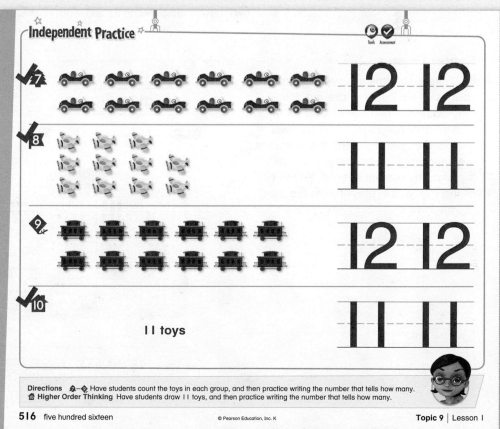

Use the **QUICK CHECK** on the previous page to prescribe differentiated instruction.

2 RtI

I **Intervention**
0–3 points on the Quick Check

O **On-Level**
4 points on the Quick Check

A **Advanced**
5 points on the Quick Check

Intervention Activity **I**

Make It, Trace It, Say It

Materials (per group)

Ten-Frame (Teaching Tool 22), 12 counters (or Teaching Tool 6), clay or modeling dough

- Give each group of students 11 counters and a ten-frame. Have them place the counters on the ten-frame with the eleventh one below it. Guide students to count the counters aloud, and then make the number using the clay.

- Repeat, using 12 counters.

- Next, have students take turns closing their eyes and tracing each clay number with a finger. Ask them to name the number they traced.

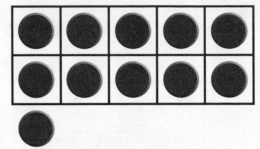

Reteach **I**

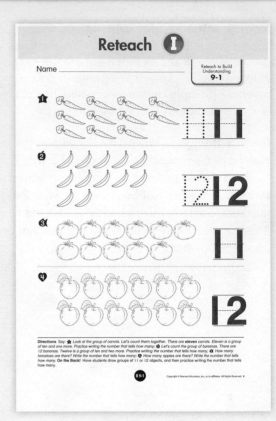

On-Level and Advanced Activity Centers **O** **A**

Center Games

Partners take turns uncovering game spaces. If the pictures are the same, they count the number of objects in one picture and keep the 2 red squares. If the pictures are different, they replace the squares. Play continues until all the pictures are uncovered. At the end of the game, the player with the most squares wins.

★ On-Level

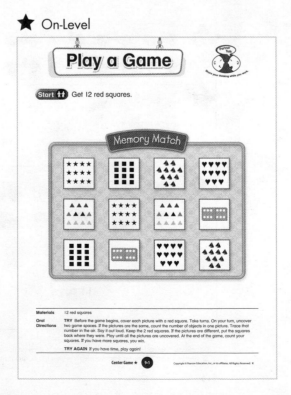

★★ Advanced

TIMING

The time allocated to Step 3 will depend on the teacher's instructional decisions and differentiation routines.

15–30 min

PEARSON realize.
PearsonRealize.com

Help Tools Games

Technology Center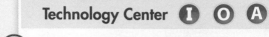

Math Tools and Math Games

A link to a specific math tools activity or math game to use with this lesson is provided at PearsonRealize.com.

Tools

Games

Leveled Assignment

I Items 1–3   **O** Items 2–4   **A** Items 3–5

Name _____

Help Tools Games

Homework & Practice 9-1
Count and Write 11 and 12

Another Look!

HOME ACTIVITY Draw groups of 11 and 12 circles, each on a separate index card. Have your child write the correct number on the back of each card. Then use the cards to practice counting and writing the numbers 11 and 12.

1

2

Directions Say: *Count the connecting cubes, and then write the number to tell how many.* ★ and ② Have students count the connecting cubes, and then write the number to tell how many.

Topic 9 | Lesson 1

Digital Resources at PearsonRealize.com

five hundred seventeen **517**

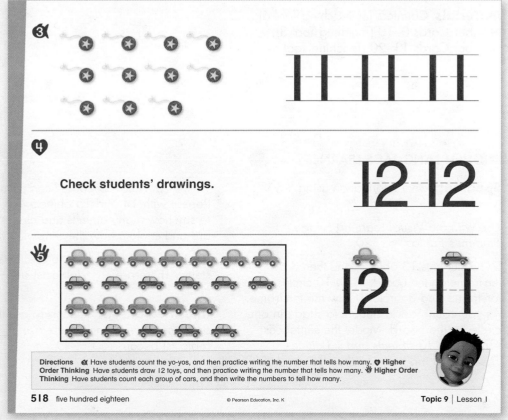

3

4

Check students' drawings.

5

Directions ✖ Have students count the yo-yos, and then practice writing the number that tells how many. ♦ Higher Order Thinking Have students draw 12 toys, and then practice writing the number that tells how many. ✋ Higher Order Thinking Have students count each group of cars, and then write the numbers to tell how many.

518 five hundred eighteen

© Pearson Education, Inc. K

Topic 9 | Lesson 1

517–518

COUNT AND WRITE 13, 14, AND 15

DIGITAL RESOURCES PearsonRealize.com

eText Student and Teacher eTexts

PD Listen and Look For Lesson Video

Think Today's Challenge

Solve Solve and Share

Learn Visual Learning Animation Plus

A-Z Glossary Animated Glossary

Tools Math Tools

Assessment Quick Check

Help Another Look Homework Video

Games Math Games

LESSON OVERVIEW FOCUS · COHERENCE · RIGOR

FOCUS

Domain K.CC Counting and Cardinality

Cluster K.CC.A Know number names and the count sequence.

Content Standard K.CC.A.3 Write numbers from 0 to 20. Represent a number of objects with a written numeral 0–20 (with 0 representing a count of no objects). Also **K.CC.B.5**

Mathematical Practices MP.3, MP.4, MP.6, MP.8

Objective Count and write the numbers 13, 14, and 15.

Essential Understanding There is a unique symbol that goes with each number word.

Vocabulary thirteen, fourteen, fifteen

Materials Counters (or Teaching Tool 6), Number Cards 0–10 (Teaching Tool 3), Number Cards 11–20 (Teaching Tool 4)

COHERENCE

In Lesson 9-1, students learned to count and write the numbers 11 and 12. In Lesson 9-2, students will count and write 13, 14, and 15. This lesson is one in a series of counting and writing double-digit numbers.

RIGOR

This lesson emphasizes **conceptual understanding** and **procedural skill**. Students build upon their understanding of numbers and the count sequence. They also work on the procedural skill of counting as they identify how many objects are in a group.

 Watch the Listen and Look For Lesson Video.
PD

MATH ANYTIME

Daily Common Core Review

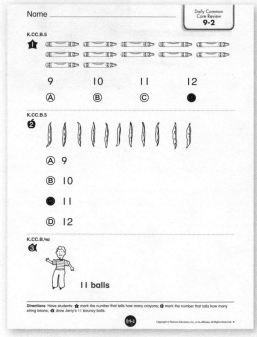

Today's Challenge

Think Use Topic 9 problems any time during this topic.

ENGLISH LANGUAGE LEARNERS

Speaking Give information using key words.

Use with the Visual Learning Bridge on Student's Edition, p. 520.

Show students 13 objects, and then draw a ten-frame on the board. Draw 10 circles in the ten-frame and 3 circles below the ten-frame. As you count, ask a student to shade in one circle on the board. Model the sentences: *"There are 13 objects and 13 circles. There are 3 more circles than 10, and that*

makes 13. I know because I can count them." Repeat with 14 and 15 objects. Ask students to say how many objects and circles there are and explain how they know.

Beginning Ask students to use the sentence stem: "There are ____ (objects) and ____ circles."

Intermediate Ask students to use the sentence stem: "I know there are ____ (objects) because ____."

Advanced Ask students to explain how they know the number of objects. Have students use complete sentences with connecting words such as *and* and *because* in their responses.

Summarize How can you explain how you know there are 13, 14, or 15 objects?

COHERENCE: Engage learners by connecting prior knowledge to new ideas.

Students use counters to count, read, and write a group of 14 objects. This prepares them for the next part of the lesson where they count, read, and write groups of 13, 14, and 15 objects.

10–15 min

Solve

 **BEFORE**

1. Pose the Solve-and-Share Problem

MP.4 Model with Math In this problem, students become familiar with multiple representations of the number 14.

Give each student 15 counters.

Say: *Carlos collected leaves to put in a scrapbook. How can Carlos show the number of leaves he collected? Use counters, and then draw them to show one way.*

2. Build Understanding

What tools do you have to show the number of leaves? [Counters] *What do you already know about ten-frames?* [If a ten-frame is filled and there are more counters below it, then there are more than 10 objects in the group.]

 DURING

3. Ask Guiding Questions As Needed

How can you find the number of leaves Carlos has? [Count the number of leaves on the scrapbook.] *What is one way to show the number of leaves Carlos has?* [Write the number 14.]

 AFTER

4. Share and Discuss Solutions

Start with students' solutions. If needed,
Solve project and analyze Charlie's work to discuss how counting 14 counters shows there are 14 leaves.

5. Transition to the Visual Learning Bridge

Counting tells how many are in a group.

When you count, the last number counted tells the number in the group.

Later in this lesson, you will learn how to count groups of 13, 14, and 15 and to write the numbers that represent those groups.

6. Extension for Early Finishers

Have students place the number card for 1 on their desk or table. Then say a number between 12 and 15 and have them place the other number card they need to make the number you said.

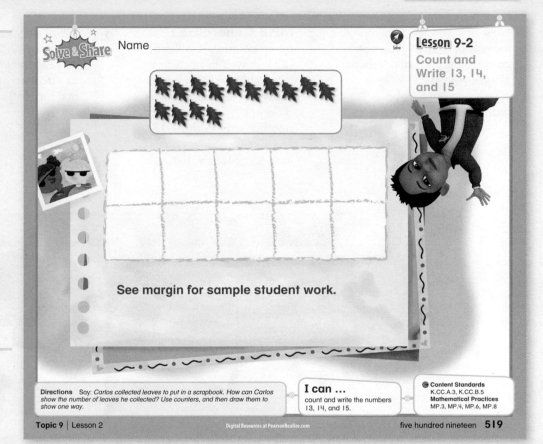

Solve & Share   Name _____

Lesson 9-2
Count and Write 13, 14, and 15

See margin for sample student work.

Directions Say: *Carlos collected leaves to put in a scrapbook. How can Carlos show the number of leaves he collected? Use counters, and then draw them to show one way.*

I can ... count and write the numbers 13, 14, and 15.

© **Content Standards** K.CC.A.3, K.CC.B.5 **Mathematical Practices** MP.3, MP.4, MP.6, MP.8

Topic 9 | Lesson 2   Digital Resources at PearsonRealize.com   five hundred nineteen **519**

Analyze Student Work

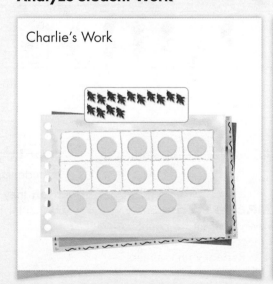

Charlie's Work

Charlie correctly places 10 counters in the ten-frame and 4 counters below the ten-frame.

Sunny's Work

Sunny places 10 counters in the ten-frame but does not put 4 counters below the ten-frame.

Learn   Glossary

The *Visual Learning Bridge* connects students' thinking in Solve & Share to important math ideas in the lesson. Use the *Visual Learning Bridge* to make these ideas explicit. Also available as a *Visual Learning Animation Plus* at PearsonRealize.com

E L L Visual Learning

How can you tell how many leaves there are? [You can count them.] *What number do you see?* [13] *Why is 13 shown?* [It tells how many leaves there are.]

MP.8 Generalize *How many counters are there?* [13] *How is this box like the first box?* [Both boxes show 13 objects.] *How is it different?* [This panel shows another way to show 13. The picture shows counters instead of leaves.]

What do you think this number will be if you trace it? [13] *Where do you start to trace the number?* [At the first top dot]

What number do you see? [13] *Why do you think this number is in this box?* [To tell how many leaves there are]

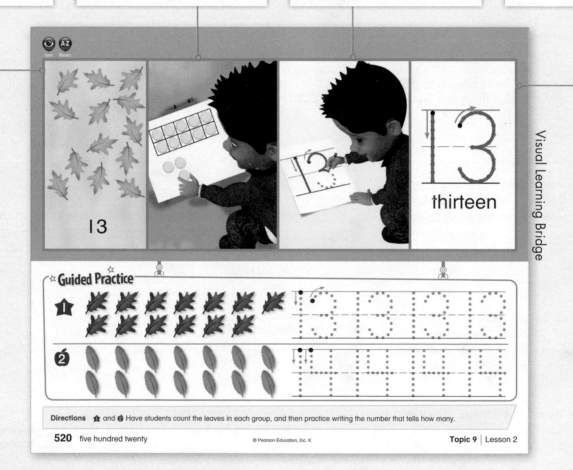

Visual Learning Bridge

☆ **Guided Practice**

Directions ⭐ and 🍂 Have students count the leaves in each group, and then practice writing the number that tells how many.

520 five hundred twenty   © Pearson Education, Inc. K   Topic 9 | Lesson 2

Complete the *Do You Understand? Show Me!* problem before starting Guided Practice.

Do You Understand? Show Me! **MP.6 Be Precise** Show a picture of a ten-frame with 10 counters drawn on it and 3 counters below it. *Which number card shows how many counters there are?* Have students hold up the number card for 13. Repeat with counters and number cards for the numbers 14 and 15.

Essential Question
Ask the following Essential Question: *Why do you write every number in a different way?* [Sample answer: Because every number has its own symbol] There is a unique symbol that goes with each number word. There are special symbols that stand for thirteen, fourteen, and fifteen. Remind students that writing numbers tells you how many objects are in a group.

Error Intervention: Item 2

If students have difficulty counting the number 14,

then they can use counters to count aloud to 14, moving 1 counter into a group for each number recited.

Tools   Assessment

✅ QUICK CHECK
Check mark indicates items for prescribing differentiation on the next page.
Items 8 and 9 are worth 1 point. Item 10 is worth up to 3 points.

20–30 min

Item 3 MP.6 Be Precise *What number can you use to represent the leaves?* [15] Have students look around the classroom or school for other representations of 15.

Items 5 and 6 If students have trouble counting the leaves, show a picture of a ten-frame with 10 counters drawn on it and 4 counters below it. *Which number card shows how many counters there are?* Have students hold up the number card for 14. Repeat with counters and the number card for the number 13.

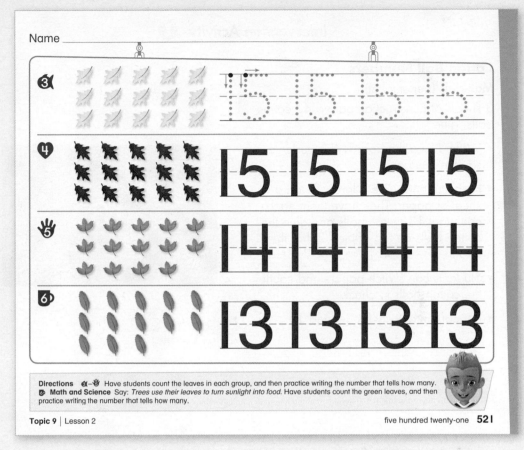

Items 7–9 MP.3 Construct Arguments Remind students that there are special symbols that stand for thirteen, fourteen, and fifteen. *How do you know how many there are in a group?* [I count the objects, and the last number I say tells how many.]

Item 10 Remind students that writing numbers tells how many are in a group. Students should draw 14 leaves. If students have difficulty drawing clearly, encourage them to pick simple shapes and draw the leaves in rows.

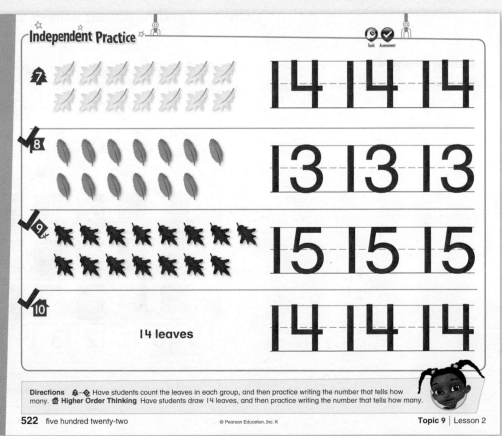

521–522

Use the **QUICK CHECK** on the previous page to prescribe differentiated instruction.

2 RtI

(I) Intervention
0–3 points on the Quick Check

(O) On-Level
4 points on the Quick Check

(A) Advanced
5 points on the Quick Check

Intervention Activity

Cotton Ball Numbers

Materials (per student)

3 sheets of construction paper, 42 cotton balls, glue

- Write *13* on the board. Ask students to say the number.

- Help students write a large 13 on a sheet of paper. Then have them each count out 13 cotton balls and glue the cotton balls on top of the 13 that they wrote.

- Students can switch papers and count the cotton balls to check.

- Repeat the activity for 14 and 15.

Reteach (I)

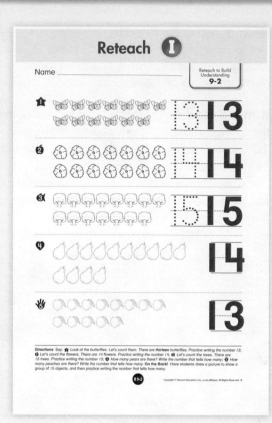

On-Level and Advanced Activity Centers (O) (A)

Center Games

Partners work together to use red and blue squares to show numbers 9 to 15.

★ On-Level

★★ Advanced

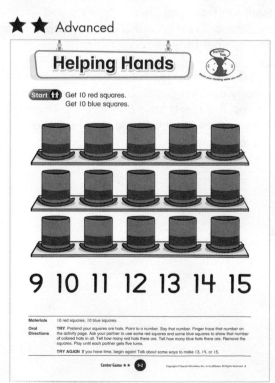

TIMING

The time allocated to Step 3 will depend on the teacher's instructional decisions and differentiation routines.

15–30 min

Help   Tools   Games

PEARSON
realize.
PearsonRealize.com

Technology Center **I** **O** **A**

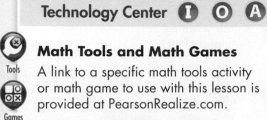

Tools

Games

Math Tools and Math Games

A link to a specific math tools activity or math game to use with this lesson is provided at PearsonRealize.com.

Leveled Assignment

I Items 1–3   **O** Items 2–4   **A** Items 3–5

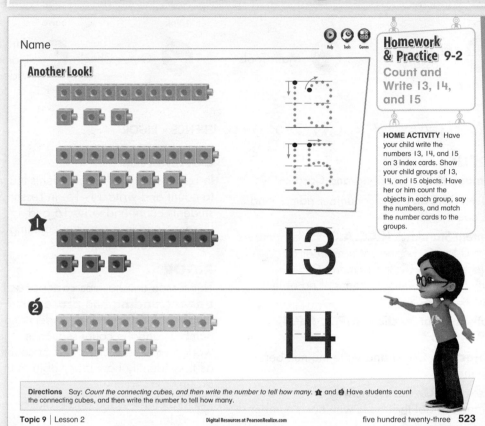

Name _____

Homework & Practice 9-2

Count and Write 13, 14, and 15

Another Look!

HOME ACTIVITY Have your child write the numbers 13, 14, and 15 on 3 index cards. Show your child groups of 13, 14, and 15 objects. Have her or him count the objects in each group, say the numbers, and match the number cards to the groups.

★ 13

② 14

Directions Say: *Count the connecting cubes, and then write the number to tell how many.* ★ and ② Have students count the connecting cubes, and then write the number to tell how many.

Topic 9 | Lesson 2   Digital Resources at PearsonRealize.com   five hundred twenty-three **523**

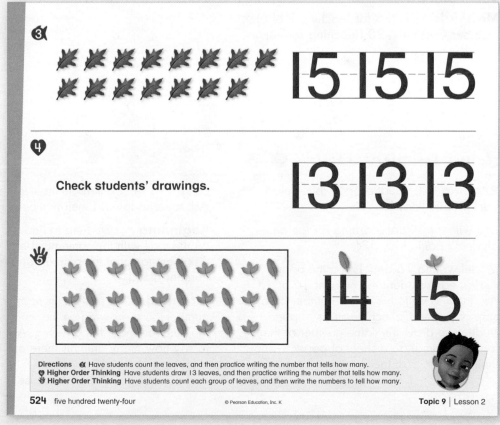

③ 15 15 15

④ **Check students' drawings.** 13 13 13

✋ 14 15

Directions ✋ Have students count the leaves, and then practice writing the number that tells how many.
Higher Order Thinking Have students draw 13 leaves, and then practice writing the number that tells how many.
Higher Order Thinking Have students count each group of leaves, and then write the numbers to tell how many.

524 five hundred twenty-four   © Pearson Education, Inc. K   Topic 9 | Lesson 2

523–524

DIGITAL RESOURCES PearsonRealize.com

 Student and Teacher eTexts
eText

 Listen and Look For Lesson Video
PD

Today's Challenge
Think

Solve and Share
Solve

 Visual Learning Animation Plus
Learn

 A-Z Animated Glossary
Glossary

 Math Tools
Tools

 Quick Check
Assessment

 Another Look Homework Video
Help

Math Games
Games

LESSON OVERVIEW FCR FOCUS • COHERENCE • RIGOR

FOCUS

Domain K.CC Counting and Cardinality

Cluster K.CC.A Know number names and the count sequence.

Content Standard K.CC.A.3 Write numbers from 0 to 20. Represent a number of objects with a written numeral 0-20 (with 0 representing a count of no objects). Also **K.CC.B.5**

Mathematical Practices MP.2, MP.4, MP.6, MP.7

Objective Count and write the numbers 16 and 17.

Essential Understanding There is a unique symbol that goes with each number word.

Vocabulary sixteen, seventeen

Materials Counters (or Teaching Tool 6), Number Cards 11–20 (Teaching Tool 4)

COHERENCE

In Lessons 9-1 and 9-2, students learned to count and write 11–15. In Lesson 9-3, students count and write 16 and 17. This lesson is one in a series of counting and writing double-digit numbers.

RIGOR

This lesson emphasizes **conceptual understanding** and **procedural skill**. Students build upon their understanding of numbers and the count sequence. They also work on the procedural skill of counting as they identify how many objects are in a group.

 Watch the Listen and Look For Lesson Video.
PD

MATH ANYTIME

Daily Common Core Review

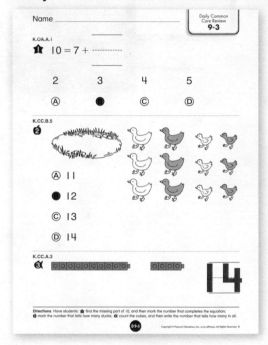

Today's Challenge

Think Use Topic 9 problems any time during this topic.

ENGLISH LANGUAGE LEARNERS ELL

Reading Use visual support to develop background knowledge.

Use with the Visual Learning Bridge on Student's Edition, p. 526.

Model writing 16 and 17 on the board. Assign each student the number 16 or 17. Ask them to write his or her number on a strip of paper. Collect the strips of paper. Ask students to draw the same number of their favorite animal on a sheet of paper to show their number. Post the drawings on a classroom wall. Distribute the number strips. Ask students to read their number strips.

Beginning Ask students to find a drawing on the wall with the same number of animals. Ask them to count the animals and read the number aloud.

Intermediate Ask students to match their numbers to a drawing on the wall and write the number under the drawing. Ask students to say how many animals there are in the drawing with the sentence frame: "This picture and number go together because ____."

Advanced Put students in pairs. Ask Student A to point to his or her number strip. Have Student B read the number and match it to a drawing on the wall. Student B should describe the picture using the number.

Summarize How do you read and write 16 and 17?

COHERENCE: Engage students by connecting prior knowledge to new ideas.
Students use counters to count, read, and write the number for a group of 16 objects. This prepares them for the next part of the lesson where they count, read, and write numbers for groups of 16 and 17 objects.

10–15 min

Solve

BEFORE

1. Pose the Solve-and-Share Problem
MP.4 Model with Math In this problem, students become familiar with multiple representations of the number 16.

Give each student 20 counters.

Say: *Jada has a collection of piggy banks. How can Carlos show the number of piggy banks Jada has? Use counters, and then draw them to show one way.*

2. Build Understanding
What are you asked to show using counters? [A way to show the number of piggy banks in the collection] *What do you already know about ten-frames?* [If a ten-frame is filled and there are more counters below it, then there are more than 10 in the group.]

DURING

3. Ask Guiding Questions As Needed
How can you find the number of piggy banks Jada has? [Touch and count the number of piggy banks.] *What tools can you use on the workmat to help you find the correct number to trace and write?* [Use the pictures of the piggy banks and the numbers that describe them.]

AFTER

4. Share and Discuss Solutions

Solve Start with students' solutions. If needed, project and analyze Kara's work to discuss how counting 16 counters shows there are 16 piggy banks.

5. Transition to the Visual Learning Bridge
Counting tells how many are in a group.

When you count, the last number counted tells the number in the group.

Later in this lesson, you will learn how to count groups of 16 and 17 and to write the numbers that represent those groups.

6. Extension for Early Finishers
Have students make a stack of 10 counters, then count on one at a time until they make 16 counters. Repeat with a stack of 10 counters and count on to 17 counters.

Solve & Share

Name _____

See margin for sample student work.

Solve

Lesson 9-3
Count and Write 16 and 17

Directions Say: *Jada has a collection of piggy banks. How can Carlos show the number of piggy banks Jada has? Use counters, and then draw them to show one way.*

I can ... count and write the numbers 16 and 17.

Content Standards K.CC.A.3, K.CC.B.5 **Mathematical Practices** MP.2, MP.4, MP.6, MP.7

Topic 9 | Lesson 3

Digital Resources at PearsonRealize.com

five hundred twenty-five **525**

Analyze Student Work

Kara's Work

Kara correctly places 10 counters in the ten-frame and 6 counters below the ten-frame.

Joel's Work

Joel places 10 counters in the ten-frame and only 5 counters below the ten-frame.

The *Visual Learning Bridge* connects students' thinking in Solve & Share to important math ideas in the lesson. Use the *Visual Learning Bridge* to make these ideas explicit. Also available as a *Visual Learning Animation Plus* at PearsonRealize.com

ELL
Visual Learning

Learn   Glossary

MP.2 Reasoning *How can you tell how many piggy banks there are?* [You can count them.] *What number do you see?* [17] *Why is 17 shown?* [It tells how many piggy banks there are.]

How many counters are there? [17] *How is this box like the first box?* [Both boxes show 17 objects.] *How is it different?* [This panel shows another way to show 17. The picture shows counters instead of piggy banks.]

What do you think this number will be if you trace it? [17] *Where do you start to trace the number?* [At the first top dot]

What number do you see? [17] *Why do you think this number is in this box?* [To tell how many piggy banks there are]

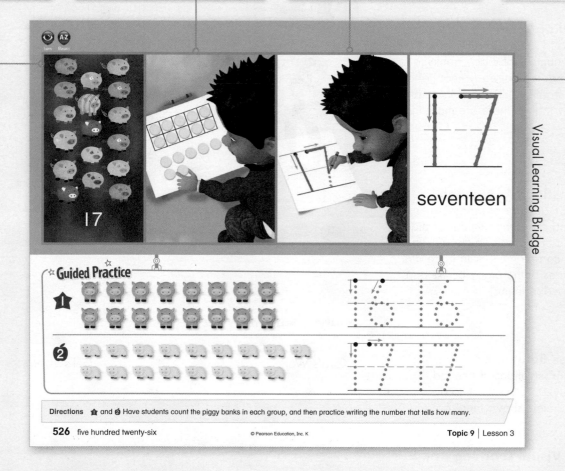

Visual Learning Bridge

Directions ★ and ② Have students count the piggy banks in each group, and then practice writing the number that tells how many.

526   five hundred twenty-six   © Pearson Education, Inc. K   **Topic 9** | Lesson 3

Complete the *Do You Understand? Show Me!* problem before starting Guided Practice.

Do You Understand? Show Me! **MP.6 Be Precise** Show a ten-frame with 10 counters on it and 6 counters in a row below it. *Which number card shows how many counters there are?* Have students hold up the number card for 16. Then show the number card for 17. Ask students to use their ten-frames to count and show 17 counters.

Essential Question

Ask the following Essential Question: *Is there another way to show how many besides drawing pictures?* [Sample answer: Yes; you can write the number.] There is a unique symbol that goes with each number word. There are special symbols that stand for sixteen and seventeen. Remind students that writing numbers tells you how many objects are in a group.

Error Intervention: Items 1–2

If students have difficulty writing the numbers 16 and 17,

then they can use full arm movements to practice writing large numbers in the air, repeating the motions until they feel confident with the shapes of the numbers. Then they can practice tracing or writing the numbers with a pencil.

✅ **QUICK CHECK**
Check mark indicates items for prescribing differentiation on the next page.
Items 8 and 9 are worth 1 point. Item 11 is worth up to 3 points.

20–30 min

Tools Assessment

Item 3 If students have difficulty, then show a picture of a ten-frame with 10 counters drawn on it and 6 counters in rows below it. *Which number card shows how many counters there are?* [The number card for 16]

Items 3–7 MP.7 Use Structure Have students look at the way the stuffed animals are organized in each item. *Do the stuffed animals line up, or are there extras in one line?* Have students count aloud to find the total number of objects in each item. Have them look for patterns in the arrangement of the stuffed animals. *Is there a pattern?* [Yes; there are 16 when the stuffed animals line up and 17 when they do not.] *How does that help you tell how many?* [It helps check my answer.]

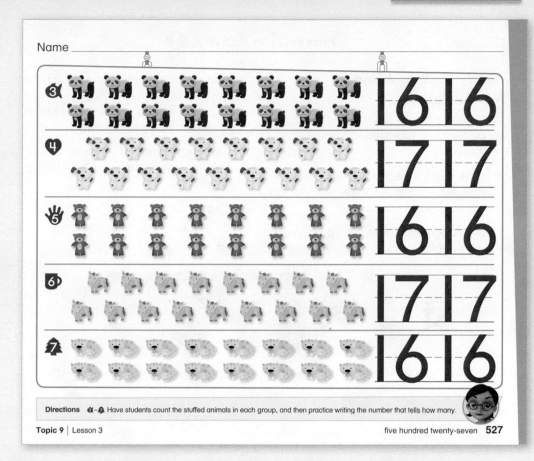

Name _____

3. 16 16
4. 17 17
5. 16 16
6. 17 17
7. 16 16

Directions 3–7 Have students count the stuffed animals in each group, and then practice writing the number that tells how many.

Topic 9 | Lesson 3   five hundred twenty-seven **527**

Items 8–10 MP.7 Use Structure Remind students that there are special symbols that stand for sixteen and seventeen. Display number cards 14 though 17 and remind students that some of these numbers were learned in a previous lesson. *Which symbol shows sixteen?* Have students pick the correct number card. Then show the number cards and have students pick the card that shows 17.

Item 11 Students can draw balls in two rows of five each, similar to a ten-frame. Then they will draw the extras below. *How many balls will you draw below if you use a ten-frame to draw 17?* [7]

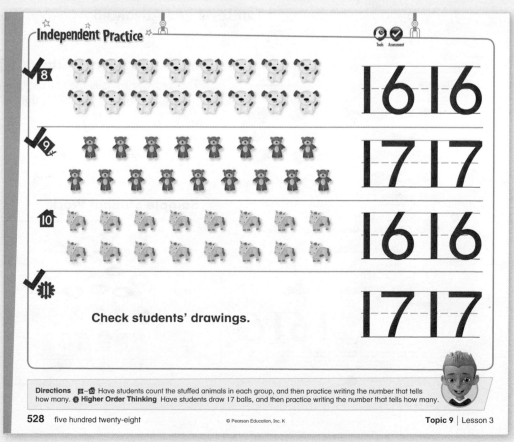

Independent Practice

8. 16 16
9. 17 17
10. 16 16

Check students' drawings.

17 17

Directions 8–10 Have students count the stuffed animals in each group, and then practice writing the number that tells how many. ✹ **Higher Order Thinking** Have students draw 17 balls, and then practice writing the number that tells how many.

528 five hundred twenty-eight   © Pearson Education, Inc. K   Topic 9 | Lesson 3

STEP 3 ASSESS AND DIFFERENTIATE

Use the **QUICK CHECK** on the previous page to prescribe differentiated instruction.

2 RtI

I Intervention
0–3 points on the Quick Check

O On-Level
4 points on the Quick Check

A Advanced
5 points on the Quick Check

Intervention Activity **I**

Sandy Seek and Find

Materials (per group)

Large tray of sand, 20 small objects such as paper clips (per student), small tray of sand

- In the large tray of sand, write the numbers 16 and 17 several times. Vary their sizes and positions.

- Ask students to count out 16 objects, and then find as many 16s as they

can in the large tray of sand and say the number aloud each time. They can use their fingers to trace the numbers already drawn in the sand.

- Then have students write 16 in their own trays and say the number each time.

- Repeat for 17.

Reteach **I**

Name _____

Reteach to Build Understanding 9-3

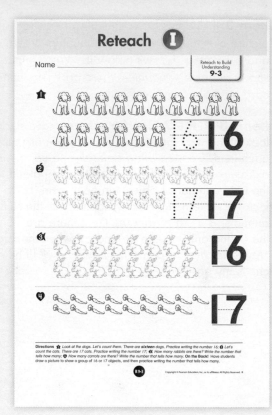

Directions ★ Look at the dogs. Let's count them. There are **sixteen** dogs. Practice writing the number 16; ❷ Let's count the cats. There are 17 cats. Practice writing the number 17; ❸ How many rabbits are there? Write the number that tells how many; ❹ How many carrots are there? Write the number that tells how many. **On the Back!** Have students draw a picture to show a group of 16 or 17 objects, and then practice writing the number that tells how many.

On-Level and Advanced Activity Centers **O** **A**

Name _____
Shelters

Math and Science Activity 9-3

❶ [mound images]

Check students' coloring.

❷ [mountain images]

16 counters

1616

Directions Say: Did you know that all living things need shelter in order to survive, no matter how big or small they are? Have students: ★ count and color 17 caves; ❷ count the ant hills, draw a group of counters with the same number, and then practice writing the number that tells how many counters. **Extension** Draw a group of 16 animal homes and another group of 17 animal homes, and then practice writing the numbers that tell how many.

Math and Science Activity **STEM**

This activity revisits the science theme, **What Can We Get From Plants?**, introduced on page 507 in the Student's Edition.

Sample Student Work

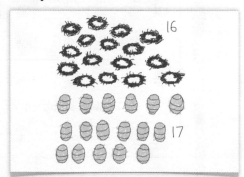

529A **Topic 9**

TIMING

The time allocated to Step 3 will depend on the teacher's instructional decisions and differentiation routines.

15–30 min

PEARSON
realize
PearsonRealize.com

Help   Tools   Games

Technology Center I O A

Tools

Games

Math Tools and Math Games

A link to a specific math tools activity or math game to use with this lesson is provided at PearsonRealize.com.

Leveled Assignment

I Items 1–3   **O** Items 1–4   **A** Items 2–5

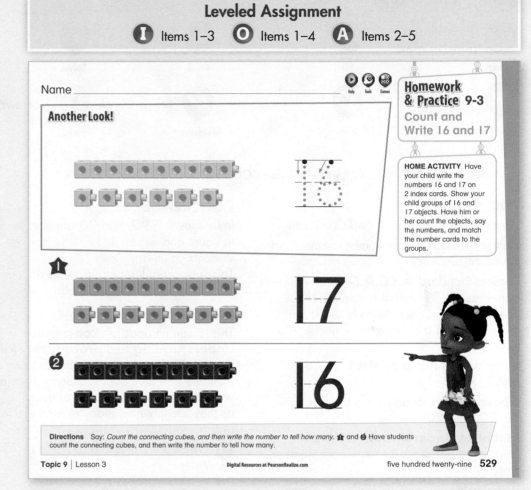

Name _____

Help Tools Games

Another Look!

Homework & Practice 9-3
Count and Write 16 and 17

HOME ACTIVITY Have your child write the numbers 16 and 17 on 2 index cards. Show your child groups of 16 and 17 objects. Have him or her count the objects, say the numbers, and match the number cards to the groups.

1

2

Directions Say: *Count the connecting cubes, and then write the number to tell how many.* ★ and ☻ Have students count the connecting cubes, and then write the number to tell how many.

Topic 9 | Lesson 3   Digital Resources at PearsonRealize.com   five hundred twenty-nine **529**

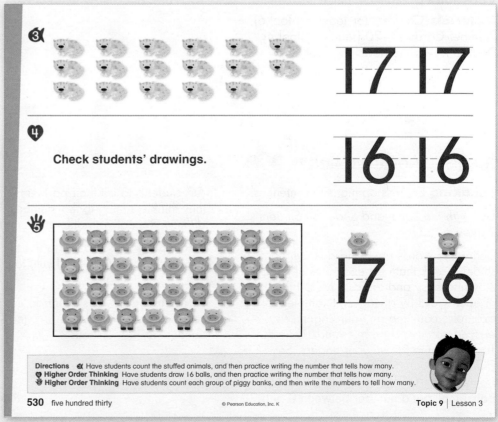

3

4

Check students' drawings.

5

Directions ☒ Have students count the stuffed animals, and then practice writing the number that tells how many. ♦ **Higher Order Thinking** Have students draw 16 balls, and then practice writing the number that tells how many. ♦ **Higher Order Thinking** Have students count each group of piggy banks, and then write the numbers to tell how many.

530 five hundred thirty   © Pearson Education, Inc. K   **Topic 9** | Lesson 3

529–530

LESSON 9-4

COUNT AND WRITE 18, 19, AND 20

LESSON OVERVIEW FCR FOCUS • COHERENCE • RIGOR

FOCUS

Domain K.CC Counting and Cardinality

Cluster K.CC.A Know number names and the count sequence.

Content Standard K.CC.A.3 Write numbers from 0 to 20. Represent a number of objects with a written numeral 0–20 (with 0 representing a count of no objects). Also **K.CC.B.5**

Mathematical Practices MP.1, MP.5, MP.7, MP.8

Objective Count and write the numbers 18, 19, and 20.

Essential Understanding There is a unique symbol that goes with each number word.

Vocabulary eighteen, nineteen, twenty

Materials Counters (or Teaching Tool 6), Number Cards 11–20 (Teaching Tool 4), Double Ten-Frame (Teaching Tool 23)

COHERENCE

In Lessons 9-1, 9-2, and 9-3, students learned to count and write 11–17. In Lesson 9-4, students count and write 18, 19, and 20. This is the final lesson in a series of counting and writing double-digit numbers.

RIGOR

This lesson emphasizes **conceptual understanding** and **procedural skill**. Students build upon their understanding of numbers and the count sequence. They also work on the procedural skill of counting as they identify how many objects are in a group.

 PD Watch the Listen and Look For Lesson Video.

MATH ANYTIME

Daily Common Core Review

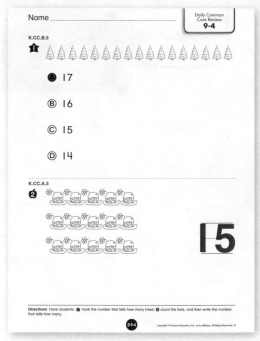

Today's Challenge

Think Use Topic 9 problems any time during this topic.

ENGLISH LANGUAGE LEARNERS ELL

Speaking Express opinions in sentences.

Use with the Solve and Share on Student's Edition p. 531.

Define the words *easy* and *difficult* for students. Ask them for examples of things they find easy and difficult. Model the use of each word by giving an example. For example, counting on your fingers, say: *It is easy to count to 5 on my hand: 1, 2, 3, 4, 5.* Try to count to 20 on your fingers. Say: *It is difficult to count to 20 on my hands because I only have 10 fingers.* Divide students into pairs. Call out a number between 0 and 20.

Ask students to tell their partners whether they think counting to that number is *easy* or *difficult*. Repeat with different numbers.

Beginning Ask students to use the sentence stem: "It is _____ (easy/difficult) to count to _____."

Intermediate Ask students to use the sentence stem: "I think it is _____ (easy/difficult) to count to _____ because _____."

Advanced Ask students to state whether they feel that counting to the number is easy or difficult. Students should explain why they feel that way.

Summarize How do you express opinions about counting to 20?

COHERENCE: Engage learners by connecting prior knowledge to new ideas.

Students use counters to count, read, and write the number for a group of 18 objects. This prepares them for the next part of the lesson where they count, read, and write numbers for groups of 18, 19, and 20 objects.

 10–15 min   Solve

BEFORE

1. Pose the Solve-and-Share Problem
MP.5 Use Appropriate Tools Strategically
In this problem, students use counters as they work to create representations of the number 18.

Give each student 20 counters.

Say: *Carlos has a collection of bird stickers in his sticker album. How can Carlos show the number of bird stickers he has? Use counters, and then draw them to show one way.*

2. Build Understanding
What are you asked to show using counters?
[The number of bird stickers in the sticker album]
What do you already know about ten-frames?
[If a ten-frame is filled, then there are at least 10 in the group.]

DURING

3. Ask Guiding Questions As Needed
What is one way to show the number of bird stickers Carlos has? [Place counters on the double ten-frame.] *What is one tool you can use on the workmat to help you find the correct number to write?* [Counters]

AFTER

4. Share and Discuss Solutions
Start with students' solutions. If needed, project and analyze Fernando's work to discuss how counting 18 counters shows there are 18 bird stickers.

5. Transition to the Visual Learning Bridge
Counting tells how many are in a group.

When you count, the last number counted tells the number in the group.

Later in this lesson, you will learn how to count groups of 19 and 20 and to write the numbers that represent those groups.

6. Extension for Early Finishers
Have students make a stack of 10 counters, and then count on from 10, 1 counter at a time, to 18 as they count aloud 10, 11, 12, ..., 18. Repeat for 19 and 20.

Solve & Share   Name _____
See margin for sample student work.

Lesson 9-4
Count and Write
18, 19, and 20

Directions Say: *Carlos has a collection of bird stickers in his sticker album. How can Carlos show the number of bird stickers he has? Use counters, and then draw them to show one way.*

I can ...
count and write the numbers 18, 19, and 20.

Content Standards
K.CC.A.3, K.CC.B.5
Mathematical Practices
MP.1, MP.5, MP.7, MP.8

Topic 9 | Lesson 4   Digital Resources at PearsonRealize.com   five hundred thirty-one **531**

Analyze Student Work

Fernando's Work

Fernando correctly places 18 counters in the double ten-frame.

Maisy's Work

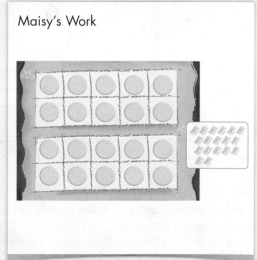

Maisy places 20 counters in the double ten-frame instead of 18 counters.

The *Visual Learning Bridge* connects students' thinking in Solve & Share to important math ideas in the lesson. Use the *Visual Learning Bridge* to make these ideas explicit. Also available as a *Visual Learning Animation Plus* at PearsonRealize.com

E L L Visual Learning

Learn   Glossary

How can you tell how many bird stickers there are? [You can count them.] *What number do you see?* [19] *Why is 19 shown?* [It tells how many bird stickers there are.]

MP.8 Generalize *How many counters are there?* [19] *How is this box like the first box?* [Both boxes show 19 objects.] *How is it different?* [This box shows another way to show 19. The picture shows counters instead of stickers.]

What do you think this number will be if you trace it? [19] *Where do you start to trace the number?* [At the first top dot]

What number do you see? [19] *Why do you think this number is in this box?* [To tell how many bird stickers there are]

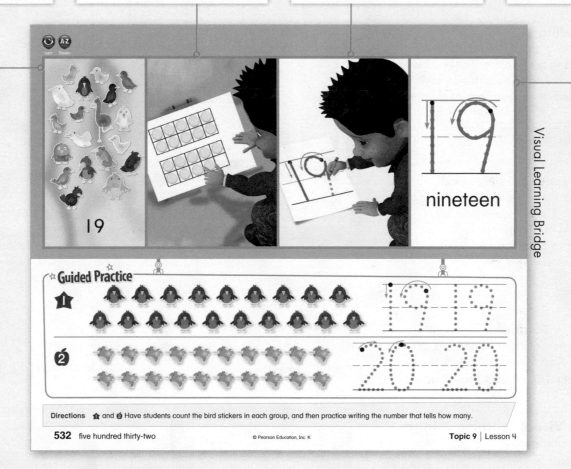

Visual Learning Bridge

nineteen

Guided Practice

① 19

② 20 20

Directions ① and ② Have students count the bird stickers in each group, and then practice writing the number that tells how many.

532 five hundred thirty-two   © Pearson Education, Inc. K   **Topic 9** | Lesson 4

Complete the *Do You Understand? Show Me!* problem before starting Guided Practice.

Do You Understand? Show Me! MP.5 Use Appropriate Tools Strategically Show a double ten-frame with 18 counters on it. *Which number card shows how many?* [18] Have students hold up the number card for 18 and say the number. Repeat, placing additional counters in the double ten-frame for the numbers 19 and 20.

Essential Question
Ask the following Essential Question: *Why does every number look different?* [Sample answer: So that we can tell them apart.] There is a unique symbol that goes with each number word. There are special symbols that stand for eighteen, nineteen, and twenty. Remind students that writing numbers tells you how many objects are in a group.

Error Intervention: Items 1 and 2

If students have difficulty counting 19 and 20 objects,

then have them count aloud as they draw 19 circles. Then have students practice counting again by putting a check mark in each circle as it is counted. Repeat for 20.

Reteaching Assign Reteaching Set A, p. 557.

☑ **QUICK CHECK**

Check mark indicates items for prescribing differentiation on the next page.
Items 9 and 10 are worth 1 point. Item 11 is worth up to 3 points.

Items 3–5 MP.1 Make Sense and Persevere
What are you trying to find? [How many stickers there are] If students lose track, have them say each number aloud as they count. *How can you keep track of objects you have counted?* [Sample answer: By placing a counter over each object as it is counted]

Items 6 and 7 If students are having trouble writing the numbers, have them use their fingers to trace the numbers on number cards.

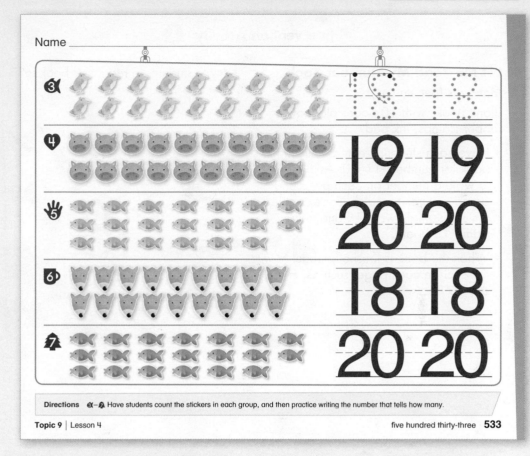

Name _____

Directions ❸–❼ Have students count the stickers in each group, and then practice writing the number that tells how many.

Topic 9 | Lesson 4   five hundred thirty-three **533**

Item 8 MP.7 Use Structure Point out to students that looking at the arrangement of a group can help you find out how many are in the group. Students can count 20 in two rows of 10. Have them practice writing this new number. This lesson is the first time they have written a 2-digit number beginning with a 2.

Items 9–11 Remind students that there are special symbols that stand for 18, 19, and 20. Show a number card for 20. *What number is this?* [20] Show the number cards for 18, 19, and 20, and ask students to identify each number.

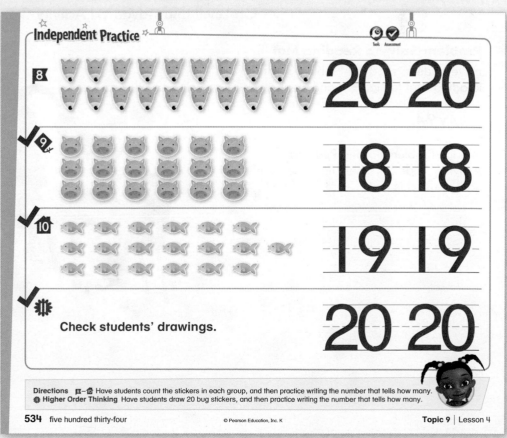

Independent Practice

Check students' drawings.

Directions ❽–❿ Have students count the stickers in each group, and then practice writing the number that tells how many.
⓫ **Higher Order Thinking** Have students draw 20 bug stickers, and then practice writing the number that tells how many.

534 five hundred thirty-four   © Pearson Education, Inc. K   Topic 9 | Lesson 4

533–534

2 RtI

Use the **QUICK CHECK** on the previous page to prescribe differentiated instruction.

I Intervention
0–3 points on the Quick Check

O On-Level
4 points on the Quick Check

A Advanced
5 points on the Quick Check

Intervention Activity **I**

Let Me Read My Number Book

Materials (per student)

Blank books with 10 pages plus cover, rubber stamps, ink pad

• Have each student create a counting book for numbers 11–20. Ask them to write a number on each page and stamp pictures to match. For example, a student might write 18 and then stamp 18 boats.

• When the book is finished, model how to describe each page, such as: *Here are 18 boats.*

• Invite students to read their book to the class.

Reteach **I**

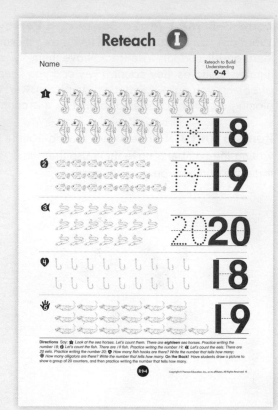

On-Level and Advanced Activity Centers **O A**

Problem-Solving Reading Mat

Have students read the Problem-Solving Reading Mat for Topic 9 and then complete Problem-Solving Reading Activity 9-4.

See the Problem-Solving Reading Activity Guide for other suggestions on how to use this mat.

TIMING

The time allocated to Step 3 will depend on the teacher's instructional decisions and differentiation routines.

15–30 min

Help   Tools   Games

Technology Center I O A

Math Tools and Math Games

Tools

Games

A link to a specific math tools activity or math game to use with this lesson is provided at PearsonRealize.com.

Leveled Assignment

I Items 1–3   O Items 2–4   A Items 3–5

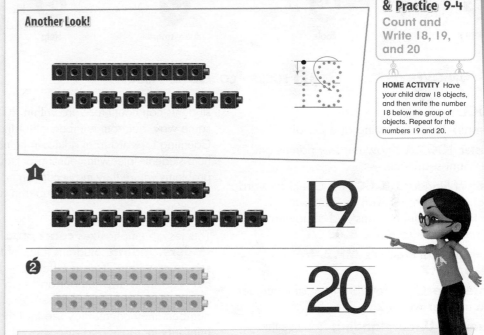

Name _____

Help Tools Games

Homework & Practice 9-4

Count and Write 18, 19, and 20

Another Look!

HOME ACTIVITY Have your child draw 18 objects, and then write the number 18 below the group of objects. Repeat for the numbers 19 and 20.

1   19

2   20

Directions Say: *Count the connecting cubes, and then write the number to tell how many.* ⭐ and 🍎 Have students count the connecting cubes, and then write the number to tell how many.

Topic 9 | Lesson 4   Digital Resources at PearsonRealize.com   five hundred thirty-five **535**

3   18 18 18

4   Check students' drawings.   19 19 19

5   18   20

Directions ❡ Have students count the stickers, and then practice writing the number that tells how many.
🟡 **Vocabulary** Have students draw **nineteen** worm stickers, and then practice writing the number that tells how many.
✋ **Higher Order Thinking** Have students count each group of stickers, and then write the numbers to tell how many.

536 five hundred thirty-six   © Pearson Education, Inc. K   Topic 9 | Lesson 4

LESSON OVERVIEW FOCUS • COHERENCE • RIGOR

FOCUS

Domain K.CC Counting and Cardinality

Cluster K.CC.A Know number names and the count sequence.

Content Standard K.CC.A.2 Count forward beginning from a given number within the known sequence (instead of having to begin at 1). Also **K.CC.B.4c**

Mathematical Practices MP.2, MP.4, MP.6, MP.7

Objective Count forward from any number to a number within 20.

Essential Understanding You use the count sequence to count from any number within 20. Numbers become greater when you count on.

Vocabulary row

Materials Counters (or Teaching Tool 6)

COHERENCE

Earlier in this topic, students extended their work with counting as they learned to count to 20. This lesson develops the understanding of the counting sequence by showing how students can count forward within 20 in the same way, but from numbers other than 1. Counting forward from a known number will help students later with counting or addition problems where they may count on from a known quantity to find the number in all.

RIGOR

This lesson emphasizes **conceptual understanding**. Students think of the count sequence within 20 in a different way; they can start from any number and then count on. As students count and then record the numbers they count, they see that these numbers increase and also show 1 more each time. Students count forward from different numbers, so they are applying this to different parts of the count sequence. This understanding can help students to count more efficiently when thinking *how many* and counting numbers of objects.

 Watch the Listen and Look For Lesson Video.
PD

MATH ANYTIME

Daily Common Core Review

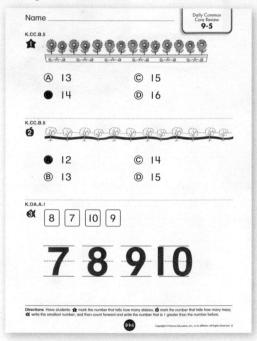

Today's Challenge

Think Use Topic 9 problems any time during this topic.

ENGLISH LANGUAGE LEARNERS

Listening Use visual support to confirm understanding.

Use with the Visual Learning Bridge on Student's Edition, p. 538.

Activity Draw a double ten-frame with numbers 1–20 written in the spaces. Put a red circle around 10. Point to 3. Say: *Listen as we count forward from 3 to 10.* Point to each number as students count. Write 3, ___, ___, ___, ___, ___, ___, 10 on the board. Point to 3. Say: *Count forward from 3 to 10 and write the missing numbers.* Point to 3

and pause at each blank. As students count forward, write the missing numbers.

Beginning Using the double ten-frame with numbers 1–20, put a red circle around 15. Point to 12. Say: *Count forward from 12 to 15.* Count forward from 12 to 15 with students. Have students work in pairs. Instruct them to take turns listening to each other count forward from 12 to 15 as they touch the numbers on the double ten-frame.

Intermediate Using the double ten-frame with numbers 1–20, put a red circle around

15. Point to 12. Say: *Listen to your partner count forward from 12 to 15, and then write the numbers.* When students have written the numbers, instruct them to read their numbers to partners.

Advanced Have students work in pairs. Have Student A identify a beginning and an end number. Student B should count forward from the beginning number, and then write the numbers, stopping at the end number. Have partners switch roles and repeat.

Summarize What is counting forward?

DEVELOP: PROBLEM-BASED LEARNING

COHERENCE: Engage students by connecting prior knowledge to new ideas.

Students set 12 counters on a ten-frame, and then add 1 more counter two times, each time recording the total number of counters. This prepares them for the next part of the lesson where they will count on from numbers other than 1.

10–15 min

Solve

BEFORE

1. Pose the Solve-and-Share Problem
MP.4 Model with Math Students write numbers to represent the number of counters on a double ten-frame. Students connect the count sequence as they see that each time they place 1 more counter, the number they have in all increases.

Distribute 14 counters to each student.

Say: *Put 12 counters on the double ten-frame. Write the number to tell how many. Put 1 more counter on the double ten-frame, and then write the number. Repeat using 1 more counter. What do you notice about the numbers? Do they get larger or smaller as you count?*

2. Build Understanding
What tools are you going to use for this problem? [Counters and a double ten-frame] *What are you asked to do?* [Put counters on the double ten-frame, count them, and write the number in all each time.]

DURING

3. Ask Guiding Questions As Needed
How many counters are you starting with? [12]
If one of the ten-frames is filled, how many counters do you know are on it? [10]

AFTER

4. Share and Discuss Solutions
Start with students' solutions. Have them share the strategies they used to solve the problem. If needed, project and analyze Martha's work to show which numbers should be recorded.

5. Transition to the Visual Learning Bridge
You have written numbers to tell how many counters. Later in this lesson, you will learn how to count forward, starting with different numbers.

6. Extension for Early Finishers
Place 2 more counters on the double ten-frame, and then write the number to tell how many. [16]

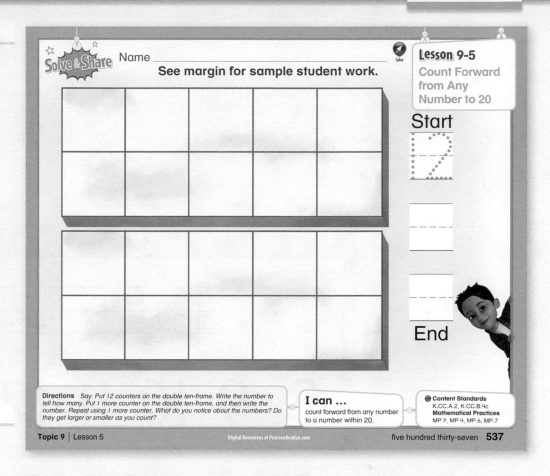

Solve & Share

Name _____

See margin for sample student work.

Lesson 9-5
Count Forward
from Any
Number to 20

Start

2

End

Directions Say: Put 12 counters on the double ten-frame. Write the number to tell how many. Put 1 more counter on the double ten-frame, and then write the number. Repeat using 1 more counter. What do you notice about the numbers? Do they get larger or smaller as you count?

I can ... count forward from any number to a number within 20.

Content Standards K.CC.A.2, K.CC.B.4c **Mathematical Practices** MP.2, MP.4, MP.6, MP.7

Topic 9 | Lesson 5

Digital Resources at PearsonRealize.com

five hundred thirty-seven **537**

Analyze Student Work

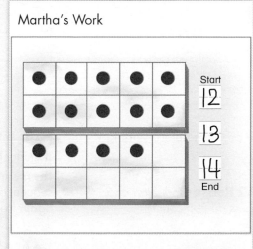

Martha's Work

Start 12
13
14 End

Carl's Work

Start 12
14
15 End

Martha counts and writes the correct numbers to tell how many each time. She recognizes that the numbers increase as she counts, and that she can count on from her previous number.

Carl places 1 more counter each time, but miscounts when finding how many, counting 1 counter twice. He does not connect placing 1 more counter to counting 1 more number. Carl recognizes the numbers increase each time he counts.

DEVELOP: VISUAL LEARNING

The *Visual Learning Bridge* connects students' thinking in Solve & Share to important math ideas in the lesson. Use the *Visual Learning Bridge* to make these ideas explicit. Also available as a *Visual Learning Animation Plus* at PearsonRealize.com

Items are in a row when they are arranged in a line side by side. This chart shows two rows of numbers. What numbers are on the top row? [1 to 10] *What numbers are on the bottom row?* [11 to 20] *Which of the numbers are you counting forward from?* [8] *Which number are you counting to?* [13] *What happens when you run out of numbers on the top row to count?* [You move to the bottom row and continue counting on left to right.]

MP.7 Use Structure *Did you count 13 numbers to get to 13?* [No] *Why not?* [I started counting from 8, so I only counted the numbers from 8 to 13.] *Which numbers did you count?* [8, 9, 10, 11, 12, 13] *What do you notice about the numbers as you count?* [Sample answer: Each number I count is 1 greater than the number before it.]

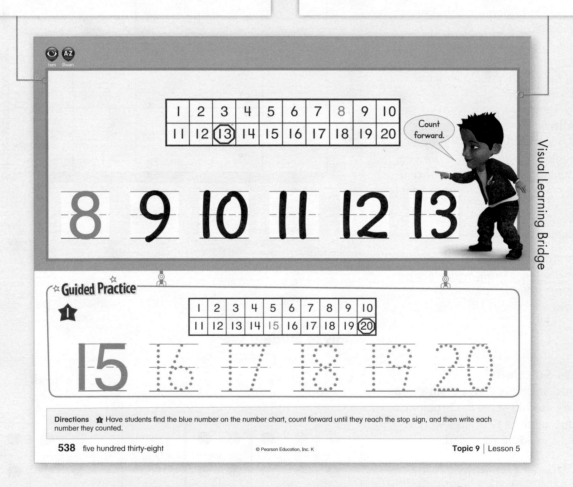

Visual Learning Bridge

Directions ★ Have students find the blue number on the number chart, count forward until they reach the stop sign, and then write each number they counted.

538 five hundred thirty-eight   © Pearson Education, Inc. K   **Topic 9** | Lesson 5

Complete the *Do You Understand? Show Me!* problem before starting Guided Practice.

Do You Understand? Show Me! MP.2 Reasoning *Start at 6. Count forward until you reach 11. What numbers do you count?* [6, 7, 8, 9, 10, 11]

 Ask the following Essential Question: *When you count from one number to another, which numbers do you count?* [Sample answer: I will count the numbers from the start number to the end number.]

Error Intervention: Item 1

If students count from 1 instead of from 15,

then explain how they can count part of the same count sequence. Use the chart to count with students from 1 to 20, then again from 15 to 20. *Both times we counted the numbers 15, 16, 17, 18, 19, and 20. The second time we just started with 15.*

1 RtI **Reteaching** Assign Reteaching Set B, p. 557.

☑ **QUICK CHECK**

Check mark indicates items for prescribing differentiation on the next page.
Items 5 and 6 are each worth 1 point. Item 8 is worth up to 3 points.

 20–30 min

Tools **Assessment**

Items 2–4 *What number will you count from?* [The blue number in the number chart] *When will you stop counting?* [When I reach the number in the stop sign in the number chart] *What numbers will you write?* [Each of the numbers I count]

Item 4 MP.7 Use Structure When students have completed Item 4, have them look at their completed page. Emphasize counting from any number within the count sequence. *Each of the items has different numbers but they are different parts of the same count sequence 1–20. Because you started counting from different numbers, you stopped at different numbers too.*

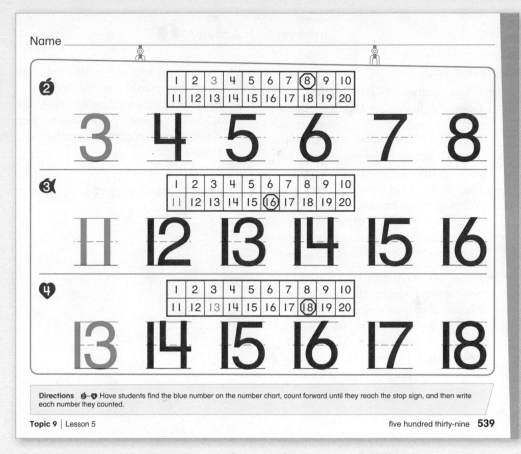

Name _____

1	2	3	4	5	6	7	⑧	9	10
11	12	13	14	15	16	17	18	19	20

❷ 3 4 5 6 7 8

1	2	3	4	5	6	7	8	9	10
11	12	13	14	15	⑯	17	18	19	20

❸ 11 12 13 14 15 16

1	2	3	4	5	6	7	8	9	10
11	12	13	14	15	16	17	⑱	19	20

❹ 13 14 15 16 17 18

Directions ❷–❹ Have students find the blue number on the number chart, count forward until they reach the stop sign, and then write each number they counted.

Topic 9 | Lesson 5

five hundred thirty-nine **539**

Items 5–8 Explain to students that the number chart can be used to help with all the items on this page, if needed. *You can find the number to count from on the number chart.* If students do use the number chart, some may need reminding, particularly for Items 5 and 6, that they count along the top row and then continue from the beginning of the next row.

Item 8 MP.6 Be Precise Students need to carefully consider the parameters of the problem. The number they pick must be within a certain range and the amount of spaces to write numbers shows how many they need to count forward. Compare different answers. Discuss similarities and differences. *Even though you picked different numbers to start with, each of the numbers you counted is 1 greater than the number before it.*

Coherence Item 8 gives students the opportunity to apply their understanding of counting on from a number. Understanding the concept of counting on from a given number, rather than counting from 1 each time, will enhance students' fluency in addition and subtraction problems in Grade 1.

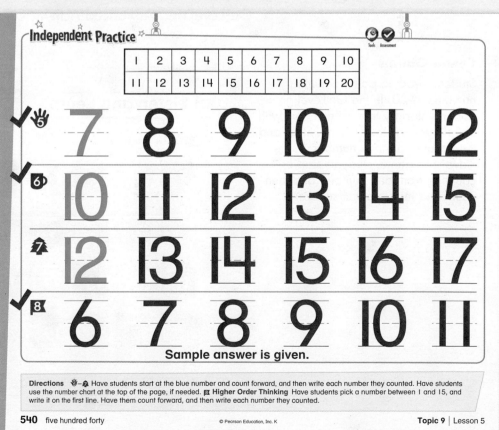

Independent Practice ☆

Tools **Assessment**

1	2	3	4	5	6	7	8	9	10
11	12	13	14	15	16	17	18	19	20

✓ **✋5** 7 8 9 10 11 12

✓ **6** 10 11 12 13 14 15

🌲7 12 13 14 15 16 17

✓ **8** 6 7 8 9 10 11

Sample answer is given.

Directions ✋–🌲 Have students start at the blue number and count forward, and then write each number they counted. Have students use the number chart at the top of the page, if needed. **8 Higher Order Thinking** Have students pick a number between 1 and 15, and write it on the first line. Have them count forward, and then write each number they counted.

540 five hundred forty

© Pearson Education, Inc. K

Topic 9 | Lesson 5

STEP 3 ASSESS AND DIFFERENTIATE

Use the **QUICK CHECK** on the previous page to prescribe differentiated instruction.

(I) Intervention
0–3 points on the Quick Check

(O) On-Level
4 points on the Quick Check

(A) Advanced
5 points on the Quick Check

Intervention Activity (I)

Count on.

- Write numbers 1–20 on the board. Count each number together. Draw a circle around 15. *What number comes just after 15 when we count?* [16] *We can count in the same way, but starting from different numbers too.* Start at 15, and then count to 20. *What number came just after 15 when I counted?* [16] *The order of the count sequence did not change, but I chose to start counting at a different number.*

- Erase the circle around 15 and circle one of the other numbers on the board. Explain that you will say this first number and then students will count forward from it, each student saying one number in turn. Pick a number that will end the count at 20 or less.

- As students become more confident, circle one number on the board and draw a square around another. Ask a student to count from the starting circled number and stop at the number with the square.

1 2 3 4 5 6 7 8 9 10 11 12 13 14 ⑮ 16 17 18 19 20

Reteach (I)

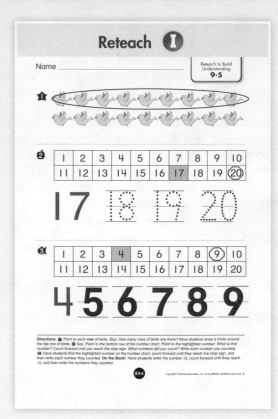

On-Level and Advanced Activity Centers (O) (A)

Center Games

Students work in pairs, counting numbers 1–20. In the On-Level game, students start by tracing numbers with their fingers as they are counted, and then count from any number. In the Advanced game, students start by counting from any number, and then count and make sets of squares.

★ On-Level

★★ Advanced

TIMING

The time allocated to Step 3 will depend on the teacher's instructional decisions and differentiation routines.

15–30 min

 Help   Tools   Games

Technology Center

Math Tools and Math Games

A link to a specific math tools activity or math game to use with this lesson is provided at PearsonRealize.com.

Leveled Assignment

I Items 1–2   **O** Items 1–3   **A** Items 1–3

Name _____

Help Tools Games

Another Look!

Homework & Practice 9-5

Count Forward from Any Number to 20

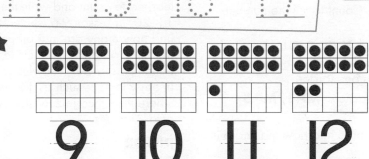

H 5 6 7

HOME ACTIVITY Pick a start number between 1 and 15. Have your child write the next four numbers. Repeat using different numbers.

1

9 10 11 12

Directions Say: *The first double ten-frame shows 14 counters. The second double ten-frame shows 1 more counter. Count the counters in each double ten-frame, and then write the numbers to tell how many. Count forward to say each number you wrote.* ★ Have students count the counters in each double ten-frame, and then write the numbers to tell how many. Then have them count forward to say each number they wrote.

Topic 9 | Lesson 5   Digital Resources at PearsonRealize.com   five hundred forty-one **541**

2

13 14 15 16

3

17 18 19 20

Directions ② Have students count the counters in each double ten-frame, and then write the numbers to tell how many. Then have them count forward to say each number they wrote. ③ **Higher Order Thinking** Have students look at the counters and the number given and find the pattern. Then have them draw the missing counters in each double ten-frame, and then write the numbers to tell how many. Have students count forward to say each number they wrote.

542 five hundred forty-two   © Pearson Education, Inc. K   Topic 9 | Lesson 5

LESSON 9-6

COUNT TO FIND HOW MANY

DIGITAL RESOURCES PearsonRealize.com

 eText Student and Teacher eTexts

PD Listen and Look For Lesson Video

 Think Today's Challenge

 Solve Solve and Share

 Learn Visual Learning Animation Plus

 Glossary Animated Glossary

 Tools Math Tools

Assessment Quick Check

Help Another Look Homework Video

 Games Math Games

LESSON OVERVIEW **FCR** FOCUS • COHERENCE • RIGOR

MATH ANYTIME

FOCUS

Domain K.CC Counting and Cardinality

Cluster K.CC.B Count to tell the number of objects.

Content Standard K.CC.B.5 Understand that each successive number name refers to a quantity that is one larger.

Mathematical Practices MP.1, MP.5, MP.7, MP.8

Objective Count to find how many are in a group.

Essential Understanding Counting tells how many are in a set, regardless of their arrangement or the order in which they were counted. The last number said when counting a set is the total. Counting is cumulative.

Materials Counters (or Teaching Tool 6)

COHERENCE

In Lessons 9-1, 9-2, 9-3, and 9-4, students learned to count and write the numbers 11–20. In Lesson 9-6, students count to find how many are in a group arranged in a line, an array, or a circle. This lesson builds on students' knowledge learned in early lessons such as 1-2 and 1-5 where they recognized groups in different arrangements.

RIGOR

This lesson emphasizes **conceptual understanding** and **procedural skill**. Students build upon their understanding of numbers and the count sequence. They also work on the procedural skill of counting as they identify how many objects are in a group.

 PD Watch the Listen and Look For Lesson Video.

Daily Common Core Review

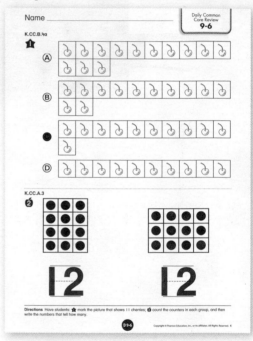

Today's Challenge

 Think Use Topic 9 problems any time during this topic.

ENGLISH LANGUAGE LEARNERS **ELL**

Reading Use visual support to develop vocabulary.

Use with Visual Learning Bridge on Student's Edition, p. 544.

Have students work in pairs. Give each pair 20 counters. Ask students to write down any number between 0 and 20 on a sheet of paper and exchange papers with their partners.

Beginning Have Student A read Student B's number and show the number with counters.

Ask students to tell the number using the sentence stem: "There are ____ counters." Have partners check each other's work.

Intermediate Ask Student A to read Student B's number and show it with counters. Have students check each other's work by grouping the counters. Ask them to explain how they checked their partner's work.

Advanced Give students 20 more counters. Have Student A read Student B's number, and then show 2 sets of counters: one with the correct number, and one with another

number. After students receive their papers, ask them to identify the set that correctly shows the number they wrote and explain how they knew which was correct.

Summarize How can you use drawings to show numbers you read?

DEVELOP: PROBLEM-BASED LEARNING

STEP 1

Solve

COHERENCE: Engage students by connecting prior knowledge to new ideas.

Students recognize that the number of objects does not change when they are rearranged or counted in another order. This prepares them for the next part of the lesson where they continue to identify and count objects in different arrangements.

10–15 min

 BEFORE

1. Pose the Solve-and-Share Problem
MP.5 Use Appropriate Tools Strategically
In this problem, students use tools to represent and communicate the number of cherries on each tray.

Give each student 25 counters.

Say: *Daniel has 13 cherries on a tray. Jada has 11 cherries on a tray. How can you show this? Use counters to show the cherries on the trays, and then draw the pictures. How can you tell that your drawings are correct?*

2. Build Understanding
What are you asked to show? [The number of cherries Daniel and Jada each have] *What do you know?* [Daniel has 13 cherries and Jada has 11 cherries.]

 **DURING**

3. Ask Guiding Questions As Needed
What should you do first? [Place 13 counters on Daniel's tray and 11 counters on Jada's tray.] *How can you use the counters to help you draw the cherries?* [Sample answer: Trace each counter to make sure I have the correct number of cherries on each tray. Then remove the counters.]

 AFTER

4. Share and Discuss Solutions
Start with students' solutions. If needed, project and analyze Benito's work to discuss the multiple representations for the number. Focus on the idea that the cherries can be counted in a variety of ways, yet the number of cherries does not change.

5. Transition to the Visual Learning Bridge
When you count, the last number counted tells the total in the group.

Later in this lesson, you will learn that the arrangement of objects in a group does not change the number of objects in the group.

6. Extension for Early Finishers
Give students 40 counters. Have them show 2 different ways to show 15 with the counters. Have them repeat with two different ways to show 20.

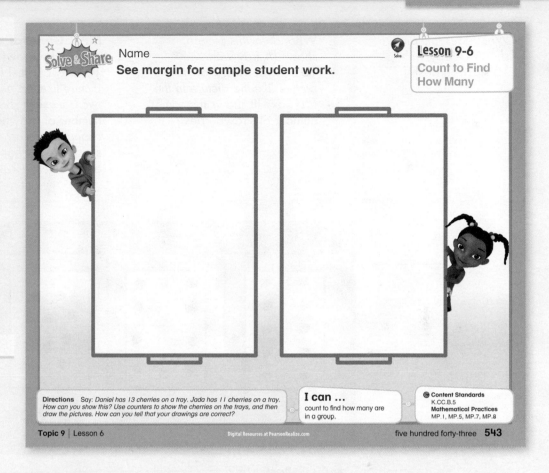

Solve & Share Name _____
See margin for sample student work.

Lesson 9-6
Count to Find How Many

Directions Say: Daniel has 13 cherries on a tray. Jada has 11 cherries on a tray. How can you show this? Use counters to show the cherries on the trays, and then draw the pictures. How can you tell that your drawings are correct?

I can … count to find how many are in a group.

Content Standards K.CC.B.5 Mathematical Practices MP.1, MP.5, MP.7, MP.8

Topic 9 | Lesson 6   Digital Resources at PearsonRealize.com   five hundred forty-three **543**

Analyze Student Work

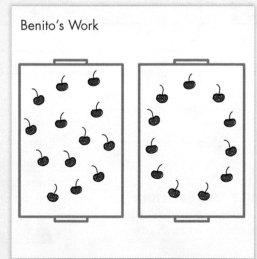

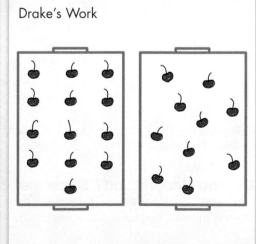

Benito correctly draws an arrangement of 13 cherries for Daniel and an arrangement of 11 cherries for Jada. He explains that he knows his drawings are correct because he counted each cherry.

Drake correctly draws an arrangement of 13 cherries for Daniel, but he draws an arrangement of 10 cherries for Jada instead of 11 cherries. Because he did not organize his arrangement of Jada's cherries, he incorrectly states that he has the correct quantity.

543

DEVELOP: VISUAL LEARNING

The *Visual Learning Bridge* connects students' thinking in Solve & Share to important math ideas in the lesson. Use the *Visual Learning Bridge* to make these ideas explicit. Also available as a *Visual Learning Animation Plus* at PearsonRealize.com

Learn   Glossary

What does this picture show? [A tray with 10 strawberries]

What does this picture show? [A tray with 10 strawberries] *How is this picture like the picture in the first box?* [It shows the same number of strawberries.]

MP.8 Generalize *What does this picture show?* [A tray with 10 strawberries] *How is this picture like the pictures in the first two boxes?* [It shows the same number of strawberries.] *Does changing the arrangement of the strawberries change the number of strawberries?* [No]

How many strawberries are in each picture? [10] *How can we check our answer?* [Count the strawberries in each picture.]

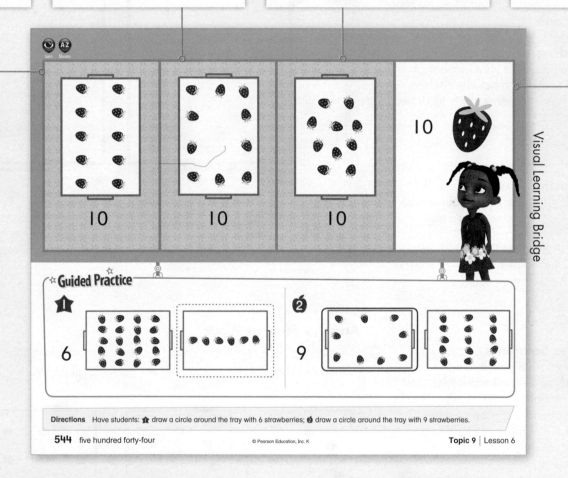

Visual Learning Bridge

Directions Have students: ★ draw a circle around the tray with 6 strawberries; ✿ draw a circle around the tray with 9 strawberries.

544 five hundred forty-four   © Pearson Education, Inc. K   **Topic 9** | Lesson 6

Complete the *Do You Understand? Show Me!* problem before starting Guided Practice.

Do You Understand? Show Me! MP.7 Use Structure

How can we arrange objects to make them easier to count? [Place objects in rows that have the same number of objects in each row.]

Ask the following Essential Question: *How do you know the number of objects does not change when you rearrange the objects?* [When I count the objects, the last number tells how many objects.] While counting tells how many objects are in a set, regardless of their arrangement, it is much easier to count when the objects are arranged. Consistent rows give a visual representation of the objects.

Error Intervention: Item 2

If students have difficulty counting the strawberries,

then have them place a counter on each strawberry, and then line the counters up to count.

Reteaching Assign Reteaching Set C, p. 558.

Tools   Assessment

✓ QUICK CHECK

Check mark indicates items for prescribing differentiation on the next page.
Items 8 and 9 are worth 1 point. Item 10 is worth up to 3 points.

20–30 min

Item 3 With practice, students develop number sense to easily identify the tray with 18 strawberries. When one number is much larger, the difference is easier to see without counting.

Item 4 MP.1 Make Sense and Persevere
What are you asked to find? [The groups with 15 bugs] The circular arrangements are trickier for students. Have them take the time to do actual counting. There are two representations that show 15 bugs. One group is closer together so it may seem visually as though there are fewer bugs.

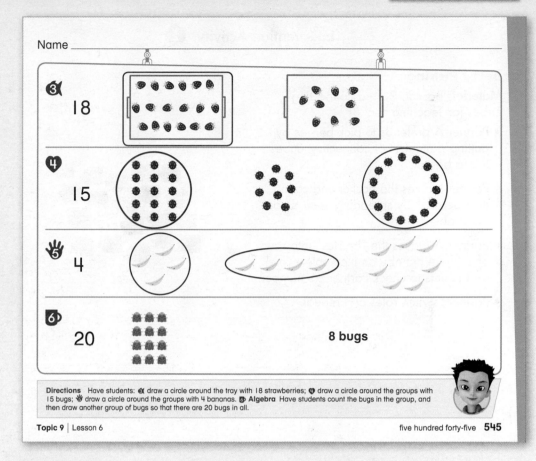

Name _____

3 18

4 15

5 4

6 20   8 bugs

Directions Have students: **3** draw a circle around the tray with 18 strawberries; **4** draw a circle around the groups with 15 bugs; **5** draw a circle around the groups with 4 bananas. **6 Algebra** Have students count the bugs in the group, and then draw another group of bugs so that there are 20 bugs in all.

Topic 9 | Lesson 6   five hundred forty-five **545**

Item 8 Since there is not much difference between the 2 flowers, students may need to count several times to ensure they are correct.

Item 10 MP.5 Use Appropriate Tools Strategically As they draw, students will need to count to know how many they have. An arrangement or organized drawing could help them keep track. To check their work, students can use 19 counters, placing the counters on top of their drawings to make sure there are 19 in each picture.

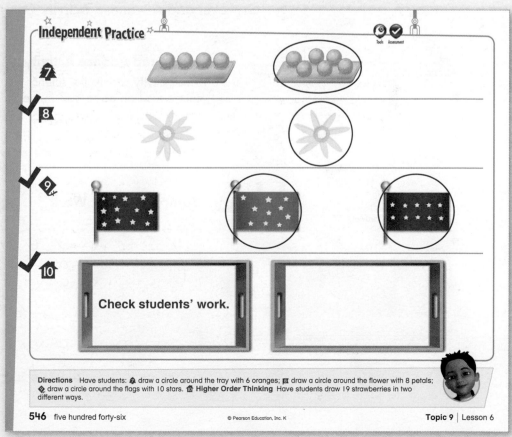

Independent Practice   Tools Assessment

7

8

9

10   Check students' work.

Directions Have students: **7** draw a circle around the tray with 6 oranges; **8** draw a circle around the flower with 8 petals; **9** draw a circle around the flags with 10 stars. **10 Higher Order Thinking** Have students draw 19 strawberries in two different ways.

546 five hundred forty-six   © Pearson Education, Inc. K   Topic 9 | Lesson 6

ASSESS AND DIFFERENTIATE

STEP 3

Use the **QUICK CHECK** on the previous page to prescribe differentiated instruction.

2 RtI

I Intervention
0–3 points on the Quick Check

O On-Level
4 points on the Quick Check

A Advanced
5 points on the Quick Check

Intervention Activity I

Berry Picking

Materials Basket, 20 red connecting cubes (or Teaching Tool 8)

• Partner A pretends to pick berries by putting a number of connecting cubes into a basket.

• Partner B takes the basket and counts the "berries" by spreading them all out on a table.

• Partner A places the "berries" into rows of 5 (there may be an incomplete row) and counts to check Partner B's number.

• Partners switch roles and repeat.

Reteach I

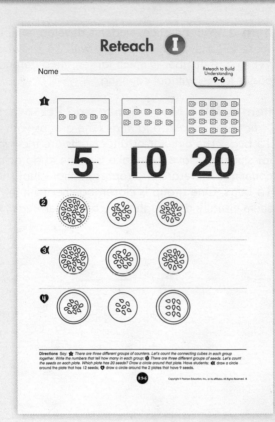

On-Level and Advanced Activity Centers O A

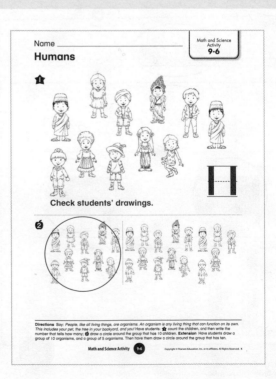

Math and Science Activity STEM

This activity revisits the science theme, What Can We Get From Plants?, introduced on page 507 in the Student's Edition.

Sample Student Work

TIMING
The time allocated to Step 3 will depend on the teacher's instructional decisions and differentiation routines.

15–30 min

 Help

 Tools

 Games

PEARSON
realize.
PearsonRealize.com

Technology Center I O A

Math Tools and Math Games

A link to a specific math tools activity or math game to use with this lesson is provided at PearsonRealize.com.

Leveled Assignment
I Items 1–3   O Items 2–4   A Items 3–5

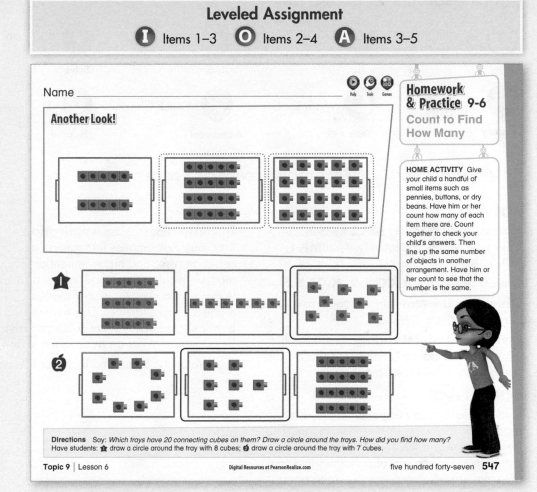

Name _____

Help Tools Games

Homework & Practice 9-6
Count to Find How Many

Another Look!

HOME ACTIVITY Give your child a handful of small items such as pennies, buttons, or dry beans. Have him or her count how many of each item there are. Count together to check your child's answers. Then line up the same number of objects in another arrangement. Have him or her count to see that the number is the same.

Directions Say: Which trays have 20 connecting cubes on them? Draw a circle around the trays. How did you find how many? Have students: ★ draw a circle around the tray with 8 cubes; ❷ draw a circle around the tray with 7 cubes.

Topic 9 | Lesson 6   Digital Resources at PearsonRealize.com   five hundred forty-seven **547**

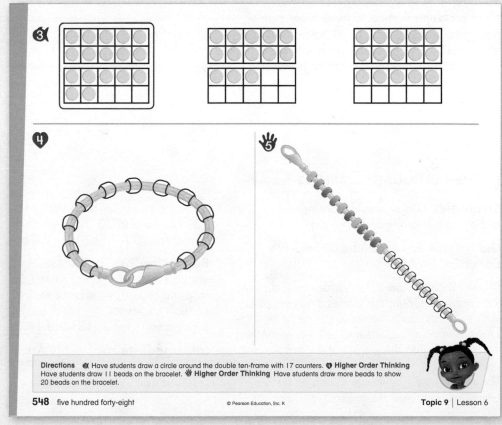

Directions ❸ Have students draw a circle around the double ten-frame with 17 counters. ❹ **Higher Order Thinking** Have students draw 11 beads on the bracelet. ❺ **Higher Order Thinking** Have students draw more beads to show 20 beads on the bracelet.

548 five hundred forty-eight   © Pearson Education, Inc. K   Topic 9 | Lesson 6

547–548

REASONING

DIGITAL RESOURCES PearsonRealize.com

 Student and Teacher eTexts eText

 Listen and Look For Lesson Video PD

 Today's Challenge Think

Solve and Share Solve

 Visual Learning Animation Plus Learn

Math Practices Animations MP

 A-Z Animated Glossary Glossary

 Math Tools Tools

 Quick Check Assessment

Another Look Homework Video Help

Math Games Games

LESSON OVERVIEW **F C R** FOCUS • COHERENCE • RIGOR

FOCUS

Mathematical Practices MP.2 Reason abstractly and quantitatively. Also **MP.1, MP.3, MP.4**

Content Standards K.CC.A.2, K.CC.B.5

Objective Use reasoning to count and write numbers to the number 20.

Essential Understanding Good math thinkers know how to think about words and numbers to solve problems.

COHERENCE

Students have many opportunities to use reasoning, including earlier in this topic. This lesson focuses on the Thinking Habits that can help to reason about problem situations. Students use what they have learned about counting as they evaluate given answers to word problems that could have more than one correct answer. Focus on having students explain why their answers work with the criteria and identifying why there is more than one correct answer.

RIGOR

This lesson emphasizes **application**. Rigorous mathematics instruction calls for the selection, use, and management of multiple mathematical practices. All of the problems in this lesson elicit the use of multiple mathematical practices. Use the thinking habits shown in the Solve & Share task to help focus thinking on MP.2 in the lesson.

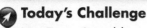 Watch the Listen and Look For Lesson Video.

MATH ANYTIME

Daily Common Core Review

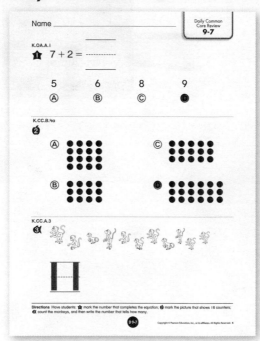

Today's Challenge
Think Use Topic 9 problems any time during this topic.

ENGLISH LANGUAGE LEARNERS **B L L**

Strategies Use strategic learning techniques: drawings/illustrations.

Use with the *Solve & Share* on Student's Edition, p. 549.

Draw 12 circles on a flat surface and display 14 counters. Count the circles and counters with students. Say: *I want to put some or all of the counters in circles.* One-by-one, move the counters into the circles. Ask: *Are there enough circles for 1 counter (7 counters, 9 counters, 12 counters)?* When all circles are filled, ask: *Are there enough circles for*

all of the counters? [No] Write 10, 11, 12, 13, 14. Point to 10. Ask: *Are there enough circles for 10 (11, 12, 13, 14) counters?*

Beginning Point to 10. Ask: *Are there enough circles for 10 counters?* Students will respond using the sentence stem: "There are enough circles for ___ counters." Continue the process for 11, 12, 13, and 14.

Intermediate Point to 11. Ask: *Are there enough circles for 11 counters?* Students will respond using the sentence stem: "There are

enough circles for ___ counters because ___." Continue the process for 12, 13, and 14.

Advanced Write 10, 11, 12, 13, and 14. Ask students to explain to partners how they know there are enough circles for 10, 11, and 12 counters. Ask partner groups to draw 15 circles. Distribute 20 counters to each partner group. Ask: *Can some or all of the counters go in the circles?* Partners will determine how many counters can go in the circles.

Summarize Why is there more than one answer?

COHERENCE: Engage students by connecting prior knowledge to new ideas.
Students circle all possible answers to a counting word problem and explain why there is more than one potential answer. This prepares them for the next part of the lesson where they will work with other word problems with multiple possible answers.

10–15 min

Solve

 BEFORE

1. Pose the Solve-and-Share Problem

MP.2 Reasoning Students count objects to identify answers to a word problem. They use reasoning to think about how the answer choices relate to the information in the problem. Students consider this context to decide which of the answers are possible and which are not.

Say: *Carlos wants to put some or all of the eggs in the carton. Draw a circle around all the numbers that tell how many eggs he could put in the carton. Explain why there could be more than one answer.*

Tell students to think about these Thinking Habits as they solve the problem.

What do the numbers stand for?

How are the numbers in the problem related?

2. Build Understanding

What do you need to find? [The numbers that tell how many eggs Carlos could put in the carton] *What do you know?* [He wants to put some or all of the eggs in the carton; the numbers that tell how many eggs: 10, 11, 12, 13, 14]

 **DURING**

3. Ask Guiding Questions As Needed

How many spaces for eggs are there in the carton? [12] *Does Carlos have to use every space in the carton?* [No] *Every egg?* [No]

 AFTER

4. Share and Discuss Solutions

Start with students' solutions. Have them share the strategies used to solve the problem. If needed, project and analyze Jonathan's work to see the possible answers.

5. Transition to the Visual Learning Bridge

You chose the numbers that show how many eggs Carlos could put in the carton and explained why. Later in this lesson, you will count to find possible answers for other word problems.

6. Extension for Early Finishers

Could Carlos put 9 eggs in the carton? [Yes] *Explain why or why not.* [Sample answer: Carlos can use some of his 14 eggs. There are 9 spaces in the carton. Carlos has 9 eggs.]

Solve & Share

Name _____

See margin for sample student work.

10 11 12 13 14

Directions Say: Carlos wants to put some or all of the eggs in the carton. Draw a circle around all the numbers that tell how many eggs he could put in the carton. Explain why there could be more than one answer.

I can ... use reasoning to count and write numbers to the number 20.

Math Practices and Problem Solving
Lesson 9-7
Reasoning

Mathematical Practices
MP.2 Also MP.1, MP.3, MP.4
Content Standards
K.CC.A.2, K.CC.B.5

Topic 9 | Lesson 7   Digital Resources at PearsonRealize.com   five hundred forty-nine **549**

Analyze Student Work

Jonathan's Work	Yasmin's Work
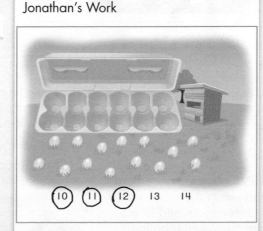	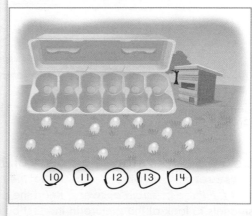

Jonathan circles 10, 11, and 12. He shares his reasoning by explaining that there are only 12 spaces in the carton, so Carlos cannot use 13 or 14 eggs. Jonathan identifies there is more than one answer because of the clue in the problem that Carlos wants to use *some* of his eggs, so any of the given numbers 12 or less will fit.

Yasmin circles all the numbers, explaining that she can count each of these numbers of eggs. Yasmin says there is more than one answer because Carlos has 14 eggs and the other numbers all come before 14 in the count sequence. Yasmin has not considered the information that the carton has only 12 spaces.

The *Visual Learning Bridge* connects students' thinking in Solve & Share to important math ideas in the lesson. Use the *Visual Learning Bridge* to make these ideas explicit. Also available as a *Visual Learning Animation Plus* at PearsonRealize.com

E L L Visual Learning

Learn   Glossary

Help Carlos solve this problem: There are some hens on a farm. Some hens are outside the barn. There are 0, 1, or 2 hens inside the barn. Could there be 10, 11, 12, 13, or 14 hens in all on the farm?

What can you see? [Hens outside the barn] *Can you see the number of hens inside the barn?* [No] *Can you find the number of hens outside the barn?* [Yes] *How?* [Count the hens I see.]

How many hens are outside the barn? [12] *If there are 0 hens in the barn, how could you find how many hens are on the farm in all?* [Count on 0 from 12.] *1 hen inside the barn?* [Count on 1 from 12.] *2 hens inside the barn?* [Count on 2 hens from 12.]

MP.2 Reasoning *Why could 10 or 11 not be possible answers?* [There are 12 hens outside the barn. This is more than 10 or 11.] *Why are there three possible answers?* [Sample answer: There are 0, 1, or 2 hens inside the barn. These are the numbers in all when I count on 0, 1, or 2 from 12.]

Visual Learning Bridge

Think. 10, 11, 12, 13, or 14?

I see 12.

⊠ ⊠ (12)(13)(14)

3 possible answers

☆ **Guided Practice**

1

8   9   (10)   (11)   (12)

Directions ⭐ Say: *There are more than 8 cows on a farm. Some cows are outside the barn. 1 or more cows are inside the barn. Count the cows that are outside of the barn, and then draw a circle around the numbers that tell how many cows there could be in all.*

Complete the *Do You Understand? Show Me!* problem before starting Guided Practice.

Do You Understand? Show Me! MP.1 Make Sense and Persevere *What were the clues from the problem that Carlos used to find the three possible answers? Read the problem again and direct students to look at the picture in the first box of the Visual Learning Bridge.* [The number of hens in the picture; 0, 1, or 2 hens inside the barn]

Essential Question

Ask the following Essential Question: *When can you get more than one possible answer to a problem when counting?* [Sample answer: If the amounts you are counting could be different, then your answers could be different too.]

Error Intervention: Item 1

If students also want to circle 9 because they can see 9 cows,

then read the directions again, emphasizing *1 or more cows are inside the barn. If there is 1 cow inside the barn, there will be more than 9.* Count: 9, 10. *If there is more than 1 cow in the barn, there will also be more than 9.*

1 RtI   **Reteaching** Assign Reteaching Set D, p. 558.

✅ QUICK CHECK

Check mark indicates items for prescribing differentiation on the next page. Items 2 and 4 are each worth 1 point. The Performance Assessment on page 552 is worth up to 3 points.

MP.2 Reasoning Listen and look for these behaviors as evidence that students are exhibiting proficiency with MP.2.

- identifies and understands the quantities in the problem
- shows and explains how quantities are related
- translates real-world contexts correctly to numbers equations, and pictorial representations
- connects equations and pictorial representations back to real-world contexts

Item 2 MP.2 Reasoning *Can you see the horses inside the stable?* [No] *Outside the stable?* [Yes] *How many horses do you see outside the stable?* [13] *Which number do you know already is not a possible answer?* [12] *Why?* [I already see 13 horses. 12 comes before 13 when I count.]

Item 4 Some students may find this problem challenging as it is different from others and includes the words *up to 15*. If needed, discuss how this means the tank can hold no more than 15 fish, not necessarily 15 fish exactly. *What will you know after you count the fish?* [The number of fish in the tank already]

Item 5 MP.2 Reasoning Students should identify the clues *greater than 11* and *less than 15*. Encourage them to explain their reasoning not only for the numbers they circled but also the numbers they marked an X on.

Item 6 MP.4 Model with Math Remind students that pictures that represent word problems do not need to be detailed. Any clear representation can work. Explain that the fact that it represents the problem accurately is more important. Connect back to the previous item. *How did you use your answer to Item 5 to help you decide the total number of cats to draw?* [Sample answer: I knew that Alex had 12, 13, or 14 cats, so those were the numbers I could choose from.]

Item 7 MP.3 Construct Arguments Students should explain how their drawing represents each part of the word problem. When students construct an argument, they should give the reasons why they made their particular choices. Also, remind students when listening to an argument that there are different ways to have shown the word problem that can all be correct. *Think about how the drawing shows the problem, not whether your drawings are the same. You may have chosen a different number of cats, put them in different places, or used a different picture to represent the cats. These can all be correct as long as the drawing shows the problem.*

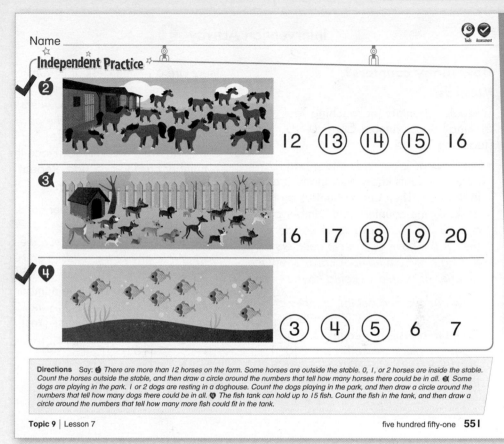

Name _____

☆ **Independent Practice** ☆

2 12 ⑬ ⑭ ⑮ 16

3 16 17 ⑱ ⑲ 20

4 ③ ④ ⑤ 6 7

Directions Say: **2** *There are more than 12 horses on the farm. Some horses are outside the stable. 0, 1, or 2 horses are inside the stable. Count the horses outside the stable, and then draw a circle around the numbers that tell how many horses there could be in all.* **3** *Some dogs are playing in the park. 1 or 2 dogs are resting in a doghouse. Count the dogs playing in the park, and then draw a circle around the numbers that tell how many dogs there could be in all.* **4** *The fish tank can hold up to 15 fish. Count the fish in the tank, and then draw a circle around the numbers that tell how many more fish could fit in the tank.*

Topic 9 | Lesson 7   five hundred fifty-one **551**

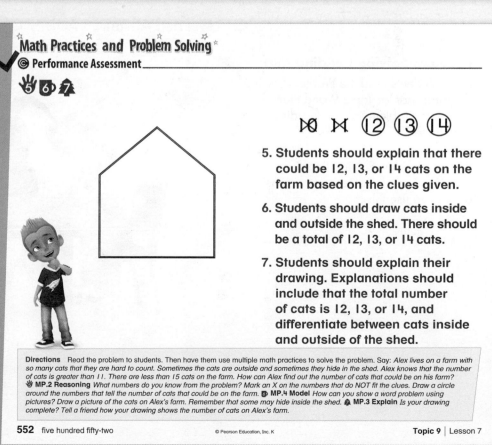

☆ **Math Practices and Problem Solving** ☆

© Performance Assessment _____

5 6 7

⋈ ⋈ ⑫ ⑬ ⑭

5. Students should explain that there could be 12, 13, or 14 cats on the farm based on the clues given.

6. Students should draw cats inside and outside the shed. There should be a total of 12, 13, or 14 cats.

7. Students should explain their drawing. Explanations should include that the total number of cats is 12, 13, or 14, and differentiate between cats inside and outside of the shed.

Directions Read the problem to students. Then have them use multiple math practices to solve the problem. Say: *Alex lives on a farm with so many cats that they are hard to count. Sometimes the cats are outside and sometimes they hide in the shed. Alex knows that the number of cats is greater than 11. There are less than 15 cats on the farm. How can Alex find out the number of cats that could be on his farm?* **MP.2 Reasoning** *What numbers do you know from the problem? Mark an X on the numbers that do NOT fit the clues. Draw a circle around the numbers that tell the number of cats that could be on the farm.* **MP.4 Model** *How can you show a word problem using pictures? Draw a picture of the cats on Alex's farm. Remember that some may hide inside the shed.* **MP.3 Explain** *Is your drawing complete? Tell a friend how your drawing shows the number of cats on Alex's farm.*

552 five hundred fifty-two   © Pearson Education, Inc. K   Topic 9 | Lesson 7

ASSESS AND DIFFERENTIATE

STEP 3

Use the **QUICK CHECK** on the previous page to prescribe differentiated instruction.

 Intervention
0–3 points on the Quick Check

On-Level
4 points on the Quick Check

Advanced
5 points on the Quick Check

Intervention Activity ⓘ

How many counters?
Materials

Two-color counters (or Teaching Tool 6), small bag, Number Cards 0–10 (Teaching Tool 3)

• Put 0, 1, or 2 counters into a bag. Do not let students know how many are in the bag. Then put 6 counters on the desk. By the counters, put number cards 6, 7, 8, 9, 10. *I have some counters on the desk. I have 0, 1, or 2 counters in this bag. Which number cards show the number of counters I could have in all?*

• *How can we find out the number of counters on the desk?* [Count them.] Count to establish 6 counters. *How many counters are in this bag?* [0, 1, or 2] *First, let's find the total number if there are 0 counters in the bag. I know*

there are 6 on the desk. *If I count on from 6 zero more, what number do I get?* [6] *So, if there are 6 counters on the desk and 0 counters in the bag, how many are there in all?* [6] *So, what is one possible answer?* [6] Place the 6 number card to one side. Repeat for 1 and 2 counters in the bag.

• Look at the remaining number cards 9 and 10. *We found the totals if there are 0, 1, or 2 counters in the bag. Were any of the totals 9 or 10?* [No] *So, these could not be possible answers.* Show students the number of counters in the bag. *Does this match one of our possible answers?* [Yes]

Reteach ⓘ

Name _____

Reteach to Build Understanding 9-7

Directions Say: ★ Let's count the fish together. There are *nineteen* fish. Write the number that tells how many; ② Look at the picture of the farm. There are more than 9 chickens on a farm. Some chickens are outside the barn. 1 or more chickens are inside the barn. How many chickens are outside of the barn? If there are 1 or more chickens inside the barn, how many chickens could be inside the barn? Draw a circle around the numbers that tell how many chickens there could be in all; ③ There are more than 10 kittens on the farm. Some kittens are outside the barn. 0, 1, or 2 kittens are inside the barn. Count the kittens outside the barn, and then draw a circle around the numbers that tell how many kittens there could be in all. **On the Back!** Have students draw from 9 to 12 objects. Have them write the number to tell how many, and then write the next three numbers.

R 9-7   Copyright © Pearson Education, Inc., or its affiliates. All Rights Reserved. K

On-Level and Advanced Activity Centers Ⓞ Ⓐ

Problem-Solving Reading Mat

Have students read the Problem-Solving Reading Mat for Topic 9 and then complete Problem-Solving Reading Activity 9-7.

See the Problem-Solving Reading Activity Guide for other suggestions on how to use this mat.

TIMING

The time allocated to Step 3 will depend on the teacher's instructional decisions and differentiation routines.

15–30 min

 Help   **Tools**   **Games**

PEARSON
realize.
PearsonRealize.com

Technology Center **I O A**

 Tools

 Games

Math Tools and Math Games

A link to a specific math tools activity or math game to use with this lesson is provided at PearsonRealize.com.

Leveled Assignment

I Items 1–5 (with help as needed)   **O** Items 1–5   **A** Items 1–5

Name _____

Homework & Practice 9-7
Reasoning

Another Look!

13 14 15 16 (17) (18)

HOME ACTIVITY Put 15 coins on a table. Say: *I have some coins on the table. I am hiding 1 or more coins in my hand. How many coins could I have in all? 13, 14, 15, 16, or 17?* Have your child count the coins on the table and then explain how he or she knows how many coins there could be in all.

1   16 17 18 (19) (20)

2   10 11 (12) (13) (14)

Directions Say: *There are 1 or more counters inside the jar. Count the yellow counters, and then draw a circle around the numbers that tell how many counters there could be in all.* ★ and ● Say: *There are 1 or more counters inside the jar. Count the counters, and then draw a circle around the numbers that tell how many counters there could be in all.*

Topic 9 | Lesson 7   Digital Resources at PearsonRealize.com   five hundred fifty-three **553**

© **Performance Assessment** _____

3 4 5

3. Students should explain that they know some bunnies are sitting in the grass and some are hiding behind the bush, and that there are 17 bunnies in all at the animal sanctuary.

4. Listen to the clues students give. Clues should include the following information: 17 bunnies in all, some are hiding behind the bush (3 bunnies), 14 bunnies are sitting in the grass.

5. Students should explain that the friend probably only counted the bunnies pictured (14 bunnies) and did not take into account that there are bunnies hiding behind the bush.

Directions Read the problem to students. Then have them use multiple math practices to solve the problem. Say: *Jada knows that there are 17 bunnies at the animal sanctuary. Some are sitting in the grass. Some are hiding behind a bush. What clues can she write to have her friends guess the number of bunnies in all?* **MP.1 Make Sense** *What do you know about the problem? How many bunnies are there in all?* **MP.2 Reasoning** *Tell your friend the clues. How many bunnies can he or she see?* **MP.3 Explain** *If your friend says there are 14 bunnies in all, what mistake did he or she probably make?*

554 five hundred fifty-four   © Pearson Education, Inc. K   **Topic 9** | Lesson 7

553–554

FLUENCY PRACTICE ACTIVITY

Games

FLUENCY PRACTICE ACTIVITY

Students practice fluently adding and subtracting within 5 during a partner activity that reinforces mathematical practices.

© Common Core Standards

Content Standard K.OA.A.5 Fluently add and subtract within 5.

Mathematical Practices MP.3, MP.6, MP.7, MP.8

Getting Started Ask students to work with a partner. Provide crayons needed for the activity. Tell students to record their answers and color the boxes on their own page. Go over the directions. Remind students to find all the sums and differences on the page.

As Students Do the Activity Remind students that each problem should be solved. When all of the boxes are colored correctly, a letter is revealed. Tell students that if the boxes they have colored do not do this, then there is an error and they need to double check their work. Remind students to compare and discuss their answers.

Another Activity Ask students to write a new addition or subtraction problem that has the same sum or difference as the original problem shown in each square. Have students record their problems along with the answers on a separate sheet of paper.

Extra Challenge *Look at the original problem and the answer you wrote in each square. If the problem is an addition problem, use the same numbers to write a correct subtraction problem. If the problem is a subtraction problem, use the numbers to write a correct addition problem. Work with a partner. Record your problems on a separate sheet of paper.*

Steps to Fluency Success To ensure all students achieve fluency, see pages 431E–431H for additional resources including practice/assessment masters on fluency subskills. You can also use the ExamView® CD-ROM to generate worksheets with multiple-choice or free-response items on fluency subskills.

Online Game The Game Center at PearsonRealize.com provides opportunities for fluency practice.

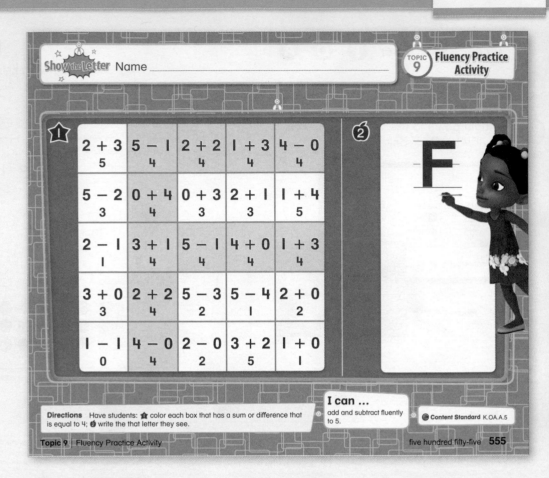

VOCABULARY REVIEW

VOCABULARY REVIEW

Students review vocabulary words used in the topic.

Oral Language Before students do the page, you might reinforce oral language through a class discussion involving one or more of the following activities.

- Have students define the terms in their own words.

- Have students say math sentences or math questions that use the words.

- Play a "What's My Word?" guessing game in which you or a student thinks about one of the words and says a clue that others listen to before they guess the word.

- Play a "Right or Wrong?" game in which you or a student says a sentence that uses one of the words correctly or incorrectly. Then others say "right" or "wrong."

Writing in Math After students do the page, you might further reinforce writing in math by doing one or more of the following activities.

- Tell students to close their books. Then you say the words and have students write them. Students trade papers to check whether the words are spelled correctly.

- Have students work with a partner. Each partner writes a math question that uses one of the words. Then they trade papers and give a written answer that uses the word.

 Online Game The Game Center at PearsonRealize.com includes a vocabulary game that students can access any time.

RtI Item Analysis for Diagnosis and Intervention				
Reteaching Sets	© Standards	Student Book Lessons	MDIS	
Set A	K.CC.A.3, K.CC.B.5	9-3, 9-4	A10	
Set B	K.CC.A.2	9-5	A8, A10	
Set C	K.CC.B.5	9-6	A10	
Set D	K.CC.A.2, K.CC.B.5, MP.2	9-7	A8, A10	

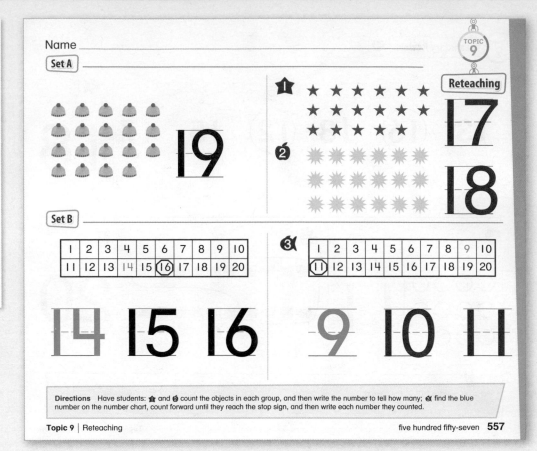

Directions Have students: ⭐ and 🍎 count the objects in each group, and then write the number to tell how many; ⬢ find the blue number on the number chart, count forward until they reach the stop sign, and then write each number they counted.

Topic 9 | Reteaching

five hundred fifty-seven **557**

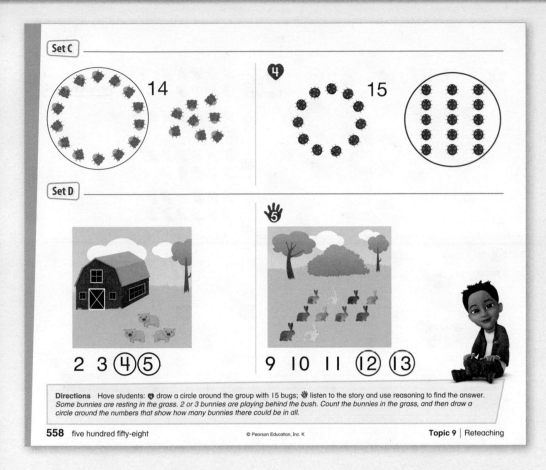

Set C _____

14

 15

Set D _____

2 3 ④⑤

9 10 11 ⑫ ⑬

Directions Have students: ✸ draw a circle around the group with 15 bugs; ✋ listen to the story and use reasoning to find the answer. *Some bunnies are resting in the grass. 2 or 3 bunnies are playing behind the bush. Count the bunnies in the grass, and then draw a circle around the numbers that show how many bunnies there could be in all.*

© Pearson Education, Inc. K   **Topic 9** | Reteaching

Response to Intervention

1 RtI

Ongoing Intervention
- Lessons with guiding questions to assess understanding
- Support to prevent misconceptions and to reteach

2 RtI

Strategic Intervention
- Targeted to small groups who need more support
- Easy to implement

3 RtI

Intensive Intervention
- Instruction to accelerate progress
- Instruction focused on foundational skills

TOPIC ASSESSMENT
COUNT NUMBERS TO 20

ANSWERING THE TOPIC ESSENTIAL QUESTION

How can numbers to 20 be counted, read, written, and pictured to tell how many?

Restate the Topic Essential Question from the Topic Opener or project it from the Student's Edition eText.

Ask students to answer the Essential Question (verbally or in writing) and give examples that support their answers. The following are key elements of the answer to the Essential Question. Be sure these are made explicit when discussing students' answers.

- Use unique number symbols to read and write numbers 11 to 20.

  Example: Thomas sees 14 ants. Write the unique number symbol to show how many ants Thomas sees. [14]

- Count on from a number other than 1.

  Example:

  17 18   19   20

- The number of objects does not change when the objects are rearranged or counted in another order.

  Example:

  15   15

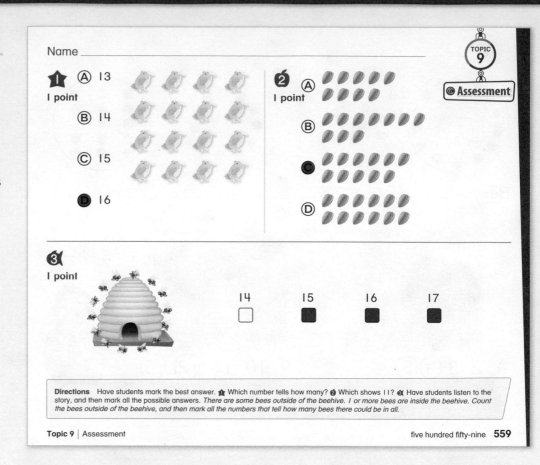

Directions Have students mark the best answer. ⭐ Which number tells how many? 🍎 Which shows 11? ❄ Have students listen to the story, and then mark all the possible answers. *There are some bees outside of the beehive. 1 or more bees are inside the beehive. Count the bees outside of the beehive, and then mark all the numbers that tell how many bees there could be in all.*

Topic 9 | Assessment   five hundred fifty-nine **559**

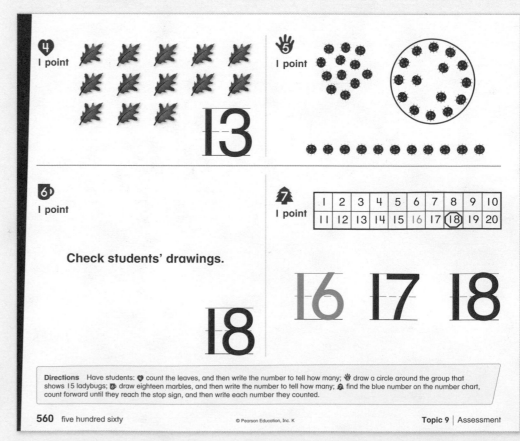

Check students' drawings.

Directions Have students: ❤ count the leaves, and then write the number to tell how many; ✋ draw a circle around the group that shows 15 ladybugs; ✊ draw eighteen marbles, and then write the number to tell how many; 🌲 find the blue number on the number chart, count forward until they reach the stop sign, and then write each number they counted.

560 five hundred sixty   © Pearson Education, Inc. K   Topic 9 | Assessment

ONLINE TOPIC ASSESSMENT
An auto-scored Topic Assessment is provided at PearsonRealize.com.

EXAMVIEW® TEST GENERATOR
ExamView can be used to create a blackline-master Topic Assessment with multiple-choice and free-response items.

Assessment

Topic Assessment Masters

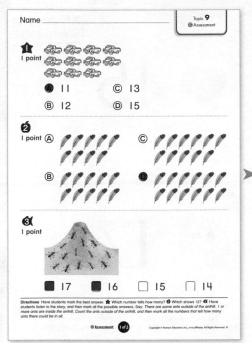

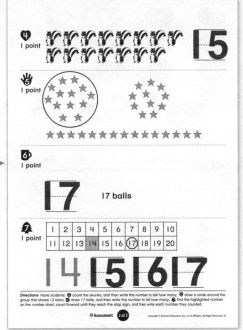

Item Analysis for Diagnosis and Intervention

Item	Standards	DOK	MDIS
1	K.CC.B.5	1	A8, A10
2	K.CC.B.5	1	A8, A10
3	K.CC.A.2, K.CC.B.5, MP.2	3	A10
4	K.CC.A.3	1	A10
5	K.CC.B.5	1	A10
6	K.CC.A.3	1	A10
7	K.CC.A.2	2	A10

The Topic Assessment Masters assess the same content item for item as the Topic Assessment in the Student's Edition.

Scoring Guide

Item	Points	Topic Assessment (Student's Edition and Masters)
1	1	Correct choice is selected.
2	1	Correct choice is selected.
3	1	Correct choices are selected.
4	1	Correct number is written.
5	1	Correct group is circled.
6	1	Correct number of items is drawn and correct number is written.
7	1	Correct numbers are written.

560A

Scoring Guide

Item	Points	Topic Performance Assessment in the Student's Edition
1	1	Correct number is written.
2	1	Correct number is written.
3	2	Draws 14 stickers in a different way.
	1	Does not draw 14 stickers in a different way, or does not draw correct number of stickers.
4	2	Correct numbers are written.
	1	Correctly writes one number.
5	2	Correct numbers are circled.
	1	Correctly circles one number.

RtI — Item Analysis for Diagnosis and Intervention

Item	Standards	DOK	MDIS
1	K.CC.A.3, K.CC.B.5	1	A10
2	K.CC.A.3, K.CC.B.5	1	A10
3	K.CC.B.5, MP.4	2	A8, A10
4	K.CC.A.2, K.CC.A.3, MP.2	3	A8, A10
5	K.CC.A.2, MP.2, MP.3	3	A10

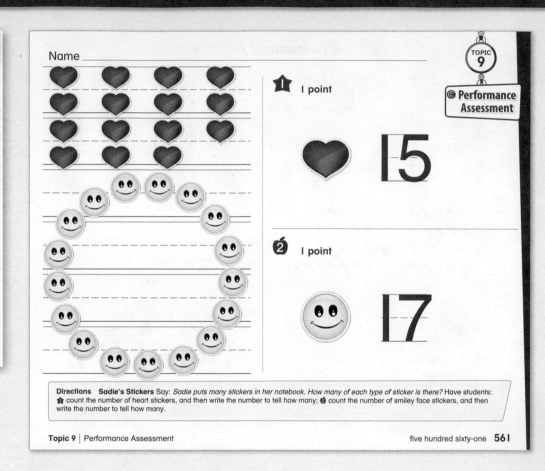

Directions Sadie's Stickers Say: *Sadie puts many stickers in her notebook. How many of each type of sticker is there?* Have students: ★ count the number of heart stickers, and then write the number to tell how many; 🍎 count the number of smiley face stickers, and then write the number to tell how many.

Topic 9 | Performance Assessment

five hundred sixty-one **561**

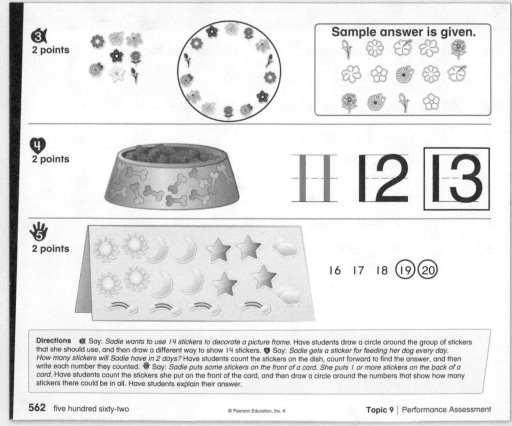

Directions ★ Say: *Sadie wants to use 14 stickers to decorate a picture frame.* Have students draw a circle around the group of stickers that she should use, and then draw a different way to show 14 stickers. 🍎 Say: *Sadie gets a sticker for feeding her dog every day. How many stickers will Sadie have in 2 days?* Have students count the stickers on the dish, count forward to find the answer, and then write each number they counted. ✋ Say: *Sadie puts some stickers on the front of a card. She puts 1 or more stickers on the back of a card.* Have students count the stickers she put on the front of the card, and then draw a circle around the numbers that show how many stickers there could be in all. Have students explain their answer.

562 five hundred sixty-two

© Pearson Education, Inc. K

Topic 9 | Performance Assessment

Topic Performance Assessment Masters

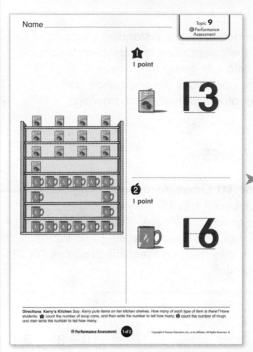

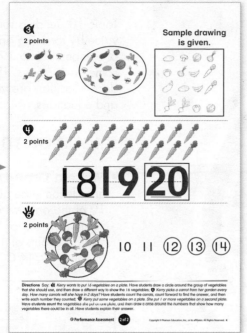

Item Analysis for Diagnosis and Intervention

Item	Standards	DOK	MDIS
1	K.CC.A.3, K.CC.B.5	1	A10
2	K.CC.A.3, K.CC.B.5	1	A10
3	K.CC.B.5, MP.4	2	A10
4	K.CC.A.2, K.CC.A.3, MP.2	3	A10
5	K.CC.A.2, MP.2, MP.3	3	A8, A10

Scoring Guide

Item	Points	Topic Performance Assessment Masters
1	1	Correct number is written.
2	1	Correct number is written.
3	2	Correct number of vegetables is circled and drawn to show a different way.
	1	Does not draw 16 vegetables in a different way, or does not circle/draw correct number of vegetables.
4	2	Correct numbers are written.
	1	Correctly writes one number.
5	2	Correct numbers are circled.
	1	Correctly circles one number.

● MAJOR CLUSTER ● SUPPORTING CLUSTER ● ADDITIONAL CLUSTER

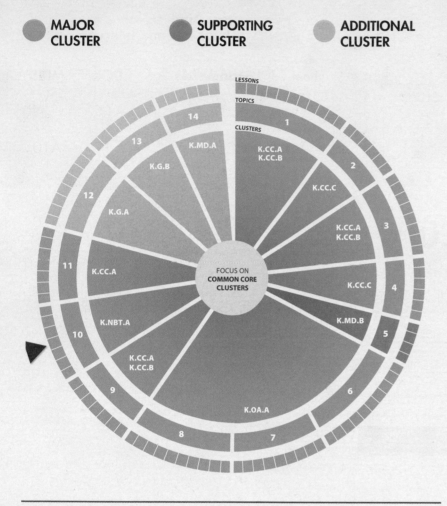

TOPIC 10 Compose and Decompose Numbers 11 to 19

TOPIC 10 FOCUSES ON

© MAJOR CLUSTER K.NBT.A
Work with numbers 11–19 to gain foundations for place value.

Content Focus in enVision math 2.0

Topic 10 builds a foundation for understanding place value by focusing on the composition and decomposition of numbers 11 to 19 into one group of 10 ones and some further ones. The operations of composition and decomposition are visualized with objects, drawings, and equations.

GROUP OF 10 ONES

• **Make a Group of 10 Ones** As students compose and decompose numbers 11 to 19, they need to visualize 10 of the ones as a group of 10 ones. They use a ten-frame or a bar of 10 objects throughout the topic to show a group of 10 ones and represent this group as the quantity 10. (K.CC.B.4a)

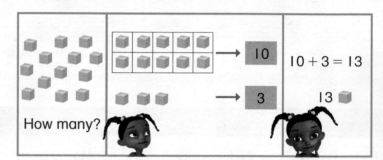

COMPOSE NUMBERS 11 TO 19

• **Make the Numbers 11 to 19** In Lessons 10-1, 10-2, and 10-3, students compose all of the teen numbers by putting together 10 ones and some more ones. They represent composition with objects, drawings, and equations. (K.NBT.A.1)

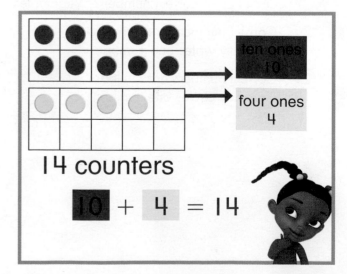

Content Focus in ёnVisionmath2.0 (continued)

• **Solve Composition Problems** Topic 10 provides many opportunities for students to solve composition problems by putting together 10 ones and extra ones to make a teen number. (K.NBT.A.1)

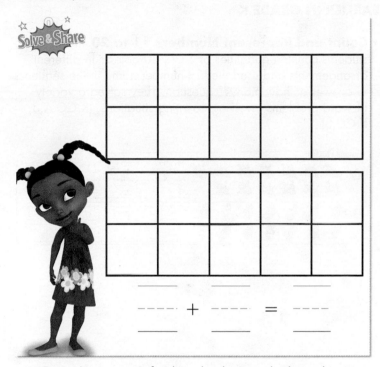

Jada made 10 prizes for the school carnival. She makes 8 more. Use counters to show how many prizes Jada made in all. Then write an equation to match the counters, and tell how the counters and equation show 10 ones and some more ones.

DECOMPOSE NUMBERS 11 TO 19

• **Find Parts of the Numbers 11 to 19** In Lessons 10-4, 10-5, and 10-6, students decompose all of the teen numbers by breaking apart the number into 10 ones and the remaining ones. They represent decomposition with objects, drawings, and equations. (K.NBT.A.1)

• **Solve Decomposition Problems** In Topic 10, students solve a variety of decomposition problems by breaking apart a teen number into 10 ones and some more ones. (K.NBT.A.1)

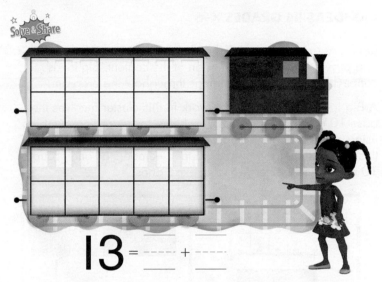

13 students wait for the train. There are only 10 seats in each train car. How many students will have to ride in a second car? Use counters to show your work. Then tell how the counters and equation show 10 ones and some more ones.

• **Professional Development Videos** Topic Overview Videos and Listen and Look For Lesson Videos present additional important information about the content of this cluster.

Content Coherence in enVisionmath2.0

Students learn best when ideas are connected in a coherent curriculum. This coherence is achieved through various types of connections including connections within clusters, across clusters, across domains, and across grades.

BIG IDEAS IN GRADES K–6

Big Ideas are the conceptual underpinnings of **enVision**math**2.0** and provide conceptual cohesion of the content. Big Ideas connect Essential Understandings throughout the program.

A Big Idea that connects the work in this cluster involves the base-10 numeration system, a scheme for recording numbers using digits 0 through 9, groups of 10, and place value. In this topic, students visualize the teen numbers as one group of 10 ones and another group of extra ones.

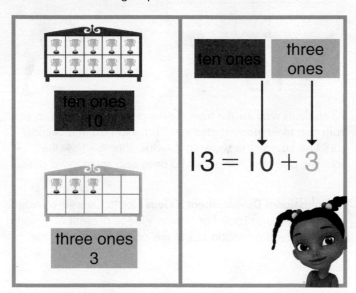

For a complete list of Big Ideas, see pages 110–111 in the *Teacher's Edition Program Overview*.

LOOK BACK

How does Topic 10 connect to what students learned earlier?

EARLIER IN GRADE K

• **Count and Represent Numbers 11 to 20** In Topic 9, students counted quantities of 11 to 20 objects in different arrangements and used the last number name in the sequence to answer a "how many?" question. They solved a variety of word problems involving counting situations. (K.CC.A.3, K.CC.B)

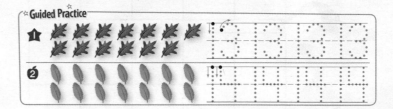

TOPIC 10

How is content connected within Topic 10?

- **Connect Composition and Decomposition** In Lessons 10-1, 10-2, and 10-3, students make teen numbers by putting together 10 ones and some extra ones and then writing the related equation.

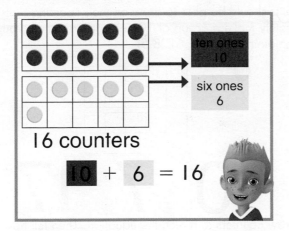

In Lessons 10-4, 10-5, and 10-6, students draw on these understandings to break apart teen numbers into 10 ones and some extra ones and then write the related equation. (K.NBT.A.1)

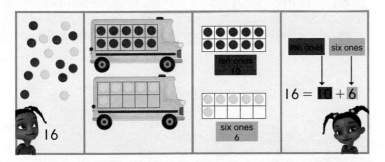

- **Problems Involving Composition and Decomposition** Throughout Topic 10, students apply the understandings they are developing about composing and decomposing the numbers 11 to 19 to solve problems involving these concepts. (K.NBT.A.1)

LOOK AHEAD

How does Topic 10 connect to what students will learn later?

LATER IN KINDERGARTEN

- **Count to 100** In Topic 11, students will count by tens or by tens and ones to various numbers up to 100. (K.CC.A.1)

GRADE 1

- **Understand Place Value** In Topic 8, students will determine how many tens and ones are in 2-digit numbers. (1.NBT.B.2)

Content Rigor in **enVision**math 2.0

A rigorous curriculum emphasizes conceptual understanding, procedural skill and fluency, and applications.

CONCEPTUAL UNDERSTANDING

• **Foundational Place-Value Concepts** For young students, the teen number 15 may look like a "1" and a "5." In Topic 10, students are presented with a correct, mathematical interpretation of 15 as group of 10 ones and 5 more ones. Students compose and decompose teen numbers using ten-frames or bars of ten objects to develop this foundational place-value concept. (K.NBT.A.1)

• **Equivalence in Composed and Decomposed Numbers** Students understand that a teen number written as one group of 10 ones and some extra ones has the same value as the 2-digit teen number. Students can count out the number of objects in each representation to show that they are the same. (K.NBT.A.1)

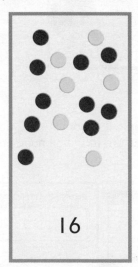

16

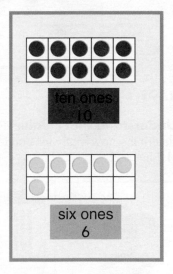

ten ones
10

six ones
6

PROCEDURAL SKILL AND FLUENCY

There are no standards in this cluster that call for fluency.

• **Make a Group of 10 Ones and Some More Ones** Students should be able to draw on their counting skills to accurately make a group of 10 ones and another group with the remaining ones. (K.CC.B.5)

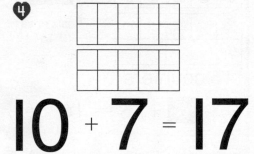

$$10 + 7 = 17$$

Draw counters to match the equation. Then tell how the picture and equation show 10 ones and some more ones.

APPLICATIONS

• **Situations Involving Composition and Decomposition** Throughout Topic 10, situations are presented that involve composition and decomposition in real-world contexts. (K.NBT.A.1)

14 students go to the zoo. The first bus takes 10 students. The rest of the students go on a second bus. Use counters to describe this situation. Then complete the equation to match the counters and tell how the counters and equation show 10 ones and some more ones.

MATH PRACTICES

Connecting Math Practices and Content Standards in énVisionmath2.0

Math practices and content standards are connected within all lessons including the lessons that focus on math practices.

MATH PRACTICES WITHIN LESSONS

- **MP.1 Make sense of problems and persevere in solving them.**

  Students make sense of problems and persevere while determining how to break apart a cube tower into two groups of cubes. (e.g., p. 598, Visual Learning Bridge)

- **MP.2 Reason abstractly and quantitatively.**

  Students use reasoning to relate ten-frames to equations involving adding 10 and a 1-digit number. (e.g., p. 576, Items 6–7)

- **MP.3 Construct viable arguments and critique the reasoning of others.**

  Students explain how they can use equations or number charts to justify their answer. (e.g., p. 606, Item 8)

- **MP.4 Model with mathematics.**

  Students use equations to model breaking apart a number into a ten and ones. (e.g., p. 597, Solve and Share)

- **MP.5 Use appropriate tools strategically.**

  Students use two-color counters strategically to solve composition and decomposition problems. (e.g., p. 594, Item 7)

- **MP.6 Attend to precision.**

  Students attend to precision when they carefully count symbols that are in two ten-frames. (e.g., p. 586, Visual Learning Bridge)

- **MP.7 Look for and make use of structure.**

  Students look for structure when they group and break apart the teen numbers by tens and ones, represent the drawings in the ten-frames, and then record the matching equations. (e.g., p. 581, Items 2–3)

- **MP.8 Look for and express regularity in repeated reasoning.**

  Students generalize that they do not need to count every item in a full ten-frame. (e.g., p. 588, Item 6)

LESSON THAT FOCUSES ON MATH PRACTICES

- **Lesson 10-7** This lesson focuses on MP.7. Students look for a pattern as they identify a single-digit number and look at the number that is 10 greater on a number chart. They then write an equation showing the composition of the number that is 10 greater than the single digit number.

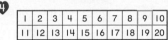

  Find the number with the blue box around it, and color the number that is 10 greater than the number in the blue box. Then write an equation to match, and then tell how the equation shows 10 ones and some more ones.

Revisit the information about MP.7 in these other resources:

- **Math Practices and Problem Solving Handbook** before Topic 1; includes Math Practices Proficiency Rubrics.

- **Math Practices Posters** to display in your classroom

  Math Practices Animations, one for each math practice, available at PearsonRealize.com.

TOPIC 10

MAJOR CLUSTER K.NBT.A

DIFFERENTIATED INSTRUCTION

 I Intervention   **O** On-Level   **A** Advanced

PEARSON realize PearsonRealize.com

Learn   Assessment   Tools   Games

Ongoing Intervention

 During the core lesson, monitor progress, reteach as needed, and extend students' thinking.

Guiding Questions

• **In the Teacher's Edition** Guiding questions are used to monitor understanding during instruction.

 Online Guiding Questions Guiding questions are also in the online Visual Learning Animation Plus.

Error Intervention: If... then...
This feature in the Teacher's Edition is provided during Guided Practice. It spotlights common errors and gives suggestions for addressing them.

Reteaching
Reteaching sets are at the end of the topic in the Student's Edition. They provide additional examples, reminders, and practice. Use these sets as needed before students do the Independent Practice.

Higher Order Thinking
These problems require students to think more deeply about the rich, conceptual knowledge developed in the lesson.

Strategic Intervention

 At the end of the lesson, assess to identify students' strengths and needs and then provide appropriate support.

Quick Check

 In the Student's Edition Assess the lesson using 2-3 items checked in the Teacher's Edition.

 Online Quick Check You can also assess the lesson using 5 online, machine-scored items.

Intervention Activity **I**
Teachers work with struggling students.

Reteach to Build Understanding **I**
This is a page of guided reteaching.

Technology Center **I O A**

 Digital Math Tools Activities reinforce the lesson content or previously taught content using a suite of digital math tools.

 Online Games provide practice on the lesson content or previously taught content.

Homework and Practice **I O A**
Use the leveled assignment to provide differentiated homework and practice.

Additional resources to support differentiated instruction for on-level and advanced students include:

On-Level and Advanced Activity Centers **O A**

• **Center Games** are provided in on-level and advanced versions.

• **Math and Science Activity** is related to the topic science theme introduced at the start of the topic.

• **Problem-Solving Reading Mat** is used with a lesson-specific activity.

Intensive Intervention

 **As needed,** provide more instruction that is on or below grade level for students who are struggling.

Math Diagnosis and Intervention System 2.0

• **Diagnosis** Use the diagnostic tests in the system. Also, use the item analysis charts given with program assessments at the start of a grade or topic, or at the end of a topic, group of topics, or the year.

• **Intervention Lessons** These two-page lessons include guided instruction followed by practice. The system includes lessons below, on, and above grade level.

• **Teacher Support** Teacher Notes provide the support needed to conduct a short lesson. The lesson focuses on vocabulary, concept development, and practice. The Teacher's Guide contains individual and class record forms and correlations to Student's Edition lessons.

Resources for Fluency Success

• A variety of print and digital resources are provided to ensure success on Common Core fluency standards. See Steps to Fluency Success on pages 431E–431H.

THE LANGUAGE OF MATH

PEARSON
realize
PearsonRealize.com

Glossary Games Story Story

English Language Learners

Provide ELL support through visual learning throughout the program, ELL instruction in every lesson, and additional ideas in an ELL Toolkit.

Visual Learning
The visual learning that is infused in **enVision**math**2.0** provides support for English language learners. This support includes a Visual Learning Animation Plus and a Visual Learning Bridge for each lesson.

English Language Learners Instruction
Lessons provide instruction for English language learners at Beginning, Intermediate, and Advanced levels of English proficiency.

English Language Learners Toolkit
This resource provides professional development and resources for supporting English language learners.

Math Vocabulary

Build math vocabulary using the vocabulary cards, vocabulary activities, vocabulary review, and glossary plus the online glossary and vocabulary game.

My Word Cards
Vocabulary cards for a topic are provided in the Student's Edition. Use the cards with students to study and learn new vocabulary words.

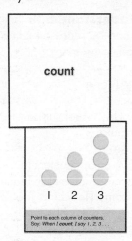

Vocabulary Activities
The Teacher's Edition provides vocabulary activities at the start of topics. These include activities for vocabulary in My Word Cards and/or activities for vocabulary in Review What You Know.

Vocabulary Review
A page of vocabulary review is provided at the end of each topic. It reviews vocabulary used in the topic.

Glossary
A glossary is provided at the back of the Student's Edition.

Animated Glossary
 An online, bilingual, animated glossary uses motion and sound to build understanding of math vocabulary.

Online Vocabulary Game
 An online vocabulary game is available in the Game Center.

Math and Reading

Connect reading and math using a data-filled reading mat for the topic with accompanying activity masters and guide. Also use topic interactive math stories.

Problem-Solving Reading Mats
There is a large, beautiful mat for each topic. At the start of the topic, help students become familiar with the mat and the vocabulary used by reading the mat aloud as students follow along. Use the Problem-Solving Reading Activity Guide for suggestions about how to use the mat.

Problem-Solving Reading Activity
At the end of some lessons, a Problem-Solving Reading Activity provides a page of math problems to solve by using the data on the mat.

Interactive Math Stories
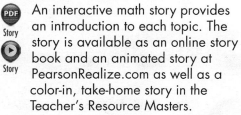 An interactive math story provides an introduction to each topic. The story is available as an online story book and an animated story at PearsonRealize.com as well as a color-in, take-home story in the Teacher's Resource Masters.

Lesson 10-1	**Lesson 10-2**	**Lesson 10-3**
MAKE 11, 12, AND 13 pp. 567–572	**MAKE 14, 15, AND 16** pp. 573–578	**MAKE 17, 18, AND 19** pp. 579–584
© Content Standard **K.NBT.A.1** Mathematical Practices **MP.2, MP.4, MP.5, MP.7**	© Content Standard **K.NBT.A.1** Mathematical Practices **MP.2, MP.3, MP.4, MP.7**	© Content Standard **K.NBT.A.1** Mathematical Practices **MP.1, MP.2, MP.4, MP.7**
Objective Use drawings and equations to make the numbers 11, 12, and 13.	**Objective** Make the numbers 14, 15, and 16.	**Objective** Make the numbers 17, 18, and 19.
Essential Understanding Numbers from 11–19 can be represented as the sum of 10 and some more.	**Essential Understanding** Numbers from 11–19 can be represented as the sum of 10 and some more.	**Essential Understanding** Numbers from 11–19 can be represented as the sum of 10 and some more.
Vocabulary How many more?	**Vocabulary** None	**Vocabulary** None
ELL Strategies: Monitor language production.	**ELL** Reading: Use visual support to develop vocabulary.	**ELL** Reading: Demonstrate comprehension by responding to questions.
Materials Two-color counters (or Teaching Tool 6), connecting cubes (or Teaching Tool 8), Ten-Frame (Teaching Tool 22)	**Materials** Two-color counters (or Teaching Tool 6), connecting cubes (or Teaching Tool 8), Ten-Frame (Teaching Tool 22), Double Ten-Frame (Teaching Tool 23), number cube (or Teaching Tool 10)	**Materials** Two-color counters (or Teaching Tool 6), connecting cubes (or Teaching Tool 8), Double Ten-Frame (Teaching Tool 23), index cards
On-Level and Advanced Activity Centers • Math and Science Activity	**On-Level and Advanced Activity Centers** • Problem-Solving Reading Mat	**On-Level and Advanced Activity Centers** • Problem-Solving Reading Mat

LESSON RESOURCES

Digital

- Student's Edition
- Daily Common Core Review
- Reteach to Build Understanding
- Center Games
- Math and Science Activity
- Problem-Solving Reading Mat
- Problem-Solving Reading Activity

Print

Digital

- Listen and Look For PD Lesson Video
- Student's Edition eText
- Today's Challenge
- Solve & Share
- Visual Learning Animation Plus

- Animated Glossary
- Math Tools
- Quick Check
- Another Look Homework Video
- Math Games

Digital

Lesson 10-4

FIND PARTS OF 11, 12, AND 13
pp. 585–590

Content Standard K.NBT.A.1
Mathematical Practices MP.4, MP.6, MP.7, MP.8

Objective Find parts of the numbers 11, 12, and 13.

Essential Understanding The numbers 11, 12, and 13 can be decomposed as the sum of ten and some ones.

Vocabulary None

ELL Listening: Learn basic/academic vocabulary.

Materials Two-color counters (or Teaching Tool 6), Ten-Frame (Teaching Tool 22), sticky notes, paper clips

On-Level and Advanced Activity Centers
- Math and Science Activity

Lesson 10-5

FIND PARTS OF 14, 15, AND 16
pp. 591–596

Content Standard K.NBT.A.1
Mathematical Practices MP.4, MP.5, MP.7, MP.8

Objective Find parts of the numbers 14, 15, and 16.

Essential Understanding The numbers 14, 15, and 16 can be decomposed as the sum of ten and some ones.

Vocabulary None

ELL Speaking: Speak using content area vocabulary in context.

Materials Two-color counters (or Teaching Tool 6), connecting cubes (or Teaching Tool 8), Double Ten-Frame (Teaching Tool 23)

On-Level and Advanced Activity Centers
- Center Games

Lesson 10-6

FIND PARTS OF 17, 18, AND 19
pp. 597–602

Content Standard K.NBT.A.1
Mathematical Practices MP.1, MP.4, MP.6, MP.8

Objective Find parts of the numbers 17, 18, and 19.

Essential Understanding The numbers 17, 18, and 19 can be decomposed as the sum of ten and some ones.

Vocabulary None

ELL Listening: Use visual support to confirm understanding.

Materials Two-color counters (or Teaching Tool 6), Connecting Cubes (Teaching Tool 8), Double Ten-Frame (Teaching Tool 23), crayons, cup

On-Level and Advanced Activity Centers
- Center Games

TOPIC RESOURCES

Digital

Print

Start of Topic
- Topic Centers
- Interactive Math Story
- Math and Science Project
- Home-School Connection
- Review What You Know
- My Word Cards

End of Topic
- Fluency Practice Activity
- Vocabulary Review
- Reteaching
- Topic Assessment
- Topic Performance Assessment

Digital

Start of Topic
- Topic Overview PD Video

End of Topic
- Math Practices Animations
- Online Topic Assessment
- ExamView® Test Generator

PearsonRealize.com

563J

Lesson 10-7

MATH PRACTICES AND PROBLEM SOLVING: LOOK FOR AND USE STRUCTURE pp. 603–608

© Mathematical Practices **MP.7, MP.3, MP.4, MP.5, MP.8**
Content Standard **K.NBT.A.1**

Objective Use patterns to make and find the parts of numbers to 19.

Essential Understanding Good math thinkers look for patterns in math to help solve problems.

Vocabulary None

ELL Strategies: Use prior experiences to understand meanings.

Materials Two-color counters (or Teaching Tool 6), Ten- Frame (Teaching Tool 22), Hundred Chart (Teaching Tool 31), crayons

On-Level and Advanced Activity Centers
- Center Games

Notes

Writing Center

We've Been Framed!

Materials
(per pair) 10 red counters, 9 yellow counters,
2 ten-frames, writing paper

- Have one student fill the top ten-frame with 10 red
  counters. Then have the student place 1 to 9 yellow
  counters in the bottom ten-frame to model any
  number from 11 to 19.

- Have a partner write an addition equation to match
  the model.

- Have partners switch roles and repeat the activity.

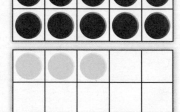

$$10 + 3 = 13$$

Building Center

Teetering Towers

Materials
(per student) 10 red connecting cubes, 9 blue
connecting cubes, writing paper

- Have each student connect 10 red connecting
  cubes and balance the tower vertically. Have
  students connect 1 blue cube to the top of
  their tower.

- Students then write an equation to match the
  cubes: $10 + 1 = 11$.

- One at a time, have students carefully add
  1 blue cube to their towers. After they
  each add a cube, have them write the
  equation that matches the red and blue cubes.

- Allow students to rebalance each tower
  if it tips over. Have them continue until their
  towers are 19 cubes tall.

$$10 + 5 = 15$$

Dramatic Play Center

Muffins for Sale!

Materials
(per class) 2 paper plates, 19 counters

- Invite volunteers to stand in front of the class to be
  "bakers." Explain that they just baked 15 muffins.
  Give 15 counters to the bakers and explain that
  each counter stands for 1 muffin. Encourage the
  bakers to pretend the counters are real muffins by
  smelling and touching them.

- Give the bakers 2 plates. Explain that the bakers
  will sell 10 of their muffins and keep the other
  muffins to take home.

- Ask students how many of the 15 muffins should
  go on the plate to sell [10]. Then ask how many
  muffins should go on the plate for the bakers to
  take home [5]. Have the bakers place the counters
  on each plate as you write the equation on the
  board: $15 = 10 + 5$.

- Repeat the activity with other volunteers and different
  numbers of muffins (from 11 to 19 muffins in all).

Bears in Two Caves

Materials
(per child) 2 index cards, brown crayon, writing paper

- Give 1 index card to each student and explain that it is a "bear cave."

- Tell students that 18 bears are looking for a cave to sleep in, but only 10 bears can fit in this cave. Have students draw 10 bears on each of their index cards, or "caves."

- When each index card has 10 bears drawn on it, give students another index card, or "cave." Explain that the other bears can sleep in this cave. Elicit how many bears are still looking for a cave [8 bears].

- When students have finished coloring the 8 bears on the index cards, guide them to see that the equation that matches their pictures is $18 = 10 + 8$.

Find Your Partner

Materials
Index cards

- On index cards, write equations that show how to decompose numbers 11 to 19: $11 = 10 + 1$, $12 = 10 + 2$, $13 = 10 + 3$, etc. On separate index cards, draw double ten-frames and counters that match each equation you wrote.

- Shuffle and distribute all the cards to students. Instruct each student to find his or her partner with the matching equation or model.

- When all cards have been matched, you can collect, shuffle, and redistribute the index cards for additional practice.

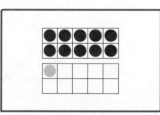

$$11 = 10 + 1$$

TOPIC 10

INTERACTIVE MATH STORY
COMPOSE AND DECOMPOSE NUMBERS 11 TO 19

PEARSON
realize
PearsonRealize.com

PDF Story   ▶ Story

Before the Story

 Picture Walk
Project the online PDF that contains a full-color version of this story. Read the title, author's name, and illustrator's name to the students. *What might Andy find on his nature walk? Let's take a look.* Page through the book. Together with students, talk about the things Andy finds on his walk and enjoy the illustrations. Point out that in each picture, Andy sees a group of objects and then some more.

Activate Prior Knowledge
Draw a ten-frame filled with circles on the board. Place 5 circles under the ten-frame. *Can someone tell how many circles the picture shows?* [15] Write the number on the board. Repeat the activity by adding or erasing circles below the ten-frame. Review several numbers from 11–19 as shown by ten and some more counters.

▶ Story Play the animated version of the story.

DURING THE STORY

This book belongs to:
Kamille

TOPIC 10 Story

Andy's Nature Walk

By Nicole S. Rouse
Illustrations by
Braj Gopal Sahoo

Andy collects 10 leaves, and then he collects some more. How many leaves does he collect in all?

$10 + \underline{2} = 12$

Topic 10 ①

Andy finds 10 rocks, and then he finds some more. How many rocks does he find in all?

$10 + \underline{5} = 15$

Topic 10 ②

READ
Read the story aloud for enjoyment. Look at the leaves on page 1. *How many leaves are on the table?* [10] *Andy finds 2 more leaves to add to the 10. How can we show this in an equation?* [Sample answer: We can show 2 being added to 10.] *How many leaves did Andy find in all?* [12] Discuss how on each page, Andy finds 10 and a single number of objects.

GESTURE
Reread the story. After reading the first page, invite a volunteer to use a finger to "draw" a circle around the leaves and the matching numbers in the equation. *Circle the leaves on the table with your finger. Now circle that number in the equation. Circle the leaves Andy is holding. Now circle that number in the equation. Circle the total number of leaves. Now circle that number in the equation.* Repeat this activity with each page in the story.

COLOR
Distribute the Interactive Math Story Books to students. On each page, have students draw a circle around the group of 10 objects. Then have them color the 2 leaves on page 1, the 5 rocks on page 2, the 4 butterflies on page 3, and the 7 ants in a line on page 4.

ANDY'S NATURE WALK

This is a story in which students use an addition equation to compose a number as 10 ones and some more ones.

Andy chases 10 butterflies, and then he chases some more. How many butterflies does he chase in all?

10 + __4__ = __14__

Topic 10 ③

Andy counts 10 ants, and then he counts some more. How many ants does he count in all?

10 + __7__ = __17__

Topic 10 ④

Extension

Take students on a nature walk. Have them work in pairs to collect items like leaves and rocks. Have the pairs count objects they see like birds or squirrels. Return to class and have the pairs create their own nature walk stories. Have them draw a picture of each different type of item they found. For example, one student may have found 10 leaves and another student 4 leaves. Have them write an equation for each picture. Invite pairs to share their stories and equations with others. Students may not always find or see 10 of one object. That is fine for this extension.

You may wish to have students take home their Interactive Math Story books and share what they have learned about adding 10 and another number.

WRITE

On each page, discuss what number of objects is being added to 10 and how to complete the equation to find the total number of objects. *What number is being added to 10?* [Answers will vary.] *How can we show the total number of objects?* [Answers will vary.] Have students complete each equation. Encourage students to share how each equation matches the story.

SPEAK

Invite students to retell each page of the story in their own words. They may start the first page with, for example, "Andy went on a nature walk. He found 10 leaves … ."

563P

TOPIC ESSENTIAL QUESTION

How can composing and decomposing numbers from 11 to 19 into ten ones and some further ones help you understand place value?

Revisit the Topic Essential Question throughout the topic, and see a note about answering the question in the Teacher's Edition for the Topic Assessment.

MATH AND SCIENCE PROJECT STEM

Science Theme The science theme for this project is **Sunlight and Earth's Surface.** This theme will be revisited in the Math and Science Activities in Lessons 10-1 and 10-4.

Discuss with students the effects of sunlight on various Earth surfaces such as a desert. Explain to students that heat from sunlight causes water to evaporate faster. The students talk to friends and relatives about sunlight and how it affects Earth.

Project-Based Learning Have students work on the **Math and Science Project** over the course of several days.

EXTENSION

Using their posters, have students show three things sunlight does for Earth. Challenge students to choose a classmate's poster and compare their information about sunlight and its effects on the Earth.

Sample Student Work for Math and Science Project

Compose and Decompose Numbers 11 to 19

TOPIC 10

Essential Question: How can composing and decomposing numbers from 11 to 19 into ten ones and some further ones help you understand place value?

A desert

Sunlight causes water to evaporate faster.

Math and Science Project: Sunlight and Earth's Surface
Directions Read the character speech bubbles to students. **Find Out!** Have students find out how sunlight affects Earth's surface. Say: *Talk to friends and relatives about sunlight and how it affects Earth.* **Journal: Make a Poster** Have students make a poster that shows 3 things sunlight does for Earth. Have them draw a sun with 16 rays. Then have them write an equation for parts of 16.

Topic 10   five hundred sixty-three **563**

Home-School Connection

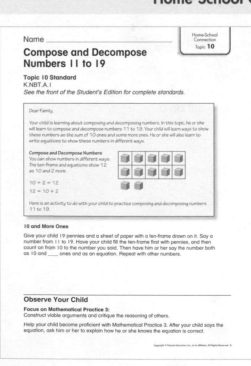

Send this page home at the start of Topic 10 to give families an overview of the content of the topic.

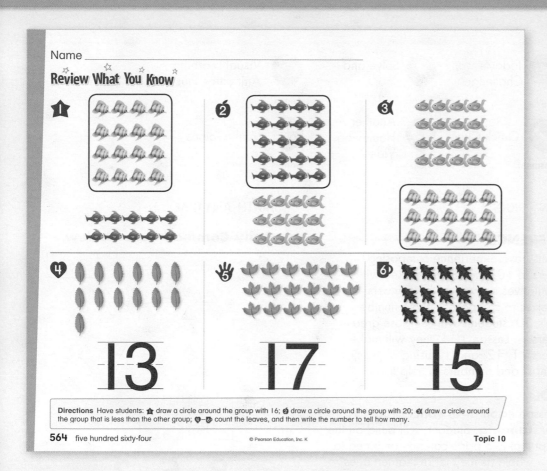

Name _____

Review What You Know

1

2

3

4

5

6

13   17   15

Directions Have students: **1** draw a circle around the group with 16; **2** draw a circle around the group with 20; **3** draw a circle around the group that is less than the other group; **4**–**6** count the leaves, and then write the number to tell how many.

Item	© Standards	MDIS
1	K.CC.A.5	A10
2	K.CC.A.5	A12
3	K.CC.C.6	A6
4	K.CC.A.3	A10
5	K.CC.A.3	A10
6	K.CC.A.3	A10

Item Analysis for Diagnosis and Intervention

Topic 10 Vocabulary Words Activity

Use the Topic 9 activity on page 508A with the Topic 10 word below.

My Word Cards **Directions** Have students cut out the vocabulary cards. Read the front of the card, and then ask them to explain what the word or phrase means.

How many more?

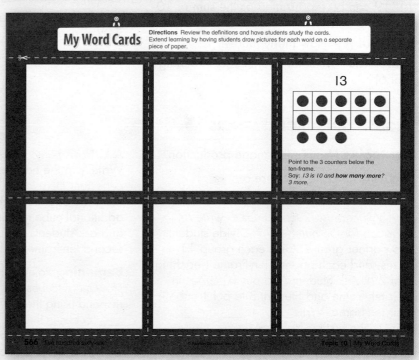

My Word Cards **Directions** Review the definitions and have students study the cards. Extend learning by having students draw pictures for each word on a separate piece of paper.

13

Point to the 3 counters below the ten-frame.
Say: *13 is 10* and **how many more**?
3 more.

LESSON 10-1

MAKE 11, 12, AND 13

LESSON OVERVIEW **FCR** FOCUS • COHERENCE • RIGOR

FOCUS

Domain K.NBT Number and Operations in Base Ten

Cluster K.NBT.A Work with numbers 11–19 to gain foundations for place value.

Content Standard K.NBT.A.1 Compose and decompose numbers from 11 to 19 into ten ones and some further ones, e.g., by using objects or drawings, and record each composition or decomposition by a drawing or equation (e.g., $18 = 10 + 8$); understand that these numbers are composed of ten ones and one, two, three, four, five, six, seven, eight, or nine ones.

Mathematical Practices MP.2, MP.4, MP.5, MP.7

Objective Use drawings and equations to make the numbers 11, 12, and 13.

Essential Understanding Numbers from 11–19 can be represented as the sum of 10 and some more.

Vocabulary How many more?

Materials Two-color counters (or Teaching Tool 6)

COHERENCE

Students have experience composing numbers to 10. They have worked with manipulatives as well as the numbers themselves to compose a given number. In Topic 10, students will compose greater numbers. In Lesson 10-1, they will make numbers 11, 12, and 13 using objects, drawings, and numbers to help them.

RIGOR

This lesson emphasizes **conceptual understanding**. Students will build on the concept that two parts can be combined to make a whole as they learn that ten ones and 1, 2, or 3 more ones combine to make a number from 11 to 13. They expand their knowledge of an equation representing a quantitative relationship. And they begin to establish a basic understanding of place value in our base-ten numeration system.

 PD Watch the Listen and Look For Lesson Video.

MATH ANYTIME

Daily Common Core Review

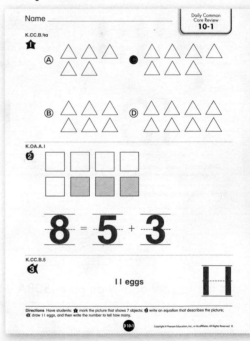

Today's Challenge

 Think Use Topic 10 problems any time during this topic.

ENGLISH LANGUAGE LEARNERS **ELL**

Strategies Monitor language production.

Use with the Solve & Share on Student's Edition p. 567.

Say: *We can use 2 ten-frames to write an equation for the number 11.* Divide students into partner groups. Give each group 11 cubes, and each partner Ten-Frame (Teaching Tool 22). Ask Student A to put 10 cubes in their ten-frame and Student B to put 1 cube in their ten-frame. Write ____ + ____ = ____. Point to the first ten-frame. Ask: *How many cubes are in this frame?* Write *10* in the equation. Point to the second ten-frame.

Ask: *How many cubes are in this frame?* Write *1* in the equation. Ask: *How many cubes are there in all?* Write *11* in the equation. Read the equation with students. Give an additional cube to each partner group and ask students to put the cube in the second ten-frame.

Beginning Point to the first ten-frame. Ask: *How many cubes are there?* Students should respond using the sentence stem: "There are ____ cubes in this ten-frame." Continue the process with the second ten-frame. Instruct students to write an equation for 12.

Intermediate Have students ask partners: *How many cubes are in each ten-frame? How many cubes in all?* Instruct students to write an equation for 12.

Advanced Ask: *How are the ten-frames used to make 12?* Students should explain to partners how the ten-frame is used to make 12, write an equation for 12, and then explain what each number in the equation represents.

Summarize How are ten-frames used to make 11 and 12?

DEVELOP: PROBLEM-BASED LEARNING

Solve

COHERENCE: Engage students by connecting prior knowledge to new ideas.

Students use counters and a ten-frame to show 10 and 1, 2, or 3 more. They write an equation to tell how many in all. This prepares them for the next part of the lesson where students draw pictures and write an equation to tell how to compose a number from 11 to 13.

10–15 min

 BEFORE

1. Pose the Solve-and-Share Problem

MP.4 Model with Math Students draw pictures to represent the number of counters using a ten-frame. Students show a quantity of 10 ones and some more ones, and then write an equation to match.

Distribute 13 counters to each student.

Say: *Use counters to fill the ten-frame. Put 1, 2, or 3 counters outside of the ten-frame. Draw all of the counters. What equation can you write to tell how many counters there are in all?*

2. Build Understanding

What are you asked to do? [Write an equation to tell how many counters in all] *What tools do you have to help you?* [Counters and ten-frame] *What does the number 10 mean in the equation?* [10 counters in the ten-frame]

 DURING

3. Ask Guiding Questions As Needed

What does the number after the plus sign represent? [The number of extra counters; the number greater than 10] *What does the number after the equal sign represent?* [How many counters in all]

 AFTER

4. Share and Discuss Solutions

Start with students' solutions. Have them share their strategies. If needed, show Gilbert's work to tell how many counters there are. Then discuss how the equation should be written.

5. Transition to the Visual Learning Bridge

You have shown that a complete ten-frame is a ten and anything left over is extra ones.

Later in this lesson, you will learn how to show 11, 12, and 13 as the sum of 10 and some extra ones.

Forming groups of tens and ones will help you to make greater numbers.

6. Extension for Early Finishers

What would the equation 1 + 10 = 11 mean? [It would mean one and one ten.] *How could it be represented as a drawing?* [A single counter and a filled ten-frame]

Solve & Share

Name _____

See margin for sample student work.

Lesson 10-1

Make 11, 12, and 13

$$10 + \underline{} = \underline{}$$

Directions Say: Use counters to fill the ten-frame. Put 1, 2, or 3 counters outside of the ten-frame. Draw all of the counters. What equation can you write to tell how many counters there are in all?

I can ... use drawings and equations to make the numbers 11, 12, and 13.

Content Standards K.NBT.A.1 Mathematical Practices MP.2, MP.4, MP.5, MP.7

Topic 10 | Lesson 1

Digital Resources at PearsonRealize.com

five hundred sixty-seven **567**

Analyze Student Work

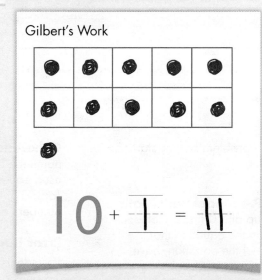

Gilbert's Work

Gilbert draws 10 counters in the ten-frame and 1 counter below it. He then correctly writes an equation to match his drawing.

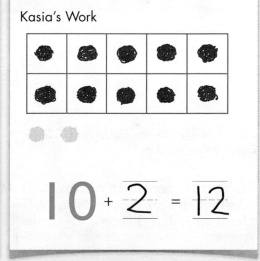

Kasia's Work

Kasia draws 10 counters in the ten-frame and 2 counters below it. She then correctly writes an equation to match her drawing.

The *Visual Learning Bridge* connects students' thinking in Solve & Share to important math ideas in the lesson. Use the *Visual Learning Bridge* to make these ideas explicit. Also available as a *Visual Learning Animation Plus* at PearsonRealize.com

E L L Visual Learning

Learn   Glossary

Jada needs to know how many boxes of t-shirts have arrived for the school fair. How can she organize them so she can count them easily? [Sample answer: She can put them in sets of ten.]

Jada put some of the boxes on the shelves in the picture. How many boxes fit on the shelves? [10; the shelves look like a filled ten-frame with 2 rows of 5.] *Are there any extra boxes that don't fit on the shelves?* [Yes.] *How many?* [3]

MP.2 Reasoning *What does the 10 represent?* [The number of boxes on the shelf; 10 ones, 1 ten] *What does the 3 mean?* [The number of extra boxes after the ten-frame was filled; 3 ones]

What does the equation say? [10 plus 3 is the same as 13; 10 plus 3 equals 13.] *What does the = sign mean?* [The amount of one side of the equation is the same as the amount on the other side.] *What is another way to say thirteen?* [1 ten and 3 ones]

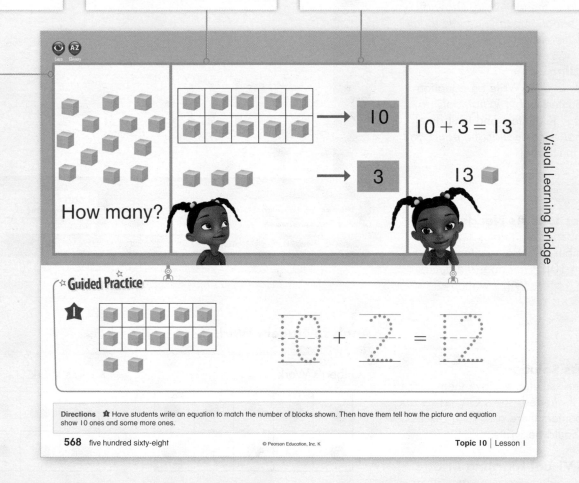

How many?

10 + 3 = 13

☆ **Guided Practice** ☆

Directions ⭐ Have students write an equation to match the number of blocks shown. Then have them tell how the picture and equation show 10 ones and some more ones.

568 five hundred sixty-eight   © Pearson Education, Inc. K   **Topic 10** | **Lesson 1**

Visual Learning Bridge

Complete the *Do You Understand? Show Me!* problem before starting Guided Practice.

Do You Understand? Show Me! MP.4 Model with Math
Have students work in pairs. Student A holds up all 10 fingers. Student B holds up 1, 2, or 3 fingers. Help students say the equation that represents the situation. As they say each part of the equation, have them touch the groups of fingers in turn.

Essential Question Ask the following Essential Question: *How can you write an equation to describe numbers that are greater than 10?* [Write the number 10 and add on the extra ones to make the number.]

Coherence This is the first lesson in a series about composing numbers. Students have the groundwork from Topic 8 where they used equations to show the two parts that make the whole. But in Topic 10, the emphasis is on the base-ten system wherein the teen numbers are composed of a 10 and some more ones.

Error Intervention: Item 1
If students are unable to tell how the picture and equation show 10 ones and some more ones,

then remind them to look at the ten-frame and count how many counters are inside the frame and how many are outside the frame.

1 RtI **Reteaching** Assign Reteaching Set A, p. 611.

✓ **QUICK CHECK**
Check mark indicates items for prescribing differentiation on the next page.
Items 7 and 8 are worth 1 point. Item 9 is worth up to 3 points.

20–30 min   Tools   Assessment

Item 2 MP.7 Use Structure Point out to students that the ten-frame provides structure for grouping ones into a ten. *Look at the red blocks in the ten-frame. How many are there?* [10] *Did you need to count them?* [No.] *You don't need to count them because the structure of the ten-frame provides 10 spaces and those 10 spaces are full.*

Items 4 and 5 Remind students to fill the ten-frame first. Explain that even though the entire ten-frame will be filled, it is important to fill it in the proper order: left to right and top to bottom. Model to students as needed.

Items 6 and 7 Point out to students that the full ten-frame is represented in the equation by the number 10. The extra counters drawn below the ten-frame are represented by the second addend in the equation. This understanding is key and should be repeated throughout Lessons 10-1, 10-2, and 10-3.

Items 8 and 9 MP.5 Use Appropriate Tools Strategically Have students use counters to plan how to fill the ten-frame and place counters below it. Using the manipulatives prior to drawing will help students organize their work.

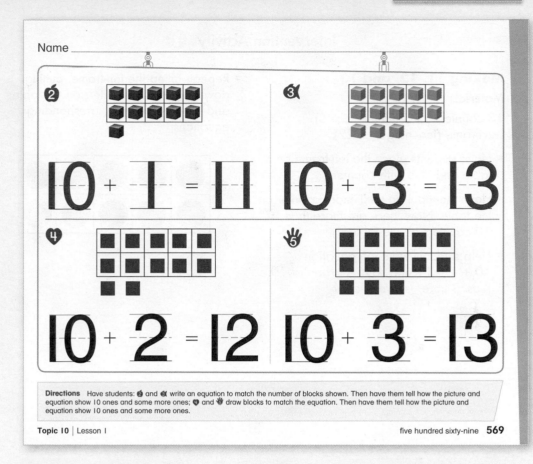

Name _____

2 10 + 1 = 11   **3** 10 + 3 = 13
4 10 + 2 = 12   **5** 10 + 3 = 13

Directions Have students: 2 and 3 write an equation to match the number of blocks shown. Then have them tell how the picture and equation show 10 ones and some more ones; 4 and 5 draw blocks to match the equation. Then have them tell how the picture and equation show 10 ones and some more ones.

Topic 10 | Lesson 1   five hundred sixty-nine **569**

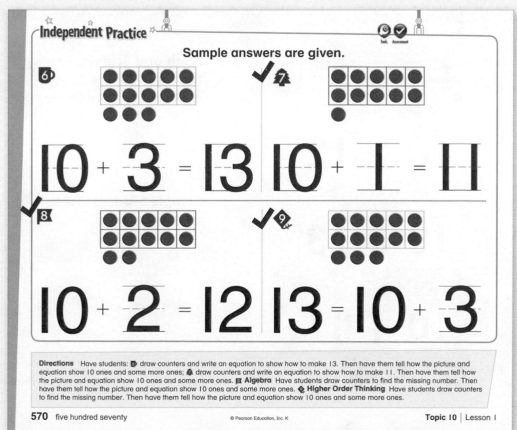

Independent Practice   Sample answers are given.

6 10 + 3 = 13   **7** 10 + 1 = 11
8 10 + 2 = 12   **9** 13 = 10 + 3

Directions Have students: 6 draw counters and write an equation to show how to make 13. Then have them tell how the picture and equation show 10 ones and some more ones; 7 draw counters and write an equation to show how to make 11. Then have them tell how the picture and equation show 10 ones and some more ones. 8 **Algebra** Have students draw counters to find the missing number. Then have them tell how the picture and equation show 10 ones and some more ones. 9 **Higher Order Thinking** Have students draw counters to find the missing number. Then have them tell how the picture and equation show 10 ones and some more ones.

570 five hundred seventy   © Pearson Education, Inc. K   Topic 10 | Lesson 1

STEP 3

ASSESS AND DIFFERENTIATE

2 RtI Use the **QUICK CHECK** on the previous page to prescribe differentiated instruction.

I Intervention
0–3 points on the Quick Check

O On-Level
4 points on the Quick Check

A Advanced
5 points on the Quick Check

Intervention Activity **I**

Making 11, 12, and 13
Materials

13 counters (or Teaching Tool 6), Ten-Frame (Teaching Tool 22)

• Have students place the ten-frame on a table and fill it with counters.

• Have them put down 1 more counter on the table. Now there are more than 10 counters on the table.

• Help students write the equation $10 + 1 = 11$ and say: *A group of 10, plus 1 more, is equal to 11.*

• Repeat, filling the ten-frame, putting down 2 (then 3) counters on the table, and then writing the corresponding equations.

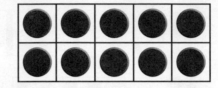

Reteach **I**

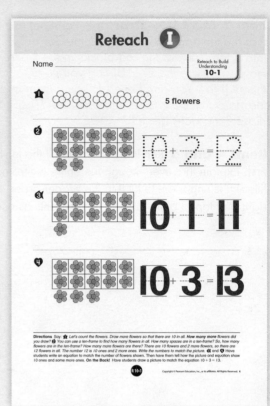

On-Level and Advanced Activity Centers **O** **A**

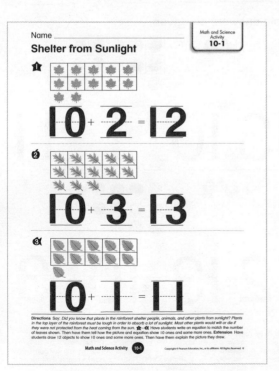

Math and Science Activity **STEM**

This activity revisits the science theme, **Sunlight and Earth's Surface,** introduced on page 563 in the Student's Edition.

Sample Student Work

TIMING

The time allocated to Step 3 will depend on the teacher's instructional decisions and differentiation routines.

15–30 min

 Help

 Tools

 Games

PEARSON
realize
PearsonRealize.com

Technology Center

 Tools

Games

Math Tools and Math Games

A link to a specific math tools activity or math game to use with this lesson is provided at PearsonRealize.com.

Leveled Assignment

 Items 1–2   Items 2–3   Items 3–4

Name _____

Help   Tools   Games

Homework & Practice 10-1

Make 11, 12, and 13

Another Look!

$$10 + 2 = 12$$

HOME ACTIVITY Have your child use pennies to model and explain how to make 11, 12, and 13 with 10 ones and some more ones.

⭐

$$10 + 3 = 13$$

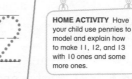

Directions Say: *You can use counters and a double ten-frame to show 12 as 10 ones and some more ones. Fill the first ten-frame with 10 counters. Then draw more counters to make 12, and write an equation to match the picture.* ⭐ Have students draw counters to make 13 and write an equation to match the picture. Then have them tell how the picture and equation show 10 ones and some more ones.

Topic 10 | Lesson 1   Digital Resources at PearsonRealize.com   five hundred seventy-one **571**

2

$$10 + 2 = 12$$

3

$$10 + 1 = 11$$

4

$$10 + 3 = 13$$
$$3 + 10 = 13$$

Directions 🌱 **Math and Science** Say: *Plants turn sunlight into food. This helps them grow. Li Mei planted 10 flowers in the sun. They grew tall. She planted 2 flowers in the shade. They did not grow as tall as the other flowers.* Have students draw flowers and write an equation to tell how many flowers Li Mei planted in all. **3** Have students draw counters to make 11 and write an equation to match the picture. Then have them tell how the picture and equation show 10 ones and some more ones. **4 Higher Order Thinking** Have students draw counters to find the missing numbers in the equations. Then have them tell how the picture and equations show 10 ones and some more ones.

572 five hundred seventy-two   © Pearson Education, Inc. K   Topic 10 | Lesson 1

LESSON 10-2

MAKE 14, 15, AND 16

LESSON OVERVIEW **FCR** FOCUS · COHERENCE · RIGOR

MATH ANYTIME

FOCUS

Domain K.NBT Number and Operations in Base Ten

Cluster K.NBT.A Work with numbers 11–19 to gain foundations for place value.

Content Standard K.NBT.A.1 Compose and decompose numbers from 11 to 19 into ten ones and some further ones, e.g., by using objects or drawings, and record each composition or decomposition by a drawing or equation (e.g., $18 = 10 + 8$); understand that these numbers are composed of ten ones and one, two, three, four, five, six, seven, eight, or nine ones.

Mathematical Practices MP.2, MP.3, MP.4, MP.7

Objective Make the numbers 14, 15, and 16.

Essential Understanding Numbers from 11–19 can be represented as the sum of 10 and some more.

Materials Two-color counters (or Teaching Tool 6)

COHERENCE

Students have experience composing numbers to 10. They have worked with manipulatives as well as the numbers themselves to compose a given number. In Lesson 10-1, students gained experience composing numbers greater than 10 into a group of ten and some more ones. In Lesson 10-2, they will continue to do so as they make numbers 14, 15, and 16. This lesson is the second in a series of three in which students work with the same concept, the focus is on different numbers in each lesson.

RIGOR

This lesson emphasizes **conceptual understanding**. Students will build on the concept that two parts can be combined to make a whole as they learn that ten ones and 4, 5 or 6 more ones combine to make a number from 14 to 16. They expand their knowledge of an equation representing a quantitative relationship.

 Watch the Listen and Look For Lesson Video.
PD

Daily Common Core Review

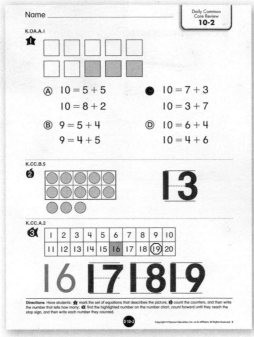

Today's Challenge
Think Use Topic 10 problems any time during this topic.

ENGLISH LANGUAGE LEARNERS **ELL**

Reading Use visual support to develop vocabulary.

Use with the Visual Learning Bridge on Student's Edition p. 574.

Divide students into partner groups. Give each student Ten-Frame (Teaching Tool 22). Distribute 14 cubes to each student. Say: *Put 10 cubes in one ten-frame, and the others in another ten-frame.* Ask: *How many cubes are in each ten-frame?* Point to the first ten-frame. Say: *10 ones.* Point to the second ten-frame. Say: *4 ones.* Ask: *What equation can be written for these ten-frames?* Give an

additional cube to each pair and ask students to put the cube in the second ten-frame.

Beginning Point to the first ten-frame. Say: *There are 10 ones.* Ask: *How many cubes are there?* Students should respond using the sentence stem: "There are __ ones in this ten-frame." Continue the process with the second ten-frame. Ask students to write an equation for 15 and read the equation to a partner.

Intermediate Ask: *How many ones are in each ten-frame? How many cubes in all?* Instruct students to write and read an equation for 15.

Advanced Ask students to use the ten-frames and cubes to write an equation for 15. Instruct students to read equations to a partner and explain what each number represents.

Summarize How are ten-frames used to make 14 and 15?

DEVELOP: PROBLEM-BASED LEARNING

COHERENCE: Engage students by connecting prior knowledge to new ideas.
Students use counters and a double ten-frame, and then write an equation to represent a number as one ten and some more ones. This prepares them for the next part of the lesson where students draw pictures and write an equation to tell how to compose a number from 14 to 16.

 10–15 min

 Solve

 **BEFORE**

1. Pose the Solve-and-Share Problem
MP.7 Use Structure Students place counters in a double ten-frame to represent a number. Students show a quantity of 10 ones and some more ones, and then write an equation to match.

Distribute 15 counters to each student.

Say: Put 15 counters in the double ten-frame to show 10 ones and some more ones. Then complete the equation to match the counters.

2. Build Understanding
What are you asked to do? [Write an equation to tell how many counters in all] *What tools do you have to help you?* [Counters and double ten-frame] *What does the number 15 mean in the equation?* [How many counters in all]

 **DURING**

3. Ask Guiding Questions As Needed
What part should you write first? [10] *What part of the double ten-frame does the 10 represent?* [The filled ten-frame at the top] *Do you need to count the counters in it?* [No.] *Why not?* [A filled ten-frame always shows 10.] *What part do you write next?* [5] *What does 15 look like on a double ten-frame?* [It is one complete ten-frame, plus one row of another ten-frame.]

 AFTER

4. Share and Discuss Solutions
 Start with students' solutions. Have them share
Solve their strategies. If needed, show Luciana's work to tell how many counters there are. Then discuss how the equation should be written.

5. Transition to the Visual Learning Bridge
You have shown that a complete ten-frame is a ten and anything left over is extra ones.

Later in this lesson, you will learn how to show 14, 15, and 16 as the sum of 10 and some extra ones.

Forming groups of tens and ones will help you to make greater numbers.

6. Extension for Early Finishers
Have pairs of students take turns counting on from 10 to 16.

Solve & Share   Name _____

See margin for sample student work.

Lesson 10-2
Make 14, 15, and 16

_ _ _ _ _ + _ _ _ _ _ = 15

Directions *Say: Put 15 counters in the double ten-frame to show 10 ones and some more ones. Then complete the equation to match the counters.*

I can ...
make the numbers 14, 15, and 16.

© **Content Standards**
K.NBT.A.1
Mathematical Practices
MP.2, MP.3, MP.4, MP.7

Topic 10 | Lesson 2   Digital Resources at PearsonRealize.com   five hundred seventy-three **573**

Analyze Student Work

Luciana's Work

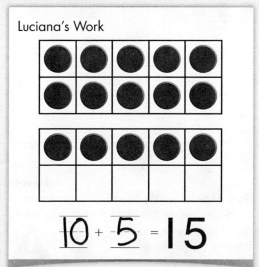

10 + 5 = 15

Luciana puts 15 counters in the double ten-frame. She then correctly writes an equation to match the counters.

Shannon's Work

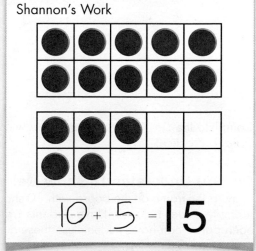

10 + 5 = 15

Shannon puts 15 counters in the double ten-frame, but she does not fill in the ten-frame from left to right. She correctly writes an equation to match the counters.

The *Visual Learning Bridge* connects students' thinking in Solve & Share to important math ideas in the lesson. Use the *Visual Learning Bridge* to make these ideas explicit. Also available as a *Visual Learning Animation Plus* at PearsonRealize.com

E L L
Visual Learning

Learn   Glossary

MP.2 Reasoning *Jada writes an equation to tell how many counters in all. She uses a double ten-frame and two-color counters to do so. Jada finds that filling a ten-frame gives her a group of 10 ones. What color is the group of 10?* [Red] *What color is the group of ones?* [Yellow] *How many extra ones are there?* [4] *What is the equation Jada wrote?* [10 + 4 = 14]

MP.3 Critique Reasoning *Alex also has a group of counters and writes an equation to tell how many counters in all. How many counters does he put into the top ten-frame?* [10] *Alex says he made a group of 10 ones. Is he correct?* [Yes; a filled ten-frame is a group of 10 ones.] *Alex places 6 counters in the bottom ten-frame. Then he writes 10 + 6 = 16. Does Alex write an equation to match his counters?* [Yes; the 10 matches the red counters and the 6 matches the yellow counters.]

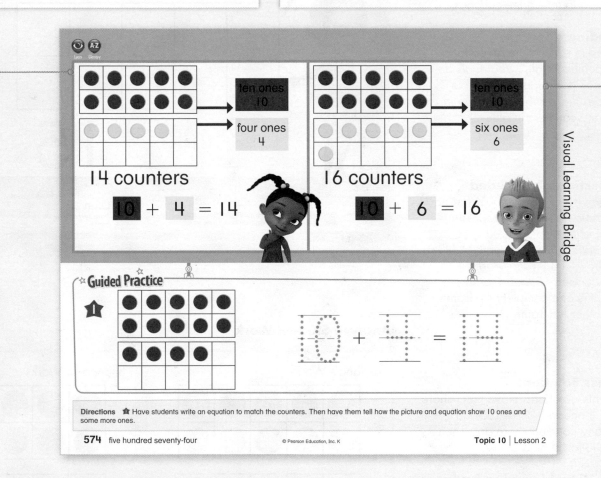

ten ones
10

four ones
4

14 counters

10 + 4 = 14

ten ones
10

six ones
6

16 counters

10 + 6 = 16

Visual Learning Bridge

☆ **Guided Practice**

1

10 + 4 = 14

Directions ☆ Have students write an equation to match the counters. Then have them tell how the picture and equation show 10 ones and some more ones.

574 five hundred seventy-four   © Pearson Education, Inc. K   **Topic 10** | Lesson 2

Complete the *Do You Understand? Show Me!* problem before starting Guided Practice.

Do You Understand? Show Me! MP.4 Model with Math
Draw a ten-frame on the board with 10 shaded circles inside it and 4 empty circles below it. Have students write the numbers next to each part. Than have students use these numbers to put together an equation: 10 + 4 = 14.

Essential Question

Ask the following Essential Question: *How can you write an equation to describe numbers that are greater than 10?* [Write the number 10 and add on the extra ones to make the number.]

Error Intervention: Item 1
If students are confused by the second ten-frame,

then have them count how many counters are in the second frame. Ask if the frame is full or not and have students explain what the second frame shows.

1
RtI
Reteaching Assign Reteaching Set B, p. 611.

☑ QUICK CHECK

Check mark indicates items for prescribing differentiation on the next page.
Items 6 and 7 are worth 1 point. Item 9 is worth up to 3 points.

20–30 min

Tools Assessment

Item 2 MP.7 Use Structure Make sure that students understand that 10 can be represented by 10 counters or by a single filled ten-frame, but that it cannot be represented by a single counter. Some students may try to represent 15 using 1 counter and 5 more counters, for example. Remind them that 15 is not 1 + 5, but rather 10 + 5. To help them, make certain that students are using the ten-frame. This can be accomplished by having students touch each counter as they read their equation.

Items 4 and 5 Point out to students that the two parts of the double ten-frame in these two items are set side by side. The double ten-frame functions in the same way, it is just positioned differently than they have seen. Explain that they should begin filling the ten-frame on the left first.

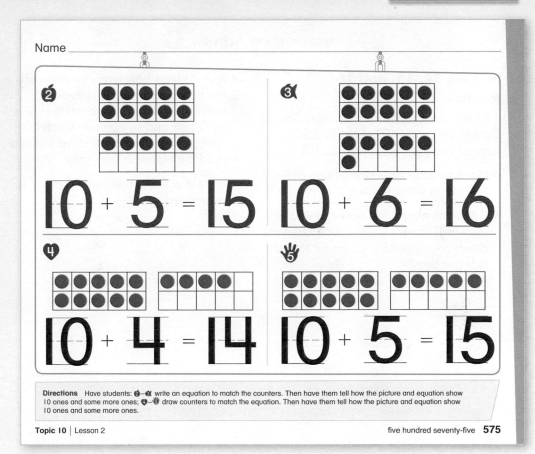

Directions Have students: ②–③ write an equation to match the counters. Then have them tell how the picture and equation show 10 ones and some more ones; ④–⑤ draw counters to match the equation. Then have them tell how the picture and equation show 10 ones and some more ones.

Topic 10 | Lesson 2   five hundred seventy-five **575**

Items 6 and 7 MP.2 Reasoning Remind students that the first number they write in the equation should be 10 to match the filled ten-frame. *What is the first number you write?* [10] *Why?* [There are 10 counters in the first ten-frame.] *What does the ten represent?* [1 ten; 10 ones] *Are there any more ones?* [Yes.] *How many extra ones are there?* [Check students' answers.]

Item 9 Ask students to focus on the given numbers and symbols in the equation before solving. *Why does the 16 come first?* [That is the total number.] *What does the equal sign mean?* [It is the balance point. Both sides of the equation show the same amount.] *If 10 is one of the parts, what does that mean for one of the ten-frames?* [The first ten-frame will be completely filled.]

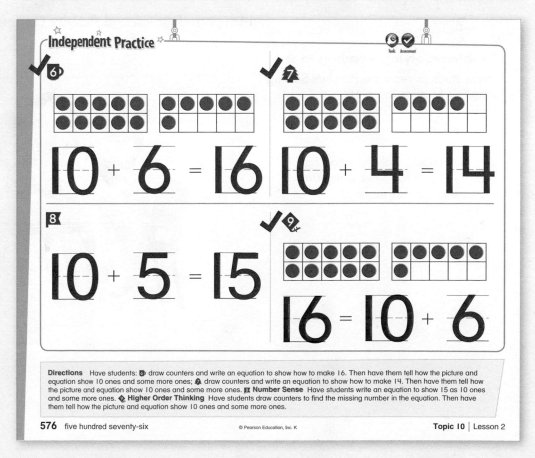

Directions Have students: ⑥ draw counters and write an equation to show how to make 16. Then have them tell how the picture and equation show 10 ones and some more ones; ⑦ draw counters and write an equation to show how to make 14. Then have them tell how the picture and equation show 10 ones and some more ones. ⑧ **Number Sense** Have students write an equation to show 15 as 10 ones and some more ones. ⑨ **Higher Order Thinking** Have students draw counters to find the missing number in the equation. Then have them tell how the picture and equation show 10 ones and some more ones.

576 five hundred seventy-six   © Pearson Education, Inc. K   Topic 10 | Lesson 2

ASSESS AND DIFFERENTIATE

STEP 3

Use the **QUICK CHECK** on the previous page to prescribe differentiated instruction.

I Intervention
0–3 points on the Quick Check

O On-Level
4 points on the Quick Check

A Advanced
5 points on the Quick Check

Intervention Activity

Making 14, 15, and 16
Materials
16 two-color counters (or Teaching Tool 6), Double Ten-Frame (Teaching Tool 23), number cube (or Teaching Tool 10)

• Have students help you fill one of the ten-frames with counters.

• Put the number cube down so 4 is showing. Have students put 4 counters down on the bottom ten-frame to show that number.

• Ask students how many counters are in the filled ten-frame. [10] Repeat for the bottom ten frame. [4] Touch the filled ten-frame and say *plus 4*. Touch both ten-frames and say *14*. Have students read the equation with you.

• Repeat with the numbers 15 and 16, as needed.

Reteach I

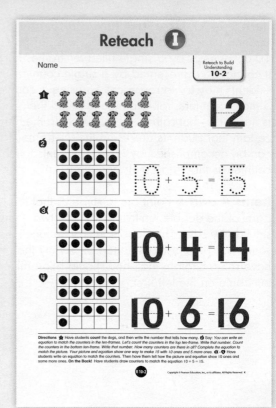

On-Level and Advanced Activity Centers O A

Problem-Solving Reading Mat

Have students read the Problem-Solving Reading Mat for Topic 10 and then complete Problem-Solving Reading Activity 10-2.

See the Problem-Solving Reading Activity Guide for other suggestions on how to use this mat.

TIMING

The time allocated to Step 3 will depend on the teacher's instructional decisions and differentiation routines.

15–30 min

 Help   Tools   Games

PEARSON
realize
PearsonRealize.com

Technology Center I O A

Math Tools and Math Games

A link to a specific math tools activity or math game to use with this lesson is provided at PearsonRealize.com.

Leveled Assignment

I Items 1–3   O Items 2–4   A Items 3–5

Name _____

Homework & Practice 10-2
Make 14, 15, and 16

Another Look!

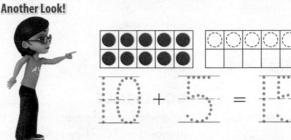

$$10 + 5 = 15$$

HOME ACTIVITY Have your child model the number 14 by drawing a big circle with 10 Xs inside the circle and 4 Xs outside the circle. Repeat with the numbers 15 and 16.

1 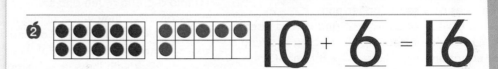 $10 + 4 = 14$

2 $10 + 6 = 16$

Directions Say: *Finish drawing counters in the ten-frame to make 15. Then write an equation to match the picture. The picture and equation show one way to make 15 with 10 ones and some more ones.* Have students: ✦ draw counters to make 14, and write an equation to match the picture. Then have them tell how the picture and equation show 10 ones and some more ones; ✌ draw counters to make 16 and write an equation to match the picture. Then have them tell how the picture and equation show 10 ones and some more ones.

---

3  $10 + 5 = 15$

4  $10 + 6 = 16$

5 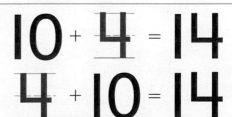 $10 + 4 = 14$

$$4 + 10 = 14$$

Directions Have students: ◑ draw counters to show how to make 15 and write an equation to match the picture. Then have them tell how the picture and equation show 10 ones and some more ones; ♦ draw counters to show how to make 16 and write an equation to match the picture. Then have them tell how the picture and equation show 10 ones and some more ones. ✋ **Higher Order Thinking** Have students draw counters to find the missing numbers in the equations. Then have them tell how the picture and equations show 10 ones and some more ones.

DIGITAL RESOURCES PearsonRealize.com

 Student and Teacher eTexts **eText**	Listen and Look For Lesson Video **PD**	Today's Challenge **Think**

Solve and Share **Solve**

 Visual Learning Animation Plus **Learn**

A-Z Animated Glossary **Glossary**

 Math Tools **Tools**

Quick Check **Assessment**

Another Look Homework Video **Help**

 Math Games **Games**

LESSON OVERVIEW **F C R** FOCUS • COHERENCE • RIGOR

FOCUS

Domain K.NBT Number and Operations in Base Ten

Cluster K.NBT.A Work with numbers 11–19 to gain foundations for place value.

Content Standard K.NBT.A.1 Compose and decompose numbers from 11 to 19 into ten ones and some further ones, e.g., by using objects or drawings, and record each composition or decomposition by a drawing or equation (e.g., $18 = 10 + 8$); understand that these numbers are composed of ten ones and one, two, three, four, five, six, seven, eight, or nine ones.

Mathematical Practices MP.1, MP.2, MP.4, MP.7

Objective Make the numbers 17, 18, and 19.

Essential Understanding Numbers from 11–19 can be represented as the sum of 10 and some more.

Materials Two-color counters (or Teaching Tool 6)

COHERENCE

Students have experience composing numbers to 10. They have worked with manipulatives as well as the numbers themselves to compose a given number. In Lessons 10-1 and 10-2, students gained experience composing numbers greater than 10 into a group of ten and some more ones. In Lesson 10-3, they will continue to do so as they make numbers 17, 18, and 19. This lesson is the final in a series of three in which students work with the same concept; the focus is on different numbers in each lesson.

RIGOR

This lesson emphasizes **conceptual understanding**. Students will build on the concept that two parts can be combined to make a whole as they learn that ten ones and 7, 8 or 9 more ones combine to make a number from 17 to 19. They expand their knowledge of an equation representing a quantitative relationship.

 Watch the Listen and Look For Lesson Video.

MATH ANYTIME

Daily Common Core Review

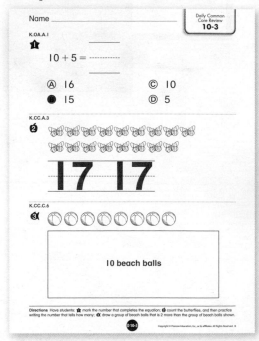

Today's Challenge

Think Use Topic 10 problems any time during this topic.

ENGLISH LANGUAGE LEARNERS **E L L**

Reading Demonstrate comprehension by responding to questions.

Use with the Solve & Share on Student's Edition p. 579.

Write and read the equation $10 + 7 = 17$. Point to 10. Say: *There is 1 ten.* Point to 7. Say: *There are 7 ones.* Point to 17. Say: *The sum is 17.* Divide students into groups of three. Distribute to each group: Double Ten-Frame (Teaching Tool 23), 19 cubes, and index cards with the following equations: $10 + 7 = 17$, $10 + 8 = 18$, $10 + 9 = 19$. Have students select a card

and read the equation. Say: *Use the ten-frames to demonstrate your equation. How many cubes will you put in each ten-frame?*

Beginning Ask: *What is the sum?* Write and read the sentence stem: "The sum is ___." Ask students to respond to the question by using the sentence stem.

Intermediate Ask: *What is the sum?* Write and read the sentence stems: "The sum is ___. I know because ___." Ask students to respond to the question using the sentence stems.

Advanced Distribute index cards with the following equations to each group: ___ $+ 7 = 17$, $10 +$ ___ $= 17$, $10 + 7 =$ ___. Have students in each group select a card and read it to group members. Ask: *How will you use a ten-frame to solve your equation?* Students should use ten-frames to explain how their equations are solved. Continue the process with equations with sums of 18 and 19.

Summarize How are ten-frames used to make 17, 18, and 19?

STEP 1 — DEVELOP: PROBLEM-BASED LEARNING

COHERENCE: Engage students by connecting prior knowledge to new ideas.

Students use counters and a double ten-frame, and then write an equation to represent a number as one ten and some more ones. This prepares them for the next part of the lesson where students draw pictures and write an equation to tell how to compose a number from 17 to 19.

 10–15 min

 Solve

 BEFORE

1. Pose the Solve-and-Share Problem

MP.4 Model with Math Students model and solve a problem using counters, a double ten-frame, and an equation. Students show a quantity of ten ones and some more ones, and then write an equation to match.

Distribute 19 counters to each student.

Say: *Jada made 10 prizes for the school carnival. She makes 8 more. Use counters to show how many prizes Jada made in all. Then write an equation to match the counters, and tell how the counters and equation show 10 ones and some more ones.*

2. Build Understanding

What are you asked to do? [Find the number of prizes Jada made in all] *What should you do first?* [Show the 10 prizes Jada made] *What tools do you have to help you?* [Counters and double ten-frame]

 DURING

3. Ask Guiding Questions As Needed

What are the two ways to represent the 10 prizes Jada made? [Put 10 counters in the top ten-frame and write 10 as the first part of the equation.] *How many more prizes does Jada make?* [8] *What does the plus sign mean?* [Add to]

 **AFTER**

4. Share and Discuss Solutions

Start with students' solutions. Have them share their strategies. If needed, show Bao's work to tell how many counters there are. Then discuss how the equation should be written.

5. Transition to the Visual Learning Bridge

You have shown that a complete ten-frame is a ten and anything left over is extra ones.

Later in this lesson, you will learn how to show 17, 18, and 19 as the sum of ten and some extra ones.

Forming groups of tens and ones will help you to make greater numbers.

6. Extension for Early Finishers

Suppose Jada had 10 prizes, but she needed to have 19 for the carnival. How could you use an equation and counters to find how many more prizes she would need to make? [Fill one ten-frame and then 9 spaces in the other ten-frame. $10 + 9 = 19$]

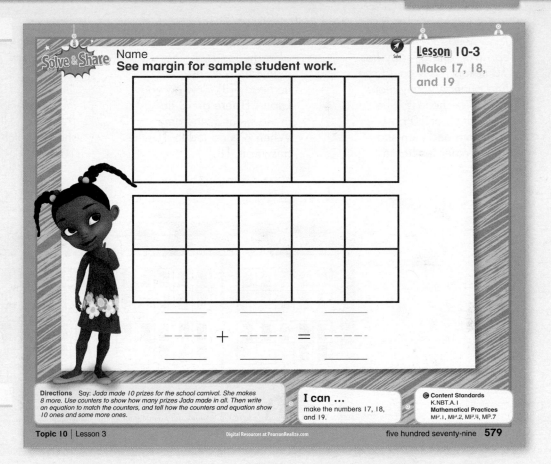

Solve & Share

Name _____
See margin for sample student work.

Lesson 10-3
Make 17, 18, and 19

____ + ____ = ____

Directions Say: *Jada made 10 prizes for the school carnival. She makes 8 more. Use counters to show how many prizes Jada made in all. Then write an equation to match the counters, and tell how the counters and equation show 10 ones and some more ones.*

I can ... make the numbers 17, 18, and 19.

Content Standards K.NBT.A.1 **Mathematical Practices** MP.1, MP.2, MP.4, MP.7

Topic 10 | Lesson 3 — Digital Resources at PearsonRealize.com — five hundred seventy-nine **579**

Analyze Student Work

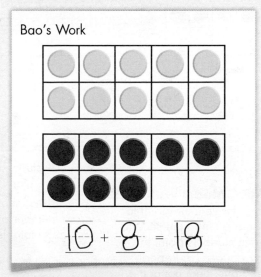

Bao's Work

$10 + 8 = 18$

Bao puts 18 counters in the double ten-frame. He then correctly writes an equation to match the counters.

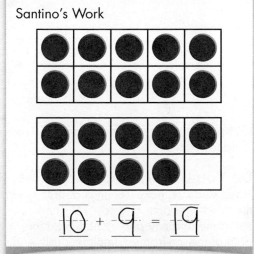

Santino's Work

$10 + 9 = 19$

Santino incorrectly puts 19 counters in the double ten-frame. He then writes an equation, however, that matches the counters.

STEP 2

DEVELOP: VISUAL LEARNING

The *Visual Learning Bridge* connects students' thinking in Solve & Share to important math ideas in the lesson. Use the *Visual Learning Bridge* to make these ideas explicit. Also available as a *Visual Learning Animation Plus* at PearsonRealize.com

ELL Visual Learning

Learn   Glossary

Jada needs 17 tickets for a carnival. She already has 10 tickets. How could she find out how many more tickets she needs? [She could think of 10 on one ten-frame and then show 7 on the other ten-frame.]

Alex needs 18 tickets. He already has 10 tickets. How many more tickets does he need? [8] How do you know? [There are 8 tickets in the second ten-frame. When 8 is added to 10, the answer is 18.]

MP.1 Make Sense and Persevere *Tell a story about this box. Begin with "Jada has 10 tickets." Use the words* How many more? [Answers will vary but should match the equation $10 + 9 = 19$.]

MP.2 Reasoning *How are these equations alike?* [They all begin with 10 and then have some ones added.] *What does the word* sum *mean?* [The total number of objects in all]

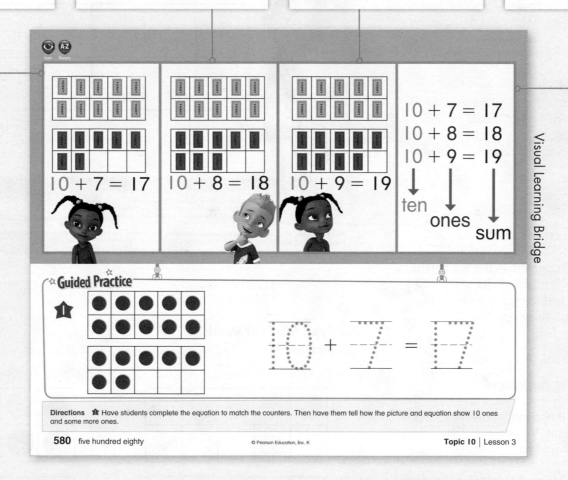

$10 + 7 = 17$
$10 + 8 = 18$
$10 + 9 = 19$
ten   ones   sum

★ Guided Practice

$$10 + 7 = 17$$

Directions ★ Have students complete the equation to match the counters. Then have them tell how the picture and equation show 10 ones and some more ones.

580 five hundred eighty   © Pearson Education, Inc. K   **Topic 10 | Lesson 3**

Visual Learning Bridge

Complete the *Do You Understand? Show Me!* problem before starting Guided Practice.

Do You Understand? Show Me! MP.4 Model with Math

Have students make 18 on a double ten-frame. Have them point to the filled ten-frame and say *10*. Then have them point to the second ten-frame and say *plus something*. Finally, have students point to both of the ten-frames simultaneously and say *equals 18*. Repeat, having students say the words with you. Then have them count the number of spaces that are filled in the second ten-frame to find the missing amount.

Essential Question Ask the following Essential Question: *How can you write an equation to describe numbers that are greater than 10?* [Write the number 10 and add on the extra ones to make the number.]

580 Topic 10

Error Intervention: Item 1

If students complete the equation by writing 17 rather than 7 in the blank,

then show them that the number added to ten must be the number of counters in the bottom ten-frame, and point out that the total is already written in the equation.

1 RtI **Reteaching** Assign Reteaching Set C, p. 612.

☑ **QUICK CHECK**
Check mark indicates items for prescribing differentiation on the next page.
Items 7 and 8 are worth 1 point. Item 9 is worth up to 3 points.

20–30 min   Tools   Assessment

Items 2 and 3 MP.7 Use Structure Remind students that a benefit of using a double ten-frame is that it provides the structure for grouping ones into a ten. *Look at the double ten-frame. Is one of the ten-frames filled?* [Yes.] *How many counters are in a filled ten-frame?* [10] *Did you need to count them?* [No.] *You don't need to count them because the structure of the ten-frame provides 10 spaces and those 10 spaces are full.*

Items 4 and 5 Allow students to use counters to help them plan their drawings. Give students 19 counters and allow them to arrange the counters as needed before they draw the counters in the book.

Item 6 MP.2 Reasoning Give students the option to use two colors to draw the counters. Guide them to use the colors to differentiate between the group of 10 ones and the extra ones. They can even use the different colors to write the addends in the equation in the matching color. *What color are the counters in the filled ten-frame?* [Sample answer: Red] *A filled ten-frame represents a group of 10 ones. What color are the counters in the other ten-frame?* [Sample answer: Yellow] *The extra counters in this ten-frame represent a group of 8 ones. What equation should you write?* [10 + 8 = 18]

Item 9 Explain to students that in this item they are trying to figure out *how many more*, not *how many in all*. This type of problem will prepare them for the next series of lessons in which they will decompose the teen numbers.

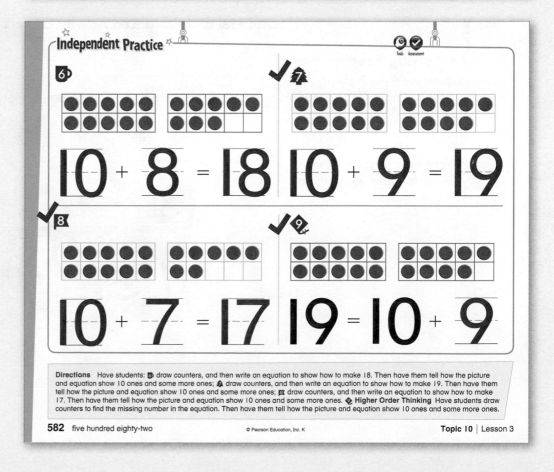

Name _____

2    $10 + 9 = 19$ 3 $10 + 8 = 18$

4    $10 + 7 = 17$ 5 $10 + 9 = 19$

Directions Have students: ② and ③ write an equation to match the counters. Then have them tell how the picture and equation show 10 ones and some more ones; ④ and ⑤ draw counters to match the equation. Then have them tell how the picture and equation show 10 ones and some more ones.

Topic 10 | Lesson 3   five hundred eighty-one **581**

Independent Practice   Tools Assessment

6   ✓7

$10 + 8 = 18$ $10 + 9 = 19$

✓8   ✓9

$10 + 7 = 17$ $19 = 10 + 9$

Directions Have students: ⑥ draw counters, and then write an equation to show how to make 18. Then have them tell how the picture and equation show 10 ones and some more ones; ⑦ draw counters, and then write an equation to show how to make 19. Then have them tell how the picture and equation show 10 ones and some more ones; ⑧ draw counters, and then write an equation to show how to make 17. Then have them tell how the picture and equation show 10 ones and some more ones. ⑨ **Higher Order Thinking** Have students draw counters to find the missing number in the equation. Then have them tell how the picture and equation show 10 ones and some more ones.

582 five hundred eighty-two   © Pearson Education, Inc. K   Topic 10 | Lesson 3

ASSESS AND DIFFERENTIATE

 Use the **QUICK CHECK** on the previous page to prescribe differentiated instruction.

I Intervention
0–3 points on the Quick Check

O On-Level
4 points on the Quick Check

A Advanced
5 points on the Quick Check

Intervention Activity **I**

Making 17, 18, and 19
Materials
19 two-color counters (or Teaching Tool 6), Double Ten-Frames (Teaching Tool 23)

• Have students fill one of the ten-frames with counters.

• Take a handful of the remaining counters. Show them to students. Ask students to estimate how many there are.

• Have students put counters down on the second ten-frame to show that number.

• Touch the filled ten-frame and say *10*. Touch the other ten-frame and say the number of counters. Have students repeat. Then help students identify how many counters there are in all.

• Repeat, taking a different number of counters. Continue with other amounts as needed.

Reteach **I**

Name _____

Reteach to Build Understanding 10-3

On-Level and Advanced Activity Centers **O** **A**

Problem-Solving Reading Mat
Have students read the Problem-Solving Reading Mat for Topic 10 and then complete Problem-Solving Reading Activity 10-3.

See the Problem-Solving Reading Activity Guide for other suggestions on how to use this mat.

TIMING

The time allocated to Step 3 will depend on the teacher's instructional decisions and differentiation routines.

15–30 min

 Help

 Tools

 Games

Technology Center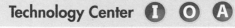

 Tools

Math Tools and Math Games

A link to a specific math tools activity or math game to use with this lesson is provided at PearsonRealize.com.

 Games

Leveled Assignment

I Items 1–3   **O** Items 2–4   **A** Items 3–5

Name _____

Another Look!

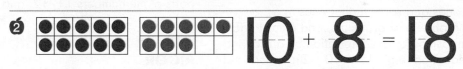

Homework & Practice 10-3

Make 17, 18, and 19

HOME ACTIVITY Place 10 marbles or other small objects in a bowl. In a second bowl, have your child count on from 10 while adding objects until there are 17 objects in all. Repeat with 19 and then 18 objects in all.

1. $10 + 7 = 17$

2. $10 + 8 = 18$

Directions Say: *Finish drawing counters in the ten-frame to show how to make 19. Then write an equation to match the picture. The picture and equation show how to make 19 with 10 ones and some more ones.* Have students: ★ *draw counters, and then write the equation to show how to make 17. Then have them tell how the picture and equation show 10 ones and some more ones;* ✿ *draw counters to show how to make 18, and then write an equation to match the picture. Then have them tell how the picture and equation show 10 ones and some more ones.*

Topic 10 | Lesson 3   Digital Resources at PearsonRealize.com   five hundred eighty-three **583**

3. $10 + 9 = 19$

4. $10 + 7 = 17$

5. $18 = 10 + 8$
$10 + 8 = 18$

Directions Have students: ★ *draw counters to make 19, and then write an equation to match the picture. Then have them tell how the picture and equation show 10 ones and some more ones;* ✿ *draw counters to make 17, and then write an equation to match the picture. Then have them tell how the picture and equation show 10 ones and some more ones.* ✋ **Higher Order Thinking** *Have students draw counters to find the missing numbers in the equations. Then have them tell how the picture and equation show 10 ones and some more ones.*

584 five hundred eighty-four   © Pearson Education, Inc. K   **Topic 10 | Lesson 3**

583–584

DIGITAL RESOURCES PearsonRealize.com

 Student and Teacher eTexts — eText

 Listen and Look For Lesson Video — PD

 Today's Challenge — Think

 Solve and Share — Solve

 Visual Learning Animation Plus — Learn

 Animated Glossary — Glossary

 Math Tools — Tools

 Quick Check — Assessment

 Another Look Homework Video — Help

 Math Games — Games

LESSON OVERVIEW   FOCUS • COHERENCE • RIGOR

FOCUS

Domain K.NBT Number and Operations in Base Ten

Cluster K.NBT.A Work with numbers 11–19 to gain foundations for place value.

Content Standard K.NBT.A.1 Compose and decompose numbers from 11 to 19 into ten ones and some further ones, e.g., by using objects or drawings, and record each composition or decomposition by a drawing or equation (e.g., 18 = 10 + 8); understand that these numbers are composed of ten ones and one, two, three, four, five, six, seven, eight, or nine ones.

Mathematical Practices MP.4, MP.6, MP.7, MP.8

Objective Find parts of the numbers 11, 12, and 13.

Essential Understanding The numbers 11, 12, and 13 can be decomposed as the sum of ten and some ones.

Materials Two-color counters (or Teaching Tool 6)

COHERENCE

Students have experience decomposing numbers to 10. They have worked with manipulatives as well as the numbers themselves to decompose a given number. In Topic 10, students will decompose greater numbers. In Lesson 10-4, they will find parts of the numbers 11, 12, and 13 using objects, drawings, and numbers to help them.

RIGOR

This lesson emphasizes **conceptual understanding**. Students will build on the concept that a number can break apart into two parts. In Topic 10, the focus is on breaking the numbers into a group of 10 ones and some more ones. Students expand their knowledge of an equation representing a quantitative relationship. Students continue to establish a basic understanding of place value in our base-ten numeration system.

 Watch the Listen and Look For Lesson Video.

MATH ANYTIME

Daily Common Core Review

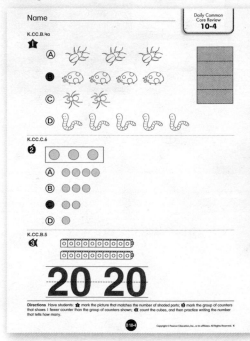

 Today's Challenge

Think Use Topic 10 problems any time during this topic.

ENGLISH LANGUAGE LEARNERS ELL

Listening Learn basic/academic vocabulary.

Use with the Visual Learning Bridge on Student's Edition p. 586.

Display 2 ten-frames. Say: *I have 12 sticky notes.* Put sticky notes on the ten-frames. Count the sticky notes in the first ten-frame with students. Write *10 ones*. Say: *There are 10 ones.* Count the sticky notes in the second ten-frame with students. Write *2 ones*. Say: *There are 2 ones.* Write *12 = 10 + 2*. Point to 12. Say: *12 is the sum.* Point to 10 and 2. Say: *There are 10 ones and 2 ones.*

Distribute 2 ten-frames and 13 counters to partner groups.

Beginning Ask students to put 10 counters in one ten-frame and 3 counters in the other. Point to the first ten-frame. Ask: *How many ones?* Have students listen to partners respond using the sentence stem: "There are __ ones." Continue the process with the second ten-frame.

Intermediate Ask students to put 10 counters in one ten-frame and 3 counters in the other. Write *13 = 10 + 3*. Have students work with partners to demonstrate

the equation using ten-frames. Ask: *Which frame shows 10 ones?* Have students listen to partners respond using the sentence stem: "This frame shows 10 ones because ____."

Advanced Write *13 = 10 + 3*. Ask students to work with partners to demonstrate the equation using ten-frames. Have students identify the sum, 10 ones, and 3 ones in the equation, and then explain how they knew.

Summarize What does 10 ones and 3 ones mean?

DEVELOP: PROBLEM-BASED LEARNING

PEARSON
realize
PearsonRealize.com

Solve

COHERENCE: Engage students by connecting prior knowledge to new ideas.

Students use counters and write an equation to show 13 in two parts. This prepares them for the next part of the lesson where they break apart 11, 12, and 13 into a group of 10 ones and 1, 2, or 3 more ones.

10–15 min

BEFORE

1. Pose the Solve-and-Share Problem

MP.7 Use Structure Students place counters in a double ten-frame to represent the two parts that make a greater number. Students show a quantity of 10 ones and some more ones, and then write an equation to match.

Distribute 13 counters to each student.

Say: *13 students wait for the train. There are only 10 seats in each train car. How many students will have to ride in a second car? Use counters to show your work. Then tell how the counters and equation show 10 ones and some more ones.*

2. Build Understanding

What are you asked to do? [Find how many students have to ride in the second train car] *What tools do you have to help you?* [Counters and double ten-frame] *What number are you breaking apart to find the answer?* [13]

DURING

3. Ask Guiding Questions As Needed

The top ten-frame represents the first train car. How many students are in the first train car? [10] *How many counters are there in all?* [13] *When you break apart 13 into a group of 10 ones and some extra ones, where can you put the extra ones?* [In the other ten-frame]

AFTER

4. Share and Discuss Solutions

 Start with students' solutions. Have them share their strategies. If needed, show Julia's work to show how to break apart 13 into a group of 10 ones and some more ones. Then discuss how the equation should be written.

5. Transition to the Visual Learning Bridge

You have shown how to break apart 13 into a group of 10 ones and a group of 3 ones.

Later in this lesson, you will learn how to break apart other numbers using drawings and equations to model your work.

6. Extension for Early Finishers

How could you break apart 14 into 10 ones and some more ones using a double ten-frame and counters? What equation would you write? [Allow students to share ideas.]

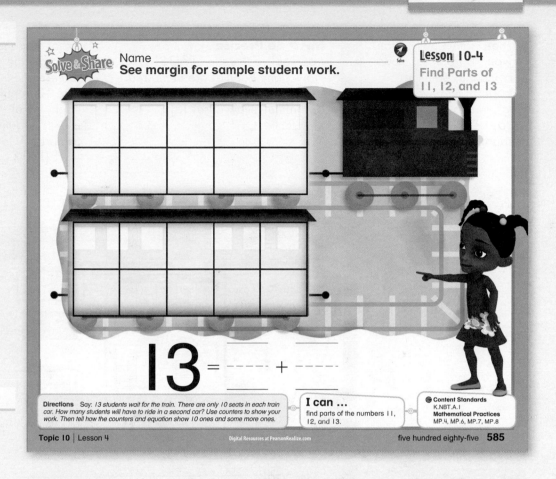

Solve & Share

Name _____
See margin for sample student work.

Lesson 10-4
Find Parts of 11, 12, and 13

$$13 = \underline{} + \underline{}$$

Directions Say: *13 students wait for the train. There are only 10 seats in each train car. How many students will have to ride in a second car? Use counters to show your work. Then tell how the counters and equation show 10 ones and some more ones.*

I can ... find parts of the numbers 11, 12, and 13.

© Content Standards K.NBT.A.1
Mathematical Practices MP.4, MP.6, MP.7, MP.8

Topic 10 | Lesson 4

Digital Resources at PearsonRealize.com

five hundred eighty-five **585**

Analyze Student Work

Julia's Work

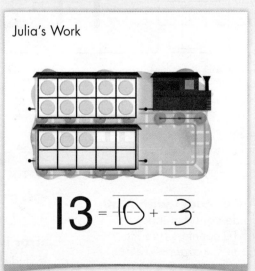

$$13 = \underline{10} + \underline{3}$$

Julia puts 13 counters in the double ten-frame. She then correctly writes an equation to match the counters.

Caleb's Work

$$13 = \underline{10} + \underline{3}$$

Caleb puts 13 counters in the double ten-frame. He then correctly writes an equation to match the counters.

The *Visual Learning Bridge* connects students' thinking in Solve & Share to important math ideas in the lesson. Use the *Visual Learning Bridge* to make these ideas explicit. Also available as a *Visual Learning Animation Plus* at PearsonRealize.com

ELL
Visual Learning

The Dolphin Swim Team won 13 trophies. How could they split the trophies into two groups to put into 2 trophy cases? [Have students share their ideas.]

MP.6 Be Precise *How many trophies are there in all?* [13] *How many trophies are in the red case?* [10] *How many trophies are in the yellow case?* [3]

What does the phrase 10 ones and the number 10 represent in the red box? [The 10 trophies in the red trophy case] *What does 3 ones and the number 3 represent in the yellow box?* [The 3 extra trophies]

Read the equation with me: 13 equals 10 plus 3. What does the 10 represent? [The group of 10 trophies; 10 ones] *What does the 3 represent?* [The group of 3 trophies; 3 ones] *Which number tells the total number of trophies?* [13]

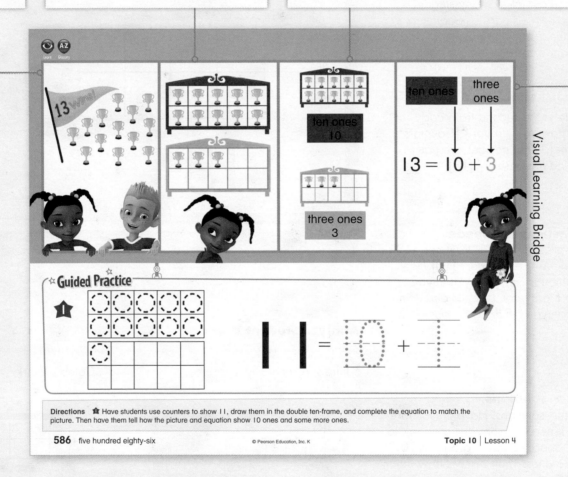

Visual Learning Bridge

Directions ★ Have students use counters to show 11, draw them in the double ten-frame, and complete the equation to match the picture. Then have them tell how the picture and equation show 10 ones and some more ones.

586 five hundred eighty-six   © Pearson Education, Inc. K   **Topic 10** | Lesson 4

Complete the *Do You Understand? Show Me!* problem before starting Guided Practice.

Do You Understand? Show Me! MP.4 Model with Math
Show students 12 two-color counters all red-side up. From those 12 counters, ask children to separate a group of 10 counters and flip them to be yellow-side up. *There are 10 ones in this group. We can call this group 1 ten. How many more counters are there?* [2] Write 12 = 10 + 2 on the board. Have students read the equation with you. Remind students that they have seen decomposition equations before in Topic 8. These types of equations are written with the total number first, then the equal sign, and then the two numbers that describe the parts with the plus sign in between them.

Essential Question
Ask the following Essential Question: *How can you write an equation to break apart numbers that are greater than 10?* [Break the number into a group of ten ones and another group of the leftover ones.]

Error Intervention: Item 1
If students do not make a group of 10 counters,

then remind them to fill up the top ten-frame entirely with 10 counters before moving on to the other ten-frame.

RtI 1
Reteaching Assign Reteaching Set D, p. 612.

☑ QUICK CHECK
Check mark indicates items for prescribing differentiation on the next page.
Items 5 and 6 are worth 1 point. Item 7 is worth up to 3 points.

Item 2 MP.4 Model with Math
Provide students with two-color counters. Encourage the use of red counters in one of the ten-frames and yellow counters in the other ten-frame. This emphasizes the concept of the numbers 11 to 13 (and up to 19 in later lessons) as a ten and some more ones.

Item 4
Listen to students' explanations as they tell how their picture matches the given equation. Answers should include words such as *break apart* and *ten-frame*. Keep alert for explanations that indicate students are developing an understanding of the base-ten numeration system.

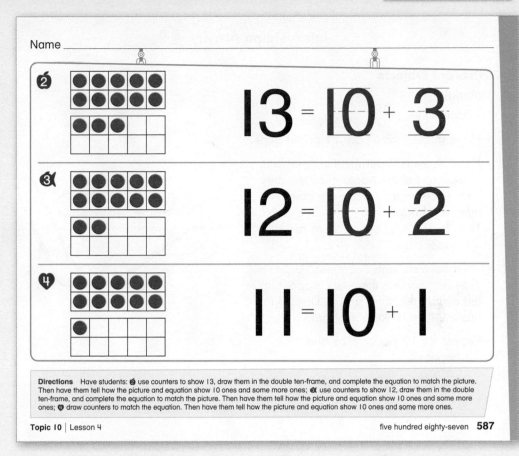

Name _____

Directions Have students: ② use counters to show 13, draw them in the double ten-frame, and complete the equation to match the picture. Then have them tell how the picture and equation show 10 ones and some more ones; ③ use counters to show 12, draw them in the double ten-frame, and complete the equation to match the picture. Then have them tell how the picture and equation show 10 ones and some more ones; ④ draw counters to match the equation. Then have them tell how the picture and equation show 10 ones and some more ones.

Topic 10 | Lesson 4   five hundred eighty-seven **587**

Item 6 MP.8 Generalize
By now students should realize that they do not need to count every single counter in a ten-frame to know that a full ten-frame has a quantity of 10. Look for students to develop automaticity in both writing 10 to tell how many counters in a full ten-frame and filling in an entire ten-frame to show 10 counters.

Item 7
Before students begin to work on this problem, point out that they should be mindful of the symbols in each equation. Students rushing quickly through their work or not paying attention to detail could make a mistake if not careful.

Coherence
Students have shifted from composing numbers 11 to 19 in Lessons 10-1 through 10-3, to decomposing numbers of the same range (11 to 19). This lesson is the first in a series of three that allows students to practice breaking apart the teen numbers into a group of tens and some more ones.

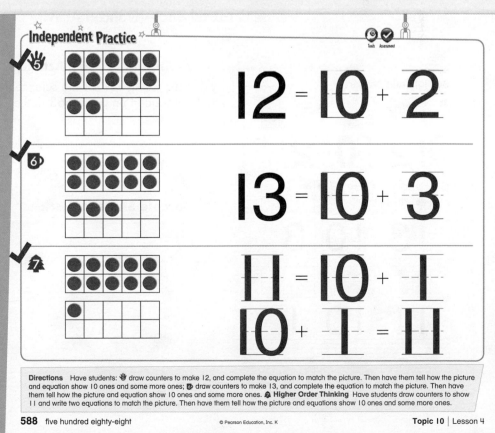

Independent Practice

Directions Have students: ⑤ draw counters to make 12, and complete the equation to match the picture. Then have them tell how the picture and equation show 10 ones and some more ones; ⑥ draw counters to make 13, and complete the equation to match the picture. Then have them tell how the picture and equation show 10 ones and some more ones. ⑦ **Higher Order Thinking** Have students draw counters to show 11 and write two equations to match the picture. Then have them tell how the picture and equations show 10 ones and some more ones.

588 five hundred eighty-eight   © Pearson Education, Inc. K   **Topic 10 | Lesson 4**

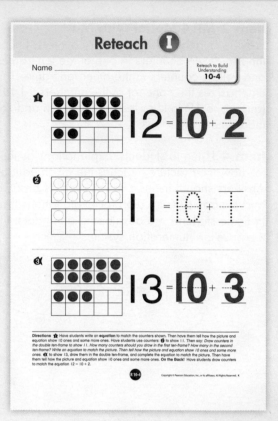

STEP 3 ASSESS AND DIFFERENTIATE

Use the **QUICK CHECK** on the previous page to prescribe differentiated instruction.

2 RtI

I Intervention
0–3 points on the Quick Check

O On-Level
4 points on the Quick Check

A Advanced
5 points on the Quick Check

Intervention Activity I

Different Objects
Materials

13 Paper clips

- Have students count out 11 paper clips.

- Have students experiment with making two groups of the paper clips. As they form each group, have them count the number of paper clips in each group. Then have them confirm there are still 11 paper clips.

- Then have students count out 10 paper clips and confirm there is 1 paper clip left over in the other group. Discuss how this situation is like a ten-frame.

- Repeat for 12 paper clips and 13 paper clips.

Reteach I

Name _____

Reteach to Build Understanding 10-4

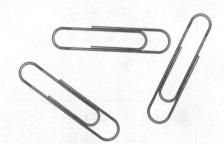

On-Level and Advanced Activity Centers O A

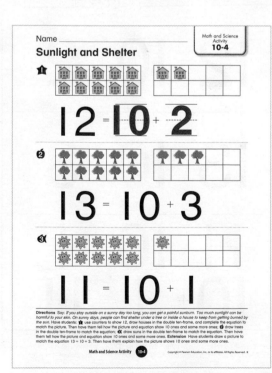

Math and Science Activity STEM

This activity revisits the science theme, **Sunlight and Earth's Surface,** introduced on page 563 in the Student's Edition.

Sample Student Work

TIMING

The time allocated to Step 3 will depend on the teacher's instructional decisions and differentiation routines.

15–30 min

Help   Tools   Games

Technology Center I O A

Math Tools and Math Games

Tools

A link to a specific math tools activity or math game to use with this lesson is provided at PearsonRealize.com

Games

Leveled Assignment

I Items 1–2   **O** Items 2–3   **A** Items 3–4

Name _____

Help   Tools   Games

Homework & Practice 10-4
Find Parts of 11, 12, and 13

Another Look!

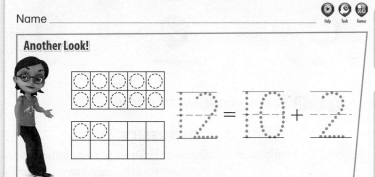

$$12 = 10 + 2$$

HOME ACTIVITY Have your child sort a group of 12 pencils into one group of 10 pencils and one group of 2 pencils. Discuss how many pencils are in each group and how many pencils there are in all. Repeat with 13 pencils and 11 pencils.

1

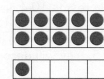

$$11 = 10 + 1$$

Directions Say: *Draw counters in the double ten-frame to show 12 and write an equation to match the picture. The picture and equation show 10 ones and some more ones.* 🡅 Have students draw counters to show 11 and write an equation to match the picture. Then have them tell how the picture and equation show 10 ones and some more ones.

Topic 10 | Lesson 4   Digital Resources at PearsonRealize.com   five hundred eighty-nine **589**

2

$$13 = 10 + 3$$

3

$$12 = 10 + 2$$

4

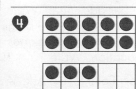

$$13 = 10 + 3$$
$$10 + 3 = 13$$

Directions Have students: 🍎 draw counters to show 13 and write an equation to match the picture. Then have them tell how the picture and equation show 10 ones and some more ones; 🦋 draw counters to show 12 and write an equation to match the picture. Then have them tell how the picture and equation show 10 ones and some more ones. 🔆 **Higher Order Thinking** Have students draw counters to show 13 and write two equations to match the picture. Then have them tell how the picture and equation show 10 ones and some more ones.

590 five hundred ninety   © Pearson Education, Inc. K   Topic 10 | Lesson 4

589–590

DIGITAL RESOURCES PearsonRealize.com

 Student and Teacher eTexts
eText

 Listen and Look For Lesson Video
PD

 Today's Challenge
Think

Solve and Share
Solve

 Visual Learning Animation Plus
Learn

A-Z Animated Glossary
Glossary

 Math Tools
Tools

 Quick Check
Assessment

 Another Look Homework Video
Help

 Math Games
Games

LESSON OVERVIEW   **F C R** FOCUS • COHERENCE • RIGOR

FOCUS

Domain K.NBT Number and Operations in Base Ten

Cluster K.NBT.A Work with numbers 11–19 to gain foundations for place value.

Content Standard K.NBT.A.1 Compose and decompose numbers from 11 to 19 into ten ones and some further ones, e.g., by using objects or drawings, and record each composition or decomposition by a drawing or equation (e.g., $18 = 10 + 8$); understand that these numbers are composed of ten ones and one, two, three, four, five, six, seven, eight, or nine ones.

Mathematical Practices MP.4, MP.5, MP.7, MP.8

Objective Find parts of the numbers 14, 15, and 16.

Essential Understanding The numbers 14, 15, and 16 can be decomposed as the sum of ten and some ones.

Materials Two-color counters (or Teaching Tool 6), connecting cubes (or Teaching Tool 8)

COHERENCE

Students have experience decomposing numbers to 10. They have worked with manipulatives as well as the numbers themselves to decompose a given number. In Topic 10, students will decompose greater numbers. In Lesson 10-4, they found parts of the numbers 11, 12, and 13 using objects, drawings, and numbers to help them. In Lesson 10-5, they will decompose 14, 15, and 16.

RIGOR

This lesson emphasizes **conceptual understanding**. Students will build on the concept that a number can break apart into two parts. In Topic 10, the focus is on breaking the numbers into a group of 10 ones and some more ones. Students expand their knowledge of an equation representing a quantitative relationship. Students continue to establish a basic understanding of place value in our base-ten numeration system.

▶ Watch the Listen and Look For Lesson Video.
PD

MATH ANYTIME

Daily Common Core Review

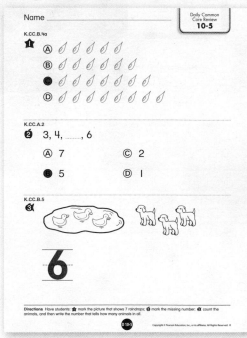

Today's Challenge
Think Use Topic 10 problems any time during this topic.

ENGLISH LANGUAGE LEARNERS **E L L**

Speaking Speak using content area vocabulary in context.

Use with the Visual Learning Bridge on Student's Edition p. 592.

Write $15 = 10 + 5$. Point to 15. Say: *This is the sum.* Point to 10. Say: *There are 10 ones.* Point to 5. Say: *There are 5 ones.* Divide students into partner groups. Distribute Double Ten-Frame (Teaching Tool 23) and 16 counters to each group. Ask students to use the ten-frames and counters to show 15. Write ____ = ____ + ____. Point to the first blank. Say: *The sum goes in this blank. What*

is the sum? Write 15 in the equation. Point to the second blank. Say: *There are 10 ones. What number goes here?* Write 10 in the equation. Point to the third blank. Say: *There are 6 ones. What number goes here?* Write 6 in the equation. Write $16 = 10 + 6$.

Beginning Point to 14. Ask: *What is this?* Students should respond using the sentence stem: *14 is the ____.* Point to 10. Ask: *What is this?* Students should respond using the sentence stem: *"10 is ____ ones."* Point to 4. Ask: *What is this?* Students should respond using the sentence stem: *"4 is ____ ones."*

Intermediate Ask students to identify the sum, 10 ones, and 4 ones in the equation using the sentence stems: "14 is the ____ because ____. 10 is ____ ones because ____. 4 is ____ ones because ____."

Advanced Ask students to identify and explain to partners what the sum, 10 ones, and 4 ones mean in the equation.

Summarize What are *sums, 10 ones,* and *4 ones?*

DEVELOP: PROBLEM-BASED LEARNING

PEARSON
realize
PearsonRealize.com

 Solve

COHERENCE: Engage students by connecting prior knowledge to new ideas.
Students use counters and write an equation to show 14 in two parts. This prepares them for the next part of the lesson where they break apart 14, 15, and 16 into a group of 10 ones and 4, 5, or 6 more ones.

10–15 min

 BEFORE

1. Pose the Solve-and-Share Problem

MP.7 Use Structure Students place counters in a double ten-frame to represent the two parts that make a greater number. Students show a quantity of ten ones and some more ones, and then write an equation to match.

Distribute 14 counters to each student.

Say: *Fourteen students go to the zoo. The first bus takes 10 students. The rest of the students go on a second bus. Use counters to describe this situation. Then complete the equation to match the counters and tell how the counters and equation show 10 ones and some more ones.*

2. Build Understanding

What are you asked to do? [Find how many students have to go on the second bus] *What tools do you have to help you?* [Counters and double ten-frame] *What number are you breaking apart to find the answer?* [14]

 DURING

3. Ask Guiding Questions As Needed

The top ten-frame represents the first bus. How many students are in the first bus? [10] *How many counters are there in all?* [14] *When you break apart 14 into a group of ten ones and some extra ones, where can you put the extra ones?* [On the second ten-frame; On the second bus] *What do you write in the equation?* [The two parts of 14; 10 and the extra ones]

 AFTER

4. Share and Discuss Solutions

 Start with students' solutions. Have them share their strategies. If needed, show Colleen's work to show how to break apart 14 into a group of ten ones and some more ones. Then discuss how the equation should be written.

5. Transition to the Visual Learning Bridge

You have shown how to break apart 14 into a group of ten ones and a group of three ones.

Later in this lesson, you will learn how to break apart other numbers using drawings and equations to model your work.

6. Extension for Early Finishers

How many more students would it take to fill the second bus, if there are now 15 students going to the zoo? [5 more] *What stays the same from 14 to 15?* [The 10] *What changes?* [The number of extra ones] *How many more students would it take to fill the second bus, if there are now 16 students going to the zoo?* [4 more]

Solve & Share   Name _See margin for sample student work._

Lesson 10-5
Find Parts of 14, 15, and 16

$$14 = \underline{} + \underline{}$$

Directions Say: *14 students go to the zoo. The first bus takes 10 students. The rest of the students go on a second bus. Use counters to describe this situation. Then complete the equation to match the counters and tell how the counters and equation show 10 ones and como more ones.*

I can ... find parts of the numbers 14, 15, and 16.

Content Standards K.NBT.A.1 **Mathematical Practices** MP.4, MP.5, MP.7, MP.8

Topic 10 | Lesson 5   Digital Resources at PearsonRealize.com   five hundred ninety-one **591**

Analyze Student Work

Colleen's Work

$$14 = 10 + 4$$

Colleen draws 10 counters in the top ten-frame and 4 counters in the bottom ten-frame. She correctly writes an equation to match her drawing.

Ollie's Work

$$14 = 8 + 6$$

Ollie draws 14 counters, but does not fill up an entire ten-frame to show a ten and some more ones. He correctly writes an equation to match his drawing.

The *Visual Learning Bridge* connects students' thinking in Solve & Share to important math ideas in the lesson. Use the *Visual Learning Bridge* to make these ideas explicit. Also available as a *Visual Learning Animation Plus* at PearsonRealize.com

Learn   Glossary

There are 16 students in Jada's class. She has represented each student with a counter. How can Jada plan where each student will sit on the bus for their next field trip? [Use a double ten-frame to show how the students will fit in the buses]

MP.4 Model with Math *Jada uses a double ten-frame to arrange the counters and fill one bus before the other. How many students are on the first bus?* [10] *How many students are on the second bus?* [6] *How many empty seats are on the second bus?* [4]

MP.8 Generalize *How is this drawing like the bus picture?* [It shows 10 in the top ten-frame and 6 in the bottom ten-frame.] *What does ten ones or 10 describe?* [How many children are on the first bus] *What does six ones or 6 describe?* [How many children are on the second bus]

How can 16 be written in two parts? [16 can be written as 10 ones and 6 ones.] *What does the 16 represent?* [The number of students in all] *How many students are on the first bus?* [10] *How many students are on the second bus?* [6]

Directions ★ Have students use counters to show 15, draw them in the double ten-frame, and complete the equation to match the picture. Then have them tell how the picture and equation show 10 ones and some more ones.

592 five hundred ninety-two   © Pearson Education, Inc. K   **Topic 10** | Lesson 5

Complete the *Do You Understand? Show Me!* problem before starting Guided Practice.

Do You Understand? Show Me! MP.5 Use Appropriate Tools Strategically Show students a single-color cube tower that is 15 cubes long. Have students count each cube in the tower with you as you point to it. *How many are there in all?* [15] Write 15 = on the board. Then break apart 5 cubes from the top of the tower. Recount each part with students. *How many cubes are in the taller tower?* [10] Write 10 + on the board. *How many cubes are in the shorter tower?* [5] Write 5 on the board to complete the equation on the board. Have students read the entire equation aloud [15 = 10 + 5].

Ask the following Essential Question: *How can you write an equation to break apart numbers that are greater than 10?* [Break the number into a group of ten ones and another group of the leftover ones]

Error Intervention: Item 1

If students place counters randomly in the bottom ten-frame instead of left to right and top to bottom,

then show them that even though their answer shows the same number of counters, it is hard to quickly count them if they are not in order. Show them the appropriate starting place in the upper left-hand corner.

Reteaching Assign Reteaching Set E, p. 613.

✔ QUICK CHECK

Check mark indicates items for prescribing differentiation on the next page.
Items 5 and 6 are worth 1 point. Item 7 is worth up to 3 points.

20–30 min   Tools   Assessment

Items 2–4 MP.4 Model with Math Remind students that each counter represents a one in the ten-frame. When they count counters in the ten-frame, it should match the number they are trying to break apart.

Item 4 MP.8 Generalize *What repeats in every Item?* [10 as one of the parts] Help students see that the full ten-frames show that there is always a group of 10 ones. Drawing the total number of counters is needed, but counting the first 10 ones is unnecessary. *What do you need to count?* [The extra ones]

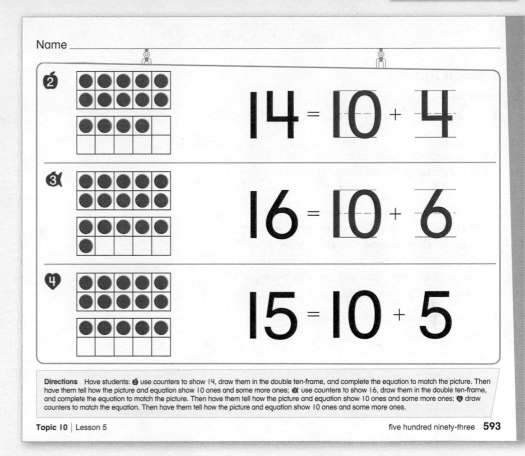

Name _____

2 $14 = 10 + 4$

3 $16 = 10 + 6$

4 $15 = 10 + 5$

Directions Have students: **2** use counters to show 14, draw them in the double ten-frame, and complete the equation to match the picture. Then have them tell how the picture and equation show 10 ones and some more ones; **3** use counters to show 16, draw them in the double ten-frame, and complete the equation to match the picture. Then have them tell how the picture and equation show 10 ones and some more ones; **4** draw counters to match the equation. Then have them tell how the picture and equation show 10 ones and some more ones.

Topic 10 | Lesson 5   five hundred ninety-three **593**

Items 5 and 6 Remind students that the full ten-frame is represented in the equation by the number 10. The counters in the bottom ten-frame are represented by the second addend in the equation.

Item 7 MP.5 Use Appropriate Tools Strategically Students will benefit from utilizing both sides of the two-color counters. Emphasize the benefit of representing the group of ten ones with one side of the counter and the group of extra ones with the other side of the counter.

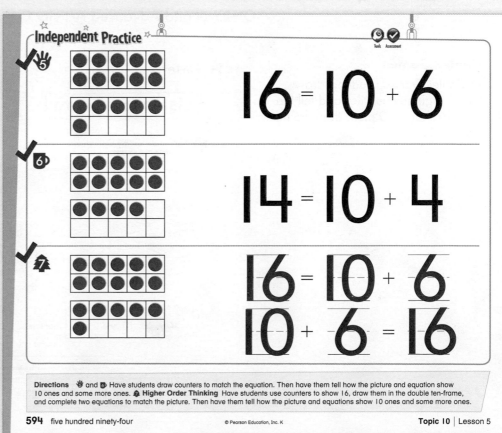

Independent Practice

5 $16 = 10 + 6$

6 $14 = 10 + 4$

7 $16 = 10 + 6$
$10 + 6 = 16$

Directions **5** and **6** Have students draw counters to match the equation. Then have them tell how the picture and equation show 10 ones and some more ones. **7 Higher Order Thinking** Have students use counters to show 16, draw them in the double ten-frame, and complete two equations to match the picture. Then have them tell how the picture and equations show 10 ones and some more ones.

594 five hundred ninety-four   © Pearson Education, Inc. K   Topic 10 | Lesson 5

STEP 3
ASSESS AND DIFFERENTIATE

Use the **QUICK CHECK** on the previous page to prescribe differentiated instruction.

2 RtI

I Intervention
0–3 points on the Quick Check

O On-Level
4 points on the Quick Check

A Advanced
5 points on the Quick Check

Intervention Activity **I**

Break It Apart

Materials

16 Connecting Cubes (or Teaching Tool 8)

- Have students make one long train with the connecting cubes. Discuss how this shows 16.

- Have students break the train so it has 10 cubes on one side and 6 cubes on the other. Discuss how this still shows 16. *What would the two trains look like on a ten-frame? How can we use the two trains to write an equation?*

- Repeat with a train of 15 cubes and then 14 cubes.

Reteach **I**

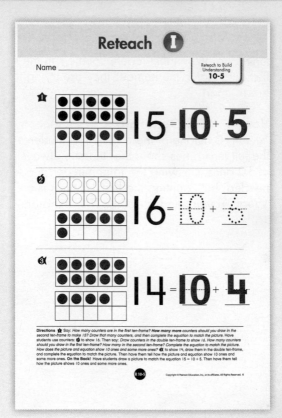

On-Level and Advanced Activity Centers **O** **A**

Center Games

In Center Games, students draw single-digit number tiles and tell the number that is 10 more than the number on the tile.

★ On-Level

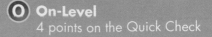
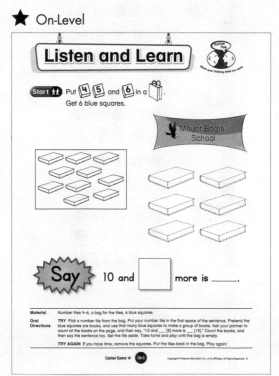

★★ Advanced

TIMING

The time allocated to Step 3 will depend on the teacher's instructional decisions and differentiation routines.

15–30 min

 Help

 Tools

 Games

PEARSON
realize.
PearsonRealize.com

Technology Center

Tools

Games

Math Tools and Math Games

A link to a specific math tools activity or math game to use with this lesson is provided at PearsonRealize.com.

Leveled Assignment

 Items 1–2   Items 2–3   Items 3–4

Name _____

Help Tools Games

Homework & Practice 10-5

Find Parts of 14, 15, and 16

Another Look!

$15 = 10 + 5$

HOME ACTIVITY Draw 14 boxes, and then shade 10 of them. Have your child tell how many boxes there are in all. Then have your child tell how many boxes are shaded and how many boxes are NOT shaded. Repeat with 16 boxes and 15 boxes.

⭐

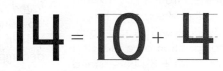

$14 = 10 + 4$

Directions Say: *Draw counters in the double ten-frame to show 15 and complete the equation to match the picture. The picture and equation show 10 ones and some more ones.* ⭐ Have students draw counters to show 14 and complete the equation to match the picture. Then have them tell how the picture and equation show 10 ones and some more ones.

Topic 10 | Lesson 5   Digital Resources at PearsonRealize.com   five hundred ninety-five **595**

---

②

$16 = 10 + 6$

③

$15 = 10 + 5$

④

$14 = 10 + 4$

$10 + 4 = 14$

Directions Have students: ② draw counters to show 16 and complete the equation to match the picture. Then have them tell how the picture and equation show 10 ones and some more ones; ③ draw counters to show 15 and complete the equation to match the picture. Then have them tell how the picture and equation show 10 ones and some more ones. ④ **Higher Order Thinking** Have students draw counters to show 14 and write two equations to match the picture. Then have them tell how the picture and equations show 10 ones and some more ones.

596 five hundred ninety-six   © Pearson Education, Inc. K   Topic 10 | Lesson 5

595–596

DIGITAL RESOURCES PearsonRealize.com

 eText Student and Teacher eTexts

 PD Listen and Look For Lesson Video

 Think Today's Challenge

 Solve Solve and Share

 Learn Visual Learning Animation Plus

 Glossary Animated Glossary

 Tools Math Tools

 Assessment Quick Check

 Help Another Look Homework Video

Games Math Games

LESSON OVERVIEW (F C R) FOCUS • COHERENCE • RIGOR

FOCUS

Domain K.NBT Number and Operations in Base Ten

Cluster K.NBT.A Work with numbers 11–19 to gain foundations for place value.

Content Standard K.NBT.A.1 Compose and decompose numbers from 11 to 19 into ten ones and some further ones, e.g., by using objects or drawings, and record each composition or decomposition by a drawing or equation (e.g., $18 = 10 + 8$); understand that these numbers are composed of ten ones and one, two, three, four, five, six, seven, eight, or nine ones.

Mathematical Practices MP.1, MP.4, MP.6, MP.8

Objective Find parts of the numbers 17, 18, and 19.

Essential Understanding The numbers 17, 18, and 19 can be decomposed as the sum of ten and some ones.

Materials Counters (or Teaching Tool 6), Double Ten-Frame (Teaching Tool 23), crayons

COHERENCE

Students have experience decomposing numbers to 10. They have worked with manipulatives as well as the numbers themselves to decompose a given number. In Topic 10, students will decompose greater numbers. In Lessons 10-4 and 10-5, they found parts of the numbers 11 through 16 using objects, drawings, and numbers to help them. In Lesson 10-6, they will decompose 17, 18, and 19.

RIGOR

This lesson emphasizes **conceptual understanding.** Students will build on the concept that a number can break apart into two parts. In Topic 10, the focus is on breaking the numbers into a group of 10 ones and some more ones. Students expand their knowledge of an equation representing a quantitative relationship. Students continue to establish a basic understanding of place value in our base-ten numeration system.

 PD Watch the Listen and Look For Lesson Video.

MATH ANYTIME

Daily Common Core Review

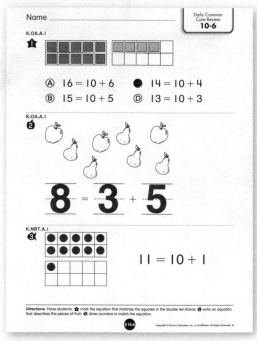

Today's Challenge

Think Use Topic 10 problems any time during this topic.

ENGLISH LANGUAGE LEARNERS (E L L)

Listening Use visual support to confirm understanding.

Use with the Visual Learning Bridge on Student's Edition p. 598.

Divide students into partner groups. Distribute 10 blue cubes and 7 red cubes to each group. Ask students to listen as you say: *I have 10 blue and 7 red cubes.* Instruct students to link the cubes. Ask: *How many cubes in all?* Count the cubes with students. Ask: *How many of the cubes are blue?* [10] *How many are red?* [7]. Write ____ = ____ + ____. Ask: *What equation can be written?*

Have students work with partners to write an equation. Distribute another red cube to each group.

Beginning Instruct students to link the cubes. Write ____ = ____ + ____. Ask students to complete the equation. When equations have been written, students will listen to partners read the equation. Point to 18. Ask: *What part of the equation is 18?* Students will respond using the sentence stem: "18 is the ____." [Sum]

Intermediate Instruct students to link the cubes and write an equation. When equations

have been written, point to 18. Ask: *What does 18 represent in the equation?* Point to the blue cubes. Ask: *What do the blue cubes represent?* Point to the red cubes. Ask: *What do the red cubes represent?* Students will listen to partners' responses.

Advanced Instruct partners to link the cubes and write an equation. Ask: *How did the cubes help you write the equation?* Students will listen to partners explain.

Summarize How does using cubes help when writing equations?

COHERENCE: Engage students by connecting prior knowledge to new ideas.
Students use a model and write an equation to show 18 in two parts. This prepares them for the next part of the lesson where they break apart 17, 18, and 19 into a group of 10 ones and 7, 8, or 9 more ones.

10–15 min

 Solve

Whole Class

BEFORE

1. Pose the Solve-and-Share Problem
MP.4 Model with Math Students color boxes to model breaking apart a number into 10 ones and some more ones. They then write an equation to match.

Give each student two crayons.

Say: *How can these 18 boxes be split into 10 ones and some more ones? Use 2 different color crayons to color the boxes to show your work. Then write an equation to match the picture.*

2. Build Understanding
What are you asked to do? [Split 18 boxes into ten ones and some more ones] *How can making a model help you solve the problem?* [The boxes can be colored to show the different parts] *What number are you breaking apart?* [18]

Small Group

DURING

3. Ask Guiding Questions As Needed
How many boxes are there in all? [18] *How can you split the boxes or break apart the boxes?* [Color some with one crayon and the others with the other crayon] *How can you show a group of 10 ones?* [Color 10 boxes]

Whole Class

AFTER

4. Share and Discuss Solutions
 Start with students' solutions. Have them share their strategies. If needed, show Ricardo's work to show how to break apart 18 into a group of ten ones and some more ones. Then discuss how the equation should be written.

5. Transition to the Visual Learning Bridge
You have shown how to break apart 18 into a group of 10 ones and a group of 8 ones.

Later in this lesson, you will learn how to break apart other numbers using drawings and equations to model your work.

6. Extension for Early Finishers
Could you use a cube train as your model? [Yes.] *Explain.* [The cube train would be 18 cubes long. You could break apart the train into a group of 10 cubes and 8 more cubes.] Give students 18 connecting cubes and allow them to experiment. *How could you use a double ten-frame to break the cube train apart?* [Put 10 cubes in the top ten-frame and the 8 extra cubes in the bottom ten-frame]

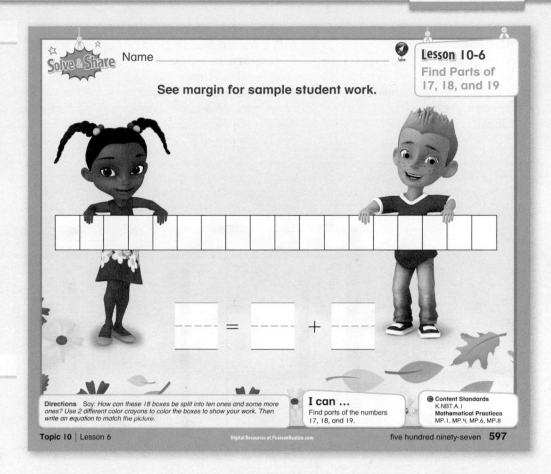

Solve & Share   Name _____

Lesson 10-6
Find Parts of 17, 18, and 19

See margin for sample student work.

____ = ____ + ____

Directions Say: How can these 18 boxes be split into ten ones and some more ones? Use 2 different color crayons to color the boxes to show your work. Then write an equation to match the picture.

I can ...
Find parts of the numbers 17, 18, and 19.

Content Standards
K.NBT.A.1
Mathematical Practices
MP.1, MP.4, MP.6, MP.8

Topic 10 | Lesson 6   Digital Resources at PearsonRealize.com   five hundred ninety-seven **597**

Analyze Student Work

Ricardo's Work

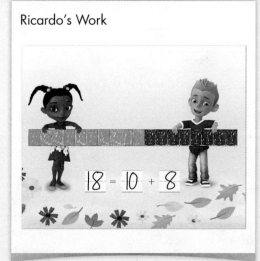

$$18 = 10 + 8$$

Ricardo colors the first 10 boxes blue and the remaining 8 boxes red. He then correctly writes the equation to match his drawing.

Tabitha's Work

$$18 = 10 + 8$$

Tabitha colors 10 boxes blue and 8 boxes red, but they are not in a row. She writes the equation to show that there is a group of 10 and some more ones.

The *Visual Learning Bridge* connects students' thinking in Solve & Share to important math ideas in the lesson. Use the *Visual Learning Bridge* to make these ideas explicit. Also available as a *Visual Learning Animation Plus* at PearsonRealize.com

Alex has a cube tower. How many cubes high is his cube tower? [17] *Why is the number 17 shown?* [Because there are 17 cubes]

MP.1 Make Sense and Persevere *Jada sees that Alex can break apart the cube tower into two groups. How many blue cubes are there?* [10] *How many red cubes are there?* [7]

Alex put the cubes in a double ten-frame. How many cubes did he put in the top ten-frame? [10] *How many cubes did he put in the bottom ten-frame?* [7] *How many cubes are there in all?* [17]

MP.6 Be Precise *Does this equation match the cubes?* [Yes.] *What does the number 17 represent?* [The number of cubes in all] *What does the 10 represent?* [The cubes in the top ten-frame] *What does the 7 represent?* [The cubes in the bottom ten-frame]

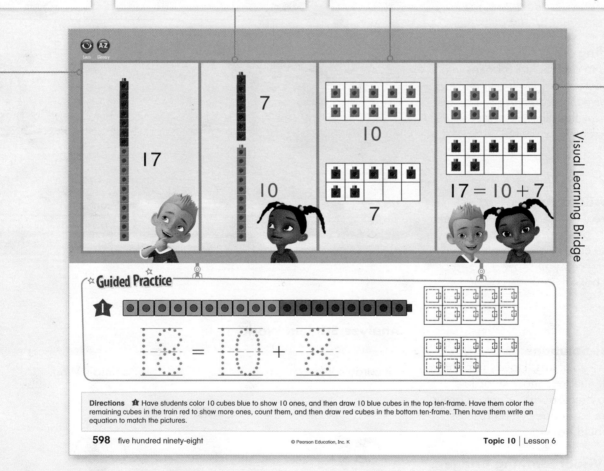

Visual Learning Bridge

★ Guided Practice ★

1.

Directions ★ Have students color 10 cubes blue to show 10 ones, and then draw 10 blue cubes in the top ten-frame. Have them color the remaining cubes in the train red to show more ones, count them, and then draw red cubes in the bottom ten-frame. Then have them write an equation to match the pictures.

598 five hundred ninety-eight   © Pearson Education, Inc. K   **Topic 10** | Lesson 6

Complete the *Do You Understand? Show Me!* problem before starting Guided Practice.

Do You Understand? Show Me! MP.4 Model with Math

Give pairs of students a double ten-frame and 18 two-color counters. Have students put 10 red counters in the first ten-frame. Then have them put 8 yellow counters in the second ten-frame. *How many counters are there in all?* [18] *How many red counters are there?* [10] *How many yellow counters are there?* [8] Write 18 = 10 + 8 on the board.

 Ask the following Essential Question: *How can you write an equation to break apart numbers that are greater than 10?* [Break the number into a group of ten ones and another group of the leftover ones.]

Coherence In the *Visual Learning Bridge*, students are shown an alternate model to represent breaking apart a number into a group of tens and ones. This links back to, and builds on, previous lessons where students decomposed numbers greater than 10 using counters. Students find that, just as there were different ways to decompose a number, there are different tools to use to model the problem.

Error Intervention: Item 1

If students have difficulty drawing the cubes,

then have them draw squares to represent the cubes in the double ten-frame.

Reteaching Assign Reteaching Set G, p. 614.

✓ QUICK CHECK

Check mark indicates items for prescribing differentiation on the next page. Items 5 and 6 are worth 1 point. Item 7 is worth up to 3 points.

20–30 min   Tools   Assessment

Item 2 MP.4 Model with Math Explain to students that they are looking to break apart 19. Some students may find it easier to write the equation before drawing the picture. Allow them this option. *What are you asked to do?* [Color the squares, show 10 ones and some more ones, and then write an equation] *Can you solve the problem by writing the equation before coloring or drawing the picture?* [Yes.]

Items 2 and 3 Have students color ten boxes in a row to show a group of 10. Some students may choose to color every other box or to attempt some sort of colorful pattern with their crayons. Encourage them to refer back to the *Visual Learning Bridge* on page 598 and see how the cubes were grouped together by color.

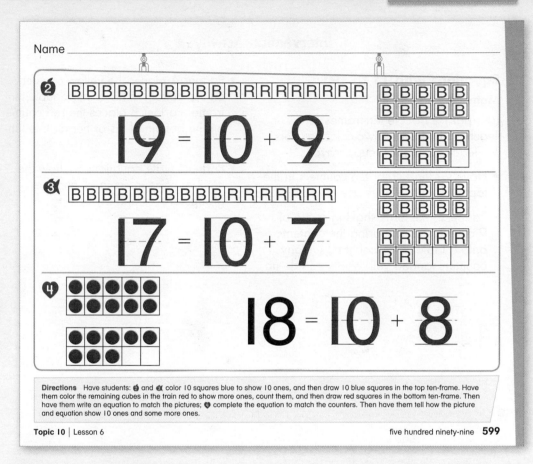

Name _____

2 $19 = 10 + 9$

3 $17 = 10 + 7$

4 $18 = 10 + 8$

Directions Have students: 2 and 3 color 10 squares blue to show 10 ones, and then draw 10 blue squares in the top ten-frame. Have them color the remaining cubes in the train red to show more ones, count them, and then draw red squares in the bottom ten-frame. Then have them write an equation to match the pictures; 4 complete the equation to match the counters. Then have them tell how the picture and equation show 10 ones and some more ones.

Topic 10 | Lesson 6   five hundred ninety-nine **599**

Items 5 and 6 MP.8 Generalize *What is the same in each item?* [The top ten-frame in the double ten-frame is always full.] Point out to students that this is because the lesson focuses on the numbers 17, 18, and 19. Most students will have grasped this concept by now. Support students who may become discouraged if they easily lose track of how many counters they have placed in a double ten-frame. For these children, you may wish to create numbered counters. This can be accomplished by placing a number sticker or a small square of masking tape (labeled 1 to 19) on each counter.

Item 7 This item has students write two different equations to match the picture and prove their work. Use this opportunity to reinforce the equal sign's role as the equation balance point. *What does the equal sign represent?* [That the amounts on either side are the same]

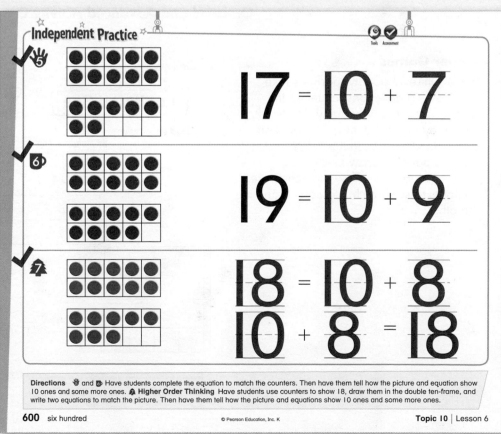

Independent Practice

5 $17 = 10 + 7$

6 $19 = 10 + 9$

7 $18 = 10 + 8$
   $10 + 8 = 18$

Directions 5 and 6 Have students complete the equation to match the counters. Then have them tell how the picture and equation show 10 ones and some more ones. 7 **Higher Order Thinking** Have students use counters to show 18, draw them in the double ten-frame, and write two equations to match the picture. Then have them tell how the picture and equations show 10 ones and some more ones.

600 six hundred   © Pearson Education, Inc. K   **Topic 10 | Lesson 6**

2
RtI

Use the **QUICK CHECK** on the previous page to prescribe differentiated instruction.

I Intervention
0–3 points on the Quick Check

O On-Level
4 points on the Quick Check

A Advanced
5 points on the Quick Check

Intervention Activity **I**

Equations with 11 to 19
Materials

(per pair) 2 double ten-frames (or Teaching Tool 23), 9 two-color counters (or Teaching Tool 6), cup, crayons

• Have students color ten counters in the top ten-frame. *This is one ten.*

• Partners take turns shaking a cup of 9 counters and pouring the contents onto a table. They count how many counters landed yellow- or red-side up.

• Partner A places the yellow counters on the bottom of his or her double ten-frame. Partner B places the red counters on the bottom of his or her double ten-frame.

• Partners write equations to show the number of counters in all and the groups of tens and ones.

Reteach **I**

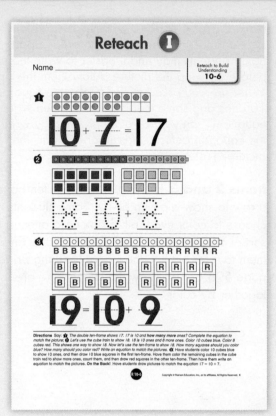

On-Level and Advanced Activity Centers **O** **A**

Center Games

In the On-Level activity, partners take turns tossing dot cubes, counting the dots, and saying how many dots in all. Then they place that many squares on a double ten-frame. In the Advanced activity, partners draw tiles to add extra ones to a ten. They then compare numbers to see which is greater than the other.

★ On-Level

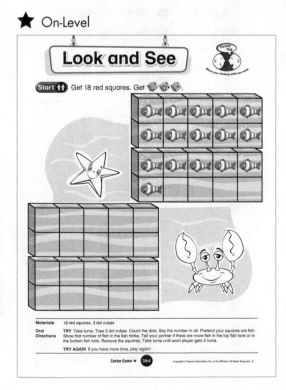

★ ★ Advanced

TIMING

The time allocated to Step 3 will depend on the teacher's instructional decisions and differentiation routines.

15–30 min

 Help   Tools   Games

Technology Center Ⓘ Ⓞ Ⓐ

Math Tools and Math Games

A link to a specific math tools activity or math game to use with this lesson is provided at PearsonRealize.com.

Leveled Assignment

Ⓘ Items 1–2   Ⓞ Items 2–3   Ⓐ Items 3–4

Name _____

Help Tools Games

Another Look!

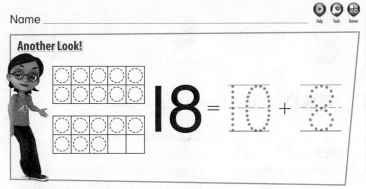

$$18 = 10 + 8$$

Homework & Practice 10-6

Find Parts of 17, 18, and 19

HOME ACTIVITY Have your child sort a group of 18 objects into a group of 10 and a group of 8. Discuss how many objects there are in each group and how many there are in all. Repeat with 17 objects and 19 objects.

★

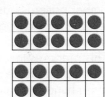

$$17 = 10 + 7$$

Directions Say: *Draw counters to show 18, and then complete the equation to match. How does the picture and equation show 10 ones and some more ones?* ★ Have students draw counters to show 17, and then complete the equation to match the picture. Then have them tell how the picture and equation show 10 ones and some more ones.

Topic 10 | Lesson 6   Digital Resources at PearsonRealize.com   six hundred one **601**

❷

$$19 = 10 + 9$$

❸

$$18 = 10 + 8$$

❹

$$17 = 10 + 7$$

$$10 + 7 = 17$$

Directions Have students: ❷ draw counters to show 19, and then complete the equation to match the picture. Then have them tell how the picture and equation show 10 ones and some more ones; ❸ draw counters to show 18, and then complete the equation to match the picture. Then have them tell how the picture and equation show 10 ones and some more ones. ❹ **Higher Order Thinking** draw counters to show 17, and then write two equations to match the picture. Then have them tell how the picture and equations show 10 ones and some more ones.

602 six hundred two   © Pearson Education, Inc. K   Topic 10 | Lesson 6

601–602

LOOK FOR AND USE STRUCTURE

DIGITAL RESOURCES PearsonRealize.com

 Student and Teacher eTexts — **eText**

 Listen and Look For Lesson Video — **PD**

 Today's Challenge — **Think**

 Solve and Share — **Solve**

 Visual Learning Animation Plus — **Learn**

 Math Practices Animations — **MP**

 Animated Glossary — **Glossary**

 Math Tools — **Tools**

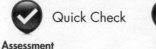 Quick Check — **Assessment**

 Another Look Homework Video — **Help**

 Math Games — **Games**

LESSON OVERVIEW **F C R** FOCUS • COHERENCE • RIGOR

FOCUS

Mathematical Practices MP.7 Look for and make use of structure. Also **MP.3, MP.4, MP.5, MP.8**

Content Standard K.NBT.A.1

Objective Use patterns to make and find the parts of numbers to 19.

Essential Understanding Good math thinkers look for patterns in math to help solve problems.

Materials Two-color counters (or Teaching Tool 6), crayons

COHERENCE

Students have used MP.7 throughout the program prior to this lesson. Use this lesson to stop and focus on the Thinking Habits good problem solvers use when they look for patterns in math. In this lesson, students look at number patterns based on place value. They compare a single-digit number with a number made with 10 and that same number. This prepares them for later work in Grade 1 on place-value and patterns in numbers on a hundred chart.

RIGOR

This lesson emphasizes **application**. Rigorous mathematics instruction calls for the selection, use, and management of multiple mathematical practices. All of the problems in this lesson elicit the use of multiple mathematical practices. Use the thinking habits shown in the Solve & Share task to help focus thinking on MP.7 in the lesson.

 Watch the Listen and Look For Lesson Video.

MATH ANYTIME

Daily Common Core Review

Today's Challenge

 Use Topic 10 problems any time during this topic.

ENGLISH LANGUAGE LEARNERS **E L L**

Strategies Use prior experiences to understand meanings.

Use with the Visual Learning Bridge on Student's Edition p. 604.

Ask: *How have you used ten-frames in the past to make a number like 13?* Have students share information with partners. Draw two ten-frames. Place counters in the ten-frames to represent 13. Point to the first ten-frame. Say: *There are 10 ones.* Point to the second ten frame. Say: *There are 3 ones.* Instruct students to look at the number chart in

Frame A. Point to 3, then 13. Say: *13 is 10 greater than 3.* Continue the process for 14.

Beginning Point to 5 and 15. Ask: *How much greater is 15?* Students should respond using the sentence stem: "15 is ____ ____ than 5."

Intermediate Ask students to look at 5 and 15 on the number chart. Ask: *How much greater is 15 than 5? How do you know?* Students should respond using the sentence stem: "15 is ___ ____ than 5 because ____."

Advanced Instruct students to work with partners to find a pattern on the number chart. Ask: *What do you notice about the top and lower numbers?* [The lower numbers are always 10 greater than the top numbers.] Instruct partners to generate equations for each number group.

Summarize On the number chart, how much greater is the lower number than the top number?

DEVELOP: PROBLEM-BASED LEARNING

COHERENCE: Engage students by connecting prior knowledge to new ideas.
Students look for a pattern between a 1-digit number and the number which is 10 more. This prepares students for later in the lesson when they will be using partial hundred charts to find patterns between 1-digit numbers and teen numbers.

10–15 min

Solve

 BEFORE

1. Pose the Solve-and-Share Problem
MP.7 Look For Patterns Students look for place-value patterns to make and compare two numbers. Each number has the same number of ones, but the blue number has a ten, too.

Distribute 10 counters to each student.

Say: *Put some counters in the red five-frame. Use a red crayon and write the number that tells how many counters are in the red frame. Put the same number of counters in the blue five-frame. Use a blue crayon and write the number that tells how many counters are in the blue frames. Show the numbers to a partner. What patterns do you see?*

Tell students to think about these Thinking Habits as they solve the problem.
Is there a pattern?
How can I describe the pattern?

2. Build Understanding
What tools do you have to work on this problem? [counters and crayons] *What are you asked to do?* [Put counters in the red five-frame and write the red number. Put the same number of counters in the blue five-frame and then write the blue number. Tell any patterns I see.]

 DURING

3. Ask Guiding Questions As Needed
What number of counters did you put in the red five-frame? [Sample answer: 3] *What number of counters did you put in the blue five-frame?* [Sample answer: 3] *What do you notice that is the same for both the red and blue numbers?* [Sample answer: Both numbers have 3 ones.]

 AFTER

4. Share and Discuss Solutions
Start with students' solutions. Have them share their strategies. If needed, show Tommy's work to discuss the patterns he found.

5. Transition to the Visual Learning Bridge
You have shown a number pattern. When you add 10 to a number of ones, the new number has the same number of ones and 1 ten.

Later in this lesson, you will look at number patterns like this also using a number chart. You will see if this same pattern works for more numbers in the number chart.

6. Extension for Early Finishers
Have students repeat the activity with different numbers of ones. If you have a hundred chart posted in the room, ask them to look for this pattern on numbers in columns on the chart.

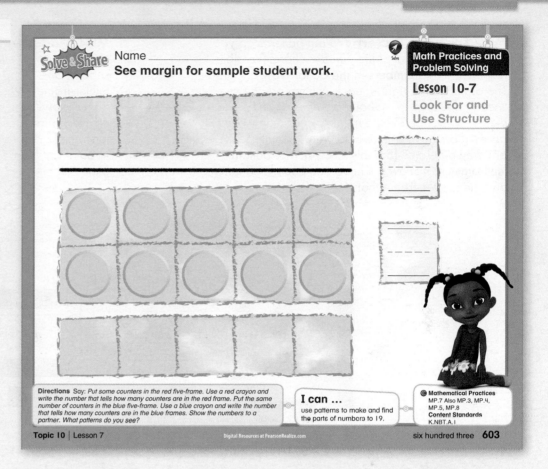

Solve & Share

Name _____
See margin for sample student work.

Solve

Directions Say: Put some counters in the red five-frame. Use a red crayon and write the number that tells how many counters are in the red frame. Put the same number of counters in the blue five-frame. Use a blue crayon and write the number that tells how many counters are in the blue frames. Show the numbers to a partner. What patterns do you see?

Math Practices and Problem Solving

Lesson 10-7
Look For and Use Structure

I can ...
use patterns to make and find the parts of numbers to 19.

Mathematical Practices
MP.7 Also MP.3, MP.4, MP.5, MP.8
Content Standards
K.NBT.A.1

Topic 10 | Lesson 7   Digital Resources at PearsonRealize.com   six hundred three **603**

Analyze Student Work

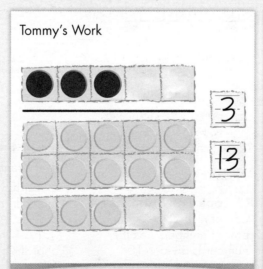

Tommy's Work

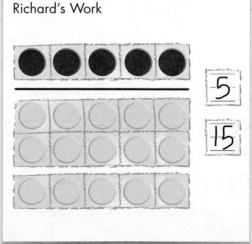

Richard's Work

Tommy places 3 counters in both the top and bottom five-frames. He counts the quantities correctly and writes the numbers. He explains that both numbers have 3 ones but that the blue number also has 1 ten. He says that this same ones, 1 ten pattern would happen if he tried different numbers of ones.

Richard places 5 counters in the top five-frame and correctly writes the number. He places a matching set of counters in the bottom five-frame as directed and writes the numbers. He says that the numbers are different but doesn't explain anything that is the same about the numbers.

STEP 2

DEVELOP: VISUAL LEARNING

PEARSON
realize.
PearsonRealize.com

Learn   Glossary

The *Visual Learning Bridge* connects students' thinking in Solve & Share to important math ideas in the lesson. Use the *Visual Learning Bridge* to make these ideas explicit. Also available as a *Visual Learning Animation Plus* at PearsonRealize.com

E L L
Visual Learning

MP.7 Look For Patterns *What patterns do you see in the two rows of the number chart?* [Possible responses: The numbers in the bottom row are greater. The digits on the right in each column are the same.] *Look at the ten-frame above the number chart and the ten-frames below the number chart. How are they alike?* [Both have a ten-frame with 4 counters.] *How are they different?* [Sample answer: The bottom ten-frames that show 14 have one completed ten-frame and the top ten-frame that shows 4 does not.]

MP.4 Model with Math *What does the yellow box show?* [One group of 10; a full ten-frame] *What do the red boxes show?* [The 4 ones; the counters in an incomplete ten-frame]. *What do you have to do to get from 4 to 14?* [Add 10]

This box shows some other number pairs where one number is just above the other on a number chart. Do these number pairs show the same pattern as 4 and 14? [Yes, the bottom number is always 10 greater than the top number.]

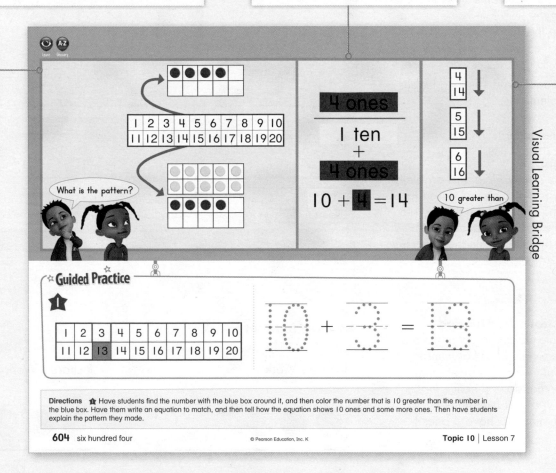

Visual Learning Bridge

☆ **Guided Practice**

Directions ★ Have students find the number with the blue box around it, and then color the number that is 10 greater than the number in the blue box. Have them write an equation to match, and then tell how the equation shows 10 ones and some more ones. Then have students explain the pattern they made.

604 six hundred four   © Pearson Education, Inc. K   **Topic 10** | Lesson 7

Complete the *Do You Understand? Show Me!* problem before starting Guided Practice.

Do You Understand? Show Me! MP.7 Look For Patterns

What number patterns do you notice as you look at 4 and 14, 5 and 15, and 6 and 16? [Sample response: Each pair of numbers has the same number of ones and 1 ten. The second number is always 10 more than the first number.] *How then would you write a number that is 10 greater than the number 2? Explain how you know.* [Sample answer: 12. The number twelve has 2 ones like the number 2 and it has one ten. So, 12 is 10 more than 2.]

Essential Question

Ask the following Essential Question: *How does seeing number patterns help you solve problems?* [Sample answer: If I can see a pattern like 10 more, I can count or add 10 faster.]

Error Intervention: Item 1

If students do not see a connection between 3 and 13,

then have them use counters and ten-frames to show each number. Have them show 3 in one ten-frame and 13 in two ten-frames. Ask them how many counters are in the ten-frame with 3. [3] Ask them how many leftover ones are in the two ten-frames that show 13. [3] Discuss how 3 and 13 have the same number of ones but that 13 has 1 ten.

RtI 1   **Reteaching** Assign Reteaching Set F, p. 613.

Tools   Assessment

☑ **QUICK CHECK**

Check mark indicates items for prescribing differentiation on the next page. Items 2 and 4 are worth 1 point. The Performance Assessment on page 606 is worth up to 3 points.

20–30 min

MP.7 Look For Patterns Listen and look for these behaviors as evidence that students are exhibiting proficiency with MP.7.

• Recognizes, describes, and uses patterns in numbers (e.g., place value when composing and decomposing numbers)

• Understands, identifies, and uses equivalent representations of numbers

• Describes how numbers and expressions are organized and put together as parts and wholes

Item 2 MP.5 Use Appropriate Tools Strategically *If needed, have students use counters and ten-frames to show the number with the blue box around it and a number that is 10 greater than that number. What number has a blue box around it?* [7] *How could you show 7 with counters on a ten-frame?* [Put 7 counters on the ten-frame] *What number is 10 more than 7 on the chart?* [17] *How could you show 17 with counters and two ten-frames?* [Show one ten-frame with 10 counters and one ten-frame with 7 counters] *How could you write an equation to show the ten-frames for 17?* [Sample answer: I could write that 10 + 7 = 17.] *What is alike and different about 7 and 17?* [Sample answer: Both have 7 ones but 17 is 10 more than 7.].

Item 5 MP.3 Construct Arguments *Look at the pattern in 10 + 1 = 11 and 10 + 2 = 12. Explain what comes next to complete the equation _____ + _____ = 13?* [Sample answer: The last equation is 10 + 3 = 13. The first equation adds 1 to 10 to get 11. The second equation adds 2 to 10 to get 12. The third equation then must add 3 more to 10 to get 13.] *What is a pattern you see?* [Sample answer: The number of ones you add and the number of ones in the whole each go up by 1.]

Item 6 MP.7 Use Structure *How can the number chart help you solve the problem?* [Sample answer: A number that is 10 more than another number is always the number right below it.]

Item 7 MP.8 Generalize *How will finding out how many cards Alex has make it easier to find out how many cards Marta has?* [Sample answer: I can see a pattern on the chart. The number 10 greater than 6 is right below 6 on the chart. So, the number 10 greater than 7 is right below 7 on the chart.]

Item 8 MP.3 Construct Arguments *How many cards will Alex have after he buys one pack of 10 cards?* [16] *How many cards will Marta have after she buys one pack of 10 cards?* [17] *How do you know you are correct?* [Sample answers: I can use the number chart or my equation to show how many cards each person has.]

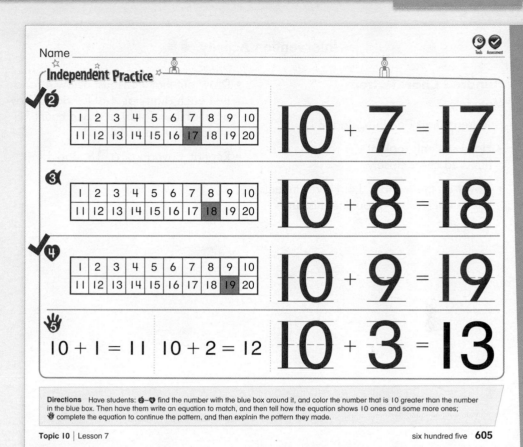

Name _____

Independent Practice

2 $10 + 7 = 17$

3 $10 + 8 = 18$

4 $10 + 9 = 19$

5 $10 + 1 = 11$ $10 + 2 = 12$ $10 + 3 = 13$

Directions Have students: 2–4 find the number with the blue box around it, and color the number that is 10 greater than the number in the blue box. Then have them write an equation to match, and then tell how the equation shows 10 ones and some more ones; ✋ complete the equation to continue the pattern, and then explain the pattern they made.

Topic 10 | Lesson 7   six hundred five **605**

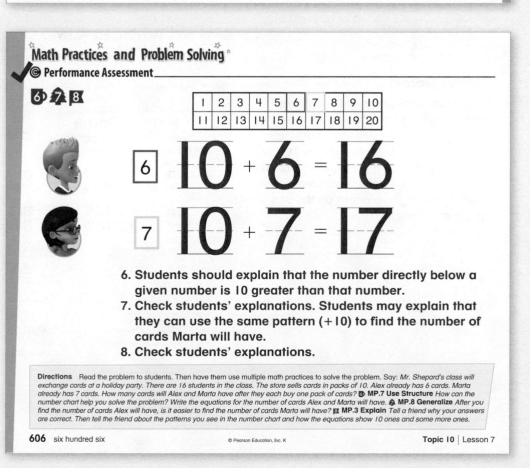

Math Practices and Problem Solving

© Performance Assessment _____

6 7 8

6 $10 + 6 = 16$

7 $10 + 7 = 17$

6. Students should explain that the number directly below a given number is 10 greater than that number.

7. Check students' explanations. Students may explain that they can use the same pattern (+10) to find the number of cards Marta will have.

8. Check students' explanations.

Directions Read the problem to students. Then have them use multiple math practices to solve the problem. Say: *Mr. Shepard's class will exchange cards at a holiday party. There are 16 students in the class. The store sells cards in packs of 10. Alex already has 6 cards. Marta already has 7 cards. How many cards will Alex and Marta have after they each buy one pack of cards?* **MP.7 Use Structure** *How can the number chart help you solve the problem? Write the equations for the number of cards Alex and Marta will have.* **MP.8 Generalize** *After you find the number of cards Alex will have, is it easier to find the number of cards Marta will have?* **MP.3 Explain** *Tell a friend why your answers are correct. Then tell the friend about the patterns you see in the number chart and how the equations show 10 ones and some more ones.*

606 six hundred six   © Pearson Education, Inc. K   Topic 10 | Lesson 7

STEP 3
ASSESS AND DIFFERENTIATE

Use the **QUICK CHECK** on the previous page to prescribe differentiated instruction.

2 RtI

I Intervention
0–3 points on the Quick Check

O On-Level
4 points on the Quick Check

A Advanced
5 points on the Quick Check

Intervention Activity **I**

Hundred Chart Pattern

Materials

Hundred Chart (Teaching Tool 31)

• Have students look at the columns in a hundred chart closely.

• Cover up the number 14. Have students talk to each other about the missing number.

• Draw out that 14 is just below 4, and that each digit has 4 at the right. Draw out that if you start at 4 and count 10 more, you end at 14.

• Repeat, covering 16, 18, and 11.

Reteach **I**

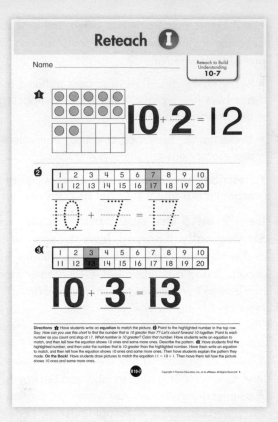

On-Level and Advanced Activity Centers **O** **A**

Center Games

In the On-Level game, partners take turns matching ten-frames that show numbers 10 to 19 with an expression to describe the number such as 10 and 5. In the Advanced game, partners take turns matching numbers with ten-frames that represent the number as ten and some more ones.

★ On-Level

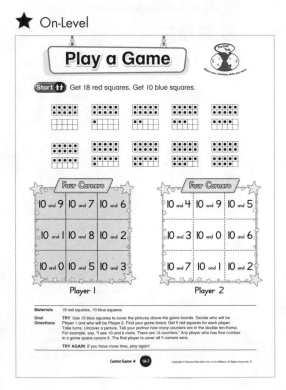

★★ Advanced

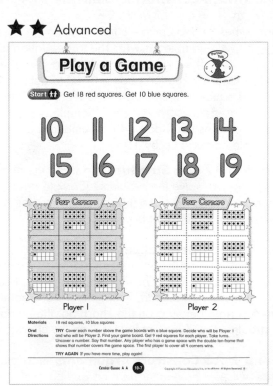

TIMING

The time allocated to Step 3 will depend on the teacher's instructional decisions and differentiation routines.

15–30 min

PEARSON
realize.
PearsonRealize.com

Help   Tools   Games

Technology Center 🄸 🄾 🄰

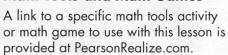

Math Tools and Math Games

A link to a specific math tools activity or math game to use with this lesson is provided at PearsonRealize.com.

Leveled Assignment

🄸 Items 1–4 (with help as needed)   🄾 Items 1–4   🄰 Items 1–4

Name _____

Homework & Practice 10-7

Look for and Use Structure

Another Look!

9

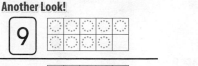

19

$$10 + 9 = 19$$

HOME ACTIVITY Take 11 pennies or other small household objects and arrange them in the following manner: two rows of 5 pennies, and a single penny underneath. Have your child write the equation that describes the number of pennies $(10 + 1 = 11)$. Repeat for quantities of 12 pennies, 13 pennies, and so on, up to 19 pennies. Have your child explain the pattern in the equations that he or she has written.

⭐

6

16

$$10 + 6 = 16$$

Directions Say: *Read the numbers on the cards, and then draw counters in the top ten-frame to show 9 and in the bottom ten-frames to show 19. Write an equation to match the drawings in the ten-frames. Tell how the picture and the equation show 10 ones and some more ones.* ⭐ *Have students read the numbers on the cards, and then draw counters in both the top and bottom ten-frames to show how many. Then have them write an equation to match the drawings in the ten-frames. Have students tell how the picture and the equation show 10 ones and some more ones.*

Ⓒ Performance Assessment

❷❸❹

1	2	3	4	5	6	7	8	9	10
11	12	13	14	15	16	17	18	19	20

Day 1

$$10 + 1 = 11$$

Day 2

$$10 + 2 = 12$$

2. Students should explain that the first two numbers in each row (1, 2, and 11, 12) will help to solve the problem.
3. Check students' work.
4. 13 apps. Check students' explanations.

Directions Read the problem to students. Then have them use multiple math practices to solve the problem. Say: *Alex got a new tablet computer. It came loaded with 10 apps. Every day, Alex is allowed to upload 1 more app. How many apps will Alex have in two days?* Ⓜ **MP.4 Model** *Can a model help you solve the problem? Write the numbers in the number chart. Which numbers will help solve this problem?* Ⓜ **MP.5 Use Tools** *How can you use the ten-frames to help? Draw counters to show how many apps there will be on Alex's tablet for each day. Then write equations to help you see the pattern.* Ⓜ **MP.7 Use Structure** *How many apps will Alex have in three days? How did seeing a pattern help you solve the problem? Explain your answer.*

TOPIC 10
FLUENCY PRACTICE ACTIVITY

PEARSON
realize
PearsonRealize.com

Games

FLUENCY PRACTICE ACTIVITY

Students practice fluently adding and subtracting within 5 during a partner activity that reinforces mathematical practices.

© Common Core Standards

Content Standard K.OA.A.5 Fluently add and subtract within 5.

Mathematical Practices MP.3, MP.6, MP.7, MP.8

Getting Started Ask students to work with a partner. Tell them to record their matches on their own page. Go over the directions. Both students should solve each problem and record their work. Tell students to take turns identifying the match.

As Students Do the Activity Remind students that each clue can be matched with only one problem. Some students may find all of the answers first and then match the clues. Allow this strategy as it provides the same fluency practice.

Another Activity Have students work together to write a new set of clues for the problems on the page. Ask them to record the new words on a separate sheet of paper.

Extra Challenge *Create your own Find a Match activity. Use the same clues on your page. Write a new problem for each clue. Then trade your activity with your partner and complete your partner's Find a Match activity.*

Steps to Fluency Success To ensure all students achieve fluency, see pages 431E–431H for additional resources including practice/assessment masters on fluency subskills. You can also use the ExamView® CD-ROM to generate worksheets with multiple-choice or free-response items on fluency subskills.

 Online Game The Game Center at PearsonRealize.com provides opportunities for fluency practice.

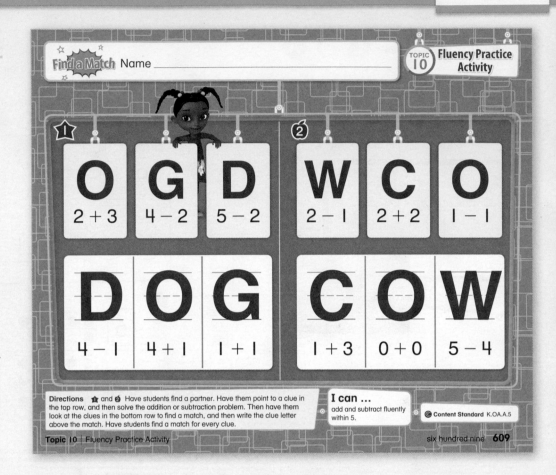

Find a Match   Name _____

TOPIC 10   Fluency Practice Activity

① | ②

O	G	D		W	C	O
---	---	---		---	---	---
2 + 3	4 − 2	5 − 2		2 − 1	2 + 2	1 − 1

D	O	G		C	O	W
---	---	---		---	---	---
4 − 1	4 + 1	1 + 1		1 + 3	0 + 0	5 − 4

Directions ① and ② Have students find a partner. Have them point to a clue in the top row, and then solve the addition or subtraction problem. Then have them look at the clues in the bottom row to find a match, and then write the clue letter above the match. Have students find a match for every clue.

I can ... add and subtract fluently within 5.

© **Content Standard** K.OA.A.5

Topic 10 | Fluency Practice Activity

six hundred nine **609**

VOCABULARY REVIEW

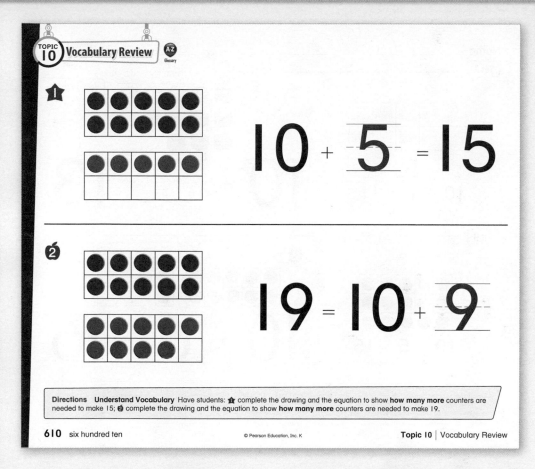

VOCABULARY REVIEW

Students review vocabulary words used in the topic.

Oral Language Before students do the page, you might reinforce oral language through a class discussion involving one or more of the following activities.

- Have students define the terms in their own words.

- Have students say math sentences or math questions that use the words.

- Play a "What's My Word?" guessing game in which you or a student thinks about one of the words and says a clue that others listen to before they guess the word.

- Play a "Right or Wrong?" game in which you or a student says a sentence that uses one of the words correctly or incorrectly. Then others say "right" or "wrong."

Writing in Math After students do the page, you might further reinforce writing in math by doing one or more of the following activities.

- Tell students to close their books. Then you say the words and have students write them. Students trade papers to check whether the words are spelled correctly.

- Have students work with a partner. Each partner writes a math question that uses one of the words. Then they trade papers and give a written answer that uses the word.

 Online Game The Game Center at PearsonRealize.com includes a vocabulary game that students can access any time.

RETEACHING
COMPOSE AND DECOMPOSE NUMBERS 11 TO 19

RtI Item Analysis for Diagnosis and Intervention				
Reteaching Sets	**© Standards**	**Student Book Lessons**	**MDIS**	
Set A	K.NBT.A.1	10-1	A10	
Set B	K.NBT.A.1	10-2	A88	
Set C	K.NBT.A.1	10-3	A10	
Set D	K.NBT.A.1	10-4	A8	
Set E	K.NBT.A.1	10-5	A88	
Set F	K.NBT.A.1, MP.7	10-7	A10	
Set G	K.NBT.A.1	10-6	A10	

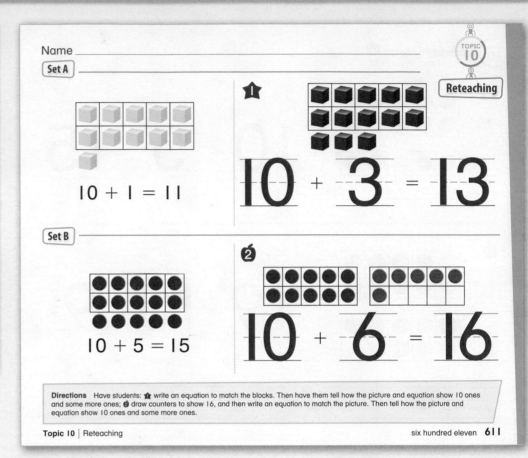

Name _____

Set A

❶

$$10 + 1 = 11$$

$$10 + 3 = 13$$

Set B

❷

$$10 + 5 = 15$$

$$10 + 6 = 16$$

Directions Have students: ❶ write an equation to match the blocks. Then have them tell how the picture and equation show 10 ones and some more ones; ❷ draw counters to show 16, and then write an equation to match the picture. Then tell how the picture and equation show 10 ones and some more ones.

Topic 10 | Reteaching

six hundred eleven **611**

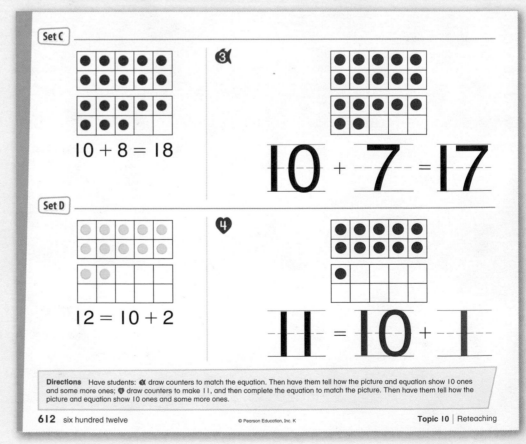

Set C

❸

$$10 + 8 = 18$$

$$10 + 7 = 17$$

Set D

❹

$$12 = 10 + 2$$

$$11 = 10 + 1$$

Directions Have students: ❸ draw counters to match the equation. Then have them tell how the picture and equation show 10 ones and some more ones; ❹ draw counters to make 11, and then complete the equation to match the picture. Then have them tell how the picture and equation show 10 ones and some more ones.

612 six hundred twelve   © Pearson Education, Inc. K   Topic 10 | Reteaching

Name _____

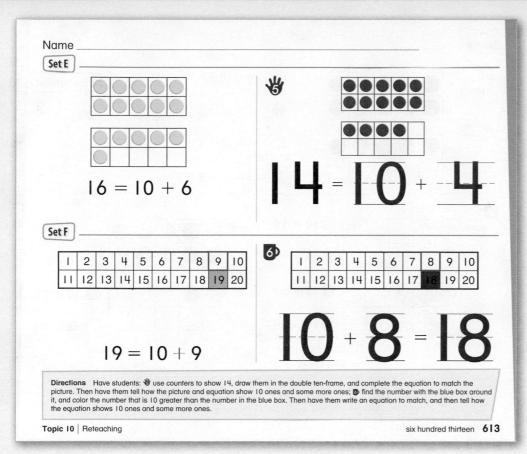

$16 = 10 + 6$

$14 = 10 + 4$

Set F

$19 = 10 + 9$

$10 + 8 = 18$

Directions Have students: ✋ use counters to show 14, draw them in the double ten-frame, and complete the equation to match the picture. Then have them tell how the picture and equation show 10 ones and some more ones; ⑥ find the number with the blue box around it, and color the number that is 10 greater than the number in the blue box. Then have them write an equation to match, and then tell how the equation shows 10 ones and some more ones.

Topic 10 | Reteaching

six hundred thirteen **613**

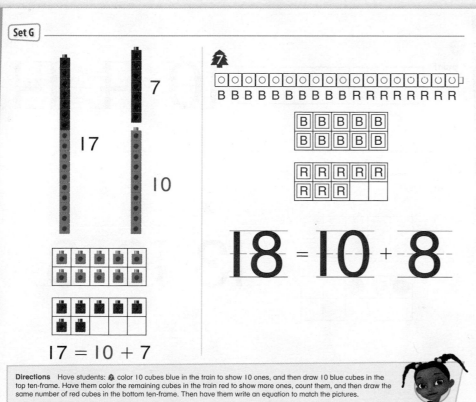

7

17

10

$17 = 10 + 7$

B B B B B B B B B B R R R R R R R R

$18 = 10 + 8$

Directions Have students: 🌲 color 10 cubes blue in the train to show 10 ones, and then draw 10 blue cubes in the top ten-frame. Have them color the remaining cubes in the train red to show more ones, count them, and then draw the same number of red cubes in the bottom ten-frame. Then have them write an equation to match the pictures.

614 six hundred fourteen

© Pearson Education, Inc. K

Topic 10 | Reteaching

1 RtI

Ongoing Intervention
- Lessons with guiding questions to assess understanding
- Support to prevent misconceptions and to reteach

2 RtI

Strategic Intervention
- Targeted to small groups who need more support
- Easy to implement

3 RtI

Intensive Intervention
- Instruction to accelerate progress
- Instruction focused on foundational skills

TOPIC ASSESSMENT
COMPOSE AND DECOMPOSE NUMBERS 11 TO 19

ANSWERING THE TOPIC ESSENTIAL QUESTION

How can composing and decomposing numbers from 11 to 19 into ten ones and some further ones help you understand place value?

Restate the Topic Essential Question from the Topic Opener or project it from the Student's Edition eText.

Ask students to answer the Essential Question (verbally or in writing) and give examples that support their answers. The following are key elements of the answer to the Essential Question. Be sure these are made explicit when discussing students' answers.

- Find the answer and write the number to tell how many. Compose the number using 10 as one of the addends.

  Example: John and Karen are playing with marbles. John has 10 marbles and Karen has 3 marbles. How many marbles are there in all? Write a number sentence with 10 that shows how you can make that number. [10 + 3 = 13]

- Compose the number as you join two numbers to make a single number with the same value, using 10 as one of the addends.

  Example: Jada counted some leaves and put them into one pile of 10. She counted 6 other leaves and put them into another pile. Write a number sentence with 10 that shows how you can make that number. [10 + 6 = 16]

- Decompose a number to make two numbers with the same total value, using 10 as one of the addends.

  Example: The coach needs 17 students for the football team. There are 10 students playing. Seven more students join the football team. How many students are on the football team altogether? How can the number 17 be represented as the sum of 10 and some more? Write an equation showing the number of students. [10 students + 7 extra students = 17 students]

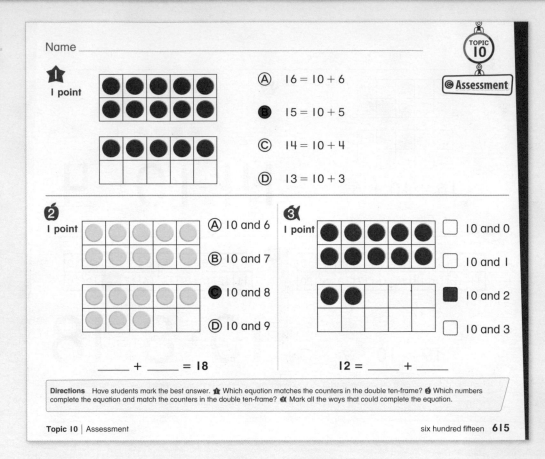

Name _____

1 I point
Ⓐ 16 = 10 + 6
Ⓑ 15 = 10 + 5
Ⓒ 14 = 10 + 4
Ⓓ 13 = 10 + 3

2 I point
Ⓐ 10 and 6
Ⓑ 10 and 7
Ⓒ 10 and 8
Ⓓ 10 and 9

____ + ____ = 18

3 I point
☐ 10 and 0
☐ 10 and 1
■ 10 and 2
☐ 10 and 3

12 = ____ + ____

Directions Have students mark the best answer. ⬆ Which equation matches the counters in the double ten-frame? ✌ Which numbers complete the equation and match the counters in the double ten-frame? ✊ Mark all the ways that could complete the equation.

Topic 10 | Assessment

six hundred fifteen **615**

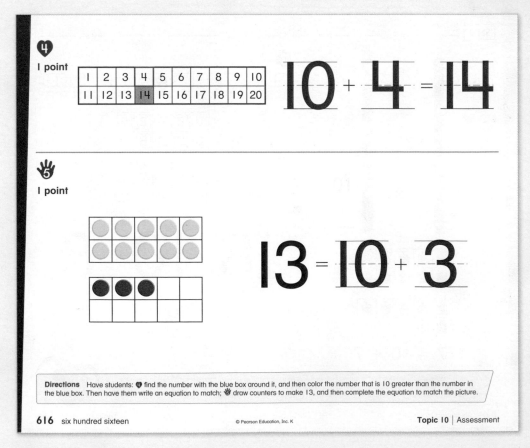

4 I point

| 1 | 2 | 3 | 4 | 5 | 6 | 7 | 8 | 9 | 10 |
| 11 | 12 | 13 | 14 | 15 | 16 | 17 | 18 | 19 | 20 |

$$10 + 4 = 14$$

5 I point

$$13 = 10 + 3$$

Directions Have students: ✋ find the number with the blue box around it, and then color the number that is 10 greater than the number in the blue box. Then have them write an equation to match; ✋ draw counters to make 13, and then complete the equation to match the picture.

616 six hundred sixteen

© Pearson Education, Inc. K

Topic 10 | Assessment

ONLINE TOPIC ASSESSMENT
An auto-scored Topic Assessment is provided
at PearsonRealize.com.

EXAMVIEW® TEST GENERATOR
ExamView can be used to create a blackline-master
Topic Assessment with multiple-choice and free-
response items.

Assessment

Name _____

6 1 point

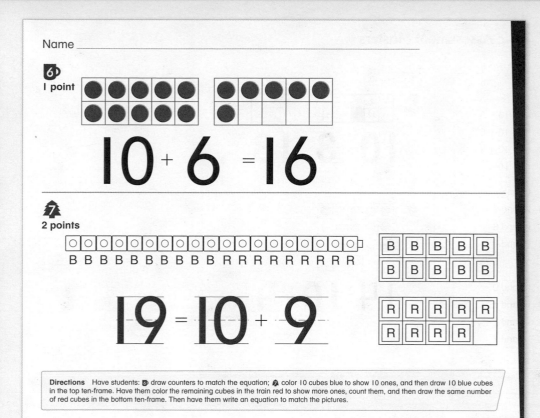

$$10 + 6 = 16$$

7 2 points

$$19 = 10 + 9$$

Directions Have students: **6** draw counters to match the equation; **7** color 10 cubes blue to show 10 ones, and then draw 10 blue cubes in the top ten-frame. Have them color the remaining cubes in the train red to show more ones, count them, and then draw the same number of red cubes in the bottom ten-frame. Then have them write an equation to match the pictures.

Topic 10 | Assessment

six hundred seventeen **617**

Item Analysis for Diagnosis and Intervention

Item	Standards	DOK	MDIS
1	K.NBT.A.1	1	A10
2	K.NBT.A.1	1	A10, A88
3	K.NBT.A.1	1	A8
4	K.NBT.A.1, MP.7	2	A10
5	K.NBT.A.1	1	A10
6	K.NBT.A.1	1	A10
7	K.NBT.A.1	2	A10, A88
8	K.NBT.A.1	1	A8, A10, A88

The Topic Assessment Masters assess the same
content item for item as the Topic Assessment in the
Student's Edition.

8 1 point

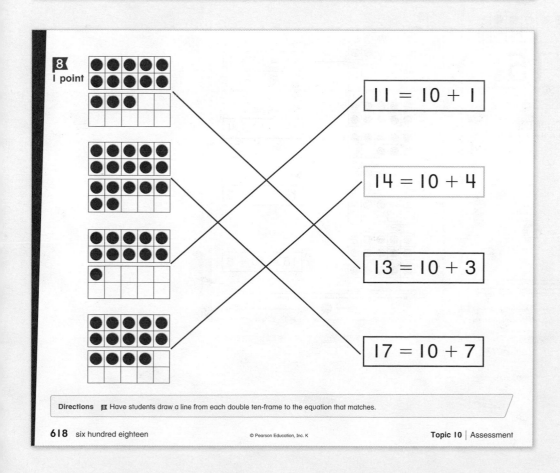

$$11 = 10 + 1$$

$$14 = 10 + 4$$

$$13 = 10 + 3$$

$$17 = 10 + 7$$

Directions **8** Have students draw a line from each double ten-frame to the equation that matches.

618 six hundred eighteen

© Pearson Education, Inc. K

Topic 10 | Assessment

Topic Assessment Masters

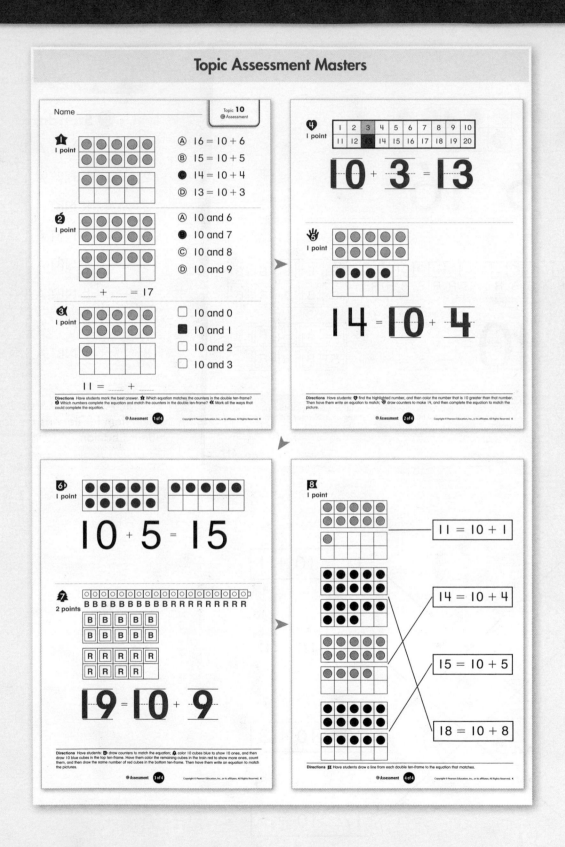

ONLINE TOPIC ASSESSMENT

An auto-scored Topic Assessment is provided at PearsonRealize.com.

EXAMVIEW® TEST GENERATOR

ExamView can be used to create a blackline-master Topic Assessment with multiple-choice and free-response items.

Scoring Guide		
Item	Points	Topic Assessment (Student's Edition and Masters)
1	1	Correct choice is selected.
2	1	Correct choice is selected.
3	1	Correct choice is selected.
4	1	Correct equation is written.
5	1	Correct number of counters are drawn and correct numbers are written.
6	1	Correct number of counters are drawn.
7	2	Correct number of cubes are drawn and correct equation is written.
	1	Correct number of cubes are drawn or correct equation is written.
8	1	Double ten-frames are matched to the correct equations.

TOPIC 10

TOPIC PERFORMANCE ASSESSMENT
COMPOSE AND DECOMPOSE NUMBERS 11 TO 19

Scoring Guide

Item	Points	Topic Performance Assessment in the Student's Edition
1	1	Correct equation is written.
2	2	Correct picture and equation are shown.
	1	Correct picture or equation is shown.
3	2	Correct picture and equations are shown.
	1	Correct picture or equations are shown.
4	2	Picture drawn and explanation is correct.
	1	Picture shown is correct, but there is no explanation.
5	2	Correct number and equation is shown.
	1	Correct number or equation is shown.

Item Analysis for Diagnosis and Intervention

Item	Standards	DOK	MDIS
1	K.NBT.A.1, MP.2	2	A8
2	K.NBT.A.1, MP.3	2	A10, A88
3	K.NBT.A.1, MP.4	3	A10, A88
4	K.NBT.A.1, MP.3	3	A10
5	K.NBT.A.1, MP.7	3	A10

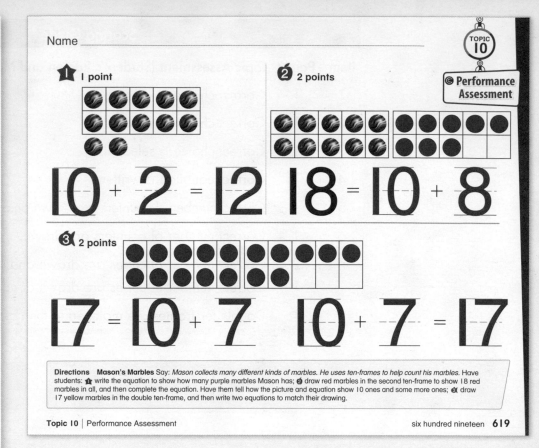

Directions **Mason's Marbles** Say: *Mason collects many different kinds of marbles. He uses ten-frames to help count his marbles.* Have students: ⭐ write the equation to show how many purple marbles Mason has; ② draw red marbles in the second ten-frame to show 18 red marbles in all, and then complete the equation. Have them tell how the picture and equation show 10 ones and some more ones; ③ draw 17 yellow marbles in the double ten-frame, and then write two equations to match their drawing.

Topic 10 | Performance Assessment   six hundred nineteen **619**

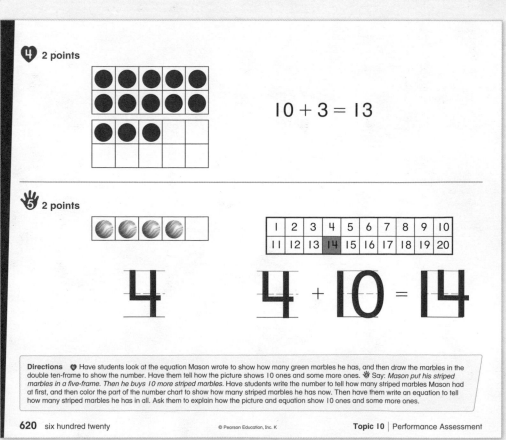

Directions ④ Have students look at the equation Mason wrote to show how many green marbles he has, and then draw the marbles in the double ten-frame to show the number. Have them tell how the picture shows 10 ones and some more ones. ⑤ Say: *Mason put his striped marbles in a five-frame. Then he buys 10 more striped marbles.* Have students write the number to tell how many striped marbles Mason had at first, and then color the part of the number chart to show how many striped marbles he has now. Then have them write an equation to tell how many striped marbles he has in all. Ask them to explain how the picture and equation show 10 ones and some more ones.

620 six hundred twenty   © Pearson Education, Inc. K   **Topic 10** | Performance Assessment

Topic Performance Assessment Masters

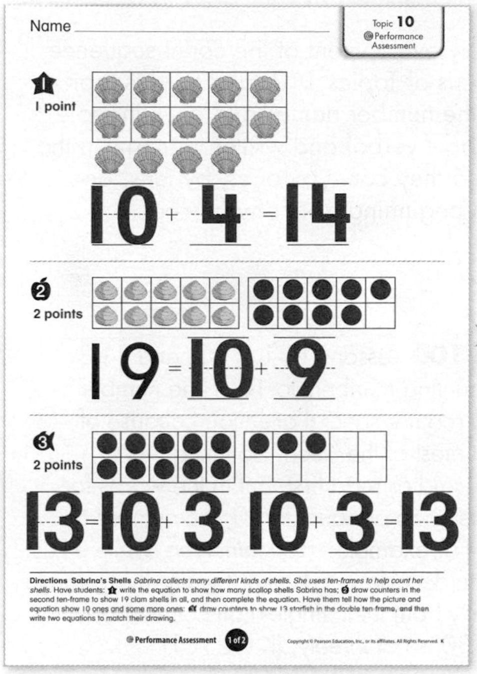

Name ______

Topic 10 Performance Assessment

1 point

10 + 4 = 14

2 points

19 = 10 + 9

2 points

13 = 10 + 3 10 + 3 = 13

Directions **Sabrina's Shells** *Sabrina collects many different kinds of shells. She uses ten-frames to help count her shells.* Have students: write the equation to show how many scallop shells Sabrina has; draw counters in the second ten-frame to show 19 clam shells in all, and then complete the equation. Have them tell how the picture and equation show 10 ones and some more ones; draw counters to show 13 starfish in the double ten-frame, and then write two equations to match their drawing.

Performance Assessment 1 of 2 Copyright © Pearson Education, Inc., or its affiliates. All Rights Reserved. K

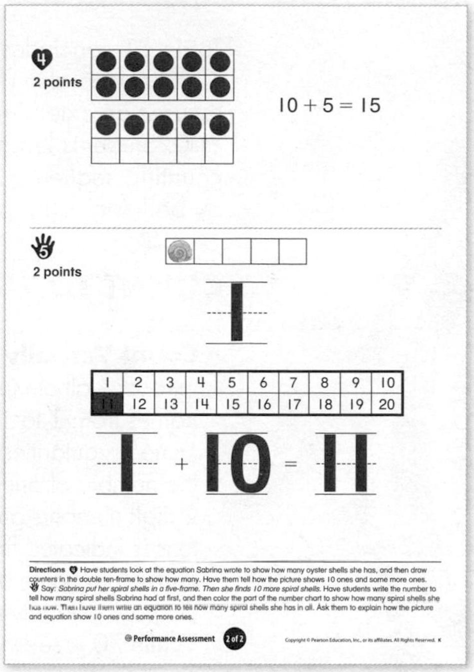

2 points

10 + 5 = 15

2 points

1

1	2	3	4	5	6	7	8	9	10
11	12	13	14	15	16	17	18	19	20

1 + 10 = 11

Directions Have students look at the equation Sabrina wrote to show how many oyster shells she has, and then draw counters in the double ten-frame to show how many. Have them tell how the picture shows 10 ones and some more ones. Say: *Sabrina put her spiral shells in a five-frame. Then she finds 10 more spiral shells.* Have students write the number to tell how many spiral shells Sabrina had at first, and then color the part of the number chart to show how many spiral shells she has now. Then have them write an equation to tell how many spiral shells she has in all. Ask them to explain how the picture and equation show 10 ones and some more ones.

Performance Assessment 2 of 2 Copyright © Pearson Education, Inc., or its affiliates. All Rights Reserved. K

RtI Item Analysis for Diagnosis and Intervention

Item	Standards	DOK	MDIS
1	K.NBT.A.1, MP.2	2	A10
2	K.NBT.A.1, MP.3	2	A10, A88
3	K.NBT.A.1, MP.4	3	A10
4	K.NBT.A.1, MP.3	3	A10
5	K.NBT.A.1, MP.7	4	A8, A10

Scoring Guide

Item	Points	Topic Performance Assessment Masters
1	1	Correct equation is written.
2	2	Correct picture and equation is shown.
	1	Correct picture or equation is shown.
3	2	Correct picture and equations are shown.
	1	Correct picture or equations are shown.
4	2	Picture drawn and explanation is correct.
	1	Picture shown is correct, but there is no explanation.
5	2	Correct number and equation is shown.
	1	Correct number or equation is shown.

FCR FOCUS | **COHERENCE** | **RIGOR**

● **MAJOR CLUSTER**   ● **SUPPORTING CLUSTER**   ● **ADDITIONAL CLUSTER**

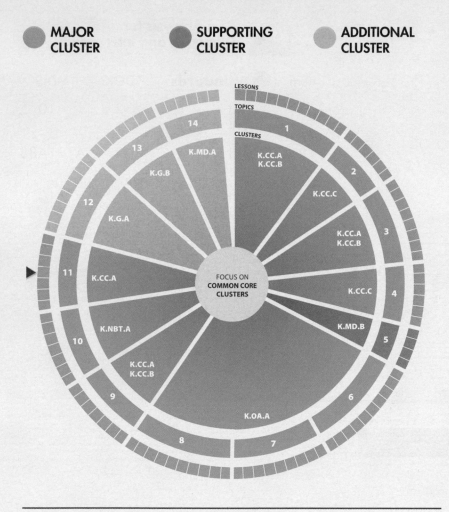

TOPIC 11 Count Numbers to 100

TOPIC 11 FOCUSES ON

Ⓒ **MAJOR CLUSTER K.CC.A**
Know number names and the count sequence.

Content Focus in enVisionmath2.0

Topic 11 concludes the development of the count sequence. K.CC.A was also a focus of Topics 1, 3, and 9. This topic focuses on extending the number names and counting to 100. Students learn about verbal and written patterns in the counting sequence, and they count by ones, by tens, and by both tens and ones beginning from any number.

COUNT TO 100

• **Count Verbally to 100** Lessons 11-1, 11-2, and 11-3 introduce all of the counting numbers to 100. The number names from 1 to 100 require special attention because of some irregularities. In most of the "teen" counting words, the number of ones is said or read first. But in the words for 2-digit numbers greater than or equal to 20, the number of tens is indicated first. For example, 19 is *nineteen*, while 39 is *thirty-nine*. Some of the decade words (ten, twenty, thirty, forty, etc.) are said differently from their single-digit counterparts. While 70 is *seventy*, 30 is not *threety*. (K.CC.A.1)

• **Count to 100 Using Visual Clues** Throughout Topic 11, the visual clues on a hundred chart help students count to 100. The columns show counting by tens, and the rows show counting by ones. (K.CC.A.1)

Content Focus in enVisionmath 2.0 (continued)

- **Count by Tens** In Lesson 11-3, students count by tens to 100. They learn about the decade numbers (10, 20, 30, and so on), count the decade numbers in order, and find missing numbers in a pattern of decade numbers. (K.CC.A.1)

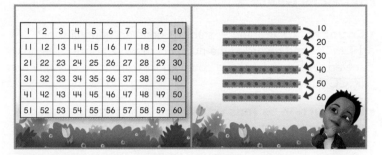

- **Count by Tens and Ones** In Lesson 11-4, students count by tens and ones to 100. They count the tens first and then continue counting the ones. This work provides a foundation for place-value concepts. (K.CC.A.1)

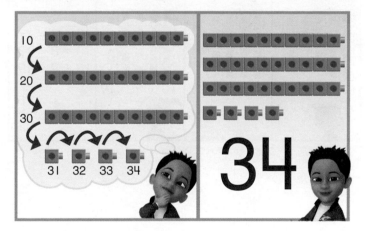

- **Count Forward Beginning with Any Number** In Lesson 11-5, students start with a beginning number other than 1 and count forward until they reach a target number. To count forward by ones, students state the beginning number and add 1 to the ones place for each subsequent number. This skill is foundational for the addition strategy of counting on. Students also count forward by tens from a given starting decade number. (K.CC.A.2)

1	2	3	4	5	6	7	8	9	10
11	12	13	14	15	16	17	18	19	20
21	22	23	24	25	26	27	28	29	30
31	32	33	34	35	36	37	38	39	40
41	42	43	44	45	46	47	48	49	50
51	52	53	54	55	56	57	58	59	60
61	62	63	64	65	66	67	68	69	70
71	72	73	74	75	76	77	78	79	80
81	82	83	84	85	86	87	88	89	90
91	92	93	94	95	96	97	98	99	100

COUNT OBJECTS

- **Solve Problems Involving Counting** In Lesson 11-4, students see that they can easily count up to 100 objects if the objects are arranged in groups of 10. They count by tens and ones to find how many. (K.CC.A.1, K.CC.A.2)

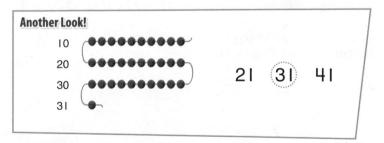

 Professional Development Videos Topic Overview Videos and Listen and Look For Lesson Videos present additional important information about the content of this cluster.

Content Coherence in enVisionmath2.0

Students learn best when ideas are connected in a coherent curriculum. This coherence is achieved through various types of connections including connections within clusters, across clusters, across domains, and across grades.

BIG IDEAS IN GRADES K–6

Big Ideas are the conceptual underpinnings of **enVision**math**2.0** and provide conceptual cohesion of the content. Big Ideas connect Essential Understandings throughout the program.

A Big Idea that connects some of the work in this cluster involves the base-10 numeration system, which is a scheme for recording numbers using digits 0 through 9, groups of 10, and place value. In this topic, as students count up to 100 objects arranged in groups of 10, they begin to visualize decade numbers as being made up of tens, and other 2-digit numbers as being made up of tens and ones.

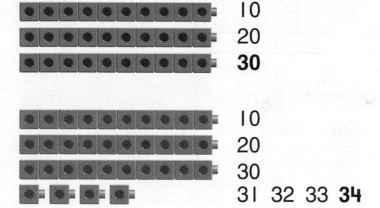

For a complete list of Big Ideas, see pages 110–111 in the *Teacher's Edition Program Overview*.

LOOK BACK

How does Topic 11 connect to what students learned earlier?

EARLIER IN GRADE K

- **Count to 20** In Topic 9, students counted quantities of 11 to 20 and recorded the numbers in written form. They also solved problems involving counting forward from any number. (K.CC.A, K.CC.B)

- **Introduction to Tens and Ones** Topics 9 and 10 began to build a foundation for understanding place value. In Topic 9, students counted objects arranged as a group of 10 ones and extra ones. Topic 10 focused on the composition and decomposition of all teen numbers into one group of 10 ones and some additional ones. (K.CC.A, K.CC.B.5, K.NBT.A.1)

TOPIC 11

How is content connected within Topic 11?

- **Extend the Count Sequence to Larger and Larger Numbers** In Lesson 11-1, students count to 30. Students use number charts to help them see and hear patterns as they count. They carry over and extend these understandings to count to 50 in Lesson 11-2. In Lesson 11-3, students continue to use patterns and number charts to count by tens to 100. (K.CC.A.1)

- **See Quantities as They Relate to 10** In order to become proficient counters, students need to understand patterns in the counting sequence. These patterns are rooted in the concepts that decade numbers are made up of tens, and other 2-digit numbers are made up of tens and ones. Throughout Topic 11, groups of 10 objects are visualized in a variety of ways. For example, on a number chart, moving down the column represents counting by tens. Cubes are arranged into bars of 10 cubes with extras shown as separate cubes. Other objects are arranged in groups of 10 with extras. (K.CC.A.1)

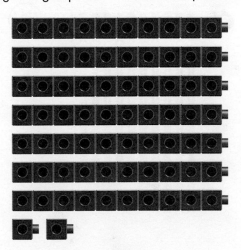

72

LOOK AHEAD

How does Topic 11 connect to what students will learn later?

GRADE 1

- **Extend the Counting Sequence to 120** In Topic 7, students will begin at any number less than 120, count to 120, and read and write numbers to 120. (1.NBT.A.1)

- **Count by Tens and Ones** In Topic 8, students will count with groups of tens and leftover ones. (1.NBT.B.2)

- **Count On to Add and Subtract** In Topics 2, 3, and 4, students will count on and count back to add and subtract within 20. In Topics 10 and 11, students will count on and count back to add and subtract 2-digit numbers. (1.OA.C.5, 1.NBT.C)

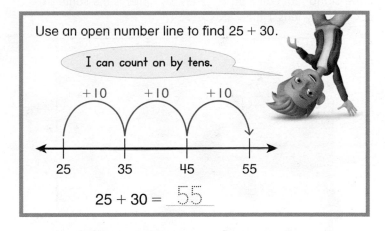

Use an open number line to find 25 + 30.

I can count on by tens.

$$25 + 30 = 55$$

MAJOR CLUSTER K.CC.A
MATH BACKGROUND: RIGOR

Content Rigor in enVisionmath2.0

A rigorous curriculum emphasizes conceptual understanding, procedural skill and fluency, and applications.

CONCEPTUAL UNDERSTANDING

- **Understand the Count Sequence** Hundred charts are used throughout the topic to help students understand the repetitive nature of counting. Just as there is a given sequence in the numbers 1 to 9, the ones digits in the other rows follow the same sequence. The right-most column highlights that after 9, they cross to the next decade number. The sequence of decade numbers, 10, 20, 30, and so on, is similar to the sequence of the ones digits, 1, 2, 3, and so on. (K.CC.A)

- **Understand that 1 Ten Is the Same as 10 Ones** A beginning concept in place value is the understanding that a 10 is made up of 10 ones. Students should come to understand that counting by ones 10 times is the same as counting by tens 1 time. (K.CC.A.1)

Carlos has some cubes. How many cubes does Carlos have? What would be a quick way to count all of the cubes? Write the number to tell how many.

- **Understand Counting Forward** To begin counting from any number, students can envision that the number they begin with represents the number of counts (by ones) that have already occurred. (K.CC.A.2)

PROCEDURAL SKILL AND FLUENCY

There are no standards in this cluster that call for fluency.

- **Count to 100** Students learn to count to 100 using the correct number words in the correct order without leaving out any numbers. (K.CC.A.1)

- **Count Forward from Any Number to 100** Students learn to count forward from any number within 100. (K.CC.A.2)

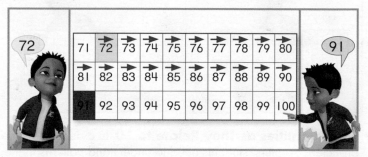

APPLICATIONS

- **Solve Problems Involving Counting** In Lesson 11-4, students count up to 100 objects arranged in groups of 10. They apply their understanding of counting by tens and ones to find how many. (K.CC.A.1, K.CC.A.2)

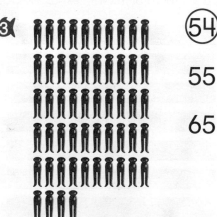

MATH PRACTICES

PEARSON
realize
PearsonRealize.com

MP

Connecting Math Practices and Content Standards in enVisionmath2.0

Math practices and content standards are connected within all lessons including the lessons that focus on math practices.

MATH PRACTICES WITHIN LESSONS

- **MP.1 Make sense of problems and persevere in solving them.**

  Students make sense of numbers that are given in a chart, and persevere in determining what numbers are missing. (e.g., p. 627, Items 3–4)

- **MP.2 Reason abstractly and quantitatively.**

  Students reason abstractly by counting by both tens and ones to identify a quantity. (e.g., p. 646, Item 9)

- **MP.3 Construct viable arguments and critique the reasoning of others.**

  Students critique reasoning involving procedures for counting decade numbers. (e.g., p. 638, Do You Understand?)

- **MP.4 Model with mathematics.**

  Students apply what they know about decade numbers to solve problems involving counting. (e.g., p. 640, Item 7)

- **MP.5 Use appropriate tools strategically.**

  Students decide when to use hundred charts to solve counting problems. (e.g., p. 656, Do You Understand?)

- **MP.6 Attend to precision.**

  Students attend to precision when they give a clear explanation for the steps they used to solve a counting problem. (e.g., p. 663, Items 5–6)

- **MP.7 Look for and make use of structure.**

  Students use the structure of the base-10 system to count on by ones and by tens from any number. (e.g., p. 661, Solve and Share)

- **MP.8 Look for and express regularity in repeated reasoning.**

  Students use repeated reasoning to generalize that the order in which the tens and ones are counted does not affect the final number. (e.g., p. 664, Item 9)

LESSON THAT FOCUSES ON MATH PRACTICES

- **Lesson 11-7** This lesson focuses on MP.7. Students identify the patterns in the tens and ones digits when counting to 100. They use the structure of the base-10 system to count on from a given number in different ways.

1	2	3	4	5	6	7	8	9	10
11	12	13	14	15	16	17	18	19	20
21	22	23	24	25	26	27	28	29	30

1	2	3	4	5	6	7	8	9	10
11	12	13	14	15	16	17	18	19	20
21	22	23	24	25	26	27	28	29	30

Count up from 3 to 18 in different ways.
One way: Count up by one 5 times, and by ten once.
Another way: Count up by ten once, and by one 5 times.

Revisit the information about MP.7 in these other resources:

- **Math Practices and Problem Solving Handbook** before Topic 1; includes Math Practices Proficiency Rubrics.

- **Math Practices Posters** to display in your classroom

- **Math Practices Animations,** one for each math practice, available at PearsonRealize.com.

MP

MAJOR CLUSTER K.CC.A

DIFFERENTIATED INSTRUCTION

 Intervention   **On-Level**   **Advanced**

 PEARSON **realize**
PearsonRealize.com

Learn **Assessment** **Tools** **Games**

Ongoing Intervention

 During the core lesson, monitor progress, reteach as needed, and extend students' thinking.

Guiding Questions

- **In the Teacher's Edition** Guiding questions are used to monitor understanding during instruction.

- **Online Guiding Questions** Guiding questions are also in the online Visual Learning Animation Plus.

Error Intervention: If... then...

This feature in the Teacher's Edition is provided during Guided Practice. It spotlights common errors and gives suggestions for addressing them.

Reteaching

Reteaching sets are at the end of the topic in the Student's Edition. They provide additional examples, reminders, and practice. Use these sets as needed before students do the Independent Practice.

Higher Order Thinking

These problems require students to think more deeply about the rich, conceptual knowledge developed in the lesson.

Strategic Intervention

 At the end of the lesson, assess to identify students' strengths and needs and then provide appropriate support.

Quick Check

✓ **In the Student's Edition** Assess the lesson using 2-3 items checked in the Teacher's Edition.

 Online Quick Check You can also assess the lesson using 5 online, machine-scored items.

Intervention Activity

Teachers work with struggling students.

Reteach to Build Understanding

This is a page of guided reteaching.

Technology Center

 Digital Math Tools Activities reinforce the lesson content or previously taught content using a suite of digital math tools.

 Online Games provide practice on the lesson content or previously taught content.

Homework and Practice

Use the leveled assignment to provide differentiated homework and practice.

Additional resources to support differentiated instruction for on-level and advanced students include:

On-Level and Advanced Activity Centers

- **Center Games** are provided in on-level and advanced versions.

- **Math and Science Activity** is related to the topic science theme introduced at the start of the topic.

- **Problem-Solving Reading Mat** is used with a lesson-specific activity.

Intensive Intervention

As needed, provide more instruction that is on or below grade level for students who are struggling.

Math Diagnosis and Intervention System 2.0

- **Diagnosis** Use the diagnostic tests in the system. Also, use the item analysis charts given with program assessments at the start of a grade or topic, or at the end of a topic, group of topics, or the year.

- **Intervention Lessons** These two-page lessons include guided instruction followed by practice. The system includes lessons below, on, and above grade level.

- **Teacher Support** Teacher Notes provide the support needed to conduct a short lesson. The lesson focuses on vocabulary, concept development, and practice. The Teacher's Guide contains individual and class record forms and correlations to Student's Edition lessons.

Resources for Fluency Success

- A variety of print and digital resources are provided to ensure success on Common Core fluency standards. See Steps to Fluency Success on pages 431E–431H.

THE LANGUAGE OF MATH

English Language Learners

Provide ELL support through visual learning throughout the program, ELL instruction in every lesson, and additional ideas in an ELL Toolkit.

Visual Learning
The visual learning that is infused in **enVision**math**2.0** provides support for English language learners. This support includes a Visual Learning Animation Plus and a Visual Learning Bridge for each lesson.

English Language Learners Instruction
Lessons provide instruction for English language learners at Beginning, Intermediate, and Advanced levels of English proficiency.

English Language Learners Toolkit
This resource provides professional development and resources for supporting English language learners.

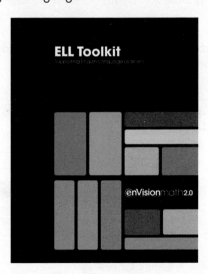

Math Vocabulary

Build math vocabulary using the vocabulary cards, vocabulary activities, vocabulary review, and glossary plus the online glossary and vocabulary game.

My Word Cards
Vocabulary cards for a topic are provided in the Student's Edition. Use the cards with students to study and learn new vocabulary words.

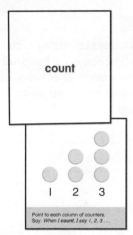

count

1 2 3

Point to each column of counters.
Say: *When I count, I say 1, 2, 3 . . .*

Vocabulary Activities
The Teacher's Edition provides vocabulary activities at the start of topics. These include activities for vocabulary in My Word Cards and/or activities for vocabulary in Review What You Know.

Vocabulary Review
A page of vocabulary review is provided at the end of each topic. It reviews vocabulary used in the topic.

Glossary
A glossary is provided at the back of the Student's Edition.

Animated Glossary
 An online, bilingual, animated glossary uses motion and sound to build understanding of math vocabulary.

Online Vocabulary Game
 An online vocabulary game is available in the Game Center.

Math and Reading

Connect reading and math using a data-filled reading mat for the topic with accompanying activity masters and guide. Also use topic interactive math stories.

Problem-Solving Reading Mats
There is a large, beautiful mat for each topic. At the start of the topic, help students become familiar with the mat and the vocabulary used by reading the mat aloud as students follow along. Use the Problem-Solving Reading Activity Guide for suggestions about how to use the mat.

Problem-Solving Reading Activity
At the end of some lessons, a Problem-Solving Reading Activity provides a page of math problems to solve by using the data on the mat.

Interactive Math Stories
  An interactive math story provides an introduction to each topic. The story is available as an online story book and an animated story at PearsonRealize.com as well as a color-in, take-home story in the Teacher's Resource Masters.

Lesson 11-1	**Lesson 11-2**	**Lesson 11-3**
COUNT USING PATTERNS TO 30 pp. 625–630	**COUNT USING PATTERNS TO 50** pp. 631–636	**COUNT BY TENS TO 100** pp. 637–642
© Content Standards **K.CC.A.1**, **K.CC.A.2** Mathematical Practices **MP.1, MP.2, MP.6, MP.7**	© Content Standards **K.CC.A.1**, **K.CC.A.2** Mathematical Practices **MP.1, MP.6, MP.7, MP.8**	© Content Standard **K.CC.A.1** Mathematical Practices **MP.2, MP.3, MP.4, MP.7**
Objective Use patterns to count to 30.	**Objective** Use patterns to count to 50.	**Objective** Skip count by tens to 100.
Essential Understanding Counting patterns can be seen on a hundred chart in both the rows and the columns. Some patterns can also be heard when counting aloud.	**Essential Understanding** Counting patterns can be seen on a hundred chart in both the rows and the columns. Some patterns can also be heard when counting aloud.	**Essential Understanding** Decade numbers such as 10, 20, … 100 are used to name groups of ten. You can count by tens to 100 by counting only the decade numbers.
Vocabulary column, ones, pattern, tens	**Vocabulary** None	**Vocabulary** decade, hundred chart
ELL Speaking: Express opinions.	**ELL Listening:** Learn new language structures.	**ELL Listening:** Demonstrate listening comprehension by following directions.
Materials Index cards, Number Cards 3–9 (use Teaching Tool 3), Hundred Chart (Teaching Tool 31)	**Materials** Index cards, counters (or Teaching Tool 6), Hundred Chart (Teaching Tool 31)	**Materials** Crayons, index cards, Hundred Chart (Teaching Tool 31)
On-Level and Advanced Activity Centers • Problem-Solving Reading Mat	**On-Level and Advanced Activity Centers** • Center Games	**On-Level and Advanced Activity Centers** • Math and Science Activity

LESSON RESOURCES

Digital

Print

- Student's Edition
- Daily Common Core Review
- Reteach to Build Understanding
- Center Games
- Math and Science Activity
- Problem-Solving Reading Mat
- Problem-Solving Reading Activity

Digital

- Listen and Look For PD Lesson Video
- Student's Edition eText
- Today's Challenge
- Solve & Share
- Visual Learning Animation Plus

- Animated Glossary
- Math Tools
- Quick Check
- Another Look Homework Video
- Math Games

Digital

<table>
<tr><th>Lesson 11-4</th><th>Lesson 11-5</th><th>Lesson 11-6</th></tr>
<tr>
<td>

COUNT BY TENS AND ONES pp. 643–648

</td>
<td>

COUNT FORWARD FROM ANY NUMBER TO 100 pp. 649–654

</td>
<td>

COUNT USING PATTERNS TO 100 pp. 655–660

</td>
</tr>
<tr>
<td>

Content Standards K.CC.A.1, K.CC.A.2
Mathematical Practices MP.1, MP.2, MP.3, MP.6

</td>
<td>

Content Standards K.CC.A.1, K.CC.A.2
Mathematical Practices MP.1, MP.5, MP.7, MP.8

</td>
<td>

Content Standards K.CC.A.2, K.CC.A.1
Mathematical Practices MP.2, MP.5, MP.6, MP.7

</td>
</tr>
<tr>
<td>

Objective Count to the number 100 by using tens and ones.

</td>
<td>

Objective Count forward from any number to 100 by ones.

</td>
<td>

Objective Count by tens and ones from any number up to 100.

</td>
</tr>
<tr>
<td>

Essential Understanding Decade numbers such as 10, 20, ... 100 are used to name groups of ten. You can count by tens to 100 by counting the decade numbers. You can also count by ones to 100.

</td>
<td>

Essential Understanding Numbers are counted and written in a specific sequence on a hundred chart.

</td>
<td>

Essential Understanding Using counting patterns on the hundred chart can help when counting on from any number from 1 to 100.

</td>
</tr>
<tr>
<td>

Vocabulary None

</td>
<td>

Vocabulary None

</td>
<td>

Vocabulary None

</td>
</tr>
<tr>
<td>

ELL Listening: Learn new academic expressions.

</td>
<td>

ELL Reading: Use support from peers and teachers to indicate, enhance and confirm understanding.

</td>
<td>

ELL Speaking: Speak using content area vocabulary in context.

</td>
</tr>
<tr>
<td>

Materials Connecting cubes (or Teaching Tool 8), crayons, straws, rubber bands

</td>
<td>

Materials Hundred Chart (Teaching Tool 31), counters (or Teaching Tool 6), crayons, index cards

</td>
<td>

Materials Hundred Chart (Teaching Tool 31)

</td>
</tr>
<tr>
<td>

On-Level and Advanced Activity Centers
• Math and Science Activity

</td>
<td>

On-Level and Advanced Activity Centers
• Center Games

</td>
<td>

On-Level and Advanced Activity Centers
• Problem-Solving Reading Mat

</td>
</tr>
</table>

TOPIC RESOURCES

Digital

Print

Start of Topic
• Topic Centers
• Interactive Math Story
• Math and Science Project
• Home-School Connection
• Review What You Know
• My Word Cards

End of Topic
• Fluency Practice Activity
• Vocabulary Review
• Reteaching
• Topic Assessment
• Topic Performance Assessment
• Cumulative Benchmark Test

Digital

Start of Topic
• Topic Overview PD Video

End of Topic
• Math Practices Animations
• Online Topic Assessment
• ExamView® Test Generator

PearsonRealize.com

Lesson 11-7

MATH PRACTICES AND PROBLEM SOLVING: LOOK FOR AND USE STRUCTURE pp. 661–666

Ⓒ Mathematical Practices **MP.7, MP.6, MP.8**

Content Standards **K.CC.A.1, K.CC.A.2**

Objective Count on from any number counting by tens and by ones.

Essential Understanding Good math thinkers look for patterns in math to solve problems.

Vocabulary None

ELL Listening: Demonstrate listening comprehension by following directions.

Materials Crayons, Hundred Chart (Teaching Tool 31)

On-Level and Advanced Activity Centers
- Center Games

Notes

Digital

PearsonRealize.com

Dramatic Play Center

How Many Beans?

Materials
Cooking pot, large spoon, measuring cup, large dried beans

- Partner A measures a cup of beans, pours it into the pot, and stirs, pretending to cook. Partner B says, "Hmm, smells good! How many beans did you cook?"

- Together the partners place the beans in groups of 10 to count them. The last group may have fewer than 10. Then students count the beans by 10s and count by 1s for the last group.

- Partners switch roles and repeat.

Technology Center

Input, Output

Materials
Computer, printer, paper

- Introduce students to the components of a computer, such as the keyboard, monitor, mouse, and printer.

- Invite students to use the number keys, the space bar, and the return key to type the numbers through 100. Have them write the numbers 1 to 10 in order, using the space bar between each number, as follows: 1 2 3 4 5 6 7 8 9 10.

- Show students how to use the return key. Then have them type the next 10 numbers. Have students type rows of 10 until they reach 100 and then print their numbers by selecting "print" from the menu bar.

- You may wish to adapt the activity. Once students have successfully typed by ones to 50, they can type by tens from 50, 51, or 52, and then count by ones, if needed, to reach 100.

Building Center

The House That Jack Built

Materials
100 blocks

- Have 10 students each build a tower with 10 blocks.

- When finished, count together by 10s to 100.

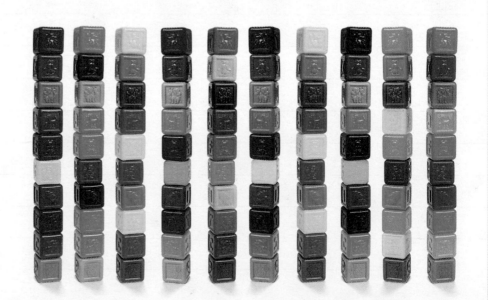

Writing Center

Letters

Materials
Large grid paper that has 100 squares, pencils

- Have students write their names on the paper. Then have them count the number of squares they used.

- Have one student, such as Henry, ask another student, Amy, to write her name on his paper. Now how many squares are used?

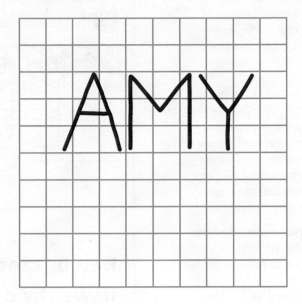

Art Center

100 Squares

Materials
Large grid paper that has 100 squares, crayons, colored pencils

- Have students draw a picture on the grid—a flower, a stick figure, a cat.

- Then have them tell how many squares their pictures take up. Have students compare the squares they used with others' pictures.

Math Center

Take a Card!

Materials
Different sets of Number Cards: Number Cards 11–20 (Teaching Tool 4) (20–30, 30–40, 40–50, 50–60, 60–70, 70–80, 80–90, 90–100)

- For example, let's say you want to give students opportunities to figure out patterns. Use one group of cards at a time. Hold up 2 cards: 34 and 37. Call on a student to take the greater number. He or she takes that number and sits down.

- Use 2 cards from another group: 47 and 49. Call on a student to take the number that shows fewer and sit down. Ensure that you pick numbers that, when chosen by students, form a pattern, such as 37, 47, 57.

- After you have played the game awhile and a number of students have chosen cards, have those students stand and hold up their cards. Have the others dictate to them to move to the right or to the left to place the numbers in their correct order: 37, 47, 57, ... *What pattern do you see?*

TOPIC 11 — INTERACTIVE MATH STORY
COUNT NUMBERS TO 100

PEARSON
realize
PearsonRealize.com

PDF Story | ▶ Story

Before the Story

Picture Walk

Project the online PDF that contains a full-color version of the story. Read the title, author's name, and illustrator's name to students. *Who is the main character in this book? How can you tell?* [Busy Bee is the main character. I can tell because the title and picture are two clues.] *Let's take a picture walk to see what Busy Bee counts.* Discuss the horses in the barn, the pigs, and the flowers that the bee counts on each of the pages.

Activate Prior Knowledge

In this story, we will count with Busy Bee. Listen as I count. Tell me the pattern I am using to count. Count by 1s from 1 to 12, then call on someone to tell how you counted.

Listen as I count again. Count by 10s from 10 to 50. Have a student tell how you counted.

Play the animated version of the story.

DURING THE STORY

This book belongs to:
Max

Busy, Busy Bee

Written by Grace Jeans
Illustrated by Garry Colby

Bee buzzes past 1 flower by a tree. We can count the flowers by 5 trees. **5** flowers!

Topic 11 1

Bee zigzags past 10 flowers by a door. Count the flowers by 2 doors. **20** flowers!

Topic 11 2

READ

Read the story aloud for enjoyment. Then read page 1 aloud. *Let's count the trees together: 1, 2, 3, 4, 5. Let's count the flowers to find out how many there are in all.* Page 2: *Let's count the flowers.* Continue by counting by 10s on pages 3 and 4.

GESTURE

Have a group of students stand in front of the class. Have the entire class count the group by 1s. Ask 5 students to come to the board. Have each student draw 10 flowers and then count by 10s to 50 together.

COLOR

Distribute the Interactive Math Story book to students along with red, yellow, and green crayons. On page 1: have students draw a circle around each flower with a red crayon; Page 2: have them color 1 set of 10 flowers yellow; Page 3: have students count and draw a circle around a group of 30 flowers in green; Page 4: have students draw a circle around 1 set of 10 in green.

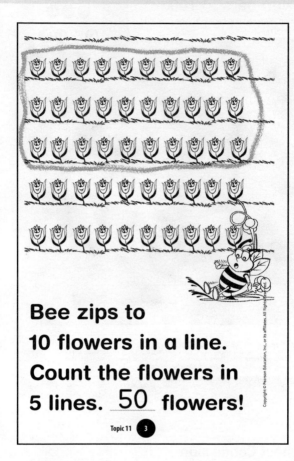

**Bee zips to
10 flowers in a line.
Count the flowers in
5 lines.** 50 **flowers!**

Topic 11 3

**Bee zooms to 10
flowers on a pen.
We can count the
flowers on 6 pens.**
60 **flowers!**

Topic 11 4

fold down

After the Story

Extension

Discuss the story's setting with students. *It seems like Busy Bee lives on or near a farm. Why do you think this is so?* [There's a barn with horses and pens with pigs.] Have students share any experiences they may have had on a farm, or anything they have learned about farms from a book, TV, or another person.

Have students draw a picture of something else on a farm that Busy Bee might count. Prompt them with questions: *Do you think there may be chickens that lay eggs? What other animals might be on a farm? Would there be vegetables growing in a garden? How about an apple tree?* Display students' pictures on a bulletin board.

You may wish to have students take home their Interactive Math Story books and share what they have learned about counting by 1s and 10s.

WRITE

Reread the first page of the story. *How many flowers are there? Let's count to find out.* Count out loud together. Have students write *5* to fill in the missing number. Follow the same procedure for the remaining pages. Read the text aloud. Ask how many. Use a pattern to count, and then have students fill in the missing numbers.

SPEAK

Invite students to retell the story in their own words, starting with "First, Busy Bee counts the flowers. Next he . . ." Encourage students to use sequence words, such as *next, then,* and *after that.*

TOPIC ESSENTIAL QUESTION

How can numbers to 100 be counted using a hundred chart?

Revisit the Topic Essential Question throughout the topic, and see a note about answering the Question in the Teacher's Edition for the Topic Assessment.

MATH AND SCIENCE PROJECT STEM

Science Theme The science theme for this project is **Ant Colonies**. This theme will be revisited in the Math and Science Activities in Lessons 11-3 and 11-4.

Ask students to discuss what the ants are doing in the photograph. Encourage them to discuss different jobs ants living in a colony might have, such as food collection or protecting the queen ant. Tell them that ants are very strong and can lift about 20 times their body weight. Talk about objects that are 20 times a student's body weight, like a small car or 20 of their friends at once.

Project-Based Learning Have students work on the **Math and Science Project** over the course of several days.

EXTENSION

Explain that some animals live alone or in small groups, like bears and jaguars, and others live in large groups, like schools of fish and colonies of bees. Then have students draw a picture of an animal that lives alone or in a small group and another animal that lives in a large group.

Sample Student Work for Math and Science Project

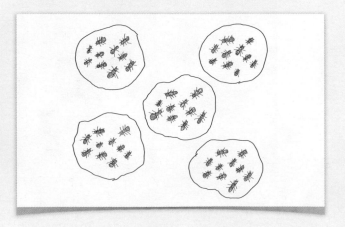

TOPIC 11 **Count Numbers to 100**
Essential Question: How can numbers to 100 be counted using a hundred chart?

Ants

Ants live in colonies.

Digital Resources
Solve Learn Glossary
Tools Assessment Help Games

Math and Science Project: Ant Colonies
Directions Read the character speech bubbles to students. **Find Out!** Have students find out how ants live and work together in colonies. Say: *Talk to friends and relatives about ant colonies. Ask about the different jobs ants in a colony might have that help them survive.* **Journal: Make a Poster** Have students make a poster. Have them draw an ant colony with 5 groups of ants. There should be 10 ants in each group. Then have them count by tens to find how many ants there are in all. Have students use a hundred chart to practice counting by tens to 50.

Topic 11   six hundred twenty-one **621**

Home-School Connection

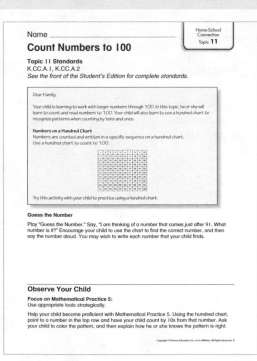

Name _____
Count Numbers to 100

Home-School Connection
Topic 11

Topic 11 Standards
K.CC.A.1, K.CC.A.2
See the front of the Student's Edition for complete standards.

Dear Family,
Your child is learning to work with larger numbers through 100. In this topic, he or she will learn to count and read numbers to 100. Your child will also learn to use a hundred chart to recognize patterns when counting by tens and ones.

Numbers on a Hundred Chart
Numbers are counted and written in a specific sequence on a hundred chart. Use a hundred chart to count to 100.

Try this activity with your child to practice using a hundred chart.

Guess the Number
Play "Guess the Number." Say, "I am thinking of a number that comes just after 91. What number is it?" Encourage your child to use the chart to find the correct number, and then say the number aloud. You may wish to write each number that your child finds.

Observe Your Child
Focus on Mathematical Practice 5:
Use appropriate tools strategically.

Help your child become proficient with Mathematical Practice 5. Using the hundred chart, point to a number in the top row and have your child count by 10s from that number. Ask your child to color the pattern, and then explain how he or she knows the pattern is right.

Send this page home at the start of Topic 11 to give families an overview of the content in the topic.

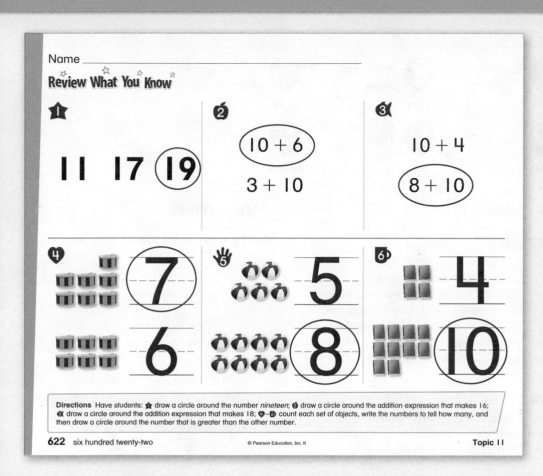

Name _____

Review What You Know

1

11 17 (19)

2

(10 + 6)

3 + 10

3

10 + 4

(8 + 10)

4 (7) (6)

5 5 (8)

6 4 (10)

Directions Have students: ★ draw a circle around the number *nineteen*; 🍎 draw a circle around the addition expression that makes 16; 🐟 draw a circle around the addition expression that makes 18; ✋–🖐 count each set of objects, write the numbers to tell how many, and then draw a circle around the number that is greater than the other number.

© Pearson Education, Inc. K

Topic 11

Topic 11 Vocabulary Words Activity

Use the Topic 9 activity on page 508A with the Topic 11 words below.

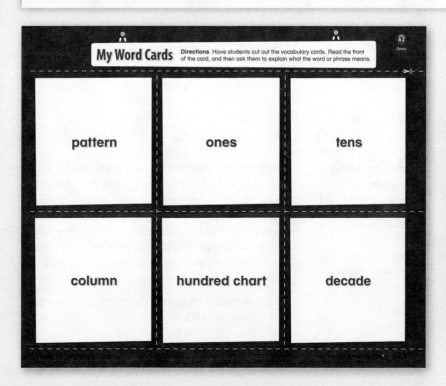

My Word Cards **Directions** Have students cut out the vocabulary cards. Read the front of the card, and then ask them to explain what the word or phrase means.

pattern

ones

tens

column

hundred chart

decade

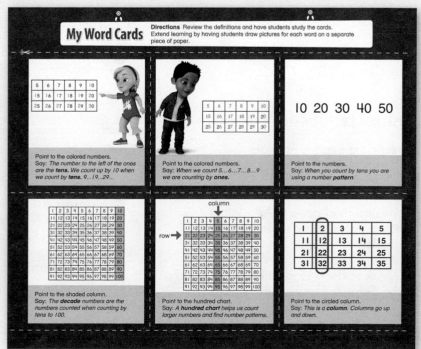

My Word Cards **Directions** Review the definitions and have students study the cards. Extend learning by having students draw pictures for each word on a separate piece of paper.

Point to the colored numbers.
Say: *The number to the left of the ones are the **tens**. We count up by 10 when we count by **tens**. 9...19...29...*

Point to the colored numbers.
Say: *When we count 5...6...7...8...9 we are counting by **ones**.*

10 20 30 40 50

Point to the numbers.
Say: *When you count by tens you are using a number **pattern**.*

Point to the shaded column.
Say: *The **decade** numbers are the numbers counted when counting by tens to 100.*

column

row →

Point to the hundred chart.
Say: *A **hundred chart** helps us count larger numbers and find number patterns.*

Point to the circled column.
Say: *This is a **column**. Columns go up and down.*

COUNT USING PATTERNS TO 30

DIGITAL RESOURCES PearsonRealize.com

 Student and Teacher eTexts
eText

 Listen and Look For Lesson Video
PD

 Today's Challenge
Think

 Solve and Share
Solve

 Visual Learning Animation Plus
Learn

 Animated Glossary
Glossary

 Math Tools
Tools

 Quick Check
Assessment

 Another Look Homework Video
Help

 Math Games
Games

LESSON OVERVIEW   **F C R** FOCUS • COHERENCE • RIGOR

FOCUS

Domain K.CC Counting and Cardinality

Cluster K.CC.A Know number names and the count sequence.

Content Standard K.CC.A.1 Count to 100 by ones and by tens. Also **K.CC.A.2**

Mathematical Practices MP.1, MP.2, MP.6, MP.7

Objective Use patterns to count to 30.

Essential Understanding Counting patterns can be seen on a hundred chart in both the rows and the columns. Some patterns can also be heard when counting aloud.

Vocabulary column, ones, pattern, tens

COHERENCE

Students have previously studied counting from a number and finding parts of a number to 20. In Lesson 11-1, students build on this work as they extend their knowledge of the counting sequence. Students use their experience of numbers to 20 to find patterns and then use those patterns to continue the count to 30.

RIGOR

This lesson emphasizes **conceptual understanding**. By broadening students' understanding of counting numbers and their relationship on a partial hundred chart, students are building their overall number sense of the patterns within the counting sequence. An understanding of these patterns will not only help students count to 30, but also develop awareness of place value as they analyze similarities and differences between tens and ones digits as they count.

 Watch the Listen and Look For Lesson Video.
PD

MATH ANYTIME

Daily Common Core Review

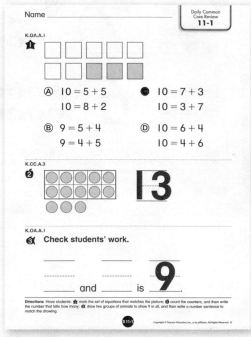

 Today's Challenge
Think Use Topic 11 problems any time during this topic.

ENGLISH LANGUAGE LEARNERS **E L L**

Speaking Express opinions.

Use with the Solve & Share on Student's Edition p. 625.

Write and read *pattern*. Ask: *What is a pattern?* Ask students to define or give examples of patterns. Say: *A pattern is something that repeats.* Write *1 1 2 1 1 2 1 1 2*. Ask students to identify the pattern. Point to the *Solve & Share* number chart. Say: *As we count from 1 to 30, see if you notice a pattern.* Instruct students to put their fingers on 1 and count to 30. Ask: *Do you see a pattern?* Instruct students to express ideas about

patterns they see in the number chart. Using index cards, instruct students to cover all but the first column in the chart. Point to 1, 11, 21.

Beginning Ask students to point to 1, 11, 21. Ask: *Do you see a pattern?* Instruct students to point to patterns they may see and respond using the sentence stem: "I see a ____." [Pattern]

Intermediate Ask students to look at 1, 11, 21. Ask: *Do you see a pattern?* Instruct students to share their opinions about patterns they may see using the sentence stem: "The ____ [Pattern] I see is ____."

Advanced Ask students to analyze 1, 11, 21. Ask: *Do you see a pattern?* Instruct students to share their opinions with partners about patterns they may see. Ask students to remove the index cards. Ask: *Do you see other patterns?* Instruct students to share their opinions with partners about patterns they may see.

Summarize What is a pattern you may see on a number chart?

DEVELOP: PROBLEM-BASED LEARNING

COHERENCE: Engage students by connecting prior knowledge to new ideas.
Students count to 30 while following the numbers on the chart. They identify any patterns they can see or hear. This prepares them for the next part of the lesson where they identify more patterns in counting numbers to 30 and use these patterns to find missing numbers.

10–15 min

 **BEFORE**

1. Pose the Solve-and-Share Problem
MP.7 Look for Patterns Students look and listen for both auditory and visual patterns as they count to 30.

Say: *Count aloud to 30 while you point to each number. What patterns do you see or hear when you count to 30 using the numbers on the chart? Color the boxes that show a pattern you find.*

2. Build Understanding
What are you asked to do? [Count to 30 using the numbers on the chart.] *What are you looking and listening for?* [Patterns that I see or hear] *What will you do when you find a pattern?* [Color the squares that show the patterns I find.]

 DURING

3. Ask Guiding Questions As Needed
What numbers do you hear repeated over and over? [Sample answer: I can hear the first row numbers (1, 2, 3...) said again in the third row numbers (21, 22, 23,...).] *What numbers, or parts of numbers, do you see repeated?* [Sample answer: The numbers going down in a line in the chart each have the same number repeated.]

 AFTER

4. Share and Discuss Solutions
 Start with students' solutions. Have them share the strategies they used to solve the problem. If needed project and analyze Darcy's work to identify a visual pattern.

5. Transition to the Visual Learning Bridge
You have described a pattern you have seen or heard. Later in this lesson, you will identify other patterns as you count to 30.

6. Extension for Early Finishers
What patterns could you find if the chart contained one more row of numbers (31 to 40)? [Sample answer: The same patterns as with 0 to 30, but you could use more numbers to show them.]

Solve & Share

Name _____

See margin for sample student work.

Lesson 11-1
Count Using
Patterns to 30

1	2	3	4	5	6	7	8	9	10
11	12	13	14	15	16	17	18	19	20
21	22	23	24	25	26	27	28	29	30

Directions Say: *Count aloud to 30 while you point to each number. What patterns do you see or hear when you count to 30 using the numbers on the chart? Color the boxes that show a pattern you find.*

I can ...
use patterns to count to 30.

Content Standards
K.CC.A.1, K.CC.A.2
Mathematical Practices
MP.1, MP.2, MP.6, MP.7

Topic 11 | Lesson 1

Digital Resources at PearsonRealize.com

six hundred twenty-five **625**

Analyze Student Work

Darcy's Work

1, 21	6, 26
2, 22	7, 27
3, 23	8, 28
4, 24	9, 29
5, 25	

Rahul's Work

Darcy explains that she heard the numbers 1 to 9 from the first row again with the numbers in the third row. She colors numbers 1 to 9 and 21 to 29 and matches 1 and 21, 2 and 22, 3 and 23, etc.

Rahul colors the numbers 5, 15 and 25 and explains that each of these numbers ends with a 5.

DEVELOP: VISUAL LEARNING

The *Visual Learning Bridge* connects students' thinking in Solve & Share to important math ideas in the lesson. Use the *Visual Learning Bridge* to make these ideas explicit. Also available as a *Visual Learning Animation Plus* at PearsonRealize.com

E L L Visual Learning

Learn   Glossary

MP.7 Look for Patterns *What is Carlos holding?* [A number chart from 1 through 30] *What else do you notice about the chart?* [Some of the numbers have been colored.] *Why have the numbers 1 and 21 been colored the same color?* [They both have *one* in the number when you say it.] *What do the other colored squares show on the chart?* [Other numbers that sound alike.] *When something is repeated, we call this a pattern. Why is the middle row not colored?* [These numbers do not sound alike.]

MP.7 Look for Patterns *What has been colored the same in this chart?* [Sample answers: The *1* in 1, 11, and 21; the *2* in 2, 12, and 22; etc.] *The part of the number that has been colored is the ones. Count by ones along the top row. What happens to the ones as you count along the row?* [They change each time] *The numbers going down are in columns. What happens to the ones in the columns?* [They stay the same.] *The part that has not been colored is the tens. What happens to the tens as you count along the row?* [They stay the same until the last one.] *Count by tens down a column. What happens to the tens in the columns?* [They change each time.] *You can use these patterns to help you count.*

Visual Learning Bridge

★ Guided Practice

1	2	3	4	5	6	7	8	9	10
11	12	13	14	15	16	17	18	19	20
21	22	23	24	25	26	27	28	29	30

Directions Have students: ★ count aloud all the numbers in the top row. Have them listen to the following numbers in the bottom row, and then draw a circle around the number in the top row and the part of the number in the bottom row that sound alike: *twenty-ONE, twenty-TWO, twenty-THREE, twenty-FOUR, twenty-FIVE, twenty-SIX.* ❷ listen to the following numbers, and then complete the numbers in the chart: *twenty-seven, twenty-eight, twenty-nine.*

626 six hundred twenty-six   © Pearson Education, Inc. K   **Topic 11 | Lesson 1**

Complete the *Do You Understand? Show Me!* problem before starting Guided Practice.

Do You Understand? Show Me! MP.2 Reasoning
Ask students to use the chart to help them count the numbers between 20 and 30. *Which numbers did you count?* [21, 22, 23, 24, 25, 26, 27, 28, 29] *What pattern can you hear?* [Sample answer: I am counting the same ones as when I count 1, 2, 3, 4 …]

Coherence In the Visual Learning Bridge students have explored both patterns they can hear and patterns they can see when they count to 30. This links back to, and builds on, work in Topic 9 where students were counting on from a number to 20.

Essential Question Ask the following Essential Question: *How can you find patterns when you count?* [Sample answer: I can listen to numbers that are repeated; I can look for numbers on a number chart that are repeated.]

Error Intervention: Item 2
If students are unable to recognize the missing numbers when you are counting aloud,

then have them say the numbers as they point to them on the number chart. Encourage students to think about the ones in each number.

1 RtI **Reteaching** Assign Reteaching Set A, p. 669.

✔ QUICK CHECK

Check mark indicates items for prescribing differentiation on the next page.
Items 7 and 8 are each worth 1 point. Item 9 is worth up to 3 points.

20–30 min

  Tools   Assessment

Items 3 and 4 MP.1 Make Sense and Persevere *How many numbers are missing on the top row?* [5] *Which numbers are NOT missing on the top row?* [6, 7, 8, 9, 10] *What are the first four numbers on the bottom row?* [21, 22, 23, 24] *How can this help you find the missing numbers?* [Sample answer: I know that the ones are the same on the top row as the bottom row because I can hear the same numbers when I count.] *How can you see which numbers are missing on the bottom row?* [Sample answer: I can look at the ones on the top row.]

Items 5 and 6 *Are the missing numbers for Item 5 in a row or a column?* [Column] *Look at the next column. What do you notice?* [All the numbers in the column end with a 5.] *Are the missing numbers for Item 6 in a column or a row?* [Row] *What changes as you move along the row?* [The ones change by 1 each time.]

Items 7 and 8 *Students use the number chart to solve the problem.* *How do you know which number is missing on the top row?* [Sample answer: I count along the row until I get to the missing number and then I know that it is the number that comes next.] *Which part of each number is missing on the bottom row?* [The ones] *Do the ones stay the same in the row or in the column?* [The column]

Item 9 MP.6 Be Precise *Are the missing numbers in the same row or the same column?* [Same row] *How could you see which numbers are missing?* [Sample answer: I can look at the numbers above and below to see the pattern in the columns.] As students count aloud the missing numbers, they may wish to follow the numbers on the top row with their finger as well as the middle row to make a connection to the pattern.

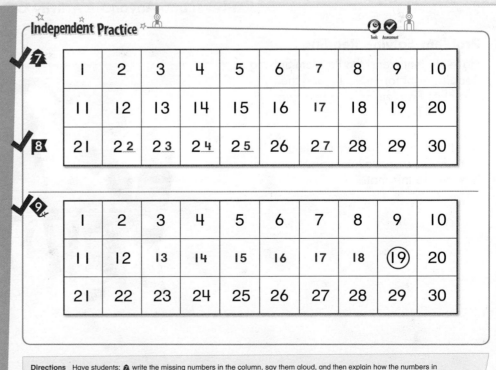

Name _____

❸

1	2	3	4	5	6	7	8	9	10
11	12	13	14	15	16	17	18	19	20

❹

21	22	23	24	2_5_	2_6_	2_7_	2_8_	2_9_	30

✋❺

1	2	3	4	5	6	7	8	9	10
11	12	13	14	15	16	17	18	19	20

☕❻

21	22	23	2_4_	25	26	27	28	29	30

Directions ✱ **Number Sense** Have students write the missing numbers, and then explain how they know the numbers are correct.
Have students: ✋ count the numbers in the bottom row aloud, and then write the missing numbers as they say them; ☕ write the missing numbers in the column, say them aloud, and then explain how the numbers in that column are alike; ☕ use the chart to find the missing numbers in the middle row, and then explain how they used the chart.

Topic 11 | Lesson 1   six hundred twenty-seven **627**

Independent Practice

Tools   Assessment

✔🌲❼

1	2	3	4	5	6	7	8	9	10
11	12	13	14	15	16	17	18	19	20

✔❽

21	2_2_	2_3_	2_4_	2_5_	26	2_7_	28	29	30

✔❾

1	2	3	4	5	6	7	8	9	10
11	12	13	14	15	16	17	18	(19)	20
21	22	23	24	25	26	27	28	29	30

Directions Have students: ❼ write the missing numbers in the column, say them aloud, and then explain how the numbers in that column are alike; ❽ count the numbers in the bottom row aloud, and then write the missing numbers as they say them aloud.
❾ **Higher Order Thinking** Have students write the missing numbers on the chart, count them aloud, and then explain the pattern they hear. Then have them draw a circle around the other number that fits the pattern.

628 six hundred twenty-eight   © Pearson Education, Inc. K   Topic 11 | Lesson 1

2 RtI Use the **QUICK CHECK** on the previous page to prescribe differentiated instruction.

I Intervention
0–3 points on the Quick Check

O On-Level
4 points on the Quick Check

A Advanced
5 points on the Quick Check

Intervention Activity I

Listen To Me Count

Materials

Number Cards 3–9 (use Teaching Tool 3), Hundred Chart (Teaching Tool 31)

- Give each student a number card. Explain that they are going to count aloud from 1 to 30 with their eyes closed. Ask students to hold up the number card they are holding if they hear it when they are counting. *How many times did you hear your number?* [Answers will vary between 2 and 3 depending on whether their number can be heard in the teen numbers or not.]

- Show a hundred chart and cover the rows for 31–100. Count again, this time following on the chart by pointing to each number. Ask students to hold up their number card when they see it on the chart as they count. Remind students that their number could be the whole number or part of a number.

- Ask students to close their eyes. Cover the number 16. Ask students to open their eyes and describe a way they could work out which number is missing. Remind students to look at both the rows and the columns. Repeat with 23 and 8.

1	2	3	4	5	6	7	8	9	10
11	12	13	14	15	■	17	18	19	20
21	22	23	24	25	26	27	28	29	30

Reteach I

Name _____

Reteach to Build Understanding 11-1

★ **5, 6, 7, 8, 9**

❷
1	2	3	4	5	6	7	8	9	10
11	12	13	14	15	16	17	18	19	20
21	22	23	24	25	26	27	28	29	30

❸
1	2	3	4	5	6	7	8	9	10
11	12	13	14	15	16	17	18	19	20
21	22	23	24	25	26	27	28	29	30

❹
11	12	13	14	15	16	17	18	19	20
21	22	23	24	25	26	27	28	29	30
31	32	33	34	35	36	37	38	39	40

Directions ★ Point to the numbers as you say them aloud. Say: *When we count 5, 6, 7, 8, and so on, we are counting by ones. Let's keep counting. What number comes next?* Have students write the next number. ❷ Say: *Listen to these numbers, and then draw a circle around the numbers in the chart that you hear: eight, eighteen, twenty-eight. How are the numbers with a circle around them alike? How are they different?* Have students: ❸ write the missing numbers, and then explain how they know the numbers are correct. ❹ write the missing numbers, say them aloud, and then explain how the numbers in that column are alike. **On the Back!** Have students write the numbers 15, 16, 17, and 18. Then have them write the next four numbers.

R 11-1   Copyright © Pearson Education, Inc., or its affiliates. All Rights Reserved. 8

On-Level and Advanced Activity Centers O A

Problem-Solving Reading Mat

Have students read the Problem-Solving Reading Mat for Topic 11 and then complete Problem-Solving Reading Activity 11-1.

See the Problem-Solving Reading Activity Guide for other suggestions on how to use this mat.

TIMING

The time allocated to Step 3 will depend on the teacher's instructional decisions and differentiation routines.

15–30 min

 Help

 Tools

 Games

 PEARSON
realize
PearsonRealize.com

Technology Center

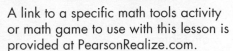 Tools

Games

Math Tools and Math Games

A link to a specific math tools activity or math game to use with this lesson is provided at PearsonRealize.com.

Leveled Assignment

I Items 1–4   **O** Items 3–6   **A** Items 3–6

Name _____

Help   Tools   Games

Homework & Practice 11-1
Count Using Patterns to 30

Another Look!

1	2	3	4	5	6	7	8	9	10
11	12	13	14	15	16	17	18	19	20
21	22	23	24	25	26	27	28	29	30

HOME ACTIVITY Tell your child a number between 1 and 10. Ask him or her to count up to 30 from that number.

1 / 2

1	2	3	4	5	6	7	8	9	10
11	12	13	14	15	16	17	18	19	20
21	22	23	24	25	26	27	28	29	30

Directions Say: *Listen to these numbers, and then draw a circle around the numbers in the chart that you hear:* nine, nineteen, twenty-nine. *What number do you see in each box of the column? What number do you hear in each number?* Have students listen to the numbers, and then draw a circle around the numbers in the chart that they hear: ⭐ four, fourteen, twenty-four; 🍎 sixteen, seventeen, eighteen, nineteen.

Topic 11 | Lesson 1   Digital Resources at PearsonRealize.com   six hundred twenty-nine **629**

3 / 4

1	2	3	4	5	6	7	8	9	10
11	12	13	14	15	16	17	18	19	20
21	22	23	24	25	26	27	28	29	30

5 / 6

1	2	3	4	5	6	7	8	9	10
11	12	13	14	15	16	17	18	19	20
21	22	23	24	25	26	27	28	29	30

Directions Have students: ⭐ write the missing numbers in the column, say them aloud, and then explain how the numbers in that column are alike; 🍎 listen to the numbers, and then draw a circle around the numbers in the chart that they hear: *twenty-seven, twenty-eight, twenty-nine, thirty.* ✋ listen to the numbers, and then draw a circle around the numbers in the chart that they hear: *twenty, twenty-one, twenty-two, twenty-three.* ☕ **Higher Order Thinking** Have students count aloud the numbers in the middle row. Have them color the boxes of the numbers that do NOT fit the pattern, and then explain why they do NOT fit the pattern.

630 six hundred thirty   © Pearson Education, Inc. K   Topic 11 | Lesson 1

629–630

LESSON 11-2

COUNT USING PATTERNS TO 50

DIGITAL RESOURCES PearsonRealize.com

eText Student and Teacher eTexts

PD Listen and Look For Lesson Video

Think Today's Challenge

Solve Solve and Share

Learn Visual Learning Animation Plus

Glossary Animated Glossary

Tools Math Tools

Assessment Quick Check

Help Another Look Homework Video

Games Math Games

LESSON OVERVIEW   **FCR** FOCUS • COHERENCE • RIGOR

FOCUS

Domain K.CC Counting and Cardinality

Cluster K.CC.A Know number names and the count sequence.

Content Standard K.CC.A.1 Count to 100 by ones and by tens. Also **K.CC.A.2**

Mathematical Practices MP.1, MP.6, MP.7, MP.8

Objective Use patterns to count to 50.

Essential Understanding Counting patterns can be seen on a hundred chart in both the rows and the columns. Some patterns can also be heard when counting aloud.

COHERENCE

Students found patterns to help them count to 30 in Lesson 11-1. They used these patterns to solve problems involving missing numbers. In Lesson 11-2, students further apply this understanding as they extend counting, and solve similar problems to 50. This continues to develop students' awareness of a greater range of numbers before they count to 100 in the next lesson.

RIGOR

This lesson emphasizes **conceptual understanding**. By furthering students' understanding of counting with a focus on patterns, this lesson deepens students' knowledge of the counting sequence. The continued use of a number chart allows students to see the relationships between the numbers they count and encourages the application of previously learned patterns, including consideration of tens and ones digits. Students are encouraged to think critically about their work as they explain how they know any missing numbers they have identified are correct.

PD Watch the Listen and Look For Lesson Video.

MATH ANYTIME

Daily Common Core Review

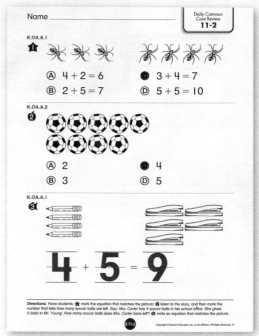

Today's Challenge

Think Use Topic 11 problems any time during this topic.

ENGLISH LANGUAGE LEARNERS **ELL**

Listening Learn new language structures.

Use with the Solve & Share on Student's Edition p. 631.

Using index cards, cover the number chart so only the second row is showing. Point to and count the numbers 11–19 with students. Ask: *How are these numbers alike/different?* Instruct students to carefully listen and give thumbs up if they agree with responses, and thumbs down if they do not agree. Continue process with 31–39 and 41–49. Cover the number chart with only the third row showing. Ask: *What numbers are missing?*

Beginning Instruct students to point to and count 21, 22. Point to the empty square. Ask: *What number is missing?* Have students listen to partners respond using the sentence stem: "The number ____ is missing." Write 23 in the square. Continue the process with the remaining missing numbers. Ask students to draw a circle around the parts of each number that sound the same.

Intermediate Point to the empty squares. Ask: *What numbers are missing?* Ask students to tell their partners the missing numbers, and then write them in the squares. Instruct students

to listen to partners count from 21–29, and then draw a circle around the parts of each number that sound the same.

Advanced Instruct students to work with partners to find the missing numbers. Ask: *How are these numbers alike/different? What parts of each number sound the same?* Have students listen to their partners' responses.

Summarize What information did you use to complete the number chart?

DEVELOP: PROBLEM-BASED LEARNING

COHERENCE: Engage students by connecting prior knowledge to new ideas.

Students identify a missing group of numbers in a number chart and explain how they know which numbers are missing by using patterns in the chart. This helps them later in the lesson when they will use different patterns to identify other missing numbers.

10–15 min

Solve

BEFORE

1. Pose the Solve-and-Share Problem
MP.7 Look for Patterns Students look for patterns on a partial hundred chart and identify the hidden numerals using counting patterns.

Say: *Look at the numbers on the chart and the parts that are underlined. Count aloud all the numbers to 50. Write and then say the numbers that are missing. Tell how you know the numbers are correct.*

2. Build Understanding
What are you asked to do? [Write and say the missing numbers.] *What will you do when you find the missing numbers?* [Tell how I know I have written the correct numbers.]

DURING

3. Ask Guiding Questions As Needed
Look at the underlined numbers. What patterns in the rows do you see? [Sample answer: The underlined numbers are the same on each row, apart from the last number.] *What patterns do you see in the numbers in the last column of the chart?* [10, 20, 30, 40, 50; each number that is underlined increases by 1.] *How do patterns help you find the missing numbers?* [Answers will vary.]

AFTER

4. Share and Discuss Solutions
 Start with students' solutions. Have them share
Solve the strategies used to solve the problem. If needed, project and analyze Lydia's work to identify a hidden number and give reasons using counting patterns.

5. Transition to the Visual Learning Bridge
You have found the missing numbers on the number chart and explained how you know you are correct.

Later in the lesson, you will find more patterns and use them to find missing numbers to 50.

6. Extension for Early Finishers
Cover 10 numbers on the chart and tell what numbers are hidden. Tell how you know. [Answers will vary.]

Solve & Share   Name _____

Lesson 11-2
Count Using Patterns to 50

See margin for sample student work.

1	2	3	4	5	6	7	8	9	10
11	12	13	14	15	16	17	18	19	20
21	22					28	29	30
31	32	33	34	35	36	37	38	39	40
41	42	43	44	45	46	47	48	49	50

Directions Say: *Look at the numbers on the chart and the parts that are underlined. Count aloud all the numbers to 50. Write and then say the numbers that are missing. Tell how you know the numbers are correct.*

I can ...
use patterns to count to 50.

© **Content Standards**
K.CC.A.1, K.CC.A.2
Mathematical Practices
MP.1, MP.6, MP.7, MP.8

Topic 11 | Lesson 2   Digital Resources at PearsonRealize.com   six hundred thirty-one **631**

Analyze Student Work

Lydia's Work

1	2	3	4	5	6	7	8	9	10
11	12	13	14	15	16	17	18	19	20
21	22	23	24	25	26	27	28	29	30
31	32	33	34	35	36	37	38	39	40
41	42	43	44	45	46	47	48	49	50

Bonnie's Work

1	2	3	4	5	6	7	8	9	10
11	12	13	14	15	16	17	18	19	20
21	22	32	42	52	62	72	28	29	30
31	32	33	34	35	36	37	38	39	40
41	42	43	44	45	46	47	48	49	50

Lydia correctly identifies the numbers 23, 24, 25, 26, and 27. She explains her numbers are correct because the tens and ones patterns match the other rows and columns. She is also able to check her numbers by counting from 21 to 30.

Bonnie correctly tells the missing numbers and counts from 21 to explain why she is correct. When she records the numbers in the chart, however, Bonnie switches the places of the tens and ones, writing 32, 42, 52, 62, 72 instead.

The *Visual Learning Bridge* connects students' thinking in Solve & Share to important math ideas in the lesson. Use the *Visual Learning Bridge* to make these ideas explicit. Also available as a *Visual Learning Animation Plus* at PearsonRealize.com

Visual Learning

Learn   Glossary

MP.1 Make Sense and Persevere *What can you see in the picture?* [A number chart; 5 counters covering some numbers on the chart] *Are the covered numbers in a row or a column?* [Column] *How does Carlos work out which numbers are missing?* [Sample answer: He looks at the numbers before and after the missing number.]

MP.8 Generalize *How many numbers have been covered on the chart?* [5] *Are the missing numbers in a row or a column?* [Row] *Which number is just before the missing numbers?* [33] *Which number is just after the missing numbers?* [39] *Name one way Carlos could work out which numbers are missing.* [Sample answers: Carlos can look at the tens in that row and the ones in each column; Carlos can count on.]

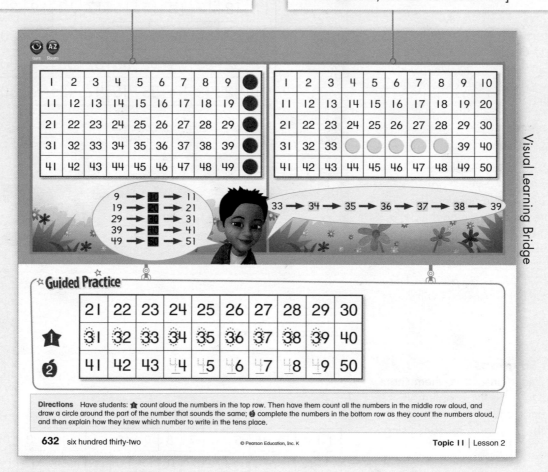

Visual Learning Bridge

632 six hundred thirty-two   © Pearson Education, Inc. K   **Topic 11** | Lesson 2

Complete the *Do You Understand? Show Me!* problem before starting Guided Practice.

Do You Understand? Show Me! MP.8 Generalize Have students cover the fourth column on the chart in Box 1 of the Visual Learning Bridge. *How can you work out which numbers are missing?* [Sample answer: I know that each number has the same ones in a column, so I can go up by ten each time after I find the top number; I can look at the numbers before and after each missing number.]

Ask the following Essential Question: *How can you use patterns to find missing numbers to 50?* [Sample answer: I can look at what comes before and after the missing number or numbers; I can think about a pattern of how the tens change when I count; I can think about a pattern of how the ones change when I count.]

Error Intervention: Item 2

If students are unable to explain how they knew which number to write in the tens place,

then have them look at the tens places in all the other rows. *What do you notice?* [The tens stay the same.]

✓ QUICK CHECK

Check mark indicates items for prescribing differentiation on the next page.
Item 8 is worth 1 point. Items 9 and 11 are each worth up to 2 points.

20–30 min   Tools   Assessment

Item 4 MP.1 Make Sense and Persevere
Students can use completed rows to help them understand the problem. *Which number on the top row has a tens place?* [10] *Which number is in the tens place?* [1] *Which number is in the ones place?* [0] *This means that there is 1 ten and 0 ones in the number 10. Which other numbers have a 1 in the tens place?* [11, 12, 13, 14, 15, 16, 17, 18, 19] *Which number in the tens place are you asked to color?* [2]

Item 7 Encourage students to look at the numbers before and after the missing numbers. *What should be in the tens places of the missing numbers?* [3] *How do you know?* [The rest of the numbers in the row apart from the last one all have a 3 in the tens place.]

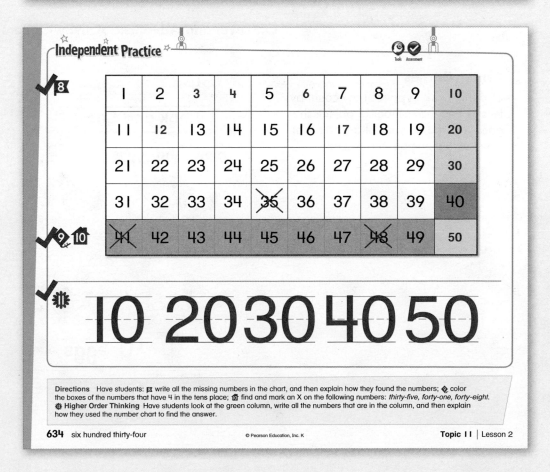

Name _____

	1	2	3	4	5	6	7	8	9	10
3	11	12	13	14	15	16	17	18	19	20
4	21	22	23	24	25	26	27	28	29	30
5	31	~~32~~	33	34				38	39	40
	41	42	43	~~44~~	45	46	47	48	49	50

6 8   **7**   34 35 36   26 36 46   ⟨35 36 37⟩

Directions Have students: ➏ write the missing numbers in the first two rows, and then explain how they found the numbers; ➍ color the boxes of the numbers that have 2 in the tens place; ✋ find and mark an X on these numbers: *thirty-two, forty-four*. ➏ **Vocabulary** Have students complete the numbers in the green column, explain the **pattern** they see in the tens place, and then write the number that is always the same in that column. ➐ Have students find the blue boxes on the chart, and then circle the set of numbers that shows the missing numbers.

Topic 11 | Lesson 2   six hundred thirty-three **633**

Item 8 MP.6 Be Precise With a range of different numbers to find, students may use a variety of patterns to solve the problem. Encourage students to think carefully about their explanations as they communicate their thinking. They may need to use different explanations to tell about the different patterns they used. *Have you explained how you found all of the numbers or just some of the numbers? Did you use different ways to find the different numbers?* [Answers will vary.]

Item 11 Students may need to follow the numbers on the chart to connect the number that is said to the numerals that represent it. *Where do you find these numbers on the chart, in a row or a column?* [Column] *Which column?* [The last one] *Look at the tens place in each number. What do you notice?* [They go up by 1 each time.]

Independent Practice

Tools Assessment

8	1	2	3	4	5	6	7	8	9	10
	11	12	13	14	15	16	17	18	19	20
	21	22	23	24	25	26	27	28	29	30
	31	32	33	34	~~35~~	36	37	38	39	40
9 10	~~41~~	42	43	44	45	46	47	~~48~~	49	50

11 10 20 30 40 50

Directions Have students: ➑ write all the missing numbers in the chart, and then explain how they found the numbers; ➒ color the boxes of the numbers that have 4 in the tens place; ➓ find and mark an X on the following numbers: *thirty-five, forty-one, forty-eight*. ✴ **Higher Order Thinking** Have students look at the green column, write all the numbers that are in the column, and then explain how they used the number chart to find the answer.

634 six hundred thirty-four   © Pearson Education, Inc. K   Topic 11 | Lesson 2

ASSESS AND DIFFERENTIATE

Use the **QUICK CHECK** on the previous page to prescribe differentiated instruction.

2 RtI

I Intervention
0–3 points on the Quick Check

O On-Level
4 points on the Quick Check

A Advanced
5 points on the Quick Check

Intervention Activity **I**

Missing Numbers

Materials

Counters (or Teaching Tool 6), Hundred Chart (Teaching Tool 31)

• Give each pair of students 5 counters and a hundred chart folded or cut in half so that only the numbers 1–50 are showing. Ask one student in each pair to cover their eyes while the other covers a number on the chart with a counter. The student who had covered their eyes must now work out the missing number. *How did you work out which number was missing?* Allow each student to explain. Make a list of different ways on the board for reference. Repeat with the other student.

• Repeat this activity but this time students place all five counters next to each other, either in a row or a column. *Which numbers are covered now? How do you know?* Encourage students to look at the patterns in the columns and the rows, the tens and the ones, as well as the numbers before and after the covered numbers. Repeat with the other student.

1	2	3	4	5	6	7	8	9	10
11	12	13	14	15	16	17	18	19	20
21	22	23	24	25	26	27	28	29	30
31	32	33	34	35	36	37	38	39	40
41	42						48	49	50

Reteach **I**

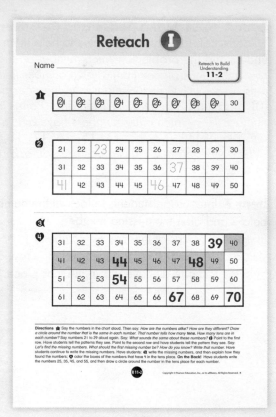

On-Level and Advanced Activity Centers **O** **A**

Center Games

Students work in pairs. They count by tens to find the number of objects that goes with the number of animals that matches the number tile picked.

★ On-Level

★★ Advanced

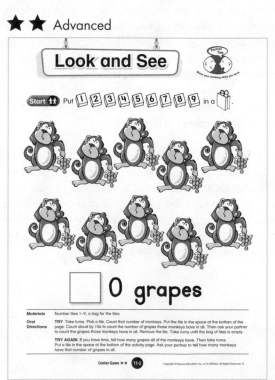

TIMING

The time allocated to Step 3 will depend on the teacher's instructional decisions and differentiation routines.

15–30 min

PEARSON realize.
PearsonRealize.com

Help Tools Games

Technology Center **I** **O** **A**

Math Tools and Math Games

A link to a specific math tools activity or math game to use with this lesson is provided at PearsonRealize.com.

Tools

Games

Name _____

Help Tools Games

Homework & Practice 11-2
Count Using Patterns to 50

Another Look!

1	2	3	4	5	6	7	8	9	10
11	12	13	14	15	16	17	18	19	20
21	22	23	24	25	26	27	28	29	30
31	32	33	34	35	36	37	38	39	40
41	42	43	44	45	46	47	48	49	50

HOME ACTIVITY Tell your child a number under 50. Ask him or her to count from that number up to 50. Repeat with different numbers.

1 **2**

1	2	3	4	5	6	7	8	9	10
11	12	13	14	15	16	17	18	19	20
21	22	23	24	25	26	27	28	29	30
31	32	33	34	35	36	37	38	39	40
41	42	43	44	45	46	47	48	49	50

Directions Have students point to the fourth row. Say: *Listen to the following numbers, and then draw a circle around the numbers in the chart that you hear*: thirty-three, thirty-four, thirty-five, thirty-six, thirty-seven. *What number do you see in almost every box of this row? What number do you hear in those numbers?* Have students listen to the numbers, draw a circle around the numbers in the chart that they hear, and then tell what is repeated in each number: **1** twenty-six, twenty-seven, twenty-eight, twenty-nine; **2** forty-one, forty-two, forty-three, forty-four.

Topic 11 | Lesson 2   Digital Resources at PearsonRealize.com   six hundred thirty-five **635**

3

1	2	3	4	5	6	7	8	9	10
11	12	13	14	15	16	17	18	19	20
21	22	23	24	25	26	27	28	29	30
31	32	33	34	35	36	37	38	39	40
41	42	43	44	45	46	47	48	49	50

4

5

10 20 30 40 50

Directions Have students: **3** write the missing numbers in the top row, say them aloud, and then explain how they know they are correct; **4** look at the numbers in the top row with a circle drawn around them. Then have them draw a circle around the tens place in each column that matches the pattern of those numbers. Have them count the numbers aloud, and then explain the pattern they hear. **5 Higher Order Thinking** Have students listen to the numbers, and then write the numbers they hear: ten, twenty, thirty, forty, fifty.

636 six hundred thirty-six   © Pearson Education, Inc. K   **Topic 11** | Lesson 2

COUNT BY TENS TO 100

DIGITAL RESOURCES PearsonRealize.com

 Student and Teacher eTexts
eText

 Listen and Look For Lesson Video
PD

 Today's Challenge
Think

 Solve and Share
Solve

 Visual Learning Animation Plus
Learn

A-Z **Animated Glossary**
Glossary

 Math Tools
Tools

✓ **Quick Check**
Assessment

 Another Look Homework Video
Help

🎮 **Math Games**
Games

LESSON OVERVIEW **FCR** FOCUS • COHERENCE • RIGOR

FOCUS

Domain K.CC Counting and Cardinality

Cluster K.CC.A Know number names and the count sequence.

Content Standard K.CC.A.1 Count to 100 by ones and by tens.

Mathematical Practices MP.2, MP.3, MP.4, MP.7

Objective Skip count by tens to 100.

Essential Understanding Decade numbers such as 10, 20, … 100 are used to name groups of ten. You can count by tens to 100 by counting only the decade numbers.

Vocabulary decade, hundred chart

COHERENCE

In Lessons 11-1 and 11-2, students used patterns to count to 30 and then 50. This work is extended in this lesson to count to 100 by tens. Similar to the work completed previously, students recognize patterns. These patterns involve the tens and ones digits as students become familiar with counting by the decade numbers. Students connect the pattern in the tens digit to the familiar counting sequence by ones.

RIGOR

This lesson emphasizes **conceptual understanding**. Students use the decade numbers to skip count by tens to 100. Counting to 100 in this way gives students an understanding of the structure of numbers greater than those they have encountered so far. Recognizing patterns within this sequence and having experience with the hundred chart will allow students to generalize about counting as they apply what they know to other numbers. This lays the foundations for counting within 100 in different ways in later lessons in this topic.

 Watch the Listen and Look For Lesson Video.

MATH ANYTIME

Daily Common Core Review

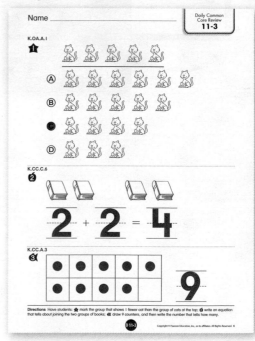

Today's Challenge

 Use Topic 11 problems any time during this topic.

ENGLISH LANGUAGE LEARNERS **ELL**

Listening Demonstrate listening comprehension by following directions.

Use with the Solve & Share on Student's Edition p. 637.

Say: *Count to 100 by ones.* Ask students to point to each number as they count from 1 to 100 by ones. Point to the decade numbers. Say: *These numbers are alike because they have a zero in the ones place.* Instruct students to color the decade numbers. Say: *Remind your partners how these numbers are alike.* Have students listen to their partners' responses. Point to 10. Demonstrate counting by tens.

Beginning Instruct students to point to 10. Say: *Start with 10 and count by tens to 100.* Count with students. Ask students to listen to the following directions: *Draw a circle around the first number. Draw a circle around the last number.* Students should circle the first and last numbers.

Intermediate Instruct students to point to 10 and count by tens to 100. Ask students to listen to the following directions: *Draw a circle around 70. Put a square around 80. Put a triangle around 20.* Students should follow the directions.

Advanced Instruct students to point to 10 and count by tens to 100. Write simple directions on 10 index cards such as: *Put a ○ around 80. Put a △ around 40.* Demonstrate reading a card. Ask students to choose a card and read the directions aloud. Have students listen as the card is read and follow the directions. Students may share responses with partners to check for accuracy. Have students take turns reading direction cards.

Summarize How do you count from 10 to 100 by tens?

DEVELOP: PROBLEM-BASED LEARNING

COHERENCE: Engage students by connecting prior knowledge to new ideas.

Students count all of the decade numbers in a hundred chart by identifying them as numbers with 0 ones. This prepares them for the next part of the lesson when they will count by tens using cubes and find missing numbers.

10–15 min

BEFORE

1. Pose the Solve-and-Share Problem
MP.7 Use Structure Students use their knowledge of place value to identify and count numbers with 0 ones on a hundred chart.

Say: *Color all the boxes of the numbers that have a zero in the ones place as you count them aloud. Tell how you know which numbers to count.*

2. Build Understanding
What are you asked to do? [Count and color the numbers with zero in the ones place.] *What number shows zero ones?* [0]

DURING

3. Ask Guiding Questions As Needed
Point to 34, or write *34* on the board. *Is this a number with zero ones? How do you know?* [No; There is a 4 in the ones place.] *What do you notice about the ones place as you read down each column?* [It is the same.]

AFTER

4. Share and Discuss Solutions
 Start with students' solutions. Have them share the strategies they used to solve the problem. If needed, project and analyze Alan's work to show which numbers to count and color.

5. Transition to the Visual Learning Bridge
You have counted by tens on this chart. Later in this lesson, you will use this pattern to continue to count by tens. You will also learn a name for these kinds of numbers.

6. Extension for Early Finishers
If you were counting by tens and the last number you said was 30, what are the next 3 numbers you would say? [40, 50, 60]

Solve & Share Name _____

See margin for sample student work.

1	2	3	4	5	6	7	8	9	10
11	12	13	14	15	16	17	18	19	20
21	22	23	24	25	26	27	28	29	30
31	32	33	34	35	36	37	38	39	40
41	42	43	44	45	46	47	48	49	50
51	52	53	54	55	56	57	58	59	60
61	62	63	64	65	66	67	68	69	70
71	72	73	74	75	76	77	78	79	80
81	82	83	84	85	86	87	88	89	90
91	92	93	94	95	96	97	98	99	100

Lesson 11-3
Count by Tens to 100

Directions Say: *Color all the boxes of the numbers that have a zero in the ones place as you count them aloud. Tell how you know which numbers to count.*

I can ... skip count by tens to 100

Content Standards K.CC.A.1 Mathematical Practices MP.2, MP.3, MP.4, MP.7

Topic 11 | Lesson 3   Digital Resources at PearsonRealize.com   six hundred thirty-seven **637**

Analyze Student Work

Alan's Work

1	2	3	4	5	6	7	8	9	10
11	12	13	14	15	16	17	18	19	20
21	22	23	24	25	26	27	28	29	30
31	32	33	34	35	36	37	38	39	40
41	42	43	44	45	46	47	48	49	50
51	52	53	54	55	56	57	58	59	60
61	62	63	64	65	66	67	68	69	70
71	72	73	74	75	76	77	78	79	80
81	82	83	84	85	86	87	88	89	90
91	92	93	94	95	96	97	98	99	100

Tevin's Work

1	2	3	4	5	6	7	8	9	10
11	12	13	14	15	16	17	18	19	20
21	22	23	24	25	26	27	28	29	30
31	32	33	34	35	36	37	38	39	40
41	42	43	44	45	46	47	48	49	50
51	52	53	54	55	56	57	58	59	60
61	62	63	64	65	66	67	68	69	70
71	72	73	74	75	76	77	78	79	80
81	82	83	84	85	86	87	88	89	90
91	92	93	94	95	96	97	98	99	100

Alan colors the boxes for 10–100 and counts them aloud. Alan explains that he knows which numbers to count because when he looks at the ones place in each of them, he sees 0 ones.

Tevin colors the boxes for 10–90, explaining that these numbers all have 0 in the ones place. Tevin does not recognize 100 as having 0 ones, so he does not color this box, as he is confused about reading the number of ones in a three-digit number.

DEVELOP: VISUAL LEARNING

Learn   Glossary

The *Visual Learning Bridge* connects students' thinking in Solve & Share to important math ideas in the lesson. Use the *Visual Learning Bridge* to make these ideas explicit. Also available as a *Visual Learning Animation Plus* at PearsonRealize.com

E L L
Visual Learning

MP.7 Look for Patterns *The chart you used before is called a hundred chart. It shows the numbers 1–100 in order. This is part of a hundred chart. It starts at 1. What number does it end at?* [60] *What numbers are colored?* [10, 20, 30, 40, 50, 60] *What do you notice about the ones place of the colored numbers?* [It is always 0.] *What do you notice about the tens place of the colored numbers?* [Sample answers: It goes up by 1 each time; They are like the numbers when I count: 1, 2, 3, 4, 5, 6.] *What number are you counting by when you count the colored numbers?* [Ten]

MP.2 Reasoning *What do you notice about these numbers and the colored numbers in the last box?* [They are the same.] *How many cubes are there in each group?* [10] *So, every time you count a group, how many more cubes are you counting on?* [10] *Decade means a group of 10, so each of these numbers can be called a decade number. What is the decade number just before 30?* [20] *Just after 50?* [60] *Before 60 but after 40?* [50]

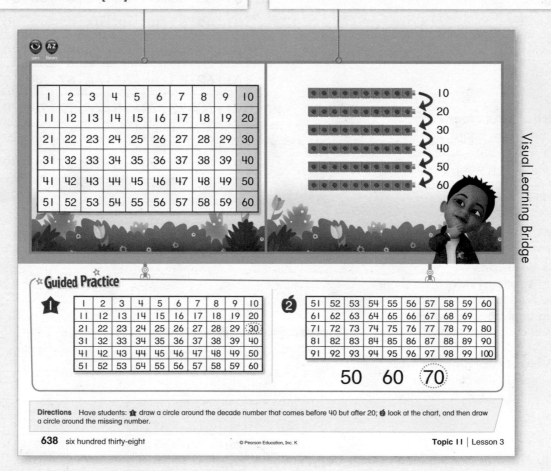

Visual Learning Bridge

Complete the *Do You Understand? Show Me!* problem before starting Guided Practice.

Do You Understand? Show Me! MP.3 Construct
Arguments *Mike counts the decade numbers to count by 10s to 40. He counts: 10, 20, 30, 35, 40. Which number should he not have counted? Why?* [35; Sample answers: The decade number after 30 is 40, not 35; The next 10 after 30 is 40.]

Ask the following Essential Question: *How can you count by tens to 100?* [Sample answer: You only say the numbers for the groups of 10: 10, 20, 30, 40, 50, 60, 70, 80, 90, 100.]

Error Intervention: Item 1

If students think they need to circle 20 and 40 as well as the dotted 30,

then give students the directions again. Explain that 20 and 40 are mentioned but emphasize the words *before* and *after*. *The number you need to circle comes after 20, so it cannot be 20. The number comes before 40, so it cannot be 40.*

Tools Assessment

✓ QUICK CHECK
Check mark indicates items for prescribing differentiation on the next page.
Items 7 and 8 are each worth 1 point. Item 9 is worth up to 3 points.

20–30 min

Item 3 MP.7 Look for Patterns Some students may wish to follow the numbers on the chart as they listen to the pattern. Others will know the pattern as they hear it. Explain that students need only circle the numbers that are missing, not every number they hear. Encourage students to compare answers with a partner as you repeat the pattern again.

Item 4 *What do you notice about the possible answers?* [Sample answers: They are all tens; They are all decade numbers; They all have 0 in the ones place.] *How many cubes are in each train?* [10] *Do you need to count every cube to find how many cubes in all?* [No] *What can you count by to find how many cubes in all?* [Tens]

Item 7 MP.4 Model with Math Students should understand that they write decade numbers to represent how many cubes in all as a running total, not 10 for each train. Encourage students to look back and connect the pattern of number of cube trains counted with the number they have written. *What number shows the number of cubes in 1 train?* [10] *2 trains?* [20] *3 trains?* [30] *Look at how the tens digit changes with each cube train.* Once 60 is established as the correct answer, extend the problem as appropriate: *If there were one more cube train of 10 cubes, what number would tell how many?* [70]

Item 9 Students should draw on their knowledge from previous items and apply it to write the decade numbers in order. You can use guiding questions to build understanding as needed. *What does it mean to write the decade numbers in order?* [Sample answer: Write them in the order that I would count.] *When you count all the decade numbers to 100, what number do you start with?* [10] *Does the ones digit change in these numbers?* [No]

Coherence In Item 9, students record the decade numbers to 100. This builds on their work in the previous lesson where students identified the decade numbers to 50 and the pattern they saw. This understanding will prepare students for the role of tens as a place value in two or more digit numbers in the next grades.

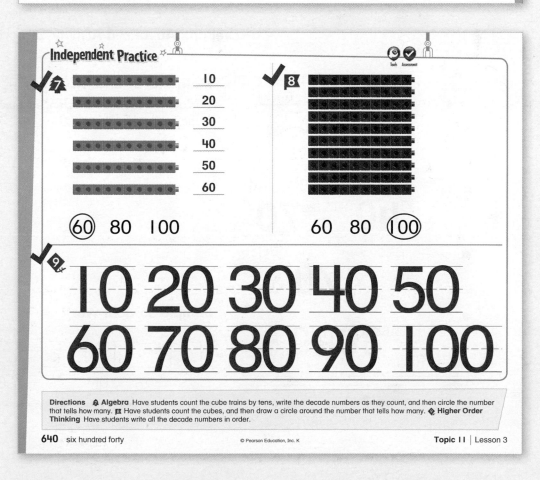

Directions Have students: ❸ draw a circle around the missing numbers in the following pattern: *ten, twenty, thirty, ____, fifty, ____, seventy, ____, ____, one hundred;* ❹–❻ count the cubes, and then draw a circle around the number that tells how many.

Topic 11 | Lesson 3
six hundred thirty-nine **639**

Independent Practice

Directions ✿ Algebra Have students count the cube trains by tens, write the decade numbers as they count, and then circle the number that tells how many. ✿ Have students count the cubes, and then draw a circle around the number that tells how many. ✿ **Higher Order Thinking** Have students write all the decade numbers in order.

640 six hundred forty   © Pearson Education, Inc. K   Topic 11 | Lesson 3

639–640

STEP 3 ASSESS AND DIFFERENTIATE

Use the **QUICK CHECK** on the previous page to prescribe differentiated instruction.

I Intervention
0–3 points on the Quick Check

O On-Level
4 points on the Quick Check

A Advanced
5 points on the Quick Check

Intervention Activity **I**

Do You Have the Number?
Materials

Hundred Chart (Teaching Tool 31)

- Give a hundred chart to each student. *Find 10 on the hundred chart. You can use the numbers in the last column to count by tens to 100.* Count down the column aloud with students until you reach 100. *You are skipping some numbers to count to 100. What are you skip counting by?* [Tens]

- Discuss the patterns students can see in the numbers. *Look at the ones place of the numbers you counted, what pattern do you see?* [There is a 0 every time.] *Look at the tens place of the numbers you counted, what pattern do you see?* [The numbers are the same as when I count by ones.]

- Ask students to choose three numbers and color the boxes in the tens column

of their hundred chart. Count by tens to 100 again as a group. Have students raise their hand when you say a number they colored. If students seem to have a good understanding of counting by tens, you can extend by asking students to raise their hands if their number matches questions you ask, such as: *Do you have the number before 70 but after 50? Do you have the missing number: 10, 20, ____, 40?*

1	2	3	4	5	6	7	8	9	10
11	12	13	14	15	16	17	18	19	20
21	22	23	24	25	26	27	28	29	30
31	32	33	34	35	36	37	38	39	40
41	42	43	44	45	46	47	48	49	50
51	52	53	54	55	56	57	58	59	60
61	62	63	64	65	66	67	68	69	70
71	72	73	74	75	76	77	78	79	80
81	82	83	84	85	86	87	88	89	90
91	92	93	94	95	96	97	98	99	100

Reteach **I**

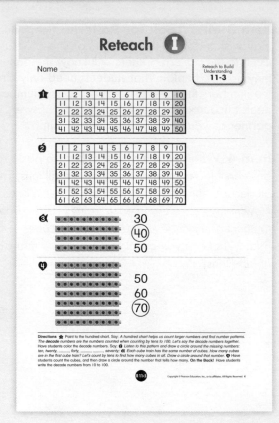

On-Level and Advanced Activity Centers **O** **A**

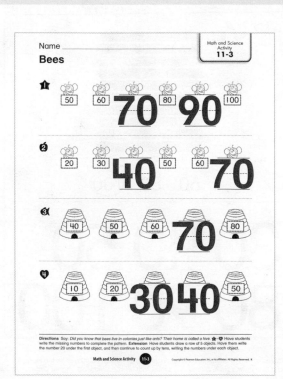

Math and Science Activity STEM

This activity revisits the science theme, **Ant Colonies**, introduced on page 621 in the Student Edition.

Sample Student Work

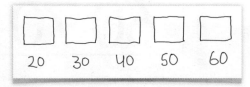

20   30   40   50   60

TIMING

The time allocated to Step 3 will depend on the teacher's instructional decisions and differentiation routines.

15–30 min   Help   Tools   Games

Technology Center

Math Tools and Math Games

Tools

Games

A link to a specific math tools activity or math game to use with this lesson is provided at PearsonRealize.com.

Leveled Assignment

I Items 1–2   **O** Items 2–4   **A** Items 3–5

Name _____   Help Tools Games

Homework & Practice 11-3

Count by Tens to 100

Another Look!

1	2	3	4	5	6	7	8	9	10
11	12	13	14	15	16	17	18	19	20
21	22	23	24	25	26	27	28	29	30
31	32	33	34	35	36	37	38	39	40
41	42	43	44	45	46	47	48	49	50
51	52	53	54	55	56	57	58	59	60
61	62	63	64	65	66	67	68	69	70
71	72	73	74	75	76	77	78	79	80
81	82	83	84	85	86	87	88	89	90
91	92	93	94	95	96	97	98	99	100

HOME ACTIVITY Arrange 30 objects, such as pennies, beads, or other small objects, in groups of 10 on a table. Ask your child to use decade numbers to count the number of objects aloud. Repeat with up to 10 groups of objects.

1	2	3	4	5	6	7	8	9	10
11	12	13	14	15	16	17	18	19	
21	22	23	24	25	26	27	28	29	
31	32	33	34	35	36	37	38	39	40
41	42	43	44	45	46	47	48	49	
51	52	53	54	55	56	57	58	59	60
61	62	63	64	65	66	67	68	69	
71	72	73	74	75	76	77	78	79	
81	82	83	84	85	86	87	88	89	90
91	92	93	94	95	96	97	98	99	

Directions Say: *Color green the boxes of the following decade numbers: ten, forty, fifty, sixty, ninety.* ⭐ Have students color orange the boxes of the following decade numbers: *twenty, thirty, fifty, seventy, eighty, one hundred.*

Topic 11 | Lesson 3   Digital Resources at PearsonRealize.com   six hundred forty-one **641**

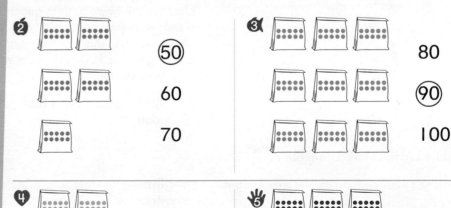

② ⑤0 / 60 / 70

③ 80 / ⑨0 / 100

④ **30**

 **80**

Directions ② and ❺ Have students count the dots, and then draw a circle around the number that tells how many. ❹ **Higher Order Thinking** Have students count the number of dots, and then write the number to tell how many. ✋ **Higher Order Thinking** Have students count the number of dots, and then write the number to tell how many.

642 six hundred forty-two   © Pearson Education, Inc. K   **Topic 11 | Lesson 3**

LESSON 11-4

COUNT BY TENS AND ONES

DIGITAL RESOURCES PearsonRealize.com

 eText Student and Teacher eTexts

 PD Listen and Look For Lesson Video

 Think Today's Challenge

 Solve Solve and Share

 Learn Visual Learning Animation Plus

A-Z **Glossary** Animated Glossary

 Tools Math Tools

 Assessment Quick Check

 Help Another Look Homework Video

 Games Math Games

LESSON OVERVIEW **F C R** FOCUS • COHERENCE • RIGOR

FOCUS

Domain K.CC Counting and Cardinality

Cluster K.CC.A Know number names and the count sequence.

Content Standard K.CC.A.1 Count to 100 by ones and by tens. Also **K.CC.A.2**

Mathematical Practices MP.1, MP.2, MP.3, MP.6

Objective Count to the number 100 by using tens and ones.

Essential Understanding Decade numbers such as 10, 20, ... 100 are used to name groups of ten. You can count by tens to 100 by counting the decade numbers. You can also count by ones to 100.

Materials Connecting cubes (or Teaching Tool 8), crayons

COHERENCE

In Lessons 11-1 and 11-2, students used patterns to count to 30 and then 50. Then students learned how to count to 100 by tens in Lesson 11-3. Each of these lessons had students recognizing patterns. In Lesson 11-4, students extend their knowledge and work with patterns of tens and ones on the hundred chart.

RIGOR

This lesson emphasizes **conceptual understanding** and **procedural skill**. Students use both ones and tens to count to 100. The understanding of both of these ways to count to 100 gives students an understanding of the structure of numbers greater than those they have encountered so far. Recognizing patterns within this sequence and having experience with the hundred chart will allow students to generalize about counting as they apply what they know to other numbers. This lays the foundations for counting within 100 in different ways in later lessons in this topic.

 PD Watch the Listen and Look For Lesson Video.

MATH ANYTIME

Daily Common Core Review

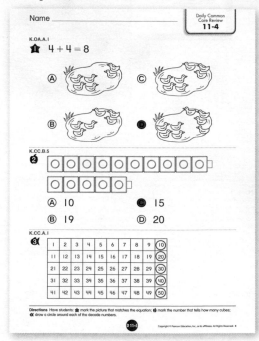

Today's Challenge

Think Use Topic 11 problems any time during this topic.

ENGLISH LANGUAGE LEARNERS **E L L**

Listening Learn new academic expressions.

Use with the Solve and Share on Student's Edition p. 643.

Model counting by tens and then by ones. Show students 33 loose cubes. Say: *Count by 10s and then count on by 1s to count big numbers quickly.* Model grouping the cubes in 10s and counting by 10s to 30. Say: *First, I count by 10s.* Show the 3 remaining cubes. Say: *Then I count on by 1s to 33.* Put students into pairs and distribute 46 cubes to each pair. Ask Student B not to look while Student A groups the cubes in 10s and some ones.

Beginning Student A tells Student B how many groups of 10 and loose cubes there are using the sentence stem: "There are ____ tens and ____ ones." Have students reverse roles using 38 cubes.

Intermediate Student A tells Student B how many groups of 10 and loose cubes there are. Student A tells the number of cubes using *count by tens* and *count on by ones* in his or her answer. Have students reverse roles using 38 cubes.

Advanced Student B asks Student A questions about the groups of 10 cubes and loose cubes. Student B tells the number and explains how he or she identified the number, using *count by tens* and *count on by ones* in his or her response.

Summarize What does it mean when you hear *count by tens* and *count on by ones*?

DEVELOP: PROBLEM-BASED LEARNING

COHERENCE: Engage learners by connecting prior knowledge to new ideas.
Students count groups of cubes to find how many. This prepares them for the next part of the lesson where they count by tens and then by ones to write the number that tells how many.

10–15 min

BEFORE

1. Pose the Solve-and-Share Problem
MP.2 Reasoning In the problem, students reason and use prior knowledge to find a quicker way to a solution.

Give each pair 55 connecting cubes.

Say: *Carlos has some cubes. How many cubes does Carlos have? What would be a quick way to count all of the cubes? Write the number to tell how many.*

2. Build Understanding
What are you asked to find? [A quick way to count all of Carlos' cubes] *What tool do you have to solve the problem?* [Connecting cubes]

DURING

3. Ask Guiding Questions As Needed
What do you think is the fastest way to count the cubes, in groups of 1, 2, 5, or 10? [10] *Why do you think counting by tens is a fast way to count?* [There are less groups to count.] *If all of the cubes cannot be put into groups of 10, how do you think you can count the extra cubes?* [I can count the extra cubes by ones.]

AFTER

4. Share and Discuss Solutions
Start with students' solutions. If needed, project and analyze Pete's work to discuss how counting by tens, and then counting on by ones is a quick way to find out how many.

5. Transition to the Visual Learning Bridge
Later in this lesson, you will learn that counting groups of 10 and then counting on by ones is a quicker way to find out how many rather than counting all of the cubes by ones.

Placing objects in groups of 10 helps you count big numbers quickly.

6. Extension for Early Finishers
Have students answer these questions: *What number is 10 more than 60?* [70] *What number is 10 more than 80?* [90] *What number is 10 less than 100?* [90]

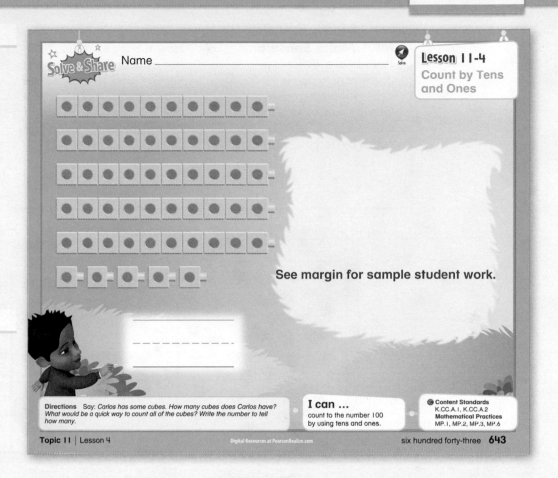

Solve & Share   Name _____   Solve

Lesson 11-4
Count by Tens and Ones

See margin for sample student work.

Directions Say: *Carlos has some cubes. How many cubes does Carlos have? What would be a quick way to count all of the cubes? Write the number to tell how many.*

I can ...
count to the number 100 by using tens and ones.

Content Standards
K.CC.A.1, K.CC.A.2
Mathematical Practices
MP.1, MP.2, MP.3, MP.6

Topic 11 | Lesson 4   Digital Resources at PearsonRealize.com   six hundred forty-three **643**

Analyze Student Work

Pete's Work

55

Pete correctly describes a quick way to find the number of cubes Carlos has by counting by tens and then counting on by ones to find 55.

Tamlyn's Work

65

Tamlyn counts by tens but makes a mistake counting and writes an incorrect number, 65.

The *Visual Learning Bridge* connects students' thinking in Solve & Share to important math ideas in the lesson. Use the *Visual Learning Bridge* to make these ideas explicit. Also available as a *Visual Learning Animation Plus* at PearsonRealize.com

E L L
Visual Learning

Learn   Glossary

MP.1 Make Sense and Persevere *What is a quick way to count these cubes?* [Sample answer: Group them by tens and then count the leftover cubes by 1s.]

How are the cubes in this box different than those in the first box? [The cubes are grouped in sets of 10.] *How can you count the groups of cubes?* [By tens] *How many cubes are left over?* [4]

MP.3 Construct Arguments *How many cubes are there?* [34] *How did Carlos count the cubes?* [He counted by tens and then counted the leftover cubes by ones.] *Why do you think counting by tens is a quick way to count?* [There are fewer groups to count.]

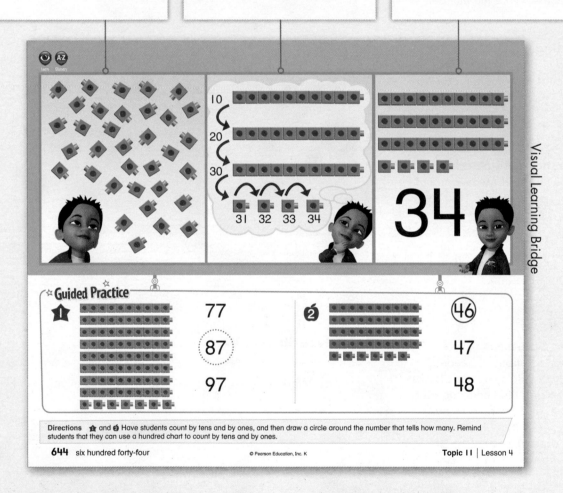

Visual Learning Bridge

Guided Practice

1. 77
   (87)
   97

2. (46)
   47
   48

Directions ★ and ② Have students count by tens and by ones, and then draw a circle around the number that tells how many. Remind students that they can use a hundred chart to count by tens and by ones.

Complete the *Do You Understand? Show Me!* problem before starting Guided Practice.

Do You Understand? Show Me! MP.1 Make Sense and Persevere
What is a quick way to count 34 cubes? [Sample answer: Count by tens and then count by ones.]

Essential Question

Ask the following Essential Question: *How can you count to any number from 10 to 100?* [You can count by ones or by tens.] You can make groups of 10 and then count on by ones. Remember that to count a large number of objects, first put the objects in groups of 10. Count by tens and then count the leftover objects by ones.

Error Intervention: Item 2
If students have difficulty counting by tens and then by ones,
then have them write the numbers (10, 20, 30, and 40) next to each group of cubes, and then count on by ones.

1 RtI
Reteaching Assign Reteaching Set B, p. 669.

☑ **QUICK CHECK**

Check mark indicates items for prescribing differentiation on the next page.
Items 7 and 8 are worth 1 point. Item 10 is worth up to 3 points.

20–30 min

Tools Assessment

Item 3 MP.6 Be Precise Remind students that they can count by tens and count on by ones to find the total number in a group. *How many are in each row besides the last row?* [10] *Let's count by tens to see how many cubes we have in the groups of 10: 10, 20, 30, 40, 50, 60, 70. We have 70 cubes in those groups. Count on from 70 by ones to count the extras. How many are there in all?* [72]

Items 4–6 Students should clearly see that there are 10 in each row in which the cubes are connected. They can count a row to be sure. If students are having trouble, count by tens with them. In Item 4, for example, count: *10, 20, 30,* and then count on by ones from there: *31, 32, 33.*

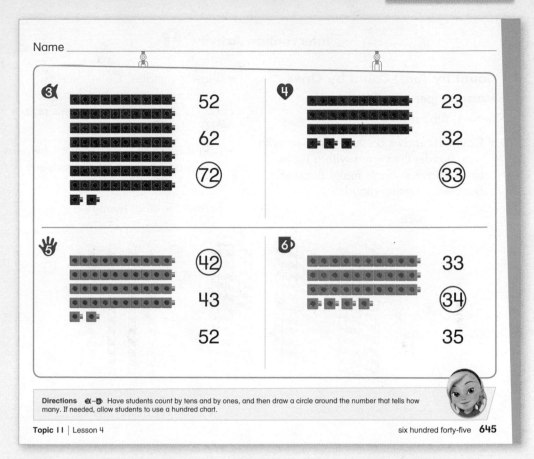

Name _____

③ 52
   62
   (72)

④ 23
   32
   (33)

⑤ (42)
   43
   52

⑥ 33
   (34)
   35

Directions ③–⑥ Have students count by tens and by ones, and then draw a circle around the number that tells how many. If needed, allow students to use a hundred chart.

Topic 11 | Lesson 4   six hundred forty-five **645**

Item 9 MP.2 Reasoning Guide students to remember that to count a large number of objects, first put objects in groups of 10. *How do you know there are 10 cubes in each row?* [Sample answer: I counted the cubes in the first row, then I saw that there is the same number of cubes in each row that has cubes connected.]

Item 10 Remind students that a quick way to count is by groups of 10. *How many cubes will you draw in a train of 10?* [10] *Will you have to draw any extras?* [I will draw 2 cube trains with 10 cubes in each train. There will be 5 extras.]

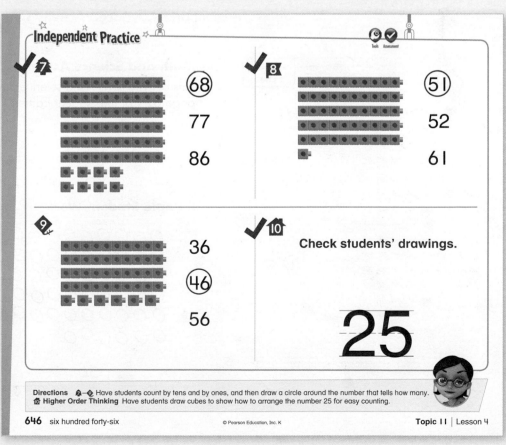

☆ Independent Practice ☆

Tools Assessment

✓⑦ (68)
    77
    86

✓⑧ (51)
    52
    61

⑨ 36
   (46)
   56

✓⑩ Check students' drawings.

   25

Directions ⑦–⑨ Have students count by tens and by ones, and then draw a circle around the number that tells how many. ⑩ **Higher Order Thinking** Have students draw cubes to show how to arrange the number 25 for easy counting.

Use the **QUICK CHECK** on the previous page to prescribe differentiated instruction.

I **Intervention**
0–3 points on the Quick Check

O **On-Level**
4 points on the Quick Check

A **Advanced**
5 points on the Quick Check

Intervention Activity **I**

Count by Tens; Count by Ones

Materials (per group)

Straws, rubber bands

• Count 10 straws as students count with you. Bundle the straws with a rubber band. Have students make 8 more bundles, counting aloud.

• Show 3 bundles. *Count by tens.* Model counting the bundles slowly: *10... 20... 30.* Have students repeat "10, 20, 30."

• Add 4 more straws. *Count on by ones.* Model counting on as students say with you: *31, 32, 33, 34.*

• Repeat for other numbers.

Reteach **I**

Name _____

Reteach to Build Understanding 11-4

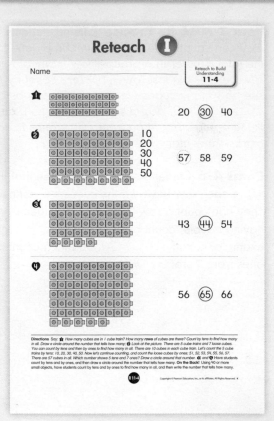

Directions Say: ★ *How many cubes are in 1 cube train? How many rows of cubes are there? Count by tens to find how many in all. Draw a circle around the number that tells how many.* ❷ *Look at the picture. There are 5 cube trains and 7 loose cubes. You can count by tens and then by ones to find how many in all. There are 10 cubes in each cube train. Let's count the 5 cube trains by tens: 10, 20, 30, 40, 50. Now let's continue counting, and count the loose cubes by ones: 51, 52, 53, 54, 55, 56, 57. There are 57 cubes in all. Which number shows 5 tens and 7 ones? Draw a circle around that number.* ❸ *and* ❹ *Have students count by tens and by ones, and then draw a circle around the number that tells how many.* **On the Back!** *Using 40 or more small objects, have students count by tens and by ones to find how many in all, and then write the number that tells how many.*

R 11-4

Copyright © Pearson Education, Inc., or its affiliates. All Rights Reserved. ❹

On-Level and Advanced Activity Centers **O** **A**

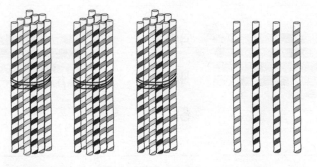

Name _____

Math and Science Activity 11-4

Ants

❶ [rows of ants] 25   34   ㉟

❷ [rows of ants] ㊼   57   74

Directions Say: *Did you know ants are social insects and live in large groups? A group of ants is called a colony.* Have students: ★ *count the rows of ants by tens and by ones, and then draw a circle around the number that tells how many;* ❷ *count the columns of ants by tens or by ones, and then draw a circle around the number that tells how many.* **Extension** *Have students draw a colony of 56 ants. They can draw circles to represent the ants if they choose. Have them draw 5 rows of 10 ants, and a row of 6 ants.*

Math and Science Activity 11-4   Copyright © Pearson Education, Inc., or its affiliates. All Rights Reserved. ❹

Math and Science Activity **STEM**

This activity revisits the science theme, **Ant Colonies,** introduced on page 621 of the Student Edition.

Sample Student Work

```
OOOOOOOOOO
OOOOOOOOOO
OOOOOOOOOO
OOOOOOOOOO
OOOOOOOOOO
OOOOOO
          56
```

TIMING

The time allocated to Step 3 will depend on the teacher's instructional decisions and differentiation routines.

15–30 min Help Tools Games

Technology Center I O A

Math Tools and Math Games

A link to a specific math tools activity or math game to use with this lesson is provided at PearsonRealize.com.

Leveled Assignment
I Items 1–4   O Items 2–5   A Items 3–6

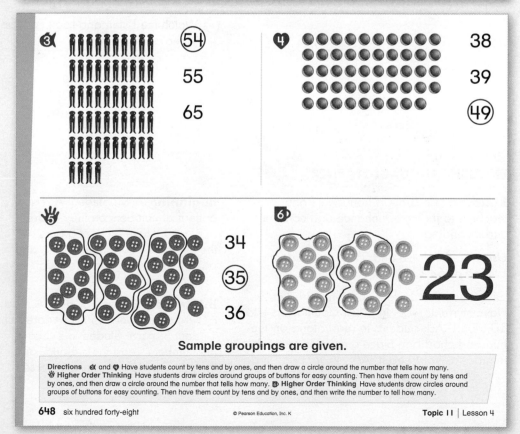

Name _____

Homework & Practice 11-4
Count by Tens and Ones

Another Look!

10
20
30
31

21 (31) 41

HOME ACTIVITY Set out a large number of pennies, beads, or other small objects. Have your child arrange the objects in groups of 10 for fast counting. Then have him or her count by tens and by ones to find how many.

⭐ 34 42 (43)

❷ (78) 87 88

Directions Say: Alex arranged his counting beads into groups of 10 for easy counting. Count the beads by tens and then by ones. How many beads are there? Draw a circle around the number that tells how many. ⭐ and ❷ Have students count the beads by tens and by ones, and then draw a circle around the number that tells how many.

Topic 11 | Lesson 4   Digital Resources at PearsonRealize.com   six hundred forty-seven **647**

❸ (54) 55 65   ❹ 38 39 (49)

❺ 34 (35) 36   ❻ **23**

Sample groupings are given.

Directions ❸ and ❹ Have students count by tens and by ones, and then draw a circle around the number that tells how many. ❺ Higher Order Thinking Have students draw circles around groups of buttons for easy counting. Then have them count by tens and by ones, and then draw a circle around the number that tells how many. ❻ Higher Order Thinking Have students draw circles around groups of buttons for easy counting. Then have them count by tens and by ones, and then write the number to tell how many.

648 six hundred forty-eight   © Pearson Education, Inc. K   Topic 11 | Lesson 4

647–648

LESSON 11-5

COUNT FORWARD FROM ANY NUMBER TO 100

DIGITAL RESOURCES PearsonRealize.com

 eText Student and Teacher eTexts

 PD Listen and Look For Lesson Video

 Think Today's Challenge

 Solve Solve and Share

 Learn Visual Learning Animation Plus

 Glossary Animated Glossary

 Tools Math Tools

 Assessment Quick Check

 Help Another Look Homework Video

 Games Math Games

LESSON OVERVIEW FOCUS • COHERENCE • RIGOR

FOCUS

Domain K.CC Counting and Cardinality

Cluster K.CC.A Know number names and the count sequence.

Content Standard K.CC.A.2 Count forward beginning from a given number within the known sequence (instead of having to begin at 1). Also **K.CC.A.1**

Mathematical Practices MP.1, MP.5, MP.7, MP.8

Objective Count forward from any number to 100 by ones.

Essential Understanding Numbers are counted and written in a specific sequence on a hundred chart.

Materials Hundred Chart (Teaching Tool 31), crayons

COHERENCE

In Lessons 11-1 and 11-2, students used patterns to count to 30 and then 50. Then students learned how to count to 100 by tens in Lesson 11-3 and by tens and ones in Lesson 11-4. Students slowly built up familiarity with patterns and working with the hundred chart. In Lesson 11-5, students move to counting on from any number on the hundred chart. This will prepare them for double-digit addition in Grade 1.

RIGOR

This lesson emphasizes **procedural skill**. Students count forward by ones until they reach a given number. As they do this on the hundred chart it deepens their understanding of number sense, counting, and patterns.

 PD Watch the Listen and Look For Lesson Video.

MATH ANYTIME

Daily Common Core Review

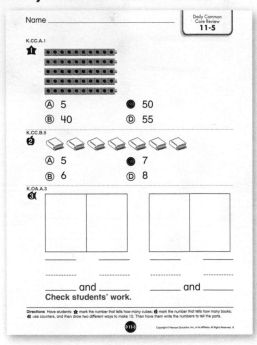

 Today's Challenge

Think Use Topic 11 problems any time during this topic.

ENGLISH LANGUAGE LEARNERS

Reading Use support from peers and teachers to indicate, enhance and confirm understanding.

Use with the Solve and Share on Student's Edition p. 649.

Give students counters and a hundred chart. Have students work in pairs. Count from 1 to 10 aloud. Ask students to read along on the hundred chart and place a counter on each number as you read it. Ask: *What pattern do you see?* [Each number is 1 more.]

Beginning Have Student A read a pattern of numbers on the hundred chart to Student B. Have Student B put counters on the numbers, read them aloud, and tell what pattern they have. Have students reverse roles and repeat.

Intermediate Have Student A read a pattern of numbers on the hundred chart to Student B. Have Student B put counters on the numbers, read them aloud, and explain the pattern. Have students reverse roles and repeat.

Advanced Ask Student A to tell Student B a pattern (e.g., count by tens). Have Student B locate the patterns on the chart and put counters on the next three numbers in the pattern. Have Student B read the pattern aloud and explain how he or she recognized the pattern. Students reverse roles and repeat.

Summarize What patterns can be seen in the hundred chart?

DEVELOP: PROBLEM-BASED LEARNING

COHERENCE: Engage learners by connecting prior knowledge to new ideas.

Students count forward by ones on a hundred chart. This prepares them for the next part of the lesson where they count forward from any number from 1 to 100, using the hundred chart to help.

10–15 min

Solve

BEFORE

1. Pose the Solve-and-Share Problem
MP.1 Make Sense and Persevere In the problem, students apply previously learned skills to solve the problem on the hundred chart.

Give each student an orange crayon.

Say: Count forward from the yellow number. Stop at the red number. Tell how many numbers you counted aloud. Color the boxes of the numbers you counted aloud to show your work.

2. Build Understanding
What are you asked to do? [To start at the yellow box and count forward to the red box] *What tool do you have to solve the problem?* [Hundred chart and crayon]

DURING

3. Ask Guiding Questions As Needed
When you count by ones, which numbers do you count? [Every number] *What number do you say first when you start counting with the yellow box?* [48] *Count forward until you get to the red box. What numbers do you say?* [48, 49, 50, 51, 52, 53, 54]

AFTER

4. Share and Discuss Solutions
Start with students' solutions. If needed, project and analyze Amelia's work to discuss the boxes that should be colored.

5. Transition to the Visual Learning Bridge
A hundred chart can be used to help you count forward by ones. Later in this lesson, you will learn that there are rules for how to count on a hundred chart.

A hundred chart can help in counting numbers to 100 by ones, beginning with any number.

6. Extension for Early Finishers
Color another yellow box on 2. Color another red box on 11. What numbers do you count when you count forward from the yellow number to the red number? [2, 3, 4, 5, 6, 7, 8, 9, 10, 11] *How many boxes did you count?* [10]

Name _____

See margin for sample student work.

Lesson 11-5
Count Forward from Any Number to 100

Directions Say: Count forward from the yellow number. Stop at the red number. Tell how many numbers you counted aloud. Color the boxes of the numbers you counted aloud to show your work.

I can ...
count forward from any number to 100 by ones.

Content Standards K.CC.A.1, K.CC.A.2 **Mathematical Practices** MP.1, MP.5, MP.7, MP.8

Topic 11 | Lesson 5

Digital Resources at PearsonRealize.com

six hundred forty-nine **649**

Analyze Student Work

Amelia's Work									
1	2	3	4	5	6	7	8	9	10
11	12	13	14	15	16	17	18	19	20
21	22	23	24	25	26	27	28	29	30
31	32	33	34	35	36	37	38	39	40
41	42	43	44	45	46	47	48	49	50
51	52	53	54	55	56	57	58	59	60
61	62	63	64	65	66	67	68	69	70
71	72	73	74	75	76	77	78	79	80
81	82	83	84	85	86	87	88	89	90
91	92	93	94	95	96	97	98	99	100

Jarek's Work									
1	2	3	4	5	6	7	8	9	10
11	12	13	14	15	16	17	18	19	20
21	22	23	24	25	26	27	28	29	30
31	32	33	34	35	36	37	38	39	40
41	42	43	44	45	46	47	48	49	50
51	52	53	54	55	56	57	58	59	60
61	62	63	64	65	66	67	68	69	70
71	72	73	74	75	76	77	78	79	80
81	82	83	84	85	86	87	88	89	90
91	92	93	94	95	96	97	98	99	100

Amelia correctly colors boxes 48, 49, 50, 51, 52, 53, 54 to show the numbers she counted. She then explains that she counted 7 numbers when counting from the yellow box to the red box.

Jarek incorrectly colors boxes 54, 55, 56, 57, 58. He explains that he counted 6 numbers because there are 6 boxes colored.

The *Visual Learning Bridge* connects students' thinking in Solve & Share to important math ideas in the lesson. Use the *Visual Learning Bridge* to make these ideas explicit. Also available as a *Visual Learning Animation Plus* at PearsonRealize.com

Visual Learning

Learn   Glossary

Carlos reads the number in the yellow box: 72 How can Carlos count forward to reach the number in the red box? [Count by ones.]

MP.5 Use Appropriate Tools Strategically *Carlos uses a crayon to help him mark the boxes as he counts. What does Carlos mark in each box?* [An arrow] *What does it show?* [The numbers he has counted] *When Carlos gets to the end of a row, where does he go next?* [To the start of the next row]

MP.7 Look for a Pattern *What do you notice about the arrows?* [There is one in each box from the yellow box to the red box.] *When counting by ones, you find the start number and count each number after it. What do you do when you get to the end of a row, like number 80?* [Move to the beginning of the next row, number 81.] *On what number does Carlos stop counting?* [91]

Visual Learning Bridge

Complete the *Do You Understand? Show Me!* problem before starting Guided Practice.

Do You Understand? Show Me! MP.7 Look for a Pattern

Give each student a Hundred Chart (Teaching Tool 31). *Start at the number 8. Count by ones. End at 15. What pattern can you see when you count by ones?* [When I start at 8 and count by ones to 15, all the numbers from 8 to 15 are marked and counted.]

Ask the following Essential Question: *How does using a hundred chart help you count from any number to another?* [It helps you keep track as you count by ones.] Counting patterns (numerical and visual) can be seen on a hundred chart. Numbers are counted and written in a specific sequence on a hundred chart.

Error Intervention: Item 2

If students color the wrong numbers,

then have them focus on just one row at a time, counting by ones and coloring the boxes. When they get to the end of the row, remind them to move down to the left hand side of the row below it. Have them continue in this manner until they reach the red box.

Reteaching Assign Reteaching Set C, p. 670.

Tools   Assessment

✓ QUICK CHECK

Check mark indicates items for prescribing differentiation on the next page.
Items 7 and 9 are worth 1 point. Item 10 is worth up to 3 points.

20–30 min

Items 3–6 MP.8 Generalize Remind students that they are counting forward from a given number in these items. *How can you tell which number to start at?* [The box is yellow.] *Does this yellow box repeat in each item?* [Yes.] *How does that help you solve the problems?* [It is easy to find the number where you have to start counting.]

Item 6 Students may suggest the strategy of counting from 56 to 76 by tens. Allow them to express how they would do this, but have them go through the process of counting by ones as well. The emphasis of this lesson is counting forward from any number to another by ones. To have them focus on counting by ones, ask them: *How many boxes did you color as you counted by ones?* [21]

Items 7–9 Remind that when counting on a hundred chart, they should move from left to right and top to bottom. Demonstrate with your finger the direction in which they should move as they progress through the hundred chart. Draw special attention to the move that is made when they get to the end of a row. *When you get to one of the decade numbers, like 10, where do you go next on the hundred chart?* [Down to the next row to 11]

Item 10 MP.7 Look for a Pattern Remind students that a quick way to count is by tens. *What pattern do you see as you look at the numbers you filled in?* [They are all decade numbers.]

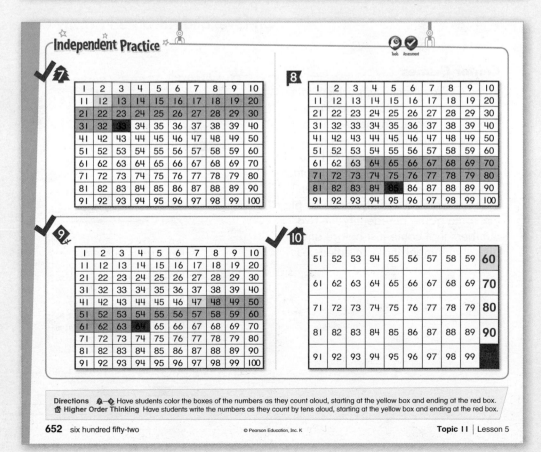

Name _____

3 / **4** / **5** / **6**

Directions ③–⑥ Have students color the boxes of the numbers as they count aloud, starting at the yellow box and ending at the red box.

Topic 11 | Lesson 5

six hundred fifty-one **651**

Independent Practice

Tools   Assessment

7 / **8** / **9** / **10**

Directions ⑦–⑨ Have students color the boxes of the numbers as they count aloud, starting at the yellow box and ending at the red box.
⑩ **Higher Order Thinking** Have students write the numbers as they count by tens aloud, starting at the yellow box and ending at the red box.

STEP 3 — ASSESS AND DIFFERENTIATE

Use the **QUICK CHECK** on the previous page to prescribe differentiated instruction.

I **Intervention**
0–3 points on the Quick Check

O **On-Level**
4 points on the Quick Check

A **Advanced**
5 points on the Quick Check

Intervention Activity **I**

Card Tricks

Materials

(per pair) Hundred Chart (Teaching Tool 31), 2 blank index cards, index cards numbered 37, 38, 39, 42, yellow crayon

• Guide students to put the number cards in a row, in order from 37 to 42. *I see that two numbers are missing. How can we use the hundred chart to find the missing numbers?*

• Have students color in the numbers with the yellow crayon on the chart. *How can you find the two missing numbers in the pattern?* [Count by ones.]

• Students use the hundred chart to find the missing numbers, and then color the numbers. Then they write those numbers on the blank index cards and put them in correct order in the row. [37, 38, 39, 40, 41, 42]

| 37 | 38 | 39 | 40 | 41 | 42 |

Reteach **I**

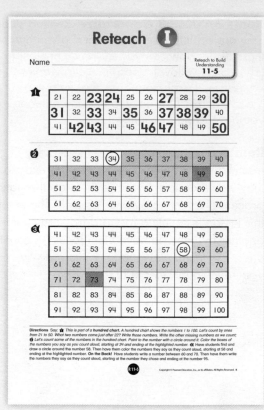

On-Level and Advanced Activity Centers **O** **A**

Center Games

In the On-Level activity, partners take turns drawing tiles to create a new two-digit number. Partner A finds that number on the hundred chart as well as the number that comes just before it. Partner B finds the number that comes just after the new two-digit number. In the Advanced activity, partners play the same game but identify the two numbers that come just before and just after the number that is created.

★ On-Level

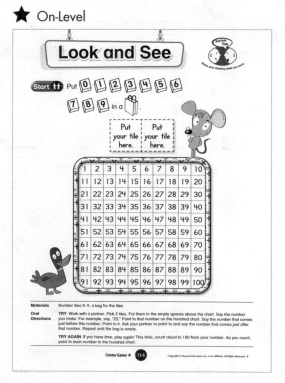

★★ Advanced

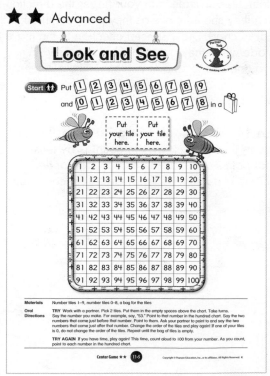

TIMING

The time allocated to Step 3 will depend on the teacher's instructional decisions and differentiation routines.

15–30 min

PEARSON
realize.
PearsonRealize.com

Help   Tools   Games

Technology Center Ⓘ Ⓞ Ⓐ

Tools

Games

Math Tools and Math Games

A link to a specific math tools activity or math game to use with this lesson is provided at PearsonRealize.com.

Leveled Assignment

Ⓘ Items 1–4   Ⓞ Items 2–5   Ⓐ Items 3–6

Name _____

Help Tools Games

Another Look!

1	2	3	4	5	6	7	8	9	10
11	12	13	14	15	16	17	18	19	20
21	22	23	24	25	26	27	28	29	30
31	32	33	34	35	36	37	38	39	40
41	42	43	44	45	46	47	48	49	50
51	52	53	54	55	56	57	58	59	60
61	62	63	64	65	66	67	68	69	70
71	72	73	74	75	76	77	78	79	80
81	82	83	84	85	86	87	88	89	90
91	92	93	94	95	96	97	98	99	100

Homework & Practice 11-5

Count Forward from Any Number to 100

HOME ACTIVITY Point to a number on a hundred chart, such as 27. Have your child count from that number to another number you have chosen. Repeat with other numbers.

1 ⭐

1	2	3	4	5	6	7	8	9	10
11	12	13	14	15	16	17	18	19	20
21	22	23	24	25	26	27	28	29	30
31	32	33	34	35	36	37	38	39	40
41	42	43	44	45	46	47	48	49	50
51	52	53	54	55	56	57	58	59	60
61	62	63	64	65	66	67	68	69	70
71	72	73	74	75	76	77	78	79	(80)
81	82	83	84	85	86	87	88	89	90
91	92	93	94	95	96	97	98	99	100

2

1	2	3	4	5	6	7	8	9	10
11	12	13	14	15	16	17	18	19	20
21	22	23	24	25	26	27	28	29	30
31	32	33	34	35	(36)	37	38	39	40
41	42	43	44	45	46	47	48	49	50
51	52	53	54	55	56	57	58	59	60
61	62	63	64	65	66	67	68	69	70
71	72	73	74	75	76	77	78	79	80
81	82	83	84	85	86	87	88	89	90
91	92	93	94	95	96	97	98	99	100

Directions Say: *You can count forward from any number. Find and draw a circle around the number* eighteen. *Count aloud until you reach the red box. Color the boxes of the numbers you counted aloud.* Have students draw a circle around the given number, and then color the boxes of the numbers as they count aloud, starting at the circled number and ending at the red box. Have them: ⭐ *draw a circle around the number* eighty; **2** *draw a circle around the number* thirty-six.

Topic 11 | Lesson 5   Digital Resources at PearsonRealize.com   six hundred fifty-three **653**

3 🐟

1	2	3	4	5	6	7	8	9	10
11	12	13	14	15	16	17	18	19	20
21	(22)	23	24	25	26	27	28	29	30
31	32	33	34	35	36	37	38	39	40
41	42	43	44	45	46	47	48	49	50
51	52	53	54	55	56	57	58	59	60
61	62	63	64	65	66	67	68	69	70
71	72	73	74	75	76	77	78	79	80
81	82	83	84	85	86	87	88	89	90
91	92	93	94	95	96	97	98	99	100

4

1	2	3	4	5	6	7	8	9	10
11	12	13	14	15	16	17	18	19	20
21	22	23	24	25	26	27	28	29	30
31	32	33	34	35	36	37	38	39	40
41	42	43	44	45	46	47	48	49	50
(51)	52	53	54	55	56	57	58	59	60
61	62	63	64	65	66	67	68	69	70
71	72	73	74	75	76	77	78	79	80
81	82	83	84	85	86	87	88	89	90
91	92	93	94	95	96	97	98	99	100

5 ✋

1	2	3	4	5	6	7	8	9	10
11	12	13	14	15	16	(17)	18	19	20
21	22	23	24	25	26	27	28	29	30
31	32	33	34	35	36	37	38	39	40
41	42	43	44	45	46	47	48	(49)	50
51	52	53	54	55	56	57	58	59	60
61	62	63	64	65	66	67	68	69	70
71	72	73	74	75	76	77	78	79	80
(81)	82	83	84	85	86	87	88	89	90
91	92	93	94	95	96	97	98	99	100

6 ✋

1	2	3	4	5	6	7	8	9	10
11	12	13	14	15	16	17	18	19	20
21	22	23	24	25	26	27	28	29	30
31	32	33	34	35	36	37	38	39	40
41	42	43	44	45	46	47	48	49	50
51	52	53	54	55	56	57	58	59	60
61	62	63	64	65	66	67	68	69	70
71	72	73	74	75	76	77	78	79	80
81	82	83	84	85	86	87	88	89	90
91	92	93	94	95	96	97	98	99	

Directions Have students draw a circle around the given number, and then color the boxes of the numbers as they count aloud, starting at the circled number and ending at the red box. Have them: 🐟 *draw a circle around the number* twenty-two; ✋ *draw a circle around the number* fifty-one. ✋ **Higher Order Thinking** Have students draw a circle around the number that comes after *sixteen*, the number that comes after *forty-eight*, and the number that comes after *eighty*. ✋ **Higher Order Thinking** Have students write the numbers as they count aloud by tens, starting at the yellow box and ending at the red box.

654 six hundred fifty-four   © Pearson Education, Inc. K   Topic 11 | Lesson 5

COUNT USING PATTERNS TO 100

DIGITAL RESOURCES PearsonRealize.com

 Student and Teacher eTexts
eText

 Listen and Look For Lesson Video
PD

 Today's Challenge
Think

 Solve and Share
Solve

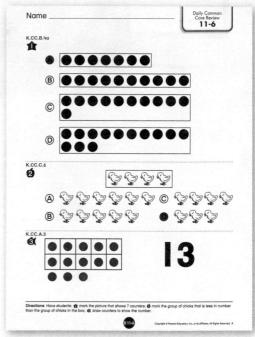 **Visual Learning Animation Plus**
Learn

 Animated Glossary
Glossary

 Math Tools
Tools

 Quick Check
Assessment

 Another Look Homework Video
Help

 Math Games
Games

LESSON OVERVIEW **FOCUS • COHERENCE • RIGOR**

FOCUS

Domain K.CC Counting and Cardinality

Cluster K.CC.A Know number names and the count sequence.

Content Standard K.CC.A.1 Count to 100 by ones and by tens. Also **K.CC.A.2**

Mathematical Practices MP.2, MP.5, MP.6, MP.7

Objective Count by tens and ones from any number up to 100.

Essential Understanding Using counting patterns on the hundred chart can help when counting on from any number from 1 to 100.

Materials Hundred Chart (Teaching Tool 31)

COHERENCE

Topic 11 lessons have had students working to count and find patterns in hundred charts. In Lessons 11-1 and 11-2, students used patterns to count to 30 and then 50. In Lesson 11-5, students moved to counting on from any number on the hundred chart. Now, in Lesson 11-6, students will find a series of missing numbers using the hundred chart for support.

RIGOR

This lesson emphasizes **conceptual understanding** and **procedural skill**. Students count forward by ones to find a set of missing numbers on the hundred chart. As they do this on the hundred chart, it deepens their understanding of number sense, counting, and patterns.

 Watch the Listen and Look For Lesson Video.
PD

MATH ANYTIME

Daily Common Core Review

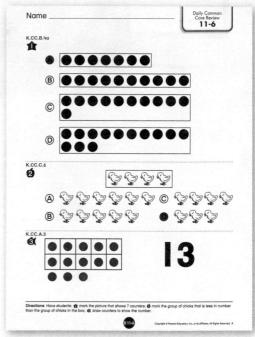

Today's Challenge

Think Use Topic 11 problems any time during this topic.

ENGLISH LANGUAGE LEARNERS E L L

Speaking Speak using content area vocabulary in context.

Use with the Visual Learning Bridge on Student's Edition p. 656.

Say *before* and *after*. Ask students to repeat. Point to the hundred chart. Say: *The order in the hundred chart tells the numbers that come before and after a number.* Give each student a hundred chart. Say: *Show me number 16.* Ask: *What number comes before 16?* [15] *What number comes after 16?* [17] Have students work with a partner.

Beginning Call out a number. Have Student A point to and say the number on the hundred chart that comes *before* the number using the sentence stem: "____ comes before ____." Have Student B point to and say the number that comes *after* the number using the sentence stem: "____ comes after ____."

Intermediate Ask Student A to call out a number. Have Student B tell which numbers come before and after that number. Have students reverse roles and repeat.

Advanced Have Student A think of a number, and tell Student B which numbers come before and after it. Have Student B use the hundred chart to tell Student A the number and explain how he or she knew the number. Have students reverse roles and repeat.

Summarize What does it mean when you speak about which number comes *before* or *after* another number?

DEVELOP: PROBLEM-BASED LEARNING

COHERENCE: Engage learners by connecting prior knowledge to new ideas.

Students find a number that is 1 more than another number on the hundred chart. This prepares them for the next part of the lesson where they count and find the missing numbers from 1 to 100 on a number chart.

 10–15 min

 BEFORE

1. Pose the Solve-and-Share Problem
MP.2 Reasoning In this problem, students use a hundred chart and their prior knowledge to determine which numbers come just after others when counting.

Say: *Carlos looks at the chart. He knows 21 comes just after 20. Draw a circle around the numbers that come just after each decade number. How do you know you are correct? What patterns do you see?*

2. Build Understanding
What are you asked to do? [Find the numbers that come just after each decade number.]
What tool do you have to solve the problem? [Hundred chart]

 DURING

3. Ask Guiding Questions As Needed
Why do you think the chart is called a hundred chart? [It has 100 numbers on it.] *When do you think you would use a hundred chart?* [Sample answer: To count numbers to 100 or to find out which numbers come just before and just after a number]

 AFTER

4. Share and Discuss Solutions
Start with students' solutions. If needed, project Solve and analyze Tricia's work to discuss how numbers can be found using a hundred chart.

5. Transition to the Visual Learning Bridge
Later in this lesson, you will learn that numbers are counted and written in a specific sequence on a hundred chart.

A hundred chart can help in counting numbers to 100 by ones beginning with any number.

6. Extension for Early Finishers
Have students work in pairs. One partner writes a number and the other tells what number comes just before and what number comes just after it. Students can use a hundred chart to check their answers.

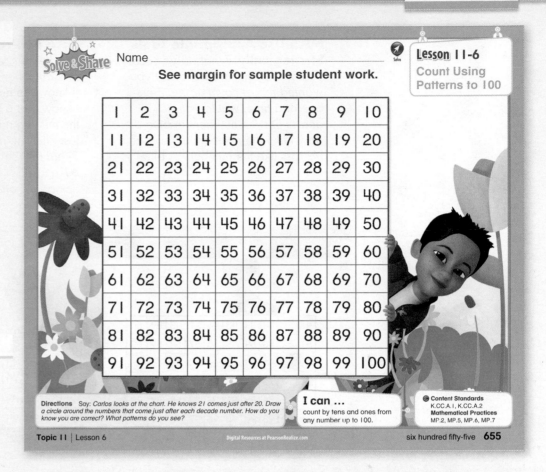

Solve & Share   Name _____   Lesson 11-6
Count Using Patterns to 100

See margin for sample student work.

1	2	3	4	5	6	7	8	9	10
11	12	13	14	15	16	17	18	19	20
21	22	23	24	25	26	27	28	29	30
31	32	33	34	35	36	37	38	39	40
41	42	43	44	45	46	47	48	49	50
51	52	53	54	55	56	57	58	59	60
61	62	63	64	65	66	67	68	69	70
71	72	73	74	75	76	77	78	79	80
81	82	83	84	85	86	87	88	89	90
91	92	93	94	95	96	97	98	99	100

Directions Say: *Carlos looks at the chart. He knows 21 comes just after 20. Draw a circle around the numbers that come just after each decade number. How do you know you are correct? What patterns do you see?*

I can ... count by tens and ones from any number up to 100.

Content Standards K.CC.A.1, K.CC.A.2 **Mathematical Practices** MP.2, MP.5, MP.6, MP.7

Topic 11 | Lesson 6   Digital Resources at PearsonRealize.com   six hundred fifty-five **655**

Analyze Student Work

Tricia's Work

1	2	3	4	5	6	7	8	9	10
(11)	12	13	14	15	16	17	18	19	20
(21)	22	23	24	25	26	27	28	29	30
(31)	32	33	34	35	36	37	38	39	40
(41)	42	43	44	45	46	47	48	49	50
(51)	52	53	54	55	56	57	58	59	60
(61)	62	63	64	65	66	67	68	69	70
(71)	72	73	74	75	76	77	78	79	80
(81)	82	83	84	85	86	87	88	89	90
(91)	92	93	94	95	96	97	98	99	100

Tricia correctly finds each of the numbers that come just after each decade number (11, 21, 31, 41, 51, 61, 71, 81, 91). She then explains that she sees a pattern in the first column.

Emerson's Work

1	2	3	4	5	6	7	8	9	10
11	12	13	14	15	16	17	18	19	20
21	22	23	24	25	26	27	28	29	(30)
31	32	33	34	35	36	37	38	39	(40)
41	42	43	44	45	46	47	48	49	(50)
51	52	53	54	55	56	57	58	59	(60)
61	62	63	64	65	66	67	68	69	(70)
71	72	73	74	75	76	77	78	79	(80)
81	82	83	84	85	86	87	88	89	(90)
91	92	93	94	95	96	97	98	99	(100)

Emerson incorrectly identifies 30 as the number that comes just after 20 and subsequently misidentifies every other decade number as coming just after the previous decade number when counting forward.

DEVELOP: VISUAL LEARNING

PEARSON
realize.
PearsonRealize.com

Learn   Glossary

The *Visual Learning Bridge* connects students' thinking in Solve & Share to important math ideas in the lesson. Use the *Visual Learning Bridge* to make these ideas explicit. Also available as a *Visual Learning Animation Plus* at PearsonRealize.com

E L L
Visual Learning

MP.5 Use Appropriate Tools Strategically *What do you see?* [A part of a hundred chart] *If you wanted to just count up numbers one at a time, would you go across like the numbers in blue or down like the numbers in yellow?* [Across like the numbers in blue]

MP.6 Be Precise *How can you use the numbers 61 and 63 to find out what number is missing?* [I know the numbers go up by 1. I know that 61 comes just before the missing number and 63 comes just after the missing number.] *What number belongs between 61 and 63?* [62] *What number comes just after 84?* [85]

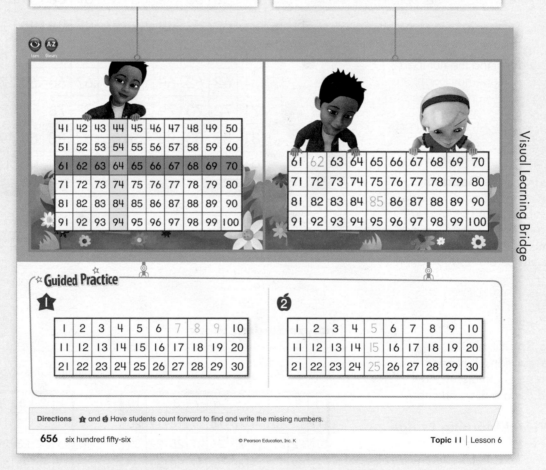

Visual Learning Bridge

☆ **Guided Practice**

❶

1	2	3	4	5	6	7	8	9	10
11	12	13	14	15	16	17	18	19	20
21	22	23	24	25	26	27	28	29	30

❷

1	2	3	4	5	6	7	8	9	10
11	12	13	14	15	16	17	18	19	20
21	22	23	24	25	26	27	28	29	30

Directions ⭐ and 🅱 Have students count forward to find and write the missing numbers.

656 six hundred fifty-six   © Pearson Education, Inc. K   **Topic 11** | Lesson 6

Complete the *Do You Understand? Show Me!* problem before starting Guided Practice.

Do You Understand? Show Me! MP.5 Use Appropriate Tools Strategically *When would you use a hundred chart?* [I would use a hundred chart to count numbers to 100 or to see which numbers come just before and just after other numbers.]

Ask the following Essential Question: *How does using a hundred chart help you count from any number to another?* [It helps you keep track as you count by ones.] Numbers are counted and written in a specific sequence on a hundred chart. Counting patterns (numerical and visual) can be seen on a hundred chart.

Error Intervention: Item 1

If students do not understand why they are writing numbers,

then remind them that the chart shows the numbers in order from 1 to 100. Students will count forward to write the numbers that are missing.

1 RtI **Reteaching** Assign Reteaching Set D, p. 670.

QUICK CHECK

Check mark indicates items for prescribing differentiation on the next page.
Items 7 and 9 are worth 1 point. Item 10 is worth up to 3 points.

20–30 min

Tools   Assessment

Item 3 MP.2 Reasoning Remind students that numbers are counted and written in a special order on a hundred chart. Call attention to the multiple choice answers below the chart. Model going through each option and asking whether or not it works as an answer before making the final selection.

Item 4 Remind students that numbers are arranged from 1 to 100 on a hundred chart. Students can practice reading rows or columns aloud to hear the number patterns.

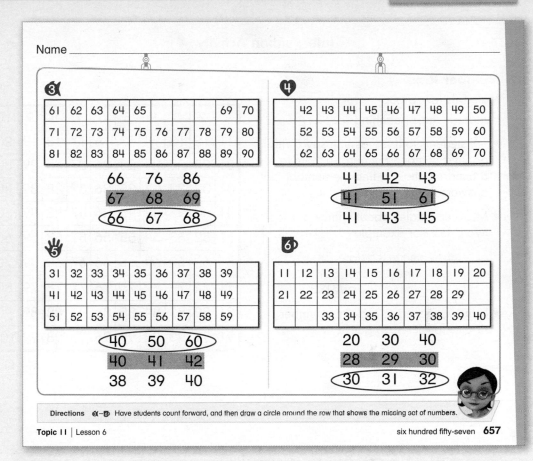

Item 7 MP.7 Look for a Pattern If students are having trouble, tell them that on a number chart, the numbers 0 to 9 are repeated in each column. *Put your finger on number 77. Trace down the column. What do you notice about the numbers?* [Sample answer: The numbers get bigger as I go down the column. All of the numbers end in 7.]

Item 10 To help students identify the column they should circle, remind them that they should look for numbers that end in 3. If needed, write a two-digit number on the board and point out the digit on the right.

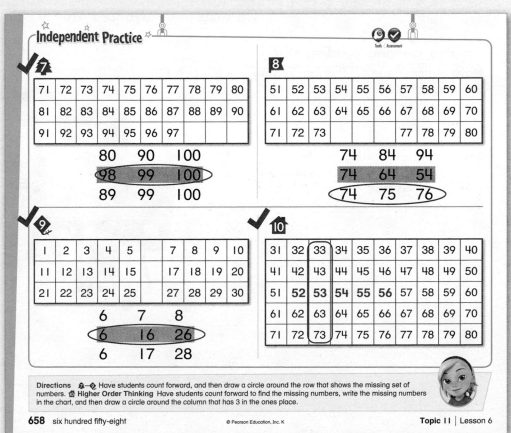

657–658

Use the **QUICK CHECK** on the previous page to prescribe differentiated instruction.

2 RtI

I Intervention
0–3 points on the Quick Check

O On-Level
4 points on the Quick Check

A Advanced
5 points on the Quick Check

Intervention Activity I

Number Riddles

Materials (per group)
Hundred Chart (Teaching Tool 31)

- Tell students to listen as you say a riddle about a number. Encourage them to use a hundred chart to find the number that answers the riddle.

- Make up riddles about numbers using two clues. For example:

  I come just before 84.
  I come just after 82.
  What number am I? [83]

- Invite volunteers to make up number riddles for others to guess.

1	2	3	4	5	6	7	8	9	10
11	12	13	14	15	16	17	18	19	20
21	22	23	24	25	26	27	28	29	30
31	32	33	34	35	36	37	38	39	40
41	42	43	44	45	46	47	48	49	50
51	52	53	54	55	56	57	58	59	60
61	62	63	64	65	66	67	68	69	70
71	72	73	74	75	76	77	78	79	80
81	82	83	84	85	86	87	88	89	90
91	92	93	94	95	96	97	98	99	100

Reteach I

Name _____

Reteach to Build Understanding 11-6

★ 10 20 30 40 50 60 70 80 90

Directions ★ Point to the row of numbers. Say: *This is a pattern. Let's count by tens together.* Draw a circle around each 0 that repeats in this pattern. ❷ Point to each number as you count aloud with students. Have them say the missing numbers as you count forward. Then have them draw a circle around the row that shows the missing set of numbers. ❸ and ❹ Have students count forward, and then draw a circle around the row that shows the missing set of numbers. **On the Back!** Have students draw a circle around a number between 1 and 20 on a hundred chart, count by tens from that number to the bottom of the chart, and then draw a circle around the numbers they counted to show a pattern.

R 11-6

Copyright © Pearson Education, Inc., or its affiliates. All Rights Reserved. K

On-Level and Advanced Activity Centers O A

Problem-Solving Reading Mat

Have students read the Problem-Solving Reading Mat for Topic 11 and then complete Problem-Solving Reading Activity 11-6.

See the Problem-Solving Reading Activity Guide for other suggestions on how to use this mat.

TIMING

The time allocated to Step 3 will depend on the teacher's instructional decisions and differentiation routines.

15–30 min

 Help   Tools   Games

Technology Center

Math Tools and Math Games

A link to a specific math tools activity or math game to use with this lesson is provided at PearsonRealize.com.

Tools

Games

Leveled Assignment

 Items 1–4   Items 2–5   Items 3–6

Name _____

Help Tools Games

Another Look!

1	2	3	4	5	6	7	8	9	10
11	12	13	14	15	16	17	18	19	20
21	22	23	24	25	26	27	28	29	30
31	32	33	34	35	36	37	38	39	40
41	42	43	44	45	46	47	48	49	50

Homework & Practice 11-6
Count Using Patterns to 100

HOME ACTIVITY Point to a hundred chart from this lesson. Take turns making up riddles and guessing the answers. For example, ask your child: *What number comes just after 31 and just before 33?* (32)

1

1	2	3	4	5	6	7	8	9	10
11	12	13	14	15	16	17	18	19	20
21	22	23	24	25	26	27	28	29	30
31	32	33	34	35	36	37	38	39	40
41	42	43	44	45	46	47	48	49	50

2

1	2	3	4	5	6	7	8	9	10
11	12	13	14	15	16	17	18	19	20
21	22	23	24	25	26	27	28	29	30
31	32	33	34	35	36	37	38	39	40
41	42	43	44	45	46	47	48	49	50
51	52	53	54	55	56	57	58	59	60

Directions Say: *Draw a circle around the column with the numbers: seven, seventeen, twenty-seven, thirty-seven, forty-seven. What pattern do you see and hear?* Have students: **1** draw a circle around the column that has 9 in the ones place, count the numbers aloud, and then explain the pattern they see and hear; **2** draw a circle around the numbers that have 3 in the tens place, count the numbers aloud, and then explain the pattern they see and hear.

Topic 11 | Lesson 6 Digital Resources at PearsonRealize.com six hundred fifty-nine **659**

3

1	2	3	4	5	6	7	8	9	10
11	12	13	14	15	16	17	18	19	20
21	22	23	24	25	26	27	28	29	30
31	32	33	34	35	36	37	38	39	40
41	42	43	44	45	46	47	48	49	50

4

41	42	43	44	45	46	47	48	49	50
51	52	52	54	55	56	57	58	59	60
61	62	63	64	65	66	67	68	69	70
71	72	73	74	75	76	77	78	79	80
81	82	83	84	85	86	87	88	89	90
91	92	93	94	95	96	97	98	99	100

5

11	12	13	14	15	16	17	18	19	20
21	22	23	24	25	26	27	28	29	30
31	32	33	34	35	36	37	38	39	40
41	42	43	44	45	46	47	48	49	50
51	52	53	54	55	56	57	58	59	60

6

51	52	53	54	55	56	57	58	59	60
61	62	63	64	65	66	67	68	69	70
71	72	73	74	75	76	77	78	79	80
81	82	83	84	85	86	87	88	89	90
91	92	93	94	95	96	97	98	99	100

Directions Have students: **3** draw a circle around the row that starts with the number *twenty-one*, count the numbers aloud, and then explain the pattern they see and hear; **4** draw a circle around the column that has 9 in the ones place, count the numbers aloud, and then explain the pattern they see and hear. **5 Higher Order Thinking** Have students count by ones to write the missing numbers, and then draw a circle around the column that has 4 in the ones place. **6 Higher Order Thinking** Have students draw a circle around the number that is 1 more than 72, and then mark an X on the number that is 1 less than 90.

660 six hundred sixty © Pearson Education, Inc. K **Topic 11 | Lesson 6**

LOOK FOR AND USE STRUCTURE

DIGITAL RESOURCES PearsonRealize.com

 Student and Teacher eTexts
eText

 Listen and Look For Lesson Video
PD

Today's Challenge
Think

Solve and Share
Solve

 Visual Learning Animation Plus
Learn

Math Practices Animations
MP

 A-Z Animated Glossary
Glossary

Math Tools
Tools

Quick Check
Assessment

Another Look Homework Video
Help

Math Games
Games

LESSON OVERVIEW   FCR FOCUS · COHERENCE · RIGOR

FOCUS

Mathematical Practices MP.7 Look for and make use of structure. Also **MP.6, MP.8**

Content Standards K.CC.A.1, K.CC.A.2

Objective Count on from any number counting by tens and by ones.

Essential Understanding Good math thinkers look for patterns in math to solve problems.

Materials crayons

COHERENCE

Students have used MP.7 earlier in this topic. Use this lesson to stop and focus on the Thinking Habits good problem solvers use when they look for and make use of structure in math. In this lesson, students show how they can use a hundred chart and patterns of counting in ones and tens to solve problems. Instruction during this lesson should focus on the structure of the tens and ones in the numbers students are using and the pattern they see in the way they choose to count.

RIGOR

This lesson emphasizes **application**. Rigorous mathematics instruction calls for the selection, use, and management of multiple mathematical practices. All of the problems in this lesson elicit the use of multiple mathematical practices. Use the thinking habits shown in the Solve & Share task to help focus thinking on MP.7 in the lesson.

 Watch the Listen and Look For Lesson Video.
PD

MATH ANYTIME

Daily Common Core Review

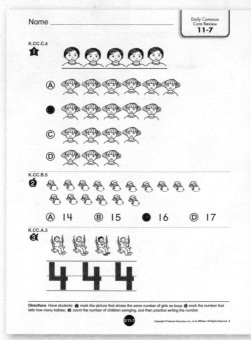

Today's Challenge

Think Use Topic 11 problems any time during this topic.

ENGLISH LANGUAGE LEARNERS ELL

Listening Demonstrate listening comprehension by following directions.

Use with the Solve & Share on Student's Edition p. 661.

Draw a number chart with numbers 1–30. Say: *Count from 2 to14. Start with 2.* Draw a circle around 2. Say: *Count by ones to 14.* Draw arrows as you count by ones from 2 to 14. Draw a circle around 14. Say: *Another way to count from 2 to 14 is using tens and ones.* Draw arrows as you count tens and ones. Ask: *What was the ending number both times?* [14]

Beginning Ask students to listen as you say: *Draw a circle around 3.* Demonstrate circling 3. Say: *Count to 18 by ones.* Demonstrate counting by ones to 18 as students count by ones to 18. Draw arrows as you count. Continue the process counting from 3 to 18 by counting by tens and ones.

Intermediate Ask partners to listen and follow directions. Pause between each direction. Say: *Draw a circle around 3. Count from 3 to 18 by ones. Draw arrows as you count.* Ask: *What is the ending number?*

Continue the process counting from 3 to 18 by counting by tens and ones.

Advanced Ask students to listen and follow directions. Say: *Draw a circle around 3. Count from 3 to 18 by ones. Draw arrows as you count.* Ask: *What is the ending number?* Continue counting from 3 to 18 by counting by tens and ones.

Summarize How are number charts used to count numbers by ones and by tens and ones?

DEVELOP: PROBLEM-BASED LEARNING

PEARSON
realize.
PearsonRealize.com

COHERENCE: Engage students by connecting prior knowledge to new ideas.

Students use their knowledge of the structure of the number system to count on in different ways. This prepares them for the next part of the lesson where they will count on from other given numbers in different ways and explain their work.

10–15 min

Solve

---

1. Pose the Solve-and-Share Problem

MP.7 Use Structure In this problem, students use the structure of the base-ten system to count on from a given number in two different ways.

Say: *Carlos's teacher gives the class a challenge. Is there more than one way to solve it? Begin at 3. Use arrows and show how you could count up 15 places. Color the number red to show where you end. Show another way to use arrows on the second chart.*

Tell students to think about these Thinking Habits as they solve the problem.

Is there a pattern?
How can I describe the pattern?

2. Build Understanding

What are you asked to do? [Show how to count up 15 places from 3 on one chart, then show another way on the other chart.] *How are you supposed to use arrows?* [To show how I am counting on]

3. Ask Guiding Questions As Needed

Which way do you move on the chart when you count by ones? [Right] *By tens?* [Down] *How many tens are in 15?* [1]

4. Share and Discuss Solutions

Start with students' solutions. Have them share the strategies they used to solve the problem. If needed, project and analyze Taylor's work to show two ways to count on 15 from 3.

5. Transition to the Visual Learning Bridge

You counted on 15 from 3 in different ways. Later in this lesson, you will count on from other numbers using tens and ones and explore the patterns you find.

6. Extension for Early Finishers

What would happen if you started at 5 rather than 3? [I would end at 20 whichever way I counted.]

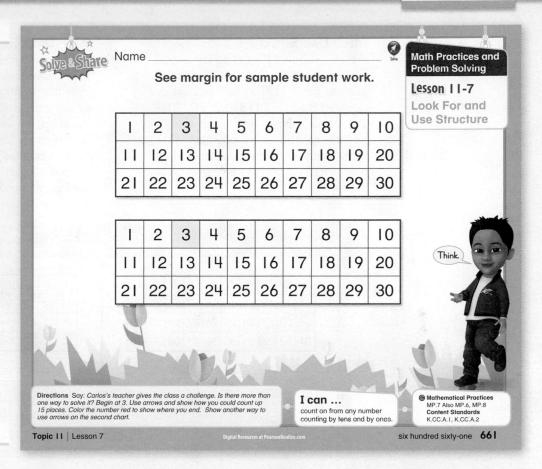

Solve & Share

Name _____

See margin for sample student work.

Solve

Math Practices and Problem Solving

Lesson 11-7
Look For and Use Structure

Think.

Directions Say: *Carlos's teacher gives the class a challenge. Is there more than one way to solve it? Begin at 3. Use arrows and show how you could count up 15 places. Color the number red to show where you end. Show another way to use arrows on the second chart.*

I can ...
count on from any number counting by tens and by ones.

Mathematical Practices
MP.7 Also MP.6, MP.8
Content Standards
K.CC.A.1, K.CC.A.2

Topic 11 | Lesson 7   Digital Resources at PearsonRealize.com   six hundred sixty-one **661**

Analyze Student Work

Taylor's Work

1	2	3	4	5	6	7	8	9	10
11	12	13	14	15	16	17	18	19	20
21	22	23	24	25	26	27	28	29	30

1	2	3	4	5	6	7	8	9	10
11	12	13	14	15	16	17	18	19	20
21	22	23	24	25	26	27	28	29	30

Taylor counts on by tens first, and then ones on the first chart. She then counts on by ones first, and then tens on the second chart.

Ryan's Work

1	2	3	4	5	6	7	8	9	10
11	12	13	14	15	16	17	18	19	20
21	22	23	24	25	26	27	28	29	30

1	2	3	4	5	6	7	8	9	10
11	12	13	14	15	16	17	18	19	20
21	22	23	24	25	26	27	28	29	30

Ryan counts by ones from 3, along 15 spaces ending at 18 on the first chart. Ryan cannot think of a second way, so he leaves the second chart blank.

The *Visual Learning Bridge* connects students' thinking in *Solve & Share* to important math ideas in the lesson. Use the *Visual Learning Bridge* to make these ideas explicit. Also available as a *Visual Learning Animation Plus* at PearsonRealize.com

E L L Visual Learning

MP.7 Use Structure *What does the chart show?* [Counting by ones first and then tens] *What number is used to start?* [17] *What numbers are counted from 17?* [18, 19, 20, 21, 22, 23, 33] *How many ones did you count?* [6] *How many tens?* [1] *How many in all did you count up from 17?* [16] *What number is at the end?* [33]

MP.7 Look for Patterns *What does the chart show?* [Counting by tens first and then ones] *What number is used to start?* [17] *What numbers are counted from 17?* [27, 28, 29, 30, 31, 32, 33] *How many tens did you count?* [1] *How many ones?* [6] *How many in all did you count up from 17?* [16] *What number is at the end?* [33] *What do you notice that is the same in both boxes?* [Both start with 17, count up 16, and end at 33.] *What is different?* [The way that 16 was counted] *Did changing the way 16 was counted on change the end number?* [No] *Why?* [Sample answer: I counted the same number of tens and ones; I still counted on the same amount, 16.]

Both ways end at 33.

Visual Learning Bridge

Guided Practice   Check students' work.

Directions   Have students: ① start at 22 and make a path to show how to count up 15 using only ones. Have them circle the number where they end, and then explain how they used the number chart to find the answer; ② start at 12 and make a path to show how to count up 14 using tens and then ones. Have them circle the number where they end, and then explain how they used the number chart to find the answer.

662   six hundred sixty-two   © Pearson Education, Inc. K   Topic 11 | Lesson 7

Complete the *Do You Understand? Show Me!* problem before starting Guided Practice.

Do You Understand? Show Me! MP.6 Be Precise *Start at 27, count to 39. What numbers do you say?* [Sample answer: 28, 29, 39] *How did you count?* [Sample answer: I counted ones first, then tens.] Students can use the number chart in Box 1 of the Visual Learning Bridge to help. Encourage students to compare their answers with a partner's.

Essential Question   Ask the following Essential Question: *Think about numbers that are made up of tens and ones. What are some ways you can count on by these numbers?* [Sample answers: Count on by ones first, then by tens; Count on by tens first, then ones; Count on just by ones.]

Error Intervention: Item 2

If students begin to count by ones from 12,

then remind students that is one way to count, but that for this item they are asked to count by tens and then by ones. *How can you show on the chart counting on 1 ten?* [Move down 1 row.] *Then, how can you show on the chart counting on 4 ones?* [Move 4 boxes to the right.]

✓ QUICK CHECK

Check mark indicates items for prescribing differentiation on the next page.
Items 3 and 5 are each worth 1 point. The Performance Assessment on page 664 is worth up to 3 points.

20–30 min

Tools   Assessment

MP.7 Look for and Make Use of Structure

Listen and look for these behaviors as evidence that students are exhibiting proficiency with MP.7.

- analyze and describe patterns in numbers
- analyze procedures to describe and work with them in different ways

Item 3 Some students may count 42 as the first number when counting by ones. Remind them of the first number to count. *What number are you starting at?* [42] *You are going to count on. You are already at 42. Do you count 42 when counting on by ones?* [No] *What is the first number you will count?* [43]

Items 5 and 6 MP.6 Be Precise *Your explanation should tell each of the steps you took to get the correct answer.* By choosing their own strategy and explaining it, students are also checking the precision of their answers and showing an understanding of tens and ones. Have students follow the path they made on their chart while explaining their work to check they have recorded accurately.

Item 7 MP.6 Be Precise Students can use the number chart for support, if needed, to find the number when counting up 18, remembering the meaning of the tens and ones places in a two-digit number.

Item 8 MP.7 Use Structure Students apply their understanding of the structure of the number 18 to count on from 7 in two different ways. They see the pattern when counting on using each way and should be able to explain the difference between the two ways. *How many ones did you count on when you counted by ones?* [18] *How many ones did you count on when you counted by tens first?* [8] *Why?* [Because I had already counted 1 ten]

Item 9 MP.8 Generalize Students should recognize counting by ones and then by tens as a third way to count on that will end at the same number. Look for students who can explain the reason why they end at 25: because the amount they are counting has not changed. These students are generalizing a rule that they will apply to counting other numbers and also later to addition and subtraction.

Independent Practice

Name _____

✓ 3

41	42	43	44	45	46	47	48	49	50
51	52	53	54	55	56	57	58	59	60
61	62	(63)	64	65	66	67	68	69	70
71	72	73	74	75	76	77	78	79	80

4

41	42	43	44	45	46	47	48	49	50
51	52	53	54	55	56	57	58	59	60
61	62	63	64	65	66	67	68	69	70
(71)	72	73	74	75	76	77	78	79	80

✓ 5 Check students' work.

61	62	63	64	65	66	67	68	69	70
71	72	73	74	75	76	77	78	79	80
81	82	83	84	85	86	87	88	89	90
91	92	93	94	95	96	97	98	(99)	100

6 Check students' work.

61	62	63	64	65	66	67	68	69	70
71	72	73	74	75	76	77	78	79	80
81	82	83	84	(85)	86	87	88	89	90
91	92	93	94	95	96	97	98	99	100

Directions Have students: ✪ start at 42 and make a path to show how to count up 21 using ones and then tens. Have them circle the number where they end, and then explain how they used the number chart to find the answer; ✪ start at 56 and make a path to show how to count up 15 using tens and ones. Have them circle the number where they end, and then explain how they used the number chart to find the answer; ✋ start at 72 and make a path to show how to count up 27 in any way they choose. Have them circle the number where they end, and then explain how they used the number chart to find the answer; ☕ start at 63 and make a path to show how to count up 22 in any way they choose. Have them draw a circle around the number where they end, and then explain how they know they are correct.

Topic 11 | Lesson 7   six hundred sixty-three **663**

Math Practices and Problem Solving

✓ Performance Assessment _____

🌲 7 8 9 Check students' work.

1	2	3	4	5	6	7	8	9	10
11	12	13	14	15	16	17	18	19	20
21	22	23	24	(25)	26	27	28	29	30
31	32	33	34	35	36	37	38	39	40

7. There is 1 ten in the number 18.
8. Counting by ones: 8, 9, 10, 11... 24, 25. Counting by tens and then by ones: 17, 18, 19, 20, 21, 22, 23, 24, 25.
9. Students should answer that they still end on 25. Whether they count by tens first or by ones first, they will end on the same number. Check students' explanations.

Directions Read the problem aloud. Then have students use multiple math practices to solve the problem. Say: *Start at 7 and count up 18 in any way you choose. Make a path to show how you counted, and then draw a circle around the number where you ended.* ✪ **MP.6 Be Precise** *How many tens are in 18?* ⬛ **MP.7 Use Structure** *What numbers would you say if you only counted by ones? What numbers would you say if you counted by tens first and then by ones?* **MP.8 Generalize** *What number would you end on if you counted by ones first and then by tens? How do you know you are correct if you did NOT count again?*

664 six hundred sixty-four   © Pearson Education, Inc. K   Topic 11 | Lesson 7

ASSESS AND DIFFERENTIATE

Use the **QUICK CHECK** on the previous page to prescribe differentiated instruction.

I Intervention
0–3 points on the Quick Check

O On-Level
4 points on the Quick Check

A Advanced
5 points on the Quick Check

Intervention Activity I

Counting On

Materials

Hundred Chart (Teaching Tool 31)

• Distribute copies of Teaching Tool 31 to each student. *Find 24 on the hundred chart. You are going to count on 13 from 24. You can count by tens first or ones first.*

• *Let's count on by tens first and then ones. How many tens are there in 13? How do you know?* [1; There is a 1 in the tens place.] Demonstrate how to count on by ten from 24 by moving down 1 row in the chart. *Now we are going to count on the 3 ones.* Ask a student to show you how to count on 3 ones. *What number do we end at?* [37] Write *37* on the board. Repeat the activity counting by ones first and then by tens. Establish that the end number is

37 both ways because the same amount, 13, is being counted on from 24.

• Give students another starting number, such as 45 and a number to count on by, such as 12. Have them work in pairs. One student counts on by tens and then ones. The other student counts on by ones and then tens. Students should mark a path on their hundred chart to show their work. Students compare their work to check they have both ended at the same number.

1	2	3	4	5	6	7	8	9	10
11	12	13	14	15	16	17	18	19	20
21	22	23	24	25	26	27	28	29	30
31	32	33	34	35	36	37	38	39	40
41	42	43	44	45	46	47	48	49	50
51	52	53	54	55	56	57	58	59	60
61	62	63	64	65	66	67	68	69	70
71	72	73	74	75	76	77	78	79	80
81	82	83	84	85	86	87	88	89	90
91	92	93	94	95	96	97	98	99	100

Reteach I

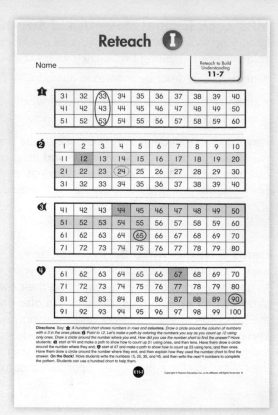

Name _____

Reteach to Build Understanding 11-7

Directions Say: ★ A hundred chart shows numbers in rows and **columns**. Draw a circle around the column of numbers with a 3 in the ones place; ❷ Point to 12. Let's make a path by coloring the numbers you say as you count up 12 using only ones. Draw a circle around the number where you end. How did you use the number chart to find the answer? Have students: ❸ start at 44 and make a path to show how to count up 21 using ones, and then tens. Have them draw a circle around the number where they end; ❹ start at 67 and make a path to show how to count up 23 using tens, and then ones. Have them draw a circle around the number where they end, and then explain how they used the number chart to find the answer. **On the Back!** Have students write the numbers 15, 25, 35, and 45, and then write the next 4 numbers to complete the pattern. Students can use a hundred chart to help them.

R 11-7   Copyright © Pearson Education, Inc., or its affiliates. All Rights Reserved. K

On-Level and Advanced Activity Centers O A

Center Games

Students work in pairs and count by ones, and then tens using the hundred chart. Advanced level students fill in any missing numbers. Students discuss the decade numbers being counted both in ones and tens.

★ On-Level

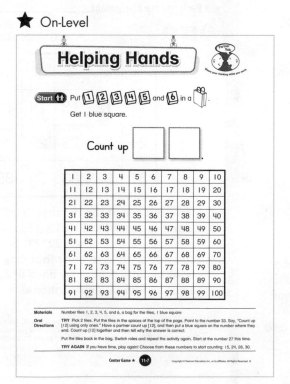

★★ Advanced

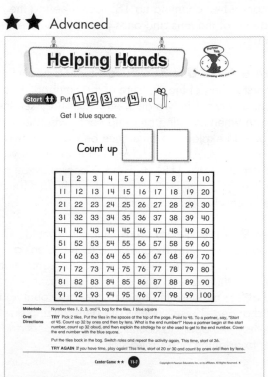

TIMING
The time allocated to Step 3 will depend on the teacher's instructional decisions and differentiation routines.

15–30 min

PEARSON
realize
PearsonRealize.com

 Help   Tools   Games

Technology Center

Tools

Games

Math Tools and Math Games

A link to a specific math tools activity or math game to use with this lesson is provided at PearsonRealize.com.

Name _____

Help Tools Games

Homework & Practice 11-7
Look For and Use Structure

Another Look!

61	62	63	64	65	66	67	68	69	70
71	72	73	74	75	76	77	78	79	80
81	82	83	84	85	86	87	88	89	90
91	92	93	94	95	96	97	98	99	100

61	62	63	64	65	66	67	68	69	70
71	72	73	74	75	76	77	78	79	80
81	82	83	84	85	86	87	88	89	90
91	92	93	94	95	96	97	98	99	100

HOME ACTIVITY Using a number chart from this lesson, give your child a start number, and then ask him or her to count up (up to 30 numbers) and tell where he or she ends. He or she should use the number chart and count by ones, by tens and then ones, or by ones and then tens. For example, your child starts at 84, counts up 11 by tens and then ones (84, 94, 95), and ends on 95.

1

1	2	3	4	5	6	7	8	9	10
11	12	13	14	15	16	17	18	19	20
21	22	23	24	25	26	27	28	29	30
31	(32)	33	34	35	36	37	38	39	40

2

41	42	43	44	45	46	47	48	49	50
51	52	53	54	55	56	57	58	59	(60)
61	62	63	64	65	66	67	68	69	70
71	72	73	74	75	76	77	78	79	80

Directions Say: *Make a path to count up 25 from 72 by tens and ones. First count up by tens and then ones. Then count up by ones and then tens. Draw a circle around the number where you end.* Have students: ★ *start at 19 and make a path to show how to count up 13 using only ones. Have them draw a circle around the number where they end, and then explain how they used the number chart to find the answer;* ② *start at 41 and make a path to show how to count up 19 using tens and ones. Have them draw a circle around the number where they end, and then explain how they used the number chart to find the answer.*

© Performance Assessment _____

3 **4** **5**

Check students' work.

61	62	63	64	65	66	67	68	69	70
71	72	73	74	75	76	77	78	79	80
81	82	83	84	85	86	(87)	88	89	90
91	92	93	94	95	96	97	98	99	100

3. There are 2 tens in 25.
4. Students should explain that they would move down the column to count by tens, and then move right across the row to count by ones.
5. Students should explain that they would still end on 25. Whether they count by tens or by ones first, they will end on the same number.

Directions Read the problem aloud. Then have students use multiple math practices to solve the problem. Say: *Start at 62 and count up 25 in any way you choose. Make a path to show how you counted, and then draw a circle around the number where you ended.* **MP.6 Be Precise** *How many tens are in 25?* **MP.7 Use Structure** *How would you use the number chart to help you count first by tens and then by ones?* **MP.8 Generalize** *What number would you end on if you counted by ones first and then by tens? How do you know you are correct if you did NOT count again?*

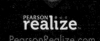

Games

FLUENCY PRACTICE ACTIVITY

Students practice fluently adding and subtracting within 5 during a partner activity that reinforces mathematical practices.

ⓒ Common Core Standards

Content Standard K.OA.A.5 Fluently add and subtract within 5.

Mathematical Practices MP.3, MP.6, MP.7, MP.8

Getting Started Ask students to work with a partner. Tell them to record their matches on their own page. Go over the directions. Both students should solve each problem and record their work. Tell students to take turns identifying the match.

As Students Do the Activity Remind students that each clue can be matched with only one problem. Some students may find all of the answers first and then match the clues. Allow this strategy as it provides the same fluency practice.

Another Activity Have students work together to write a new set of clues for the problems on the page. Ask them to record the new words on a separate sheet of paper.

Extra Challenge *Create your own Find a Match activity. Use the same clue letters on your page. Write a new problem for each clue. Then trade your activity with your partner and complete your partner's Find a Match activity.*

Steps to Fluency Success To ensure all students achieve fluency, see pages 431E–431H for additional resources including practice/assessment masters on fluency subskills. You can also use the ExamView® CD-ROM to generate worksheets with multiple-choice or free-response items on fluency subskills.

 Online Game The Game Center at PearsonRealize.com provides opportunities for fluency practice.

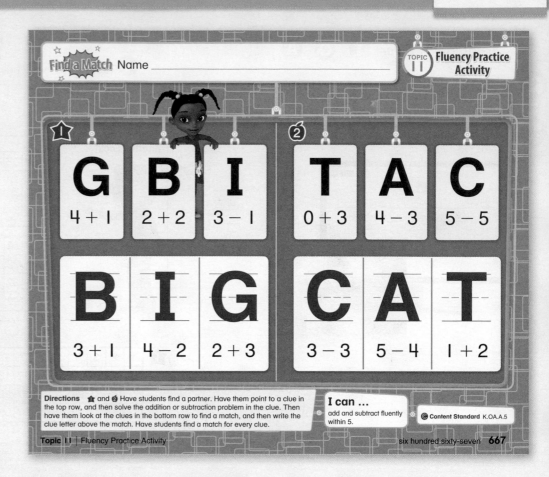

VOCABULARY REVIEW

Glossary Games

1	2	3	4	5	6	7	8	9	10
11	12	13	14	15	16	17	18	19	20
21	22	23	24	25	26	27	28	29	30
31	32	33	34	35	36	37	38	39	40
41	42	43	44	45	46	47	48	49	50
51	52	53	54	55	56	57	58	59	60
61	62	63	64	65	66	67	68	69	70
71	72	73	74	75	76	77	78	79	80
81	82	83	84	85	86	87	88	89	90
91	92	93	94	95	96	97	98	99	100

Directions Understand Vocabulary Have students: ⭐ draw a circle around the part of the number in the orange column that is the **ones** place; ❷ draw a circle around the part of the number in the blue column that is the **tens** place; ❸ color the **decade** numbers yellow.

668 six hundred sixty-eight   © Pearson Education, Inc. K   **Topic 11** | Vocabulary Review

VOCABULARY REVIEW

Students review vocabulary words used in the topic.

Oral Language Before students do the page, you might reinforce oral language through a class discussion involving one or more of the following activities.

- Have students define the terms in their own words.

- Have students say math sentences or math questions that use the words.

- Play a "What's My Word?" guessing game in which you or a student thinks about one of the words and says a clue that others listen to before they guess the word.

- Play a "Right or Wrong?" game in which you or a student says a sentence that uses one of the words correctly or incorrectly. Then others say "right" or "wrong."

Writing in Math After students do the page, you might further reinforce writing in math by doing one or more of the following activities.

- Tell students to close their books. Then you say the words and have students write them. Students trade papers to check whether the words are spelled correctly.

- Have students work with a partner. Each partner writes a math question that uses one of the words. Then they trade papers and give a written answer that uses the word.

 Online Game The Game Center at PearsonRealize.com includes a vocabulary game that students can access any time.

RETEACHING
COUNT NUMBERS TO 100

RtI	Item Analysis for Diagnosis and Intervention			
Reteaching Sets	**© Standards**	**Student Book Lessons**	**MDIS**	
Set A	K.CC.A.1	11-1	A12	
Set B	K.CC.A.1, K.CC.A.2	11-4	A13	
Set C	K.CC.A.2	11-5	A13	
Set D	K.CC.A.1, K.CC.A.2	11-6	A13	

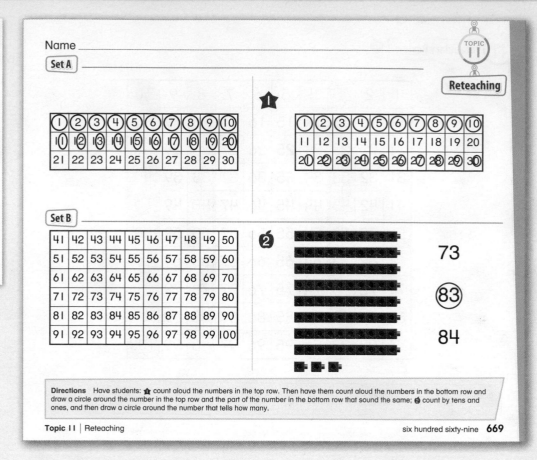

Name

Set A

Reteaching

Set B

Directions Have students: ★ count aloud the numbers in the top row. Then have them count aloud the numbers in the bottom row and draw a circle around the number in the top row and the part of the number in the bottom row that sound the same; ❷ count by tens and ones, and then draw a circle around the number that tells how many.

Topic 11 | Reteaching

six hundred sixty-nine **669**

Set C

1	2	3	4	5	6	7	8	9	10
11	12	13	14	15	16	17	18	19	20
21	22	23	24	25	26	27	28	29	30
31	32	33	34	35	36	37	38	39	40
41	42	43	44	45	46	47	48	49	50

51	52	53	54	55	56	57	58	59	60
61	62	63	64	65	66	67	68	69	70
71	72	73	74	75	76	77	78	79	80
81	82	83	84	85	86	87	88	89	90
91	92	93	94	95	96	97	98	99	100

Set D

1	2	3	4	5	6	7	8	9	10
11	12	13	14	15	16	17	18	19	20
21	22	23	24	25	26	27	28	29	30
			34	35	36	37	38	39	40
41	42	43	44	45	46	47	48	49	50

31   32   33

51	52	53	54	55	56	57	58	59	60
61	62	63	64	65	66	67	68	69	70
71	72	73	74	75		77	78	79	80
81	82	83	84	85		87	88	89	90
91	92	93	94	95		97	98	99	100

75   76   77
76   86   90
76   86   96

Directions Have students: ❸ color the boxes of the numbers as they count aloud by ones, starting at the yellow box and ending at the red box; ❹ count forward, and then draw a circle around the row that shows the missing set of numbers.

© Pearson Education, Inc. K   **Topic 11** | Reteaching

Response to Intervention

Ongoing Intervention
1 RtI
- Lessons with guiding questions to assess understanding
- Support to prevent misconceptions and to reteach

Strategic Intervention
2 RtI
- Targeted to small groups who need more support
- Easy to implement

Intensive Intervention
3 RtI
- Instruction to accelerate progress
- Instruction focused on foundational skills

TOPIC ASSESSMENT
COUNT NUMBERS TO 100

ANSWERING THE TOPIC ESSENTIAL QUESTION

How can numbers to 100 be counted using a hundred chart?

Restate the Topic Essential Question from the Topic Opener or project it from the Student's Edition eText.

Ask students to answer the Essential Question (verbally or in writing) and give examples that support their answers. The following are key elements of the answer to the Essential Question. Be sure these are made explicit when discussing students' answers.

- Move right on a hundred chart to count by 1s.
  Example: What number is between 37 and 39? [38 is in between 37 and 39.]

- A quick way to count groups of objects is to count by 10s, and then count on by 1s.
  Example: What is a quick way to count 53 connecting cubes? Make 5 groups of 10 cubes. [Count the groups by 10s, and then count on by 1s: 10, 20, 30, 40, 50, 51, 52, 53.]

- Number words follow patterns starting at 20.
  Example: Which number comes next in the sequence: thirty-two, thirty-three, thirty-four, _____? The number words *two*, *three*, and *four* increase by 1. [The next number is thirty-five, or 35.]

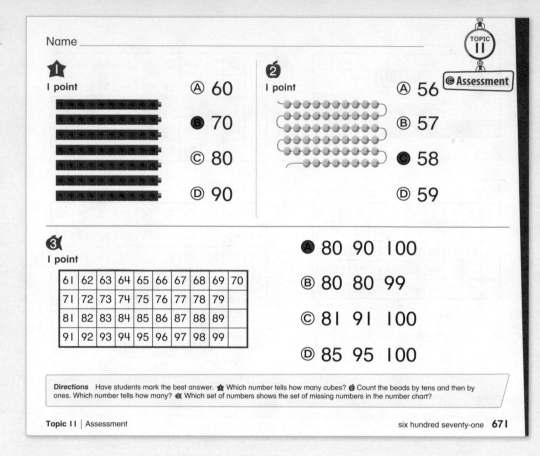

Name _____

⊜ Assessment

1 I point
Ⓐ 60
Ⓑ **70**
Ⓒ 80
Ⓓ 90

2 I point
Ⓐ 56
Ⓑ 57
Ⓒ **58**
Ⓓ 59

3 I point

61	62	63	64	65	66	67	68	69	70
71	72	73	74	75	76	77	78	79	
81	82	83	84	85	86	87	88	89	
91	92	93	94	95	96	97	98	99	

Ⓐ **80 90 100**
Ⓑ 80 80 99
Ⓒ 81 91 100
Ⓓ 85 95 100

Directions Have students mark the best answer. ⭐ Which number tells how many cubes? 🍎 Count the beads by tens and then by ones. Which number tells how many? 🎄 Which set of numbers shows the set of missing numbers in the number chart?

Topic 11 | Assessment

six hundred seventy-one **671**

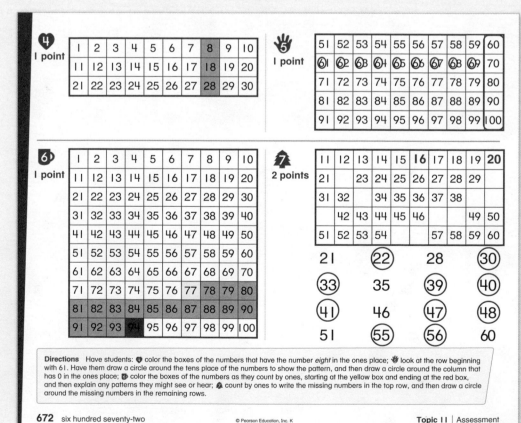

4 I point

1	2	3	4	5	6	7	**8**	9	10
11	12	13	14	15	16	17	**18**	19	20
21	22	23	24	25	26	27	**28**	29	30

5 I point

51	52	53	54	55	56	57	58	59	60
61	62	63	64	65	66	67	68	69	70
71	72	73	74	75	76	77	78	79	80
81	82	83	84	85	86	87	88	89	90
91	92	93	94	95	96	97	98	99	100

6 I point

1	2	3	4	5	6	7	8	9	10
11	12	13	14	15	16	17	18	19	20
21	22	23	24	25	26	27	28	29	30
31	32	33	34	35	36	37	38	39	40
41	42	43	44	45	46	47	48	49	50
51	52	53	54	55	56	57	58	59	60
61	62	63	64	65	66	67	68	69	70
71	72	73	74	75	76	77	78	79	80
81	82	83	84	85	86	87	88	89	90
91	92	93	94	95	96	97	98	99	100

7 2 points

11	12	13	14	15	**16**	17	18	19	**20**
21		23	24	25	26	27	28	29	
31	32		34	35	36	37	38		
	42	43	44	45	46			49	50
51	52	53	54			57	58	59	60

21   ㉒   28   ㉚
㉝   35   ㊰   ㊵
㊶   46   ㊼   ㊽
51   �55   ㊴   60

Directions Have students: ❹ color the boxes of the numbers that have the number *eight* in the ones place; ✋ look at the row beginning with 61. Have them draw a circle around the tens place of the numbers to show the pattern, and then draw a circle around the column that has 0 in the ones place; ❻ color the boxes of the numbers as they count by ones, starting at the yellow box and ending at the red box, and then explain any patterns they might see or hear; 🎄 count by ones to write the missing numbers in the top row, and then draw a circle around the missing numbers in the remaining rows.

672 six hundred seventy-two

© Pearson Education, Inc. K

Topic 11 | Assessment

ONLINE TOPIC ASSESSMENT

An auto-scored Topic Assessment is provided at PearsonRealize.com.

EXAMVIEW® TEST GENERATOR

ExamView can be used to create a blackline-master Topic Assessment with multiple-choice and free-response items.

Assessment

Topic Assessment Masters

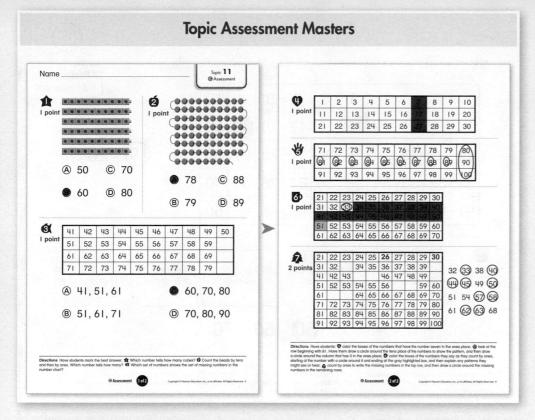

Item Analysis for Diagnosis and Intervention

Item	© Standards	DOK	MDIS
1	K.CC.A.1	1	A16
2	K.CC.A.1	1	A13
3	K.CC.A.1, K.CC.A.2	1	A16
4	K.CC.A.1, MP.7	1	A12, A13
5	K.CC.A.1, MP.7	2	A13
6	K.CC.A.2	1	A13
7	K.CC.A.2	2	A13

The Topic Assessment Masters assess the same content item for item as the Topic Assessment in the Student's Edition.

Scoring Guide

Item	Points	Topic Assessment (Student's Edition and Masters)
1	1	Correct choice is selected.
2	1	Correct choice is selected.
3	1	Correct choice is selected.
4	1	Correct numbers are colored.
5	1	Correct digits and correct column are circled.
6	1	Correct numbers are colored.
7	2	Correct numbers are written in chart and circled.
	1	Correct numbers are written in chart or circled.

Scoring Guide

Item	Points	Topic Performance Assessment in the Student's Edition
1	1	Correct number is circled.
2	1	Correct number is circled.
3	2	Correct circles are made around groups of crackers and correct number is circled.
	1	Correct circles made around crackers or correct number is circled.
4	1	Correct set of numbers is circled.
5	2	Correctly shows the path to count up 18 in any way and clear explanation is given.
	1	Correctly shows path, but explanation is not clear.

RtI Item Analysis for Diagnosis and Intervention

Item	© Standards	DOK	MDIS
1	K.CC.A.1, K.CC.A.2, MP.7	2	A13
2	K.CC.A.1	2	A16
3	K.CC.A.1, K.CC.A.2, MP.4	3	A13
4	K.CC.A.2, MP.7	2	A13
5	K.CC.A.1, K.CC.A.2, MP.3	3	A13

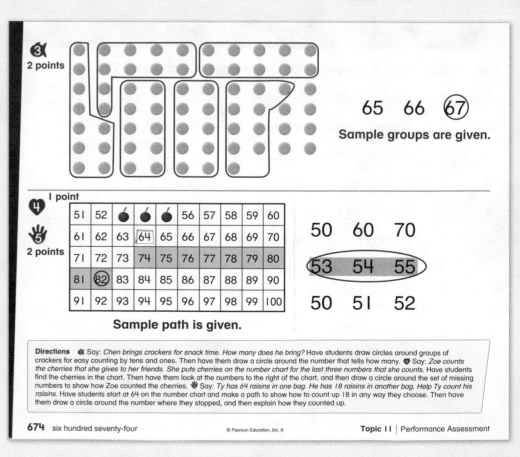

Name _____

TOPIC 11

© Performance Assessment

⭐ 1 point

1	2	3	4	5	6	7	8	9	10
11	12	13	14	15	16	17	18	●	20
21	22	23	24	25	26	27	28	29	30
31	32	33	34	35	36	37	38	39	40
41	42	43	44	45	46	47	48	49	50

9 ⑲ 20

✌ 2 1 point

⑤⓪ 60 70

Directions **School Snacks** Say: *It's snack time for the Kindergarten class!* ⭐ Say: *Keisha puts a grape on the hundred chart to show how many grapes she has in her snack bag.* Have students look at the numbers that come just before and just after the grape, and then at the numbers that are just above and just below it. Have them draw a circle around the missing number that tells how many grapes Keisha has. ✌ Have students count the pretzels that Liam and his friends share for their snack. Have them draw a circle around the number that tells how many. If needed, students can use the hundred chart to help.

Topic 11 | Performance Assessment   six hundred seventy-three **673**

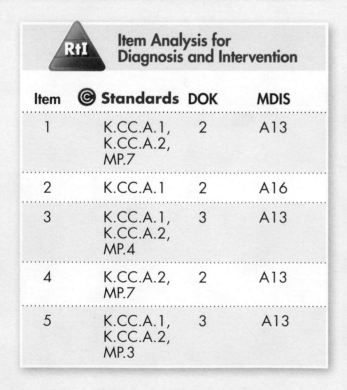

✊ 3 2 points

65 66 ㊻⑦

Sample groups are given.

✋ 4 1 point / ✋ 5 2 points

51	52	●	●	●	56	57	58	59	60
61	62	63	[64]	65	66	67	68	69	70
71	72	73	74	75	76	77	78	79	80
81	⑧②	83	84	85	86	87	88	89	90
91	92	93	94	95	96	97	98	99	100

50 60 70

（53 54 55）

50 51 52

Sample path is given.

Directions ✊ Say: *Chen brings crackers for snack time. How many does he bring?* Have students draw circles around groups of crackers for easy counting by tens and ones. Then have them draw a circle around the number that tells how many. ✋ Say: *Zoe counts the cherries that she gives to her friends. She puts cherries on the number chart for the last three numbers that she counts.* Have students find the cherries in the chart. Then have them look at the numbers to the right of the chart, and then draw a circle around the set of missing numbers to show how Zoe counted the cherries. ✋ Say: *Ty has 64 raisins in one bag. He has 18 raisins in another bag. Help Ty count his raisins.* Have students start at 64 on the number chart and make a path to show how to count up 18 in any way they choose. Then have them draw a circle around the number where they stopped, and then explain how they counted up.

Topic Performance Assessment Masters

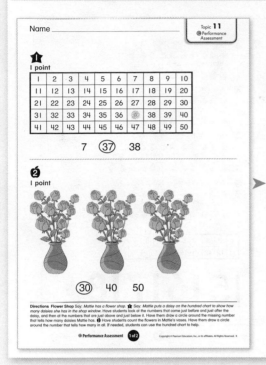

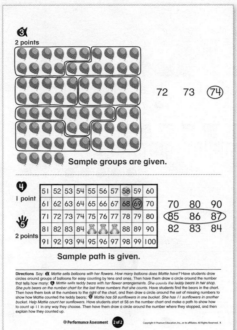

Item Analysis for Diagnosis and Intervention

RtI

Item	© Standards	DOK	MDIS
1	K.CC.A.1, K.CC.A.2, MP.7	2	A13
2	K.CC.A.1	2	A16
3	K.CC.A.1, K.CC.A.2, MP.4	3	A13
4	K.CC.A.2, MP.7	2	A13
5	K.CC.A.1, K.CC.A.2, MP.3	3	A13

Scoring Guide

Item	Points	Topic Performance Assessment Masters
1	1	Correct number is circled.
2	1	Correct number is circled.
3	2	Correct circles are made around the groups of balloons and correct number is circled.
	1	Correct circles are made around the groups of balloons or correct number is circled.
4	1	Correct set of numbers is circled.
5	2	Correctly shows the path to count up 11 in any way and clear explanation is given.
	1	Correctly shows path, but explanation is not clear.

Topics 1–11 Cumulative/Benchmark Assessment

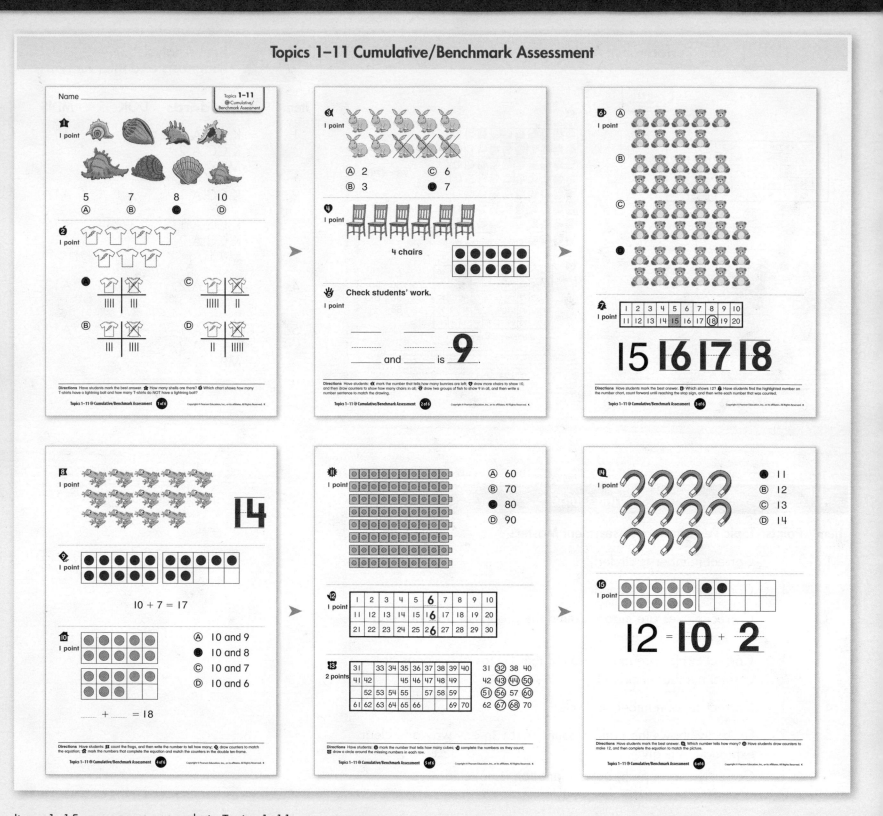

Items 1–15 assess content taught in Topics 1–11.

ONLINE CUMULATIVE/BENCHMARK ASSESSMENT

An auto-scored Cumulative/Benchmark Assessment is provided at PearsonRealize.com.

RtI   Item Analysis for Diagnosis and Intervention

Item	© Standards	DOK	MDIS	Item	© Standards	DOK	MDIS	Item	© Standards	DOK	MDIS
1	K.CC.B.4a	1	A3	7	K.CC.A.2	1	A19	12	K.CC.A.1, MP.7	1	A13
2	K.MD.B.3	1	D48	8	K.CC.B.5, K.CC.A.3	1	A10	13	K.CC.A.1, K.CC.A.2, MP.6	2	A13
3	K.OA.A.1	1	B8	9	K.NBT.A.1, MP.2	1	A18, B28				
4	K.OA.A.4	1	B11					14	K.CC.B.5	1	A3
5	K.OA.A.3, MP.4	2	B10	10	K.NBT.A.1	1	B28	15	K.NBT.A.1, MP.4	2	B15, B17
6	K.CC.B.5	1	A8	11	K.CC.A.1	1	A16				

For items worth 1 point, responses should be completely correct to get a score of 1 point. For other items, use the Scoring Guide below.

Scoring Guide

Item	Points	Topics 1–11 Cumulative/Benchmark Assessment
13	2	All 9 missing numbers are circled.
	1	6–8 missing numbers are circled.

TOPIC 12

ADDITIONAL CLUSTER K.G.A
MATH BACKGROUND: FOCUS

F C R FOCUS   COHERENCE   RIGOR

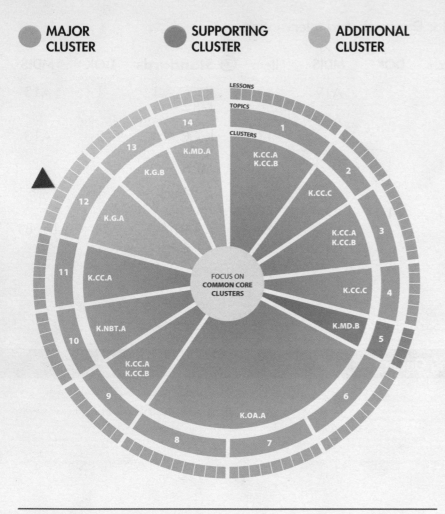

● MAJOR CLUSTER   ● SUPPORTING CLUSTER   ● ADDITIONAL CLUSTER

TOPIC 12 Identify and Describe Shapes

TOPIC 12 FOCUSES ON

© ADDITIONAL CLUSTER K.G.A

Identify and describe shapes (squares, circles, triangles, rectangles, hexagons, cubes, cones, cylinders, and spheres).

Content Focus in enVisionmath 2.0

Topic 12 formally introduces many geometric ideas by asking students to: (1) identify shapes as two-dimensional (flat) or three-dimensional (solid), (2) name squares, circles, triangles, rectangles, hexagons, cubes, cones, cylinders, and spheres regardless of orientation and size, and (3) use terms such as "above," "below," "beside," "next to," "in front of," and "behind" to describe the relative position of shapes in their environments.

TWO- AND THREE-DIMENSIONAL SHAPES

- **Flat or Solid** In Lesson 12-1, students see a variety of geometric shapes and real-world objects and sort them by indicating if they are flat (two-dimensional) or solid (three-dimensional). (K.G.A.3)

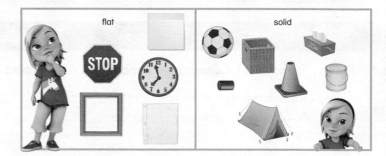

NAME SHAPES

- **Circles and Triangles** In Lesson 12-2, students identify circles (round flat shapes) and triangles (flat shapes with 3 sides and 3 vertices). (K.G.A.2)

Content Focus in enVisionmath 2.0 (continued)

- **Squares and Other Rectangles** In Lesson 12-3, students are exposed to the idea that a shape can belong to two categories when they learn that a square is also a rectangle. Students identify these shapes regardless of orientation or size. Students are at a "visual" level of geometric thinking (e.g., a rectangle "looks like a door") and moving to a "descriptive" level where they perceive properties (e.g., a triangle has 3 sides). (K.G.A.2)

Color the rectangles. Then mark an X on each rectangle that is also a square.

- **Hexagons** In Lesson 12-4, students identify hexagons regardless of orientation or size. (K.G.A.2)

Color the hexagons.

- **Names of Solids** In Lesson 12-5, students name three-dimensional shapes, such as cylinders, cones, spheres, and cubes, regardless of orientation. (K.G.A.2)

Name the solid figure on the left. Draw a circle around the solid figure on the right that is the same shape.

- **Shapes in the Environment** In Lesson 12-6, students name shapes for both flat and solid objects shown in a real-world environment. (K.G.A.1, K.G.A.2, K.G.A.3)

DESCRIBE RELATIVE POSITIONS OF SHAPES

- **Positional Language** In Lesson 12-7, students describe the relative positions of shapes in an environment using positional language such as "above," "below," "next to," "beside," "in front of," and "behind." (K.G.A.1)

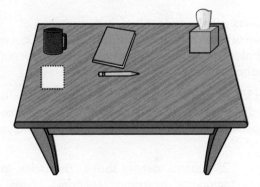

Mark an X on the object next to the pencil that looks like a rectangle. Draw an object that looks like a square in front of the mug.

- **Professional Development Videos** Topic Overview Videos and Listen and Look For Lesson Videos present additional important information about the content of this cluster.

Content Coherence in enVisionmath2.0

Students learn best when ideas are connected in a coherent curriculum. This coherence is achieved through various types of connections including connections within clusters, across clusters, across domains, and across grades.

BIG IDEAS IN GRADES K–6

Big Ideas are the conceptual underpinnings of **enVision**math**2.0** and provide conceptual cohesion of the content. Big Ideas connect Essential Understandings throughout the program.

A Big Idea that connects the work in this cluster is that two- and three-dimensional geometric objects with or without curved surfaces can be described, classified, and analyzed based on their attributes.

In Topic 12, students identify shapes as circles, triangles, squares, rectangles, hexagons, cylinders, cones, spheres, and cubes based on their attributes, and students see how a given shape can be classified in more than one category.

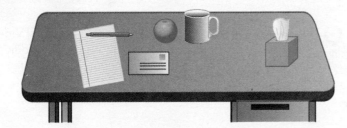

Point to objects in the picture and name their shape. Draw a circle around objects that are flat. Then mark an X on objects that are solid.

For a complete list of Big Ideas, see pages 110–111 in the *Teacher's Edition Program Overview.*

LOOK BACK

How does Topic 12 connect to what students learned earlier?

BEFORE ENTERING SCHOOL

- **Two- and Three-Dimensional Shapes** Students have early experiences with flat and solid shapes. Typically, students have some experience naming shapes such as squares, spheres, and cubes. However, many students enter school with a wealth of experience working with and exploring two- and three-dimensional shapes.

EARLIER IN GRADE K

- **Count Objects** In Topics 1, 2, 3, and 4, students learned to count and conserve the cardinality of sets of objects. This understanding of number is critical when counting sides and vertices of shapes. (K.CC.B.4a, K.CC.B.5)

- **Sort Objects** In Topic 5, students sorted items in a data set based on attributes. This laid the foundation for students to sort and name geometric shapes based on attributes. (K.MD.B.3)

Draw a circle around the animals that have feathers. Then mark an X on the animals that do NOT have feathers.

TOPIC 12

How is content connected within Topic 12?

- **Classify and Further Classify** In Lesson 12-1, students classify shapes as flat or solid. (K.G.A.3) This lays a foundation for further classifying flat shapes in Lessons 12-2, 12-3, and 12-4, and for further classifying solid shapes in Lesson 12-5. (K.G.A.2)

- **Pull Ideas Together** Lesson 12-6 pulls ideas together as students describe shapes for objects in an environment. They use names of shapes and identify the shapes as flat or solid. (K.G.A.1, K.G.A.2, K.G.A.3) Lesson 12-7 pulls ideas together as students describe the relative positions of objects and name the shapes of the objects. (K.G.A.1, K.G.A.2)

Point to objects in the picture and name their shape. Then draw a circle around objects that are flat, and mark an X on objects that are solid.

- **Name Shapes Regardless of Orientation or Size** A connecting thread throughout Topic 12 is having students name shapes based on attributes, regardless of the orientation or overall size of the shapes. (K.G.A.2)

- **Identify and Analyze** Lessons 12-2, 12-3, 12-4, and 12-5 also develop Additional Cluster K.G.B by asking students to analyze two- and three-dimensional shapes, in different sizes and orientations, using informal language to describe their parts (e.g., number of sides and vertices) and other attributes (e.g., having sides of equal length). (K.G.B.4)

LOOK AHEAD

How does Topic 12 connect to what students will learn later?

LATER IN GRADE K

- **Analyze, Compare, Create, and Compose Shapes** In Topic 13, students will name shapes in order to help them analyze, compare, create, and compose shapes. (K.G.B.4)

What solid figures do you see?
What does an object have to look like to roll?
Why can these figures be stacked?
Which solid figures slide?

GRADE 1

- **Identify Defining and Non-Defining Attributes** In Topic 14, students will use what they have learned about attributes of shapes to help them distinguish between defining attributes (e.g., triangles are closed and three-sided) versus non-defining attributes (e.g., color, orientation, overall size). (1.G.A.1)

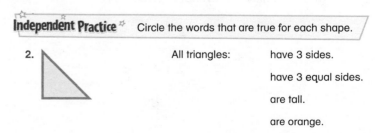

Independent Practice   Circle the words that are true for each shape.

2.

All triangles: have 3 sides.

have 3 equal sides.

are tall.

are orange.

Content Rigor in enVisionmath2.0

A rigorous curriculum emphasizes conceptual understanding, procedural skill and fluency, and applications.

CONCEPTUAL UNDERSTANDING

- **Two-Dimensional and Three-Dimensional Shapes**
  The distinction between two- and three-dimensional shapes is a crucial concept in Topic 12 because students first decide if a shape is flat or solid before looking at other attributes. (K.G.A.3)

    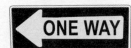

Mark an X on the objects that are solid. Then draw a circle around the objects that are flat.

- **Name Shapes Regardless of Orientation or Size**
  Topic 12 introduces students to the concept that names of geometric shapes are based on attributes of the shapes. Topic 12 also introduces students to the concept that the overall size of a shape and the orientation of the shape (how it is positioned) are not defining attributes (not affecting the name of the shape). (K.G.A.2)

- **Relative Positions of Shapes** Topic 12 reinforces spatial reasoning by having students describe the relative positions of objects. For example, if a cylinder is in front of a sphere, the sphere also is behind the cylinder. (K.G.A.1)

PROCEDURAL SKILL AND FLUENCY

There are no standards in this cluster that call for fluency, and there are no procedural skills taught in Topic 12.

APPLICATIONS

- **Real-World Applications** Topic 12 shows flat and solid geometric figures represented by real-world objects, such as street signs, household objects, classroom objects, toys, food containers, and sports equipment. (K.G.A)

Point to objects in the picture and name each shape. Draw a circle around the objects that look like a cylinder. Mark an X on objects that look like a cone.

Connecting Math Practices and Content Standards in enVisionmath2.0

Math practices and content standards are connected within all lessons including the lessons that focus on math practices.

MATH PRACTICES WITHIN LESSONS

- **MP.1 Make sense of problems and persevere in solving them.**

  Students plan out what they will draw before they begin drawing shapes in an environment, and persevere by considering each position separately. (e.g., p. 723, Item 2)

- **MP.2 Reason abstractly and quantitatively.**

  Students use reasoning when they consider attributes to decide what a shape is. (e.g., p. 699, Item 3)

- **MP.3 Construct viable arguments and critique the reasoning of others.**

  Students justify whether a real-world object resembles a two-dimensional or three-dimensional shape. (e.g., p. 687, Items 2–4)

- **MP.4 Model with mathematics.**

  Students model with mathematics by looking for and finding objects in their classroom that are shaped like geometric solids. (e.g., p. 709, Solve and Share)

- **MP.5 Use appropriate tools strategically.**

  Students use pattern blocks to help draw shapes. (e.g., p. 706, Item 8)

- **MP.6 Attend to precision.**

  Students use clear language and precise definitions to describe the relative position of shapes in their environment. (e.g., p. 727, Solve and Share)

- **MP.7 Look for and make use of structure.**

  Students describe, identify, and compare rectangles and squares based on their attributes. (e.g., p. 697, Solve and Share)

- **MP.8 Look for and express regularity in repeated reasoning.**

  Students use repeated reasoning to identify different forms that a particular shape can have while still keeping its defining attributes. (e.g., p. 700, Items 6–9)

LESSON THAT FOCUSES ON MATH PRACTICES

- **Lesson 12-8** This lesson focuses on MP.6. Students use precise language to describe the position of shapes in the environment. This lesson requires students to use mathematical names to describe three-dimensional shapes.

Thinking Habits

Am I using numbers, units, and symbols correctly?

Am I using the correct definitions?

Is my answer clear?

Revisit the information about MP.6 in these other resources:

- **Math Practices and Problem Solving Handbook** before Topic 1; includes Math Practices Proficiency Rubrics.

- **Math Practices Posters** to display in your classroom

- **Math Practices Animations,** one for each math practice, available at PearsonRealize.com.

TOPIC 12

ADDITIONAL CLUSTER K.G.A

DIFFERENTIATED INSTRUCTION

 Intervention   **On-Level**   **Advanced**

PEARSON realize
PearsonRealize.com

Learn Assessment Tools Games

Ongoing Intervention

 During the core lesson, monitor progress, reteach as needed, and extend students' thinking.

Guiding Questions

- **In the Teacher's Edition** Guiding questions are used to monitor understanding during instruction.

 Online Guiding Questions Guiding questions are also in the online Visual Learning Animation Plus.

Error Intervention: If... then...
This feature in the Teacher's Edition is provided during Guided Practice. It spotlights common errors and gives suggestions for addressing them.

Reteaching
Reteaching sets are at the end of the topic in the Student's Edition. They provide additional examples, reminders, and practice. Use these sets as needed before students do the Independent Practice.

Higher Order Thinking
These problems require students to think more deeply about the rich, conceptual knowledge developed in the lesson.

Strategic Intervention

 At the end of the lesson, assess to identify students' strengths and needs and then provide appropriate support.

Quick Check

 In the Student's Edition Assess the lesson using 2-3 items checked in the Teacher's Edition.

 Online Quick Check You can also assess the lesson using 5 online, machine-scored items.

Intervention Activity
Teachers work with struggling students.

Reteach to Build Understanding
This is a page of guided reteaching.

Technology Center

 Digital Math Tools Activities reinforce the lesson content or previously taught content using a suite of digital math tools.

 Online Games provide practice on the lesson content or previously taught content.

Homework and Practice
Use the leveled assignment to provide differentiated homework and practice.

Additional resources to support differentiated instruction for on-level and advanced students include:

On-Level and Advanced Activity Centers

- **Center Games** are provided in on-level and advanced versions.

- **Math and Science Activity** is related to the topic science theme introduced at the start of the topic.

- **Problem-Solving Reading Mat** is used with a lesson-specific activity.

Intensive Intervention

 As needed, provide more instruction that is on or below grade level for students who are struggling.

Math Diagnosis and Intervention System 2.0

- **Diagnosis** Use the diagnostic tests in the system. Also, use the item analysis charts given with program assessments at the start of a grade or topic, or at the end of a topic, group of topics, or the year.

- **Intervention Lessons** These two-page lessons include guided instruction followed by practice. The system includes lessons below, on, and above grade level.

- **Teacher Support** Teacher Notes provide the support needed to conduct a short lesson. The lesson focuses on vocabulary, concept development, and practice. The Teacher's Guide contains individual and class record forms and correlations to Student's Edition lessons.

Resources for Fluency Success

- A variety of print and digital resources are provided to ensure success on Common Core fluency standards. See Steps to Fluency Success on pages 431E–431H.

PEARSON
realize.
PearsonRealize.com

Glossary   Games   Story   Story

English Language Learners

Provide ELL support through visual learning throughout the program, ELL instruction in every lesson, and additional ideas in an ELL Toolkit.

Visual Learning
The visual learning that is infused in **enVision**math**2.0** provides support for English language learners. This support includes a Visual Learning Animation Plus and a Visual Learning Bridge for each lesson.

English Language Learners Instruction
Lessons provide instruction for English language learners at Beginning, Intermediate, and Advanced levels of English proficiency.

English Language Learners Toolkit
This resource provides professional development and resources for supporting English language learners.

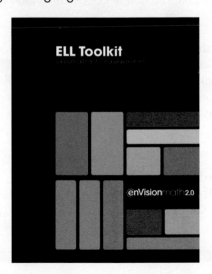

ELL Toolkit

enVision math 2.0

Math Vocabulary

Build math vocabulary using the vocabulary cards, vocabulary activities, vocabulary review, and glossary plus the online glossary and vocabulary game.

My Word Cards
Vocabulary cards for a topic are provided in the Student's Edition. Use the cards with students to study and learn new vocabulary words.

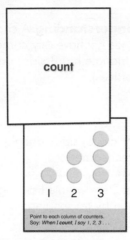

count

Point to each column of counters.
Say: *When I count, I say 1, 2, 3 . . .*

Vocabulary Activities
The Teacher's Edition provides vocabulary activities at the start of topics. These include activities for vocabulary in My Word Cards and/or activities for vocabulary in Review What You Know.

Vocabulary Review
A page of vocabulary review is provided at the end of each topic. It reviews vocabulary used in the topic.

Glossary
A glossary is provided at the back of the Student's Edition.

Animated Glossary
 An online, bilingual, animated glossary uses motion and sound to build understanding of math vocabulary.

Online Vocabulary Game
 On online vocabulary game is available in the Game Center.

Math and Reading

Connect reading and math using a data-filled reading mat for the topic with accompanying activity masters and guide. Also use topic interactive math stories.

Problem-Solving Reading Mats
There is a large, beautiful mat for each topic. At the start of the topic, help students become familiar with the mat and the vocabulary used by reading the mat aloud as students follow along. Use the Problem-Solving Reading Activity Guide for suggestions about how to use the mat.

Problem-Solving Reading Activity
At the end of some lessons, a Problem-Solving Reading Activity provides a page of math problems to solve by using the data on the mat.

Interactive Math Stories
  An interactive math story provides an introduction to each topic. The story is available as an online story book and an animated story at PearsonRealize.com as well as a color-in, take-home story in the Teacher's Resource Masters.

Lesson 12-1

TWO-DIMENSIONAL (2-D) AND THREE-DIMENSIONAL (3-D) SHAPES pp. 685–690

Ⓒ **Content Standard K.G.A.3**
Mathematical Practices MP.3, MP.6, MP.7

Objective Name shapes as flat or solid.

Essential Understanding Objects have shape. Some objects, such as a sheet of paper or a photograph, are two-dimensional, or flat, shapes. Some objects, such as a ball, can, box, or jar, are three-dimensional, or solid, shapes.

Vocabulary sort, two-dimensional shape (flat), three-dimensional shape (solid)

ELL Reading: Use support from peers/teachers to enhance/confirm understanding.

Materials 2-D and 3-D Shapes (Teaching Tool 37), index cards, pencil box

On-Level and Advanced Activity Centers
• Problem-Solving Reading Mat

Lesson 12-2

CIRCLES AND TRIANGLES pp. 691–696

Ⓒ **Content Standards K.G.A.2, K.G.B.4**
Mathematical Practices MP.2, MP.5, MP.6, MP.7

Objective Identify and describe circles and triangles.

Essential Understanding A circle is round and does not have any corners (vertices). A triangle has 3 sides and 3 corners (vertices).

Vocabulary circle, side, triangle, vertex/vertices (corner)

ELL Listening: Demonstrate listening comprehension by responding to questions.

Materials Circles (Teaching Tool 32), Triangles (Teaching Tool 33), Squares (Teaching Tool 34), colored pencils, construction paper, drawing paper, blunt-tipped scissors, stapler, magazine pictures of objects with circular and triangular shapes, glue

On-Level and Advanced Activity Centers
• Center Games

Lesson 12-3

SQUARES AND OTHER RECTANGLES pp. 697–702

Ⓒ **Content Standards K.G.A.2, K.G.B.4**
Mathematical Practices MP.2, MP.6, MP.7, MP.8

Objective Identify and describe squares and other rectangles.

Essential Understanding Flat shapes called rectangles have 4 sides and 4 vertices that look the same. A rectangle looks like a door. Squares are special rectangles because their sides are all the same length.

Vocabulary rectangle, square

ELL Strategies: Use strategies when speaking, such as synonyms. **Speaking:** Share information in cooperative learning interactions.

Materials Rectangles (Teaching Tool 35), Squares (Teaching Tool 34), attribute blocks (or Teaching Tool 46), construction paper in assorted colors, glue, blunt-tipped scissors

On-Level and Advanced Activity Centers
• Center Games

LESSON RESOURCES

Digital

• Student's Edition
• Daily Common Core Review
• Reteach to Build Understanding
• Center Games
• Math and Science Activity
• Problem-Solving Reading Mat
• Problem-Solving Reading Activity

Print

Digital

• Listen and Look For PD Lesson Video
• Student's Edition eText
• Today's Challenge
• Solve & Share
• Visual Learning Animation Plus

• Animated Glossary
• Math Tools
• Quick Check
• Another Look Homework Video
• Math Games

Lesson 12-4

HEXAGONS pp. 703–708

Content Standards K.G.A.2, K.G.B.4
Mathematical Practices MP.3, MP.5, MP.6, MP.7

Objective Describe and identify hexagons.

Essential Understanding Six-sided flat shapes are called hexagons. These shapes can be found in objects made by people and in nature.

Vocabulary hexagon

ELL Strategies: Use known, accessible language to learn new/essential language in the process.

Materials Hexagons (Teaching Tool 36), pattern blocks (or Teaching Tool 41), attribute blocks (or Teaching Tool 46), paper bag

On-Level and Advanced Activity Centers
• Math and Science Activity

Lesson 12-5

SOLID FIGURES pp. 709–714

Content Standards K.G.A.2, K.G.B.4
Mathematical Practices MP.2, MP.4, MP.6, MP.7

Objective Describe and identify solid figures.

Essential Understanding Spheres, cylinders, cones, and cubes are solid figures. Many everyday objects closely approximate these figures.

Vocabulary cone, cube, cylinder, sphere

ELL Strategies: Use known, accessible language to learn new/essential language in the process. **Speaking:** Speak using content area vocabulary in context.

Materials 3-D Shapes and Real Life Objects (Teaching Tool 39), classroom objects in the shape of solid figures, geometric solids

On-Level and Advanced Activity Centers
• Center Games

Lesson 12-6

DESCRIBE SHAPES IN THE ENVIRONMENT pp. 715–720

Content Standards K.G.A.1, K.G.A.2, K.G.A.3
Mathematical Practices MP.1, MP.3, MP.6, MP.7

Objective Describe shapes in the environment.

Essential Understanding Objects have shape. Some objects look like flat shapes or solid shapes, including squares, rectangles, triangles, circles, hexagons, spheres, cubes, cylinders, and cones.

Vocabulary None

ELL Strategies: Use prior knowledge to understand meanings.

Materials Attribute blocks (or Teaching Tool 46), paper bag, ball, chart paper

On-Level and Advanced Activity Centers
• Math and Science Activity

TOPIC RESOURCES

Digital

Print

Start of Topic
• Topic Centers
• Interactive Math Story
• Math and Science Project
• Home-School Connection
• Review What You Know
• My Word Cards

End of Topic
• Fluency Practice Activity
• Vocabulary Review
• Reteaching
• Topic Assessment
• Topic Performance Assessment

Digital

Start of Topic
• Topic Overview PD Video

End of Topic
• Math Practices Animations
• Online Topic Assessment
• ExamView® Test Generator

Lesson 12-7	Lesson 12-8
DESCRIBE THE POSITION OF SHAPES IN THE ENVIRONMENT pp. 721–726	**MATH PRACTICES AND PROBLEM SOLVING: PRECISION** pp. 727–732
ⓒ Content Standard **K.G.A.1** Mathematical Practices **MP.1, MP.2, MP.3, MP.6**	ⓒ Mathematical Practices **MP.6, MP.2, MP.3** Content Standard **K.G.A.1**
Objective Describe positions of shapes in the environment.	**Objective** Describe positions of shapes in the environment.
Essential Understanding The positions of objects in relation to surrounding objects can be described using words such as *above, below, beside, in front of, behind,* and *next to.*	**Essential Understanding** Good math thinkers are careful about what they write and say, so their ideas about math are clear.
Vocabulary above, behind, below, beside, in front of, next to	**Vocabulary** none
ELL Listening: Demonstrate listening comprehension by following directions.	**ELL** Speaking: Speak using content area vocabulary in context.
Materials sticky notes, green construction paper, tape, pencil, pencil box	**Materials** Connecting cubes (or Teaching Tool 8), two-color counters (or Teaching Tool 6)
On-Level and Advanced Activity Centers • Center Games	**On-Level and Advanced Activity Centers** • Problem Solving Reading Mat

Notes

_____

_____

_____

_____

_____

Social Studies Center

Along the Way

Materials
Chart paper, crayons, cardboard shapes to match pictures

• Draw a picture of a stop sign on chart paper. Also, draw a one way sign, a speed limit sign, and a school zone sign.

• Provide partners with cardboard shapes that match the shapes of the traffic signs. Then have students take turns counting the number of sides of each shape.

• Partners can trace the cardboard shapes that have the same shapes as traffic signs and draw inside the outlines to make each sign.

Movement Center

Act It Out!

Materials
Attribute blocks (or Teaching Tool 46), paper bag

• Place the attribute blocks in the bag. Have students choose the blocks one at a time and identify the shape.

• Ask them to model the shape using their hands or working with other students to form the shape with their bodies.

• Ask students to describe the shape they formed using the words *side* and *vertex* (or *corner*).

Building Center

Group Them

Materials
(per pair) Attribute blocks: 3 squares, 3 triangles, 3 circles (or Teaching Tool 46)

• Have students sort the shapes into groups. Have students discuss what they are doing by answering your questions.

• *Think about the shapes for one group. How are they alike? Think about number of sides for another group. Do all the blocks have the same number of sides?*

• Have students draw pictures of their groups to share with others.

Dramatic Play Center

Cookie Fun

Materials
Clay, glitter, cookie cutters in various shapes

- Have students use clay to bake "cookies" in different shapes—circles, squares, triangles, and rectangles.

- Then have students act out a party scene.

Art Center

Shaping Up

Materials
Colored yarn, dark construction paper, glue, blunt-tipped scissors

- Have students make a yarn collage of different shapes. They might overlap two circles or squares or add rectangles and triangles to the picture.

- Some students might make a simple animal with the yarn shapes.

- Then have students describe the shapes in their designs using the words *side* and *vertex/ vertices.*

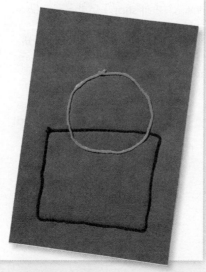

Building Center

Animal Shapes

Materials
Pattern blocks (or Teaching Tool 41)

- Have students use pattern blocks to build animals.

- Have them present what they have built, describing the shapes they used to build their animals.

TOPIC **12**

INTERACTIVE MATH STORY
IDENTIFY AND DESCRIBE SHAPES

PEARSON
realize.
PearsonRealize.com

PDF Story   ▶ Story

Before the Story

PDF Story

Picture Walk
Project the online PDF that contains a full-color version of this story. Read the title, author's name, and illustrator's name to students. *This is a story about exploring outside places and finding things. Let's look and see what we can discover in each outdoor scene.* As you page through the story, invite students to point to the plants, animals, buildings, and toy equipment they see. Encourage students to name each of the things they point out. Ask students also to find the two turtles in each picture.

Activate Prior Knowledge
We will be looking for two-dimensional shapes in this story. Let's look at some shapes together. Draw a rectangle, triangle, circle, and square on the board. Point to the rectangle and invite a volunteer to name the shape. *What shape is this?* [Rectangle] Then have the class repeat the name of the shape together. Continue identifying and reviewing the remaining shapes.

▶ Story
Play the animated version of the story.

DURING THE STORY

This book belongs to:
Deandre

TOPIC **12** Story

Shape Hop

Written by Cindy Frink
Illustrated by Luciana Navarro-Powell

Hop in the door!
Find a ☐.
Draw one more.

Topic 12 **1**

Hop in the door!
Find a △.
Draw one more.

Topic 12 **2**

READ
Read the story aloud for enjoyment. Point to the turtle opening the door on each page. *This big turtle is telling the story. He's inviting the little turtle and the frog to hop in the door. He's also asking you to find certain shapes on the page.* As you read about each shape, ask students to name it. Then have them name things they see that have the same shape.

GESTURE
Have students point to the turtle at the door on each page as you reread the story. *Who is telling the story?* [The big turtle] As you read about each shape, invite students to use their fingers to draw that shape in the air. *Use your finger to draw a small rectangle in the air. Can you draw a medium size rectangle? Now draw a large rectangle!* Have volunteers trace the shapes in the pictures that students find.

COLOR
Distribute Interactive Math Story Books to students. On the first page, students should use the same crayon to color two objects: the rectangle outline shown in the text and the rectangle they find in the picture. Guide students to use different color crayons to color, identify, and draw two-dimensional shapes on each of the remaining pages as appropriate. The colors students choose will vary.

SHAPE HOP

This is a story in which students will identify and name
two-dimensional shapes.

Hop in the door!
Find a ◯ .
Draw one more. _____

Topic 12 **3**

Hop in the door!
Find a ☐ .
Draw one more. _____

Topic 12 **4**

WRITE

Work with students to
locate and draw a two-
dimensional shape. *What
shape are you looking
for?* [First page: rectangle]
*Where is the shape in
the story?* [Students may
point or explain that the
outline of the shape is
in the second sentence.]
*Draw your own rectangle.
Use the same color crayon
you used before. You may
draw the shape on the line
or in the space next to the
words.*

SPEAK

Invite students to retell the
story as a conversation
between the two turtles.
Each time the first turtle
makes a statement or
request, the second turtle
responds. For example, the
first turtle can say, "Hop
in the door." Then, the
second turtle can answer,
"I hopped in the door and
now I'm on a _____!"
[First page, country road;
second page, farm; third
page, field; fourth page,
playground]

After the Story

Extension

As a class, create a large
outdoor scene on mural paper to
show the shapes students found
in the story. Cut out rectangles,
triangles, circles, and squares of
different sizes from construction
paper. Have each student
choose a shape and glue it on
background paper, and then
use crayons or markers to add
details to turn the shape into an
outdoor object. Students can
also draw background scenery.

You may wish to have students
take home their Interactive
Math Story books and share
what they have learned about
identifying shapes with a family
member.

TOPIC ESSENTIAL QUESTION

How can two- and three-dimensional shapes be identified and described?

Revisit the Topic Essential Question throughout the topic, and see a note about answering the question in the Teacher's Edition for the Topic Assessment.

MATH AND SCIENCE PROJECT **STEM**

The science theme for this project is **Pushing and Pulling Objects**. This theme will be revisited in the Math and Science Activities in Lessons 12-4 and 12-6.

Talk with students about how shapes are everywhere: outside, inside, at school, in the grocery store, at home, and in nature. Ask students to describe the shapes they see in the photograph.

Project-Based Learning Have students work on the **Math and Science Project** over the course of several days.

EXTENSION

Ask students to choose one shape (e.g., circle, square, triangle) and find five examples of this shape in their world. Students can compile their lists by drawing, writing, and/or photographing shapes and looking for examples at school, home, and places in between.

Sample of Student Work for Math and Science Project

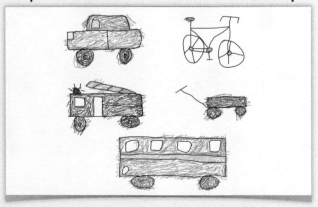

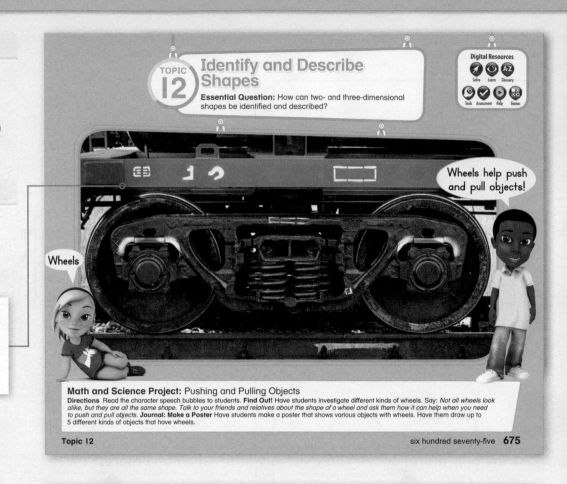

Math and Science Project: Pushing and Pulling Objects
Directions Read the character speech bubbles to students. **Find Out!** Have students investigate different kinds of wheels. Say: *Not all wheels look alike, but they are all the same shape. Talk to your friends and relatives about the shape of a wheel and ask them how it can help when you need to push and pull objects.* **Journal: Make a Poster** Have students make a poster that shows various objects with wheels. Have them draw up to 5 different kinds of objects that have wheels.

Topic 12   six hundred seventy-five **675**

Home-School Connection

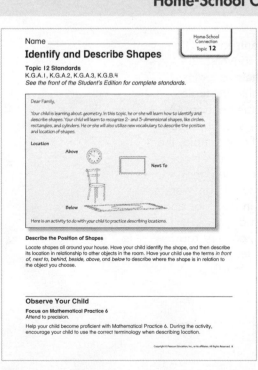

Send this page home at the start of Topic 12 to give families an overview of the content in the topic.

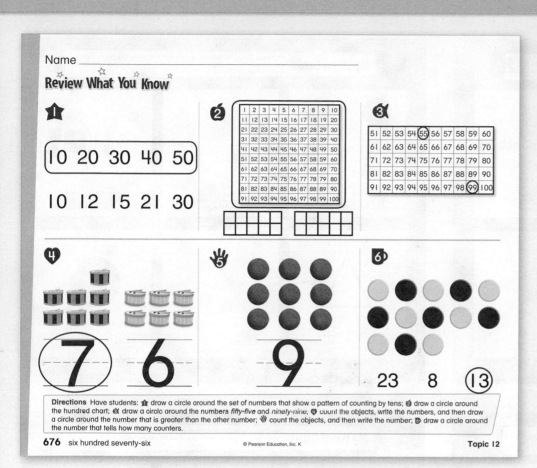

Name _____

Review What You Know

1

| 10 | 20 | 30 | 40 | 50 |

10 12 15 21 30

2

1	2	3	4	5	6	7	8	9	10
11	12	13	14	15	16	17	18	19	20
21	22	23	24	25	26	27	28	29	30
31	32	33	34	35	36	37	38	39	40
41	42	43	44	45	46	47	48	49	50
51	52	53	54	55	56	57	58	59	60
61	62	63	64	65	66	67	68	69	70
71	72	73	74	75	76	77	78	79	80
81	82	83	84	85	86	87	88	89	90
91	92	93	94	95	96	97	98	99	100

3

51	52	53	54	55	56	57	58	59	60
61	62	63	64	65	66	67	68	69	70
71	72	73	74	75	76	77	78	79	80
81	82	83	84	85	86	87	88	89	90
91	92	93	94	95	96	97	98	99	100

4

7

5

6

9

6

23   8   13

Directions Have students: **1** draw a circle around the set of numbers that show a pattern of counting by tens; **2** draw a circle around the hundred chart; **3** draw a circle around the numbers *fifty-five* and *ninety-nine*, **4** count the objects, write the numbers, and then draw a circle around the number that is greater than the other number; **5** count the objects, and then write the number; **6** draw a circle around the number that tells how many counters.

© Pearson Education, Inc. K

Topic 12

Item Analysis for Diagnosis and Intervention

Item	Ⓒ Standards	MDIS
1	K.CC.A.1	A16
2	K.CC.A.1	A13
3	K.CC.A.1	A13
4	K.CC.A.3, K.CC.C.7	A3, A7
5	K.CC.A.3	A3
6	K.CC.B.5	A10, A12

Topic 12 Vocabulary Words Activity

What Does It Mean to You?

Pass out copies of the Vocabulary: Word Chart (Teaching Tool 49) to students. On the board, draw a vocabulary chart for students to see. Write three new vocabulary words in the New Word column. Ask students to give you everyday or mathematical meanings of the words and write those meanings in the What It Means column. Tell students to write down the words and meanings as you write them on the board. Then tell students that they will learn more about these words in this topic.

For example, write the word *vertex* in the New Word column. Write students' definitions such as *corner* in the What It Means column.

TOPIC 12

TOPIC OPENER

IDENTIFY AND DESCRIBE SHAPES

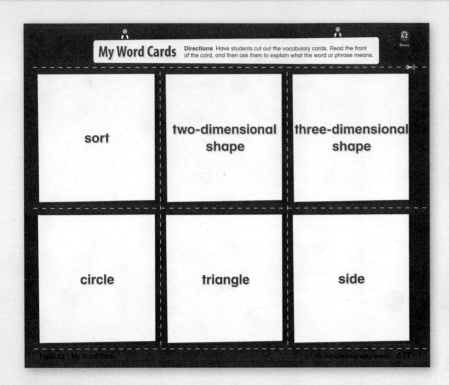

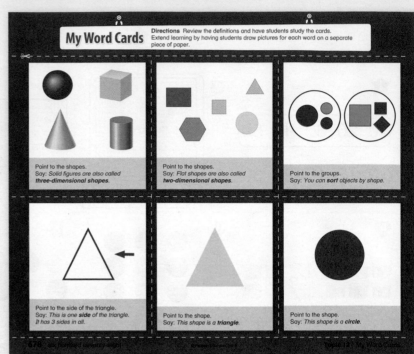

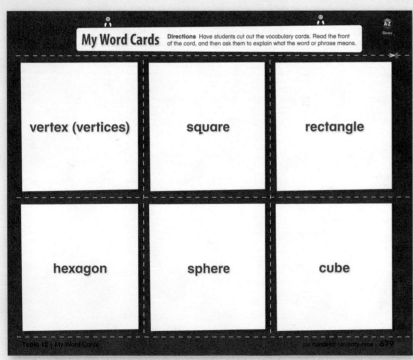

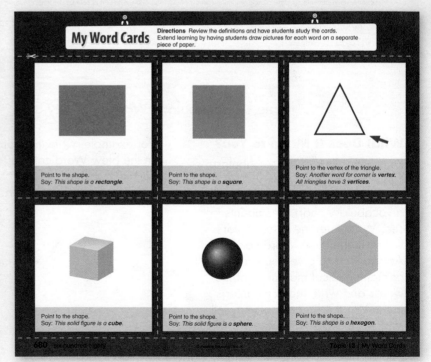

My Word Cards

Directions Have students cut out the vocabulary cards. Read the front of the card, and then ask them to explain what the word or phrase means.

cone	cylinder	in front of
behind	next to	above

My Word Cards

Directions Review the definitions and have students study the cards. Extend learning by having students draw pictures for each word on a separate piece of paper.

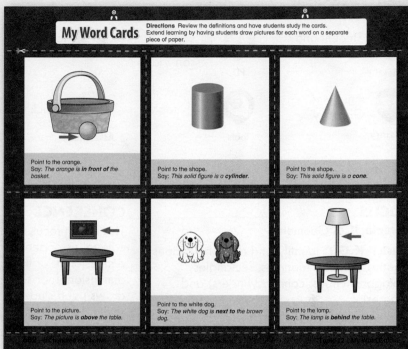

Point to the orange.
Say: *The orange is **in front of** the basket.*

Point to the shape.
Say: *This solid figure is a **cylinder**.*

Point to the shape.
Say: *This solid figure is a **cone**.*

Point to the picture.
Say: *The picture is **above** the table.*

Point to the white dog.
Say: *The white dog is **next to** the brown dog.*

Point to the lamp.
Say: *The lamp is **behind** the table.*

My Word Cards

Directions Have students cut out the vocabulary cards. Read the front of the card, and then ask them to explain what the word or phrase means.

below	beside	

My Word Cards

Directions Review the definitions and have students study the cards. Extend learning by having students draw pictures for each word on a separate piece of paper.

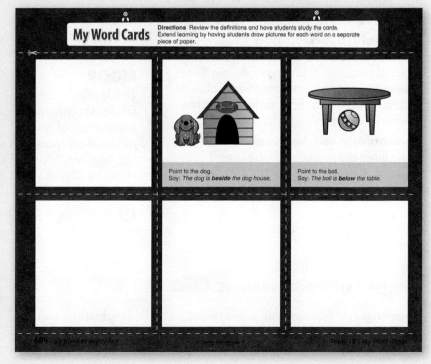

Point to the dog.
Say: *The dog is **beside** the dog house.*

Point to the ball.
Say: *The ball is **below** the table.*

TWO-DIMENSIONAL (2-D) AND THREE-DIMENSIONAL (3-D) SHAPES

 Student and Teacher eTexts
eText

 Listen and Look For Lesson Video
PD

Today's Challenge
Think

Solve and Share
Solve

 Visual Learning Animation Plus
Learn

 Animated Glossary
Glossary

 Math Tools
Tools

Quick Check
Assessment

 Another Look Homework Video
Help

Math Games
Games

LESSON OVERVIEW **FCR** FOCUS • COHERENCE • RIGOR

FOCUS

Domain K.G Geometry

Cluster K.G.A Identify and describe shapes (squares, circles, triangles, rectangles, hexagons, cubes, cones, cylinders, and spheres).

Content Standard K.G.A.3 Identify shapes as two-dimensional (lying in a plane, "flat") or three-dimensional ("solid").

Mathematical Practices MP.3, MP.6, MP.7

Objective Name shapes as flat or solid.

Essential Understanding Objects have shape. Some objects, such as a sheet of paper or a photograph, are two-dimensional, or flat, shapes. Some objects, such as a ball, can, box, or jar, are three-dimensional, or solid, shapes.

Vocabulary sort, two-dimensional shape (flat), three-dimensional shape (solid)

Materials 2-D and 3-D Shapes (Teaching Tool 37)

COHERENCE

This lesson focuses on identifying two categories of geometric figures: two-dimensional, or flat, shapes and three-dimensional, or solid, shapes. The lesson draws upon students' prior knowledge by relating the concepts of flat and solid to common objects in students' environments. In the remaining lessons in this topic, students will learn to identify and describe certain two- and three-dimensional shapes by their sides and vertices. Then, in Topic 13, students will analyze, compare, and build two- and three-dimensional shapes.

RIGOR

This lesson emphasizes **conceptual understanding**. Students begin their exploration of geometric shapes and learn to differentiate two types of shapes: solid and flat. Students identify both examples and nonexamples of solids and flats to deepen their understanding.

 Watch the Listen and Look For Lesson Video.
PD

MATH ANYTIME

Daily Common Core Review

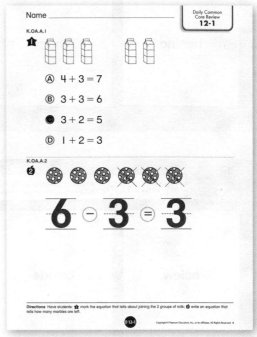

Today's Challenge
Think Use Topic 12 problems any time during this topic.

ENGLISH LANGUAGE LEARNERS **ELL**

Reading Use support from peers/teachers to enhance/confirm understanding.

Use with the Visual Learning Bridge on Student's Edition, p. 686.

Write *flat* and *solid*. Point to and read each term. Ask students to run their hands over the tops of their tables. Say: *This table top is flat.* Ask students to hold up their pencil boxes. Say: *The pencil box is solid.* Ask students to tell about the differences between flat and solid objects.

Beginning Write the words *flat* and *solid* on index cards. Distribute them to students. Instruct students to point to and read *flat* and *solid*. Hold up various classroom items that are flat or solid. Ask: *Is this flat or solid?* Have students hold up and read the correct card.

Intermediate Instruct students to write *flat* and *solid* on index cards. Divide students into partner groups. Have Student A show an object to Student B. Student A should ask: *"Is this flat or solid?"* Student B should hold up and read the correct card. Have students reverse roles and repeat.

Advanced Instruct students to write *flat* and *solid* on index cards. Divide students into partner groups. Have Student A show an object to Student B. Student A should ask: *"Is this flat or solid?"* Student B should hold up and read the correct card and respond using the sentence stem: "It is [flat, solid] because ___." Have students reverse roles and repeat.

Summarize How are flat and solid objects different?

DEVELOP: PROBLEM-BASED LEARNING

COHERENCE: Engage students by connecting prior knowledge to new ideas.
Students observe and sort shapes using any attribute. This prepares students to sort and classify shapes as solids or flats in the next part of the lesson.

 10–15 min

 Solve

BEFORE

1. Pose the Solve-and-Share Problem
MP.7 Use Structure Students look for common attributes as they sort a group of shapes.

Provide each student with 2-D and 3-D Shapes (Teaching Tool 37).

Say: *Pick six shapes from a bag. Put the shapes into two groups. Tell how the groups are different. Then draw a picture of the shapes you put on each table.*

2. Build Understanding
Help students observe and compare attributes.
What shapes do you have? [Answers will vary.]
What do you need to do with these shapes?
[Sample answer: Put the shapes into two groups.]

DURING

3. Ask Guiding Questions As Needed
In what ways are two or more of the shapes the same? [Answers will vary. Sample answer: Some of the shapes have corners. Others do not.] *What are some of the ways you could put these shapes into two groups?* [Answers will vary. Sample answer: One group could be flat shapes. The other group could be solid shapes.]

AFTER

4. Share and Discuss Solutions
 Start with students' solutions. Have them share
Solve the strategies used to solve the problem. If needed, project and analyze Calvin's work to discuss one way to sort the shapes into two groups.

5. Transition to the Visual Learning Bridge
You put shapes into two groups and described how they are different and how they are the same.

Later in this lesson, you will learn about one way to sort shapes.

6. Extension for Early Finishers
Invite students to draw a new shape for one of the groups. The shape may be the same shape as an existing shape in a different size or orientation, or it may be a different shape altogether. Have students explain why the new shape belongs in the group.

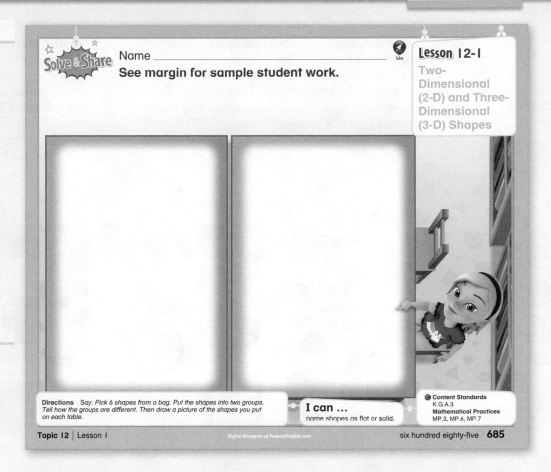

Solve & Share

Name _____
See margin for sample student work.

Lesson 12-1
Two-Dimensional (2-D) and Three-Dimensional (3-D) Shapes

Directions Say: *Pick 6 shapes from a bag. Put the shapes into two groups. Tell how the groups are different. Then draw a picture of the shapes you put on each table.*

I can ... name shapes as flat or solid.

Content Standards K.G.A.3 Mathematical Practices MP.3, MP.6, MP.7

Topic 12 | Lesson 1   Digital Resources at PearsonRealize.com   six hundred eighty-five **685**

Analyze Student Work

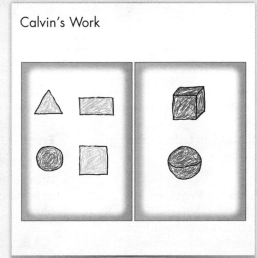

Calvin's Work

Alisha's Work

Calvin sorts the shapes as 2-D shapes and 3-D shapes. He says that 3-D shapes are harder to draw than 2-D shapes.

Alisha sorts shapes into shapes with corners and shapes without corners.

STEP 2

DEVELOP: VISUAL LEARNING

The *Visual Learning Bridge* connects students' thinking in Solve & Share to important math ideas in the lesson. Use the *Visual Learning Bridge* to make these ideas explicit. Also available as a *Visual Learning Animation Plus* at PearsonRealize.com

 Visual Learning

 Learn Glossary

What objects do you see? [Sticky note, paper, stop sign, clock, picture frame] *What word does Emily use to describe these objects?* [Flat] *In what ways are these objects the same?* [Sample answer: They are flat. They are things we use.] *What is another object Emily could put in this box?* [Sample answer: A poster] *Why?* [Sample answer: A poster is a flat shape.]

MP.7 Use Structure *What objects do you see in this box?* [Soccer ball, basket, tissue box, curved block, traffic cone, can, tent] *How are the objects in this box different from the objects in the first box?* [The objects in this box are thicker.] *The objects in this box are solid shapes. What is another object Emily could put in this box?* [Sample answer: An orange] *Why?* [Sample answer: An orange has thickness; it is a solid shape.]

Visual Learning Bridge

☆ **Guided Practice**

Directions ★ Have students draw a circle around the objects that are flat, and mark an X on the objects that are solid.

686 six hundred eighty-six   © Pearson Education, Inc. K   **Topic 12** | Lesson 1

Complete the *Do You Understand? Show Me!* problem before starting Guided Practice.

Do You Understand? Show Me! MP.6 Be Precise

Have students use the terms *flat* and *solid* to describe objects in the classroom. Point to two or three different objects and each time provide verbal clues: *Does this (book) have a flat or solid shape?* Then point silently to objects and have students respond by saying either *flat* or *solid. You can call a flat shape a two-dimensional shape and a solid shape a three-dimensional shape.*

 Ask the following Essential Question: *How are objects that have solid shapes different from objects that have flat shapes?* [Sample answer: Objects with solid shapes have thickness.]

Error Intervention: Item 1

If students identify a plate as a solid,

then allow students to explain their choice. It could be that plates at home or school are more three-dimensional than the pictured plate.

 Reteaching Assign Reteaching Set A, p. 735.

686 Topic 12

☑ **QUICK CHECK**

Check mark indicates items for prescribing differentiation on the next page.
Items 6 and 7 are each worth 1 point. Item 8 is worth up to 3 points.

20–30 min

Tools   Assessment

Items 2–4 MP.3 Construct Arguments In order to use real objects to model plane figures in the primary grades, we have to tolerate some thickness (third dimension). Some students may need guidance on how flat an object has to be to be called *flat*. If so, open up a class discussion and guide students to a consensus.

Items 4 and 5 To deepen understanding, students identify nonexamples. In these dichotomous groupings, either an object belongs in the category or it does not. To prepare students for the change in language structure, hold up a flat object in one hand and a solid object in another. *Which object is NOT flat?* Raise the solid object. *Can you name another object that is NOT flat?* [Sample answers: Ball; book]

Item 6 MP.7 Look for Patterns If students compare the pictures of the pipe and the can, they might wonder whether the space inside the open pipe is an important attribute: The sides of the pipe are thin. Direct students to find pictures of other open and/or hollow solids in the lesson (the ice cream cone, party hat, and pencil box) to help them decide.

Item 8 If students struggle to come up with ideas, give students hints by asking guiding questions to spark their imagination. *Is your solid something you see inside or outside? At school? At home? Is it big or small?*

Coherence Identifying whether a shape is flat or solid will help students in later lessons accurately name two- and three-dimensional shapes.

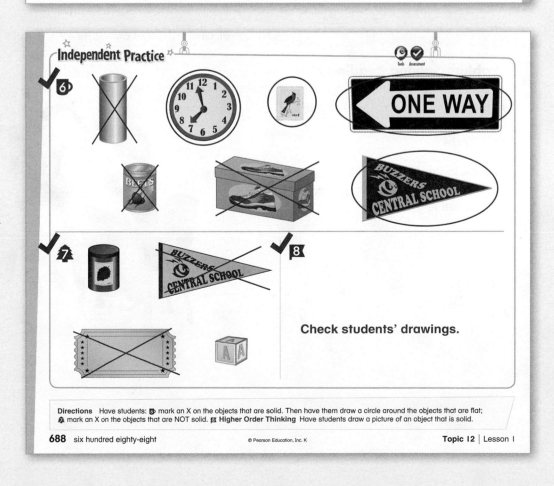

687–688

2 RtI

Use the **QUICK CHECK** on the previous page to prescribe differentiated instruction.

I Intervention
0–3 points on the Quick Check

O On-Level
4 points on the Quick Check

A Advanced
5 points on the Quick Check

Intervention Activity

Concentration Game
Materials

Index cards with matching pairs of two- and three-dimensional objects

• Shuffle the cards and place them facedown in rows.

• The first player turns over 2 cards and tells whether the pictures are the same or different.

• If the pictures are the same, the player tells how they are the same and keeps the cards. Otherwise, the player tells how they are different and turns the cards facedown.

• The second player then gets to turn over 2 cards. Play continues until all matches are made.

Reteach

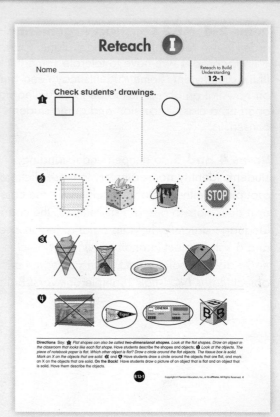

On-Level and Advanced Activity Centers

Problem-Solving Reading Mat

Have students read the Problem-Solving Reading Mat for Topic 12 and then complete Problem-Solving Reading Activity 12-1.

See the Problem-Solving Reading Activity Guide for other suggestions on how to use this mat.

TIMING

The time allocated to Step 3 will depend on the teacher's instructional decisions and differentiation routines.

15–30 min

PEARSON
realize.
PearsonRealize.com

Help   Tools   Games

Technology Center I O A

Math Tools and Math Games

A link to a specific math tools activity or math game to use with this lesson is provided at PearsonRealize.com.

Leveled Assignment
I Items 1–3   O Items 2–4   A Items 3–5

Name _____

Help   Tools   Games

Homework & Practice 12-1
Two-Dimensional (2-D) and Three-Dimensional (3-D) Shapes

Another Look!

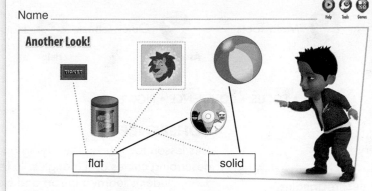

flat   solid

HOME ACTIVITY Point to various objects throughout your house. Have your child tell whether the object is flat or solid. Then have him or her draw a flat object and a solid object that can be found in the kitchen.

⭐ 1

Directions Say: *The DVD is flat. What other objects are flat? Draw a line from the objects that are flat to the box labeled* flat. *The beach ball is solid. Draw a line from other objects that are solid to the box labeled* solid. ⭐ Have students draw a circle around the objects that are flat, and then mark an X on the objects that are solid.

Topic 12 | Lesson 1   Digital Resources at PearsonRealize.com   six hundred eighty-nine **689**

2

3

4   5

Check students' drawings.   **Check students' drawings.**

Directions 🍎 and ✖ Have students mark an X on the objects that are NOT flat. 🍎 **Higher Order Thinking** Have students identify an object in a bedroom that is solid, and then draw a picture of that object. ✋ **Higher Order Thinking** Have students identify an object in a kitchen that is flat, and then draw a picture of that object.

690 six hundred ninety   © Pearson Education, Inc. K   Topic 12 | Lesson 1

DIGITAL RESOURCES PearsonRealize.com

 Student and Teacher eTexts
eText

 Listen and Look For Lesson Video
PD

 Today's Challenge
Think

 Solve and Share
Solve

Visual Learning Animation Plus
Learn

 Animated Glossary
Glossary

Math Tools
Tools

 Quick Check
Assessment

 Another Look Homework Video
Help

 Math Games
Games

LESSON OVERVIEW FCR FOCUS • COHERENCE • RIGOR

FOCUS

Domain K.G Geometry

Cluster K.G.A Identify and describe shapes (squares, circles, triangles, rectangles, hexagons, cubes, cones, cylinders, and spheres).

Content Standard K.G.A.2 Correctly name shapes regardless of their orientations or overall size. Also **K.G.B.4**.

Mathematical Practices MP.2, MP.5, MP.6, MP.7

Objective Identify and describe circles and triangles.

Essential Understanding A circle is round and does not have any corners (vertices). A triangle has 3 sides and 3 corners (vertices).

Vocabulary circle, triangle, side, vertex/vertices (corner)

Materials Circles (Teaching Tool 32), Triangles (Teaching Tool 33), Squares (Teaching Tool 34)

COHERENCE

This lesson focuses on identifying and describing circles and triangles. In Lesson 12-1, students learned to sort and classify shapes as flat or solid. In this lesson, students learn that they can further classify flat shapes as circles or triangles. In differentiating circles and triangles, students informally sort and classify non-polygons (circles) and polygons (triangles). In the next lesson, students learn that they can sort into even more groups through the introduction of rectangles and special rectangles, squares.

RIGOR

This lesson emphasizes **conceptual understanding**. Students learn that they can categorize flat shapes as circles and triangles. Because circles and triangles have unique attributes, students can use these attributes to identify other circles and triangles regardless of size.

 Watch the Listen and Look For Lesson Video.
PD

MATH ANYTIME

Daily Common Core Review

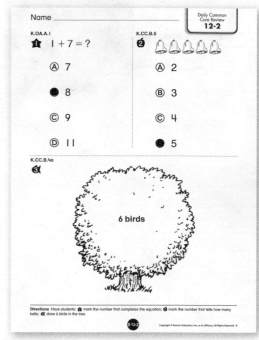

Today's Challenge

Think Use Topic 12 problems any time during this topic.

ENGLISH LANGUAGE LEARNERS ELL

Listening Demonstrate listening comprehension by responding to questions.

Use with the Visual Learning Bridge on Student's Edition, p. 692.

Distribute paper and colored pencils to students. Ask each student to draw a secret object that has the shape of a circle or triangle (e.g., a wheel or a roof). Have students work in pairs. Have Student A try to guess the object and its shape in Student B's secret drawing. Student A should listen while Student B describes attributes of the

secret object. Help students as needed with descriptions and shape names. Encourage students to use the words *side, corner, circle,* and *triangle* in their responses. After Student A correctly guesses the object and shape, have students switch roles.

Beginning Describe a shape to students using the words *sides* and *corner*. *What is the shape?* Have students respond using the sentence stem: "It is a ____."

Intermediate Ask students to respond using complete sentences to describe the shape and guess the object.

Advanced Ask Student B to include descriptions of the object's shape and size. Student A should explain how he or she knew the shape.

Summarize What information can you use to describe a shape?

STEP 1

DEVELOP: PROBLEM-BASED LEARNING

COHERENCE: Engage learners by connecting prior knowledge to new ideas.

Students tell how triangle and circle shapes look different. This prepares them for the next part of the lesson where they learn about the attributes of circles and triangles.

10–15 min

 Solve

BEFORE

1. Pose the Solve-and-Share Problem
MP.7 Use Structure. In the problem, students analyze in their own words how triangles and circles are different. Students observe patterns that help to define triangles and circles; for example, circles are round, and triangles have three sides.

Provide each student with a cutout of a circle, triangle, and square (use Teaching Tools 32–34).

Say: *The zoo has a polar animals exhibit. There are polar bears and penguins. Place the shapes in the animal pens that are the same shape. Tell how the shapes you placed in the pen on the left are different from the shapes you placed in the pen on the right.*

2. Build Understanding
What are you asked to do with your shapes? [Place the shapes in the pens that are the same shape.] *What are you asked to tell about the shapes in the pens?* [Tell how they are different.]

DURING

3. Ask Guiding Questions As Needed
Will you use all three shapes? [No] *How do you know?* [There are only 2 pens and I have 3 shapes.] *Look at the penguins' pen. How many points does this pen have?* [0] *Look at the polar bears' pen. How many points does this pen have?* [3]

AFTER

4. Share and Discuss Solutions
 Start with students' solutions. If needed,
Solve project Chloe's work to discuss the different attributes of circles and triangles.

5. Transition to the Visual Learning Bridge
You can use a name to describe shapes that are alike.

Later in the lesson, you will learn that some shapes can be compared by the number of sides and the number of corners.

6. Extension for Early Finishers
Does the size of a shape change what type of shape it is? [No] *Why?* [Because size does not change how many points a shape has; it just means bigger or smaller]

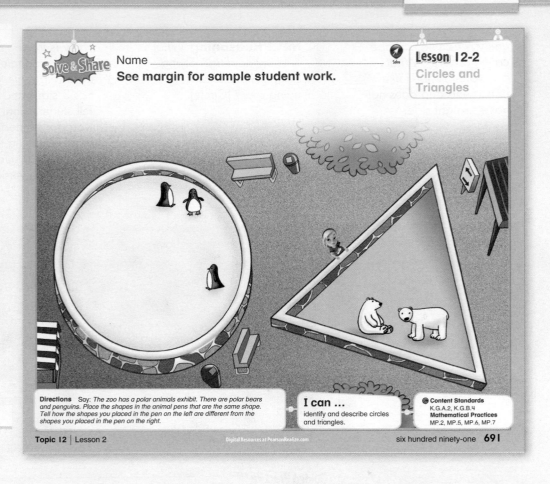

Solve & Share Name _____

See margin for sample student work.

Lesson 12-2
Circles and Triangles

Directions Say: *The zoo has a polar animals exhibit. There are polar bears and penguins. Place the shapes in the animal pens that are the same shape. Tell how the shapes you placed in the pen on the left are different from the shapes you placed in the pen on the right.*

I can ...
identify and describe circles and triangles.

Content Standards
K.G.A.2, K.G.B.4
Mathematical Practices
MP.2, MP.5, MP.6, MP.7

Topic 12 | Lesson 2   Digital Resources at PearsonRealize.com   six hundred ninety-one **691**

Analyze Student Work

Chloe's Work

Chloe correctly places a matching shape in each pen. She says the shapes are different because one shape is round and the other shape has three points.

Arthur's Work

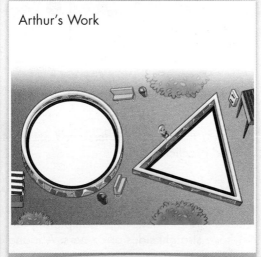

Arthur places a matching shape in each pen. He says the shapes are different because one shape has points and the other one doesn't.

STEP 2

DEVELOP: VISUAL LEARNING

PEARSON
realize.
PearsonRealize.com

Learn   Glossary

The *Visual Learning Bridge* connects students' thinking in Solve & Share to important math ideas in the lesson. Use the *Visual Learning Bridge* to make these ideas explicit. Also available as a *Visual Learning Animation Plus* at PearsonRealize.com

Visual Learning

Emily is tracing a shape called a circle. What does a circle look like? [It is round and does not have straight sides or corners.]

MP.2 Reasoning *What is Emily holding?* [Flying disc] *What shape is the flying disc?* [Circle]

Emily is tracing a shape called a triangle. What does a triangle look like? [It has 3 sides and 3 corners.] Tell students that another word for corners is *vertices*. Practice saying the word *vertices* with students as you point to the vertices of the triangle.

What shape is Emily pointing to on the sailboat? [Triangle] *How do you know?* [It has 3 sides and 3 vertices.]

Visual Learning Bridge

☆ **Guided Practice** ★

1

2

Directions ★ and ✿ Have students color the circle in each row, and then mark an X on each triangle.

692 six hundred ninety-two   © Pearson Education, Inc. K   **Topic 12** | Lesson 2

Complete the *Do You Understand? Show Me!* problem before starting Guided Practice.

Do You Understand? Show Me! MP.6 Be Precise *Use the words* sides, corners, *and* vertices *to tell what a circle looks like and what a triangle looks like.* [Sample answer: A circle is round. It does not have straight sides or corners. A triangle has 3 straight sides and 3 vertices.]

Essential Question
Ask the following Essential Question: *How do you tell the difference between a circle and a triangle?* [A circle is round. A triangle has 3 sides and 3 vertices.]

Error Intervention: Item 1

If students confuse triangles and stars,

then remind them that triangles have only 3 sides and 3 corners, or vertices.

Reteaching Assign Reteaching Set B, p. 735.

✓ QUICK CHECK
Check mark indicates items for prescribing differentiation on the next page.
Items 6 and 7 are each worth 1 point. Item 10 is worth up to 3 points.

20–30 min   Tools Assessment

Item 3 Suggest that students take their time and examine each object presented in the item. Direct students' attention to the square and ask: *Is it a circle? Explain.* [No; It has straight sides.] *Is it a triangle? How do you know?* [No; It has too many sides and corners to be a triangle.] Repeat, asking the same questions about the rectangle.

Item 5 MP.5 Use Appropriate Tools Strategically Picturing real objects shows students how objects that are part of our everyday lives are shaped like circles and triangles. Students can hold the objects, feel the vertices, count the sides, and explore the different attributes. Make sure to give students the two-dimensional objects that show these shapes.

Item 7 MP.7 Look for Patterns Students can trace the shapes to help them count the sides or vertices. Students may be able to distinguish the triangle and circle by sight. Encourage them to tell how they know. *How do you know this is a triangle?* [Sample answer: I counted 3 sides and 3 vertices.]

Items 8 and 9 These items contain more than 1 circle or more than 1 triangle in each row. This requires students to examine each individual shape. Remind students that triangles have exactly 3 sides. If students have trouble keeping track, then have them trace each side as they count.

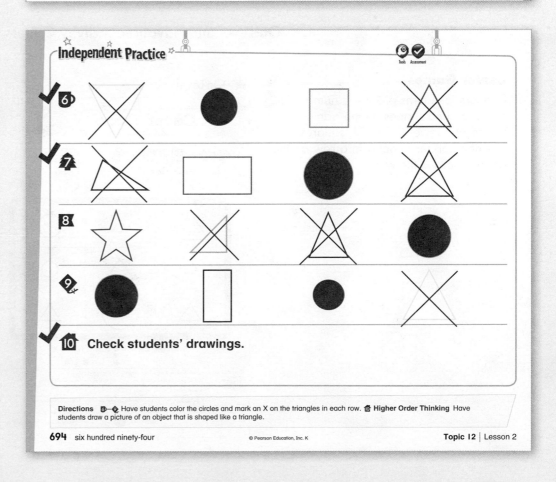

ASSESS AND DIFFERENTIATE

Use the **QUICK CHECK** on the previous page to prescribe differentiated instruction.

2 RtI

ⓘ Intervention
0–3 points on the Quick Check

Ⓞ On-Level
4 points on the Quick Check

Ⓐ Advanced
5 points on the Quick Check

Intervention Activity

Circle- and Triangle-Shaped Books
Materials

(per student)

Construction paper, drawing paper, blunt-tipped scissors, stapler, magazine pictures of objects with circular and triangular shapes, glue

• Make a triangle-shaped book by cutting out 6 matching triangles. Cut

2 from construction paper and 4 from drawing paper. Staple the pages cut from drawing paper between the construction paper covers to form a book. Make a similar circle-shaped book.

• Have students glue a matching picture onto each page of the appropriately shaped book.

My Triangle Book

My Circle Book

Reteach ⓘ

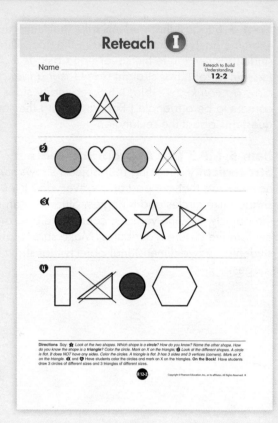

Name _____

Reteach to Build Understanding
12-2

Directions Say: ① Look at the two shapes. Which shape is a *circle*? How do you know? Name the other shape. How do you know the shape is a *triangle*? Color the circle. Mark an X on the triangle; ② Look at the different shapes. A *circle* is flat. It does NOT have any sides. Color the circles. A triangle is flat. It has 3 sides and 3 vertices (corners). Mark an X on the triangle. ③ and ④ Have students color the circles and mark an X on the triangles. **On the Back!** Have students draw 3 circles of different sizes and 3 triangles of different sizes.

On-Level and Advanced Activity Centers Ⓞ Ⓐ

Center Games

Partners take turns picking a number tile. They find shapes on the game board and cover them with squares. The first partner to get 3 in a row on the game board is the winner.

★ On-Level

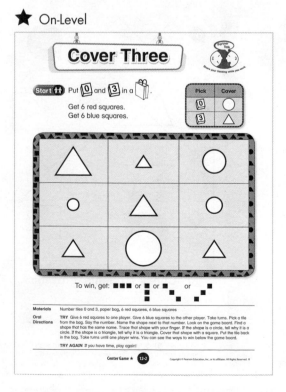

★★ Advanced

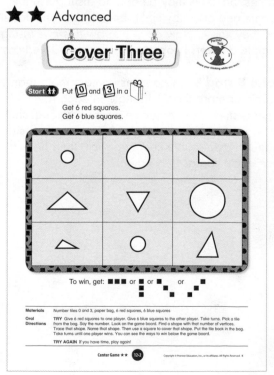

TIMING

The time allocated to Step 3 will depend on the teacher's instructional decisions and differentiation routines.

15–30 min

Help **Tools** **Games**

PEARSON
realize
PearsonRealize.com

Technology Center I O A

Tools
Games

Math Tools and Math Games

A link to a specific math tools activity or math game to use with this lesson is provided at PearsonRealize.com.

Leveled Assignment

I Items 1–5 **O** Items 2–6 **A** Items 3–7

Name _____

Homework & Practice 12-2
Circles and Triangles

Another Look!

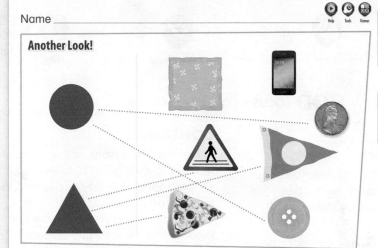

HOME ACTIVITY Look through a magazine with your child. Ask him or her to find pictures of objects that look like a circle or a triangle.

⭐

Directions Say: *A circle is round. Draw a line from the objects that look like a circle to the blue circle on the left. A triangle has 3 sides and 3 vertices. Draw a line from the objects that look like a triangle to the blue triangle on the left.* ⭐ Have students draw a circle around the objects that look like a triangle and mark an X on the objects that look like a circle.

Topic 12 | Lesson 2   Digital Resources at PearsonRealize.com   six hundred ninety-five **695**

2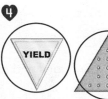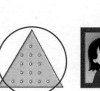

3

4

5

6
Check students' drawings.

7
Check students' drawings.

Directions Have students: **2** and **3** mark an X on the objects that look like a circle; **4** and **5** draw a circle around the objects that look like a triangle. **6 Higher Order Thinking** Have students draw a large red circle and a small blue triangle. **7 Higher Order Thinking** Have students draw a picture using at least 2 circles and 1 triangle. Have them tell a partner what they drew using the names of the shapes.

696 six hundred ninety-six   © Pearson Education, Inc. K   **Topic 12 | Lesson 2**

695–696

SQUARES AND OTHER RECTANGLES

DIGITAL RESOURCES PearsonRealize.com

 Student and Teacher eTexts
eText

 Listen and Look For Lesson Video
PD

 Today's Challenge
Think

 Solve and Share
Solve

 Visual Learning Animation Plus
Learn

 Animated Glossary
Glossary

 Math Tools
Tools

 Quick Check
Assessment

 Another Look Homework Video
Help

 Math Games
Games

LESSON OVERVIEW **FCR** FOCUS • COHERENCE • RIGOR

FOCUS

Domain K.G Geometry

Cluster K.G.A Identify and describe shapes (squares, circles, triangles, rectangles, hexagons, cubes, cones, cylinders, and spheres).

Content Standard K.G.A.2 Correctly name shapes regardless of their orientations or overall size. Also **K.G.B.4**.

Mathematical Practices MP.2, MP.6, MP.7, MP.8

Objective Identify and describe squares and other rectangles.

Essential Understanding Flat shapes called rectangles have 4 sides and 4 vertices that look the same. A rectangle looks like a door. Squares are special rectangles because their sides are all the same length.

Vocabulary rectangle, square

Materials Squares (Teaching Tool 34), Rectangles (Teaching Tool 35)

COHERENCE

In the first two lessons of this topic, students learned to distinguish between flat and solid shapes, and to identify circles and triangles from an assortment of flat shapes. In this lesson, students learn that some flat shapes belong to more than one category: some rectangles are also squares. Students will continue to classify shapes, based on shared attributes, throughout the elementary grades.

RIGOR

This lesson emphasizes **conceptual understanding**. Students learn to recognize rectangles, figures with 4 sides and 4 vertices that look the same. If the sides are the same length, the figure is also a square. Angle measurement is introduced in Grade 2, where students will learn about right angles.

 Watch the Listen and Look For Lesson Video.
PD

MATH ANYTIME

Daily Common Core Review

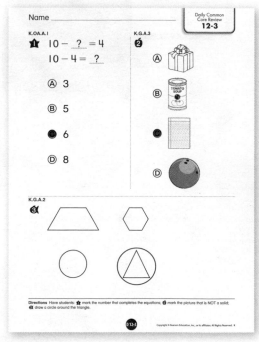

Today's Challenge

Think Use Topic 12 problems any time during this topic.

ENGLISH LANGUAGE LEARNERS **ELL**

Strategies Use strategies when speaking, such as synonyms.

Speaking Share information in cooperative learning interactions.

Use with the Do You Understand? on Teacher's Edition, p. 698.

After discussing the Do You Understand? problem, draw a two-column chart on the board with a square in one column and a rectangle in the other. Ask students to think of an object that is a square or a rectangle.

Have each student stand and name his or her object or describe it. Ask the class to identify the shape. Draw the object in the correct column. Have the class confirm the shape by describing the sides and vertices .

Beginning If students do not know the name of the shape, have them describe their classmates' objects with one of the following sentence stems: "The shape has ____ sides. The shape has ____ corners."

Intermediate Ask students to use complete sentences to tell about their objects. Ask them

to describe their classmates' shapes using the sentence stem: "I know the shape is a ____ because ____."

Advanced Ask students to include the words *sides* and *vertices* in their descriptions.

Summarize How can information you are given help you talk about an object's shape?

DEVELOP: PROBLEM-BASED LEARNING

PEARSON
realize.
PearsonRealize.com

COHERENCE: Engage learners by connecting prior knowledge to new ideas.

Students match a rectangle or a square shape with a similar shape in a picture. This prepares them for the next part of the lesson where they learn about the attributes of rectangles and squares.

10–15 min

Solve

 BEFORE

1. Pose the Solve-and-Share Problem

MP.7 Use Structure Students describe, identify, and compare rectangles and squares based on their attributes.

Say: *Emily is holding two shapes. Pick either the red or the blue shape. Draw a line from that shape to something in the room that has the same shape.*

2. Build Understanding

What are you asked to do with the shapes Emily is holding and the picture of the room? [Draw a line from one shape to a shape in the room that it looks like.] *What do you know about the shapes Emily is holding?* [Sample answer: Both shapes have 4 sides and 4 vertices.]

 **DURING**

3. Ask Guiding Questions As Needed

Does the blue shape have sides that are all the same length? [Yes] *What object in the room looks like it has sides with the same length?* [The rug] *Does the red shape have sides that are all the same length?* [No]

 AFTER

4. Share and Discuss Solutions

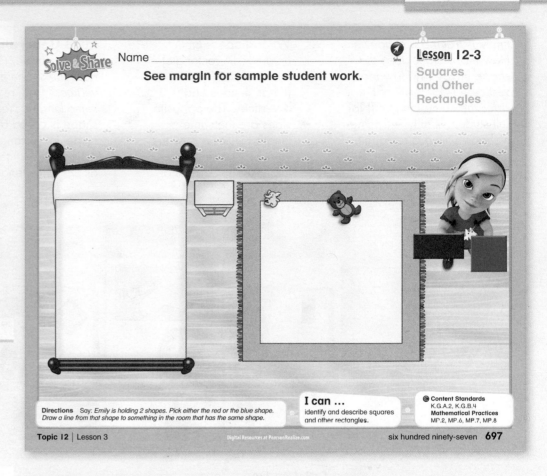

 Start with students' solutions. If needed, project Denzel's work to discuss the shapes he matched and described. Use Laurel's work as a preview of how squares and rectangles are alike but different.

5. Transition to the Visual Learning Bridge

Geometric shapes can be matched to objects in the real world.

Later in the lesson, you will learn to identify and describe squares and other rectangles.

6. Extension for Early Finishers

Have students look around the room for shapes that look like the red and blue shapes. Have them tell why shapes in the room are the same as each of these shapes.

Solve & Share
Name _____
See margin for sample student work.

Lesson 12-3
Squares and Other Rectangles

Directions Say: Emily is holding 2 shapes. Pick either the red or the blue shape. Draw a line from that shape to something in the room that has the same shape.

I can ... identify and describe squares and other rectangles.

Content Standards K.G.A.2, K.G.B.4 **Mathematical Practices** MP.2, MP.6, MP.7, MP.8

Topic 12 | Lesson 3   Digital Resources at PearsonRealize.com   six hundred ninety-seven **697**

Analyze Student Work

Denzel's Work

Denzel draws a line from the blue shape to the rug. He says that both shapes have 4 sides that are the same length.

Laurel's Work

Laurel draws a line from the red shape to the rug. She says that both shapes have 4 corners and 4 sides.

The *Visual Learning Bridge* connects students' thinking in Solve & Share to important math ideas in the lesson. Use the *Visual Learning Bridge* to make these ideas explicit. Also available as a *Visual Learning Animation Plus* at PearsonRealize.com

Emily is tracing a shape. How many sides does the shape have? [4] *How many vertices?* [4] *Are all of the sides the same length?* [No] Tell students Emily is tracing a shape called a rectangle.

What shape is Emily holding? [A rectangle] *How do you know?* [It has 4 sides and 4 vertices. The opposite sides are the same length.] Discuss how the vertices of a rectangle look like the corners of a door.

MP.8 Generalize *Emily is tracing another shape. How many sides does the shape have?* [4] *How many vertices?* [4] *Are all of the sides the same length?* [Yes] Tell students this shape is called a square, which is a special rectangle because it has 4 sides, 4 vertices, and its sides are all the same length.

What shape is Emily holding? [A square] *How do you know?* [It has 4 sides and 4 vertices. The 4 sides are the same length.] Discuss how the vertices of a square also look like the corners of a door.

Visual Learning Bridge

☆ **Guided Practice**

1

2

Directions 🌟 and 🍎 Have students color the rectangles in each row, and then mark an X on each rectangle that is also a square.

698 six hundred ninety-eight   © Pearson Education, Inc. K   **Topic 12** | Lesson 3

Complete the *Do You Understand? Show Me!* problem before starting Guided Practice.

Do You Understand? Show Me! MP.6 Be Precise Draw a circle, a square, and a rectangle on the board. *Which shapes are rectangles? How do you know?* [The rectangles have 4 sides and 4 corners, or vertices. The vertices look like the corners of a door. The opposite sides are the same length. There are 2 rectangles on the board. One is also a square.]

Coherence This lesson expands the geometric figure hierarchy to include rectangles and squares as a subset of rectangles. In later grades, students classify triangles, rectangles, and squares as polygons, and rectangles and squares as quadrilaterals.

Essential Question Ask the following Essential Question: *What makes a square a special rectangle?* [All 4 sides of a square are the same length.]

Error Intervention Item 2

If students do not understand that a square is a rectangle,

then place a square next to a rectangle. Talk about the attributes they have in common, and the ways that they differ.

RtI 1 **Reteaching** Assign Reteaching Set C, p. 736.

✔ **QUICK CHECK**
Check mark indicates items for prescribing differentiation on the next page.
Items 6 and 8 are each worth 1 point. Item 10 is worth up to 3 points.

20–30 min

Item 3 MP.2 Reasoning Make sure students understand that a rectangle is still a rectangle even if it is tilted. For each shape, have students check for 4 sides and 4 vertices that look the same. If the shape has both attributes, it is a rectangle. To decide if it is a square, remind students to look at the lengths of the sides to see whether they are equal.

Item 5 Point out to students that the objects pictured are things that they might see in everyday life. Have them explore the classroom to find objects shaped like squares and rectangles.

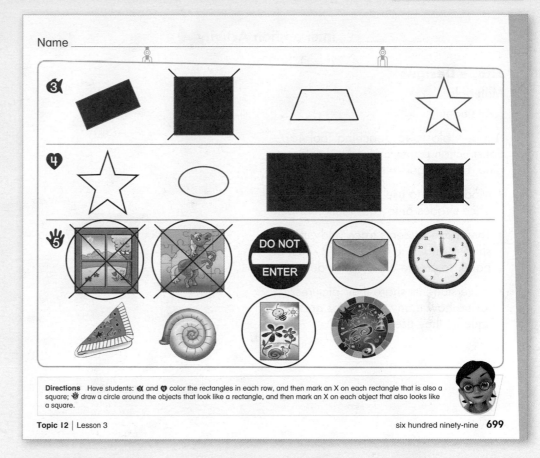

Name

Directions Have students: ③ and ④ color the rectangles in each row, and then mark an X on each rectangle that is also a square; ✋ draw a circle around the objects that look like a rectangle, and then mark an X on each object that also looks like a square.

Topic 12 | Lesson 3   six hundred ninety-nine **699**

Items 6–9 MP.8 Generalize It may be confusing to students that two shapes can look different but have the same name. Remind students that a shape with 4 sides that are all the same length is a special rectangle called a square. Have students describe a rectangle that is not a square, in particular the length of its sides.

Item 10 Students demonstrate their understanding of rectangles and squares by drawing the shapes themselves. Students can find an object to trace if necessary. Have them count the number of sides aloud as they draw.

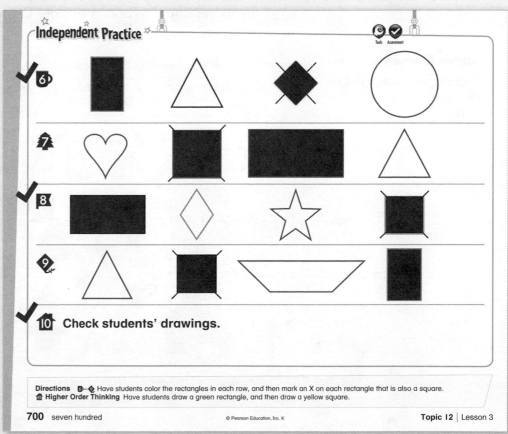

Independent Practice

10 Check students' drawings.

Directions ⑥–⑨ Have students color the rectangles in each row, and then mark an X on each rectangle that is also a square. 🏠 **Higher Order Thinking** Have students draw a green rectangle, and then draw a yellow square.

700 seven hundred   © Pearson Education, Inc. K   Topic 12 | Lesson 3

2 RtI

Use the **QUICK CHECK** on the previous page to prescribe differentiated instruction.

I **Intervention**
0–3 points on the Quick Check

O **On-Level**
4 points on the Quick Check

A **Advanced**
5 points on the Quick Check

Intervention Activity **I**

Shape Designs

Materials

(per student)

Attribute blocks (or Teaching Tool 46), construction paper in assorted colors, glue, blunt-tipped scissors

• Model how to use attribute blocks to trace shapes onto construction paper.

• Then have students trace and cut out shapes and glue them onto a sheet of paper to create a picture or design.

• Have students share their pictures, telling how many rectangles and squares they used.

Reteach **I**

Name _____

Reteach to Build Understanding
12-3

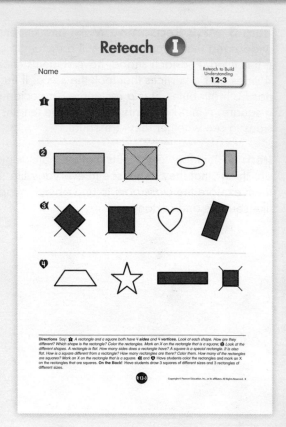

Directions Say: ★ A rectangle and a square both have 4 *sides* and 4 *vertices*. Look at each shape. How are they different? Which shape is the rectangle? Color the rectangles. Mark an X on the rectangle that is a square; ❷ Look at the different shapes. A rectangle is flat. How many sides does a rectangle have? A square is a special rectangle. It is also flat. How is a square different from a rectangle? How many rectangles are there? Color them. How many of the rectangles are squares? Mark an X on the rectangle that is a square. ❸ and ❹ Have students color the rectangles and mark an X on the rectangles that are squares. **On the Back!** Have students draw 3 squares of different sizes and 3 rectangles of different sizes.

R 12-3   Copyright © Pearson Education, Inc., or its affiliates. All Rights Reserved. K

On-Level and Advanced Activity Centers **O** **A**

Center Games

Students find rectangles and decide whether that rectangle is or is not a square.

★ On-Level

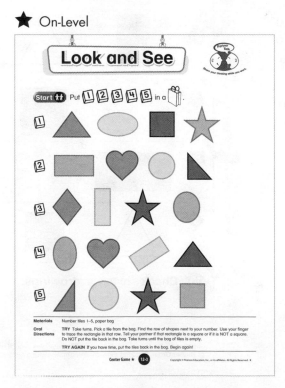

Look and See

Partner Tool

Start 👥 Put 1 2 3 4 5 in a 📖.

Materials Number tiles 1–5, paper bag

Oral Directions **TRY** Take turns. Pick a tile from the bag. Find the row of shapes next to your number. Use your finger to trace the rectangle in that row. Tell your partner if that rectangle is a square or if it is NOT a square. Do NOT put the tile back in the bag. Take turns until the bag of tiles is empty.

TRY AGAIN If you have time, put the tiles back in the bag. Begin again!

Center Game ★   12-3   Copyright © Pearson Education, Inc., or its affiliates. All Rights Reserved. K

★★ Advanced

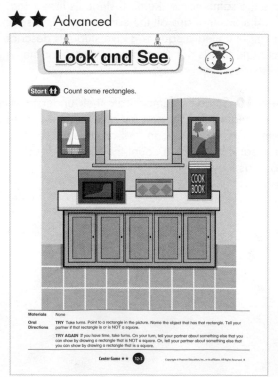

Look and See

Partner Tool

Start 👥 Count some rectangles.

Materials None

Oral Directions **TRY** Take turns. Point to a rectangle in the picture. Name the object that has that rectangle. Tell your partner if that rectangle is or is NOT a square.

TRY AGAIN If you have time, take turns. On your turn, tell your partner about something else that you can show by drawing a rectangle that is NOT a square. Or, tell your partner about something else that you can show by drawing a rectangle that is a square.

Center Game ★★   12-3   Copyright © Pearson Education, Inc., or its affiliates. All Rights Reserved. K

TIMING

The time allocated to Step 3 will depend on the teacher's instructional decisions and differentiation routines.

15–30 min   Help   Tools   Games

PEARSON
realize.
PearsonRealize.com

Technology Center 🅘 🅞 🅐

Tools

Games

Math Tools and Math Games

A link to a specific math tools activity or math game to use with this lesson is provided at PearsonRealize.com.

Leveled Assignment
🅘 Items 1–5   🅞 Items 2–6   🅐 Items 3–7

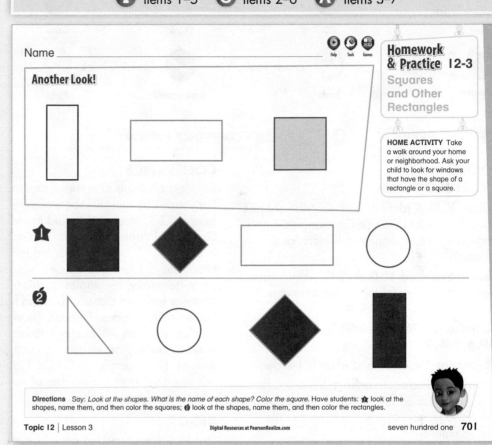

Name _____

Help Tools Games

Homework & Practice 12-3
Squares and Other Rectangles

Another Look!

HOME ACTIVITY Take a walk around your home or neighborhood. Ask your child to look for windows that have the shape of a rectangle or a square.

Directions Say: *Look at the shapes. What is the name of each shape? Color the square.* Have students: ⭐ look at the shapes, name them, and then color the squares; 🍎 look at the shapes, name them, and then color the rectangles.

Topic 12 | Lesson 3   Digital Resources at PearsonRealize.com   seven hundred one **701**

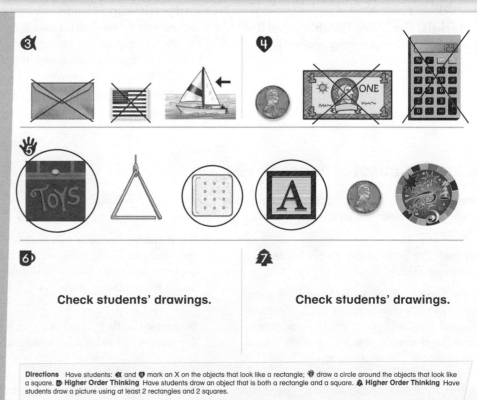

Check students' drawings.   **Check students' drawings.**

Directions Have students: ❸ and ❹ mark an X on the objects that look like a rectangle; ✋ draw a circle around the objects that look like a square. 🍎 **Higher Order Thinking** Have students draw an object that is both a rectangle and a square. 🌲 **Higher Order Thinking** Have students draw a picture using at least 2 rectangles and 2 squares.

702 seven hundred two   © Pearson Education, Inc. K   Topic 12 | Lesson 3

DIGITAL RESOURCES PearsonRealize.com

 eText Student and Teacher eTexts

 PD Listen and Look For Lesson Video

 Think Today's Challenge

 Solve Solve and Share

 Learn Visual Learning Animation Plus

 Glossary Animated Glossary

 Tools Math Tools

 Assessment Quick Check

 Help Another Look Homework Video

 Games Math Games

LESSON OVERVIEW FOCUS • COHERENCE • RIGOR

FOCUS

Domain K.G Geometry

Cluster K.G.A Identify and describe shapes (squares, circles, triangles, rectangles, hexagons, cubes, cones, cylinders, and spheres).

Content Standard K.G.A.2 Correctly name shapes regardless of their orientations or overall size. Also **K.G.B.4**.

Mathematical Practices MP.3, MP.5, MP.6, MP.7

Objective Describe and identify hexagons.

Essential Understanding Six-sided flat shapes are called hexagons. These shapes can be found in objects made by people and in nature.

Vocabulary hexagon

Materials Hexagons (Teaching Tool 36), pattern blocks (or Teaching Tool 41)

COHERENCE

Students continue to sort and classify flat shapes by their numbers of sides. In Lesson 12-2, students learned to identify circles and three-sided shapes, triangles. In Lesson 12-3, students learned to identify two types of four-sided shapes: squares and, more generally, rectangles. In this lesson, students sort and classify six-sided figures, known as hexagons. Through the elementary grades, students will continue to learn new ways to classify an increasing number of flat shapes. For example, in Grade 1, students will learn to count the number of vertices when classifying flat shapes.

RIGOR

This lesson emphasizes **conceptual understanding**. Students learn that flat shapes can have 6 sides and that six-sided flat shapes are called hexagons. Students learn to recognize hexagons in nature and in objects made by people.

 PD Watch the Listen and Look For Lesson Video.

MATH ANYTIME

Daily Common Core Review

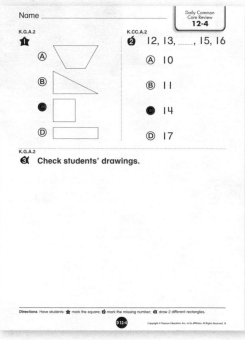

Today's Challenge

 Think Use Topic 12 problems any time during this topic.

ENGLISH LANGUAGE LEARNERS

Strategies Use known, accessible language to learn new/essential language in the process.

Use with the Solve & Share on Student's Edition p. 703.

Write *Shapes*. Point to and read the term. Say: *We've learned about circles, rectangles, squares, and triangles.* Instruct students to draw the shapes in the air as each shape is mentioned. Draw a hexagon. Say: *This is a hexagon.* Count the number of sides of the hexagon with students. Say: *There are 6 sides on a hexagon.* Instruct students to draw a hexagon in the air.

Beginning Recount the number of sides of the hexagon. Ask: *How many sides does a hexagon have?* Students should respond using the sentence stem: "A ___ has ___ sides."

Intermediate Instruct students to recount the number of sides of a hexagon. Ask: *How do you know when a shape is a hexagon?* Students should respond using the sentence stem: "I know a shape is a ___ because ___."

Advanced Say: *Describe a hexagon to a partner.* Students should describe the characteristics of a hexagon to partners.

Summarize What is a hexagon?

DEVELOP: PROBLEM-BASED LEARNING

COHERENCE: Engage students by connecting prior knowledge to new ideas.

Students learn to recognize six-sided figures, called hexagons. This prepares students to identify hexagons within collections of various shapes and familiar objects.

10–15 min

Solve

BEFORE

1. Pose the Solve-and-Share Problem

MP.3 Construct Arguments Students discuss which pieces of art contain six-sided shapes. Some students may argue that the figures must be similar to the regular yellow pattern block. Others may argue that the side lengths can be different. Point out that the sides of a hexagon do not have to have the same length.

Provide each student with a yellow hexagon pattern block (or Teaching Tool 41) and Hexagons (Teaching Tool 36).

Emily wants to buy art that has six-sided shapes in it like the yellow pattern block. Draw a circle around all the pieces of art that she can buy.

2. Build Understanding

What kind of art do you see in this store? [Pictures, sculptures, and a mobile] *What do the pictured pieces of art have in common?* [They all have shapes in them.]

DURING

3. Ask Guiding Questions As Needed

Have students identify a side on one of the hexagons on the workmat. *Point to a side.* [Check students' fingers.] *How can you find out which pieces of art have six-sided shapes in them?* [Count the sides of each shape]

AFTER

4. Share and Discuss Solutions

Solve Start with students' solutions. Have them share the strategies used to solve the problem. If needed, project and analyze London's work to discuss how to find six-sided shapes in the art store.

5. Transition to the Visual Learning Bridge

You counted sides of flat shapes and identified those shapes that have six sides. Later in the lesson, you will learn a name for six-sided figures.

6. Extension for Early Finishers

Have students draw a picture that includes at least one six-sided shape. Suggest that students incorporate one or more hexagons from Teaching Tool 36 in their artwork. [Check students' work.]

Solve & Share

Name **See margin for sample student work.**

 Solve

Lesson 12-4
Hexagons

Directions Say: *Emily wants to buy art that has six-sided shapes in it like the yellow pattern block. Draw a circle around all the pieces of art that she can buy.*

I can ... describe and identify hexagons.

Content Standards K.G.A.2, K.G.B.4 **Mathematical Practices** MP.3, MP.5, MP.6, MP.7

Analyze Student Work

London's Work

London counts both regular and irregular six-sided figures. She considers the knot in the pictured man's tie, but decides that the top of the knot is too curved to count as a side.

Cooper's Work

Cooper counts only regular hexagons. He argues that the six-sided shapes must look exactly like the yellow pattern block.

STEP 2

DEVELOP: VISUAL LEARNING

Learn   Glossary

The *Visual Learning Bridge* connects students' thinking in Solve &
Share to important math ideas in the lesson. Use the *Visual Learning
Bridge* to make these ideas explicit. Also available as a *Visual Learning
Animation Plus* at PearsonRealize.com

E L L
Visual Learning

Emily is tracing a shape called a hexagon. How many sides does a hexagon have? [6 sides] *How many vertices does a hexagon have?* [6 vertices]

MP.6 Be Precise *What do you see?* [Honeycomb] *What shape is traced in the honeycomb?* [Hexagon] *How do you know?* [It has 6 sides and 6 vertices.]

What do you see? [A window] *What shape is the window?* [Hexagon] *How do you know?* [It has 6 sides and 6 vertices.]

What do you see? [A nut] *What shape is the nut?* [Hexagon] *How do you know?* [It has 6 sides and 6 vertices.]

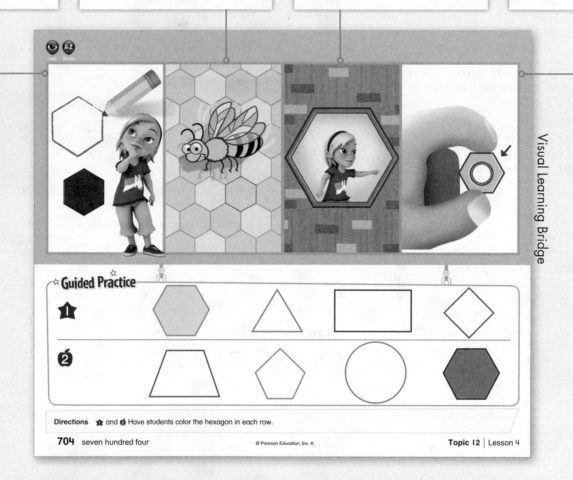

Visual Learning Bridge

☆ **Guided Practice**

1

2

Directions ★ and ❻ Have students color the hexagon in each row.

704 seven hundred four   © Pearson Education, Inc. K   **Topic 12 | Lesson 4**

Complete the *Do You Understand? Show Me!* problem before starting Guided Practice.

Do You Understand? Show Me! **MP.5 Use Appropriate Tools Strategically** Provide students with pattern blocks or with drawings of different shapes including circles, triangles, rectangles, squares, and hexagons. *Find a shape that is a hexagon. Tell how you know which shape is a hexagon.* [I count the number of sides of each shape. If the last number I say for a shape is 6, the shape is a hexagon.]

Coherence Students link what they have learned about triangle and rectangle sides and vertices to hexagon sides and vertices.

 Ask the following Essential Question: *How do you know whether a shape is a hexagon?* [A hexagon has 6 sides and 6 vertices.]

Error Intervention: Item 2

If students color the pentagon,

then have them touch or place a tick mark on each side as they count its sides.

 Reteaching Assign Reteaching Set D, p. 736.

Tools **Assessment**

20–30 min

QUICK CHECK

Check mark indicates items for prescribing differentiation on the next page.
Item 7 is worth 2 points. Item 8 is worth up to 3 points.

Item 3 MP. 7 Use Structure Ask students guiding questions to help them see the structure of the implied groups: example of a hexagon and non-examples. *How is the hexagon the same as the other shapes in this item?* [All the shapes have sides and vertices.] *How is the hexagon different from the other shapes in this item?* [The hexagon is the only shape with 6 sides and 6 vertices.]

Item 5 Have students name the objects pictured in the item. [Napkin, plate, purse, button] Point out that in the real world some objects come in more than one shape. *What other shapes can a button be?* [Circle]

Item 7 Show students a real penny and have them find the classroom clock. *What shape does the penny and clock have?* [Circles] *How is a circle different from a hexagon?* [A circle has no sides and no vertices. A hexagon has 6 sides and 6 vertices.]

Item 8 MP.5 Use Appropriate Tools Strategically If students can't think of what to draw, have them either glue a hexagon from Teaching Tool 36 or trace a hexagon pattern block.

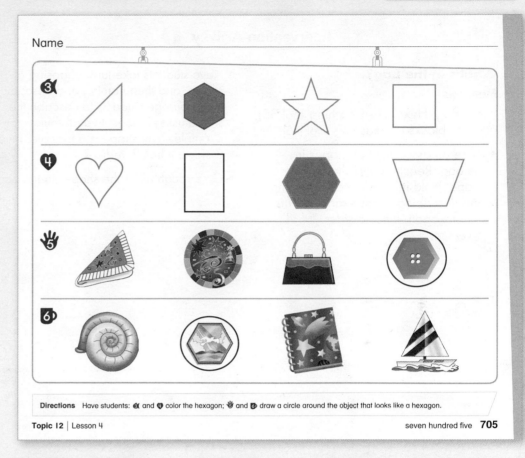

Name _____

Directions Have students: ❸ and ❹ color the hexagon; ✋ and ❻ draw a circle around the object that looks like a hexagon.

Topic 12 | Lesson 4   seven hundred five **705**

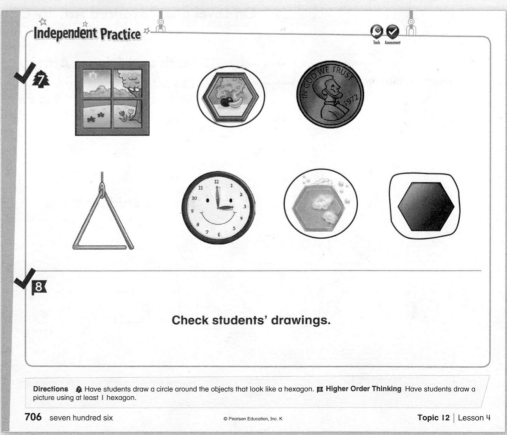

Independent Practice

Check students' drawings.

Directions 🐟 Have students draw a circle around the objects that look like a hexagon. ⬛ **Higher Order Thinking** Have students draw a picture using at least 1 hexagon.

706 seven hundred six   © Pearson Education, Inc. K   Topic 12 | Lesson 4

705–706

ASSESS AND DIFFERENTIATE

2 RtI

Use the **QUICK CHECK** on the previous page to prescribe differentiated instruction.

Ⓘ Intervention
0–3 points on the Quick Check

Ⓞ On-Level
4 points on the Quick Check

Ⓐ Advanced
5 points on the Quick Check

Intervention Activity Ⓘ

What's in the Bag?

Materials

Paper bag, Hexagons (Teaching Tool 36), attribute blocks (or Teaching Tool 46)

• Place an assortment of shapes in the bag. Reach in and choose one shape. Hold it up and model naming and describing it. For example, *This is a hexagon. It has 6 sides. It has 6 vertices.*

• Have students take turns choosing a shape, and then naming and describing it. Encourage students to describe the shape using at least two attributes, for example, "My shape is a triangle. It has 3 sides. It has 3 vertices."

• Go through all of the shapes in the bag.

Reteach Ⓘ

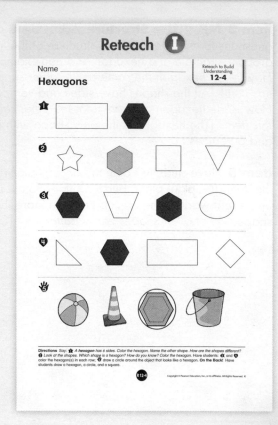

On-Level and Advanced Activity Centers Ⓞ Ⓐ

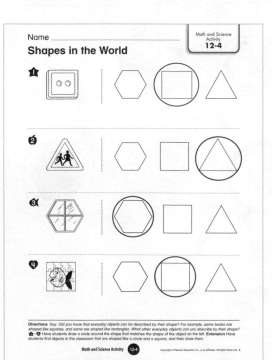

Math and Science Activity STEM

This activity revisits the science theme, **Pushing and Pulling Objects,** introduced on page 675 in the Student's Edition.

Sample Student Work

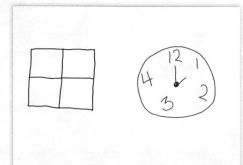

TIMING

The time allocated to Step 3 will depend on the teacher's instructional decisions and differentiation routines.

15–30 min

 Help Tools Games

PEARSON
realize
PearsonRealize.com

Technology Center

Tools

Games

Math Tools and Math Games

A link to a specific math tools activity or math game to use with this lesson is provided at PearsonRealize.com.

Leveled Assignment

I Items 1–3 **O** Items 2–4 **A** Items 3–5

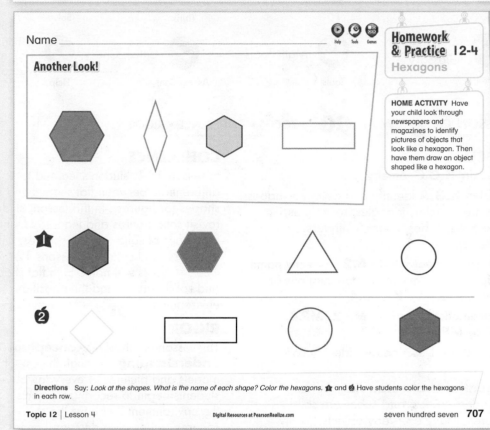

Name _____

Help Tools Games

Homework & Practice 12-4

Hexagons

Another Look!

HOME ACTIVITY Have your child look through newspapers and magazines to identify pictures of objects that look like a hexagon. Then have them draw an object shaped like a hexagon.

1

2

Directions Say: *Look at the shapes. What is the name of each shape? Color the hexagons.* ★ and 🍎 Have students color the hexagons in each row.

Topic 12 | Lesson 4   Digital Resources at PearsonRealize.com   seven hundred seven **707**

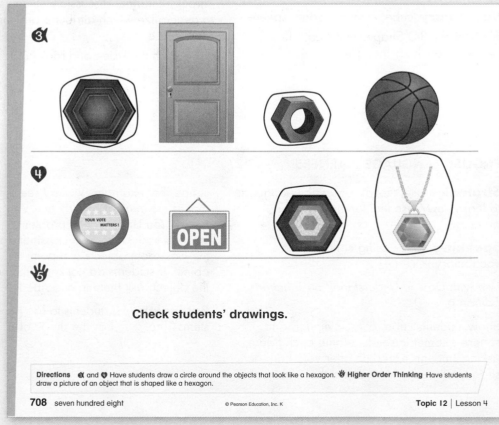

3

4

✋5

Check students' drawings.

Directions ◀ and ♥ Have students draw a circle around the objects that look like a hexagon. ✋ **Higher Order Thinking** Have students draw a picture of an object that is shaped like a hexagon.

708 seven hundred eight   © Pearson Education, Inc. K   **Topic 12 | Lesson 4**

LESSON 12-5
SOLID FIGURES

DIGITAL RESOURCES PearsonRealize.com

eText Student and Teacher eTexts

PD Listen and Look For Lesson Video

Think Today's Challenge

Solve Solve and Share

Learn Visual Learning Animation Plus

Glossary Animated Glossary

Tools Math Tools

Assessment Quick Check

Help Another Look Homework Video

Games Math Games

LESSON OVERVIEW **FCR** FOCUS • COHERENCE • RIGOR

MATH ANYTIME

FOCUS

Domain K.G Geometry

Cluster K.G.A Identify and describe shapes (squares, circles, triangles, rectangles, hexagons, cubes, cones, cylinders, and spheres).

Content Standard K.G.A.2 Correctly name shapes regardless of their orientations or overall size. Also **K.G.B.4**.

Mathematical Practices MP.2, MP.4, MP.6, MP.7

Objective Describe and identify solid figures.

Essential Understanding Spheres, cylinders, cones, and cubes are solid figures. Many everyday objects closely approximate these figures.

Vocabulary cube, cylinder, cone, sphere

Materials 3-D Shapes and Real Life Objects (Teaching Tool 39)

COHERENCE

In Lesson 12-1, students learned to differentiate between flat shapes and solid shapes (or figures). In this lesson, students revisit solid figures and learn to identify four types of solid figures: spheres, cubes, cylinders, and cones. In Lessons 12-6 and 12-7, students will name both flat shapes and solid figures, and their positions in the environment.

RIGOR

This lesson emphasizes **conceptual understanding**. Through the use of models and pictures of everyday objects, students begin to recognize objects in the environment that have the shapes of spheres, cubes, cylinders, and cones. Through informal discussion, students begin to generalize which attributes are unique to each figure.

PD Watch the Listen and Look For Lesson Video.

Daily Common Core Review

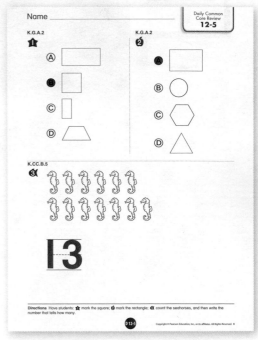

Today's Challenge

Think Use Topic 12 problems any time during this topic.

ENGLISH LANGUAGE LEARNERS ELL

Strategies Use known, accessible language to learn new/essential language in the process.

Speaking Speak using content area vocabulary in context.

Use with Do You Understand? on Teacher's Edition p. 710.

Show students cube, cone, cylinder, and sphere geometric solids. Name each figure, asking students to repeat after you. For each shape, tell students an object that is the same

shape. For example, *When I see a cone, it makes me think of a party hat.* Work through the Do You Understand? problem. Ask students to listen to their classmates tell about the classroom objects and point to each object. If students do not know the name of the object, ask them to describe it.

Beginning Ask students to use the sentence stem: "The ____ has the shape of a ____."

Intermediate Ask students to use complete sentences to tell the shape of the object.

Advanced Ask students to explain how the object's shape is the same as the geometric solid.

Summarize How can you describe the shape of objects?

PEARSON
realize.
PearsonRealize.com

COHERENCE: Engage students by connecting prior knowledge to new ideas.
Students learn about the shapes of many classroom objects. This prepares them for the next part of the lesson where they learn about these solid figures: cube, cylinder, cone, and sphere.

10–15 min

Solve

BEFORE

1. Pose the Solve-and-Share Problem
MP.4 Model with Math In this problem, students use real objects to draw a connection to three-dimensional solids.

Display a set of geometric solids: cone, cylinder, sphere, cube.

Jackson wants to find objects that have the same shape as the solid figures. How can he find objects that have the same shape? Draw objects below each solid figure that have the same shape.

2. Build Understanding
What are you asked to find? [Other objects that look like the solid figures] *What tools do you have to solve the problem?* [Geometric solids]

DURING

3. Ask Guiding Questions As Needed
Hold up different solids and ask students the following questions: *Does this shape have flat sides? Does it have any corners? What objects in our classroom have this shape?*

AFTER

4. Share and Discuss Solutions
Start with students' solutions. If needed, **Solve** project and analyze Kennedy's work to discuss how real-world objects relate to solid figures.

5. Transition to the Visual Learning Bridge
You found objects that have the same shapes as the pictured figures. Later in the lesson, you will identify the shapes of everyday objects.

6. Extension for Early Finishers
Show students various classroom objects shaped like solid figures. Have them complete this sentence for each object: "This object is shaped like a _____." [sphere, cube, cone, or cylinder]

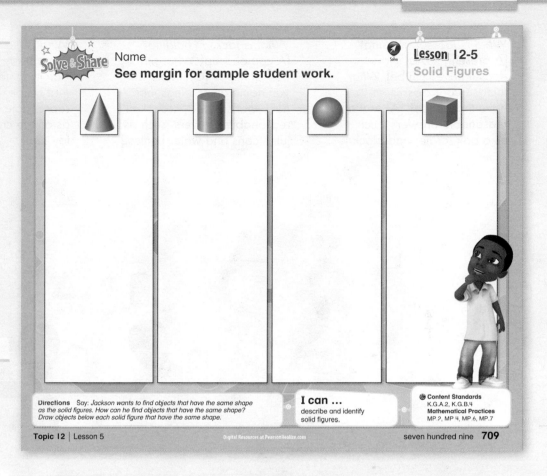

Solve & Share

Name _____

See margin for sample student work.

Solve

Lesson 12-5
Solid Figures

Directions Say: *Jackson wants to find objects that have the same shape as the solid figures. How can he find objects that have the same shape? Draw objects below each solid figure that have the same shape.*

I can ...
describe and identify solid figures.

Content Standards
K.G.A.2, K.G.B.4
Mathematical Practices
MP.2, MP.4, MP.6, MP.7

Topic 12 | Lesson 5

Digital Resources at PearsonRealize.com

seven hundred nine **709**

Analyze Student Work

Kennedy's Work

Derek's Work

Kennedy draws real-world shapes that match the three-dimensional solids shown.

Derek draws shapes that do not match the three-dimensional solids shown.

STEP 2

DEVELOP: VISUAL LEARNING

The *Visual Learning Bridge* connects students' thinking in Solve & Share to important math ideas in the lesson. Use the *Visual Learning Bridge* to make these ideas explicit. Also available as a *Visual Learning Animation Plus* at PearsonRealize.com

E L L Visual Learning

Learn   Glossary

What is Jackson holding? [A present] *What shape does it have?* [Cube] *What things in our classroom have that shape?* [Accept all reasonable answers, such as a box, crate, and block.]

What is Jackson holding? [A can of soup] *What shape does it have?* [Cylinder] *Can you name other things that have that shape?* [Accept all reasonable answers, such as juice cans and water bottles.]

What solid figure looks like a party hat? [A cone] *Name something with that shape.* [Accept all reasonable answers, such as an ice cream cone and toy top.]

MP.7 Use Structure *What shape does a ball have?* [It is round and has no flat sides.] *What solid figure looks like a ball?* [A sphere] *Can you name other things that have that shape?* [Accept all reasonable answers, such as planet Earth, the sun, and peas.]

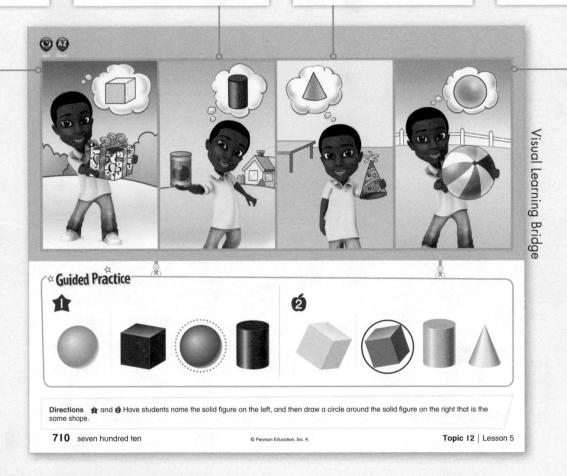

Visual Learning Bridge

Guided Practice

1

2

Directions ★ and ② Have students name the solid figure on the left, and then draw a circle around the solid figure on the right that is the same shape.

710 seven hundred ten   © Pearson Education, Inc. K   **Topic 12** | Lesson 5

Complete the *Do You Understand? Show Me!* problem before starting Guided Practice.

Do You Understand? Show Me! MP.2 Reasoning
Display the geometric solids and hold up a cube. *Name something in our classroom that has the shape of a cube.* [Accept all reasonable answers.] Repeat for cone, cylinder, and sphere.

Coherence In the Visual Learning Bridge, students learn to identify the shapes of some solid objects. This links back to their work in Lessons 12-2 through 12-4, where students identified the shapes of certain flat objects.

Essential Question Ask the following Essential Question: *How are spheres, cubes, cylinders, and cones the same?* [They are solid figures.]

Error Intervention: Item 2

If students are confused by the size, color, or orientation of a solid figure,

then have them compare models with matching classroom objects that students can hold in their hands. Have them focus on the attributes of one shape at a time.

1 RtI **Reteaching** Assign Reteaching Set E, p. 737.

QUICK CHECK

Check mark indicates items for prescribing differentiation on the next page.
Items 10 and 11 are worth 1 point. Item 12 is worth up to 3 points.

20–30 min

Tools Assessment

Items 3–8 Remind students that matching shapes do not need to be the same size, direction or orientation, or color.

Item 6 MP.6 Be Precise To help students identify the object that matches the shape, ask them to describe the attributes of the cone, such as it is flat at one end, has a point at the other end, and is curvy in between. Then have them consider each object one by one. *Explain why each object does or does not match the attributes of the cone.* [Sample answer: The ball does not have a flat side or a point at one end.]

Items 9–12 MP.2 Reasoning Remind students that solid figures can be turned in different directions or orientations, but they are still the same objects.

Item 10 Show students something that is shaped like a cube. Help students describe the object. *Is the object round?* [No.] *Is it curvy?* [No.] *Does it have any flat sides?* [Yes.] Help students conclude that all sides of the cube are flat. Then help them locate the solid that only has flat sides. Tell students to remember to look for flat sides when describing and matching solids.

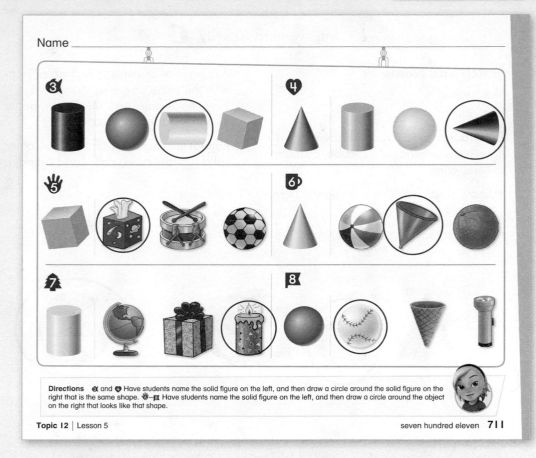

Directions ❸ and ❹ Have students name the solid figure on the left, and then draw a circle around the solid figure on the right that is the same shape. ❺–❽ Have students name the solid figure on the left, and then draw a circle around the object on the right that looks like that shape.

Topic 12 | Lesson 5

seven hundred eleven **711**

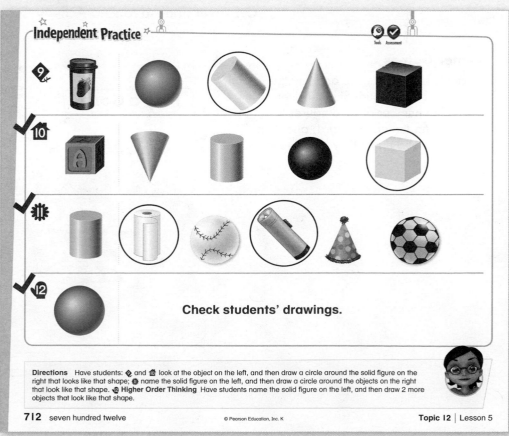

Independent Practice

Check students' drawings.

Directions Have students: ❾ and ❿ look at the object on the left, and then draw a circle around the solid figure on the right that looks like that shape; ⓫ name the solid figure on the left, and then draw a circle around the objects on the right that look like that shape. ⓬ **Higher Order Thinking** Have students name the solid figure on the left, and then draw 2 more objects that look like that shape.

712 seven hundred twelve   © Pearson Education, Inc. K   **Topic 12 | Lesson 5**

711–712

Use the **QUICK CHECK** on the previous page to prescribe differentiated instruction.

I **Intervention**
0–3 points on the Quick Check

O **On-Level**
4 points on the Quick Check

A **Advanced**
5 points on the Quick Check

Intervention Activity **I**

Match and Name

Materials

(per pair)

Classroom objects in the shape of solid figures, geometric solids: cube, cylinder, sphere, cone

- Show a sphere. *This is a sphere.* Have students repeat "sphere."

- Model describing a sphere: *A sphere is round like a ball. It has no flat surfaces.*

- Ask pairs of students to find an object with the same shape as the sphere. Have each pair show the object, name it, and describe the shape.

- Repeat that activity with the three other solid figures: cube, cone, and cylinder.

Reteach **I**

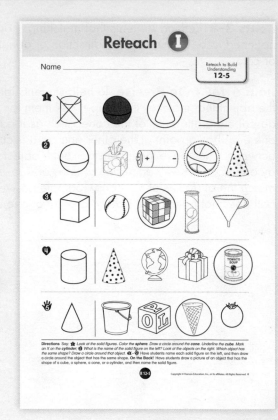

On-Level and Advanced Activity Centers **O** **A**

Center Games

Students toss a dot cube and say the number of dots aloud. Students then count that number of solid figures to move along the game board, and then name the solid figure they land on.

★ On-Level

★★ Advanced

TIMING

The time allocated to Step 3 will depend on the teacher's instructional decisions and differentiation routines.

15–30 min

 Help Tools Games

PEARSON
realize
PearsonRealize.com

Technology Center

 Tools

 Games

Math Tools and Math Games

A link to a specific math tools activity or math game to use with this lesson is provided at PearsonRealize.com.

Leveled Assignment

 Items 1–4   Ⓞ Items 2–5   Ⓐ Items 3–6

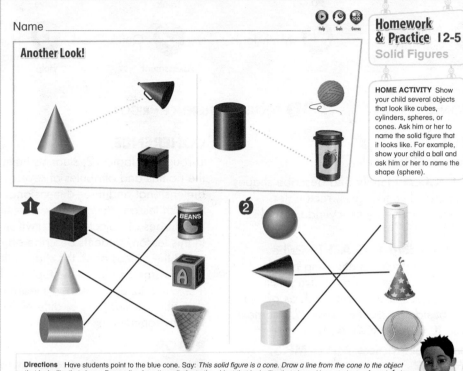

Name _____

Help Tools Games

Homework & Practice 12-5
Solid Figures

Another Look!

HOME ACTIVITY Show your child several objects that look like cubes, cylinders, spheres, or cones. Ask him or her to name the solid figure that it looks like. For example, show your child a ball and ask him or her to name the shape (sphere).

Directions Have students point to the blue cone. Say: *This solid figure is a cone. Draw a line from the cone to the object that looks like that shape. Draw a line from the cylinder to the object that looks like that shape.* Have students: ★ and ② draw a line from each solid figure to the object that looks like that shape.

Topic 12 | Lesson 5   Digital Resources at PearsonRealize.com   seven hundred thirteen **713**

Check students' drawings.

Directions ❸ and ❹ Have students draw a circle around the 4 objects in each row that look like the same shape, and then name the shape. ✋ **Math and Science** Say: *Pushing on an object can make it move. Some shapes are easier to push than others.* Have students draw a circle around the object that is easier to push. ❻ **Higher Order Thinking** Have students draw 2 objects that do NOT look like a sphere. Tell a partner what shapes the objects look like.

714 seven hundred fourteen   © Pearson Education, Inc. K   Topic 12 | Lesson 5

LESSON 12-6

DESCRIBE SHAPES IN THE ENVIRONMENT

LESSON OVERVIEW   F C R FOCUS • COHERENCE • RIGOR

FOCUS

Domain K.G Geometry

Cluster K.G.A Identify and describe shapes (squares, circles, triangles, rectangles, hexagons, cubes, cones, cylinders, and spheres).

Content Standard K.G.A.1 Describe objects in the environment using names of shapes, and describe the relative positions of these objects using terms such as *above, below, beside, in front of, behind,* and *next to.* Also **K.G.A.2, K.G.A.3.**

Mathematical Practices MP.1, MP.3, MP.6, MP.7

Objective Describe shapes in the environment.

Essential Understanding Objects have shape. Some objects look like flat shapes or solid shapes, including squares, rectangles, triangles, circles, hexagons, spheres, cubes, cylinders, and cones.

COHERENCE

Throughout Topic 12, students have learned the names and attributes of several two-dimensional and three-dimensional shapes. In each lesson, students have identified the shapes of objects in the environment. In this lesson, students describe objects using the names of all the shapes that they have learned so far in the topic. In Lessons 12-7 and 12-8, students will learn how to describe the positions of different objects in the environment.

RIGOR

This lesson emphasizes **conceptual understanding** and **application**. Students review and generalize defining attributes of different shapes. They use these concepts and related vocabulary to describe the shapes in the environment.

 Watch the Listen and Look For Lesson Video.
PD

MATH ANYTIME

Daily Common Core Review

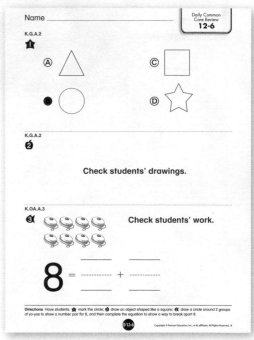

Today's Challenge
Think Use Topic 12 problems any time during this topic.

ENGLISH LANGUAGE LEARNERS E L L

Strategies Use prior knowledge to understand meanings.

Use with the Visual Learning Bridge on Student's Edition p. 716.

Write *flat* and *solid.* Say: *We've worked with flat and solid objects in the past. Describe to your partner an object that is flat and an object that is solid.* Point to the wall. Ask: *Is the wall a flat or solid object?*

Beginning Point to a ball. Ask: *Is the ball flat or solid?* Students will respond using the sentence stem: "The ball is ___." Continue the process with other objects in the classroom.

Intermediate Point to a ball. Ask: *Is the ball flat or solid? How do you know?* Students will respond using the sentence stem: "The ball is ___ because ___." Continue the process with other objects in the classroom.

Advanced Draw a T-Chart on chart paper. On one side of the T-Chart, label *Flat* and on the other, label *Solid.* Instruct students to identify objects in the classroom as flat or solid and draw pictures of or write words for the objects on the T-Chart. Ask students to explain to partners why certain objects are flat and others are solid.

Summarize How would you describe objects that are flat and objects that are solid?

COHERENCE: Engage students by connecting prior knowledge to new ideas.
Students review the names of flat and solid shapes and look for an example of one of these shapes in the classroom. This prepares students to describe an object by its shape.

10–15 min

 Solve

BEFORE

1. Pose the Solve-and-Share Problem
MP.7 Use Structure Students identify a shape and look for an example of the shape in the environment.

Say: *Draw a circle around one of the shapes on the workmat. Name the shape. Can you find that shape in your classroom? Draw a picture of the object and its surroundings.*

2. Build Understanding
Look at the shapes on the page. Which are flat? [Students indicate shapes on the right.] *Which are solid?* [Students indicate shapes on the left.] *Let's say the names of the shapes together.* Name the shapes with students starting at the top of the left hand column to the bottom and then the right hand column from top to bottom. [cone, sphere, cube, cylinder, hexagon, circle, triangle, square, rectangle]

DURING

3. Ask Guiding Questions As Needed
Which shapes do you see in the classroom? [Answers will vary.] *Which shapes do you NOT see in the classroom?* [Answers will vary.] Depending upon students' answers, ask questions that draw students' attention to objects with these shapes.

AFTER

4. Share and Discuss Solutions
 Solve Start with students' solutions. Have them share the strategies used to solve the problem. If needed, project and analyze Felipe's work to discuss an example of a shape in the environment.

5. Transition to the Visual Learning Bridge
You identified a shape and found an object that had that shape. Later in this lesson, you will learn to describe objects by their shapes.

6. Extension for Early Finishers
Have students repeat the activity using a different shape on their workmat. Have students describe how the two shapes or objects are alike or different.

Solve & Share

Name _____

See margin for sample student work.

 Solve

Directions Say: *Draw a circle around one of the shapes on the workmat. Name the shape. Can you find that shape in your classroom? Draw a picture of the object and its surroundings.*

I can ...
describe shapes in the environment.

Content Standards
K.G.A.1, K.G.A.2, K.G.A.3
Mathematical Practices
MP.1, MP.3, MP.6, MP.7

Topic 12 | Lesson 6   Digital Resources at PearsonRealize.com   seven hundred fifteen **715**

Analyze Student Work

Felipe's Work

Ursula's Work

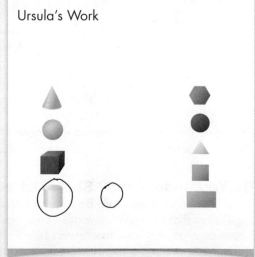

Felipe chooses a cone from the workmat. At first he has trouble finding a cone in the classroom, but he finds that there was a cone in his hand the whole time—his pencil tip.

Ursula chooses a cylinder. She draws a circle that represents a circle that she sees on the bulletin board. Ursula matches the circle to the face on the cylinder instead of looking for the solid.

DEVELOP: VISUAL LEARNING

STEP 2

PEARSON
realize
PearsonRealize.com

Learn   Glossary

The *Visual Learning Bridge* connects students' thinking in Solve & Share to important math ideas in the lesson. Use the *Visual Learning Bridge* to make these ideas explicit. Also available as a *Visual Learning Animation Plus* at PearsonRealize.com

ELL
Visual Learning

What objects do you see in the classroom? [Clock, blackboard, table, ball, tissue box] *Which objects have flat shapes?* [Clock, blackboard, tabletop] *Which objects have solid shapes?* [Ball, tissue box]

MP.6 Be Precise Explain to students that they can describe the objects using the names of shapes. *Follow the blue arrows from the first picture. What shape can you use to describe the clock?* [Circle] *The blackboard?* [Rectangle] *The ball?* [Sphere] *The tissue box?* [Cube]

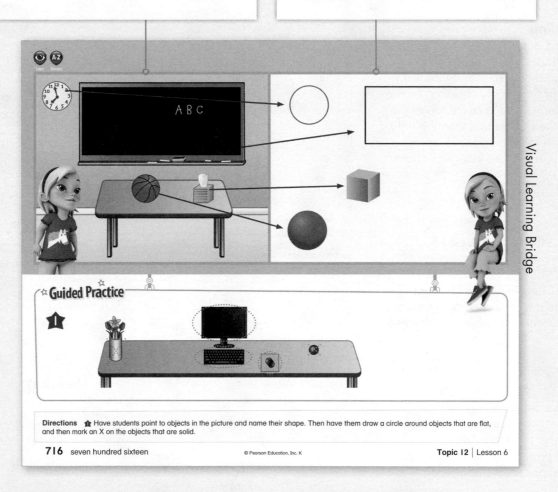

Visual Learning Bridge

☆ **Guided Practice**

Directions ★ Have students point to objects in the picture and name their shape. Then have them draw a circle around objects that are flat, and then mark an X on the objects that are solid.

716 seven hundred sixteen   © Pearson Education, Inc. K   **Topic 12 | Lesson 6**

Complete the *Do You Understand? Show Me!* problem before starting Guided Practice.

Do You Understand? Show Me! MP.3 Critique Reasoning

Direct students' attention to Box 1 in the Visual Learning Bridge. *Keith says that the tabletop looks like a triangle. Is Keith correct? Show or explain.* [Sample answer: No, Keith is wrong. The tabletop looks like a rectangle because it has 4 sides. A triangle has 3 sides.]

Essential Question

Ask the following Essential Question: *What shapes can you use to describe objects in the environment?* [Sample answers: squares, rectangles, triangles, circles, hexagons, spheres, cubes, cylinders, and cones]

Error Intervention: Item 1

If students identify the computer as being solid,

then explain that we're thinking of the flat screen as a flat shape, just as we are thinking of the blackboard as a flat shape.

1 RtI

Reteaching Assign Reteaching Set F, p. 737.

✓ **QUICK CHECK**
Check mark indicates items for prescribing differentiation on the next page.
Item 3 is worth 2 points. Item 4 is worth up to 3 points.

20–30 min

Tools Assessment

Item 2 MP.6 Be Precise *What shapes do you see in the picture?* [Cylinders, squares, circles, rectangles] *Which are two-dimensional shapes and which are three-dimensional shapes?* [The squares, circles, and rectangles are two-dimensional. The cylinders are three-dimensional.]

Challenge students to draw an additional two- or three-dimensional shape on the picture. *Draw an object on the picture whose shape you know. What is the object?* [Sample answer: a ball] *What is its shape?* [Sample answer: a sphere]

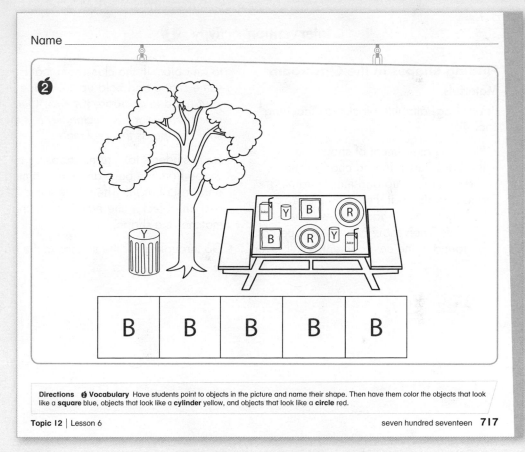

Name _____

2

| B | B | B | B | B |

Directions ✐ **Vocabulary** Have students point to objects in the picture and name their shape. Then have them color the objects that look like a **square** blue, objects that look like a **cylinder** yellow, and objects that look like a **circle** red.

Topic 12 | Lesson 6   seven hundred seventeen **717**

Item 3 *How are the pennant and the funnel different?* [The pennant is a flat shape; it is a triangle. The funnel is a solid shape; it is a cone.] *How can you describe the tire?* [The tire has a shape like a circle.]

Item 4 MP.1 Make Sense and Persevere
Activate students' prior knowledge so that they can focus on the math in the item. *What parks have you visited? What objects did you see in the parks? What will you draw in your picture of the park?* [Answers will vary.] This will help them make sense of the problem and work through the steps needed to complete the task.

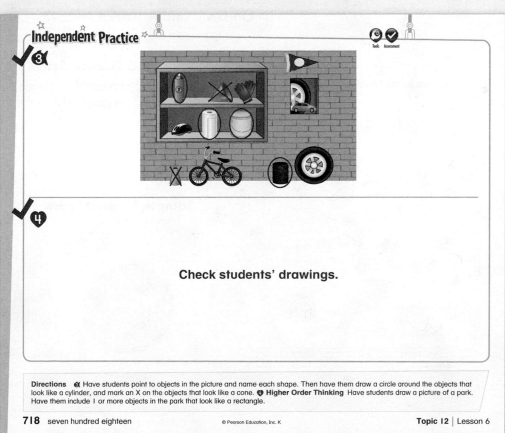

Independent Practice

3

4

Check students' drawings.

Directions ✐ Have students point to objects in the picture and name each shape. Then have them draw a circle around the objects that look like a cylinder, and mark an X on the objects that look like a cone. ❶ **Higher Order Thinking** Have students draw a picture of a park. Have them include 1 or more objects in the park that look like a rectangle.

718 seven hundred eighteen   © Pearson Education, Inc. K   Topic 12 | Lesson 6

717–718

Use the **QUICK CHECK** on the previous page to prescribe differentiated instruction.

ⓘ Intervention
0–3 points on the Quick Check

Ⓞ On-Level
4 points on the Quick Check

Ⓐ Advanced
5 points on the Quick Check

Intervention Activity ⓘ

Finding Shapes in the Classroom
Materials
Paper bag, attribute blocks (or Teaching Tool 46)

• Place an assortment of shapes in the bag. Reach in and choose one shape. Hold it up and model naming and describing it. For example, *This is a rectangle. It has 4 sides. It has 4 vertices.* Then show how this shape can be found in the environment. Walk over to an object in the classroom that is the same shape and hold up the shape in your hand to compare the two. *Our classroom door is a rectangle. It is the same shape as this rectangle.*

• Have students take turns choosing a shape from the bag, and then naming and describing it. Then have them find an object in the environment that matches the shape.

• Go through all of the shapes in the bag.

Reteach ⓘ

Name _____

Reteach to Build Understanding
12-6

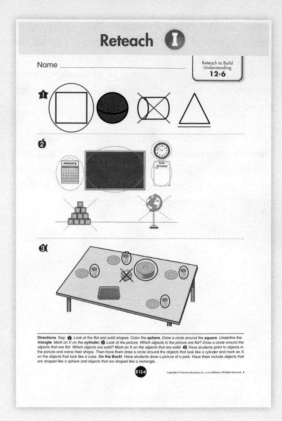

Directions Say: ☆ *Look at the flat and solid shapes. Color the sphere. Draw a circle around the square. Underline the triangle. Mark an X on the cylinder.* ❶ *Look at the picture. Which objects in the picture are flat? Draw a circle around the objects that are flat. Which objects are solid? Mark an X on the objects that are solid.* ❷ *Have students point to objects in the picture and name their shape. Then have them draw a circle around the objects that look like a cylinder and mark an X on the objects that look like a cube.* **On the Back!** *Have students draw a picture of a park. Have them include objects that are shaped like a sphere and objects that are shaped like a rectangle.*

R 12-6   Copyright © Pearson Education, Inc., or its affiliates. All Rights Reserved. K

On-Level and Advanced Activity Centers Ⓞ Ⓐ

Name _____
Objects in the Environment

Math and Science Activity
12-6

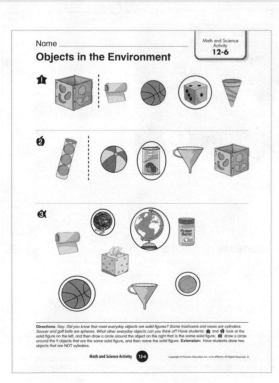

Directions Say: *Did you know that most everyday objects are solid figures? Some trashcans and vases are cylinders. Soccer and golf balls are spheres. What other everyday objects can you think of?* Have students: ☆ and ❶ *look at the solid figure on the left, and then draw a circle around the object on the right that is the same solid figure.* ❷ *draw a circle around the 4 objects that are the same solid figure, and then name the solid figure.* **Extension:** *Have students draw two objects that are NOT cylinders.*

Math and Science Activity   12-6   Copyright © Pearson Education, Inc., or its affiliates. All Rights Reserved. K

Math and Science Activity STEM
This activity revisits the science theme, **Pushing and Pulling Objects**, introduced on page 675 in the Student's Edition.

Sample Student Work

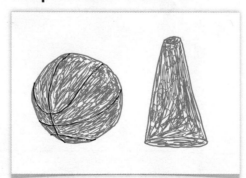

TIMING

The time allocated to Step 3 will depend on the teacher's instructional decisions and differentiation routines.

15–30 min

 Help   Tools   Games

PEARSON
realize.
PearsonRealize.com

Technology Center I O A

 Tools

Math Tools and Math Games

A link to a specific math tools activity or math game to use with this lesson is provided at PearsonRealize.com.

Games

Leveled Assignment

I Items 1–2   O Items 2–3   A Items 1–3

Name _____

 Help Tools Games

Another Look!

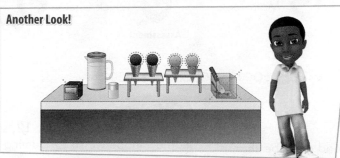

Homework & Practice 12-6
Describe Shapes in the Environment

HOME ACTIVITY Have your child identify and name objects in your house that look like a circle, square, rectangle, triangle, hexagon, sphere, cube, cylinder, and cone. Have them tell where each object is located in the house.

 1

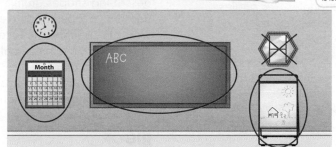

Directions Say: *Point to a scoop of ice cream. What shape is the scoop of ice cream? Find other objects in the picture that look like a sphere and draw a circle around them. Can you find an object that looks like a cube? Mark an X on the objects that look like a cube.*
⭐ Have students point to objects in the picture and name each shape. Then have them draw a circle around the objects that look like a rectangle, and then mark an X on the object that looks like a hexagon.

Topic 12 | Lesson 6   Digital Resources at PearsonRealize.com   seven hundred nineteen **719**

2

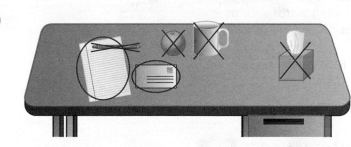

3

Check students' drawings.

Directions Have students point to objects in the picture and name their shape. Have them draw a circle around objects that are flat, and then mark an X on objects that are solid. ⭐ **Higher Order Thinking** Have students draw a picture of a playground. Have them draw at least 1 object that looks like a sphere and 1 object that looks like a rectangle.

720 seven hundred twenty   © Pearson Education, Inc. K   **Topic 12** | Lesson 6

DESCRIBE THE POSITION OF SHAPES IN THE ENVIRONMENT

DIGITAL RESOURCES PearsonRealize.com

 eText Student and Teacher eTexts

 PD Listen and Look For Lesson Video

 Think Today's Challenge

 Solve Solve and Share

 Learn Visual Learning Animation Plus

 Glossary Animated Glossary

 Tools Math Tools

 Assessment Quick Check

 Help Another Look Homework Video

 **Games** Math Games

LESSON OVERVIEW   FCR FOCUS • COHERENCE • RIGOR

FOCUS

Domain K.G Geometry

Cluster K.G.A Identify and describe shapes (squares, circles, triangles, rectangles, hexagons, cubes, cones, cylinders, and spheres).

Content Standard K.G.A.1 Describe objects in the environment using names of shapes, and describe the relative positions of these objects using terms such as *above, below, beside, in front of, behind,* and *next to.*

Mathematical Practices MP.1, MP.2, MP.3, MP.6

Objective Describe positions of shapes in the environment.

Essential Understanding The positions of objects in relation to surrounding objects can be described using words such as *above, below, beside, in front of, behind,* and *next to.*

Vocabulary in front of, behind, next to, above, below, beside

COHERENCE

In previous lessons in Topic 12, students learned shape words for naming and describing shapes. In this lesson, students use that vocabulary as well as position words to describe the location of shapes. Being able to communicate position is important in all math topics. For example, in Grade 1 Topic 8, students will learn about the importance of position in numbers when they study place value to 100.

RIGOR

This lesson emphasizes **conceptual understanding** and **application**. Students practice using shape and position words to describe the location of objects and shapes.

 PD Watch the Listen and Look For Lesson Video.

MATH ANYTIME

Daily Common Core Review

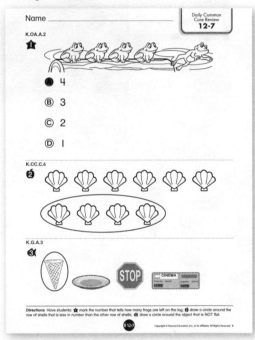

Today's Challenge

 Think Use Topic 12 problems any time during this topic.

ENGLISH LANGUAGE LEARNERS ELL

Listening Demonstrate listening comprehension by following directions.

Use with the Visual Learning Bridge on Student's Edition, p. 722.

Say: *Listen carefully and follow directions.* Ask students to hold their pencil above their heads, in front of their noses, next to their elbows, behind their knees, and next to their ear. Write *next to, in front, above,* and *behind.* Say: *Use these words to describe positions of shapes in our classroom.* On a table, display a sticky note next to a cup. Say: *The square is next to the cup.*

Beginning Move the sticky note in front of the cup. Say: *The square is in front of the cup.* Move the sticky note behind the cup. Say: *The square is behind the cup.* Ask students to put their pencil boxes on their desks. Distribute sticky notes to each student. Give students directions, such as, *Put the square next to your pencil box.*

Intermediate Ask students to look around the room to find the objects being described. Say: *I'm thinking of a rectangle that is next to the wall. What am I thinking about?* [Sample answer: flag] Continue providing

clues for finding shapes in the environment using *next to, in front of,* and *behind* in the directions.

Advanced Divide students into partner groups. Have Student A describe a shape's position in the room using *next to, in front,* or *behind.* Student B should find the objects being described. Have students reverse roles and repeat.

Summarize What do *next to, in front of,* and *behind* mean?

DEVELOP: PROBLEM-BASED LEARNING

COHERENCE: Engage students by connecting prior knowledge to new ideas.

Students use their everyday language to describe the positions of objects in the picture. This prepares them for the next part of the lesson, where students practice using words that describe the positions of objects.

 10–15 min

 Solve

 **BEFORE**

1. Pose the Solve-and-Share Problem

MP.1 Make Sense and Persevere Students review what they know about shapes. They choose a location for a horse and informally talk about the location of the horse.

Emily feeds the animals on the farm. Look at the objects in the picture. Color and name the shapes you see. Draw a horse on the farm. Describe the position of the horse.

2. Build Understanding

Talk about the word *position*. Students might be familiar with its meaning as the way a person sits or stands, such as sitting in a cross-legged position. Explain that position can refer to locations of individual people or objects. *What position do we get into to go to the cafeteria?* [Into a line with people in front and behind]

 **DURING**

3. Ask Guiding Questions As Needed

Encourage students to verbalize the locations of shapes and objects using their own words. *What is next to the dog?* [A pail] *What is under the rooster?* [An object shaped like a cube]

 AFTER

4. Share and Discuss Solutions

Start with students' solutions. Have them share the strategies used to solve the problem. If needed, project and analyze Teo's work or Bristol's work to discuss one approach.

5. Transition to the Visual Learning Bridge

You used words to talk about positions of shapes and objects. Later in this lesson, you will learn more words that can help you describe position.

6. Extension for Early Finishers

Have students draw a pig or a cow in the farm picture. Ask them to describe what the animal is doing and what its position is relative to other shapes in the picture.

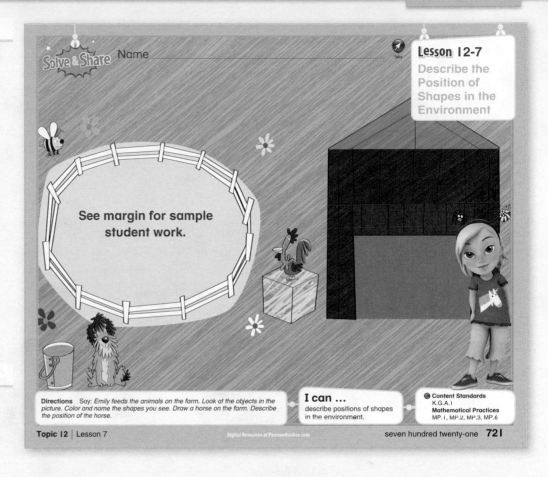

Solve & Share   Name _____

See margin for sample student work.

Lesson 12-7
Describe the Position of Shapes in the Environment

Directions Say: Emily feeds the animals on the farm. Look at the objects in the picture. Color and name the shapes you see. Draw a horse on the farm. Describe the position of the horse.

I can ... describe positions of shapes in the environment.

Content Standards K.G.A.1 **Mathematical Practices** MP.1, MP.2, MP.3, MP.6

Topic 12 | Lesson 7   Digital Resources at PearsonRealize.com   seven hundred twenty-one **721**

Analyze Student Work

Teo's Work

Teo colors and names 1 circle, 1 cube, 2 rectangles, and 1 triangle, and then draws a horse in the corral.

Bristol's Work

Bristol colors and names 1 circle, 1 cube, 1 square, and 1 triangle, and then draws a horse in front of the barn.

DEVELOP: VISUAL LEARNING

The *Visual Learning Bridge* connects students' thinking in Solve & Share to important math ideas in the lesson. Use the *Visual Learning Bridge* to make these ideas explicit. Also available as a *Visual Learning Animation Plus* at PearsonRealize.com

Visual Learning

Learn Glossary

MP.6 Be Precise *Look at the objects in the picture. What shapes do the objects have?* [Sample answers: Circle, sphere, rectangle, cylinder] *Which object is behind the chair, the yarn or the cat?* [The cat] *Where is the girl standing?* [Sample answers: Next to the chair; behind the table]

Continue using vocabulary words and providing opportunities for students to use the vocabulary words. *Where is the girl standing now?* [Behind the table] *Who is sitting in front of the chair?* [The boy]

Visual Learning Bridge

☆ **Guided Practice**

Directions ★ Have students mark an X on the object next to the pencil that looks like a rectangle. Have students draw an object that looks like a square in front of the mug. Then have them draw an object that looks like a cone next to the table.

722 seven hundred twenty-two   © Pearson Education, Inc. K   **Topic 12** | Lesson 7

Complete the *Do You Understand? Show Me!* problem before starting Guided Practice.

Do You Understand? Show Me! MP.2 Reasoning Place
about five different objects on a desk. Stack two of the objects. Point to an object and have students name the object and describe its position. Have students suggest another way to describe the object's position.

Ask the following Essential Question: *What words can you use to describe the position of shapes in the environment?* [Sample answers: *Above, below, beside, in front of, behind,* and *next to*]

Error Intervention: Item 1

If students draw a cube instead of a cone,

then show them a model of each to compare. *How are the words cube and cone alike?* [Both start with the same sound.] *How can you remember which is which?* [Sample answer: I can think of an ice cube and an ice cream cone.]

1 RtI **Reteaching** Assign Reteaching Set G, p. 738.

☑ **QUICK CHECK**
Check mark indicates items for prescribing differentiation on the next page.
Item 3 is worth up to 5 points.

20–30 min

Tools   Assessment

Item 2 MP.2 Reasoning *Where will you draw the rectangle? Is there more than one place where you can draw a rectangle that is beside the sandbox?* [Sample answer: Yes, the rectangle can be on any side of the sandbox, though *beside* is often used to mean to the right or left.]

MP.1 Make Sense and Persevere Students need to make sense of the directions before they can begin drawing. They need to plan out what they will draw and where it goes. It will help students if each part of the directions is read separately, so that students understand what is being asked of them.

Name _____

Check students' drawings.

Directions 🍎 Have students name the shape of the objects in the picture and use position words to describe their location. Then have them draw an X on the object in front of the sandcastle that looks like a cylinder. Have students draw an object that looks like a sphere beside Jackson, and then an object that looks like a rectangle beside the sandbox.

Topic 12 | Lesson 7   seven hundred twenty-three   **723**

Item 3 MP.3 Construct Arguments *What other word can you use to describe the shape of the object you drew above the tree?* [A circle] *Explain why this is true.* [When you draw a sphere it can also look like a two-dimensional circle.]

Some students may say the apples on the tree are spheres. Discuss with students why the apples are similar to and different from spheres. [They are round around the middle but not on the top and bottom.]

Independent Practice

✓ 3

Check students' drawings.

Directions 👆 **Higher Order Thinking** Have students mark an X on the object below the tree that looks like a rectangle. Have students draw an object that looks like a sphere above the tree, and then an object that looks like a triangle behind the fence. Then have them name the shape of the objects in the picture and use position words to describe their location.

724 seven hundred twenty-four   © Pearson Education, Inc. K   Topic 12 | Lesson 7

STEP 3 ASSESS AND DIFFERENTIATE

Use the **QUICK CHECK** on the previous page to prescribe differentiated instruction.

2 RtI

I Intervention
0–3 points on the Quick Check

O On-Level
4 points on the Quick Check

A Advanced
5 points on the Quick Check

Intervention Activity **I**

Lily Pad Hop

Materials

2 sheets of green construction paper, tape

- Tape a sheet of green construction paper to the floor. Tell students they are hopping frogs and this is their lily pad.

- Model each action as you call out directions. *Hop in front of the lily pad. Hop next to the lily pad. Hop behind the lily pad.* Hold the other sheet of paper above your head. *Hop below the lily pad.*

- Then, one at a time, have students act out different directions you give them. Use a variety of position words learned in the lesson.

Reteach **I**

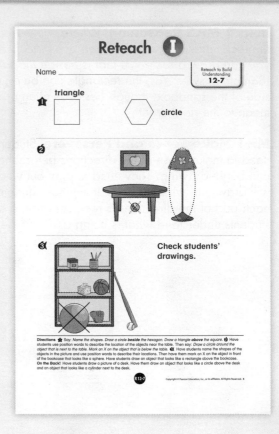

On-Level and Advanced Activity Centers **O** **A**

Center Games

For the On-Level game, a number tile is drawn to determine which player gets to name an object that is either "in front of" or "behind" the fence and places a square on that object. In the Advanced game, a tile is drawn to determine how many objects a player chooses and says whether each object is "in front of" or "behind" another object and places a square on each object. In both games, play continues until one player uses all of his or her squares.

TIMING

The time allocated to Step 3 will depend on the teacher's instructional decisions and differentiation routines.

15–30 min

 Help Tools Games

PEARSON
realize
PearsonRealize.com

Technology Center

 Tools
 Games

Math Tools and Math Games

A link to a specific math tools activity or math game to use with this lesson is provided at PearsonRealize.com.

Leveled Assignment

I Items 1–2   **O** Items 2–3   **A** Items 1–3

Name _____ Help Tools Games

Homework & Practice 12-7
Describe the Position of Shapes in the Environment

Another Look!

 City Park

HOME ACTIVITY Have your child name the shapes of several items in the kitchen, and then tell where they are located using the following position words: *above, below, in front of, behind, next to,* and *beside.*

Directions Say: *Look at the shapes on the left. Then look at the picture. Find the object that is below the tree, and then mark an X on the shape that it looks like. Then draw circles around the objects in the picture that look like circles.* ⭐ Have students find the object that is behind the cone, and then mark an X on the solid figure that it looks like on the left. Then have students draw circles around the objects in the picture that are shaped like spheres.

Topic 12 | Lesson 7   Digital Resources at PearsonRealize.com   seven hundred twenty-five **725**

 sphere

cube   cone

Directions ✏ Have students find the object that is above the table, and then mark an X on the solid figure that it looks like on the left. Then have students draw circles around the objects in the picture that are shaped like spheres. ✦ **Higher Order Thinking** Have students draw an object shaped like a cube below an object shaped like a sphere, and beside an object shaped like a cone.

726 seven hundred twenty-six   © Pearson Education, Inc. K   **Topic 12 | Lesson 7**

PRECISION

DIGITAL RESOURCES PearsonRealize.com

 Student and Teacher eTexts
eText

 Listen and Look For Lesson Video
PD

Today's Challenge
Think

Solve and Share
Solve

 Visual Learning Animation Plus
Learn

 Math Practices Animations
MP

 A-Z Animated Glossary
Glossary

 Math Tools
Tools

 Quick Check
Assessment

 Another Look Homework Video
Help

 Math Games
Games

LESSON OVERVIEW 🄕🄲🄡 FOCUS • COHERENCE • RIGOR

FOCUS

Mathematical Practices MP.6 Attend to precision. Also **MP.2, MP.3**

Content Standard K.G.A.1

Objective Describe positions of shapes in the environment.

Essential Understanding Good math thinkers are careful about what they write and say, so their ideas about math are clear.

Materials Connecting cubes (or Teaching Tool 8), two-color counters (or Teaching Tool 6)

COHERENCE

In Lessons 12-1 through 12-6, students learned shape words for naming and describing two- and three-dimensional shapes. In Lesson 12-7, students learned position words to describe the location of shapes. In this lesson, students continue to verbally describe the location of objects clearly and accurately. Starting in Grade 1, students learn to communicate their understanding through writing.

RIGOR

This lesson emphasizes **application**. Students continue to use the vocabulary they have learned to describe the position and shape of two-dimensional and three-dimensional objects in the environment. The use of clear communication can help students develop a deeper understanding of the math content.

 Watch the Listen and Look For Lesson Video.
PD

MATH ANYTIME

Daily Common Core Review

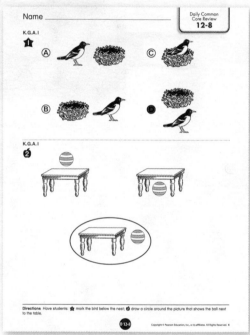

Today's Challenge

Think Use Topic 12 problems any time during this topic.

ENGLISH LANGUAGE LEARNERS 🄔🄛🄛

Speaking Speak using content area vocabulary in context.

Use with the Solve & Share on Student's Edition p. 727.

Write *above, next to, in front of, below,* and *behind.* Point to and read each term. Ask students to tell their partners the meanings of the terms. Instruct students to put their hands on their tables. Give students directions to demonstrate understanding of the terms, such as: *Put your right hand above your left hand.*

Beginning Distribute a cube to each student. Say: *Put the cube above the cow.* Students should place the cube in the correct position. Ask: *Where is the cube?* Have students respond using the sentence stem: "The cube is ___ the cow." [Above] Continue the activity by asking students to place the cube in various places in the picture.

Intermediate Distribute 2 cubes to each student. Have Student A place his/her cubes in the picture, and then describe the position of 1 cube using the sentence stem: "The cube is ___ the ___." Have Student B point to the

cube being described. Have students switch roles and repeat.

Advanced Distribute 4 cubes to each student. Have Student A place his/her cubes in the picture, and then describe the position of 1 cube using the terms *above, next to, in front of, below,* or *behind.* Have Student B identify the cube and explain how she or he knew which cube was described. Have students switch roles and repeat.

Summarize What words are used to describe positions of shapes?

DEVELOP: PROBLEM-BASED LEARNING

COHERENCE: Engage students by connecting prior knowledge to new ideas.

Students play a game that requires them to give clear directions to find an object on a workmat showing a farm scene. This game prepares them for the next part of the lesson, in which they must use precise language and defend their reasoning.

 10–15 min

 Solve

 BEFORE

1. Pose the Solve-and-Share Problem

MP.6 Be Precise Students give directions for finding an object. To be successful, students must use clear communication, using definitions precisely.

Provide each pair of students with 1 blue cube, 1 red cube, 1 yellow counter, and 1 red counter.

Emily's teacher teaches her class a game. She uses 1 blue cube, 1 red cube, 1 yellow counter, and 1 red counter and puts each of them somewhere on the farm picture. Play this game with a partner. Place the tools on the page, and then describe where one of them is located. Do NOT tell your partner which one you are talking about. How can your partner tell which one you are describing? Change places and play again.

Tell students to think about these Thinking Habits as they solve the problem.

Am I using the correct definitions?

Is my answer clear?

2. Build Understanding

What do you see on the page? [Sample answer: A barn, a cow, a scarecrow, a fence, corn, the sun] *Where can you place the tools?* [Sample answers: Next to the barn; in front of the fence; below the scarecrow]

 **DURING**

3. Ask Guiding Questions As Needed

What words can help you find the tool? [Answers will vary.] *How else can you describe the position of the tool?* [Answers will vary.]

 AFTER

4. Share and Discuss Solutions

 Start with students' solutions. Have them share the strategies used to solve the problem. If needed, project and analyze Bronte's and Marlee's work to discuss two approaches.

5. Transition to the Visual Learning Bridge

You gave careful directions so that your partner could find objects. Later in this lesson, you will explain how you know you are correct.

6. Extension for Early Finishers

With a partner, describe the object without naming it, and describe the location. Have the partner pick out the shape and place it in the correct location.

Solve & Share

Name _____

See margin for sample student work.

Math Practices and Problem Solving

Lesson 12-8
Precision

Think.

Directions Say: *Emily's teacher teaches her class a game. She uses 1 blue cube, 1 red cube, 1 yellow counter, and 1 red counter and puts each of them somewhere on the farm picture. Play this game with a partner. Place the tools on the page, and then describe where one of them is located. Do NOT tell your partner which one you are talking about. How can your partner tell which one you are describing? Change places and play again.*

I can ...
describe positions of shapes in the environment.

Ⓖ **Mathematical Practices**
MP.6 Also MP.3, MP.2
Content Standards
K.G.A.1

Topic 12 | Lesson 8

Digital Resources at PearsonRealize.com

seven hundred twenty-seven **727**

Analyze Student Work

Bronte's Work

Bronte tells Seth that the object is next to the cow and in front of the barn. Though Seth needs only one of those clues, he is glad to have a second clue to confirm his thinking. Seth correctly chooses the red cube.

Marlee's Work

Marlee tells Devon that the object is on top of the scarecrow. Devon correctly chooses the blue cube.

STEP 2

DEVELOP: VISUAL LEARNING

The *Visual Learning Bridge* connects students' thinking in Solve & Share to important math ideas in the lesson. Use the *Visual Learning Bridge* to make these ideas explicit. Also available as a *Visual Learning Animation Plus* at PearsonRealize.com

E L L Visual Learning

PEARSON realize.
PearsonRealize.com

👁 Learn   A-Z Glossary

MP.6 Be Precise *Emily is looking for something in her room. Which shape is Emily thinking of?* [Sphere] *Do you see an object that looks like a sphere on the shelf? How do you know?* [No; one object is a puzzle that is shaped like a cube, and one object is a can shaped like a cylinder.] *Where else in Emily's room can she look for an object shaped like a sphere?* [Next to, beside, or below the bed]

MP.3 Critique Reasoning *Emily found a ball under her bed. How do you know that Emily chose the correct object?* [The ball looks just like a sphere. Both the sphere and the ball have a curved shape.] *Where is the ball?* [The ball is below the bed.]

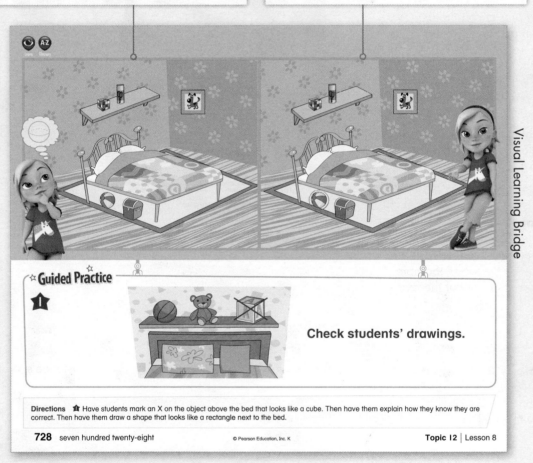

Visual Learning Bridge

☆ **Guided Practice**

Check students' drawings.

Directions ☆ Have students mark an X on the object above the bed that looks like a cube. Then have them explain how they know they are correct. Then have them draw a shape that looks like a rectangle next to the bed.

728 seven hundred twenty-eight   © Pearson Education, Inc. K   **Topic 12** | Lesson 8

Complete the *Do You Understand? Show Me!* problem before starting Guided Practice.

Do You Understand? Show Me! **MP.6 Be Precise** *The girl said that the can on the shelf above the bed is also a sphere because it has a round surface. Is she correct? Explain.* [No; the can is shaped like a cylinder. It has two flat surfaces. A sphere does not have flat surfaces.]

Coherence In the Visual Learning Bridge, students learn that they need to support their answers with precise explanations. This links back to the last two lessons, where students described solids in the environment (Lessons 12-6 and 12-7) and the locations of the solids (Lesson 12-7).

Essential Question Ask the following Essential Question: *Why is it important to explain your answers?* [Sample answer: So that my ideas about math are clear]

Error Intervention: Item 1

If students draw a rectangle but can't name the object,

then they might not recognize the head of the bed as being part of a whole bed. *What kinds of objects might be next to your bed?* [Sample answer: Table, alarm clock] *Which of those objects look like a rectangle?* [Sample answer: Table, alarm clock]

1 RtI **Reteaching** Assign Reteaching Set H, p. 738.

✓ **QUICK CHECK**

Check mark indicates items for prescribing differentiation on the next page. Items 2 and 3 are each worth 1 point. The Performance Assessment on page 730 is worth up to 3 points.

20–30 min   Tools Assessment

MP.6 Be Precise Listen and look for these behaviors as evidence that students are exhibiting proficiency with MP.6.

• Accurately uses problem-solving strategies

• Decides whether an exact answer or estimate is needed

Item 2 Point out to students that these items are sporting goods. Some students may be unfamiliar with the shuttlecock or may only know it as a birdie. You may want to provide background knowledge that this cone-shaped object is hit over a net in the racket sport of badminton. *What object is the shuttlecock in front of?* [The bowling ball]

Item 3 MP.2 Reasoning *Why is the sphere NOT the correct answer?* [It is beside the box of tissues. I need to find objects that are not next to the box of tissues.]

Item 4 MP.6 Be Precise Take this opportunity to show students the similarity between *next to* and *beside*. *What other position words can you use to identify the tennis balls?* [Next to]

Item 5 MP.2 Reasoning Explain to students that there is often more than one way to describe the location of an object. This is because it can be described in relation to multiple other objects. Help students answer the question by looking at the water bottle in relation to the soccer ball. Then have them focus on the water bottle in relation to the bench.

Item 6 MP.3 Critique Reasoning *Carlos describes the soccer ball as being in front of the bench. Do you agree or disagree? Explain how you know you are correct.* [I disagree. The soccer ball is below the bench. Also, it is behind the water bottle, and the water bottle is below the bench.]

Name _____

☆ Independent Practice ☆

✓ 2

✓ 3

Directions ✎ Have students name the shapes of the objects in the picture. Then have them mark an X on the object that is behind another object, and is next to the object that looks like a cylinder. Have them explain how they decided which shape to mark. ✖ Have students find the object in the picture that is NOT beside the box of tissues, and then mark an X on the solid it looks like on the left. Have them explain why a sphere is NOT the right answer. Then have them name the shape of the objects in the picture.

Topic 12 | Lesson 8   seven hundred twenty-nine **729**

☆ Math Practices and Problem Solving ☆

© Performance Assessment

4. Tennis ball can; Students should explain that the shape words *cylinder* and *cube* and position word *beside* helped identify the tennis ball can.

5. Sample answer is given. The water bottle is in front of the soccer ball.

6. Students should explain that the poster is positioned below the clock.

Directions Read the problem to students. Then have them use multiple math practices to solve the problem. Say: *Carlos wants to tell a friend about different things in the locker room and where they are located. What words can he use?* ❶ **MP.6 Be Precise** Mark an X on the object that looks like a cylinder that is beside the object that looks like a cube. What words helped you find the correct object? ❷ **MP.2 Reason** Carlos says the soccer ball is behind the water bottle. What is another way to explain where the water bottle is? ❸ **MP.3 Explain** Carlos describes the rectangle poster as being above the circle clock. Do you agree or disagree? Explain how you know you are correct.

730 seven hundred thirty   © Pearson Education, Inc. K   **Topic 12 | Lesson 8**

2 RtI

Use the **QUICK CHECK** on the previous page to prescribe differentiated instruction.

I Intervention
0–3 points on the Quick Check

O On-Level
4 points on the Quick Check

A Advanced
5 points on the Quick Check

Intervention Activity **I**

Charades

• Have students act out a task for the rest of the group, focusing the directions both on a shape and a position word. Some examples: *Put a cylinder on my desk. Hold a sphere and stand to the left of the bookshelf. Hold a cube in front of you.*

• Whisper a direction to a student and then have him or her act out the task. The rest of the group has to guess what the student is doing. Encourage students to identify the shape of the object and its position.

• Repeat the activity, giving as many students as possible a chance to act out a task.

Reteach **I**

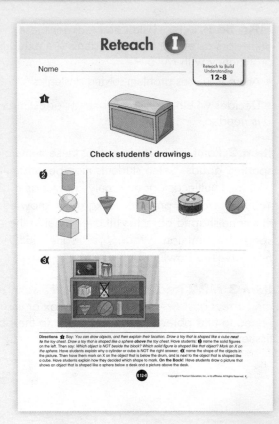

Name _____

Reteach to Build Understanding 12-8

Check students' drawings.

On-Level and Advanced Activity Centers **O** **A**

Problem-Solving Reading Mat

Have students read the Problem-Solving Reading Mat for Topic 12 and then complete Problem-Solving Reading Activity 12-8.

See the Problem-Solving Reading Activity Guide for other suggestions on how to use this mat.

TIMING

The time allocated to Step 3 will depend on the teacher's instructional decisions and differentiation routines.

15–30 min   Help   Tools   Games

PEARSON realize PearsonRealize.com

Technology Center

Tools

Games

Math Tools and Math Games

A link to a specific math tools activity or math game to use with this lesson is provided at PearsonRealize.com.

Leveled Assignment

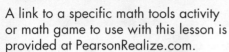 Items 1–4 (with help as needed)   **O** Items 1–4   **A** Items 1–4

Name _____   Help Tools Games

Homework & Practice 12-8
Precision

Another Look!

HOME ACTIVITY Place several items on a table, such as a plate, spoon, fork, cup, and napkin. Have your child tell the position of each object using the following words: *above, below, beside, next to, in front of,* and *behind.* For example, a child might say, "The spoon is beside the plate."

❶

Check students' work.

Directions Say: *Look at the objects in the picture. Name the shapes of the objects you see. Now draw a circle around the shapes that you see. Name the object above the basketball. Mark an X on that object. Draw a circle around the object that is next to the basketball and below the block.* ★ *Have students mark an X on the object that looks like a sphere below the picnic table. Then have them draw a circle around the object that looks like a cylinder beside the tree.*

Topic 12 | Lesson 8   Digital Resources at PearsonRealize.com   seven hundred thirty-one **731**

© **Performance Assessment** _____

 2. Soup can; Students should explain that the shape words *cylinder* and *cone* and position word *behind* helped identify the soup can.

3. Sample answers are given. The ice cream cone is in front of the soup can. The ice cream cone is beside the sugar cube.

4. Students should explain that the door is both a rectangle and positioned below the clock.

Directions Read the problem to students. Then have them use multiple math practices to solve the problem. Say: *Marta wants to tell a friend about different things in the kitchen and where they are located. What words can she use?* ✷ **MP.6 Be Precise** *Mark an X on the object that looks like a cylinder that is behind the object that looks like a cone. What words helped you find the correct object?* ✷ **MP.2 Reason** *The ice cream cone is next to the sugar cube. What is another way to explain where the ice cream cone is?* ✷ **MP.3 Explain** *Marta describes the door as looking like a rectangle. She also says it is below the clock. Do you agree or disagree? Explain how you know you are correct.*

732 seven hundred thirty-two   © Pearson Education, Inc. K   Topic 12 | Lesson 8

TOPIC 12

FLUENCY PRACTICE ACTIVITY

Games

FLUENCY PRACTICE ACTIVITY

Students practice fluently adding and subtracting within 5 during a partner activity that reinforces mathematical practices.

© Common Core Standards

Content Standard K.OA.A.5 Fluently add and subtract within 5.
Mathematical Practices MP.3, MP.6, MP.7, MP.8

Getting Started Ask students to work with a partner. Provide crayons needed for the activity. Tell students to record their answers and color the boxes on their own page. Go over the directions. Remind students to find all the sums and differences on the page.

As Students Do the Activity Remind students that each problem should be solved. When all of the boxes are colored correctly, a letter is revealed. Tell students that if the boxes they have colored do not do this, then there is an error and they need to double check their work. Remind students to compare and discuss their answers.

Another Activity Provide students with a five-by-five grid similar to the grid on the Student's Edition page. Have them create a new game board for the letter T where the sums or differences are equal to 3.

Extra Challenge *Look at the blank paper I gave you. I want you to think of addition and subtraction problems with a sum or difference of 4. I want you to make a game board where you color the boxes with a sum or difference of 4. And I want the coloring to spell the letter T. All the other spaces on the board not used for the T should have a sum or difference that is not 4.*

Steps to Fluency Success To ensure all students achieve fluency, see pages 431E– 431H for additional resources including practice/assessment masters on fluency subskills. You can also use the ExamView® CD-ROM to generate worksheets with multiple-choice or free-response items on fluency subskills.

 Online Game The Game Center at PearsonRealize.com provides opportunities for fluency practice.

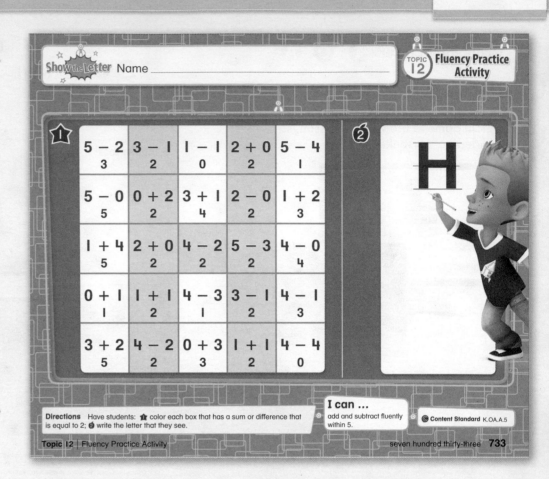

VOCABULARY REVIEW

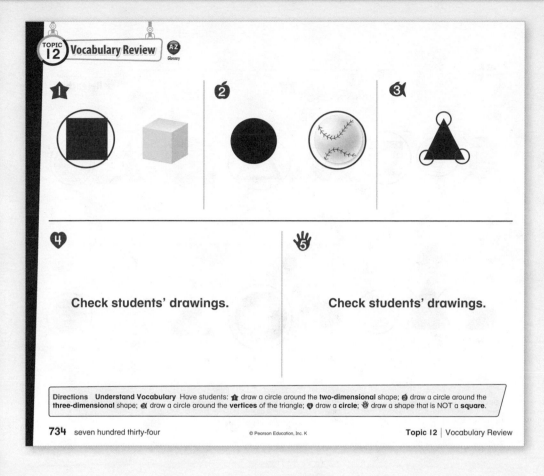

VOCABULARY REVIEW

Students review vocabulary words used in the topic.

Oral Language Before students do the page, you might reinforce oral language through a class discussion involving one or more of the following activities.

- Have students define the terms in their own words.

- Have students say math sentences or math questions that use the words.

- Play a "What's My Word?" guessing game in which you or a student thinks about one of the words and says a clue that others listen to before they guess the word.

- Play a "Right or Wrong?" game in which you or a student says a sentence that uses one of the words correctly or incorrectly. Then others say "right" or "wrong."

Writing in Math After students do the page, you might further reinforce writing in math by doing one or more of the following activities.

- Tell students to close their books. Then you say the words and have students write them. Students trade papers to check whether the words are spelled correctly.

- Have students work with a partner. Each partner writes a math question that uses one of the words. Then they trade papers and give a written answer that uses the word.

 Online Game The Game Center at PearsonRealize.com includes a vocabulary game that students can access any time.

RtI Item Analysis for Diagnosis and Intervention			
Reteaching Sets	© **Standards**	**Student Book Lessons**	**MDIS**
Set A	K.G.A.3	12-1	D29, D31
Set B	K.G.A.2	12-2	D29
Set C	K.G.A.2	12-3	D29
Set D	K.G.A.2	12-4	D30
Set E	K.G.A.2	12-5	D31
Set F	K.G.A.1, K.G.A.3	12-6	D29, D31
Set G	K.G.A.1, MP.6	12-7	D28
Set H	K.G.A.1, MP.6	12-8	D28

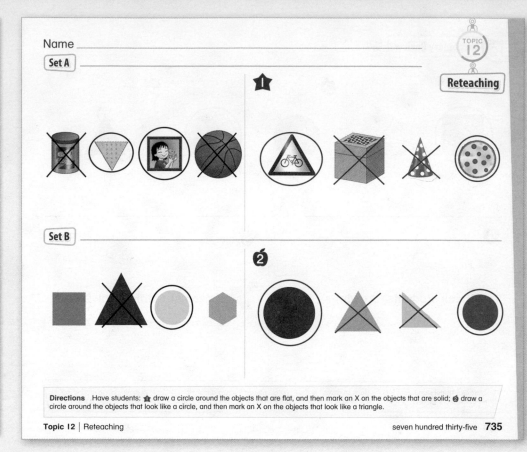

Name _____

Set A

Set B

Directions Have students: ❶ draw a circle around the objects that are flat, and then mark an X on the objects that are solid; ❷ draw a circle around the objects that look like a circle, and then mark an X on the objects that look like a triangle.

Topic 12 | Reteaching   seven hundred thirty-five **735**

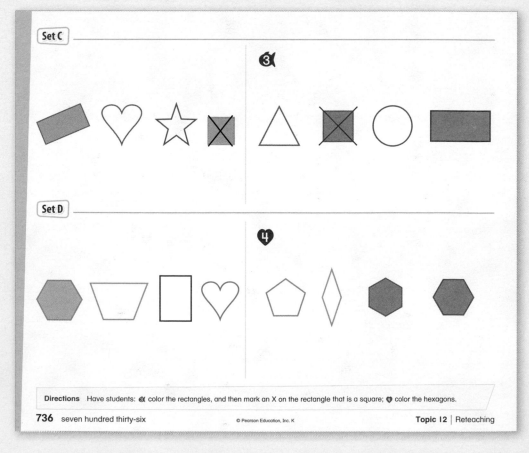

Set C

Set D

Directions Have students: ❸ color the rectangles, and then mark an X on the rectangle that is a square; ❹ color the hexagons.

736 seven hundred thirty-six   © Pearson Education, Inc. K   **Topic 12** | Reteaching

Name _____

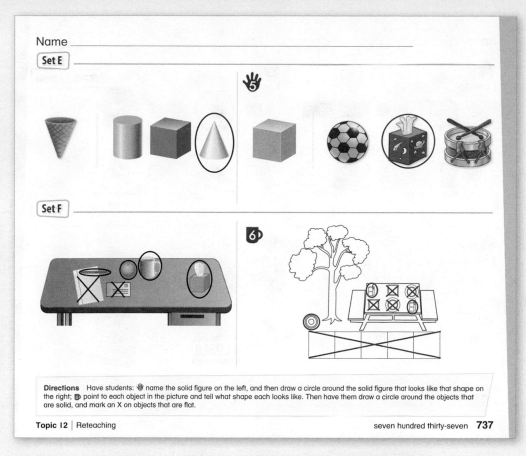

Set F

Directions Have students: 🖐 name the solid figure on the left, and then draw a circle around the solid figure that looks like that shape on the right; 👆 point to each object in the picture and tell what shape each looks like. Then have them draw a circle around the objects that are solid, and mark an X on objects that are flat.

1 RtI

Ongoing Intervention
- Lessons with guiding questions to assess understanding
- Support to prevent misconceptions and to reteach

2 RtI

Strategic Intervention
- Targeted to small groups who need more support
- Easy to implement

3 RtI

Intensive Intervention
- Instruction to accelerate progress
- Instruction focused on foundational skills

Set G

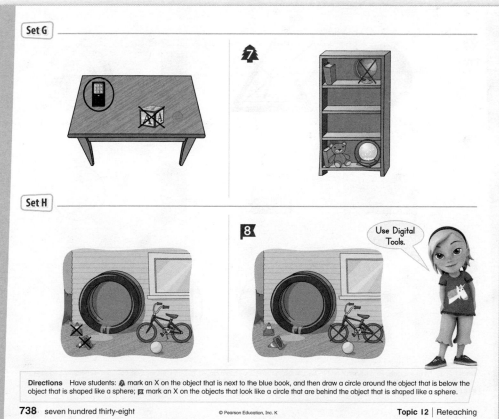

Set H

Use Digital Tools.

Directions Have students: 🔲 mark an X on the object that is next to the blue book, and then draw a circle around the object that is below the object that is shaped like a sphere; 🔳 mark an X on the objects that look like a circle that are behind the object that is shaped like a sphere.

TOPIC ASSESSMENT

IDENTIFY AND DESCRIBE SHAPES

ANSWERING THE TOPIC ESSENTIAL QUESTION

How can two- and three-dimensional shapes be identified and described?

Restate the Topic Essential Question from the Topic Opener or project it from the Student's Edition eText.

Ask students to answer the Essential Question (verbally or in writing) and give examples that support their answers. The following are key elements of the answer to the Essential Question. Be sure these are made explicit when discussing students' answers.

- Name shapes by their attributes.

  Example: Mark is looking at a magazine. He finds a picture of an object that has no corners. He finds a picture of an object that has 3 sides and 3 corners. What shapes did he see? [Circle; triangle]

- There are everyday objects that have the same shapes as flat shapes or solid figures.

  Example: Think about items you see in your kitchen. Draw two of these items. Which shapes do they remind you of? [Answers will vary.]

- Describe the position of shapes.

  Example: Use solid figures. Put a cube beside a sphere. Put a cone behind the cube. [Check students' answers.]

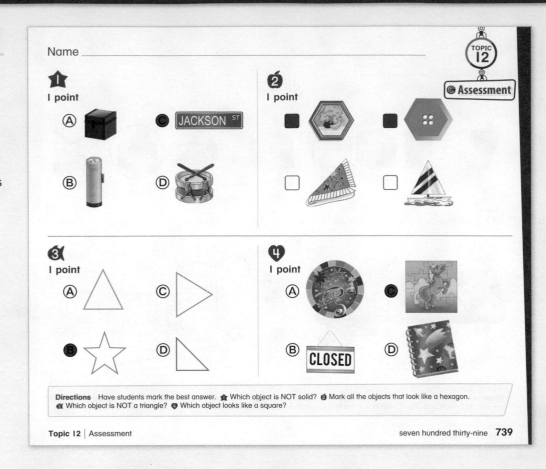

Directions Have students mark the best answer. 🏠 Which object is NOT solid? 🍎 Mark all the objects that look like a hexagon. ③ Which object is NOT a triangle? ④ Which object looks like a square?

Topic 12 | Assessment

seven hundred thirty-nine **739**

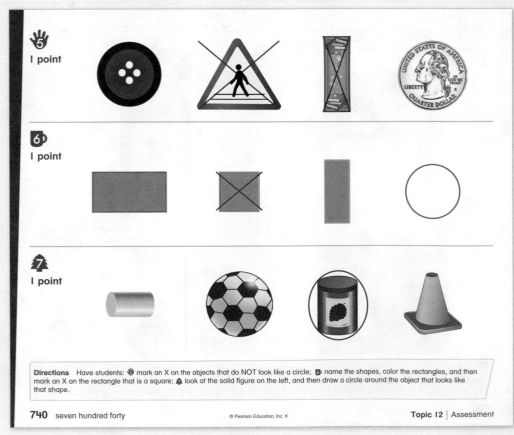

Directions Have students: ✋ mark an X on the objects that do NOT look like a circle; ⑥ name the shapes, color the rectangles, and then mark an X on the rectangle that is a square; 🌲 look at the solid figure on the left, and then draw a circle around the object that looks like that shape.

740 seven hundred forty

© Pearson Education, Inc. K

Topic 12 | Assessment

Assessment

ONLINE TOPIC ASSESSMENT
An auto-scored Topic Assessment is provided at PearsonRealize.com.

EXAMVIEW® TEST GENERATOR
ExamView can be used to create a blackline-master Topic Assessment with multiple-choice and free-response items.

Name _____

8 2 points

Check students' drawings.

9 1 point

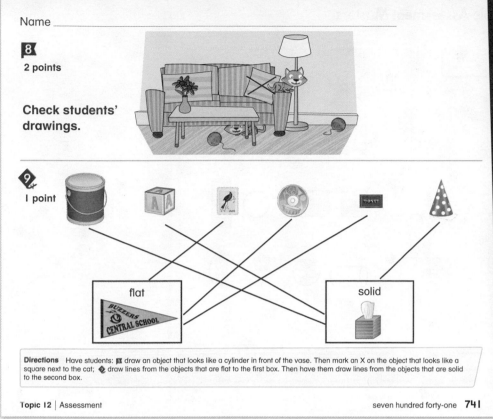

flat

solid

Directions Have students: ⓧ draw an object that looks like a cylinder in front of the vase. Then mark an X on the object that looks like a square next to the cat; ⓨ draw lines from the objects that are flat to the first box. Then have them draw lines from the objects that are solid to the second box.

Topic 12 | Assessment

seven hundred forty-one **741**

---

10 2 points

book

sphere   cup

11 2 points

Check students' drawings.

12 2 points

Directions Have students: ⓾ draw a picture of an object that looks like a sphere below a book and next to a cup; ⓫ draw a picture of an object that is flat. Then have them draw an object that is solid; ⓬ draw a circle around the objects that look like a circle, and then mark an X on the objects that look like a rectangle.

742 seven hundred forty-two   © Pearson Education, Inc. K   Topic 12 | Assessment

---

RtI Item Analysis for Diagnosis and Intervention

Item	Ⓒ Standards	DOK	MDIS
1	K.G.A.3	1	D29, D31
2	K.G.A.2	1	D29, D30
3	K.G.A.2	1	D29
4	K.G.A.2	1	D29
5	K.G.A.2	1	D29
6	K.G.A.2	1	D29
7	K.G.A.2	1	D31
8	K.G.A.1	1	D28, D29, D31
9	K.G.A.3	1	D29, D31
10	K.G.A.1, MP.6	2	D28
11	K.G.A.3	2	D29, D31
12	K.G.A.1, K.G.A.2	2	D29

The Topic Assessment Masters assess the same content item for item as the Topic Assessment in the Student's Edition.

741–742

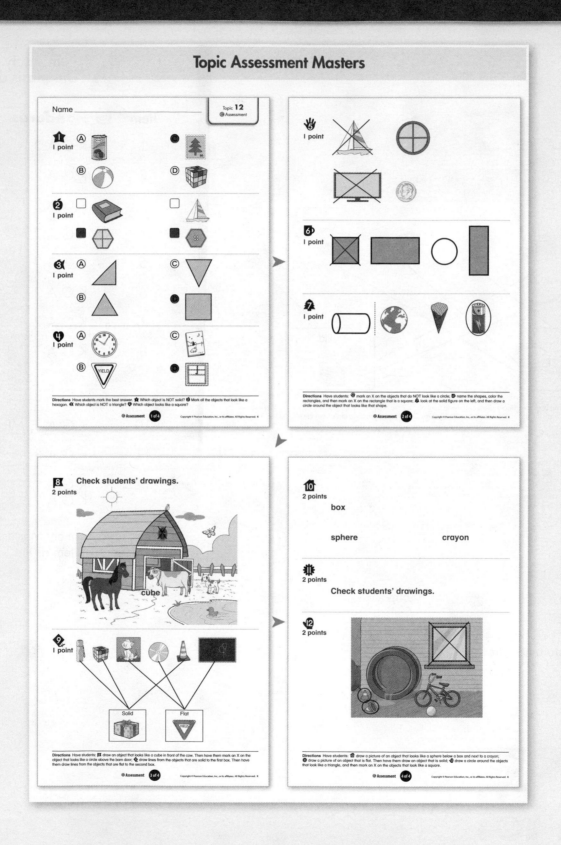

Topic Assessment Masters

ONLINE TOPIC ASSESSMENT

An auto-scored Topic Assessment is provided at PearsonRealize.com.

EXAMVIEW® TEST GENERATOR

ExamView can be used to create a blackline-master Topic Assessment with multiple-choice and free-response items.

Scoring Guide

Item	Points	Topic Assessment (Student's Edition and Masters)
1	1	Correct choice is selected.
2	1	Correct choices are selected.
3	1	Correct choice is selected.
4	1	Correct choice is selected.
5	1	Correct objects are crossed out.
6	1	All three rectangles are colored and the square is crossed out.
7	1	Correct object is circled.
8	2	Object is drawn in the correct position and correct object is crossed out.
	1	Object is drawn in the correct position or correct object is crossed out.
9	1	Objects are correctly identified as *flat* or *solid*.
10	2	All three objects are drawn in the correct position.
	1	One or two objects are drawn in the correct position.
11	2	One flat and one solid object is drawn.
	1	One flat or one solid object is drawn.
12	2	Circles and rectangles are correctly identified.
	1	One circle and one rectangle are correctly identified.

Scoring Guide

Item	Points	Topic Performance Assessment in the Student's Edition
1	1	Correct choices are selected.
2	1	Correct choices are selected.
3	1	Correct object is crossed out.
4	1	Correct object is drawn in the correct position.
5	1	Correct object is circled.

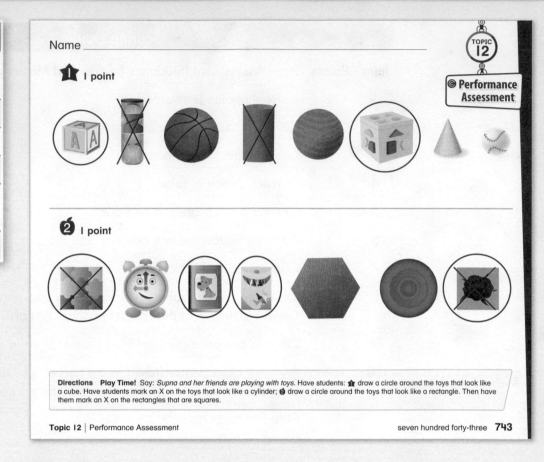

Name _____

TOPIC 12

© Performance Assessment

⭐ 1 point

② 1 point

Directions **Play Time!** Say: *Supna and her friends are playing with toys.* Have students: ⭐ draw a circle around the toys that look like a cube. Have students mark an X on the toys that look like a cylinder; ② draw a circle around the toys that look like a rectangle. Then have them mark an X on the rectangles that are squares.

Topic 12 | Performance Assessment   seven hundred forty-three **743**

Item Analysis for Diagnosis and Intervention

Item	© Standards	DOK	MDIS
1	K.G.A.2	2	D31
2	K.G.A.2	2	D29
3	K.G.A.2	2	D29, D30
4	K.G.A.1, K.G.A.2, MP.6	3	D28, D31
5	K.G.A.1, K.G.A.2, MP.6	3	D28, D31

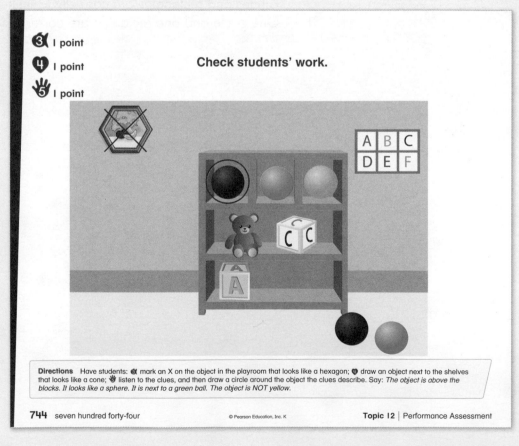

③ 1 point

④ 1 point

✋ 1 point

Check students' work.

A B C
D E F

Directions Have students: ③ mark an X on the object in the playroom that looks like a hexagon; ④ draw an object next to the shelves that looks like a cone; ✋ listen to the clues, and then draw a circle around the object the clues describe. Say: *The object is above the blocks. It looks like a sphere. It is next to a green ball. The object is NOT yellow.*

744 seven hundred forty-four   © Pearson Education, Inc. K   Topic 12 | Performance Assessment

Topic Performance Assessment Masters

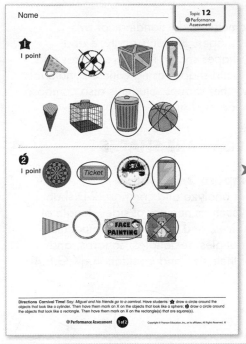

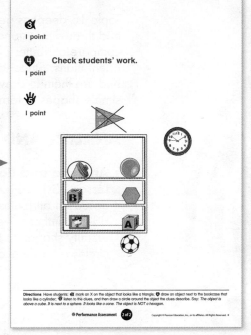

Item Analysis for Diagnosis and Intervention

Item	© Standards	DOK	MDIS
1	K.G.A.2	2	D31
2	K.G.A.2	2	D29
3	K.G.A.2	2	D29
4	K.G.A.1, K.G.A.2, MP.6	3	D31
5	K.G.A.1, K.G.A.2, MP.6	3	D29, D30, D31

Scoring Guide

Item	Points	Topic Performance Assessment Masters
1	1	Correct choices are selected.
2	1	Correct choices are selected.
3	1	Correct object is crossed out.
4	1	Correct object is drawn in the correct position.
5	1	Correct object is circled.

F C R FOCUS   COHERENCE   RIGOR

● **MAJOR CLUSTER**   ● **SUPPORTING CLUSTER**   ● **ADDITIONAL CLUSTER**

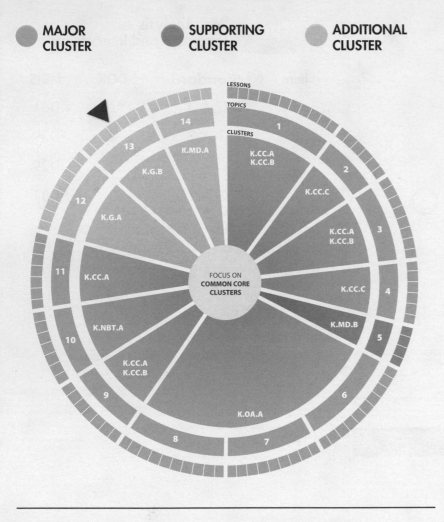

TOPIC 13   Analyze, Compare, and Create Shapes

TOPIC 13 FOCUSES ON

© ADDITIONAL CLUSTER K.G.B
Analyze, compare, create, and compose shapes.

Content Focus in ⒺnVisionmath 2.0

Topic 13 deepens geometric understandings of two- and three-dimensional shapes. Students analyze and compare attributes of shapes shown in different sizes and orientations. Students build shapes using concrete materials, and use them to draw other shapes. Students also compose simple shapes to form larger shapes.

ANALYZE AND COMPARE SHAPES

- **Analyze and Compare 2-D Shapes** In Lesson 13-1, students analyze and compare 2-D shapes based on attributes, such as number of sides, length of sides, number of vertices, and being round. Students identify shapes as triangles, rectangles, squares, and circles regardless of their size and orientation. (K.G.B.4)

Mark an X on the shapes that do NOT fit the clues, draw a circle around the shape that the clues describe, and then tell how the shapes you marked with an X are different than the shape you drew a circle around.

Clues: I am NOT round. I have less than 4 sides. What shape am I?

- **Analyze and Compare 3-D Shapes** In Lesson 13-2, students analyze and compare 3-D shapes based on the attributes of whether the shapes roll, slide, and/or stack. Students identify cubes, cylinders, cones, and spheres. (K.G.B.4)

Draw a circle around the solid figures that slide and roll.

Content Focus in **enVision**math 2.0 (continued)

• **Find 2-D Shapes on 3-D Shapes** In Lesson 13-3, students match 2-D shapes (squares and circles) with solid figures that have a flat surface with that shape. (K.G.B.4)

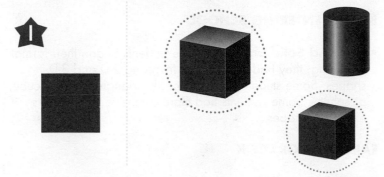

Look at the shape on the left, and then draw a circle around the solid figures that have a flat surface with that shape.

CREATE AND COMPOSE SHAPES

• **Compose 2-D Shapes to Form Larger 2-D Shapes**
In Lesson 13-5, students compose simple 2-D shapes to form larger shapes. (K.G.B.6)

Use the pattern block shown to cover the shape, draw the lines, and then write the number that tells how many pattern blocks to use.

• **Create 2-D Shapes** In Lesson 13-6, students draw 2-D shapes. They also build 2-D shapes from materials such as pipe cleaners, yarn, and straws. Building shapes encourages students to focus on attributes. (K.G.B.4, K.G.B.5)

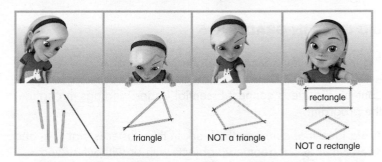

To build a triangle, students need 3 straws for the side. The straws can be different lengths.

• **Create 3-D Shapes** In Lesson 13-7, students use materials such as straws, clay, craft sticks, and paper to build 3-D shapes. Students also build shapes by composing two or more 3-D shapes. Building shapes encourages students to focus on attributes. (K.G.B.5, K.G.B.6)

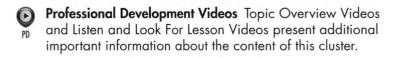

Use tools to build the solid figure shown.

 Professional Development Videos Topic Overview Videos and Listen and Look For Lesson Videos present additional important information about the content of this cluster.

Content Coherence in enVisionmath2.0

Students learn best when ideas are connected in a coherent curriculum. This coherence is achieved through various types of connections including connections within clusters, across clusters, across domains, and across grades.

BIG IDEAS IN GRADES K–6

Big Ideas are the conceptual underpinnings of **enVision**math**2.0** and provide conceptual cohesion of the content. Big Ideas connect Essential Understandings throughout the program.

A Big Idea that connects the work in this cluster is that two- and three-dimensional geometric objects with or without curved surfaces can be described, classified, and analyzed based on their attributes. In Topic 13, students analyze and compare 2-D shapes and 3-D shapes based on their attributes. An understanding of attributes is also reinforced when students build shapes, draw shapes, and combine simple shapes to form larger shapes.

Use tools to build the shape on the left, and then draw a circle around the solid figures that build the shape.

For a complete list of Big Ideas, see pages 110–111 in the *Teacher's Edition Program Overview*.

LOOK BACK

How does Topic 13 connect to what students learned earlier?

BEFORE ENTERING SCHOOL

• **Flat and Solid Shapes** Before students began their formal schooling, they had experiences involving 2-D and 3-D shapes. Some students knew terms like triangle, square, cube, or sphere. Some students had more extensive experiences exploring shapes.

EARLIER IN GRADE K

• **Sort Objects** In Topic 5, students sorted items in a data set based on attributes. This laid the foundation for students to understand how to sort geometric shapes based on their attributes. (K.MD.B.3)

Draw a circle around the dogs that have spots, and then mark an X on the dogs that do NOT have spots.

• **Name Flat and Solid Shapes** In Topic 12, students used attributes to name flat shapes as squares, circles, triangles, rectangles, or hexagons, and solid shapes as cubes, cones, cylinders, or spheres. Students also describe the relative position of shapes as above, below, beside, next to, in front of, or behind. (K.G.A)

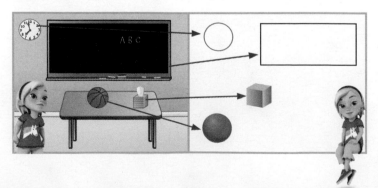

TOPIC 13

How is content connected within Topic 13?

- **Connect 2-D and 3-D Shapes** Lesson 13-1 focuses on 2-D shapes. Lesson 13-2 focuses on 3-D shapes. Lesson 13-3 makes connections between these shapes by asking students to identify 2-D shapes on flat surfaces of 3-D shapes. (K.G.B.4)

- **Use Attributes When Creating and Composing Shapes** In Lessons 13-1, 13-2, and 13-3, students analyze and compare shapes based on their attributes. (K.G.B.4) Students draw on this work with attributes when they compose, build, and draw shapes in Lessons 13-5, 13-6, and 13-7. (K.G.B.5, K.G.B.6)

- **Ways to Represent Shapes** Throughout Topic 13, students work with different representations of 2-D and 3-D shapes. Students build them, draw them, and see pictures of them. (K.G.B.4, K.G.B.5)

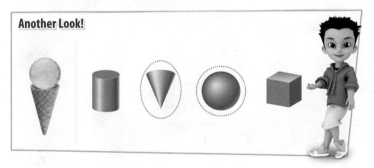

Another Look!

Look at the object on the left. Draw a circle around the solid figures that make the shape.

- **Name Shapes Regardless of Orientation or Size** Throughout Topic 13, students use attributes to name shapes regardless of their orientation or overall size. (K.G.B.4)

LOOK AHEAD

How does Topic 13 connect to what students will learn later?

LATER IN GRADE K

- **Describe Measurable Attributes of an Object** In Topic 14, students will be asked to describe which attributes are measurable in a given object. (K.MD.A.1)

Look at the object on the left, identify the attributes that can be measured, and then draw a circle around the tools that could be used to tell about those attributes.

GRADE 1

- **Understand Defining Attributes and Compose Shapes** In Topic 14, students will distinguish between defining attributes of shapes (e.g., number and length of sides) and non-defining attributes (e.g., color, size, orientation). (1.G.A.1) Students will also create 2-D and 3-D composite shapes, and they will compose new shapes from the composite shapes. (1.G.A.2)

☆ **Guided Practice** ☆ Write how many faces or flat surfaces and vertices each 3-D shape has.

	3-D shape	Number of faces or flat surfaces	Number of vertices	Number of edges
1.		6	8	12
2.				

Content Rigor in  **2.0**

A rigorous curriculum emphasizes conceptual understanding, procedural skill and fluency, and applications.

CONCEPTUAL UNDERSTANDING

- **Understand Attributes of Shapes** Topic 13 deepens students' understanding that names of geometric shapes are based on attributes of the shapes. The work with analyzing, comparing, building, and drawing shapes forces students to focus on attributes, and that helps students visually determine when a certain two- or three-dimensional figure is or is not a shape with a specific name. (K.G.B.4, K.G.B.5)

- **Non-Defining Attributes of Shapes** Topic 13 reinforces the concept that the overall size of a shape and the orientation of the shape are not defining attributes. The positioning of a shape does not affect the name of that shape. (K.G.B.3)

- **Compose Shapes** When students first combine shapes to make larger shapes, they use trial and error. Gradually they consider side length and gain an intuitive appreciation of angle size, translations, reflections, and rotations. (K.G.B.6)

Triangles can be combined to compose a hexagon.

PROCEDURAL SKILL AND FLUENCY

There are no standards in this cluster that call for fluency. There are no procedural skills taught in this cluster.

APPLICATIONS

- **Real-World Applications** Topic 13 shows 2-D and 3-D geometric figures represented by real-world objects including toys, household items, classroom items, sports equipment, and food. (K.G.B)

Look at the shape at the left, and then draw a circle around the objects that have a flat surface with that shape.

MP

Connecting Math Practices and Content Standards in enVisionmath2.0

Math practices and content standards are connected within all lessons including the lessons that focus on math practices.

MATH PRACTICES WITHIN LESSONS

- **MP.1** Make sense of problems and persevere in solving them.

  Students make sense of the solution to geometry problems by checking whether their answers are reasonable. (e.g., p. 787, Item 4)

- **MP.2** Reason abstractly and quantitatively.

  Students use reasoning to identify shapes based on their attributes. (e.g., p. 749, Solve and Share)

- **MP.3** Construct viable arguments and critique the reasoning of others.

  Students construct arguments by telling the name of two shapes they build and explaining how these shapes are different from one another. (e.g., p. 779, Solve and Share)

- **MP.4** Model with mathematics.

  Students use what they know about geometric shapes to model real-world objects. (e.g., p. 785, Solve and Share)

- **MP.5** Use appropriate tools strategically.

  Students can use real-world materials to model 2-D and 3-D shapes. (e.g., p. 788, Item 10)

- **MP.6** Attend to precision.

  Students use precise language to describe the flat surfaces of 3-D objects. (e.g., p. 762, Do You Understand?)

- **MP.7** Look for and make use of structure.

  Students look for a relationship between whether an object has a flat or curved surface, and whether that object will stack or roll. (e.g., p. 756, Do You Understand?)

- **MP.8** Look for and express regularity in repeated reasoning.

  Students use repeated reasoning to make generalizations about composed shapes. (e.g., p. 776, Item 6)

LESSON THAT FOCUSES ON MATH PRACTICES

- **Lesson 13-4** This lesson focuses on MP.1. It is intentionally placed in the middle of this topic to help bridge from the students' work on analyzing and comparing two- and three-dimensional shapes to the work they will do on building and composing shapes. In this lesson, students work on making sense of the problem and persevering in solving it. When students guess a shape based on given attributes from a partner, they are working to persevere in solving problems by using the information given to determine the shape.

Thinking Habits

What do I need to find?

What do I know?

What's my plan for solving the problem?

What else can I try if I get stuck?

How can I check that my solution make sense?

Revisit the information about MP.1 in these other resources:

- **Math Practices and Problem Solving Handbook** before Topic 1; includes Math Practices Proficiency Rubrics.

- **Math Practices Posters** to display in your classroom

- **Math Practices Animations,** one for each math practice, available at PearsonRealize.com.
  MP

TOPIC 13

ADDITIONAL CLUSTER K.G.B

DIFFERENTIATED INSTRUCTION

 I Intervention   **O** On-Level   **A** Advanced

 PEARSON **realize.** PearsonRealize.com

Learn   Assessment   Tools   Games

Ongoing Intervention

 1 RtI **During the core lesson,** monitor progress, reteach as needed, and extend students' thinking.

Guiding Questions
• **In the Teacher's Edition** Guiding questions are used to monitor understanding during instruction.

 Online Guiding Questions Guiding questions are also in the online Visual Learning Animation Plus.

Error Intervention: If... then...
This feature in the Teacher's Edition is provided during Guided Practice. It spotlights common errors and gives suggestions for addressing them.

Reteaching
Reteaching sets are at the end of the topic in the Student's Edition. They provide additional examples, reminders, and practice. Use these sets as needed before students do the Independent Practice.

Higher Order Thinking
These problems require students to think more deeply about the rich, conceptual knowledge developed in the lesson.

Strategic Intervention

 2 RtI **At the end of the lesson,** assess to identify students' strengths and needs and then provide appropriate support.

Quick Check
✓ **In the Student's Edition** Assess the lesson using 2-3 items checked in the Teacher's Edition.

 Online Quick Check You can also assess the lesson using 5 online, machine-scored items.

Intervention Activity
Teachers work with struggling students.

Reteach to Build Understanding
This is a page of guided reteaching.

Technology Center
 Digital Math Tools Activities reinforce the lesson content or previously taught content using a suite of digital math tools.

 Online Games provide practice on the lesson content or previously taught content.

Homework and Practice
Use the leveled assignment to provide differentiated homework and practice.

Additional resources to support differentiated instruction for on-level and advanced students include:

On-Level and Advanced Activity Centers
• **Center Games** are provided in on-level and advanced versions.

• **Math and Science Activity** is related to the topic science theme introduced at the start of the topic.

• **Problem-Solving Reading Mat** is used with a lesson-specific activity.

Intensive Intervention

 3 RtI **As needed,** provide more instruction that is on or below grade level for students who are struggling.

Math Diagnosis and Intervention System 2.0
• **Diagnosis** Use the diagnostic tests in the system. Also, use the item analysis charts given with program assessments at the start of a grade or topic, or at the end of a topic, group of topics, or the year.

• **Intervention Lessons** These two-page lessons include guided instruction followed by practice. The system includes lessons below, on, and above grade level.

• **Teacher Support** Teacher Notes provide the support needed to conduct a short lesson. The lesson focuses on vocabulary, concept development, and practice. The Teacher's Guide contains individual and class record forms and correlations to Student's Edition lessons.

Resources for Fluency Success
• A variety of print and digital resources are provided to ensure success on Common Core fluency standards. See Steps to Fluency Success on pages 431E–431H.

PEARSON
realize.
PearsonRealize.com

Glossary   **Games**   **Story**   **Story**

English Language Learners

Provide ELL support through visual learning throughout the program, ELL instruction in every lesson, and additional ideas in an ELL Toolkit.

Visual Learning
The visual learning that is infused in **enVision**math**2.0** provides support for English language learners. This support includes a Visual Learning Animation Plus and a Visual Learning Bridge for each lesson.

English Language Learners Instruction

Lessons provide instruction for English language learners at Beginning, Intermediate, and Advanced levels of English proficiency.

English Language Learners Toolkit
This resource provides professional development and resources for supporting English language learners.

Math Vocabulary

Build math vocabulary using the vocabulary cards, vocabulary activities, vocabulary review, and glossary plus the online glossary and vocabulary game.

My Word Cards
Vocabulary cards for a topic are provided in the Student's Edition. Use the cards with students to study and learn new vocabulary words.

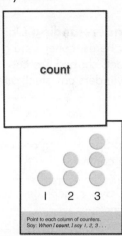

Vocabulary Activities
The Teacher's Edition provides vocabulary activities at the start of topics. These include activities for vocabulary in My Word Cards and/or activities for vocabulary in Review What You Know.

Vocabulary Review
A page of vocabulary review is provided at the end of each topic. It reviews vocabulary used in the topic.

Glossary
A glossary is provided at the back of the Student's Edition.

Animated Glossary

An online, bilingual, animated glossary uses motion and sound to build understanding of math vocabulary.

Online Vocabulary Game

On online vocabulary game is available in the Game Center.

Math and Reading

Connect reading and math using a data-filled reading mat for the topic with accompanying activity masters and guide. Also use topic interactive math stories.

Problem-Solving Reading Mats
There is a large, beautiful mat for each topic. At the start of the topic, help students become familiar with the mat and the vocabulary used by reading the mat aloud as students follow along. Use the Problem-Solving Reading Activity Guide for suggestions about how to use the mat.

Problem-Solving Reading Activity
At the end of some lessons, a Problem-Solving Reading Activity provides a page of math problems to solve by using the data on the mat.

Interactive Math Stories

An interactive math story provides an introduction to each topic. The story is available as an online story book and an animated story at PearsonRealize.com as well as a color-in, take-home story in the Teacher's Resource Masters.

TOPIC PLANNER

ANALYZE, COMPARE, AND CREATE SHAPES

Lesson 13-1

ANALYZE AND COMPARE TWO-DIMENSIONAL (2-D) SHAPES pp. 749–754

Ⓒ **Content Standard K.G.B.4**
Mathematical Practices MP.2, MP.4, MP.6, MP.7

Objective Analyze and compare 2-D shapes.

Essential Understanding 2-D shapes can be sorted and identified by their attributes.

Vocabulary None

ELL Speaking: Ask and give information using key words/expressions.

Materials Attribute blocks (or Teaching Tool 46), classroom objects

On-Level and Advanced Activity Centers
• Math and Science Activity

Lesson 13-2

ANALYZE AND COMPARE THREE-DIMENSIONAL (3-D) SHAPES pp. 755–760

Ⓒ **Content Standard K.G.B.4**
Mathematical Practices MP.1, MP.2, MP.3, MP.7

Objective Analyze and compare 3-D shapes.

Essential Understanding Objects shaped like spheres, cones, and cylinders can roll. Objects shaped like cubes, cones, and cylinders can stack and slide.

Vocabulary roll, slide, stack

ELL Speaking: Speak using content area vocabulary in context.

Materials Crayons, geometric solids, classroom objects

On-Level and Advanced Activity Centers
• Math and Science Activity

Lesson 13-3

COMPARE 2-D AND 3-D SHAPES pp. 761–766

Ⓒ **Content Standard K.G.B.4**
Mathematical Practices MP.2, MP.5, MP.6

Objective Analyze and compare 2-D and 3-D shapes.

Essential Understanding The flat surfaces of many solid figures have specific 2-D shapes.

Vocabulary flat surface

ELL Speaking: Ask for and give information using key words.

Materials Modeling clay, rolling pin, geometric solids, classroom objects

On-Level and Advanced Activity Centers
• Problem-Solving Reading Mat

LESSON RESOURCES

Digital
• Student's Edition
• Daily Common Core Review
• Reteach to Build Understanding
• Center Games
• Math and Science Activity
• Problem-Solving Reading Mat
• Problem-Solving Reading Activity

Print

Digital
• Listen and Look For PD Lesson Video
• Student's Edition eText
• Today's Challenge
• Solve & Share
• Visual Learning Animation Plus

• Animated Glossary
• Math Tools
• Quick Check
• Another Look Homework Video
• Math Games

Lesson 13-4

MATH PRACTICES AND PROBLEM SOLVING: MAKE SENSE AND PERSEVERE pp. 767–772

ⓒ Mathematical Practices **MP.1, MP.3, MP.5, MP.6**
Content Standards **K.G.A.3, K.G.B.4**

Objective Analyze, compare, and make different 2-D and 3-D shapes using math.

Essential Understanding Good math thinkers know what the problem is about. They have a plan to solve it. They keep trying if they get stuck.

Vocabulary None

ELL Listening: Demonstrate listening comprehension by taking notes.

Materials Attribute blocks (or Teaching Tool 46), geometric solids, small classroom objects, 3-column chart with top row illustrating actions of *roll, stack,* and *slide*

On-Level and Advanced Activity Centers
• Center Games

Lesson 13-5

MAKE 2-D SHAPES FROM OTHER 2-D SHAPES pp. 773–778

ⓒ Content Standard **K.G.B.6**
Mathematical Practices **MP.1, MP.4, MP.5, MP.7, MP.8**

Objective Make 2-D shapes using other 2-D shapes.

Essential Understanding You can make 2-D shapes by putting together two or more 2-D shapes.

Vocabulary None

ELL Reading: Develop basic [math] sight vocabulary.

Materials Construction paper right triangles, pattern blocks (or Teaching Tool 41), Triangles (Teaching Tool 33), index cards, paper

On-Level and Advanced Activity Centers
• Center Games

Lesson 13-6

BUILD 2-D SHAPES pp. 779–784

ⓒ Content Standards **K.G.B.5, K.G.B.4**
Mathematical Practices **MP.2, MP.3, MP.4, MP.7**

Objective Build 2-D shapes that match given attributes.

Essential Understanding When building a given 2-D shape, the shape must exhibit all of the attributes of the shape.

Vocabulary None

ELL Speaking: Speak using content area vocabulary in context.

Materials Yarn, string, pipe cleaners, straws, scissors, tape, dry pasta, index cards

On-Level and Advanced Activity Centers
• Problem-Solving Reading Mat

TOPIC RESOURCES

Digital

Print

Start of Topic
• Topic Centers
• Interactive Math Story
• Math and Science Project
• Home-School Connection
• Review What You Know
• My Word Cards

End of Topic
• Fluency Practice Activity
• Vocabulary Review
• Reteaching
• Topic Assessment
• Topic Performance Assessment

Digital

Start of Topic
• Topic Overview PD Video

End of Topic
• Math Practices Animations
• Online Topic Assessment
• ExamView® Test Generator

TOPIC PLANNER

ANALYZE, COMPARE, AND CREATE SHAPES

Lesson 13-7

BUILD 3-D SHAPES pp. 785–790

Content Standards **K.G.B.5, K.G.B.6**
Mathematical Practices **MP.1, MP.2, MP.4, MP.5, MP.6**

Objective Use materials to build 3-D shapes.

Essential Understanding 3-D shapes can be combined to make other 3-D shapes.

Vocabulary None

ELL Listening: Learn basic/academic vocabulary.

Materials Small cubes, clay, craft sticks, geometric solids, Building with Solid Figures (Teaching Tool 40), straws, yarn, pipe cleaners, paper, index cards

On-Level and Advanced Activity Centers
- Center Games

Notes

Dramatic Play Center

I Spy

Materials
Classroom objects

- Have students play *I Spy* with classroom objects. Have one student spy an object that resembles a solid figure. Have that student give clues about the object's shape until his or her classmates identify the object.

- Have other students take turns spying objects and giving clues.

Math Center

Shapes in a Bag

Materials
Paper bag, geometric solids

- Have students take turns reaching into the bag and identifying a shape by touch. They can self-check by looking at the shape.

Sand and Water Center

Guess It!

Materials
Sand, spray bottle with water, tray or shallow pan, geometric solids: cube, cone, cylinder

- Place sand in a tray and spray it gently with water.

- Partner A covers his or her eyes. Partner B chooses a solid and presses each of the flat surfaces into the sand. When all flat surfaces have been imprinted, Partner A looks and decides which solid shape made the impressions.

- Partners take turns pressing the flat surfaces of a solid into the sand and naming the solid that made the impressions.

Social Studies Center

Deconstructing Shapes

Materials
Construction paper, magazines, blunt-tipped scissors, glue, geometric solids: cone, cube, cylinder

- Stack 2 geometric solids to make a new shape, and show the shape to the class.

- Have students find pictures in magazines that are the same shape as the solid figures used to make the new shape. Then have them cut out and glue the pictures onto a sheet of paper. Students should attempt to replicate the new shape and should glue the pictures in a way that shows the two shapes stacked together.

- Repeat the activity, stacking different geometric solids each time.

Art Center

Finding Flat Surfaces

Materials
Construction paper, crayons, classroom objects

- Have students find a classroom object that resembles a cone, a cube, or a cylinder.

- Then have them trace a flat surface of that object on the construction paper.

- Have students share their objects and describe the shape of the object and its flat surface(s).

Building Center

Building Specs

Materials
Various blocks of different shapes, prepared index cards with number and kinds of blocks indicated

- Have pairs of students select a card and build something that includes the assigned number and kinds of blocks. They can also use other building blocks, but the aim is to include the assigned number of blocks within their structure.

- Have partners present their structures to others, pointing out how they incorporated the assigned blocks.

TOPIC
13
INTERACTIVE MATH STORY

ANALYZE, COMPARE, AND CREATE SHAPES

PEARSON
realize
PearsonRealize.com

PDF
Story

Story

Before the Story

PDF
Story

Picture Walk

Project the online PDF that contains a full-color version of this story. Read the title, author's name, and illustrator's name to students. Ask students to look at the pages. *Where does this story take place?* [Lin's room] *Who are the main characters?* [Lin and her mom] *What do you think Lin's mother wants Lin to do?* [Clean her messy room] *Why is the room messy?* [Toys are all over the floor.]

Activate Prior Knowledge

In this story, we identify solid figures. Hold up a ball and a block. *How are these shapes different from each other?* [Sample answers: One is round and one is shaped like a box; One has corners and the other is smooth all around.]

Story
Play the animated version of the story.

DURING THE STORY

This book belongs to:
Malcolm

TOPIC 13 Story

Lin's Messy Room
Written by Joyce Mallery Illustrated by Paul Sharp

Lin's room is a mess!
That is clear.
What should she put here?

Topic 13 1

Lin's room is a mess!
That is clear.
What should she put here?

Topic 13 2

fold up

READ

Read the story aloud for enjoyment. Explain that Lin's mother wants the toys to be placed on the shelf she points to. Page 1: *What toys belong on the bottom shelf?* [Round things] Direct students' attention to the objects in the boxes. *Which should Lin place on the bottom shelf, the ball or the puzzle?* [Ball] Continue in this manner.

GESTURE

Ask students to point to specific shapes on each page. Point out that the blocks are cubes, the hats are cones, and the balls are spheres. Refer to one page and have students find squares and rectangles hidden on the toys or in other places in the room.

Finally have students point to where Lin should place her rag doll and stuffed elephant. [Bed]

COLOR

Distribute the Interactive Math Story books to students. Read the story aloud page by page. Have students color the correct part of the bookshelf yellow on each page— page 1: bottom shelf page 2: middle shelf pages 3 and 4: top shelf

LIN'S MESSY ROOM

This is a story in which students identify solid figures and categorize them.

Lin's room is a mess!

That is clear.

What should she put here?

Topic 13   3

The work is done.

It's time for fun!

Lin can play with the clay.

Where is it?

Topic 13   4

fold down

WRITE

Reread the story to students. This time have them circle the answer to the question raised in the text—page 1: the ball; page 2: the cone hat; page 3: the puzzle; page 4: the jars of clay.

SPEAK

Invite students to retell the story in their own words. Encourage them to include the correct shape words in their retellings. Prompt them with questions. *What solid shapes did Lin put on the middle shelf?* [Cones] *The bottom shelf?* [Spheres]

Extension

Play a guessing game with students. For example: *I see something in the classroom that is a cylinder. It holds something we use. It holds a liquid. It can be one of many colors. What is it?* [Jar of paint] Then call on a volunteer to do the same. Have him or her select an object and give clues describing it. If needed, prompt the student with descriptions by whispering in his or her ear.

You may wish to have students take home their Interactive Math Story books and share what they have learned about solid figures.

TOPIC ESSENTIAL QUESTION

How can solid figures be named, described, compared, and composed?

Revisit the Topic Essential Question throughout the topic, and see a note about answering the question in the Teacher's Edition for the Topic Assessment.

MATH AND SCIENCE PROJECT STEM

The science theme for this project is **How Do Objects Move?** This theme will be revisited in the Math and Science Activities in Lessons 13-1 and 13-2.

> Balls in sports are designed so that they move, bounce, and behave in certain ways. Baseballs have 108 stitches. How a baseball is thrown changes how the stitches "grab" the air, making the ball fly straight or curve.

Project-Based Learning Have students work on the **Math and Science Project** over the course of several days.

EXTENSION

Label 3 boxes *Roll, Stack,* and *Slide.* Ask students to find 2 everyday objects and place them into the appropriate box. Challenge students to identify the objects that may belong in more than one box and explain why. Use shape vocabulary throughout the exercise.

Sample Student Work for Math and Science Project

Math and Science Project: How Do Objects Move?
Directions Read the character speech bubbles to students. **Find Out!** Have students observe and describe how objects move using the terms *roll, stack,* and *slide.* Say: *Objects move in different ways. Talk to your friends and relatives about everyday objects that are cones, cylinders, spheres, or cubes. Ask them how each one moves and whether they roll, stack, or slide.* **Journal: Make a Poster** Have students make a poster that shows everyday objects that are cones, cylinders, spheres, and cubes, and then tell how each one moves.

Topic 13   seven hundred forty-five **745**

Home-School Connection

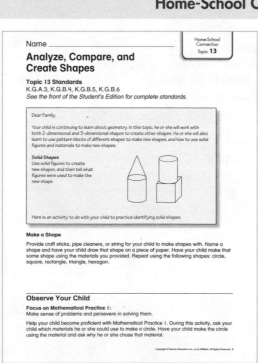

Send this page home at the start of Topic 13 to give families an overview of the content in the topic.

Name _____

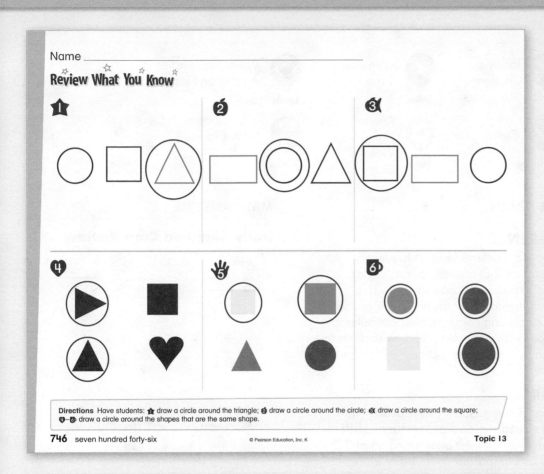

⭐ Review What You Know

Directions Have students: ⭐ draw a circle around the triangle; 🍎 draw a circle around the circle; 🦅 draw a circle around the square; ❤️—6️⃣ draw a circle around the shapes that are the same shape.

RtI	Item Analysis for Diagnosis and Intervention	
Item	**© Standards**	**MDIS**
1	K.G.A.2	D29
2	K.G.A.2	D29
3	K.G.A.2	D29
4	K.G.A.2	D29
5	K.G.A.2	D29
6	K.G.A.2	D29

Topic 13 Vocabulary Words Activity

Use the Topic 12 activity on page 676 with the Topic 13 words below.

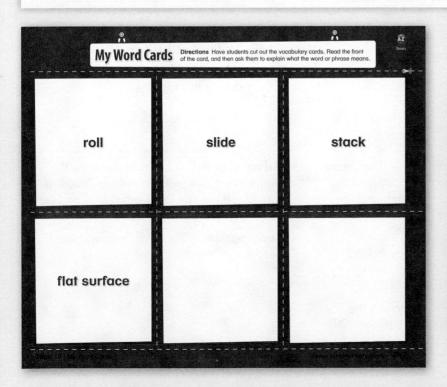

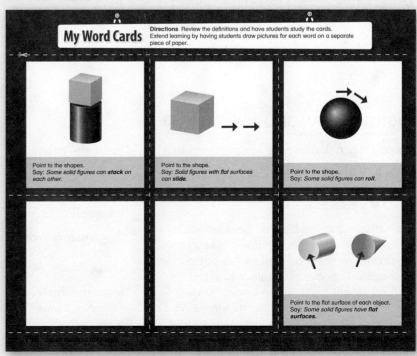

ANALYZE AND COMPARE TWO-DIMENSIONAL (2-D) SHAPES

DIGITAL RESOURCES PearsonRealize.com

 Student and Teacher eTexts
eText

 Listen and Look For Lesson Video
PD

Today's Challenge
Think

Solve and Share
Solve

 Visual Learning Animation Plus
Learn

A-Z Animated Glossary
Glossary

Math Tools
Tools

Quick Check
Assessment

Another Look Homework Video
Help

Math Games
Games

LESSON OVERVIEW  FOCUS • COHERENCE • RIGOR

FOCUS

Domain K.G Geometry

Cluster K.G.B Analyze, compare, create, and compose shapes.

Content Standard K.G.B.4 Analyze and compare two- and three-dimensional shapes, in different sizes and orientations, using informal language to describe their similarities, differences, parts (e.g., number of sides and vertices/"corners"), and other attributes (e.g., having sides of equal length).

Mathematical Practices MP.2, MP.4, MP.6, MP.7

Objective Analyze and compare 2-D shapes.

Essential Understanding 2-D shapes can be sorted and identified by their attributes.

Materials Attribute blocks (or Teaching Tool 46)

COHERENCE

In Topic 12, students learned to identify and describe 2-D shapes such as circles, triangles, rectangles, and squares. This lesson brings together those 2-D shapes so that students can compare their attributes. This work with attributes prepares students to analyze and compare 2-D and 3-D shapes throughout Topic 13.

RIGOR

This lesson emphasizes **conceptual understanding** and **procedural skill**. Students deepen their understanding of 2-D shapes by comparing attributes of triangles, circles, rectangles, and squares. Students also identify shapes when given attributes as clues. The clues prompt students to identify examples of shapes and nonexamples of shapes.

 Watch the Listen and Look For Lesson Video.
PD

MATH ANYTIME

Daily Common Core Review

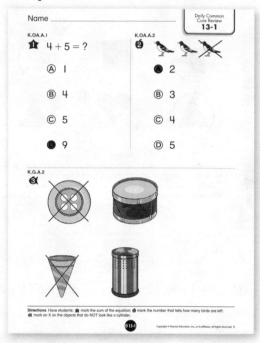

Today's Challenge

Think Use Topic 13 problems any time during this topic.

ENGLISH LANGUAGE LEARNERS

Speaking Ask and give information using key words/expressions.

Use with the Do You Understand? on Teacher's Edition p. 750.

After discussing the Do You Understand? problem with students, review the key terms *sides* and *vertices*, as well as the name of shapes. Call on a volunteer to stand with his or her back to the board. Draw a circle, triangle, square, or rectangle on the board and above the volunteer so that

he or she cannot see the shape. The shape should be visible to the other students. Ask students to give the volunteer information about the shape. Have the volunteer use the information to guess the shape.

Beginning Prompt students by asking questions, such as: *How many sides does the shape have? How many vertices?*

Intermediate Ask students to use the sentence stems: "It has ____. It does NOT have ____."

Advanced Ask students to describe the shape using complete sentences. Students should use the key terms *sides* and *vertices* in their descriptions.

Summarize What words can you use to describe different shapes?

COHERENCE: Engage learners by connecting prior knowledge to new ideas.

Students apply what they have learned about the names and attributes of shapes to identify a shape. This prepares them for the next part of the lesson where they identify other shapes based on their attributes.

10–15 min

Solve

 hole Class **BEFORE**

1. Pose the Solve-and-Share Problem
MP.2 Reasoning In the problem, students use logical reasoning to identify a two-dimensional shape based on its attributes.

Give each student a rectangle, square, circle, and triangle attribute block.

Say: *Emily wants to figure out what shape is behind the door. The shape has 4 vertices and 4 equal sides. Use the shapes above the door to help you find the mystery shape. Draw the shape on the door.*

2. Build Understanding
What do you know about the shape behind the door? [It has 4 vertices and 4 equal sides.]
What tools do you have to find out what shape it is? [Sample answers: Shapes on the page; attribute blocks]

 mall roup **DURING**

3. Ask Guiding Questions As Needed
How many sides does a rectangle have? [4]
Are a rectangle's 4 sides always the same length? [No]

hole Class **AFTER**

4. Share and Discuss Solutions
Start with students' solutions. Have them share Solve the strategies they used to solve the problem. If needed, project and analyze Caroline's work to show how to identify the shape by its attributes.

5. Transition to the Visual Learning Bridge
You identified a shape by a description of its sides and vertices. Later in this lesson, you will learn how to identify shapes using other clues about their attributes.

6. Extension for Early Finishers
Have students work in pairs. Each partner takes turns giving clues about a shape until his or her partner guesses the shape.

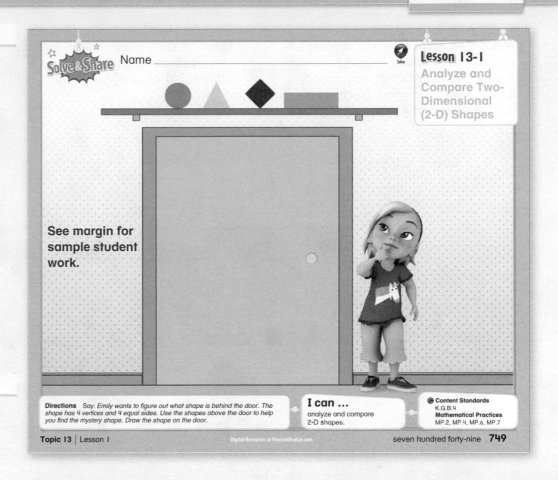

Solve & Share   Name _____

See margin for sample student work.

Directions Say: Emily wants to figure out what shape is behind the door. The shape has 4 vertices and 4 equal sides. Use the shapes above the door to help you find the mystery shape. Draw the shape on the door.

Topic 13 | Lesson 1

Lesson 13-1
Analyze and Compare Two-Dimensional (2-D) Shapes

I can ...
analyze and compare 2-D shapes.

Content Standards
K.G.B.4
Mathematical Practices
MP.2, MP.4, MP.6, MP.7

Digital Resources at PearsonRealize.com   seven hundred forty-nine **749**

Analyze Student Work

Caroline's Work

Caroline correctly identifies the mystery shape as a square and draws it on the door.

Grayson's Work

Grayson incorrectly identifies the mystery shape as a rectangle and draws it on the door.

STEP 2

DEVELOP: VISUAL LEARNING

The *Visual Learning Bridge* connects students' thinking in Solve & Share to important math ideas in the lesson. Use the *Visual Learning Bridge* to make these ideas explicit. Also available as a *Visual Learning Animation Plus* at PearsonRealize.com

 Visual Learning

  Learn Glossary

MP.7 Use Structure *We need to use the attributes of these shapes to identify the rectangles. What do you already know about rectangles?* [Rectangles have 4 sides and 4 vertices.]

Why did Emily mark an X on the first shape? [Because it does not have 4 sides and 4 vertices]

Why did Emily draw a circle around the two shapes? [They are rectangles.] *How do you know?* [They have 4 sides and 4 vertices.]

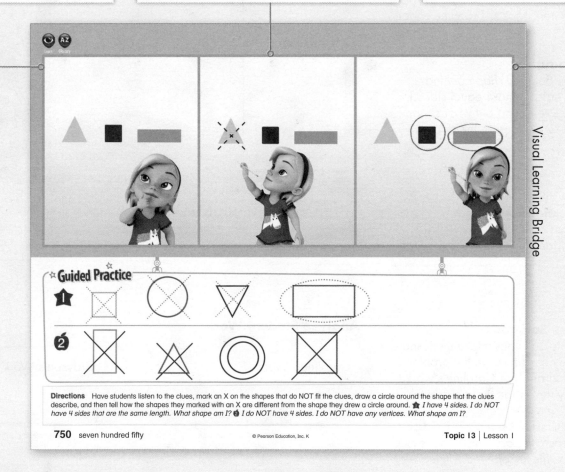

Visual Learning Bridge

Guided Practice

Directions Have students listen to the clues, mark an X on the shapes that do NOT fit the clues, draw a circle around the shape that the clues describe, and then tell how the shapes they marked with an X are different from the shape they drew a circle around. ⭐ *I have 4 sides. I do NOT have 4 sides that are the same length. What shape am I?* ❷ *I do NOT have 4 sides. I do NOT have any vertices. What shape am I?*

750 seven hundred fifty   © Pearson Education, Inc. K   **Topic 13** | Lesson 1

Complete the *Do You Understand? Show Me!* problem before starting Guided Practice.

Do You Understand? Show Me! MP.6 Be Precise *Which shapes have 4 sides and 4 vertices: squares, rectangles, circles, or triangles?* [Squares and rectangles]

Coherence In the Visual Learning Bridge, students compare the attributes of three shapes. This links back to their previous work in Topic 12, where students learned to identify triangles, rectangles, and squares.

Ask the following Essential Question: *What information can help you identify a 2-D shape?* [Sample answer: Knowing the number of sides and/or the number of vertices can help you identify a shape.]

Error Intervention: Item 2

If students have difficulty identifying attributes of shapes,

then have them use paper shapes to identify the attributes in the clues.

 Reteaching Assign Reteaching Set A, p. 793.

✓ QUICK CHECK

Check mark indicates items for prescribing differentiation on the next page.
Items 7 and 8 are worth 1 point. Item 10 is worth up to 3 points.

20–30 min   Tools Assessment

Item 3 Have students mark an X on any shapes that can be eliminated as soon as each clue is read. Waiting until all of the clues have been read to eliminate shapes may be too difficult for some students.

Items 3–5 MP.6 Be Precise Students will hear riddles phrased slightly differently. They need to listen actively for clues. If needed, remind students that the words *corners* and *vertices* refer to the same thing.

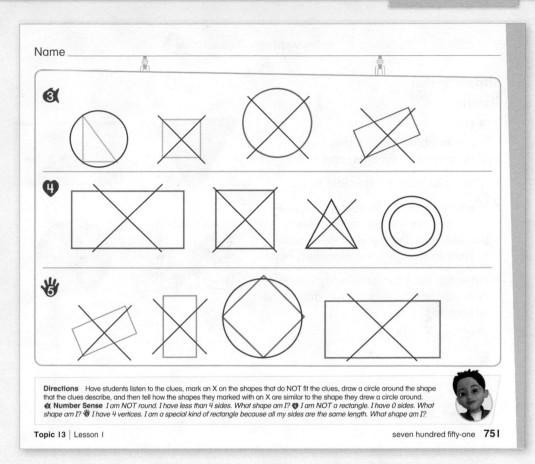

Item 7 MP.4 Model with Math The reference to a real object, such as a classroom door, will solidify the attributes of the shape for some students. If needed, point out the classroom door. *How many sides does it have?* [4] *Are they all the same size?* [No] Have students use this information to look for a shape with 4 sides that are not all the same length.

Item 8 Some students will want to hear all of the clues before drawing, while others will want to draw as soon as they think they know what the shape is. Encourage students to listen to all of the clues before drawing.

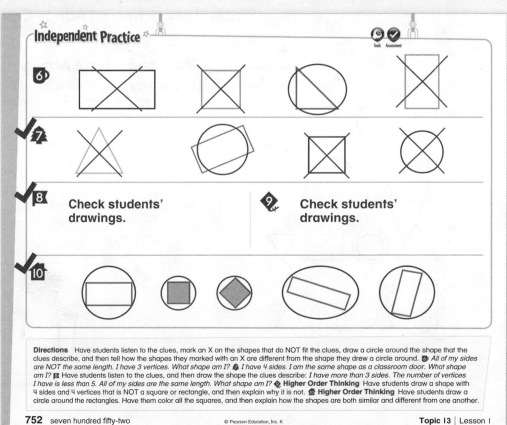

Use the **QUICK CHECK** on the previous page to prescribe differentiated instruction.

I **Intervention**
0–3 points on the Quick Check

O **On-Level**
4 points on the Quick Check

A **Advanced**
5 points on the Quick Check

Intervention Activity **I**

Shape Sorter

Materials

(per pair)

Classroom objects in the shapes of circles, triangles, squares, and rectangles

• Display objects for the class to see.

• Have one partner in each pair cover his or her eyes while you identify a shape in the display. Ask the second partner to describe the identified object.

• Have the first partner identify the object that matches the description and name the shape.

Reteach **I**

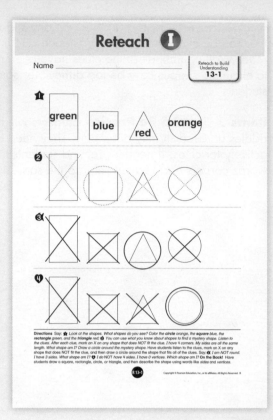

Name _____

Reteach to Build Understanding 13-1

Directions Say: ★ *Look at the shapes. What shapes do you see? Color the **circle** orange, the **square** blue, the **rectangle** green, and the **triangle** red;* ❶ *You can use what you know about shapes to find a mystery shape. Listen to the clues. After each clue, mark an X on any shape that does NOT fit the clue. I have 4 corners. My sides are all the same length. What shape am I? Draw a circle around the mystery shape. Have students listen to the clues, mark an X on any shape that does NOT fit the clue, and then draw a circle around the shape that fits all of the clues. Say:* ❷ *I am NOT round. I have 3 sides. What shape am I?* ❸ *I do NOT have 4 sides. I have 0 vertices. Which shape am I?* **On the Back!** *Have students draw a square, rectangle, circle, or triangle, and then describe the shape using words like sides and vertices.*

On-Level and Advanced Activity Centers **O** **A**

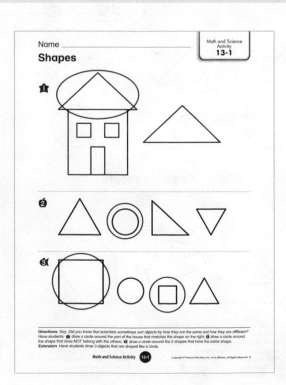

Name _____

Shapes

Math and Science Activity 13-1

Directions Say: *Did you know that scientists sometimes sort objects by how they are the same and how they are different?* Have students: ★ *draw a circle around the part of the house that matches the shape on the right;* ❶ *draw a circle around the shape that does NOT belong with the others;* ❷ *draw a circle around the 2 shapes that have the same shape.* **Extension** Have students draw 3 objects that are shaped like a circle.

Math and Science Activity 13-1

Copyright © Pearson Education, Inc., or its affiliates. All Rights Reserved. K

Math and Science Activity **STEM**

This activity revisits the science theme, **How Do Objects Move?**, introduced on page 745 in the Student's Edition.

Sample Student Work

TIMING

The time allocated to Step 3 will depend on the teacher's instructional decisions and differentiation routines.

15–30 min

Help Tools Games

Technology Center Ⅰ Ⓞ Ⓐ

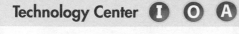
Tools

Games

Math Tools and Math Games

A link to a specific math tools activity or math game to use with this lesson is provided at PearsonRealize.com.

Leveled Assignment

Ⅰ Items 1–4   Ⓞ Items 2–6   Ⓐ Items 3–7

Name _____

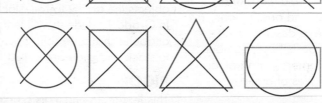

Homework & Practice 13-1

Analyze and Compare Two-Dimensional (2-D) Shapes

Another Look!

HOME ACTIVITY Play *What Object Am I?* with your child. Think of an object in the house, such as a window or a door, and give clues about it. For example: "I have 4 sides and 4 vertices. All of my sides are the same length. What shape am I?" Then have your child give you clues about an object.

1

2

Directions Say: *Listen to the clues. After each clue, mark an X on any shape that does NOT fit the clue. I have 4 sides. I am a special kind of rectangle because all of my sides are the same length. Draw a circle around the shape that fits all of the clues.* Have students listen to the clues, mark an X on the shapes that do NOT fit the clues, draw a circle around the shape that the clues describe, and then tell how the shapes they marked with an X are similar to the shape they drew a circle around. **★** *I do NOT have 4 vertices. I have 3 sides. What shape am I?* **✿** *I have 4 vertices. My sides are NOT all the same length. What shape am I?*

Topic 13 | Lesson 1   Digital Resources at PearsonRealize.com   seven hundred fifty-three **753**

3

4

5

6

Check students' drawings.

7

Directions Have students listen to the clues to find the mystery object in each row. Have students mark an X on the objects that do NOT fit the clues, draw a circle around the object that the clues describe, and then tell how the shape of the objects they marked with an X are different from the shape of the object they draw a circle around. **★** *I do NOT have 3 sides. I am round. What shape do I look like?* **✿** *I am NOT round. I have 4 sides that are the same length. What shape do I look like?* **✋** Have students write the number that tells how many vertices the shape has. **✿ Higher Order Thinking** Have students draw a picture of an object in the classroom that has 0 sides and 0 corners. **✿ Higher Order Thinking** Have students draw a circle around the circles, and then mark an X on the other shapes. Have them explain why the others are NOT circles.

LESSON 13-2

ANALYZE AND COMPARE THREE-DIMENSIONAL (3-D) SHAPES

DIGITAL RESOURCES PearsonRealize.com

 Student and Teacher eTexts
eText

 Listen and Look For Lesson Video
PD

 Today's Challenge
Think

 Solve and Share
Solve

 Visual Learning Animation Plus
Learn

 Animated Glossary
Glossary

 Math Tools
Tools

 Quick Check
Assessment

 Another Look Homework Video
Help

 Math Games
Games

LESSON OVERVIEW FCR FOCUS • COHERENCE • RIGOR

FOCUS

Domain K.G Geometry

Cluster K.G.B Analyze, compare, create, and compose shapes.

Content Standard K.G.B.4 Analyze and compare two- and three-dimensional shapes, in different sizes and orientations, using informal language to describe their similarities, differences, parts (e.g., number of sides and vertices/"corners"), and other attributes (e.g., having sides of equal length).

Mathematical Practices MP.1, MP.2, MP.3, MP.7

Objective Analyze and compare 3-D shapes.

Essential Understanding Objects shaped like spheres, cones, and cylinders can roll. Objects shaped like cubes, cones, and cylinders can stack and slide.

Vocabulary roll, slide, stack

Materials Geometric solids, crayons

COHERENCE

In Topic 12, students learned to identify spheres, cylinders, cones, and cubes, and to find objects that have those shapes in the environment. In this lesson, students learn that some attributes of solid figures give objects the ability to roll, stack, or slide. In Grade 1, students will learn that the attributes that give solid figures the ability to stack and slide are called *faces*.

RIGOR

This lesson emphasizes **conceptual understanding**. Students learn to identify 3-D shapes based on common attributes. These include the attributes that allow solid figures to roll, stack, or slide.

 Watch the Listen and Look For Lesson
PD Video.

MATH ANYTIME

Daily Common Core Review

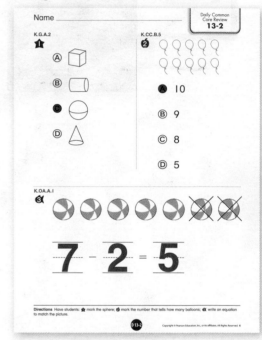

Today's Challenge

Think Use Topic 13 problems any time during this topic.

ENGLISH LANGUAGE LEARNERS ELL

Speaking Speak using content area vocabulary in context.

Use with the Visual Learning Bridge on Student's Edition p. 756.

Review the words *roll*, *stack*, and *slide* by demonstrating each action with geometric solids. Ask students to repeat each word. Show students a sphere. *Can you roll this solid figure? Slide? Stack?* Give each student a cube, sphere, cone, or cylinder geometric solid. Have students work in pairs. Ask each student to describe to his or her partner what

action or actions he or she can and cannot do with the solid figure. (e.g., I can slide it; I cannot stack it.)

Beginning Ask students to use the following sentence stems: "I can _____ it, and I can _____ it. I can _____ it, but I cannot _____ it."

Intermediate Ask students to use complete sentences to talk about at least two actions that can or cannot be done with the solid figure. Students should use *and* and *but* in their responses.

Advanced Ask students to include the name of the solid figure in their descriptions and use connecting words such as *and*, *but*, and *or*.

Summarize What words can you use to describe two actions a solid figure can do?

DEVELOP: PROBLEM-BASED LEARNING

PEARSON
realize
PearsonRealize.com

COHERENCE: Engage learners by connecting prior knowledge to new ideas.

Students use clues to color solid figures that match a given description. This prepares them for the next part of the lesson where students learn which solid figures roll, stack, and slide.

10–15 min

Solve

 BEFORE

1. Pose the Solve-and-Share Problem

MP.1 Make Sense and Persevere In this problem, students plan a solution pathway to determine which of the given shapes to color.

Provide groups of students with geometric solids and crayons.

Say: Jackson wants to find a solid figure. The solid figure has flat sides and it rolls. Color the solid figures that match the description.

2. Build Understanding

The shapes on this page are all solid figures. What are you asked to find? [Solid figures that have flat sides and that can roll] *What do you already know?* [Sample answers: Spheres are round; cubes have flat sides; cones have a flat side and a vertex.]

 **DURING**

3. Ask Guiding Questions As Needed

How does knowing which shapes are NOT round or NOT curved help you find the solution to this problem? [I can forget about the figures that are NOT round or NOT curved and focus on those that are.]

 AFTER

4. Share and Discuss Solutions

 Start with students' solutions. If needed, Solve project and analyze Fabian's work to discuss which solid figures have flat sides and can roll.

5. Transition to the Visual Learning Bridge

You identified solid figures that have flat sides and can roll. Later in this lesson, you will learn about solid figures that slide and solid figures that stack.

6. Extension for Early Finishers

Have students find objects in the classroom in the shape of a sphere, a cube, a cone, and a cylinder.

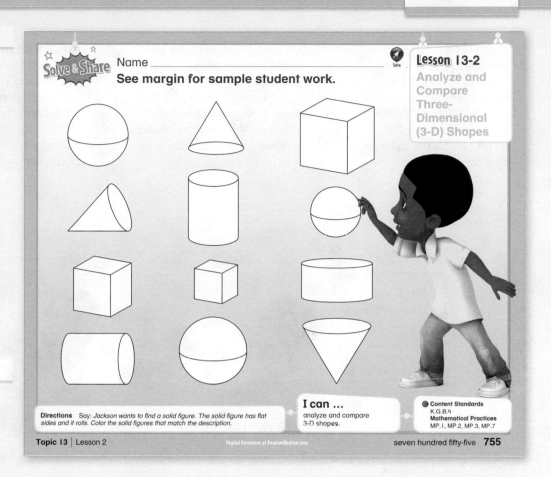

Solve & Share

Name _____

See margin for sample student work.

Solve

Lesson 13-2

Analyze and Compare Three-Dimensional (3-D) Shapes

Directions Say: Jackson wants to find a solid figure. The solid figure has flat sides and it rolls. Color the solid figures that match the description.

I can ...
analyze and compare 3-D shapes.

Content Standards K.G.B.4 **Mathematical Practices** MP.1, MP.2, MP.3, MP.7

Topic 13 | Lesson 2

Digital Resources at PearsonRealize.com

seven hundred fifty-five **755**

Analyze Student Work

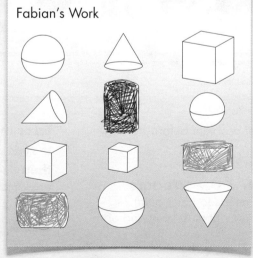

Fabian's Work

Fabian correctly colors the cylinders.

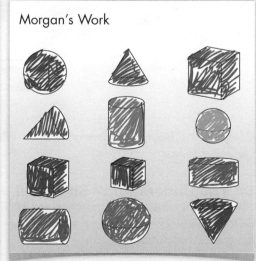

Morgan's Work

Morgan incorrectly colors all of the solid figures.

The *Visual Learning Bridge* connects students' thinking in Solve & Share to important math ideas in the lesson. Use the *Visual Learning Bridge* to make these ideas explicit. Also available as a *Visual Learning Animation Plus* at PearsonRealize.com

E L L
Visual Learning

Learn

Glossary

What solid figures do you see? [Cube, sphere, cone, cylinder] *Which solid figure has 2 or more vertices?* [Cube] *Which solid figures have flat surfaces?* [Cube, cylinder, and cone]

Which solid figures do you see? [Sphere, cone, cylinder] *What movement is each figure doing?* [Rolling] *What does an object have to look like to roll?* [It must be round or have a curved surface.]

MP.2 Reasoning *What do you see?* [A cube and cylinder are stacked.] *Why can these solid figures be stacked?* [They have flat surfaces.] *Can you stack a cone?* [Yes, but only when its flat surface is on top of another figure.]

Which solid figures slide? [Cube, cone, cylinder] *Which can stack, slide, and roll?* [Cylinder, cone]

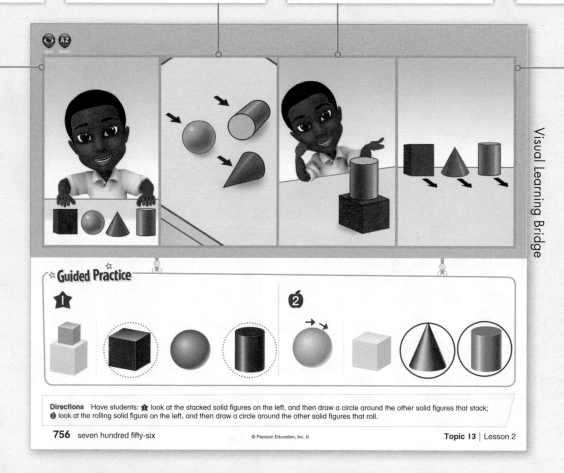

Visual Learning Bridge

☆ **Guided Practice**

Directions Have students: 1⃣ look at the stacked solid figures on the left, and then draw a circle around the other solid figures that stack; 2⃣ look at the rolling solid figure on the left, and then draw a circle around the other solid figures that roll.

756 seven hundred fifty-six   © Pearson Education, Inc. K   **Topic 13** | Lesson 2

Complete the *Do You Understand? Show Me!* problem before starting Guided Practice.

Do You Understand? Show Me! MP.7 Use Structure

How do you know if an object will stack? [It needs to have a flat surface.] *How do you know if an object will roll?* [It must be round or have a curved surface.]

Essential
Question

Ask the following Essential Question: *Which 3-D shapes can roll? Which can stack? Which can slide?* [A cylinder, sphere, or cone can roll. A cylinder, cone, or cube can stack. A cube, cone, or cylinder can slide.]

Error Intervention: Item 2

If students confuse roll, stack, and slide,

then have them handle and experiment with each solid figure to see which ones roll, stack, and/or slide.

RtI

Reteaching Assign Reteaching Set B, p. 793.

✓ QUICK CHECK

Check mark indicates items for prescribing differentiation on the next page.
Items 9 and 10 are worth 1 point. Item 11 is worth up to 3 points.

Tools Assessment

20–30 min

Item 3 MP.7 Use Structure Remind students that solid figures have properties that make them different from one another, such as the number of flat surfaces. Students may also notice other attributes, such as the number of sides and vertices/corners of each solid.

Item 7 Remind students that solids can roll, slide, and stack. Ask students to think about the shape of each object. *What attribute allows an object to slide or stack?* [At least 1 flat surface] Guide students as they determine which objects have flat surfaces that allow them to slide and stack.

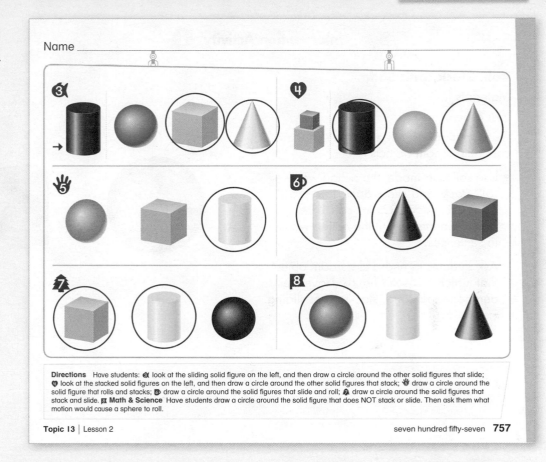

Name _____

Directions Have students: ❸ look at the sliding solid figure on the left, and then draw a circle around the other solid figures that slide; ❹ look at the stacked solid figures on the left, and then draw a circle around the other solid figures that stack; ❺ draw a circle around the solid figure that rolls and stacks; ❻ draw a circle around the solid figures that slide and roll; ❼ draw a circle around the solid figures that stack and slide. ❽ **Math & Science** Have students draw a circle around the solid figure that does NOT stack or slide. Then ask them what motion would cause a sphere to roll.

Topic 13 | Lesson 2   seven hundred fifty-seven **757**

Item 9 If students have difficulty, remind them that an object must have a round surface in order to roll.

Item 11 MP.3 Construct Arguments If students have difficulty, point to an object and ask them: *Does this object have a flat surface?* Have them practice stacking objects in the classroom. *Why can't you stack a sphere?* [It does not have any flat surfaces. It rolls.] *Can a cone be on the bottom of a stack? Explain.* [No, a cone cannot be on the bottom of a stack because you cannot stack an object on its point. Stacked objects cannot balance with a point on the bottom. However, a cone can be stacked on top of a cube or cylinder.]

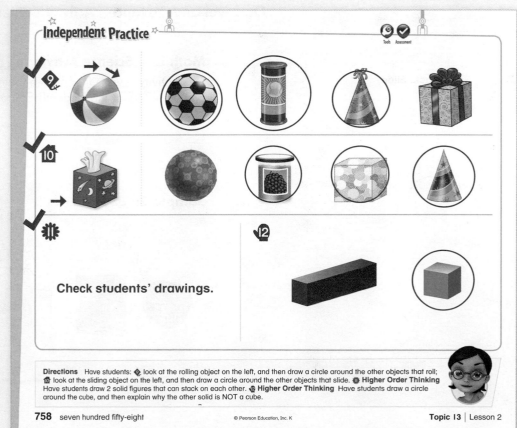

Independent Practice

Check students' drawings.

Directions Have students: ❾ look at the rolling object on the left, and then draw a circle around the other objects that roll; ❿ look at the sliding object on the left, and then draw a circle around the other objects that slide. ⓫ **Higher Order Thinking** Have students draw 2 solid figures that can stack on each other. ⓬ **Higher Order Thinking** Have students draw a circle around the cube, and then explain why the other solid is NOT a cube.

758 seven hundred fifty-eight   © Pearson Education, Inc. K   Topic 13 | Lesson 2

Use the **QUICK CHECK** on the previous page to prescribe differentiated instruction.

2 RtI

I Intervention
0–3 points on the Quick Check

O On-Level
4 points on the Quick Check

A Advanced
5 points on the Quick Check

Intervention Activity **I**

Roll, Stack, and Slide
Materials
(per group)
Geometric solids: cube, cylinder, sphere, cone; classroom objects

- Use solids to model the action words *roll*, *stack*, and *slide*. *Spheres can roll. Cubes can stack. Cones can slide.* Have students repeat the action words in sentences.

- Ask students to find a classroom object that matches a solid figure. Have them demonstrate rolling, stacking, or sliding.

Reteach **I**

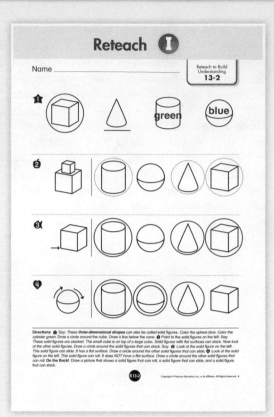

On-Level and Advanced Activity Centers **O A**

Math and Science Activity STEM

This activity revisits the science theme, **How Do Objects Move?**, introduced on page 745 of the Student's Edition.

Sample Student Work

Help **Tools** **Games**

15–30 min

TIMING

The time allocated to Step 3 will depend on the teacher's instructional decisions and differentiation routines.

Technology Center I O A

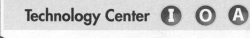

Tools

Games

Math Tools and Math Games

A link to a specific math tools activity or math game to use with this lesson is provided at PearsonRealize.com.

Leveled Assignment

I Items 1–4   **O** Items 2–5   **A** Items 3–6

Name _____

Help Tools Games

Another Look!

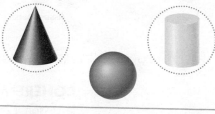

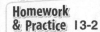

Homework & Practice 13-2

Analyze and Compare Three-Dimensional (3-D) Shapes

HOME ACTIVITY Show your child a ball, a can, and a cube-shaped block. Ask him or her to compare the features of each object, such as which objects can stack, which can roll, and which can slide. Have your child point to the flat surfaces on each of the objects.

1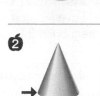

2

Directions Say: *A cube can stack on top of another cube. Draw a circle around the other solid figures that can also be stacked on top of a cube.* Have students: ★ look at the solid figure on the left that can roll, and then draw a circle around the other solid figures that can roll; ✿ look at the solid figure on the left that can slide, and then draw a circle around the other solid figures that can slide.

Topic 13 | Lesson 2   Digital Resources at PearsonRealize.com   seven hundred fifty-nine **759**

3

4

5

Check students' drawings.

6

Check students' drawings.

Directions Have students: ★ mark an X on the solid figures that can both roll and slide; ✿ mark an X on the solid figure that is NOT a sphere, and then explain how it is similar to and different from a sphere. ✋ **Higher Order Thinking** Have students draw 2 solid figures that can roll. ☕ **Higher Order Thinking** Have students use all of the 3 solid figures that can stack to draw a castle made of blocks. Then have them explain why cones can only stack on top of other shapes.

760 seven hundred sixty   © Pearson Education, Inc. K   **Topic 13** | Lesson 2

LESSON 13-3

COMPARE 2-D AND 3-D SHAPES

LESSON OVERVIEW · FCR · FOCUS · COHERENCE · RIGOR

FOCUS

Domain K.G Geometry

Cluster K.G.B Analyze, create, compare, and compose shapes.

Content Standard K.G.B.4 Analyze and compare two- and three-dimensional shapes, in different sizes and orientations, using informal language to describe their similarities, differences, parts (e.g., number of sides and vertices/"corners"), and other attributes (e.g., having sides of equal length).

Mathematical Practices MP.2, MP.5, MP.6

Objective Analyze and compare 2-D and 3-D shapes.

Essential Understanding The flat surfaces of many solid figures have specific 2-D shapes.

Vocabulary flat surface

Materials Geometric solids

COHERENCE

In Lesson 12-1, students differentiated between flat shapes and solid figures. In this lesson, students connect flat and solid figures by identifying 2-D shapes in the flat surfaces of 3-D shapes. In Lesson 13-7, students will use what they have learned about flat surfaces to help them build 3-D shapes.

RIGOR

This lesson emphasizes **conceptual understanding**. Students relate 2-D shapes to the shapes of the flat surfaces in 3-D shapes, and vice versa. Students learn to recognize that a cube's flat surfaces are squares, and that a cone's and cylinder's flat surfaces are circles.

 Watch the Listen and Look For Lesson Video.
PD

MATH ANYTIME

Daily Common Core Review

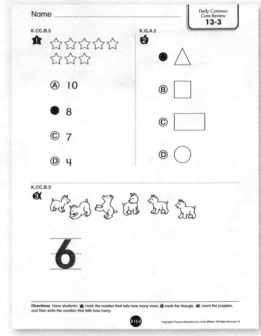

Today's Challenge

Think Use Topic 13 problems any time during this topic.

ENGLISH LANGUAGE LEARNERS ELL

Speaking Ask for and give information using key words.

Use with the Do You Understand? on Teacher's Edition p. 762.

Say the words *flat surface*, and illustrate their meaning by pointing out objects in the room with flat surfaces. Ask students to repeat the words. Point to a book. *Does a book have a flat surface?* [Yes] Point to different objects and ask students whether or not the objects have flat surfaces. Have students works in pairs.

Beginning Have Student A point to an object and ask: "Does ___ have a flat surface?" Student B should respond with: "Yes, it does, or No, it does not." Have students reverse roles and repeat.

Intermediate Have Student A ask Student B whether or not various objects in the classroom have flat surfaces. Student B should respond in complete sentences. Have students reverse roles and repeat.

Advanced Have partners ask each other what objects in their homes have flat surfaces. Students should respond in complete sentences.

Summarize How can you ask about the surface of an object?

DEVELOP: PROBLEM-BASED LEARNING

COHERENCE: Engage learners by connecting prior knowledge to new ideas.
Students identify real-world objects and solid figures that have a flat surface that is a circle. This prepares students for the next part of the lesson where they learn to use flat surfaces to classify solids.

10–15 min

Solve

BEFORE

1. Pose the Solve-and-Share Problem
MP.5 Use Appropriate Tools Strategically
In this problem, students use geometric solids to help them identify flat surfaces that are circles.

Provide groups of students with cube, cone, sphere, and cylinder geometric solids.

Say: *Jackson needs to find a circle that is a flat surface of a solid figure. What solid figures have a circle as a part of the figure? Draw a circle around the solid figures that have a circle as a part. Mark an X on the solid figures that do NOT.*

2. Build Understanding
What are you asked to do? [Find solid figures that have at least one flat surface that is a circle.] *What tools can you use to help you solve the problem?* [Geometric solids]

DURING

3. Ask Guiding Questions As Needed
Which solid figure has a side that is shaped like a circle? [Sample answer: Cone] *What should you do to check?* [Trace around the solid figure.] *Are there any other solid figures with a side that is shaped like a circle?* [Yes] *Which solid figure?* [Sample answer: Cylinder]

AFTER

4. Share and Discuss Solutions
Solve ➤ Start with students' solutions. If needed, project Everett's work to discuss the two-dimensional components of the three-dimensional objects.

5. Transition to the Visual Learning Bridge
You learned that some 3-D objects have flat surfaces that are circles. Later in this lesson, you will learn that some 3-D objects have flat surfaces that are squares.

6. Extension for Early Finishers
Have students trace a flat side of each solid on the board and ask students to name the shapes they drew.

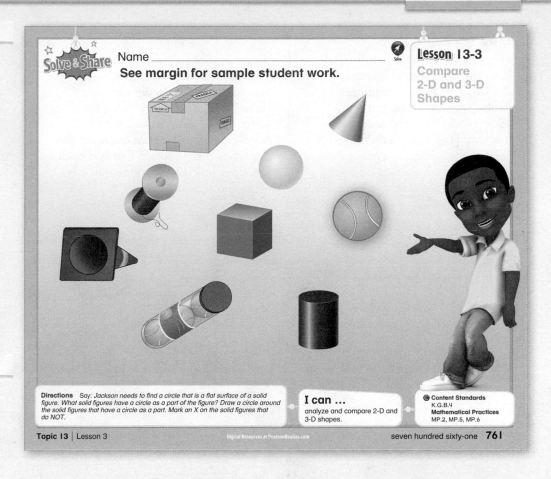

Solve & Share

Name _____

See margin for sample student work.

 Solve

Lesson 13-3
Compare 2-D and 3-D Shapes

Directions Say: *Jackson needs to find a circle that is a flat surface of a solid figure. What solid figures have a circle as a part of the figure? Draw a circle around the solid figures that have a circle as a part. Mark an X on the solid figures that do NOT.*

I can ...
analyze and compare 2-D and 3-D shapes.

Content Standards
K.G.B.4
Mathematical Practices
MP.2, MP.5, MP.6

Topic 13 | Lesson 3

Digital Resources at PearsonRealize.com

seven hundred sixty-one **761**

Analyze Student Work

Everett's Work

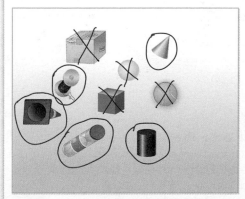

Cara's Work

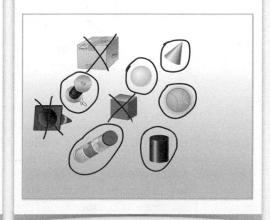

Everett correctly circles all of the cones and cylinders. He draws an X on objects that are not cones or cylinders.

Cara includes spheres because they appear to be a circle when drawn in two dimensions. She excludes the traffic cone, saying that the circle is a hole, not a surface.

The *Visual Learning Bridge* connects students' thinking in Solve & Share to important math ideas in the lesson. Use the *Visual Learning Bridge* to make these ideas explicit. Also available as a *Visual Learning Animation Plus* at PearsonRealize.com

E L L
Visual Learning

MP.6 Be Precise *What shape is Jackson holding?* [Square] *What solid figure has flat surfaces that are squares?* [Cube] *Are all of the flat surfaces on the cube squares? Explain.* [Yes; each side of the cube is the same.]

Jackson wants to find objects that have a square, flat surface in his classroom. What objects does Jackson see in the classroom? [Sample answers: Calendar, clock, door] *What flat surfaces do these objects have? Describe them.* [Sample answers: The clock has a flat surface that is a circle. The door has a flat surface that is a rectangle.]

Jackson identifies a square flat surface in 2 classroom objects. Which objects have a square flat surface? [The calendar and the window in the door] *A student says that the calendar's flat surface is not the same shape as the square because the calendar is tilted. Is the student correct? Explain.* [No; tilting an object does not change its shape. The calendar is still shaped like a square.]

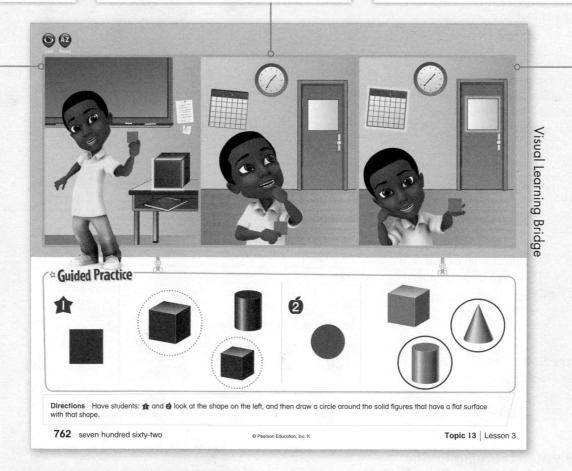

Visual Learning Bridge

☆ **Guided Practice**

Directions Have students: ★ and ✿ look at the shape on the left, and then draw a circle around the solid figures that have a flat surface with that shape.

762 seven hundred sixty-two   © Pearson Education, Inc. K   **Topic 13** | Lesson 3

Complete the *Do You Understand? Show Me!* problem before starting Guided Practice.

Do You Understand? Show Me! MP.6 Be Precise Show students the flat surface of a cube and the flat surface of a cylinder. Ask students what type of surface each shape is. [Each shape is a flat surface.] Now ask them the shape of each flat surface. [The shape of the cube's flat surface is a square, and the shape of the cylinder's flat surface is a circle.]

Coherence In the Visual Learning Bridge, students examine the flat surfaces of 3-D shapes. This connects to their previous work with 2-D shapes in Topic 12.

Essential Question

Ask the following Essential Question: *How do 3-D shapes contain 2-D shapes?* [Some flat surfaces of 3-D shapes are squares; some flat surfaces are circles.]

Error Intervention: Item 2

If students have difficulty with the orientation of shapes,

then provide real objects as they complete the items.

☑ **QUICK CHECK**

Check mark indicates items for prescribing differentiation on the next page.
Items 7 and 8 are each worth 1 point. Item 9 is worth up to 3 points.

20–30 min

Item 3 *Look at the circled figures. How many flat surfaces do you count in all?* [3 flat surfaces] *How many flat surfaces do you need to draw? Why?* [1 flat surface; all of the flat surfaces of these shapes are circles.]

Item 4 MP.5 Use Appropriate Tools Strategically Remind students that shapes can be in different positions. Give students geometric solids to hold and manipulate. *Turn your solid until you can identify the flat surface. Then see if the flat surface matches the shape at the beginning of the row.* Students can identify that the shape at the start of the row is a square. Then have them look for objects that have square-shaped sides.

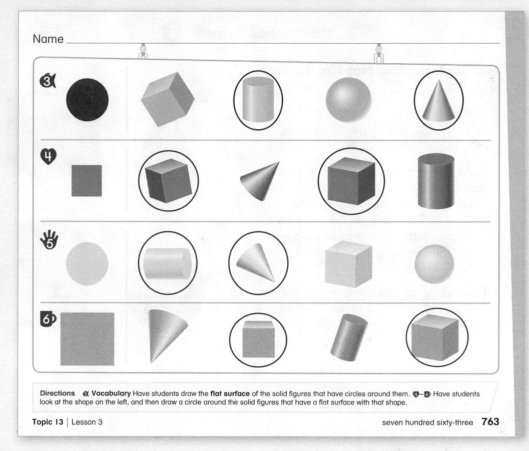

Name _____

Directions ❸ Vocabulary Have students draw the **flat surface** of the solid figures that have circles around them. ❹–❻ Have students look at the shape on the left, and then draw a circle around the solid figures that have a flat surface with that shape.

Topic 13 | Lesson 3   seven hundred sixty-three **763**

Item 8 Some students might think the baseball matches the shape of the orange circle. Remind students: *Many objects have flat sides that are called flat surfaces. Although the baseball is round, it does not have any round flat surfaces.*

Item 9 MP.2 Reasoning Students can use reasoning to help them draw the shape of the flat surfaces of the circled figures. *What is the name for the solid figures that are circled?* [Cube] *If the solid figures are both cubes, why do they look different?* [Sample answer: The solid figures are drawn from different positions.] *What do you know about the flat surfaces of a cube?* [The flat surfaces are squares.] *What does this tell you about the shape you should draw?* [I should draw a square.]

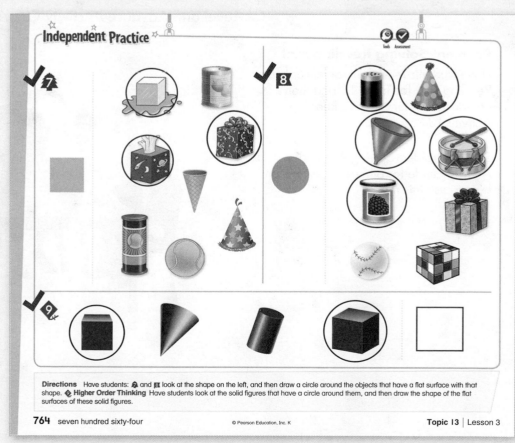

Independent Practice

Directions Have students: ❼ and ❽ look at the shape on the left, and then draw a circle around the objects that have a flat surface with that shape. ❾ **Higher Order Thinking** Have students look at the solid figures that have a circle around them, and then draw the shape of the flat surfaces of these solid figures.

764 seven hundred sixty-four   © Pearson Education, Inc. K   Topic 13 | Lesson 3

STEP 3 ASSESS AND DIFFERENTIATE

Use the **QUICK CHECK** on the previous page to prescribe differentiated instruction.

 RtI

I **Intervention**
0–3 points on the Quick Check

O **On-Level**
4 points on the Quick Check

A **Advanced**
5 points on the Quick Check

Intervention Activity

Flat Surfaces and Not-Flat Surfaces

Materials
(per pair)

Modeling clay, rolling pin, geometric solids: cube, cylinder, sphere, cone

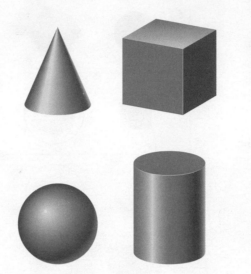

- Hold up the cube and rub your palm across the sides. *These are flat surfaces.* Hold up the sphere, cupping your hand around it. *There are no flat surfaces on a sphere.* Ask students to pick up each shape and verbally identify the flat and curved surfaces.

- Have partners make imprints of the flat surfaces in rolled-out modeling clay.

Reteach

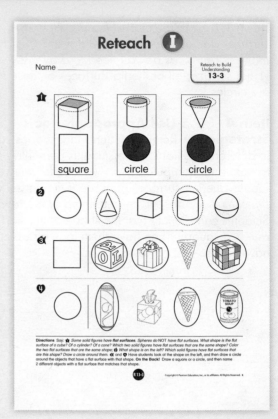

On-Level and Advanced Activity Centers **O** **A**

Problem-Solving Reading Mat

Have students read the Problem-Solving Reading Mat for Topic 13 and then complete Problem-Solving Reading Activity 13-3.

See the Problem-Solving Reading Activity Guide for other suggestions on how to use this mat.

765A   Topic 13

TIMING

The time allocated to Step 3 will depend on the teacher's instructional decisions and differentiation routines.

15–30 min

 Help

 Tools

 Games

PEARSON
realize
PearsonRealize.com

Technology Center

Math Tools and Math Games

A link to a specific math tools activity or math game to use with this lesson is provided at PearsonRealize.com.

Tools

Games

Leveled Assignment

I Items 1–3 **O** Items 2–4 **A** Items 3–5

Name _____

Help Tools Games

Homework & Practice 13-3
Compare 2-D and 3-D Shapes

Another Look!

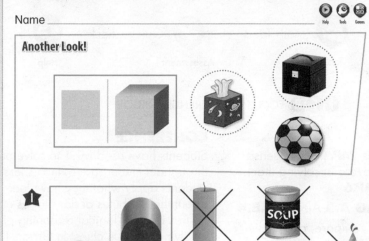

HOME ACTIVITY Show your child a can and ask him or her to identify the flat surfaces (circles). Show your child a box shaped like a cube and ask him or her to identify the flat surfaces (squares). Take turns identifying other objects that have flat surfaces that are circles or squares.

1

Directions Say: *A cube has square flat surfaces. Draw a circle around the objects that have a square flat surface.* ★ Have students look at the cylinder and cone in the blue box, identify the shape of their flat surfaces, and then mark an X on the objects that have a flat surface with that shape.

Topic 13 | Lesson 3   Digital Resources at PearsonRealize.com   seven hundred sixty-five **765**

2

3

4

5

Directions Have students: 🍎 and 🎈 look at the object on the left, and then draw a circle around the shape of its flat surfaces; 🍎 and ✋ look at the objects, and then draw the shape of their flat surfaces.

766 seven hundred sixty-six   © Pearson Education, Inc. K   **Topic 13 | Lesson 3**

765–766

MAKE SENSE AND PERSEVERE

DIGITAL RESOURCES PearsonRealize.com

 Student and Teacher eTexts
eText

 Listen and Look For Lesson Video
PD

 Today's Challenge
Think

 Solve and Share
Solve

 Visual Learning Animation Plus
Learn

 Math Practices Animations
MP

 Animated Glossary
Glossary

 Math Tools
Tools

 Quick Check
Assessment

 Another Look Homework Video
Help

 Math Games
Games

LESSON OVERVIEW   FOCUS • COHERENCE • RIGOR

FOCUS

Mathematical Practices MP.1 Make sense of problems and persevere in solving them. Also **MP.3, MP.5, MP.6**

Content Standards K.G.A.3 Also **K.G.B.4**

Objective Analyze, compare, and make different 2-D and 3-D shapes using math.

Essential Understanding Good math thinkers know what the problem is about. They have a plan to solve it. They keep trying if they get stuck.

Materials Attribute blocks (or Teaching Tool 46), geometric solids

COHERENCE

Students have used MP.1 to solve problems throughout kindergarten. In this lesson, students apply what they have learned about the attributes of flat shapes and solid figures to solve logical reasoning problems involving multiple clues. In Grade 1, students continue to develop perseverance as they solve two-step and multi-step problems.

RIGOR

This lesson emphasizes **application**. Students apply what they have learned about 2-D and 3-D shapes and use MP.1 to make sense of problems. The problems in this lesson promote the use of multiple mathematical practices, but the emphasis is on MP.1 and perseverance as students identify a mystery shape by considering multiple clues.

 Watch the Listen and Look For Lesson Video.
PD

MATH ANYTIME

Daily Common Core Review

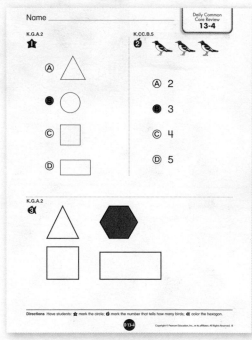

Today's Challenge

Think Use Topic 13 problems any time during this topic.

ENGLISH LANGUAGE LEARNERS

Listening Demonstrate listening comprehension by taking notes.

Use with Do You Understand? on Teacher's Edition p. 768.

Distribute copies of a 3-column chart with the top row illustrating the actions of *roll, stack,* and *slide.* Show a sphere, a cone, and a cube in the left column. Alternatively, draw the chart on the board for students to copy. Work through the activity with students. Ask

them to listen carefully to your descriptions and use the chart to take notes. Model an example of how to fill in the chart.

Beginning Ask students to use their notes to tell what shape it is, using this sentence stem: "You are thinking of a ____."

Intermediate Ask students to use their notes to tell you what the shape is. Students should use complete sentences in their responses.

Advanced Ask students to use their notes to tell you what the shape is and to answer questions about the shape (e.g., Can it be rolled?).

Summarize How can you use notes to help you understand the clues you hear about a shape?

DEVELOP: PROBLEM-BASED LEARNING

COHERENCE: Engage learners by connecting prior knowledge to new ideas.
Students sort two- and three-dimensional shapes. This prepares them for the next part of the lesson, where students identify solid figures from given clues.

10–15 min

Solve

BEFORE

1. Pose the Solve-and-Share Problem
MP.1 Make Sense and Persevere In this problem, students analyze given information and formulate a plan to determine and justify a solution to the problem.

Provide each group of students with attribute blocks and geometric solids.

Using attribute blocks, show a small square, a large rectangle, a large and a small triangle, and a small circle. Using geometric solids, show the cube, the cylinder, the sphere, and the cone.

Say: *Jackson wants to put flat shapes behind Door 1 and solid figures behind Door 2. Draw a line from each shape to the correct door to show how he should sort the shapes.*

Tell students to think about these Thinking Habits as they solve the problem.
What do I need to find?
What do I know?
What's my plan for solving the problem?
How can I check that my solution makes sense?

2. Build Understanding
What are you asked to do? [Sort flat shapes and solid figures.] *What tools do you have to solve the problem?* [Attribute blocks, geometric solids]

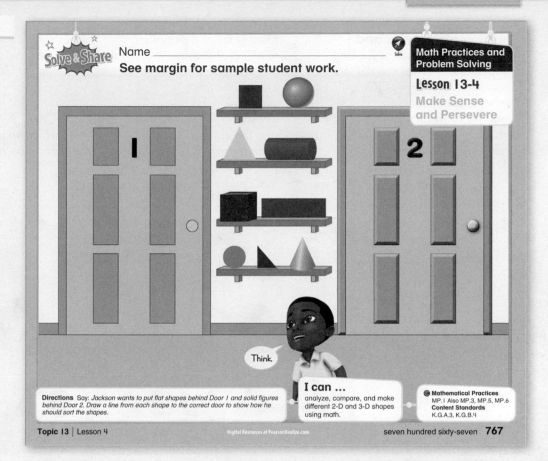

Solve & Share

Name _____
See margin for sample student work.

1

2

Think.

I can ...
analyze, compare, and make different 2-D and 3-D shapes using math.

Directions Say: Jackson wants to put flat shapes behind Door 1 and solid figures behind Door 2. Draw a line from each shape to the correct door to show how he should sort the shapes.

Topic 13 | Lesson 4

Digital Resources at PearsonRealize.com

Math Practices and Problem Solving

Lesson 13-4
Make Sense and Persevere

Mathematical Practices
MP.1 Also MP.3, MP.5, MP.6
Content Standards
K.G.A.3, K.G.B.4

seven hundred sixty-seven **767**

DURING

3. Ask Guiding Questions As Needed
How would you describe each shape or figure? [Answers will vary.] *How are the shapes and solid figures alike? Different?* [Answers will vary.]

AFTER

4. Share and Discuss Solutions
Start with students' solutions. If needed, project and analyze Ruby's work to discuss how knowing the different attributes of shapes can help students figure out which shape is being described.

5. Transition to the Visual Learning Bridge
You sorted objects as flat shapes and solid figures. Later in this lesson, you will use clues to identify flat shapes and solid figures.

6. Extension for Early Finishers
In pairs, have students take turns giving clues about a shape until their partners guess the shape.

Analyze Student Work

Ruby's Work

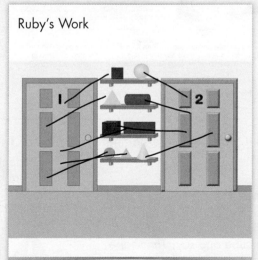

Ruby correctly sorts the two- and three-dimensional shapes.

Stefan's Work

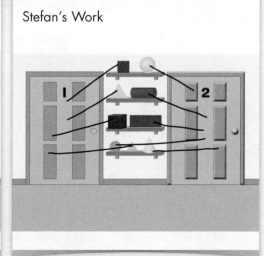

Stefan incorrectly sorts the two- and three-dimensional shapes.

The *Visual Learning Bridge* connects students' thinking in Solve & Share to important math ideas in the lesson. Use the *Visual Learning Bridge* to make these ideas explicit. Also available as a *Visual Learning Animation Plus* at PearsonRealize.com

E L L
Visual Learning

MP.1 Make Sense and Persevere *Jackson is looking at 3 shapes. What are the names of the shapes?* [Cube, sphere, cone] *Jackson's teacher is giving him clues about one of the shapes. He has to figure out which shape the teacher is describing.*

Here is the first clue: I am thinking of a shape that rolls. What shape am I? Can you tell which shape is being described by that clue? [No] *Why not?* [Both the sphere and the cone can roll.] *Why is there an X on the cube?* [The cube is the only shape that cannot roll.]

Here is the second clue: The shape I am thinking of looks like a baseball. Which shape does not fit that clue? [Cone] *Now can you tell which shape is being described?* [Yes]

MP.3 Construct Arguments *Which shape is Jackson holding up?* [Sphere] *How do you know the sphere is the shape his teacher is describing?* [It rolls, and it looks like a baseball, so it fits both clues.]

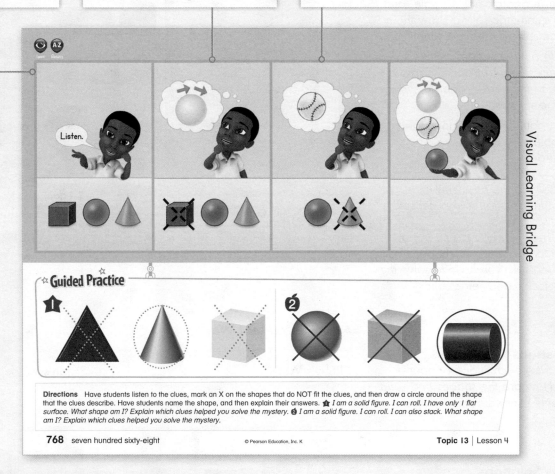

Visual Learning Bridge

Guided Practice

Directions Have students listen to the clues, mark an X on the shapes that do NOT fit the clues, and then draw a circle around the shape that the clues describe. Have students name the shape, and then explain their answers. ⭐ *I am a solid figure. I can roll. I have only 1 flat surface. What shape am I? Explain which clues helped you solve the mystery.* ② *I am a solid figure. I can roll. I can also stack. What shape am I? Explain which clues helped you solve the mystery.*

768 seven hundred sixty-eight   © Pearson Education, Inc. K   **Topic 13** | Lesson 4

Complete the *Do You Understand? Show Me!* problem before starting Guided Practice.

Do You Understand? Show Me! MP.1 Make Sense and Persevere
Show the students 3 shapes (sphere, cone, and cube) and say: *I am thinking of a shape that rolls. Which shape could it be?* [It could be a sphere or a cone.] Remove the cube and say: *The shape I am thinking of can stack on top of another shape. Which shape am I thinking of now?* [You are thinking of a cone.]

Essential Question
Ask the following Essential Question: *How can you use clues to identify a shape?* [Sample answer: Use each clue to eliminate choices. Check that the remaining choice fits all the clues.]

Error Intervention: Item 2
If students have difficulty identifying the cylinder as a shape that can stack,

then use a geometric solid to show how the cylinder can be rotated to stand on one of its flat surfaces.

Reteaching Assign Reteaching Set C, p. 794.

20–30 min

Tools **Assessment**

✓ QUICK CHECK

Check mark indicates items for prescribing differentiation on the next page. Items 3 and 6 are each worth 1 point. The Performance Assessment on page 770 is worth up to 3 points.

MP.1 Make Sense and Persevere Listen and look for these behaviors as evidence that students are exhibiting proficiency with MP.1.

• gives a good explanation of the problem

• thinks about a plan before jumping into the solution

• identifies likely strategies for solving the problem

• makes sure the answer makes sense before stopping work

Items 3–8 MP.5 Use Appropriate Tools Strategically Make geometric solids and attribute blocks (or Teaching Tool 46) available to students. Have them choose from among these tools, as needed, as they solve the problems.

Item 5 Some students may not understand the difference between rolling and sliding. Guide them to understand the difference. *On what kind of surface does an object slide?* [Flat surface] *Roll?* [Round, curvy, or non-flat surface] Then have students consider the cone and the sphere. *Both have a curvy surface, but only the cone has a flat surface. This is why it can do both—roll and slide.*

Item 9 MP.1 Make Sense and Persevere Point out that students can use their answers to "What makes it special?" to help them make up clues.

Item 10 MP.6 Be Precise *What makes good clues different from a list of attributes of the shape?* [Good clues help you get the answer correct.]

Item 11 MP.3 Construct Arguments Help students think of additional clues or better clues as needed. *What is an attribute that makes a cylinder different from a sphere? Explain.* [Sample answer: A cylinder can stack, but a sphere cannot, since the sphere does not have a flat surface.]

Name _____

☆ ☆ ☆
Independent Practice ☆

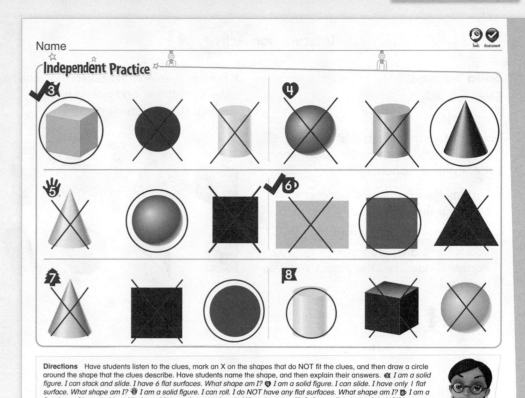

Directions Have students listen to the clues, mark an X on the shapes that do NOT fit the clues, and then draw a circle around the shape that the clues describe. Have students name the shape, and then explain their answers. ❸ *I am a solid figure. I can stack and slide. I have 6 flat surfaces. What shape am I?* ❹ *I am a solid figure. I can slide. I have only 1 flat surface. What shape am I?* ✋ *I am a solid figure. I can roll. I do NOT have any flat surfaces. What shape am I?* ❻ *I am a flat shape. I have 4 sides. All of my sides are the same length. What shape am I?* ❼ *I am a flat shape. I do NOT have any straight sides. What shape am I?* ❽ *I am a solid figure. I can roll. I have 2 flat surfaces. What shape am I?*

Topic 13 | **Lesson 4**   seven hundred sixty-nine **769**

☆ ☆ ☆ ☆
Math Practices and Problem Solving ☆
✓ © **Performance Assessment** _____

9. 10. 11.

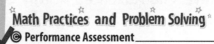

9. Cylinder; Students should explain that it is a solid figure. They may also include information about its flat surfaces and its ability to stack, slide, and roll.

10. Sample answer: I am a solid figure. I can slide, stack, and roll.

11. Students should explain that more specific clues can be given. For example, students might say that the shape has the same shape as a can of soup.

Directions Read the problem to students. Then have them use multiple math practices to solve the problem. Have students look at the shape at the top of the page. Say: *Emily's teacher teaches the class a game. They have to give a classmate clues about the mystery shape. What clues can Emily give about this shape?* ❾ **MP.1 Make Sense** *What is the shape? What makes it special?* 🔟 **MP.6 Be Precise** *What clues can you give about the shape? Think about how it looks, and whether or not it can roll, stack, or slide.* ⚡ **MP.3 Explain** *What if your classmate gives you the wrong answer? Can you give more clues to help him or her?*

770 seven hundred seventy   © Pearson Education, Inc. K   **Topic 13** | **Lesson 4**

STEP 3 ASSESS AND DIFFERENTIATE

 Use the **QUICK CHECK** on the previous page to prescribe differentiated instruction.

2 RtI

I Intervention
0–3 points on the Quick Check

O On-Level
4 points on the Quick Check

A Advanced
5 points on the Quick Check

Intervention Activity **I**

Solid Sorter

Materials

(per pair)

Small classroom objects that look like geometric solids, geometric solids: cone, cube, cylinder, sphere

• Display the objects and geometric solids for the class.

• Partner A covers his or her eyes while you remove a shape from the display. Partner B describes the object that was removed.

• Partner A selects the object that matches the description and names it to tell which shape is missing.

Reteach **I**

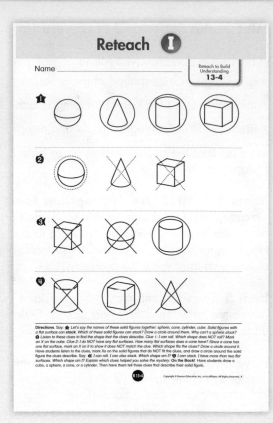

On-Level and Advanced Activity Centers **O** **A**

Center Games

In the On-Level activity, partners take turns picking a tile and then finding a shape that has a certain number of flat surfaces. They cover that shape on the game board and the first player to cover all the shapes on their board wins. In the Advanced activity, players uncover game spaces to reveal a pair of three-dimensional shapes. They analyze the shapes' flat surfaces and collect a certain number of blue squares. The first player to collect 10 blue squares wins.

★ On-Level

★★ Advanced

TIMING

The time allocated to Step 3 will depend on the teacher's instructional decisions and differentiation routines.

15–30 min

PEARSON
realize
PearsonRealize.com

Help   Tools   Games

Technology Center

Math Tools and Math Games

A link to a specific math tools activity or math game to use with this lesson is provided at PearsonRealize.com.

Leveled Assignment

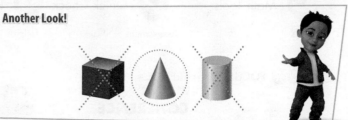

I Items 1–7 (with help as needed)   **O** Items 1–7   **A** Items 1–7

Name _____   Help Tools Games

Homework & Practice 13-4
Make Sense and Persevere

Another Look!

HOME ACTIVITY Pick an object in the room that is a cube, sphere, cone, or cylinder. Give your child clues about its shape, and ask him or her to guess which object you are thinking about. For example, a clue could be "Its flat surface is shaped like a square." (cube) Then invite your child to take a turn picking an object and giving you clues.

Directions Say: *Listen to the clues. After each clue, mark an X on any shape that does NOT fit the clue. I can roll. I do NOT have 2 flat surfaces. What shape am I? Draw a circle around the shape that fits all of the clues.* Read the clues to students. Have them mark an X on the shapes that do NOT fit the clues and draw a circle around the shape that the clues describe. Have students explain which clues helped them get the answer. ★ *I can roll. I CANNOT stack. What shape am I?* ② *I can stack. I can slide. What shape am I?* ③ *I can roll. I have only 1 flat surface. What shape am I?* ④ *I can stack. I CANNOT roll. What shape am I?*

Topic 13 | Lesson 4   Digital Resources at PearsonRealize.com   seven hundred seventy-one **771**

ⓒ Performance Assessment _____

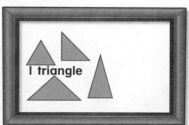
1 triangle

3 rectangles

5. Outside: rectangle, hexagon, square, circle; Inside: triangles
6. Students should explain that all the shapes inside the frame have 3 sides and 3 vertices.

Directions Read the problem to students. Then have them use multiple math practices to solve the problem. Say: *Jackson is trying to solve a mystery. How are the shapes inside the frame similar? How can you find the answer?* ✋ **MP.1 Make Sense** *What shapes are outside of the frame? What shapes are inside the frame?* ⑥ **MP.6 Be Precise** *What attribute do all of the shapes inside the frame have? Draw another shape like it inside the frame.* 🌲 **MP.5 Use Tools** *Listen to the clues, and then draw 3 shapes inside the bottom frame that match the clues. I have 4 sides and 4 vertices. My sides are NOT the same length. What shape am I?*

772 seven hundred seventy-two   © Pearson Education, Inc. K   Topic 13 | Lesson 4

MAKE 2-D SHAPES FROM OTHER 2-D SHAPES

DIGITAL RESOURCES PearsonRealize.com

 Student and Teacher eTexts — eText

 Listen and Look For Lesson Video — PD

Today's Challenge — Think

Solve and Share — Solve

Visual Learning Animation Plus — Learn

 Animated Glossary — Glossary

Math Tools — Tools

Quick Check — Assessment

Another Look Homework Video — Help

Math Games — Games

LESSON OVERVIEW F C R FOCUS • COHERENCE • RIGOR

FOCUS

Domain K.G Geometry

Cluster K.G.B Analyze, compare, create, and compose shapes.

Content Standard K.G.B.6 Compose simple shapes to form larger shapes.

Mathematical Practices MP.1, MP.4, MP.5, MP.7, MP.8

Objective Make 2-D shapes using other 2-D shapes.

Essential Understanding You can make 2-D shapes by putting together two or more 2-D shapes.

Materials Construction paper right triangles, pattern blocks (or Teaching Tool 41)

COHERENCE

Early in Kindergarten, students learned about numbers. In Topics 12 and 13, students learned the names and attributes of flat shapes. In this lesson, students count shapes and use them to make a larger shape. In Grade 1, students will learn to partition rectangles into equal shares.

RIGOR

This lesson emphasizes **conceptual understanding** and **procedural skill**. Students develop the understanding that they can combine shapes to make new shapes. Students follow the process of using pattern blocks to cover shapes, drawing the lines to show how this was done, and then writing how many pattern blocks they used.

 Watch the Listen and Look For Lesson Video.

MATH ANYTIME

Daily Common Core Review

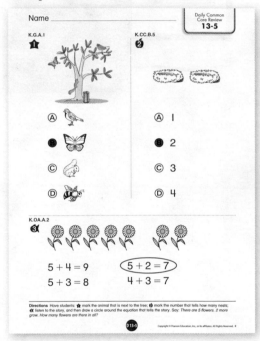

Today's Challenge

Think Use Topic 13 problems any time during this topic.

ENGLISH LANGUAGE LEARNERS E L L

Reading Develop basic [math] sight vocabulary.

Use with the Visual Learning Bridge on Student's Edition p. 774.

Draw a triangle. Ask: *What is this shape?* Write the word "triangle" under the shape. Point to and read *triangle* with students. Continue the process with the following shapes: circle, square, rectangle, hexagon. Display 6 triangles. Say: *I can make a hexagon using 6 triangles.* Demonstrate making a hexagon. Distribute index cards to students with the words and illustrations:

triangle △, circle ○, square □, rectangle □, hexagon ⬡.

Beginning Display a triangle. Ask: *What is this shape?* Students will hold up and read the correct card. Using 6 triangles, make a hexagon. Ask: *What is this shape?* Students will hold up and read the correct card. Continue the process using squares to make rectangles.

Intermediate Distribute 6 triangles and 6 squares. Instruct students to find and read the hexagon card. Say: *Make a hexagon using triangles. How many triangles did you*

use? Continue the process using squares to make rectangles.

Advanced Instruct students to read the shape cards to partners. Turn the cards face down. Divide students into partner groups. Distribute 6 triangles and 6 squares to each group. Student A will select a card and read it to Student B. Student B will determine if the shape can be made using the squares/triangles and, if so, will use the squares/triangles to make the shape. Students will reverse roles.

Summarize How are triangles used to make a hexagon?

DEVELOP: PROBLEM-BASED LEARNING

Solve

COHERENCE: Engage students by connecting prior knowledge to new ideas.
Students use two triangles to make one familiar shape. This prepares them for the next part of the lesson, which involves using a greater number and variety of shapes to make new shapes.

10–15 min

BEFORE

1. Pose the Solve-and-Share Problem
MP.1 Make Sense and Persevere Students combine 2 triangles to make a shape they know.

Provide each student with 2 right triangles made from construction paper. The right triangles should be the same size, and two of the sides of each triangle should be the same length.

Say: *Emily has 2 triangles. She thinks she can use them to make a 2-D shape she has learned—a circle, triangle, square, or rectangle. Try to make one of these shapes with your triangles. Tell what shape you made.*

2. Build Understanding
What are you asked to do? [Make a circle, triangle, square, or rectangle.] *What will you use to make the shape?* [2 triangles]

DURING

3. Ask Guiding Questions As Needed
How can you move your triangles to make a new shape? [Flip, slide, or turn the triangles.] *What is the name of the new shape?* [Square or triangle] Remind students that a square is a special type of rectangle with all sides having the same length. Therefore, *rectangle* would be correct also. *Is it one of the shapes that Emily wants to make?* [Yes] Have students trace their new shape and compare their drawings with others. *Is there more than one answer? Explain.* [Sample answer: Yes, we can make a square or a triangle.]

AFTER

4. Share and Discuss Solutions
Start with students' solutions. If needed, **Solve** project and analyze Tia's work to talk about how she made a square with the 2 triangles. Discuss how the 2 triangles could have also formed a larger triangle.

5. Transition to the Visual Learning Bridge
You used 2 triangles to make either a square or a triangle. Later in this lesson, you will learn to make more new shapes using triangles and squares.

6. Extension for Early Finishers
Can you make a circle using 2 triangles? Why or why not? [No, because circles do not have straight sides and triangles do.]

Solve & Share   Name _____   Solve

Lesson 13-5
Make 2-D Shapes from Other 2-D Shapes

See margin for sample student work.

Directions Say: *Emily has 2 triangles. She thinks she can use them to make a 2-D shape she has learned—a circle, triangle, square, or rectangle. Try to make one of these shapes with your triangles. Tell what shape you made.*

I can … make 2-D shapes using other 2-D shapes.

Content Standards K.G.B.6 **Mathematical Practices** MP.1, MP.4, MP.5, MP.7, MP.8

Topic 13 | Lesson 5   Digital Resources at PearsonRealize.com   seven hundred seventy-three **773**

Analyze Student Work

Tia's Work

Tia puts the long sides of the triangles together. She says she made a square.

Elijah's Work

Elijah incorrectly puts the 2 triangles on top of each other and says it is still a triangle.

The *Visual Learning Bridge* connects students' thinking in the *Solve & Share* to important math ideas in the lesson. Use the *Visual Learning Bridge* to make these ideas explicit. Also available as a *Visual Learning Animation Plus* at PearsonRealize.com

E L L Visual Learning

Learn   Glossary

What pattern block matches this shape? [Hexagon] *How many corners does a hexagon have?* [6 corners] *How many sides does a hexagon have?* [6 sides] *Emily wants to make the hexagon out of pattern blocks.*

MP.4 Model with Math *Emily decides to use triangle pattern blocks to make the hexagon. How does the length of a side of the triangle compare to the length of a side of the hexagon?* [They are the same.] *How many corners does a triangle have?* [3 corners] *How many sides does a triangle have?* [3 sides]

MP.7 Use Structure *Emily continues to fill the hexagon with triangle pattern blocks. How many triangle pattern blocks has Emily used so far?* [3 triangle pattern blocks] *How many more triangles does Emily need to complete the hexagon?* [3 triangle pattern blocks]

Emily finishes making the hexagon. How many triangle pattern blocks does Emily use to make the hexagon? [6 triangles] *Is the hexagon completely filled?* [Yes]

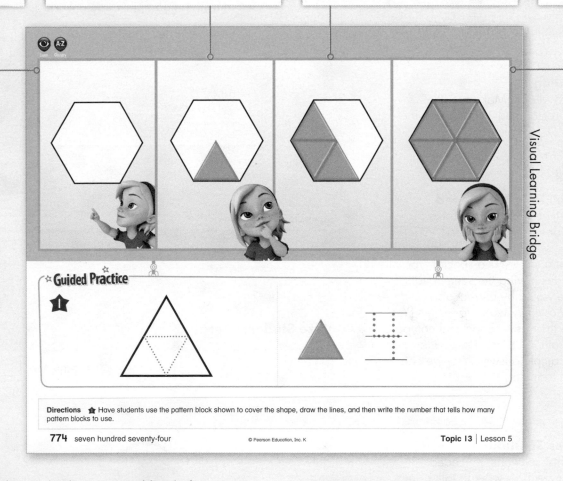

Visual Learning Bridge

☆ **Guided Practice**

1

Directions ★ Have students use the pattern block shown to cover the shape, draw the lines, and then write the number that tells how many pattern blocks to use.

774   seven hundred seventy-four   © Pearson Education, Inc. K   **Topic 13** | Lesson 5

Complete the *Do You Understand? Show Me!* problem before starting Guided Practice.

Do You Understand? Show Me! MP.7 Use Structure

Invite students to use two or more pattern block triangles to make a larger shape. Have students name or describe the new shape. Ask them to count and name the number of triangles they used.

Ask the following Essential Question: *How can you make a new shape by putting together smaller shapes?* [Sample answer: I can make a new shape by putting the sides of other shapes together.]

Error Intervention: Item 1

If students use too many or too few triangles,

then explain that they should fit the triangles together snugly so that there are no overlaps or gaps.

✓ QUICK CHECK
Check mark indicates items for prescribing differentiation on the next page.
Items 5 and 7 are each worth 1 point. Item 9 is worth up to 3 points.

20–30 min

Tools   Assessment

Item 2 MP.5 Use Appropriate Tools *What tool can you use to solve the problem?* [A square pattern block] *What shape will you make?* [A rectangle] Remind students to write the number of pattern blocks they use.

Item 4 *What does a fish look like?* [It has a head, body, and tail.] *Which block could you use for its tail?* [Sample answer: A triangle] *Which block will you use for its body?* [Sample answer: A triangle and a square] Students may need to be reminded that shapes do not always have to connect at their sides. You may want to have students compare the fish they create.

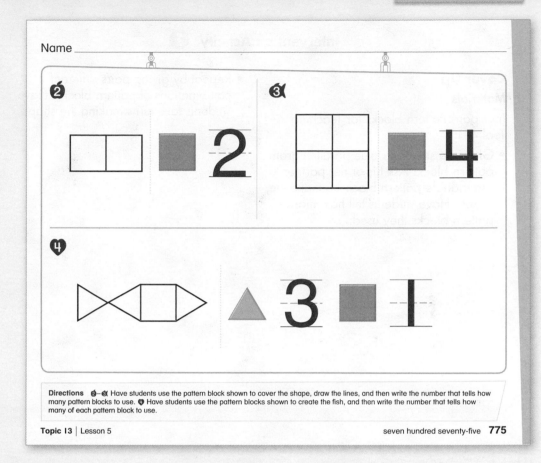

Name _____

Directions 𝟚–𝟛 Have students use the pattern block shown to cover the shape, draw the lines, and then write the number that tells how many pattern blocks to use. 𝟜 Have students use the pattern blocks shown to create the fish, and then write the number that tells how many of each pattern block to use.

Topic 13 | Lesson 5   seven hundred seventy-five **775**

Item 6 MP.8 Generalize *How is this large shape like the shape you made in Item 1 of Guided Practice?* [Sample answer: It is the same shape. Here a point is at the bottom instead of at the top.] *How can you use what you learned in Item 1 to help you with Item 6?* [Sample answer: I can use the same number of triangles.]

Items 7–9 Provide students with scrap paper as necessary for large shapes or designs.

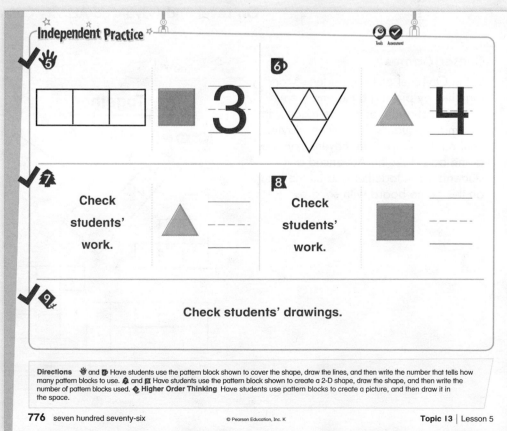

Independent Practice

5 Check students' work.

7 Check students' work.

8 Check students' work.

9 Check students' drawings.

Directions ✋ and 𝟞 Have students use the pattern block shown to cover the shape, draw the lines, and then write the number that tells how many pattern blocks to use. 𝟟 and 𝟠 Have students use the pattern block shown to create a 2-D shape, draw the shape, and then write the number of pattern blocks used. 𝟡 **Higher Order Thinking** Have students use pattern blocks to create a picture, and then draw it in the space.

776 seven hundred seventy-six   © Pearson Education, Inc. K   Topic 13 | Lesson 5

STEP 3 ASSESS AND DIFFERENTIATE

Use the **QUICK CHECK** on the previous page to prescribe differentiated instruction.

2 RtI

I Intervention
0–3 points on the Quick Check

O On-Level
4 points on the Quick Check

A Advanced
5 points on the Quick Check

Intervention Activity **I**

Cover Up

Materials

(per pair) Pattern blocks (or Teaching Tool 41)

• Give one student a blue parallelogram pattern block. Ask his or her partner to use triangle pattern blocks to make the shape. Have students tell how many pattern blocks they used.

• Repeat by giving pairs different combinations of pattern blocks. Have students take turns making the shape.

Reteach **I**

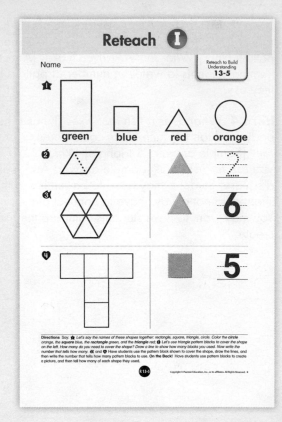

On-Level and Advanced Activity Centers **O** **A**

Center Games

In the On-Level activity, students work together by picking a tile and then finding a shape that can be made with that many squares. They keep playing until all the shapes are covered on the game board. In the Advanced activity, students work together and fill the letters on the game board with squares.

★ On-Level

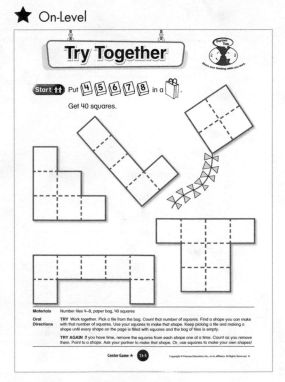

★★ Advanced

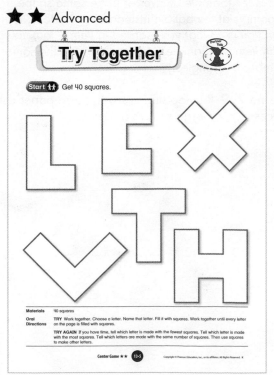

TIMING

The time allocated to Step 3 will depend on the teacher's instructional decisions and differentiation routines.

15–30 min

 Help   Tools   Games

Technology Center Ⓘ Ⓞ Ⓐ

Math Tools and Math Games

Tools

Games

A link to a specific math tools activity or math game to use with this lesson is provided at PearsonRealize.com.

Leveled Assignment

Ⓘ Items 1–2 Ⓞ Items 2–3 Ⓐ Items 3–4

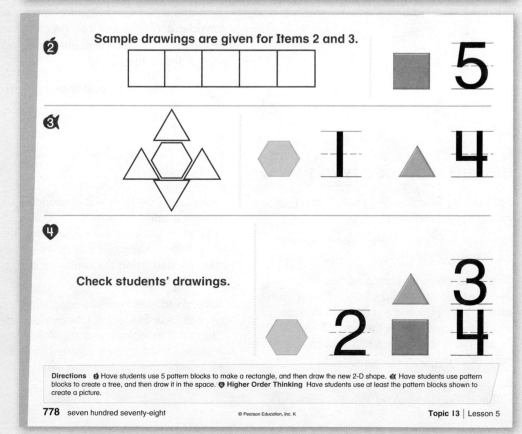

Name _____

Help Tools Games

Homework & Practice 13-5

Make 2-D Shapes from Other 2-D Shapes

Another Look!

6

HOME ACTIVITY Give your child paper, pencil, and a small square shape, such as a square cracker or a square sticky-note. Ask him or her to draw another shape, such as a rectangle, using the square. Repeat with other shapes.

★ Check students' drawings. **9**

Directions Say: *What shape is the pattern block? Use 6 pattern blocks to make a rectangle. Draw the new shape you made.* ★ Have students use 9 pattern blocks to make a triangle, and then draw the new 2-D shape.

Topic 13 | Lesson 5   Digital Resources at PearsonRealize.com   seven hundred seventy-seven **777**

② Sample drawings are given for Items 2 and 3.   **5**

③   **I**   **4**

④ Check students' drawings.   **3**   **2**   **4**

Directions ② Have students use 5 pattern blocks to make a rectangle, and then draw the new 2-D shape. ③ Have students use pattern blocks to create a tree, and then draw it in the space. ④ **Higher Order Thinking** Have students use at least the pattern blocks shown to create a picture.

778 seven hundred seventy-eight   © Pearson Education, Inc. K   Topic 13 | Lesson 5

BUILD 2-D SHAPES

DIGITAL RESOURCES PearsonRealize.com

 Student and Teacher eTexts — eText

 Listen and Look For Lesson Video — PD

 Today's Challenge — Think

 Solve and Share — Solve

 Visual Learning Animation Plus — Learn

 Animated Glossary — Glossary

 Math Tools — Tools

 Quick Check — Assessment

 Another Look Homework Video — Help

Math Games — Games

LESSON OVERVIEW FOCUS • COHERENCE • RIGOR

MATH ANYTIME

FOCUS

Domain K.G Geometry

Cluster K.G.B Analyze, compare, create, and compose shapes.

Content Standard K.G.B.5 Model shapes in the world by building shapes from components (e.g., sticks and clay balls) and drawing shapes. Also **K.G.B.4**.

Mathematical Practices MP.2, MP.3, MP.4, MP.7

Objective Build 2-D shapes that match given attributes.

Essential Understanding When building a given 2-D shape, the shape must exhibit all of the attributes of the shape.

Materials yarn, string, pipe cleaners, straws, scissors, tape

COHERENCE

This lesson focuses on building 2-D shapes with given attributes. In Lesson 13-1, students learned about these attributes as they analyzed and compared 2-D shapes. Students will apply what they learned to help them build shapes correctly in this lesson. In Lesson 13-7, students will extend the process to building 3-D shapes.

RIGOR

This lesson emphasizes **conceptual understanding**. Students deepen their understanding of 2-D shapes when they build or draw shapes with given attributes. For example, building a rectangle requires students to think carefully about the essential characteristics that must be present in any rectangle they make. Students must also consider attributes that can be changed, such as size or color, without changing the type of shape they build.

 Watch the Listen and Look For Lesson Video.

Daily Common Core Review

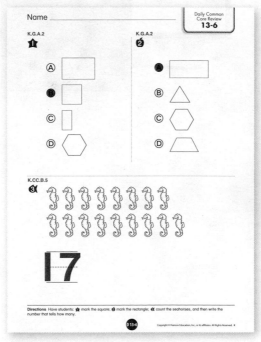

Directions Have students: ★ mark the square; ✦ mark the rectangle; ❋ count the seahorses, and then write the number that tells how many.

 Today's Challenge

Think Use Topic 13 problems any time during this topic.

ENGLISH LANGUAGE LEARNERS ELL

Speaking Speak using content area vocabulary in context.

Use with the Solve & Share on Student's Edition p. 779.

Display a piece of yarn or string. Demonstrate making a circle with the yarn/string. Say: *This is a circle.* Demonstrate making a square with the yarn/string. Say: *This is not a circle. This is a square.* Distribute yarn or string to each student.

Beginning Say: *Make a circle.* Students will make a circle. Ask: *What shape did you make?* Students will respond using the sentence stem: "I made a ___." Say: *Make a square.* Students will make a square. Ask: *What shape did you make?* Students will respond using the sentence stem: "I made a ___."

Intermediate Divide students into partner groups. Ask Student A to make a circle and Student B to make a square. Ask: *How are the circle and square different?* Students will respond using the sentence stem: "The ___ and ___ are different because ___."

Advanced Divide students into partner groups. Provide students with index cards of drawings of varying sizes of circles, squares, rectangles, and triangles. Turn the cards over. Each student will draw a card and make the shape using the yarn/string. Students will explain to partners how the shapes are the same/different. Continue the process with the remaining cards.

Summarize How are circles and squares different?

COHERENCE: Engage students by connecting prior knowledge to new ideas.
Students use what they have learned about attributes of shapes to build a circle and to build a shape that is not a circle. This prepares them for the next part of the lesson, where they build other shapes that do or do not have specified attributes.

10–15 min

Solve

BEFORE

1. Pose the Solve-and-Share Problem
MP.3 Construct Arguments In this problem, students construct an argument to explain how the two shapes they created are different from each other.

Provide each group of students with yarn, string, pipe cleaners, and straws.

Say: *Use yarn, string, or pipe cleaners to build a circle. Then use yarn, string, pipe cleaners, or straws to build a shape that is NOT a circle, and then tell what shape you built. Explain how the shapes you built are different from one another.*

2. Build Understanding
What are you asked to do? [Build a shape that is a circle and a shape that is not a circle.] *What materials do you have to solve the problem?* [Yarn, string, pipe cleaners, and straws]

DURING

3. Ask Guiding Questions As Needed
What is true about every circle? [Sample answer: They have no vertices.] *What are the names of some other 2-D shapes you know?* [Sample answer: Triangle, rectangle, square]

AFTER

4. Share and Discuss Solutions
Start with students' solutions. Have them share the strategies they used to solve the problem. If needed, project and analyze Juan's work to discuss one way to build a circle and a shape that is not a circle.

5. Transition to the Visual Learning Bridge
You solved a word problem that involved building a circle and a shape that is not a circle. Later in this lesson, you will use what you know about triangles, rectangles, and squares to build examples of other shapes.

6. Extension for Early Finishers
Use your materials to build a different circle. How is it similar to and different from the first circle you made? [Sample answer: Both circles have no vertices. The circles are different sizes.]

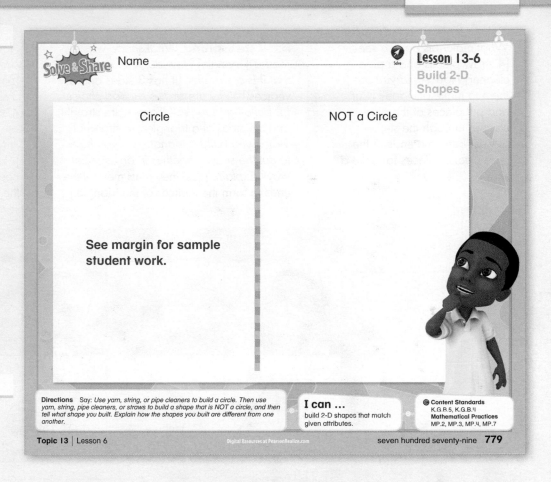

Solve & Share   Name _____

Lesson 13-6
Build 2-D Shapes

Circle   NOT a Circle

See margin for sample student work.

Directions Say: *Use yarn, string, or pipe cleaners to build a circle. Then use yarn, string, pipe cleaners, or straws to build a shape that is NOT a circle, and then tell what shape you built. Explain how the shapes you built are different from one another.*

I can ...
build 2-D shapes that match given attributes.

Content Standards K.G.B.5, K.G.B.4 **Mathematical Practices** MP.2, MP.3, MP.4, MP.7

Topic 13 | Lesson 6   Digital Resources at PearsonRealize.com   seven hundred seventy-nine **779**

Analyze Student Work

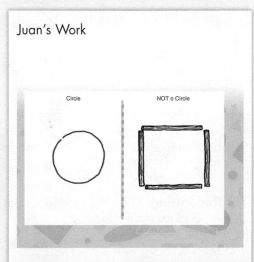

Juan's Work

Circle   NOT a Circle

Juan builds a circle from string. He uses straws to make a square, and he correctly names both shapes. He correctly explains that the shapes are different from each other because the circle has no vertices, while the square has four vertices.

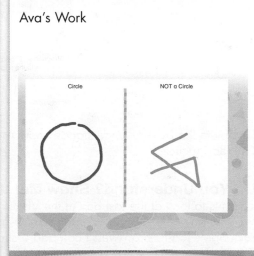

Ava's Work

Circle   NOT a Circle

Ava builds a circle by bending a pipe cleaner. Then she bends another pipe cleaner to form an abstract shape. She correctly states that the first shape is a circle but is not able to name the second shape since it is not one of the common 2-D shapes that students should be able to name.

DEVELOP: VISUAL LEARNING

PEARSON
realize.
PearsonRealize.com

The *Visual Learning Bridge* connects students' thinking in Solve & Share to important math ideas in the lesson. Use the *Visual Learning Bridge* to make these ideas explicit. Also available as a *Visual Learning Animation Plus* at PearsonRealize.com

E L L
Visual Learning

👁 A-Z
Learn Glossary

What materials do you see? [4 straw pieces and a pipe cleaner] *How could you use them to make a shape?* [Cut and put pieces of the pipe cleaner through the straw pieces. Bend the ends of the pipe cleaner pieces to make a shape.]

MP.2 Reasoning *What shape was made?* [Triangle] *How do you know that it is a triangle?* [It has 3 sides and 3 vertices.] *Why are straws a good choice for building triangles?* [Straws are straight, and the sides of a triangle are straight.] *When you build a triangle, do you have to put the straws together in any special way? Explain.* [Yes; they must meet at the ends to form the vertices of the triangle.]

How do you know that this shape is NOT a triangle? [Because a triangle has 3 sides and this shape has 4 sides] *If you take away one of the straws, will you be left with a triangle? Explain.* [No; the ends of the straws need to meet so they form the vertices of the triangle.]

MP.7 Use Structure *The shape on the top is a rectangle because it has 4 sides and 4 square corners. Why is the shape on the bottom NOT a rectangle?* [The corners are not square.]

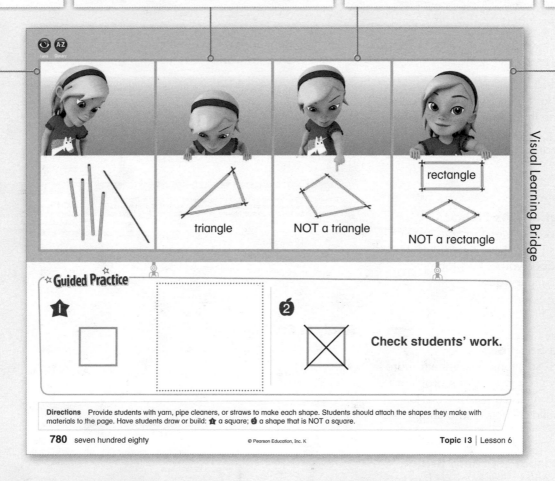

Visual Learning Bridge

triangle

NOT a triangle

rectangle

NOT a rectangle

☆ **Guided Practice** ☆

1

2 Check students' work.

Directions Provide students with yarn, pipe cleaners, or straws to make each shape. Students should attach the shapes they make with materials to the page. Have students draw or build: 🏠 a square; 🍎 a shape that is NOT a square.

Complete the *Do You Understand? Show Me!* problem before starting Guided Practice.

Do You Understand? Show Me! MP.2 Reasoning

Ask students to look at the last box in the Visual Learning Bridge. *How can you use straws to show a different way to build a shape that is not a rectangle?* [Sample answer: I can add a straw to build a shape with 5 sides.]

Essential Question

Ask the following Essential Question: *How do you build a given 2-D shape?* [Sample answer: Name the important attributes of the shape. Then use materials to build a shape that has those attributes.]

Error Intervention: Item 2

If students make a square with a different orientation,

then tell students that the way a shape is turned on the page does not change the kind of shape it is.

1 RtI

Reteaching Assign Reteaching Set D, p. 794.

✔ QUICK CHECK

Item 3 MP.4 Model with Math A rectangle is a mathematical model for many real-world objects. You may wish to have students use this connection to help them build their rectangle. *What is an example of a real-world rectangle?* [Sample answer: A classroom window] *How can you use the real-world rectangle to check that you built your shape correctly?* [Sample answer: I can compare my shape to the classroom window.]

Item 4 There are essentially three ways Kindergarten students might build a shape that is not a rectangle. Students might change the angles (e.g., by building a parallelogram), they might change the side lengths (e.g., by building a trapezoid), or they might change the number of sides (e.g., by building a triangle or a pentagon). If students have difficulty getting started, you might want to suggest one of these routes as a starting point.

Item 9 MP.3 Construct Arguments After students solve the problem, ask them how they know the shape they drew is a square. For example, students might show that the corner of an index card or sheet of paper fits into the four corners of the shape they drew. Students might also show that the shape has four equal sides by comparing the sides to a known length (e.g., "All of the sides are about the same length as my finger.").

Item 10 Guide students to think about the connection between the materials they use and the types of shapes they can build. *If you use straws to build a shape, what will be true about the sides of the shape? Why?* [Sample answer: The sides will be straight, since the straws are straight.] *How are yarn, string, and pipe cleaners different from straws?* [Sample answer: You can bend yarn, string, and pipe cleaners to make curves, but straws stay straight.] *How is a circle different from a rectangle, triangle, and square?* [Sample answer: A circle has no straight sides.] *What does that tell you about the materials you should use for building a circle?* [Sample answer: It is best to use yarn, string, or pipe cleaners so that you can bend them.]

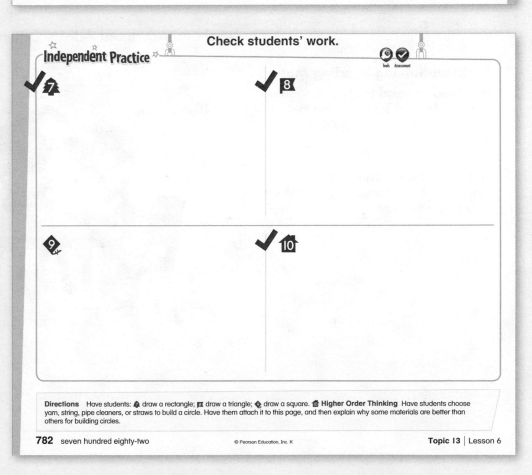

2 RtI

Use the **QUICK CHECK** on the previous page to prescribe differentiated instruction.

I **Intervention**
0–3 points on the Quick Check

O **On-Level**
4 points on the Quick Check

A **Advanced**
5 points on the Quick Check

Intervention Activity **I**

Shape Riddles

Materials

(per pair) String, pipe cleaners, dry pasta

- Put students in pairs. Whisper the name of a shape to Partner A.

- Have Partner A give clues, one at a time, to Partner B until he or she guesses that shape.

- Have both partners work together to create the shape with string, pipe cleaners, or dry pasta.

- Have partners switch roles and repeat the activity with a different shape.

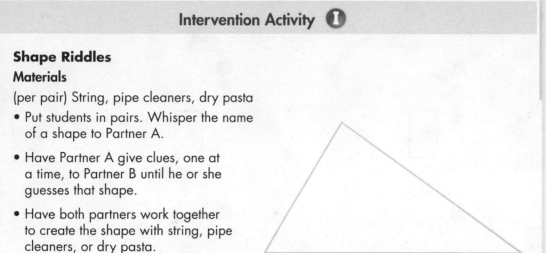

Reteach **I**

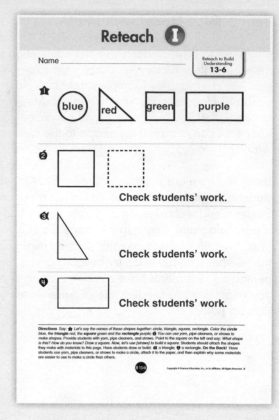

Name _____

Reteach to Build Understanding 13-6

1. blue | red | green | purple

2. [square] [dashed square]
Check students' work.

3. [triangle]
Check students' work.

4. [rectangle]
Check students' work.

Directions Say: ★ *Let's say the names of these shapes together: circle, triangle, square, rectangle. Color the circle blue, the triangle red, the square green and the rectangle purple.* ❷ *You can use yarn, pipe cleaners, or straws to make shapes. Provide students with yarn, pipe cleaners, and straws. Point to the square on the left and say: What shape is this? How do you know? Draw a square. Now, let's use [straws] to build a square. Students should attach the shapes they make with materials to this page. Have students draw or build:* ❸ *a triangle;* ❹ *a rectangle.* **On the Back!** *Have students use yarn, pipe cleaners, or straws to make a circle, attach it to the paper, and then explain why some materials are easier to use to make a circle than others.*

R 13-6

Copyright © Pearson Education, Inc., or its affiliates. All Rights Reserved. B

On-Level and Advanced Activity Centers **O** **A**

Problem-Solving Reading Mat

Have students read the Problem-Solving Reading Mat for Topic 13 and then complete Problem-Solving Reading Activity 13-6.

See the Problem-Solving Reading Activity Guide for other suggestions on how to use this mat.

TIMING

The time allocated to Step 3 will depend on the teacher's instructional decisions and differentiation routines.

15–30 min

 Help

 Tools

 Games

PEARSON
realize
PearsonRealize.com

Technology Center

Tools

Games

Math Tools and Math Games

A link to a specific math tools activity or math game to use with this lesson is provided at PearsonRealize.com.

Leveled Assignment

Ⓘ Items 1–5   Ⓞ Items 2–6   Ⓐ Items 3–7

Name _____

Another Look!

Homework & Practice 13-6
Build 2-D Shapes

HOME ACTIVITY Take a look around your kitchen. With your child, look for materials that can be used to build different 2-D shapes. For example, your child can build shapes from dough, wooden spoons, or string.

1

Directions Say: *This is a square. How do you know it is a square? Let's practice drawing a square.* Have students listen to the story:
1 Avery built shapes out of pipe cleaners. Mark an X on the triangle.

Topic 13 | Lesson 6   Digital Resources at PearsonRealize.com   seven hundred eighty-three **783**

2

3

4 Check students' drawings.   **5** Check students' drawings.

6 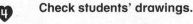 Check students' drawings.   **7** Check students' drawings.

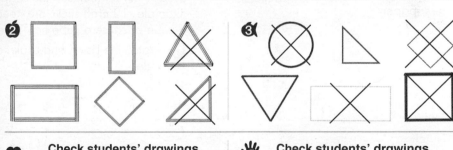

Directions Have students listen to each story: **2** Diego built 6 shapes out of straws. Mark an X on the shapes that are NOT rectangles. **3** Destiny built 6 shapes out of pipe cleaners. Mark an X on the shapes that are NOT triangles. Have students: **4** draw a circle; **5** draw a triangle. **6** **Higher Order Thinking** Have students draw a rectangle that is NOT a square. **7** **Higher Order Thinking** Have students draw a rectangle that is also a square.

784 seven hundred eighty-four   © Pearson Education, Inc. K   Topic 13 | Lesson 6

DIGITAL RESOURCES PearsonRealize.com

 Student and Teacher eTexts — **eText**

Listen and Look For Lesson Video — **PD**

Today's Challenge — **Think**

Solve and Share — **Solve**

Visual Learning Animation Plus — **Learn**

 Animated Glossary — **Glossary**

Math Tools — **Tools**

Quick Check — **Assessment**

Another Look Homework Video — **Help**

Math Games — **Games**

LESSON OVERVIEW **FCR** FOCUS • COHERENCE • RIGOR

FOCUS

Domain K.G Geometry

Cluster K.G.B Analyze, compare, create, and compose shapes.

Content Standard K.G.B.5 Model shapes in the world by building shapes from components (e.g., sticks and clay balls) and drawing shapes. Also **K.G.B.6.**

Mathematical Practices MP.1, MP.2, MP.4, MP.5, MP.6

Objective Use materials to build 3-D shapes.

Essential Understanding 3-D shapes can be combined to make other 3-D shapes.

Materials Small cubes, clay, craft sticks, geometric solids, Building with Solid Figures (Teaching Tool 40), straws, yarn, pipe cleaners, paper

COHERENCE

This lesson focuses on building 3-D shapes. In Lesson 13-2, students learned to identify 3-D shapes that can stack and 3-D shapes that can roll. Now students apply and extend these ideas as they use 3-D shapes to build new 3-D shapes. In Grade 1, students will compose new shapes from composite shapes they have made.

RIGOR

This lesson emphasizes **conceptual understanding**. Students investigate 3-D shapes that can be composed to make new shapes. Understanding the attributes of 2-D shapes and 3-D shapes is critical for this task. In addition, as students use materials to build 3-D shapes, they connect the materials used to the attributes of the shape. For example, 12 craft sticks are needed to build a cube because a cube has 12 edges.

▶ Watch the Listen and Look For Lesson
PD Video.

MATH ANYTIME

Daily Common Core Review

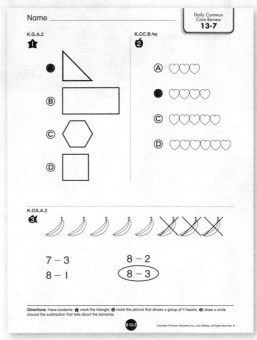

Today's Challenge

Think Use Topic 13 problems any time during this topic.

ENGLISH LANGUAGE LEARNERS **ELL**

Listening Learn basic/academic vocabulary.

Use with the Solve & Share on Student's Edition p. 785.

Display a cube, cone, cylinder, and sphere. Point to the cube. Say: *This is a cube.* Write *cube*. Continue the process with other solid figures. Point to the illustration in *Solve & Share*. Ask: *What 3-D shapes could be used to make this building?*

Beginning Distribute index cards to students with the words and illustrations as follows:

cube , cone , cylinder , and

sphere . Point to the illustration in the *Solve & Share*. Ask: *What 3-D shapes are used?* Students should respond by displaying the correct index cards.

Intermediate Distribute 4 index cards to students and ask them to write and illustrate the following words: cube, cone, cylinder, sphere. Point to the illustration in *Solve & Share*. Ask: *What 3-D shapes are used to make this building?* Students should respond by displaying the correct index cards and using the sentence stem: "The ___ and ___ are used to make the building."

Advanced Distribute 4 index cards to students and ask them to write and illustrate the following words: cube, cone, cylinder, sphere. Point to the illustration in the *Solve & Share*. Ask: *What 3-D shapes are used to make this building? How are they used to make the building?* Students should display the correct cards and use the vocabulary in sentences as they describe how the shapes are used to make the building to partners.

Summarize How are a cylinder and cone used to make a 3-D building?

STEP 1

DEVELOP: PROBLEM-BASED LEARNING

COHERENCE: Engage students by connecting prior knowledge to new ideas.

Students use what they have learned about the attributes of cones and cylinders to build a 3-D shape. This prepares them for the next part of the lesson when they consider other ways of building new 3-D shapes from existing 3-D shapes.

10–15 min

Solve

 BEFORE

1. Pose the Solve-and-Share Problem
MP.4 Model with Math Students use geometric solids to model a real-world object.

Provide each group of students with geometric solids (sphere, cube, cone, cylinder).

Say: *Jackson wants to build this building with solid figures. Which solid figures can he use? Tell how you know.*

2. Build Understanding
What are you asked to do? [Decide which solid figures can be used to build the building shown on the page.] *What materials do you have to solve the problem?* [Geometric solids]

 DURING

3. Ask Guiding Questions As Needed
Which 3-D shapes roll? [Sphere, cone, cylinder] *Can any of those 3-D shapes stack? Explain.* [Yes; the cylinder and the cone stack because they each have a flat surface.]

 AFTER

4. Share and Discuss Solutions
Start with students' solutions. Have them share the strategies used to solve the problem. If needed, project and analyze Naoko's work to discuss how a cylinder and a cone can be stacked to build the building.

5. Transition to the Visual Learning Bridge
You stacked a cylinder and cone to build a model of a building. Later in this lesson, you will learn how other 3-D shapes can be put together to form new 3-D shapes.

6. Extension for Early Finishers
How could you make the building taller? What 3-D shape or shapes could you use? How would you use them? [Sample answer: To make the building taller, you can stack 2 cylinders and then stack a cone on top of the cylinders.]

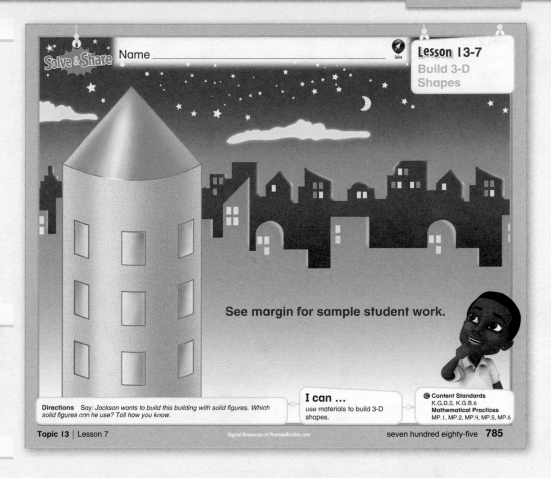

Name

Lesson 13-7
Build 3-D Shapes

See margin for sample student work.

Directions Say: *Jackson wants to build this building with solid figures. Which solid figures can he use? Tell how you know.*

I can ... use materials to build 3-D shapes.

Content Standards K.G.D.5, K.G.B.6 **Mathematical Practices** MP.1, MP.2, MP.4, MP.5, MP.6

Topic 13 | Lesson 7 · Digital Resources at PearsonRealize.com · seven hundred eighty-five **785**

Analyze Student Work

Naoko's Work

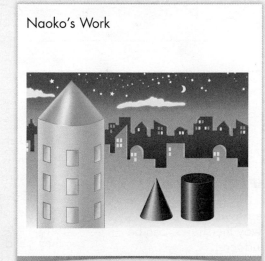

Naoko chooses a cone and a cylinder from the set of geometric solids. She is able to visualize how these 3-D shapes are related to the 2-D representation of the building on the student page. She recognizes that the flat surface of the cone means that it can be stacked on top of the cylinder.

Teagan's Work

Teagan draws a triangle and a rectangle. He may not understand that the drawing of the building is a model of a 3-D object, so he breaks down the component shapes of the building into similar 2-D shapes.

STEP 2
DEVELOP: VISUAL LEARNING

PEARSON
realize
PearsonRealize.com

Learn   Glossary

The *Visual Learning Bridge* connects students' thinking in the Solve & Share to important math ideas in the lesson. Use the *Visual Learning Bridge* to make these ideas explicit. Also available as a *Visual Learning Animation Plus* at PearsonRealize.com

E L L
Visual Learning

MP.2 Reasoning Have students use small cubes to build the 3-D shape. *How would you describe the shape Jackson built?* [Cube] *How many small cubes did Jackson use to make the large cube?* [8] *Does the picture in the book show all 8 of the small cubes? Why or why not?* [No; it only shows 7 small cubes because one of them is hidden in the back.]

Have students use craft sticks and clay to build the 3-D shape. *This is the frame of a building. It only has edges. What shape could you use to help count the edges?* [Cube] *When you were building this cube, what 2-D shape did you make first? Explain.* [Sample answer: I made a square first because each flat surface of the cube is a square.]

Have students use geometric solids to build the 3-D shape. *What solid figures did you use to make this shape?* [Cone, cylinder] *Why is the cylinder turned this way?* [So the cone can be stacked on top of its flat surface] *What would happen if the cylinder were turned onto its side?* [You wouldn't be able to stack the cone on top.]

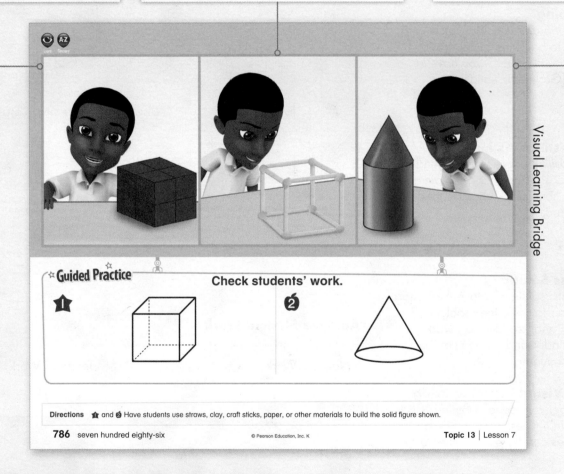

Visual Learning Bridge

☆ **Guided Practice**

Check students' work.

1️⃣

2️⃣

Directions ⭐ and 2️⃣ Have students use straws, clay, craft sticks, paper, or other materials to build the solid figure shown.

Complete the *Do You Understand? Show Me!* problem before starting Guided Practice.

Do You Understand? Show Me! MP.6 Be Precise *How can you make a 3-D shape using a cube and a cone? Is there more than one way? Explain your answer.* [Sample answer: I can stack the cone on top of the cube. This is the only way the shapes can be stacked because the cone only has one flat surface.]

Coherence In the Visual Learning Bridge, students consider the flat surfaces of 3-D shapes as they learn different ways to build 3-D shapes. This links back to their previous work with attributes of 2-D shapes.

Essential Question

Ask the following Essential Question: *How can you combine 3-D shapes to make other 3-D shapes?* [Sample answer: Use the flat surfaces to stack the 3-D shapes.]

Error Intervention: Item 1

If students have trouble building a cube with the correct number of flat surfaces or edges,

then have students begin by examining a geometric solid that is a model of a cube. Ask them to count the number of flat surfaces and the number of edges. Remind students that the solid figure they build should have the same number of flat surfaces and the same number of edges as the model.

✔ QUICK CHECK

Check mark indicates items for prescribing differentiation on the next page.
Items 7 and 8 are worth 1 point. Item 10 is worth up to 3 points.

20–30 min

Tools   Assessment

Item 4 MP.1 Make Sense and Persevere

Remind students that an important part of solving any problem is asking whether the answer makes sense. To that end, ask students how they can check that their answer to this item is correct. For example, students might find geometric solids for the shapes they circled and check whether the solids can be stacked as shown in the given figure.

Item 5 *What 3-D shapes are given on the left side of the page?* [Cylinder, cube] *Can these solid figures be stacked? If so, how?* [Sample answer: Yes; you can put the cube on the bottom and the cylinder on top, or you can put the cylinder on the bottom and the cube on top.] *Can these solid figures be used to build the first shape on the right side of the page? Why or why not?* [Sample answer: No; you need 2 cubes to build the shape.] *Can these solid figures be used to build the last shape on the right side of the page? Why or why not?* [Sample answer: No; you need a cylinder and a cone to build the shape.]

Item 7 Be sure students understand that some problems have more than one correct answer. Students may circle one of the shapes that the given solid figures can build without looking further to see whether there is another possible answer among the choices. To help students uncover additional correct answers, it may be helpful to have them compare and discuss their work with one or more classmates.

Item 10 MP.5 Use Appropriate Tools

Strategically *How would you describe the shape you are asked to build?* [Sample answer: It is built from 2 cubes that are next to each other.] *What tools or materials have you already used to build a cube?* [Sample answer: Craft sticks and clay] *Can you use those same tools or materials to build this shape? Explain.* [Sample answer: Yes; you can use craft sticks and clay to build 1 cube, and then add another cube on one side of it.] *How many craft sticks do you need to build this shape?* [20]

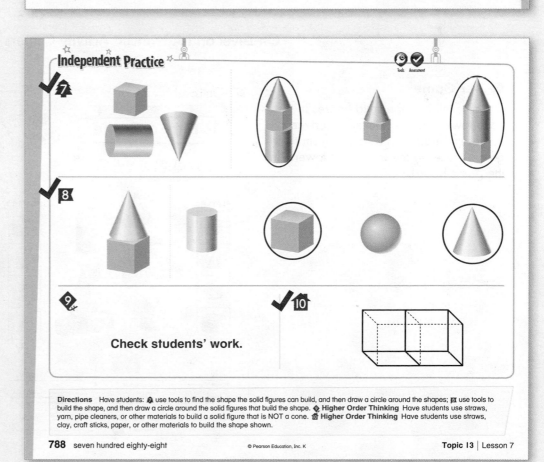

Name _____

Directions Have students: ❸ and ❹ use tools to build the shape, and then draw a circle around the solid figures that build the shape; ✋ and ❻ use tools to find the shape the solid figures can build, and then draw a circle around the shape.

Topic 13 | Lesson 7   seven hundred eighty-seven   **787**

Independent Practice

Check students' work.

Directions Have students: 🌲 use tools to find the shape the solid figures can build, and then draw a circle around the shapes; 🌲 use tools to build the shape, and then draw a circle around the solid figures that build the shape. ✿ **Higher Order Thinking** Have students use straws, yarn, pipe cleaners, or other materials to build a solid figure that is NOT a cone. 🏠 **Higher Order Thinking** Have students use straws, clay, craft sticks, paper, or other materials to build the shape shown.

788 seven hundred eighty-eight   © Pearson Education, Inc. K   Topic 13 | Lesson 7

Use the **QUICK CHECK** on the previous page to prescribe differentiated instruction.

2 RtI

I Intervention
0–3 points on the Quick Check

O On-Level
4 points on the Quick Check

A Advanced
5 points on the Quick Check

Intervention Activity **I**

Cut and Paste Buildings

Materials

Building with Solid Figures (Teaching Tool 40), geometric solids: cube, cone, cylinder

• Give groups of students one of the 6 different cards showing line drawings of solid figures.

• Have students work together to build the shape on the card using geometric solids.

• Repeat by giving groups different cards. Have students take turns building.

Reteach **I**

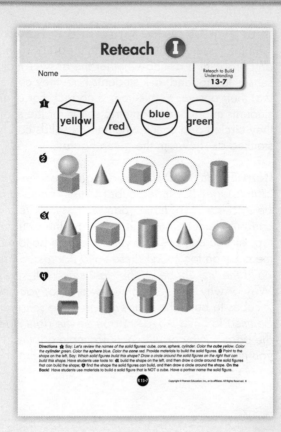

On-Level and Advanced Activity Centers **O** **A**

Center Games

Students tell why the solid figures in each tower can be stacked. Then they name and match solid figures from their game spaces to the individual towers on the game board.

★ On-Level

★★ Advanced

TIMING

The time allocated to Step 3 will depend on the teacher's instructional decisions and differentiation routines.

15–30 min

realize
PearsonRealize.com

Help   Tools   Games

Technology Center I O A

Math Tools and Math Games

A link to a specific math tools activity or math game to use with this lesson is provided at PearsonRealize.com.

Tools

Games

Leveled Assignment

I Items 1–4   O Items 2–5   A Items 3–6

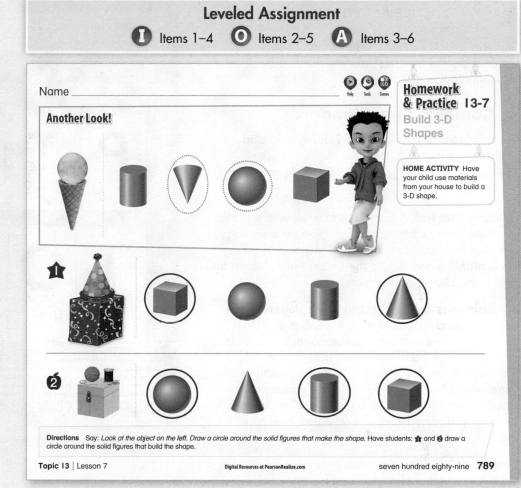

Name _____

Another Look!

Homework & Practice 13-7
Build 3-D Shapes

HOME ACTIVITY Have your child use materials from your house to build a 3-D shape.

1

2

Directions Say: *Look at the object on the left. Draw a circle around the solid figures that make the shape.* Have students: 🎈 and 🍎 draw a circle around the solid figures that build the shape.

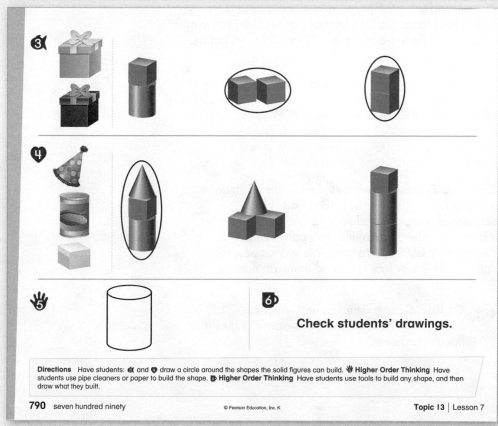

3

4

✋5

6 **Check students' drawings.**

Directions Have students: ✋ and 🎈 draw a circle around the shapes the solid figures can build. ✋ **Higher Order Thinking** Have students use pipe cleaners or paper to build the shape. 🍎 **Higher Order Thinking** Have students use tools to build any shape, and then draw what they built.

TOPIC **13**

FLUENCY PRACTICE ACTIVITY

PEARSON
realize
PearsonRealize.com

Games

FLUENCY PRACTICE ACTIVITY

Students practice fluently adding and subtracting within 5 during a partner activity that reinforces mathematical practices.

Ⓒ Common Core Standards

Content Standard K.OA.A.5 Fluently add and subtract within 5.

Mathematical Practices MP.3, MP.6, MP.7, MP.8

Getting Started Ask students to work with a partner. Tell them to record their matches on their own page. Go over the directions. Both students should solve each problem and record their work. Tell students to take turns identifying the match.

As Students Do the Activity As students work on Item 1 and Item 2, remind them that each clue can be matched with only one problem. Some students may find all of the answers first and then match the clues. Allow this strategy as it provides the same fluency practice. Remind students to compare and discuss their answers. Have them read each word. Draw and discuss the object revealed by the clues, top hat.

Another Activity Have students work together to write a new set of clues below PTO and THA on Items 1 and 2 on the page. Ask them to record the new rules on a separate sheet of paper. The problems should be different but should still result in top hat as the two words.

Extra Challenge *Look at your paper. Think about how you can change the problems under P, T, and O and still spell the same word below. Write down your new clues on another piece of paper. Then, look at T, H, and A. Write new clues for each letter. The new clues should still give you the same word below.*

Steps to Fluency Success To ensure all students achieve fluency, see pages 431E–431H for additional resources including practice/assessment masters on fluency subskills. You can also use the ExamView® CD-ROM to generate worksheets with multiple-choice or free-response items on fluency subskills.

Online Game The Game Center at PearsonRealize.com provides opportunities for fluency practice.

VOCABULARY REVIEW

A-Z Glossary **Games**

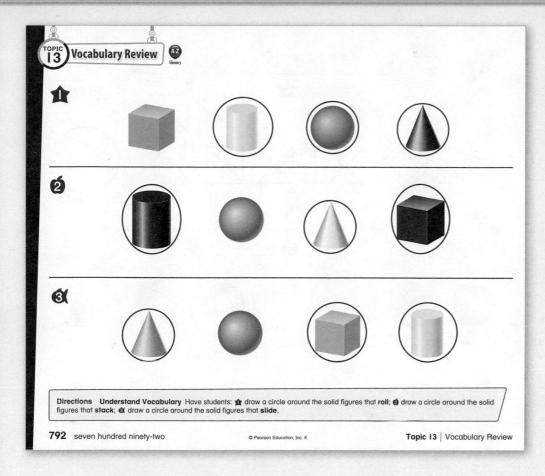

Directions **Understand Vocabulary** Have students: ★ draw a circle around the solid figures that **roll**; ❷ draw a circle around the solid figures that **stack**; ❸ draw a circle around the solid figures that **slide**.

792 seven hundred ninety-two   © Pearson Education, Inc. K   **Topic 13** | Vocabulary Review

VOCABULARY REVIEW

Students review vocabulary words used in the topic.

Oral Language Before students do the page, you might reinforce oral language through a class discussion involving one or more of the following activities.

- Have students define the terms in their own words.

- Have students say math sentences or math questions that use the words.

- Play a "What's My Word?" guessing game in which you or a student thinks about one of the words and says a clue that others listen to before they guess the word.

- Play a "Right or Wrong?" game in which you or a student says a sentence that uses one of the words correctly or incorrectly. Then others say "right" or "wrong."

Writing in Math After students do the page, you might further reinforce writing in math by doing one or more of the following activities.

- Tell students to close their books. Then you say the words and have students write them. Students trade papers to check whether the words are spelled correctly.

- Have students work with a partner. Each partner writes a math question that uses one of the words. Then they trade papers and give a written answer that uses the word.

 Online Game The Game Center at PearsonRealize.com includes a vocabulary game that students can access any time.

RtI **Item Analysis for Diagnosis and Intervention**			
Reteaching Sets	© **Standards**	**Student Book Lessons**	**MDIS**
Set A	K.G.B.4	13-1	D30
Set B	K.G.B.4	13-2	D31
Set C	K.G.B.4	13-4	D30, D31
Set D	K.G.B.4	13-6	D29

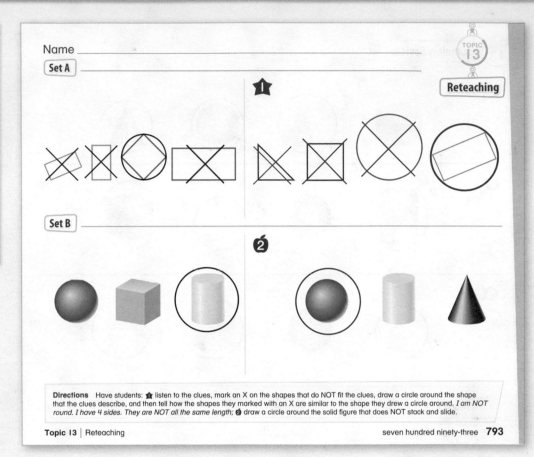

Directions Have students: ★ listen to the clues, mark an X on the shapes that do NOT fit the clues, draw a circle around the shape that the clues describe, and then tell how the shapes they marked with an X are similar to the shape they drew a circle around. *I am NOT round. I have 4 sides. They are NOT all the same length;* 🍎 draw a circle around the solid figure that does NOT stack and slide.

Topic 13 | Reteaching

seven hundred ninety-three **793**

Set C

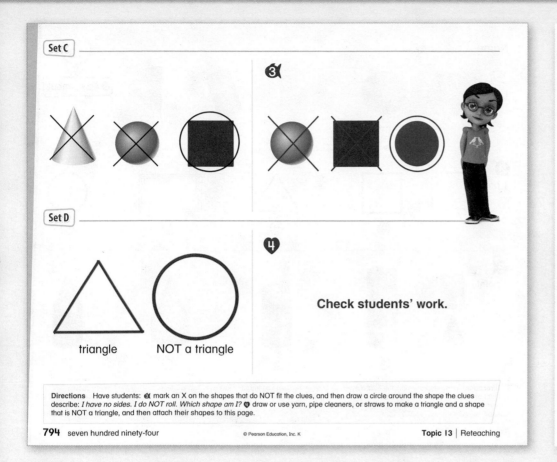

③

Set D

④

triangle   NOT a triangle

Check students' work.

Directions Have students: ③ mark an X on the shapes that do NOT fit the clues, and then draw a circle around the shape the clues describe: *I have no sides. I do NOT roll. Which shape am I?* ④ draw or use yarn, pipe cleaners, or straws to make a triangle and a shape that is NOT a triangle, and then attach their shapes to this page.

Response to Intervention

Ongoing Intervention
- Lessons with guiding questions to assess understanding
- Support to prevent misconceptions and to reteach

Strategic Intervention
- Targeted to small groups who need more support
- Easy to implement

Intensive Intervention
- Instruction to accelerate progress
- Instruction focused on foundational skills

TOPIC ASSESSMENT

ANALYZE, COMPARE, AND CREATE SHAPES

ANSWERING THE TOPIC ESSENTIAL QUESTION

How can solid figures be named, described, compared, and composed?

Restate the Topic Essential Question from the Topic Opener or project it from the Student's Edition eText.

Ask students to answer the Essential Question (verbally or in writing) and give examples that support their answers. The following are key elements of the answer to the Essential Question. Be sure these are made explicit when discussing students' answers.

• Name shapes by their attributes.

  Example: Karen is playing with Sara. Karen says: At home I have an object that has 4 sides and 4 vertices. All the sides are the same length. What shape is it? [Square]

• There are everyday objects that have the same shapes as solids.

  Example: Show to Jovan a can and ask him to identify the flat surfaces. [Circles] Show to Ana a box shaped like a cube and ask her to identify the flat surfaces. [Squares]

• Shapes can be identified and named by attributes.

  Example: Naheem is using materials from his classroom to build solid figures. What figures is he building? [Cylinders, cones, cubes]

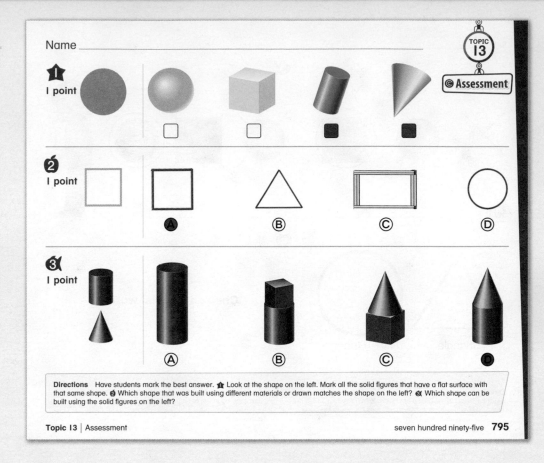

Directions Have students mark the best answer. ★ Look at the shape on the left. Mark all the solid figures that have a flat surface with that same shape. ② Which shape that was built using different materials or drawn matches the shape on the left? ③ Which shape can be built using the solid figures on the left?

Topic 13 | Assessment seven hundred ninety-five **795**

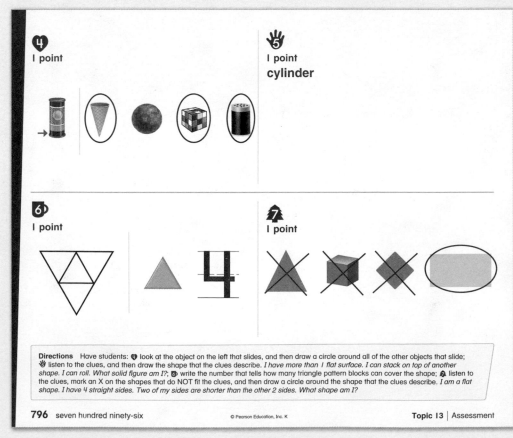

Directions Have students: ④ look at the object on the left that slides, and then draw a circle around all of the other objects that slide; ⑤ listen to the clues, and then draw the shape that the clues describe. *I have more than 1 flat surface. I can stack on top of another shape. I can roll. What solid figure am I?*; ⑥ write the number that tells how many triangle pattern blocks can cover the shape; ⑦ listen to the clues, mark an X on the shapes that do NOT fit the clues, and then draw a circle around the shape that the clues describe. *I am a flat shape. I have 4 straight sides. Two of my sides are shorter than the other 2 sides. What shape am I?*

ONLINE TOPIC ASSESSMENT

An auto-scored Topic Assessment is provided at PearsonRealize.com.

EXAMVIEW® TEST GENERATOR

ExamView can be used to create a blackline-master Topic Assessment with multiple-choice and free-response items.

Assessment

Topic Assessment Masters

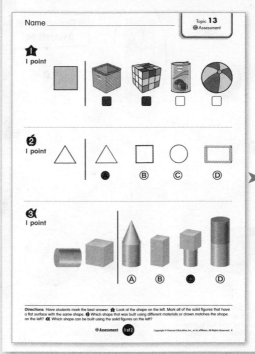

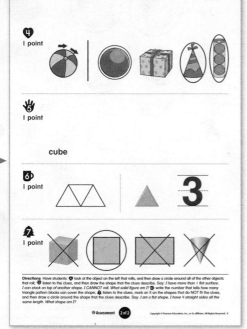

RtI Item Analysis for Diagnosis and Intervention

Item	© Standards	DOK	MDIS
1	K.G.B.4	1	D32
2	K.G.B.5, K.G.B.4	1	D29, D30
3	K.G.B.6	1	D31
4	K.G.B.4	1	D31
5	K.G.B.4	2	D31, D32
6	K.G.B.6	1	D33
7	MP.1, K.G.A.3, K.G.B.4	2	D30

The Topic Assessment Masters assess the same content item for item as the Topic Assessment in the Student's Edition.

Scoring Guide

Item	Points	Topic Assessment Masters
1	1	Correct choices selected.
2	1	Correct choice selected.
3	1	Correct choice selected.
4	1	Correct objects circled.
5	1	Correct solid figure drawn.
6	1	Correct number written.
7	1	Correct shape circled and X marked on other 3 shapes.

Scoring Guide

Item	Points	Topic Performance Assessment in the Student's Edition
1	1	Correct choices selected.
2	1	Correct flat surface drawn and name written.
3	1	Correct solid figures circled.
4	2	Correct pattern blocks shown to cover puzzle and correct numbers written for each pattern block used.
	1	Correct pattern blocks shown to cover puzzle or correct numbers written for each pattern block used.
5	2	Correct object circled and correct name of shape given, and X marked on other objects.
	1	Correct object circled and X marked on other objects or correct name of shape given for object.

RtI Item Analysis for Diagnosis and Intervention

Item	© Standards	DOK	MDIS
1	K.G.B.4	3	D31
2	K.G.B.4	3	D32
3	K.G.B.5, K.G.B.6	2	D31
4	K.G.B.6	3	D33
5	MP.1, K.G.A.3, K.G.B.4	4	D30, D31

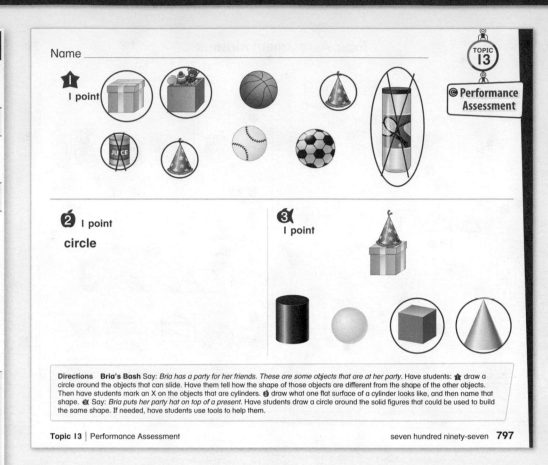

Name _____

1 I point

2 I point

circle

3 I point

Directions   Bria's Bash Say: *Bria has a party for her friends. These are some objects that are at her party.* Have students: **1** draw a circle around the objects that can slide. Have them tell how the shape of those objects are different from the shape of the other objects. Then have students mark an X on the objects that are cylinders. **2** draw what one flat surface of a cylinder looks like, and then name that shape. **3** Say: *Bria puts her party hat on top of a present.* Have students draw a circle around the solid figures that could be used to build the same shape. If needed, have students use tools to help them.

Topic 13 | Performance Assessment   seven hundred ninety-seven **797**

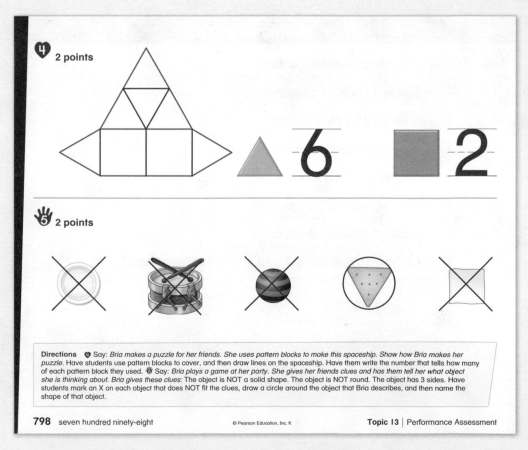

4 2 points

5 2 points

Directions   4 Say: *Bria makes a puzzle for her friends. She uses pattern blocks to make this spaceship.* Show how Bria makes her puzzle. Have students use pattern blocks to cover, and then draw lines on the spaceship. Have them write the number that tells how many of each pattern block they used. **5** Say: *Bria plays a game at her party. She gives her friends clues and has them tell her what object she is thinking about. Bria gives these clues: The object is NOT a solid shape. The object is NOT round. The object has 3 sides.* Have students mark an X on each object that does NOT fit the clues, draw a circle around the object that Bria describes, and then name the shape of that object.

798 seven hundred ninety-eight   © Pearson Education, Inc. K   **Topic 13** | Performance Assessment

Topic Performance Assessment Masters

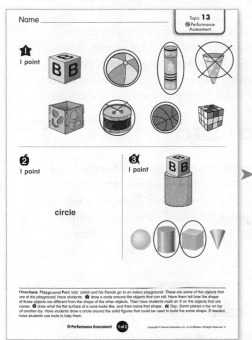

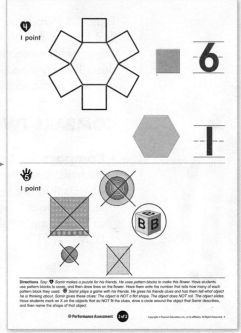

Item	© Standards	DOK	MDIS
1	K.G.B.4	3	D31
2	K.G.B.4	3	D32
3	K.G.B.5, K.G.B.6	2	D31
4	K.G.B.6	3	D33
5	MP.1, K.G.A.3, K.G.B.4	4	D31, D30

Scoring Guide

Item	Points	Topic Performance Assessment Masters
1	1	Correct choices selected.
2	1	Correct flat surface drawn and name written.
3	1	Correct solid figures circled.
4	2	Correct pattern blocks shown to cover puzzle and correct numbers written for each pattern block used.
	1	Correct pattern blocks shown to cover puzzle or correct numbers written for each pattern block used.
5	2	Correct object circled and correct name of shape given, and X marked on other objects.
	1	Correct object circled and X marked on other objects or correct name of shape given for object.

MATH BACKGROUND: FOCUS

F C R FOCUS COHERENCE RIGOR

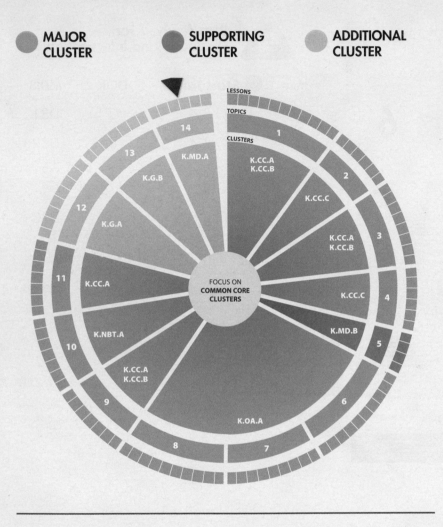

● **MAJOR CLUSTER**   ● **SUPPORTING CLUSTER**   ● **ADDITIONAL CLUSTER**

TOPIC 14 Describe and Compare Measurable Attributes

TOPIC 14 FOCUSES ON

© **ADDITIONAL CLUSTER K.MD.A**

Describe and compare measurable attributes.

Topic 14 introduces measurement by teaching students that objects can be directly compared by length, height, capacity, or weight. Students learn that objects can be described by measurable attributes and that some objects can be described by more than one measurable attribute.

COMPARE TWO OBJECTS

- **Compare by Length and Height** In Lesson 14-1, students compare the lengths or heights of two pictured objects that are lined up at one end. Then they use the terms "longer," "shorter," "taller," "the same length," or "the same height" to tell how the objects compare. (K.MD.A.2)

Mark an X on the shorter object.

- **Compare by Capacity** In Lesson 14-2, students compare the capacities of two pictured containers. Then they use the terms "holds more," "holds less," or "holds the same amount" to tell how the containers compare. (K.MD.A.2)

Draw a circle around the cup that holds more and mark an X on the cup that holds less, or underline the cups if they hold the same amount.

Content Focus in **enVision**math **2.0** (continued)

- **Compare by Weight** In Lesson 14-3, students compare the weights of two pictured objects, record the comparison on a balance scale, and use the terms "heavier," "lighter," or "the same weight" to tell how the objects compare. Students come to understand that the heavier object is on the lower side of the scale, and the lighter object is on the higher side of the scale. (K.MD.A.2)

DESCRIBE MEASURABLE ATTRIBUTES

- **Distinguish and Describe the Length or Height, Capacity, and Weight of Objects** In Lesson 14-4, students learn about measurable attributes by developing an understanding of tools that can be used to measure those attributes. They learn that length can be measured with connecting cubes, capacity can be measured with a measuring cup, and weight can be measured with a balance scale. Students also learn that some objects have only certain measurable attributes. (K.MD.A.1)

Look at the object on the left, identify the attributes that can be measured, and then draw a circle around the tools that could be used to tell about those attributes.

- **Describe Measurable Attributes of a Single Object** In Lesson 14-5, students describe an object by one or more of its measurable attributes. They indicate the tools that could be used to tell about those attributes and the tools that could not be used. (K.MD.A.1)

  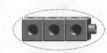 

Look at the object on the left and identify the attributes that can be measured. Then draw a circle around the tool(s) that could be used to tell about those attributes and mark an X on the tool(s) that could not.

Professional Development Videos Topic Overview Videos and Listen and Look For Lesson Videos present additional important information about the content of this cluster.

Content Coherence in enVisionmath2.0

Students learn best when ideas are connected in a coherent curriculum. This coherence is achieved through various types of connections including connections within clusters, across clusters, across domains, and across grades.

BIG IDEAS IN GRADES K–6

Big Ideas are the conceptual underpinnings of **enVision**math**2.0** and provide conceptual cohesion of the content. Big Ideas connect Essential Understandings throughout the program.

A Big Idea that connects the work in this cluster is that some attributes of objects are measurable. In this topic, students learn that the attributes of length, height, capacity, and weight can be measured. Objects can be compared by comparing those attributes.

Draw a circle around each container that holds more and mark an X on each container that holds less, or underline the containers if they hold the same amount.

For a complete list of Big Ideas, see pages 110–111 in the *Teacher's Edition Program Overview*.

LOOK BACK

How does Topic 14 connect to what students learned earlier?

BEFORE ENTERING SCHOOL

• **Use Observations to Compare** Before entering school, children likely observed that some things are bigger than others. For example, young children understand that a bus is bigger than a car. They might also have begun to develop a sense of specific attributes. They may have noticed that their parents' shoes are longer than their shoes, a pumpkin is heavier than an apple, and a milk jug holds more milk than a single-serving glass.

EARLIER IN GRADE K

• **Compare Quantities** In Topics 2 and 4, students determined whether the number of objects in one group is greater than, less than, or equal to the number of objects in another group. This involved comparing discrete attributes. The cardinal number of a group of objects is a discrete attribute because it is possible to count exactly how many are in the group. The measurement attributes introduced in Topic 14 are continuous attributes because they can always be subdivided into smaller units. Measurements of continuous attributes are always approximations. "More than" and "less than" comparisons can be made for both continuous and discrete attributes. (K.CC.C.6)

Count the monkey and banana stickers, and then write the numbers to tell how many. Draw a circle around the number that is greater than the other number and mark an X on the number that is less than the other number.

TOPIC 14

How is content connected within Topic 14?

- **Build on the Concept of Measurable Attributes** In Lessons 14-1, 14-2, and 14-3, students are introduced to the specific measurable attributes of length or height, capacity, and weight. They directly compare common objects by one of these attributes. Students use these concepts in Lessons 14-4, 14-5, and 14-6, as they describe an object by all of the measurable attributes that apply to the object. They learn that tools can be used to measure how long or tall something is, how heavy something is, or how much something holds. (K.MD.A.1, K.MD.A.2)

Another Look!

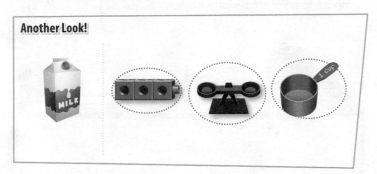

What attributes does a carton of milk have? Draw a circle around the tools that could be used to tell about these attributes.

- **Compare Objects by Attribute** In Lessons 14-1, 14-2, and 14-3, students are deciding which object has "more of" or "less of" a particular measurable attribute. (K.MD.A.2)

LOOK AHEAD

How does Topic 14 connect to what students will learn later?

GRADE 1

- **Comparison of Three Objects by Length** In Topic 12, students will develop the concept of transitivity and comparing three, rather than two, objects by length. To describe the comparison, they use the words "longest" or "shortest." (1.MD.A.1)

- **Indirect Measurement** In Topic 12, students will use string to indirectly compare the lengths of two objects that are not placed together. (1.MD.A.1)

- **Use Units to Measure Length** In Topic 12, students will be introduced to measuring length by iterating length units such as cubes, paper clips, and pennies. (1.MD.A.2)

Content Rigor in enVisionmath2.0

A rigorous curriculum emphasizes conceptual understanding, procedural skill and fluency, and applications.

CONCEPTUAL UNDERSTANDING

- **Conservation of Length and Height** Students may believe that the length of an object changes when the object changes orientation, e.g., a stick is longer when it is horizontal than when it is vertical, or a ribbon is shorter when it is curled. The topic includes common objects shown in various orientations to help students begin to understand that length is conserved. Classroom demonstrations with real objects can help to underscore the concept. (K.MD.A.2)

- **Understand That an Object Can Have More Than One Measurable Attribute** Students may believe that an object has just one measurable attribute, and so they always describe one object as being bigger or smaller than another object. In this topic, students are introduced to three measurable attributes: length or height, capacity, and weight. They learn that some objects can have two or three of these attributes. (K.MD.A.1)

- **Understand That a Comparison Depends on the Attribute Being Measured** As students progress through the topic, you might want to encourage exploration of the concept that one object may be "more" than another object when measuring the length and yet may not be "more" when measuring weight. (K.MD.A.2)

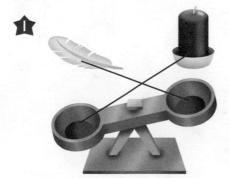

The feather is longer than the candle.
The candle is heavier than the feather.

PROCEDURAL SKILL AND FLUENCY

There are no standards in this cluster that call for fluency. There are no procedural skills in this cluster.

APPLICATIONS

- **Real-World Contexts** In everyday situations, measurement involves real-world objects. Throughout the topic, students apply their understanding of measurable attributes to describe and compare familiar, real-world objects. (K.MD.A.1, K.MD.A.2)

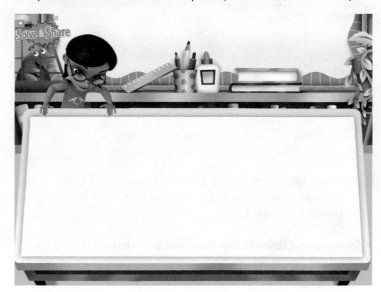

Choose an object in your classroom to draw. Describe all the ways you could measure it. Then draw the tools you could use to measure the object.

Connecting Math Practices and Content Standards in ënVisionmath2.0

Math practices and content standards are connected within all lessons including the lessons that focus on math practices.

MATH PRACTICES WITHIN LESSONS

- **MP.1 Make sense of problems and persevere in solving them.**

  Students make sense of which attributes apply for a given item, and persevere as they consider different possible means of measurement. (e.g., p. 826, Item 8)

- **MP.2 Reason abstractly and quantitatively.**

  Students use reasoning when considering the relationship between two objects for a particular measurable attribute. (e.g., p. 817, Solve and Share)

- **MP.3 Construct viable arguments and critique the reasoning of others.**

  Students critique procedures that others use to measure length. (e.g., p. 838, Item 10)

- **MP.4 Model with mathematics.**

  Students apply what they know about balance scales to solve comparative weight problems. (e.g., p. 820, Item 16)

- **MP.5 Use appropriate tools strategically.**

  Students decide which tools can be used to compare objects by their measurable attributes. (e.g., p. 823, Solve and Share)

- **MP.6 Attend to precision.**

  Students use the correct definitions and terms of comparison when they give clear explanations about measurable attributes. (e.g., p. 838, Item 9)

- **MP.7 Look for and make use of structure.**

  Students look for patterns in which attributes are measurable and which are not measurable. (e.g., p. 831, Item 5)

- **MP.8 Look for and express regularity in repeated reasoning.**

  Students use repeated reasoning when they consider a measurable attribute in identical copies of an object. (e.g., p. 819, Item 5)

LESSON THAT FOCUSES ON MATH PRACTICES

- **Lesson 14-6** This lesson focuses on MP.6. Students compare two lengths, one length that is a cube rod of a specific number and another length with no marked units. Students use the exact number of cubes correctly to create the rod length and do the subsequent comparison.

5

Revisit the information about MP.6 in these other resources:

- **Math Practices and Problem Solving Handbook** before Topic 1; includes Math Practices Proficiency Rubrics.

- **Math Practices Posters** to display in your classroom

- **Math Practices Animations,** one for each math practice, available at PearsonRealize.com.

MP

Learn Assessment Tools Games

Ongoing Intervention

 During the core lesson, monitor progress, reteach as needed, and extend students' thinking.

Guiding Questions
- **In the Teacher's Edition** Guiding questions are used to monitor understanding during instruction.

 Online Guiding Questions Guiding questions are also in the online Visual Learning Animation Plus.

Error Intervention: If... then...
This feature in the Teacher's Edition is provided during Guided Practice. It spotlights common errors and gives suggestions for addressing them.

Reteaching
Reteaching sets are at the end of the topic in the Student's Edition. They provide additional examples, reminders, and practice. Use these sets as needed before students do the Independent Practice.

Higher Order Thinking
These problems require students to think more deeply about the rich, conceptual knowledge developed in the lesson.

Strategic Intervention

 At the end of the lesson, assess to identify students' strengths and needs and then provide appropriate support.

Quick Check
✓ **In the Student's Edition** Assess the lesson using 2-3 items checked in the Teacher's Edition.

 Online Quick Check You can also assess the lesson using 5 online, machine-scored items.

Intervention Activity **I**
Teachers work with struggling students.

Reteach to Build Understanding **I**
This is a page of guided reteaching.

Technology Center **I O A**
 Digital Math Tools Activities reinforce the lesson content or previously taught content using a suite of digital math tools.

 Online Games provide practice on the lesson content or previously taught content.

Homework and Practice **I O A**
Use the leveled assignment to provide differentiated homework and practice.

Additional resources to support differentiated instruction for on-level and advanced students include:

On-Level and Advanced Activity Centers **O A**
- **Center Games** are provided in on-level and advanced versions.
- **Math and Science Activity** is related to the topic science theme introduced at the start of the topic.
- **Problem-Solving Reading Mat** is used with a lesson-specific activity.

Intensive Intervention

 As needed, provide more instruction that is on or below grade level for students who are struggling.

Math Diagnosis and Intervention System 2.0
- **Diagnosis** Use the diagnostic tests in the system. Also, use the item analysis charts given with program assessments at the start of a grade or topic, or at the end of a topic, group of topics, or the year.
- **Intervention Lessons** These two-page lessons include guided instruction followed by practice. The system includes lessons below, on, and above grade level.
- **Teacher Support** Teacher Notes provide the support needed to conduct a short lesson. The lesson focuses on vocabulary, concept development, and practice. The Teacher's Guide contains individual and class record forms and correlations to Student's Edition lessons.

Resources for Fluency Success
- A variety of print and digital resources are provided to ensure success on Common Core fluency standards. See Steps to Fluency Success on pages 431E–431H.

Glossary Games Story Story

PEARSON realize.
PearsonRealize.com

English Language Learners

Provide ELL support through visual learning throughout the program, ELL instruction in every lesson, and additional ideas in an ELL Toolkit.

Visual Learning
The visual learning that is infused in **enVision**math**2.0** provides support for English language learners. This support includes a Visual Learning Animation Plus and a Visual Learning Bridge for each lesson.

English Language Learners Instruction
Lessons provide instruction for English language learners at Beginning, Intermediate, and Advanced levels of English proficiency.

English Language Learners Toolkit
This resource provides professional development and resources for supporting English language learners.

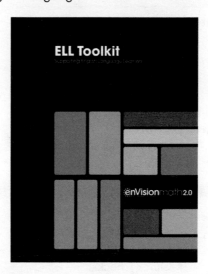

ELL Toolkit
Supporting English Language Learners

enVision math 2.0

Math Vocabulary

Build math vocabulary using the vocabulary cards, vocabulary activities, vocabulary review, and glossary plus the online glossary and vocabulary game.

My Word Cards
Vocabulary cards for a topic are provided in the Student's Edition. Use the cards with students to study and learn new vocabulary words.

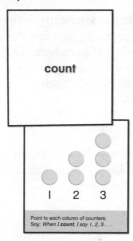

count

1 2 3

Point to each column of counters.
Say: When I *count*, I say 1, 2, 3 . . .

Vocabulary Activities
The Teacher's Edition provides vocabulary activities at the start of topics. These include activities for vocabulary in My Word Cards and/or activities for vocabulary in Review What You Know.

Vocabulary Review
A page of vocabulary review is provided at the end of each topic. It reviews vocabulary used in the topic.

Glossary
A glossary is provided at the back of the Student's Edition.

Animated Glossary
An online, bilingual, animated glossary uses motion and sound to build understanding of math vocabulary.

Online Vocabulary Game
On online vocabulary game is available in the Game Center.

Math and Reading

Connect reading and math using a data-filled reading mat for the topic with accompanying activity masters and guide. Also use topic interactive math stories.

Problem-Solving Reading Mats
There is a large, beautiful mat for each topic. At the start of the topic, help students become familiar with the mat and the vocabulary used by reading the mat aloud as students follow along. Use the Problem-Solving Reading Activity Guide for suggestions about how to use the mat.

Problem-Solving Reading Activity
At the end of some lessons, a Problem-Solving Reading Activity provides a page of math problems to solve by using the data on the mat.

Interactive Math Stories
An interactive math story provides an introduction to each topic. The story is available as an online story book and an animated story at PearsonRealize.com as well as a color-in, take-home story in the Teacher's Resource Masters.

Lesson 14-1

COMPARE BY LENGTH AND HEIGHT
pp. 805–810

ⓒ Content Standard **K.MD.A.2**
Mathematical Practices **MP.2, MP.5, MP.6, MP.7**

Objective Compare objects by length and height.

Essential Understanding When you compare by length or height, you are thinking about how long or tall objects are. Objects can be compared by length or height to see which is longer/taller and which is shorter.

Vocabulary height, length, longer, shorter, taller

ELL Speaking: Speak using content area vocabulary in context.

Materials Connecting cubes (or Teaching Tool 8), Cube Trains (Teaching Tool 11), masking tape, classroom objects, pencils (same/different lengths), objects (same/different lengths)

On-Level and Advanced Activity Centers
• Problem-Solving Reading Mat

Lesson 14-2

COMPARE BY CAPACITY
pp. 811–816

ⓒ Content Standard **K.MD.A.2**
Mathematical Practices **MP.2, MP.3, MP.6, MP.8**

Objective Compare objects by capacity.

Essential Understanding When you compare by capacity, you are thinking about how much objects hold. Objects can be compared by capacity to see which holds more and which holds less.

Vocabulary capacity

ELL Reading: Demonstrate comprehension by retelling information.

Materials Different-sized cups or mugs, glue, assortment of play teacups, pitcher of water, pan

On-Level and Advanced Activity Centers
• Center Games

Lesson 14-3

COMPARE BY WEIGHT
pp. 817–822

ⓒ Content Standard **K.MD.A.2**
Mathematical Practices **MP.2, MP.3, MP.4, MP.8**

Objective Compare objects by weight.

Essential Understanding When you compare by weight, you are thinking about how heavy objects are. Objects can be compared by weight to see which is heavier and which is lighter.

Vocabulary balance scale, heavier, lighter, weighs, weight

ELL Listening: Use contextual support to confirm understanding.

Materials Balance scale, paper bag, objects (same/different weights)

On-Level and Advanced Activity Centers
• Problem-Solving Reading Mat

LESSON RESOURCES

Digital

• Student's Edition
• Daily Common Core Review
• Reteach to Build Understanding
• Center Games
• Math and Science Activity
• Problem-Solving Reading Mat
• Problem-Solving Reading Activity

Print

Digital

• Listen and Look For PD Lesson Video
• Student's Edition eText
• Today's Challenge
• Solve & Share
• Visual Learning Animation Plus

• Animated Glossary
• Math Tools
• Quick Check
• Another Look Homework Video
• Math Games

Lesson 14-4

DESCRIBE OBJECTS BY ATTRIBUTES
pp. 823–828

Content Standard K.MD.A.1
Mathematical Practices MP.1, MP.2, MP.5, MP.6

Objective Use attributes to describe different objects.

Essential Understanding Objects have measurable attributes that can be recognized and described.

Vocabulary attribute

ELL Strategies: Use prior experiences to understand meanings.
Speaking: Express ideas in single words and short phrases.

Materials Connecting cubes (or Teaching Tool 8), measuring cup, books, construction paper, blunt-tipped scissors, crayons, classroom objects, pencil, water bottle

On-Level and Advanced Activity Centers
• Math and Science Activity

Lesson 14-5

DESCRIBE OBJECTS BY MEASURABLE ATTRIBUTES pp. 829–834

Content Standard K.MD.A.1
Mathematical Practices MP.4, MP.5, MP.6, MP.7

Objective Use words to describe how an object can be measured.

Essential Understanding Objects have measurable attributes that can be recognized and described.

Vocabulary None

ELL Speaking: Speak using content area vocabulary in context.

Materials Classroom objects, balance scale, colored pencils, connecting cubes (or Teaching Tool 8), measuring cup, sticky notes, marker

On-Level and Advanced Activity Centers
• Math and Science Activity

Lesson 14-6

MATH PRACTICES AND PROBLEM SOLVING: PRECISION pp. 835–840

Mathematical Practices MP.6, MP.3, MP.4, MP.5

Content Standard K.MD.A.2

Objective Solve math problems about objects with measurable attributes by using precision.

Essential Understanding Good math thinkers are careful about what they write and say, so their ideas about math are clear.

Vocabulary None

ELL Listening: Demonstrate listening comprehension by following directions.

Materials Connecting cubes (or Teaching Tool 8), classroom objects

On-Level and Advanced Activity Centers
• Center Games

TOPIC RESOURCES

Digital

Print

Start of Topic
• Topic Centers
• Interactive Math Story
• Math and Science Project
• Home-School Connection
• Review What You Know
• My Word Cards

End of Topic
• Fluency Practice Activity
• Vocabulary Review
• Reteaching
• Topic Assessment
• Topic Performance Assessment
• Cumulative/Benchmark Assessment
• End-Of-Year Assessment

Digital

Start of Topic
• Topic Overview PD Video

End of Topic
• Math Practices Animations
• Online Topic Assessment
• ExamView® Test Generator

PearsonRealize.com

Dramatic Play Center

Taller Than Teddy?

Materials
Teddy bear and other large dolls, trucks, building blocks

- Have students sit a teddy bear on the floor and then build a tower that is as tall as "Teddy," the bear.

- Help students use comparative language. For example, they can say, "My tower is *as tall as* Teddy."

- Repeat with toy trucks and block towers.

Sand and Water Center

How Many Cups?

Materials
Medium-sized cup, smaller cup, bowl, water in a pitcher

- Have partners use 2 different-sized containers to count how many cups it takes to fill a bowl.

- Have students record with tallies how many of each container it takes to fill the bowl.

Social Studies Center

Line Up the Family

Materials
Construction paper, crayons, photos, glue

- Have students list members of their families, including their pets.

- Then have them draw pictures of family members according to height. *Who is the tallest in the family? Draw that person at the far left of the paper. Who is the shortest in the family? Draw that person on the far right.*

- Students might also bring in photos of family members to glue onto paper.

- Have partners describe their work using comparative language. For example, a student might say, "My sister is *taller* than I am."

Art Center

Paper Chains

Materials
Strips of paper of the same length, glue

- Have 2 different groups or pairs of students make a paper chain. Give them a set time to do this: about 3 minutes.

- After the time is up, have students compare the 2 chains. *Which is longer than the other?*

- Have students use direct comparison to order the chains by length.

- Display the chains along with some math statistics in the room.

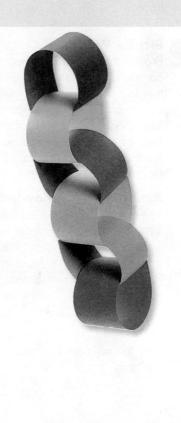

Movement Center

Long, Longer, Longest

Materials
Masking tape

- Tape 3 different lengths of masking tape onto the floor.

- Direct a student to stand at the beginning of the longest tape. Then have a student stand on the middle tape, and finally another student stand on the shortest tape.

- Have students "walk" the tape paths and stand still when they reach the end.

- Have them decide which tape path is the longest and which is the shortest.

Science Center

Plant Heights

Materials
(per pair) 2 picture books about plants, potted plants in the classroom

- As a group, have students talk about different kinds of plants they have seen.

- Give each pair 2 picture books. Have each student find a picture of a plant in his or her book. Then have them place the books next to each other and compare the heights of their plant pictures. Ask students to point to the taller plant and say aloud the word *taller*.

- Next, have partners compare the heights of potted plants in the classroom. If 2 plants are available, have students compare the heights using the words *shorter* and *taller*. If 3 plants are available, have them order the plants from shortest to tallest.

PEARSON
realize.
PearsonRealize.com

 PDF Story    Story

Before the Story

 Picture Walk
PDF Story
Project the online PDF that contains a full-color version of this story. Read the title, author's name, and illustrator's name to students. *What kind of animal is Bob?* [Buffalo] *Where do you think this story takes place?* [In a store]

Activate Prior Knowledge
In this story, we shop with Bob. We will help him pick out the sizes he needs or wants. We will compare sizes, too. Hold up 2 pieces of chalk or 2 pencils of different lengths. *Which one is longer than the other?*

Play the animated version of the story.
Story

DURING THE STORY

This book belongs to:
Marcia

TOPIC 14 | Story

When Bob Shops

Written by Carolyn Fleck   Illustrated by Jenny B. Harris

Bob wants the biggest bear. Which bear does Bob buy?

Topic 14 ①

Bob needs a smaller size. Which shirt does Bob buy?

Topic 14 ②

fold up

READ
Read the story aloud for enjoyment. Then read each page aloud and wait for students to respond to the text. Have them point to the biggest bear, the smaller shirt, the longest sandwich, and the largest umbrella.

GESTURE
Use props from the classroom, such as 3 stuffed animals or 3 toys of various sizes. Call on volunteers to role-play a store clerk and a buyer like Bob. Have others in the class tell Bob which toy he should buy, the smallest or the biggest. Give opportunities for other students to role-play various shopping roles, always picking out the smaller or bigger of 2 objects or the biggest or longest of 3 objects.

COLOR
Distribute the Interactive Math Story books to students. Have students follow these directions: *Color the biggest bear brown. Color the smallest shirt green. Color the longest sandwich yellow. Color the largest umbrella blue.*

This is a story in which students compare and order by size, such as from big to biggest and from long to longest.

Bob wants the longest sandwich. Please don't forget the mayo! Which sandwich does Bob buy?

Topic 14 **3**

Bob wants the largest umbrella. Which one will he buy?

Topic 14 **4**

WRITE
In large letters on the board or chart paper, write *big* and *bigger*. Read the words aloud. Draw a happy face next to *big*, and a bigger one next to *bigger*.

Then invite volunteers to draw other pictures under the labels, such as a big flower and a bigger flower.

SPEAK
Invite students to retell the story in their own words, starting with "First Bob buys ____, and then he buys ____," and so on until students have included all the items: the teddy bear, the shirt, the sandwich, and the umbrella.

After the Story

Extension
On chart paper, write an extension of "When Bob Shops" with students. Have them suggest what other things Bob would buy in a big department store—possibly shoes, pants, a sweater, or a hat. Then read aloud the story to students and display it so students can revisit it another day.

You may wish to have students take home their Interactive Math Story books and share what they have learned about measurement.

799N

DESCRIBE AND COMPARE MEASURABLE ATTRIBUTES

TOPIC ESSENTIAL QUESTION

How can objects be compared by length, height, capacity, and weight?

Revisit the Topic Essential Question throughout the topic, and see a note about answering the question in the Teacher's Edition for the Topic Assessment.

MATH AND SCIENCE PROJECT (STEM)

The science theme for this project is **Using Materials to Create Shade.** This theme will be revisited in the Math and Science Activities in Lessons 14-4 and 14-5.

Ask students to describe what they see in the photograph. Tell them that the post and the fabric of the umbrella are materials used to create shade. Encourage students to discuss what materials they have used to make shade.

Project-Based Learning Have students work on the **Math and Science Project** over the course of several days.

EXTENSION

After students have drawn three different objects, challenge them to compare two objects at a time by weight. *Which of the objects is lighter?* Have students look at a different pair of objects that they drew. *Which of the objects is heavier?*

Sample Student Work for Math and Science Project

Math and Science Project: Using Materials to Create Shade
Directions Read the character speech bubbles to students. **Find Out!** Have students find out different ways to create shade. Say: *We can use materials to create shade. Talk to your friends and relatives about different ways humans create shade from the sun.* **Journal: Make a Poster** Have students make a poster that shows various objects humans use to create shade. Have them draw three different ways humans create shade.

Topic 14   seven hundred ninety-nine **799**

Home-School Connection

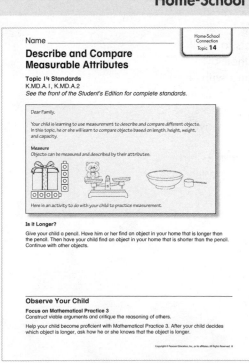

Send this page home at the start of Topic 14 to give families an overview of the content in the topic.

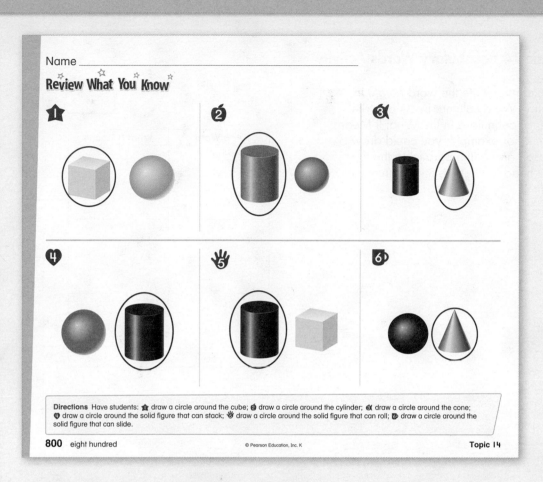

Name _____

Review What You Know

1

2

3

4

5

6

Directions Have students: **1** draw a circle around the cube; **2** draw a circle around the cylinder; **3** draw a circle around the cone; **4** draw a circle around the solid figure that can stack; **5** draw a circle around the solid figure that can roll; **6** draw a circle around the solid figure that can slide.

800 eight hundred

© Pearson Education, Inc. K

Topic 14

Item Analysis for Diagnosis and Intervention

Item	© Standards	MDIS
1	K.G.A.2	D31
2	K.G.A.2	D31
3	K.G.A.2	D31
4	K.G.B.4	D31
5	K.G.B.4	D31
6	K.G.B.4	D31

Vocabulary Review Activity

Use the Vocabulary Frayer Model (Teaching Tool 47) as a graphic organizer to help students look at words in different ways in order to fully understand their meanings. Have students write one of the vocabulary review words (solid figure) in the center oval. Then have them write the definition, characteristics, examples, and non-examples of the word. Students can use words and pictures to complete the model. You may wish to have students work in groups or an aide to help students to complete Frayer models for the different vocabulary review words.

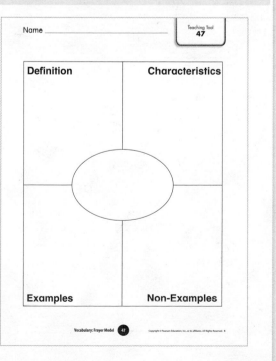

Topic 14 Vocabulary Words Activity

What Does It Mean to You?

Pass out copies of the Vocabulary: Word Chart (Teaching Tool 49) to students. On the board, draw a vocabulary chart for students to see. Write three new vocabulary words in the New Word column. Ask students to give you everyday or mathematical meanings of the words and write those meanings in the What It Means column. Tell students to write down the words and meanings as you write them on the board. Then tell students that they will learn more about these words in this topic.

For example, write the word *height* in the New Word column. Draw or write students' definitions in the What It Means column. For example, you could draw a person and a line parallel to the top of the head to illustrate the meaning of *height*.

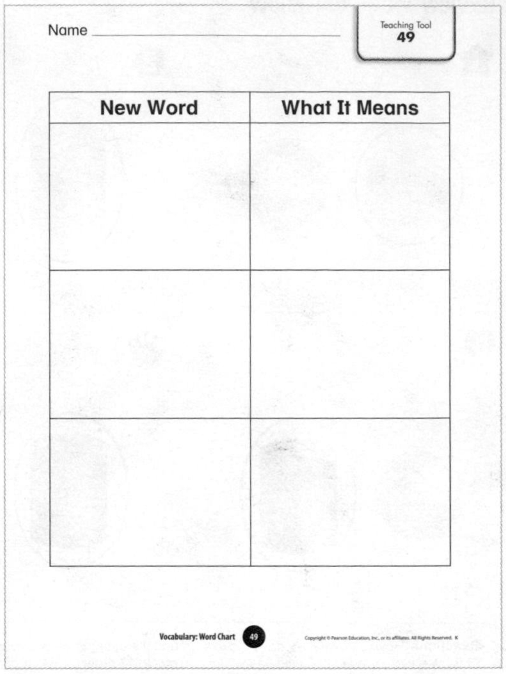

Name _____

Teaching Tool 49

New Word	What It Means

Vocabulary: Word Chart 49 Copyright © Pearson Education, Inc., or its affiliates. All Rights Reserved. B

My Word Cards

length	longer	shorter
height	taller	capacity

My Word Cards

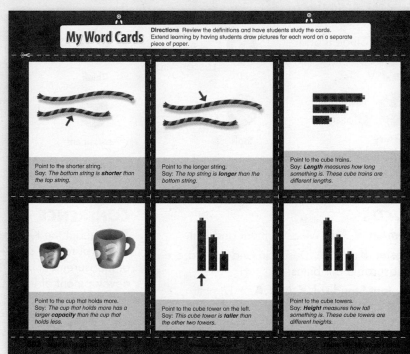

Point to the shorter string.
Say: *The bottom string is shorter than the top string.*

Point to the longer string.
Say: *The top string is longer than the bottom string.*

Point to the cube trains.
Say: *Length measures how long something is. These cube trains are different lengths.*

Point to the cup that holds more.
Say: *The cup that holds more has a larger capacity than the cup that holds less.*

Point to the cube tower on the left.
Say: *This cube tower is taller than the other two towers.*

Point to the cube towers.
Say: *Height measures how tall something is. These cube towers are different heights.*

My Word Cards

weight	weighs	heavier
lighter	attribute	balance scale

My Word Cards

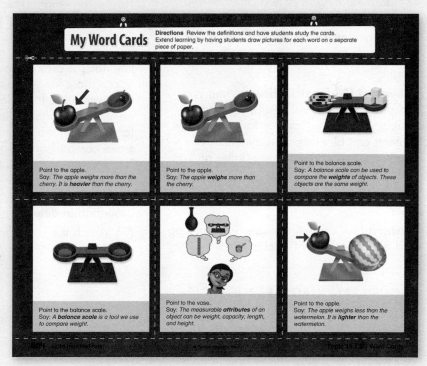

Point to the apple.
Say: *The apple weighs more than the cherry. It is heavier than the cherry.*

Point to the apple.
Say: *The apple weighs more than the cherry.*

Point to the balance scale.
Say: *A balance scale can be used to compare the weights of objects. These objects are the same weight.*

Point to the balance scale.
Say: *A balance scale is a tool we use to compare weight.*

Point to the vase.
Say: *The measurable attributes of an object can be weight, capacity, length, and height.*

Point to the apple.
Say: *The apple weighs less than the watermelon. It is lighter than the watermelon.*

LESSON 14-1

COMPARE BY LENGTH AND HEIGHT

LESSON OVERVIEW   FCR FOCUS • COHERENCE • RIGOR

FOCUS

Domain K.MD Measurement and Data

Cluster K.MD.A Describe and compare measurable attributes.

Content Standard K.MD.A.2 Directly compare two objects with a measurable attribute in common, to see which object has "more of/less of" the attribute, and describe the difference. *For example, directly compare the heights of two children and describe one child as taller/shorter.*

Math Practices MP.2, MP.5, MP.6, MP.7

Objective Compare objects by length and height.

Essential Understanding When you compare by length or height, you are thinking about how long or tall objects are. Objects can be compared by length or height to see which is longer/taller and which is shorter.

Vocabulary height, length, longer, shorter, taller

Materials Connecting cubes (or Teaching Tool 8), Cube Trains (Teaching Tool 11)

COHERENCE

Throughout the K–2 years, length plays a central role in students' understanding of measurement. In this lesson, the development of length measurement begins with comparisons and progresses, in later grades, through the use of physical units and eventually rulers and standard units.

RIGOR

This lesson emphasizes **conceptual understanding** and **procedural skill**. Students see the similarities and differences between the concepts of length and height. Emphasis is also placed on using the appropriate language when comparing these attributes for different objects. Students identify the longer/taller and shorter objects (or objects that are the same length) as they make comparisons throughout this lesson. This not only develops their understanding of length/height as an attribute, but also how the length or height relationship can be described in different ways.

 Watch the Listen and Look For Lesson Video.

MATH ANYTIME

Daily Common Core Review

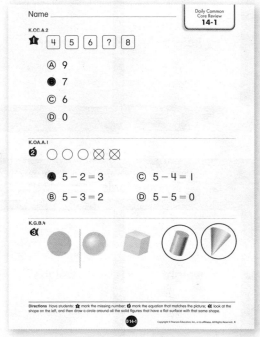

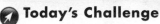

 Today's Challenge
Think Use Topic 14 problems any time during this topic.

ENGLISH LANGUAGE LEARNERS ELL

Speaking Speak using content area vocabulary in context.

Use with the Visual Learning Bridge on Student's Edition p. 806.

When introducing new vocabulary, say the words *length, longer,* and *shorter* for students to repeat. Show students 2 pencils of the same length and 2 pencils of different lengths. Say: *When you want to know how long something is, you talk about its length.* Show the pencils of the same length and say: *The length of these pencils is the same.* Show the longer pencil and say: *This pencil*

is longer than the other pencil. Show the shorter pencil and say: *This pencil is shorter in length.* Give students objects of the same and different lengths. Ask: *Which object is longer? Shorter? The same length?*

Beginning Ask students to hold up the object and use the sentence stem: "The ____ (object) is ____."

Intermediate Ask students to hold up the object and say which is longer/shorter/the same length.

Advanced Ask students to hold up the object that is longer/shorter/the same length and explain how they know which is longer and which is shorter.

Summarize What does it mean when you say *longer, shorter,* and *the same length*?

COHERENCE: Engage students by connecting prior knowledge to new ideas.
Students compare objects by length. This prepares them for the next part of the lesson where they compare other objects and identify which are longer or taller, and which are shorter.

10–15 min

Solve

 Whole Class

BEFORE

1. Pose the Solve-and-Share Problem
MP.5 Use Appropriate Tools Strategically
In this problem, students use real objects to solve problems about length.

Give each student 10 connecting cubes.

Say: Marta makes a cube train with 4 cubes. Is her cube train bigger or smaller than the crayon? Is her cube train bigger or smaller than the pencil? How can you find out?

2. Build Understanding
What are you asked to do? [Tell if the cube train is bigger or smaller than the crayon and the pencil.] *What tools do you have to solve the problem?* [Connecting cubes]

 Small Group

DURING

3. Ask Guiding Questions As Needed
How can you use your cubes to make the same cube train as Marta? [Connect 4 cubes together.] *How do you know if an object will be bigger or smaller than 4 connecting cubes?* [Line up the object and the cube train.]

 Whole Class

AFTER

4. Share and Discuss Solutions
 Start with students' solutions. If needed, project Solve and analyze Monica's work to discuss what it means to compare objects by length.

5. Transition to the Visual Learning Bridge
You have compared a cube train to two different objects. Later in this lesson, you will compare other objects in a similar way. You will learn ways to describe these objects.

6. Extension for Early Finishers
Have students make two 8-cube trains. *How can you compare these trains?* [You can place them side-by-side or count the number of cubes in each train.]

Solve & Share   Name _____   Solve   Lesson 14-1
Compare by Length and Height

See margin for sample student work.

Directions Say: Marta makes a cube train with 4 cubes. Is her cube train bigger or smaller than the crayon? Is her cube train bigger or smaller than the pencil? How can you find out?

I can … compare objects by length and height.

Content Standards K.MD.A.2
Mathematical Practices MP.2, MP.5, MP.6, MP.7

Topic 14 | Lesson 1   Digital Resources at PearsonRealize.com   eight hundred five **805**

Analyze Student Work

Monica's Work

Denise's Work

Monica explains that she can line up the cube train with the crayon and the pencil to find out which is bigger and which is smaller. Based on this, Monica identifies that the cube train is bigger than the crayon and smaller than the pencil.

Denise understands that she can put the cube train by the objects to compare. She does not, however, line up the cube train with the objects. This causes an error as Denise points to the overlapping cubes to the left of the crayon and the right of the pencil to explain that the cube train is bigger than both objects.

The *Visual Learning Bridge* connects students' thinking in Solve & Share to important math ideas in the lesson. Use the *Visual Learning Bridge* to make these ideas explicit. Also available as a *Visual Learning Animation Plus* at PearsonRealize.com

Visual Learning

Learn   Glossary

Length is the measure of an object from end to end. Are these spoons the same length? [No] *An object is longer if it has a greater length. Marta compares the spoons. Which is longer?* [The top spoon] *How do you know?* [The end sticks out farther than the other spoon.]

Height is the measure of an object from bottom to top. Are these spoons the same height? [No] *An object is taller if it has a greater height. Marta compares the spoons. Which is taller?* [The left spoon] *How do you know?* [The end sticks up higher than the right spoon.]

Marta compares the refrigerator and the chair. Is she comparing their height or their length? [Height] *Which is taller?* [The refrigerator] *How do you know?* [The refrigerator sticks up higher than the chair.]

MP.6 Be Precise *When an object is not as long or as tall as another, you can say it is shorter. What word would you use to describe the height of the chair compared to the height of the refrigerator?* [Shorter] *Why?* [The chair is not as tall as the refrigerator.] *How does lining up the ends of the objects help you compare them?* [If the ends are lined up, I can look at the other end to compare the length or height.]

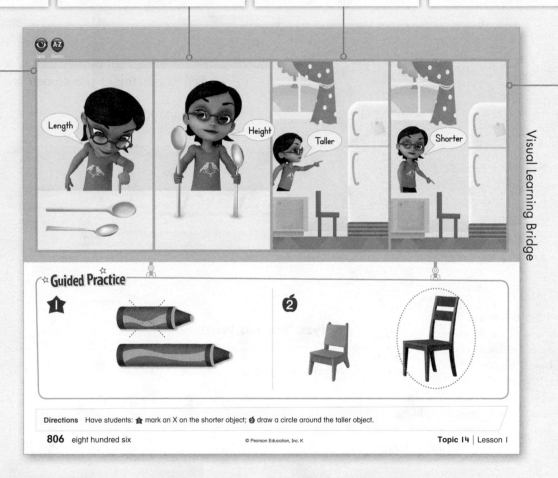

Visual Learning Bridge

☆ **Guided Practice** ☆

1

2

Directions Have students: ★ mark an X on the shorter object; ⊘ draw a circle around the taller object.

806 eight hundred six   © Pearson Education, Inc. K   **Topic 14** | Lesson 1

Complete the *Do You Understand? Show Me!* problem before starting Guided Practice.

Do You Understand? Show Me! MP.7 Use Structure
Distribute 8 connecting cubes to each student. *Use some or all of your cubes to make 2 cube trains.* Then have students explain to a partner which cube train is longer, shorter, or if the trains are the same length/height.

Essential Question

Ask the following Essential Question: *What does it mean to compare the lengths or heights of objects?* [Compare how long or tall they are; Find which object is taller/longer and which is shorter, or if they are the the same length/height.]

Error Intervention: Item 2

If students are unsure why they are not marking the smaller object as they did in Item 1,

then read the directions for each item again. Emphasize the words *shorter* and *taller*. Discuss the definition of each. Use cube trains to help demonstrate the definitions as needed.

Reteaching Assign Reteaching Set A, p. 843.

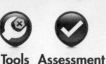
✓ QUICK CHECK

Check mark indicates items for prescribing differentiation on the next page.
Item 7 is worth 1 point. Items 9 and 10 are each worth up to 2 points.

20–30 min

Item 3 MP.5 Use Appropriate Tools Strategically Some students will closely examine these objects to see if one is minutely shorter or longer than the other. Encourage students to use connecting cubes to check the length of the pencils. *Make a cube train to show the length of each pencil, and then compare the cube trains.* Have students count the number of cubes in each train. *Are there more cubes in one train than the other, or do both trains have the same number of cubes?* [Both trains have the same number of cubes.] *What does that tell you about the pencils?* [They are the same length.]

Items 4 and 5 By marking both the shorter and longer objects in different ways, students can express their understanding of comparing objects.

Items 7 and 8 MP.2 Reasoning Students may be able to tell which is longer or shorter by sight. Ask students to explain how they decided which to circle, to draw an X on, or to underline: *How do you know which is shorter? How can you tell which is longer? Why did you underline these 2 objects?* [Answers will vary.]

Items 9 and 10 Ask students how they made sure that their drawn objects are the correct length. Remind students to line up one end of their drawing with the end of the object to compare. They may make a cube train the length of the object and compare it to their drawing to check their answers.

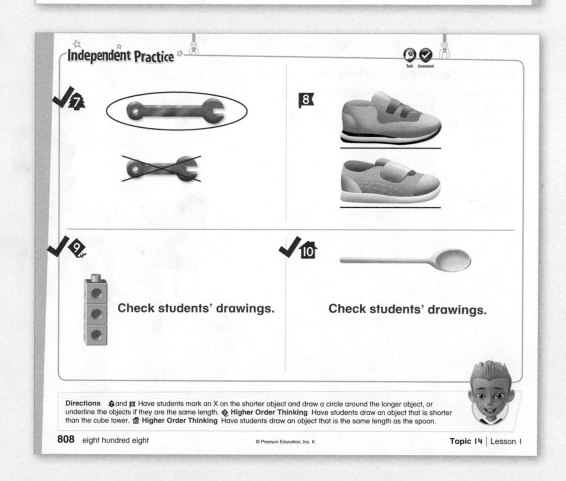

Name _____

3

4

5

6

Directions Have students: **3** and **4** draw a circle around the longer object or underline the objects if they are the same length; **5** and **6** mark an X on the shorter object or underline the objects if they are the same height.

Topic 14 | Lesson 1

eight hundred seven **807**

Independent Practice

7

8

9
Check students' drawings.

10
Check students' drawings.

Directions **7** and **8** Have students mark an X on the shorter object and draw a circle around the longer object, or underline the objects if they are the same length. ◆ **Higher Order Thinking** Have students draw an object that is shorter than the cube tower. **10** **Higher Order Thinking** Have students draw an object that is the same length as the spoon.

808 eight hundred eight   © Pearson Education, Inc. K   Topic 14 | Lesson 1

Use the **QUICK CHECK** on the previous page to prescribe differentiated instruction.

I Intervention
0–3 points on the Quick Check

O On-Level
4 points on the Quick Check

A Advanced
5 points on the Quick Check

Intervention Activity **I**

Match and Name
Materials
Masking tape, classroom objects

- Use masking tape to make a vertical starting line on a desk or table.

- Ask 2 students to each choose an object.

- Model lining up the 2 objects on the starting line.

- Ask students to decide which object is longer and which is shorter.

- Repeat for comparing height with a different pair of objects and a horizontal line of tape. Continue with other objects.

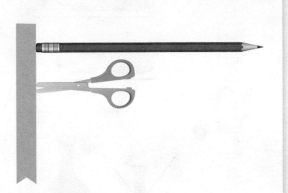

Reteach **I**

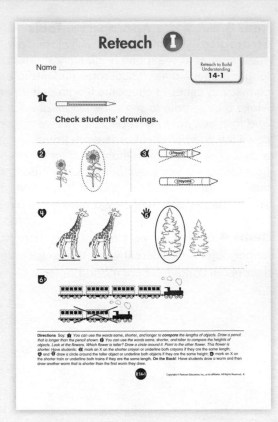

On-Level and Advanced Activity Centers **O** **A**

Problem-Solving Reading Mat

Have students read the Problem-Solving Reading Mat for Topic 14 and then complete Problem-Solving Reading Activity 14-1.

See the Problem-Solving Reading Activity Guide for other suggestions on how to use this mat.

TIMING

The time allocated to Step 3 will depend on the teacher's instructional decisions and differentiation routines.

15–30 min

 Help

 Tools

 Games

Technology Center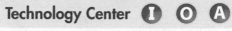

 Tools

 Games

Math Tools and Math Games

A link to a specific math tools activity or math game to use with this lesson is provided at PearsonRealize.com.

Leveled Assignment

I Items 1–6   **O** Items 2–7   **A** Items 2–8

Name _____

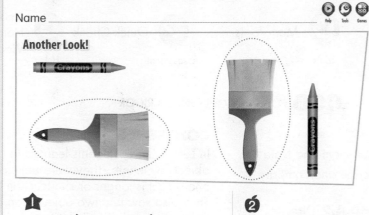

Another Look!

1

2

Homework & Practice 14-1
Compare by Length and Height

HOME ACTIVITY Set a kitchen spoon on a table. Ask your child to find 2 kitchen items that are longer than the spoon and 2 kitchen items that are shorter than the spoon. Then set a vase on the table. Ask your child to find 2 household objects that are taller than the vase and 2 household objects that are shorter than the vase.

Directions Say: *Compare the objects on the left by length. Which object is longer? Draw a circle around the longer object. Now compare the objects by height. Draw a circle around the taller object. How are length and height related?* Have students: **1** mark an X on the shorter object or underline the objects if they are the same length; **2** draw a circle around the taller object or underline the objects if they are the same height.

Topic 14 | Lesson 1   Digital Resources at PearsonRealize.com   eight hundred nine **809**

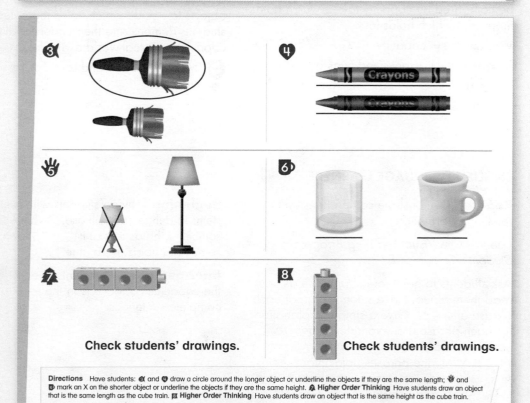

3

4

5

6

7   Check students' drawings.

8   Check students' drawings.

Directions Have students: **3** and **4** draw a circle around the longer object or underline the objects if they are the same length; **5** and **6** mark an X on the shorter object or underline the objects if they are the same height. **7 Higher Order Thinking** Have students draw an object that is the same length as the cube train. **8 Higher Order Thinking** Have students draw an object that is the same height as the cube train.

810 eight hundred ten   © Pearson Education, Inc. K   **Topic 14** | Lesson 1

DIGITAL RESOURCES PearsonRealize.com

  eText Student and Teacher eTexts

 PD Listen and Look For Lesson Video

  Think Today's Challenge

 Solve Solve and Share

  Learn Visual Learning Animation Plus

 Glossary Animated Glossary

Tools Math Tools

Assessment Quick Check

Help Another Look Homework Video

Games Math Games

LESSON OVERVIEW **FCR** FOCUS • COHERENCE • RIGOR

FOCUS

Domain K.MD Measurement and Data

Cluster K.MD.A Describe and compare measurable attributes.

Content Standard K.MD.A.2 Directly compare two objects with a measurable attribute in common, to see which object has "more of/less of" the attribute, and describe the difference. *For example, directly compare the heights of two children and describe one child as taller/shorter.*

Math Practices MP.2, MP.3, MP.6, MP.8

Objective Compare objects by capacity.

Essential Understanding When you compare by capacity, you are thinking about how much objects hold. Objects can be compared by capacity to see which holds more and which holds less.

Vocabulary capacity

Materials Different-sized cups or mugs, glue

COHERENCE

In Lesson 14-1, students learned to compare objects by length. They were able to tell if one object is longer or shorter than another. They also saw that two objects can be the same length. In this lesson, students learn about another measurable attribute, capacity, using pictures in a similar way to identify objects that hold more, hold less, or hold the same. This lays foundations for measuring capacity in later grades.

RIGOR

This lesson emphasizes **conceptual understanding** and **procedural skill**. Students learn the meaning of capacity, considering how it is relative with different objects. By comparing the capacities of two objects to decide which holds more/less, students demonstrate their understanding of capacity with real-world examples.

 PD Watch the Listen and Look For Lesson Video.

MATH ANYTIME

Daily Common Core Review

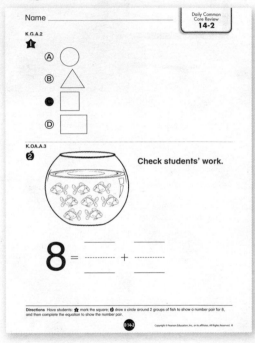

 Today's Challenge

Think Use Topic 14 problems any time during this topic.

ENGLISH LANGUAGE LEARNERS **ELL**

Reading Demonstrate comprehension by retelling information.

Use with the Visual Learning Bridge on Student's Edition p. 812.

Ask students to point to each phrase as you read them aloud. Have students repeat each phrase after you. Give a simple explanation for each phrase. For example: *When something holds more, it is larger. More can fit in it.* Write the phrases *holds more, holds less,* and *holds the same* on the board. Point to each one and ask students to explain what it means in their own words.

Beginning Provide students with sentence stems to define each phrase: "When something holds less, it is ____. When something holds more, it is ____."

Intermediate Ask students to describe the capacities of objects in the room using complete sentences.

Advanced Ask students to define each phrase and provide an example to illustrate each. Ask students to use pictures or objects to illustrate their definition. Students compare these phrases of measurement with other phrases of measure they have learned (e.g., longer, shorter, taller).

Summarize How can you explain in your own words what the phrases *holds more, holds less,* and *holds the same* mean?

DEVELOP: PROBLEM-BASED LEARNING

PEARSON
realize.
PearsonRealize.com

COHERENCE: Engage students by connecting prior knowledge to new ideas.
Students compare objects by capacity. This prepares them for the next part of the lesson where students decide which container holds more and which holds less.

10–15 min

 Solve

BEFORE

1. Pose the Solve-and-Share Problem
MP.2 Reasoning In this problem, students compare the capacities of real-world objects. They consider the comparative sizes of the cups to decide which holds more and explain how this can be determined.

Display 2 different-sized cups or mugs.

Say: Marta has 2 cups. She wants to use the cup that holds more. How can she find out which cup holds more? Glue the cup that holds less on the left side of the workmat and the cup that holds more on the right side.

2. Build Understanding
What are you asked to do? [Find out which cup holds more.] *What tools do you have to solve the problem?* [Cups]

 ## DURING

3. Ask Guiding Questions As Needed
What do you notice that is different about the two cups? [Sample answers: Different color, different sizes] *Fill the larger cup with water. What will happen if I try to pour this water into the other cup? Will it all fit?* [No, it will overflow.]

 ## AFTER

4. Share and Discuss Solutions
Start with students' solutions. If needed, **Solve** project Will's work to discuss the relationships of object capacity.

5. Transition to the Visual Learning Bridge
You have decided which cup holds more and which cup holds less. Later in this lesson, you will compare other objects to decide which holds more and which holds less. How much something holds is called its capacity.

6. Extension for Early Finishers
Display different items such as a small pot and a vase. *Which object do you think holds more? How can we find out?* [Sample answer: We can pour water from one container into the other to see if the water fits or spills out.]

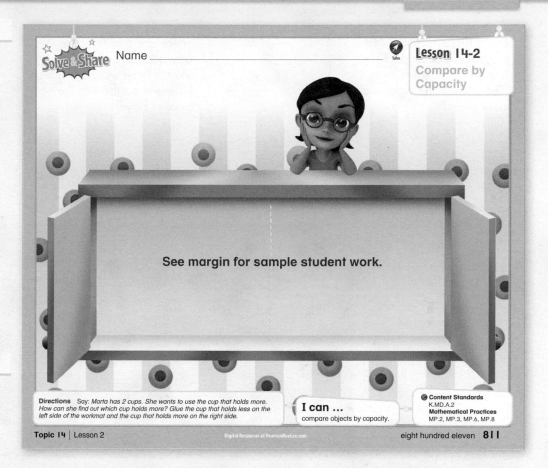

Solve & Share Name _____

 Solve

Lesson 14-2
Compare by Capacity

See margin for sample student work.

Directions Say: Marta has 2 cups. She wants to use the cup that holds more. How can she find out which cup holds more? Glue the cup that holds less on the left side of the workmat and the cup that holds more on the right side.

I can ...
compare objects by capacity.

⊙ **Content Standards**
K.MD.A.2
Mathematical Practices
MP.2, MP.3, MP.6, MP.8

Topic 14 | Lesson 2   Digital Resources at PearsonRealize.com   eight hundred eleven **811**

Analyze Student Work

Will 's Work

Anna's Work

Will correctly identifies which cup holds more and glues that cup on the right. He glues the cup that holds less on the left. Will explains that if the larger cup was full with water, this could not be poured into the smaller cup without overflowing.

Anna correctly identifies which cup holds more, but she glues the cups in the wrong places on the mat.

DEVELOP: VISUAL LEARNING

The *Visual Learning Bridge* connects students' thinking in Solve & Share to important math ideas in the lesson. Use the *Visual Learning Bridge* to make these ideas explicit. Also available as a *Visual Learning Animation Plus* at PearsonRealize.com

ELL Visual Learning

Learn   Glossary

There are 2 glasses. Are the glasses full or empty? [Full] *Which glass holds more?* [The one on the right; the taller glass]

There are 2 bowls. Are the bowls full or empty? [Empty] *Which bowl would hold less?* [The one on the left; the smaller bowl]

MP.2 Reasoning *There are 2 pitchers. Are the pitchers full or empty?* [Full] *Do the pitchers hold the same amount or does one hold more?* [They hold the same amount.]

Holds more   Holds less   Holds the same

Visual Learning Bridge

☆ Guided Practice

1   **2**

Directions ☆ and ⑳ Have students draw a circle around the cup that holds more and mark an X on the cup that holds less, or underline the cups if they hold the same amount.

812 eight hundred twelve   © Pearson Education, Inc. K   **Topic 14** | Lesson 2

Complete the *Do You Understand? Show Me!* problem before starting Guided Practice.

Do You Understand? Show Me! MP.3 Construct
Arguments Hold up 2 glasses of different sizes. *Which glass holds more than the other?* [Answers will vary.] Encourage students to justify their response. *How do you know?* [Sample answer: This cup is larger; it has more space. So, if the cups are both full, it will hold more.] *How can you check to see whether a glass holds more or less?* [You can pour water from one glass to the other to see if water spills over or if the water does not fill the glass.]

Essential Question Ask the following Essential Question: *What does it mean to compare the capacities of objects?* [Compare how much they can hold; Find which object can hold more and which can hold less, or if they can hold the same.]

Error Intervention: Items 1 and 2

If students have difficulty using the pictures to compare capacity,

then have them use real containers and sand or rice to compare. Then relate the pictures to the containers.

1 RtI   **Reteaching** Assign Reteaching Set B, p. 843.

☑ **QUICK CHECK**

Check mark indicates items for prescribing differentiation on the next page.
Items 7 and 9 are each worth 1 point. Item 10 is worth up to 3 points.

20–30 min

Tools   Assessment

Item 3 Remind students that they need to mark both the pot that holds more and the pot that holds less. *How can you tell which pot holds more?* [Sample answer: The bigger pot holds more than the smaller one because it has more space inside.]

Item 5 MP.8 Generalize When objects are the same size and have the same dimensions, then they will have the same capacities. Students can explore pouring water or sand between 2 identical containers to show that the same amount will fit in each.

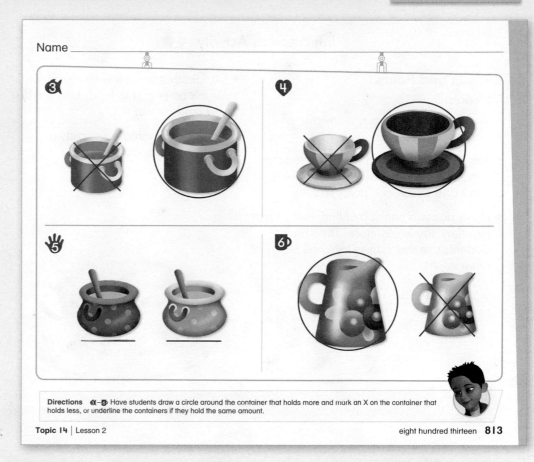

Name

Directions ❸–❻ Have students draw a circle around the container that holds more and mark an X on the container that holds less, or underline the containers if they hold the same amount.

Topic 14 | Lesson 2   eight hundred thirteen **813**

Item 8 MP.6 Be Precise Students demonstrate their understanding of the word *capacity* in a problem context. Encourage students to use the words *holds more* and *holds less* to communicate their conclusions about the capacities.

Item 10 Some students will draw a smaller version of the given object. Other students will draw an entirely new object. Ask students to explain how their drawings show an object that holds less. [Sample answer: The object I drew is shorter and not as wide, so it has less space inside.]

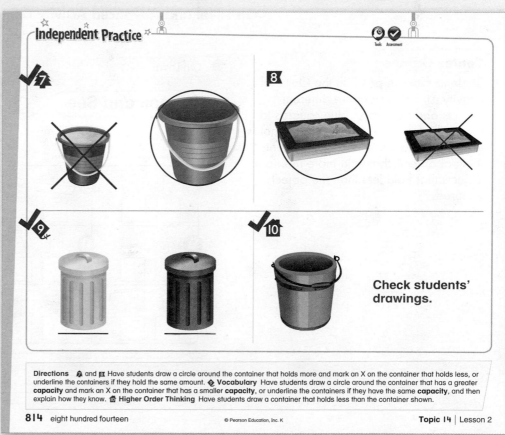

Independent Practice

Tools Assessment

Check students' drawings.

Directions ❼ and ❽ Have students draw a circle around the container that holds more and mark an X on the container that holds less, or underline the containers if they hold the same amount. ❾ **Vocabulary** Have students draw a circle around the container that has a greater **capacity** and mark an X on the container that has a smaller **capacity**, or underline the containers if they have the same **capacity**, and then explain how they know. ❿ **Higher Order Thinking** Have students draw a container that holds less than the container shown.

814 eight hundred fourteen   © Pearson Education, Inc. K   **Topic 14 | Lesson 2**

2 RtI

Use the **QUICK CHECK** on the previous page to prescribe differentiated instruction.

I Intervention
0–3 points on the Quick Check

O On-Level
4 points on the Quick Check

A Advanced
5 points on the Quick Check

Intervention Activity **I**

Carrots and Pears
Materials

Assortment of play teacups, pitcher of water, pan

- Ask 2 students to each choose a teacup. Have students decide which one holds more and which one holds less.

- Have students check by filling the cup they say holds more. Then have students use that cup to try to fill the other cup.

- Explain that if there is too much water for the other cup to hold, then the first cup holds more.

- Continue by using other cups and comparing capacities.

Reteach **I**

Name _____

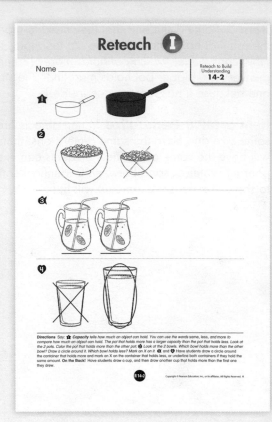

Reteach to Build Understanding 14-2

Directions Say: ★ *Capacity tells how much an object can hold. You can use the words same, less, and more to compare how much an object can hold. The pot that holds more has a larger capacity than the pot that holds less. Look at the 2 pots. Color the pot that holds more than the other pot* ② *Look at the 2 bowls. Which bowl holds more than the other bowl? Draw a circle around it. Which bowl holds less? Mark an X on it.* ③ *and* ④ *Have students draw a circle around the container that holds more and mark an X on the container that holds less, or underline both containers if they hold the same amount.* **On the Back!** *Have students draw a cup, and then draw another cup that holds more than the first one they draw.*

R 14-2

Copyright © Pearson Education, Inc., or its affiliates. All Rights Reserved. K

On-Level and Advanced Activity Centers **O A**

Center Games

Students work in pairs. In the On-Level activity, students compare different objects and use red or blue squares to label which holds more and which holds less. In the Advanced activity, students think of objects that hold more than and objects that hold less than the objects pictured.

★ On-Level

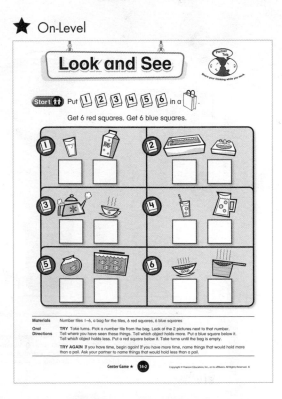

★★ Advanced

TIMING
The time allocated to Step 3 will depend on the teacher's instructional decisions and differentiation routines.

15–30 min

 Help Tools  Games

PEARSON
realize
PearsonRealize.com

Technology Center

 Tools

 Games

Math Tools and Math Games

A link to a specific math tools activity or math game to use with this lesson is provided at PearsonRealize.com.

Leveled Assignment

I Items 1–3 **O** Items 1–4 **A** Items 2–5

Name _____

Homework & Practice 14-2
Compare by Capacity

Another Look!

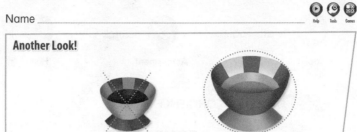

HOME ACTIVITY Set 2 pots that can hold different capacities on the table. Ask your child which one holds more and which one holds less. Check the answer by filling each with water. You can repeat using different containers.

⭐

Directions Say: *Which bowl holds more? How do you know? Draw a circle around it. Then mark an X on the bowl that holds less.* ⭐ Have students draw a circle around each container that holds more and mark an X on each container that holds less, or underline the containers if they hold the same amount.

Topic 14 | Lesson 2   Digital Resources at PearsonRealize.com   eight hundred fifteen **815**

2

3

Check students' drawings.

4

Check students' drawings.

5

Check students' drawings.

Directions Have students: ❷ draw a circle around the container that holds more and mark an X on the container that holds less, or underline the containers if they hold the same amount; ❸ draw a container that holds less than the basket. ❹ **Higher Order Thinking** Have students draw a bowl, and then draw another bowl that holds more. ❺ **Higher Order Thinking** Have students draw a cup, draw another cup that holds more, and then draw another cup that holds less.

816 eight hundred sixteen   © Pearson Education, Inc. K   Topic 14 | Lesson 2

DIGITAL RESOURCES PearsonRealize.com

 eText Student and Teacher eTexts

 PD Listen and Look For Lesson Video

 Think Today's Challenge

 Solve Solve and Share

 Learn Visual Learning Animation Plus

 Glossary Animated Glossary

 Tools Math Tools

 Assessment Quick Check

 Help Another Look Homework Video

 Games Math Games

LESSON OVERVIEW 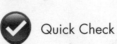 FOCUS • COHERENCE • RIGOR

FOCUS

Domain K.MD Measurement and Data

Cluster K.MD.A Describe and compare measurable attributes.

Content Standard K.MD.A.2 Directly compare two objects with a measurable attribute in common, to see which object has "more of/less of" the attribute, and describe the difference. *For example, directly compare the heights of two children and describe one child as taller/shorter.*

Math Practices MP.2, MP.3, MP.4, MP.8

Objective Compare objects by weight.

Essential Understanding When you compare by weight, you are thinking about how heavy objects are. Objects can be compared by weight to see which is heavier and which is lighter.

Vocabulary heavier, lighter, weighs, weight, balance scale

Materials Balance scale

COHERENCE

Students have previously compared objects by length, height, and capacity. Students adopt a similar approach as they compare objects by weight in this lesson. Students will connect comparison terms they have used before as they learn about heavier and lighter. An understanding of how to compare objects by weight and the introduction to the use of a balance scale build toward measuring weight in later grades.

RIGOR

This lesson emphasizes **conceptual understanding**. Students think about an object in terms of weight and how this can relate in different ways to the weight of another object. Students often think that a larger object always weighs more than a smaller object. To address this misconception, provide many hands-on experiences so that students can compare the weight of a larger, lightweight object with a smaller, heavier object.

 PD Watch the Listen and Look For Lesson Video.

MATH ANYTIME

Daily Common Core Review

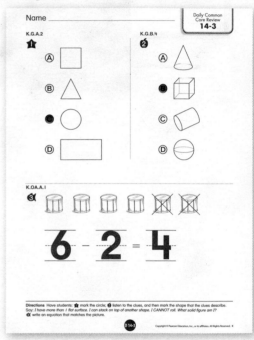

Today's Challenge

Think Use Topic 14 problems any time during this topic.

ENGLISH LANGUAGE LEARNERS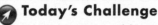

Listening Use contextual support to confirm understanding.

Use before the Visual Learning Bridge on Student's Edition p. 818.

Show students a balance scale with 2 objects that weigh the same. Show how the scale works by adding an object to one side. Ask: *Which side is heavier? Which side is lighter?* Repeat with other objects in the classroom. Ask volunteers to come to the front of the room with an object to compare to one of the objects on the scale. Instruct the student to ask the class: "Which object

is heaver? Lighter?" Students should predict which object is heavier/lighter before they are weighed.

Beginning Ask students to point to the object and respond using the sentence stem: "The _____ is heavier/lighter."

Intermediate Ask students to explain their predictions. Ask the group if they agree or disagree.

Advanced Ask students to explain their predictions. Ask the class if they agree or disagree. Show students 2 additional objects and ask: *What will happen if we put 1 object on each side of the scale?* Students answer and explain their reasoning. Ask the group if they agree or disagree.

Summarize What does it mean when you talk about *heavier* and *lighter* weight?

DEVELOP: PROBLEM-BASED LEARNING

COHERENCE: Engage students by connecting prior knowledge to new ideas.

Students compare objects by weight. This prepares them for the next part of the lesson where they compare to decide which objects are heavier, lighter, or the same weight.

10–15 min

Solve

BEFORE

1. Pose the Solve-and-Share Problem
MP.2 Reasoning In this problem, students consider the relationship of two objects in terms of weight to determine which object is heavier and which object is lighter.

Display how a balance scale works in front of the class. Say: *Marta has a pencil and a book. She wants to put the lighter object in her backpack. How can she figure out which object is lighter? Draw the objects where they belong on the balance scale.*

2. Build Understanding
What are you asked to find? [A way to tell which object is lighter] *What tool can be used to tell which object is lighter?* [Balance scale]

DURING

3. Ask Guiding Questions As Needed
Would the heavier or lighter object go on the lower side of the balance scale? [The heavier object] *Would the heavier or lighter object go on the higher side of the balance scale?* [The lighter object]

AFTER

4. Share and Discuss Solutions
Start with students' solutions. If needed, project Solve and analyze Maddie's work to discuss how to compare objects by weight.

5. Transition to the Visual Learning Bridge
You have compared 2 objects to decide which is heavier and which is lighter. Later in this lesson, you will compare other objects to decide if they are heavier, lighter, or the same weight.

6. Extension for Early Finishers
Which object is heavier—a red connecting cube or a blue connecting cube? [They weigh about the same.]

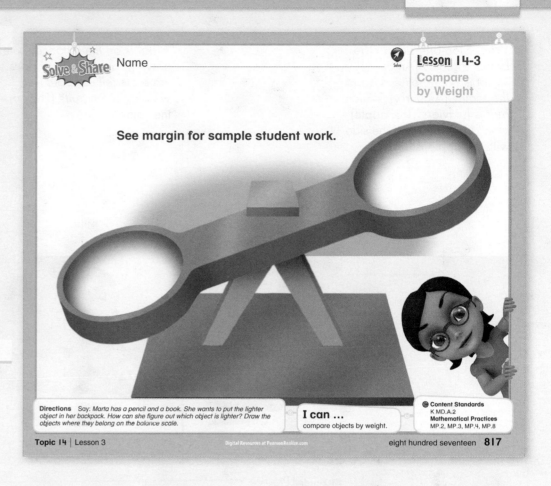

Solve & Share   Name _____   Solve   **Lesson 14-3**
Compare by Weight

See margin for sample student work.

Directions Say: Marta has a pencil and a book. She wants to put the lighter object in her backpack. How can she figure out which object is lighter? Draw the objects where they belong on the balance scale.

I can ... compare objects by weight.

Content Standards K.MD.A.2 **Mathematical Practices** MP.2, MP.3, MP.4, MP.8

Topic 14 | Lesson 3   Digital Resources at PearsonRealize.com   eight hundred seventeen **817**

Analyze Student Work

Maddie's Work

Lumen's Work

Maddie says Marta can use a balance scale to figure out which object is lighter. She correctly draws a book on the lower side of the balance scale and a pencil on the higher side of the balance scale.

Lumen says Marta can use a balance scale to figure out which object is lighter. She incorrectly draws a pencil on the lower side of the balance scale and a book on the higher side of the balance scale.

DEVELOP: VISUAL LEARNING

PEARSON
realize
PearsonRealize.com

The *Visual Learning Bridge* connects students' thinking in Solve & Share to important math ideas in the lesson. Use the *Visual Learning Bridge* to make these ideas explicit. Also available as a *Visual Learning Animation Plus* at PearsonRealize.com

ELL Visual Learning

👁 Learn   A-Z Glossary

What is on one side of the balance scale? [An apple] *What is on the other side of the scale?* [A cherry] *Which fruit is heavier?* [The apple] *How do you know?* [The side with the apple is lower.]

What is on the balance scale now? [2 apples] *What does the scale tell us about the weights of the fruit?* [They are the same.]

MP.3 Construct Arguments
Which fruit is lighter? [The apple] *How do you know?* [The side with the apple is higher.] *Which fruit is heavier?* [The melon] *How do you know?* [The side with the melon is lower.]

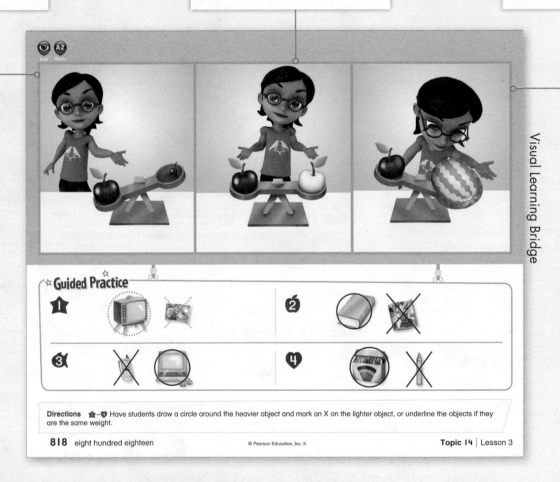

Visual Learning Bridge

☆ Guided Practice

Directions ⭐–❹ Have students draw a circle around the heavier object and mark an X on the lighter object, or underline the objects if they are the same weight.

818 eight hundred eighteen   © Pearson Education, Inc. K   **Topic 14** | Lesson 3

Complete the *Do You Understand? Show Me!* problem before starting Guided Practice.

Do You Understand? Show Me! MP.2 Reasoning *What animal is heavier than you? What animal is lighter than you?* [Accept reasonable responses.]

Essential Question

Ask the following Essential Question: *What does it mean to compare the weight of objects?* [Compare how heavy they are; Find which object is heavier and which is lighter, or if they weigh about the same.]

Error Intervention: Item 2

If students are confused between comparing size and weight,

then have them hold and compare the weights of a large bag of plastic foam peanuts and a small bag of pennies.

✅ **QUICK CHECK**
Check mark indicates items for prescribing differentiation on the next page.
Items 12 and 14 are each worth 1 point. Item 16 is worth up to 3 points.

20–30 min

Item 5 MP.8 Generalize Since the slices of bread are the same thing and the same size, they will weigh the same. You can give students other objects to compare, such as 2 identical crayons or 2 staplers. They can hold them and feel that they are the same weight.

Item 8 Objects may have attributes that are the same, such as similar appearances or similar purposes, and attributes that are different, such as weight. If students have trouble comparing the weights of the clocks, point out that an alarm clock could sit on a night stand in a bedroom, while a grandfather clock could be so heavy that a grown-up could not pick it up.

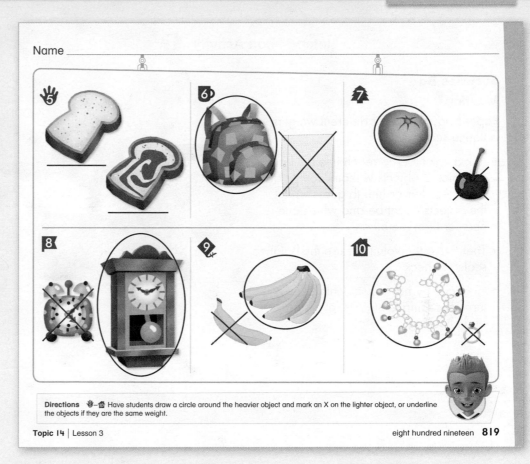

Name _____

Directions 👋–🔟 Have students draw a circle around the heavier object and mark an X on the lighter object, or underline the objects if they are the same weight.

Topic 14 | Lesson 3   eight hundred nineteen **819**

Item 14 While there is a greater quantity of grapes, clearly the watermelon weighs more. Students may have to rely on their prior experiences to know what the objects are and to have an idea of how much they weigh.

Item 16 MP.4 Model with Math Students must not only come up with a lighter object and a heavier object, but they must also match that a balance scale tips down for the heavier object. If students have trouble drawing an object that is heavier than another, suggest that they think of an object they could easily hold in one hand and another object they would not be able to carry, even if they used both hands. Then guide students as they draw the objects on the correct sides of the scale.

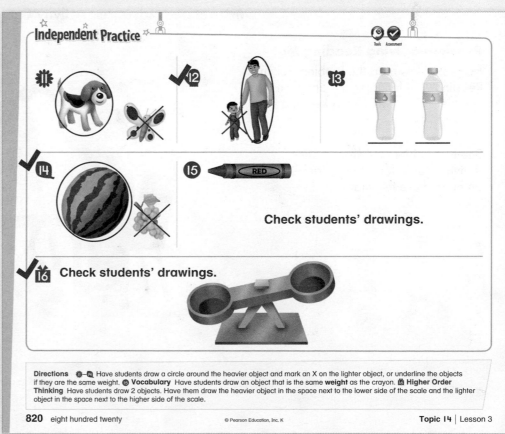

Independent Practice

Check students' drawings.

16 Check students' drawings.

Directions 1️⃣1️⃣–1️⃣4️⃣ Have students draw a circle around the heavier object and mark an X on the lighter object, or underline the objects if they are the same weight. 1️⃣5️⃣ **Vocabulary** Have students draw an object that is the same **weight** as the crayon. 1️⃣6️⃣ **Higher Order Thinking** Have students draw 2 objects. Have them draw the heavier object in the space next to the lower side of the scale and the lighter object in the space next to the higher side of the scale.

820 eight hundred twenty   © Pearson Education, Inc. K   Topic 14 | Lesson 3

ASSESS AND DIFFERENTIATE

 2 RtI

Use the **QUICK CHECK** on the previous page to prescribe differentiated instruction.

I Intervention
0–3 points on the Quick Check

O On-Level
4 points on the Quick Check

A Advanced
5 points on the Quick Check

Intervention Activity **I**

Surprise Bag

Materials

Paper bag, objects of different weights, balance scale

- Ask a volunteer to reach into the bag and pick 2 objects without looking at them. Ask her or him to guess what the objects might be and which one is heavier than the other.

- Then have the volunteer use the balance scale to check.

- Continue by having students take turns choosing 2 objects, guessing, and checking.

Reteach **I**

Name _____

Reteach to Build Understanding 14-3

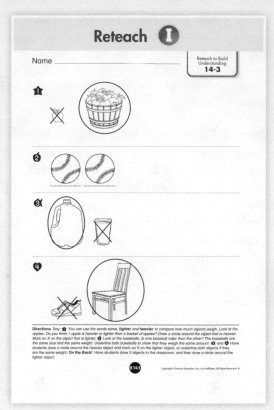

Directions Say: ☆ You can use the words same, lighter and heavier to compare how much objects weigh. Look at the apples. Do you think 1 apple is heavier or lighter than a basket of apples? Draw a circle around the object that is heavier. Mark an X on the object that is lighter. ❶ Look at the baseballs. Is one baseball taller than the other? The baseballs are the same size and the same weight. Underline both baseballs to show that they weigh the same amount. ❷ and ❸ Have students draw a circle around the heavier object and mark an X on the lighter object, or underline both objects if they are the same weight. **On the Back!** Have students draw 2 objects in the classroom, and then draw a circle around the lighter object.

On-Level and Advanced Activity Centers **O** **A**

Problem-Solving Reading Mat

Have students read the Problem-Solving Reading Mat for Topic 14 and then complete Problem-Solving Reading Activity 14-3.

See the Problem-Solving Reading Activity Guide for other suggestions on how to use this mat.

TIMING

The time allocated to Step 3 will depend on the teacher's instructional decisions and differentiation routines.

15–30 min

Help **Tools** **Games**

PEARSON
realize.
PearsonRealize.com

Technology Center **I** **O** **A**

Tools

Games

Math Tools and Math Games

A link to a specific math tools activity or math game to use with this lesson is provided at PearsonRealize.com.

Leveled Assignment

I Items 1–5   **O** Items 3–7   **A** Items 3–8

Name _____

Another Look!

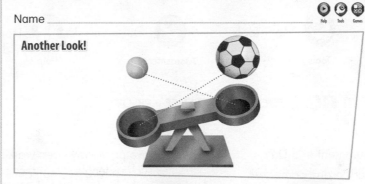

Homework & Practice 14-3
Compare by Weight

HOME ACTIVITY Ask your child to hold a slice of bread. Then ask your child to find something in your kitchen that is heavier than the slice of bread and then something that is lighter than the slice of bread.

1

2

Directions Say: *Compare the objects. Which ball is heavier? Draw a line from the heavier ball to the lower side of the scale and a line from the lighter ball to the higher side of the scale.* ★ and ❷ Have students compare the objects, and then match the heavier object to the lower side of the scale and the lighter object to the higher side of the scale.

Topic 14 | Lesson 3   Digital Resources at PearsonRealize.com   eight hundred twenty-one **821**

3

4
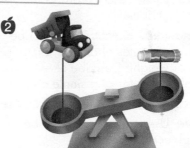

5

6

7

8

Check students' drawings.   Check students' drawings.

Directions ✂ **Math & Science** Have students tell which provides more shade, and then have them discuss what man-made objects protect them from the sun. ❺–❻ Have students draw a circle around the heavier object and mark an X on the lighter object. ❼ **Higher Order Thinking** Have students draw one object that is light and one object that is heavy. ❽ **Higher Order Thinking** Have students draw 2 objects that are the same weight.

822 eight hundred twenty-two   © Pearson Education, Inc. K   Topic 14 | Lesson 3

821–822

LESSON 14-4

DESCRIBE OBJECTS BY ATTRIBUTES

DIGITAL RESOURCES PearsonRealize.com

 Student and Teacher eTexts
eText

 Listen and Look For Lesson Video
PD

 Today's Challenge
Think

 Solve and Share
Solve

 Visual Learning Animation Plus
Learn

 Animated Glossary
Glossary

 Math Tools
Tools

 Quick Check
Assessment

 Another Look Homework Video
Help

 Math Games
Games

LESSON OVERVIEW   FOCUS • COHERENCE • RIGOR

FOCUS

Domain K.MD Measurement and Data

Cluster K.MD.A Describe and compare measurable attributes.

Content Standard K.MD.A.1 Describe measurable attributes of objects, such as length or weight. Describe several measurable attributes of a single objects.

Math Practices MP.1, MP.2, MP.5, MP.6

Objective Use attributes to describe different objects.

Essential Understanding Objects have measurable attributes that can be recognized and described.

Vocabulary attribute

Materials Books

COHERENCE

Students have previously been working with attributes such as length, height, capacity, and weight. In this lesson, students identify the attributes of an object that can be measured and determine appropriate tools that could be used to describe them. Students will likely use these and other tools when they eventually measure these attributes of objects.

RIGOR

This lesson emphasizes **conceptual understanding**. Students see that objects can be described by more than one of the attributes they have been using and consider the appropriate tool to measure. Previously they have been thinking of these attributes individually when comparing. This is an important step in understanding how attributes describe objects, focusing on what defines the object and understanding that not every object can necessarily be described by every attribute.

 Watch the Listen and Look For Lesson Video.
PD

MATH ANYTIME

Daily Common Core Review

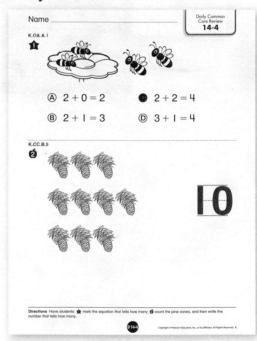

Today's Challenge

Think Use Topic 14 problems any time during this topic.

ENGLISH LANGUAGE LEARNERS

Strategies Use prior experiences to understand meanings.

Speaking Express ideas in single words and short phrases.

Use with the Solve and Share on Student's Edition p. 823.

Show students a cube train and a measuring cup. Hold up a pencil. Ask: *Which of these objects tells how long the pencil is?* [Cube train] Hold up a bottle of water. Ask: *Which of these objects will tell how much water I have?* [Cup] Ask students to name different objects that each tool can measure.

Beginning Ask students to use one-word responses or simple phrases when they speak. They can use the sentence stems: "A cube train can measure ____. A cup can measure ____."

Intermediate Ask students to use complete sentences to describe what objects can be measured by the cube train and the cup.

Advanced Ask students to use complete sentences to describe what objects can be measured by the cube train and the cup. Ask them to explain how they know what attribute they can measure.

Summarize How can you describe what different tools measure?

STEP 1

DEVELOP: PROBLEM-BASED LEARNING

PEARSON
realize
PearsonRealize.com

Solve

10–15 min

COHERENCE: Engage students by connecting prior knowledge to new ideas.
Students consider what attributes can be measured by two given tools and provide examples. This prepares them for the next part of the lesson where students choose from three given tools as they describe attributes of different objects.

BEFORE

1. Pose the Solve-and-Share Problem
MP.5 Use Appropriate Tools Strategically
In this problem, students use tools and describe the attributes of an everyday object.

Say: *These are 2 tools for measuring. What can you measure with the cup? What can you measure with the cube train? Draw an object you can measure with each tool.*

2. Build Understanding
What are you asked to do? [Draw an object that can be measured by a cup and an object that can be measured by a cube train.]
What information do you already know? [The cube train and the measuring cup are tools that can be used to measure.]

DURING

3. Ask Guiding Questions As Needed
What can you measure with connecting cubes? [How long something is] *What can you measure using a measuring cup?* [How much a container can hold]

AFTER

4. Share and Discuss Solutions
 Start with students' solutions. If needed, project
Solve and analyze Raul's work to discuss objects that can be measured with each tool.

5. Transition to the Visual Learning Bridge
You have found examples of objects that can be measured with connecting cubes and with a measuring cup. Later in this lesson, you will identify attributes of different objects that can be measured.

6. Extension for Early Finishers
Ask students to name another object that can hold something. [Sample answers: Water bottle, fish tank, bowl]

Solve & Share   Name _____   Lesson 14-4
Describe Objects by Attributes

See margin for sample student work.

Directions Say: These are 2 tools for measuring. What can you measure with the cup? What can you measure with the cube train? Draw an object you can measure with each tool.

I can ...
use attributes to describe different objects.

Content Standards
K.MD.A.1
Mathematical Practices
MP.1, MP.2, MP.5, MP.6

Topic 14 | Lesson 4   Digital Resources at PearsonRealize.com   eight hundred twenty-three **823**

Analyze Student Work

Raul's Work

Tricia's Work

Raul correctly identifies a bowl as an object that can be measured with the cup and a crayon as an object that can be measured with the cube train. Raul draws both objects in the correct places.

Tricia correctly identifies a plastic cup as an object that can be measured with the cup and also with the cube train. Tricia correctly draws the object in both places.

STEP 2

DEVELOP: VISUAL LEARNING

PEARSON
realize
PearsonRealize.com

The *Visual Learning Bridge* connects students' thinking in Solve & Share to important math ideas in the lesson. Use the *Visual Learning Bridge* to make these ideas explicit. Also available as a *Visual Learning Animation Plus* at PearsonRealize.com

Visual Learning

Learn   Glossary

What words can you use to describe this water bottle? [Sample answers: Tall, long, full, heavy, clear, round] *Which attributes do these words describe?* [Sample answers: *Long describes* length, and *heavy describes* weight.] *What tools do you see?* [Cube train, balance scale, and measuring cup]

MP.5 Use Appropriate Tools Strategically *The tools can help us find out how long, tall, or how heavy something is. Tools can also tell us how much an object holds. Which tool would be best for finding out the length of the water bottle?* [Cube train]

MP.5 Use Appropriate Tools Strategically *Which tool should we use to find out how heavy the water bottle is?* [Balance scale] *Which weighs more, the water bottle or the apple?* [The water bottle] *How do you know?* [The side with the water bottle is lower.]

Which looks like it can hold more, the water bottle or the measuring cup? [The water bottle] *The measuring cup is a tool we can use to find out how much the water bottle can hold.*

Visual Learning Bridge

☆ **Guided Practice**

1

Directions ★ Have students look at the object on the left, identify the attributes that can be measured, and then draw a circle around the tools that could be used to tell about those attributes.

824 eight hundred twenty-four   © Pearson Education, Inc. K   **Topic 14** | **Lesson 4**

Complete the *Do You Understand? Show Me!* problem before starting Guided Practice.

Do You Understand? Show Me! MP.2 Reasoning Display a large book and a small book next to each other. *An attribute is what we use to describe an object, for example, size, shape, color.* Ask students to tell the attributes that can be measured for each book and explain how they know. Help students to see that the size of the object does not affect the attributes that can be measured.

 Ask the following Essential Question: *What attributes can you use to describe objects?* [Sample answers: Length, height, weight, capacity]

Coherence In the Visual Learning Bridge, students see how tools can describe different attributes of the same object. This links back to the previous lessons in this topic where student learned to use these tools to compare each of the attributes discussed.

Error Intervention: Item 1

If students have difficulty identifying which tool they could use,

then talk through the steps to analyze that length and weight are attributes of the pencil that can be measured, while the capacity of a pencil cannot be measured using a measuring cup.

Check mark indicates items for prescribing differentiation on the next page.
Items 6 and 8 are each worth 1 point. Item 9 is worth up to 3 points.

20–30 min

Tools Assessment

Items 2–5 Students may notice that the measuring cup is only circled for the cup and jar. Ask them to consider the function of the cup and the jar to help make sense of this.

Item 2 MP.6 Be Precise Guide students to notice that the cup can be filled, the cup can be weighed, and the height of the cup can be measured. Encourage students to state how each tool can be used to measure the cup. *What does the cube train tell you about the cup?* [How tall it is] *The balance scale?* [Whether it is heavier or lighter than another object] *The measuring cup?* [How much it can hold]

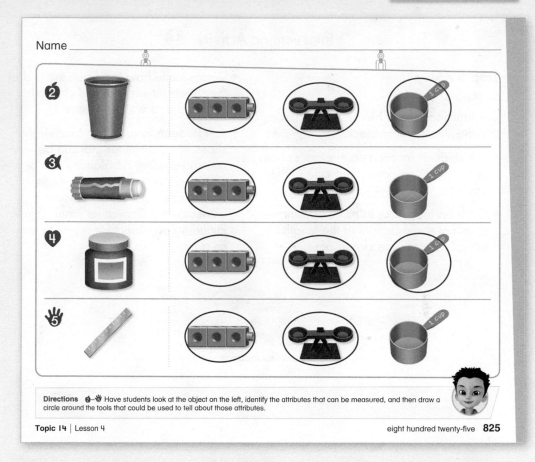

Item 8 MP.1 Make Sense and Persevere Students might have difficulty understanding why a measuring cup cannot be used. *Remember that a measuring cup tells how much a container holds.* Have students share some examples of containers with measurable capacity, such as jars, pitchers, and bottles. *Is a crayon a container that can hold something inside?* [No] *This means that a crayon does not have capacity for a measuring cup to measure.* Generally, if an object can have its capacity measured with a measuring cup, then the attributes of length and weight can be measured.

Item 9 Although students should draw new objects rather than repeat those from previous items, it will help them to think about previous work with balance scales to identify the attribute needed.

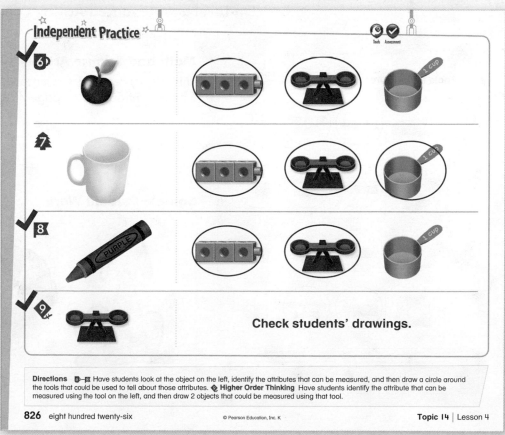

STEP 3 ASSESS AND DIFFERENTIATE

 RtI 2

Use the **QUICK CHECK** on the previous page to prescribe differentiated instruction.

I Intervention 0–3 points on the Quick Check

O On-Level 4 points on the Quick Check

A Advanced 5 points on the Quick Check

Intervention Activity **I**

Step by Step

Materials

Construction paper, blunt-tipped scissors, crayons, classroom objects

- Ask students to trace each other's shoes on construction paper and cut out the tracings.

- Have partners take turns comparing the length of the shoeprint to the length of other objects in the classroom.

- Demonstrate how to line up the end of the shoeprint with the end of another object to find which is longer.

- Ask students to consider whether their shoes have attributes that can be measured using a balance scale or a measuring cup. They can explain how to use the tools to measure as necessary. Repeat for other objects, including an object for capacity, such as a jar.

Reteach **I**

Name _____

Reteach to Build Understanding 14-4

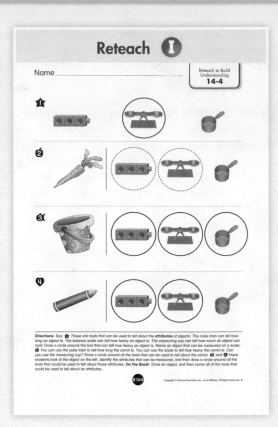

Directions Say: These are tools that can be used to tell about the **attributes** of objects. The cube train can tell how long an object is. The balance scale can tell how heavy an object is. The measuring cup can tell how much an object can hold. Draw a circle around the tool that can tell how heavy an object is. Name an object that can be measured on a scale; ❶ You can use the cube train to tell how long the carrot is. You can use the scale to tell how heavy the carrot is. Can you use the measuring cup? Draw a circle around all the tools that can be used to tell about the carrot. ❷ and ❸ Have students look at the object on the left, identify the attributes that can be measured, and then draw a circle around all the tools that could be used to tell about those attributes. **On the Back!** Draw an object, and then name all of the tools that could be used to tell about its attributes.

On-Level and Advanced Activity Centers **O A**

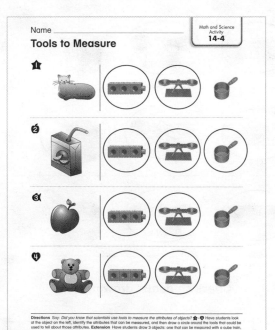

Name _____

Tools to Measure

Math and Science Activity 14-4

Directions Say: Did you know that scientists use tools to measure the attributes of objects? ❶–❹ Have students look at the object on the left, identify the attributes that can be measured, and then draw a circle around the tools that could be used to tell about those attributes. **Extension** Have students draw 3 objects: one that can be measured with a cube train, one that can be measured with a balance scale, and one that can be measured with a cup.

Math and Science Activity 14-4

Math and Science Activity STEM

This activity revisits the science theme, **Using Materials to Create Shade,** introduced on page 799 of the Student's Edition.

Sample Student Work

TIMING

The time allocated to Step 3 will depend on the teacher's instructional decisions and differentiation routines.

15–30 min

 Help

 Tools

 Games

PEARSON
realize.
PearsonRealize.com

Technology Center I O A

Tools

Games

Math Tools and Math Games

A link to a specific math tools activity or math game to use with this lesson is provided at PearsonRealize.com.

Leveled Assignment

I Items 1–4   O Items 2–5   A Items 3–6

Name _____

 Help Tools Games

Homework & Practice 14-4

Describe Objects by Attributes

Another Look!

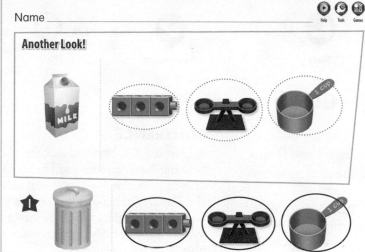

HOME ACTIVITY Choose a few small objects, such as a cup, a book, and a spoon. Ask your child to describe each object, and then name tools that could be used to tell about different attributes of the object (e.g., balance scale, cube trains, measuring cup).

Directions Say: *Attributes, like how long something is, how heavy something is, or how much something holds, can be measured using tools. What attributes does a carton of milk have? Draw a circle around the tools that could be used to tell about these attributes.* ★ and ✿ Have students look at the object on the left, identify the attributes that can be measured, and then draw a circle around the tools that could be used to tell about those attributes.

    Check students' drawings.

    Check students' drawings.

Directions ✸ and ✿ Have students identify what attribute the tool on the left can measure, and then draw a circle around the object or objects that could be measured with that tool. ✋ **Higher Order Thinking** Have students identify the attribute that can be measured using the tool on the left, and then draw 2 objects that could be measured using that tool. ☕ **Higher Order Thinking** Have students draw an object that could be measured by the attributes of length, weight, and capacity.

LESSON 14-5

DESCRIBE OBJECTS BY MEASURABLE ATTRIBUTES

LESSON OVERVIEW   FOCUS • COHERENCE • RIGOR

FOCUS

Domain K.MD Measurement and Data

Cluster K.MD.A Describe and compare measurable attributes.

Content Standard K.MD.A.1 Describe measurable attributes of objects, such as length or weight. Describe several measurable attributes of a single object.

Mathematical Practices MP.4, MP.5, MP.6, MP.7

Objective Use words to describe how an object can be measured.

Essential Understanding Objects have measurable attributes that can be recognized and described.

COHERENCE

In Lesson 14-4, students thought about how attributes can be used to describe objects and identified tools that could help. This lesson continues work on this concept and also considers attributes that cannot be measured with tools, such as color of the object.

RIGOR

This lesson emphasizes **conceptual understanding**. By identifying nonexamples as well as examples, students are gaining a deeper understanding of what it means to describe measurable attributes. They see measurable attributes as distinct from other attributes of objects, which builds towards understanding the measurements students will work with when they measure objects in Grades 1 and 2.

 PD Watch the Listen and Look For Lesson Video.

MATH ANYTIME

Daily Common Core Review

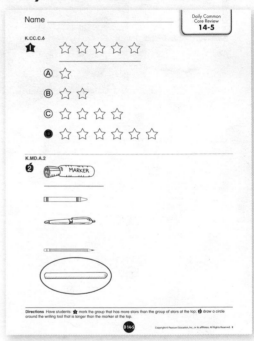

 Today's Challenge

Think Use Topic 14 problems any time during this topic.

ENGLISH LANGUAGE LEARNERS

Speaking Speak using content area vocabulary in context.

Use with the Solve & Share on Student's Edition p. 829.

Display a measuring cup, connecting cubes, balance scale. Point to the measuring cup. Say: *A measuring cup can be used to measure liquids.* Ask students to point to examples in the classroom of what a measuring cup can be used to measure. Point to the cubes. Say: *Cubes can be used to measure length.* Ask students to identify examples in the classroom of what cubes

can be used to measure. Point to the scales. Say: *Balance scales can be used to measure weight.* Ask students to identify examples of what scales can be used to measure.

Beginning Point to the measuring cup, cubes, and scale. Display a marker. Ask: *What will be used to measure a marker?* Students will respond using the sentence stem: "___ will be used to measure." [Cubes] Continue the process with objects found in the classroom.

Intermediate Display a marker. Ask: *What will be used to measure a marker? Why?*

Students will respond using the sentence stem: "___ [Cubes] will be used to measure because ___." Continue the process with objects found in the classroom.

Advanced Instruct students to work with partners to find objects in the classroom that can be measured using a measuring cup, cubes, and scales. Ask partner groups to explain to other partner groups why the measuring cup, cubes, or scales are used to measure the objects.

Summarize What is a measuring cup, cubes, and a balance scale used to measure?

DEVELOP: PROBLEM-BASED LEARNING

PEARSON
realize
PearsonRealize.com

COHERENCE: Engage students by connecting prior knowledge to new ideas.

Students describe the different ways an object can be measured. They also think about the tools they would use to measure it. This prepares students for the next part of the lesson where they select tools from given options as they identify attributes that can be measured for different objects.

10–15 min

Solve

Whole Class

BEFORE

1. Pose the Solve-and-Share Problem
MP.5 Use Appropriate Tools Strategically
In this problem, students think about which attributes of an object they can measure. They choose tools based on whether they are appropriate to measure these attributes.

Say: *Choose an object in your classroom to draw. Describe all the ways you could measure it. Then draw the tools you could use to measure the object.*

2. Build Understanding
What are you asked to do? [Choose an object and describe all the ways it can be measured; Draw tools I can use to measure the object.] *What attributes can describe objects?* [Sample answers: Length, height, weight, capacity]

Small Group

DURING

3. Ask Guiding Questions As Needed
Can some objects be measured in more than one way? [Yes] *Is the same tool always helpful for measuring every attribute?* [No; Sample answer: Some tools are only helpful for measuring certain attributes.]

Whole Class

AFTER

4. Share and Discuss Solutions
Start with students' solutions. Have them share the strategies they used to solve the problem. If needed, project and analyze Kiera's work to show different tools that can be used to measure attributes of an object.

5. Transition to the Visual Learning Bridge
You have thought about how an object can be measured and which tools you can use to measure it. Later in this lesson, you choose tools and tell attributes that can be measured for different objects.

6. Extension for Early Finishers
Name an object (or another object if one was already chosen) that you can measure its length, weight, and capacity. Explain how you would measure each of these attributes. [Answers will vary.]

Solve & Share   Name _____

Lesson 14-5
Describe Objects by Measurable Attributes

See margin for sample student work.

Directions Say: *Choose an object in your classroom to draw. Describe all the ways you could measure it. Then draw the tools you could use to measure the object.*

I can ...
use my words to describe how an object can be measured.

Content Standards
K.MD.A.1
Mathematical Practices
MP.4, MP.5, MP.6, MP.7

Topic 14 | Lesson 5   Digital Resources at PearsonRealize.com   eight hundred twenty-nine **829**

Analyze Student Work

Kiera's Work

Adrian's Work

Kiera chooses a pencil and explains that she can measure its length and its weight. Kiera explains she will not measure the capacity of the pencil because she cannot fill it with anything. Kiera draws appropriate tools to tell about the two attributes she identified.

Adrian chooses a pencil jar and explains that he can measure how tall it is and also how much it holds. He draws appropriate tools to tell about the two attributes he identified. Adrian did not consider that weight is also a measurable attribute of the pencil jar.

DEVELOP: VISUAL LEARNING

The *Visual Learning Bridge* connects students' thinking in Solve & Share to important math ideas in the lesson. Use the *Visual Learning Bridge* to make these ideas explicit. Also available as a *Visual Learning Animation Plus* at PearsonRealize.com

Visual Learning

Learn   Glossary

MP.6 Be Precise *What object is Marta looking at?* [Vase] *What attributes of the vase could Marta measure?* [Height, weight, capacity] *What does it mean to measure the height of the vase?* [Find how tall the vase is.] *The weight of the vase?* [How heavy the vase is] *The capacity of the vase?* [How much it holds]

MP.5 Use Appropriate Tools Strategically *Marta is thinking about three tools she can use to measure the vase. Which tool would Marta use to tell about the height of the vase?* [Cubes] *The weight of the vase?* [Balance scale] *The capacity of the vase?* [Measuring cup]

What attributes of the vase is Marta thinking about? [The color; a use for the vase] *Can Marta use any of the tools to tell about these attributes?* [No]

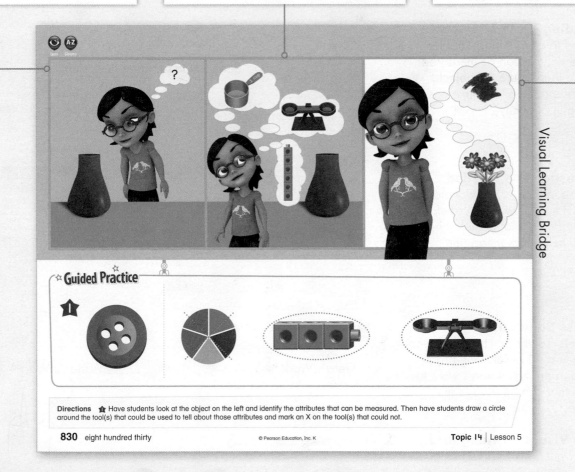

Visual Learning Bridge

Guided Practice

1

Directions ★ Have students look at the object on the left and identify the attributes that can be measured. Then have students draw a circle around the tool(s) that could be used to tell about those attributes and mark an X on the tool(s) that could not.

830 eight hundred thirty   © Pearson Education, Inc. K   **Topic 14** | Lesson 5

Complete the *Do You Understand? Show Me!* problem before starting Guided Practice.

Do You Understand? Show Me! **MP.5 Use Appropriate Tools Strategically** Ask students to choose one of the tools and explain how Marta will use it to measure an attribute of the vase.

 Ask the following Essential Question: *How can you use tools to describe attributes of objects?* [Sample answer: I can use cubes to tell about length or height, a balance scale to tell about weight, and a measuring cup to tell about capacity.]

Error Intervention: Item 1

If students do not see why the color wheel cannot be used to tell about a measurable attribute,

then remind students to think about attributes that can be measured such as length, height, weight, and capacity. *Could you use this tool to find how long the button is? How heavy it is? How much it holds?* [No]

1 RtI **Reteaching** Assign Reteaching Set C, p. 844.

✔ QUICK CHECK

Check mark indicates items for prescribing differentiation on the next page.
Items 6 and 8 are worth 1 point. Item 9 is worth up to 3 points.

Items 2–5 If students seem to grasp the concept quickly, ask about other tools that can be used instead of, or in addition to, the tools they circled, such as cubes for Item 2 or paper cups for Item 5. *There are different tools you can use to tell about attributes of objects. The tools you are circling are examples of some of these tools.*

Item 5 MP.7 Look for Patterns Ask students to look back at the color wheel tool in each item. *What do you notice about your answers?* [The color wheel tool is always marked with an X.] *Why is this?* [This does not tell about an attribute that can be measured.]

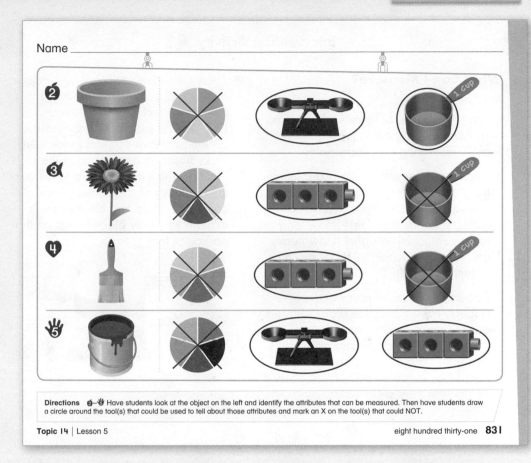

Name _____

Directions 👆–✋ Have students look at the object on the left and identify the attributes that can be measured. Then have students draw a circle around the tool(s) that could be used to tell about those attributes and mark an X on the tool(s) that could NOT.

Topic 14 | Lesson 5

eight hundred thirty-one **831**

Item 6 Ask students to explain the attributes they identified based on the tools they circled. *What attribute can you tell about with the cubes?* [Length or height] *What attribute can you tell about with the balance scale?* [Weight]

Items 8 and 9 MP.4 Model with Math Students draw a picture to demonstrate their understanding of how tools can be used to describe measurable attributes of an object. Students should consider the context of the items as they talk about their drawings. For Item 8, *Think about the attributes you are describing with the tools you chose.* For Item 9, *Can you draw the same object for both answers?* [No, one object can be measured with cubes. The other object cannot be measured with cubes.] Students can compare their answers with a partner. Discuss how they know whether their answers are reasonable.

Coherence Item 8 builds on work completed in this lesson and Lesson 14-4 by switching the steps students have typically taken on most other items in these lessons. This focuses thinking on attributes of objects in a different way. Students think of an object they could measure with the tools rather than choosing which tools could measure a given object.

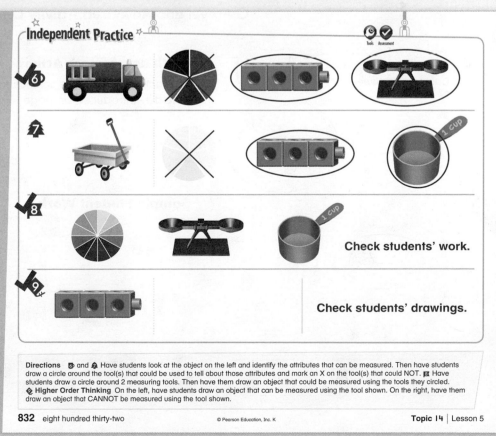

Independent Practice

Check students' work.

Check students' drawings.

Directions 6 and 7 Have students look at the object on the left and identify the attributes that can be measured. Then have students draw a circle around the tool(s) that could be used to tell about those attributes and mark an X on the tool(s) that could NOT. 8 Have students draw a circle around 2 measuring tools. Then have them draw an object that could be measured using the tools they circled. ♦ **Higher Order Thinking** On the left, have students draw an object that can be measured using the tool shown. On the right, have them draw an object that CANNOT be measured using the tool shown.

832 eight hundred thirty-two

© Pearson Education, Inc. K

Topic 14 | Lesson 5

2 RtI

Use the **QUICK CHECK** on the previous page to prescribe differentiated instruction.

I Intervention
0–3 points on the Quick Check

O On-Level
4 points on the Quick Check

A Advanced
5 points on the Quick Check

Intervention Activity **I**

What Can I Measure?
Materials
Classroom objects, balance scale, colored pencils, connecting cubes (or Teaching Tool 8), measuring cup, sticky notes

- Discuss the measurable attributes: length, height, weight, and capacity. *What are you describing if you describe an object's length or height?* [How long or tall an object is] *Weight?* [How heavy an object is] *Capacity?* [How much an object can hold]

- Distribute two sticky notes to each student. Put the balance scale, colored pencil, cubes, and measuring cup in a group. Put the classroom objects in another group. Have each student choose a classroom object and draw it on each of their sticky notes.

- *Think about the attributes we discussed and which of those can be measured for your object. Which of these tools can be used to tell about those attributes?* Have students place their sticky notes on one or two of the tools that they think can be used to tell about the attributes of their object. Look at each sticky note and have students explain why they placed them on that particular tool.

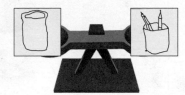

Reteach **I**

Name _____

Reteach to Build Understanding
14-5

Check students' drawings.

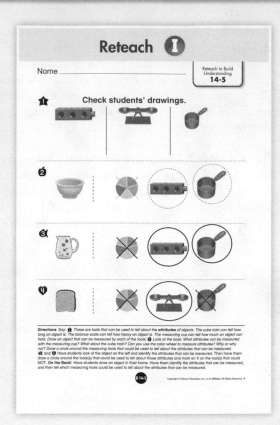

Directions Say: ★ These are tools that can be used to tell about the **attributes** of objects. The cube train can tell how long an object is. The balance scale can tell how heavy an object is. The measuring cup can tell how much an object can hold. Draw an object that can be measured by each of the tools. ❷ Look at the bowl. What attributes can be measured with the measuring cup? What about the cube train? Can you use the color wheel to measure attributes? Why or why not? Draw a circle around the measuring tools that could be used to tell about the attributes that can be measured. ❸ and ❹ Have students look at the object on the left and identify the attributes that can be measured. Then have them draw a circle around the tool(s) that could be used to tell about those attributes and mark an X on the tool(s) that could NOT. **On the Back!** Have students draw an object in their home. Have them identify the attributes that can be measured, and then tell which measuring tools could be used to tell about the attributes that can be measured.

B 14-5   Copyright © Pearson Education, Inc., or its affiliates. All Rights Reserved. K

On-Level and Advanced Activity Centers **O** **A**

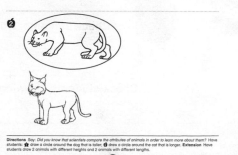

Name _____

Compare Attributes of Animals

Math and Science Activity
14-5

Directions Say: Did you know that scientists compare the attributes of animals in order to learn more about them? Have students: ★ draw a circle around the dog that is taller; ❷ draw a circle around the cat that is longer. **Extension** Have students draw 2 animals with different heights and 2 animals with different lengths.

Math and Science Activity   14-5   Copyright © Pearson Education, Inc., or its affiliates. All Rights Reserved. K

Math and Science Activity **STEM**
This activity revisits the science theme, **Using Materials to Create Shade,** introduced on page 799 of the Student's Edition.

Sample Student Work

TIMING
The time allocated to Step 3 will depend on the teacher's instructional decisions and differentiation routines.

15–30 min

 Help   Tools   Games

PEARSON
realize
PearsonRealize.com

Technology Center

Tools

Games

Math Tools and Math Games

A link to a specific math tools activity or math game to use with this lesson is provided at PearsonRealize.com.

Leveled Assignment

 Items 1–4   Items 2–5   Items 3–6

Name _____

Homework & Practice 14-5

Describe Objects by Measurable Attributes

Another Look!

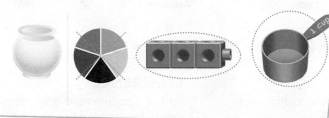

HOME ACTIVITY Show your child several household objects, such as a plate or a mug. Have him or her describe each object, and then name the tool(s) that could be used to tell about the different attributes. Then have him or her name an attribute that could NOT be measured by one of the tools.

1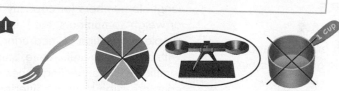

2

Directions Say: *Attributes, like how tall something is, how heavy something is, or how much something holds, can be measured using tools. What attributes does a bowl have? Draw a circle around the tool(s) that could be used to tell about these attributes. Then mark an X on the tool(s) that could NOT.* ✿ and ❷ Have students look at the object on the left and identify the attributes that can be measured. Then have students draw a circle around the tool(s) that could be used to tell about those attributes and mark an X on the tool(s) that could NOT.

Topic 14 | Lesson 5   Digital Resources at PearsonRealize.com   eight hundred thirty-three **833**

3

4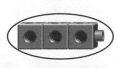

5    **Check students' work.**

6   **Check students' drawings.**

Directions ❸ and ❹ Have students look at the object on the left and identify the attributes that can be measured. Then have students draw a circle around the tool(s) that could be used to tell about those attributes and mark an X on the tool(s) that could NOT. ✋ **Higher Order Thinking** Have students draw a circle around 2 measuring tools. Then have them draw an object that could be measured using those tools. ❻ **Higher Order Thinking** On the left, have students draw an object that can be measured using the tool shown. On the right, have them draw an object that CANNOT be measured using the tool shown.

834 eight hundred thirty-four   © Pearson Education, Inc. K   Topic 14 | Lesson 5

PRECISION

DIGITAL RESOURCES PearsonRealize.com

 Student and Teacher eTexts
eText

 Listen and Look For Lesson Video
PD

 Today's Challenge
Think

 Solve and Share
Solve

 Visual Learning Animation Plus
Learn

 Math Practices Animations
MP

 Animated Glossary
Glossary

 Math Tools
Tools

 Quick Check
Assessment

 Another Look Homework Video
Help

 Math Games
Games

LESSON OVERVIEW **FCR** FOCUS • COHERENCE • RIGOR

FOCUS

Math Practices MP.6 Attend to Precision.
Also **MP.3, MP.4, MP.5**

Content Standard K.MD.A.2

Objective Solve math problems about objects with measurable attributes by using precision.

Essential Understanding Good math thinkers are careful about what they write and say, so their ideas about math are clear.

Materials Connecting cubes (or Teaching Tool 8)

COHERENCE

Part of measurement is the conversion of length to numbers (or capacity to numbers, or weight to numbers, etc.). It starts with the simple connection of measuring an object with repeatable units. Here, students are familiar with connecting cubes and can compare cube trains of differing lengths with objects. They are not measuring yet, but comparing, an important step toward measuring using numbers.

RIGOR

This lesson emphasizes **application**. Rigorous mathematics instruction calls for the selection, use, and management of multiple mathematical practices. All of the problems in this lesson elicit the use of multiple mathematical practices. Use the thinking habits shown in the Solve & Share task to help focus thinking on MP.6 in the lesson.

 Watch the Listen and Look For Lesson Video.
PD

MATH ANYTIME

Daily Common Core Review

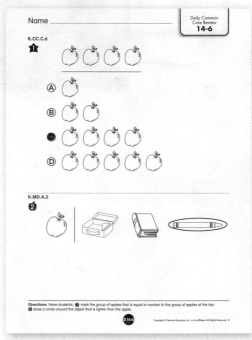

Today's Challenge

Think Use Topic 14 problems any time during this topic.

ENGLISH LANGUAGE LEARNERS

Listening Demonstrate listening comprehension by following directions.

Use with the Solve and Share on Student's Edition p. 835.

Distribute connecting cubes to students. Ask students to choose an object (e.g., book, pencil) and to build a cube train. Put students in groups of 4. Ask students to put their objects in the middle of the group for all to see. Students should compare the objects to their cube train. Have the group ask and answer

questions about each object's length to compare the objects and identify one of the objects (e.g., Is the object longer than my cube train?).

Beginning Have students use the following sentence stems to answer: "This ___ [object] is longer than/shorter than/the same length as the ____. [cube train]"

Intermediate Ask students to use complete sentences to describe, compare, and identify the objects.

Advanced Ask students to compare the objects using the words *longer, shorter,* and *the same length.* Ask students to explain how they identified each object.

Summarize How can you identify an object from a description of its length?

COHERENCE: Engage students by connecting prior knowledge to new ideas.
Students compare by length to identify the shorter object. This prepares them for the next part of the lesson where they build cube towers and cube trains of given lengths and compare them with objects to identify which is taller/longer or shorter.

10–15 min

Solve

BEFORE

1. Pose the Solve-and-Share Problem
MP.6 Be Precise In this problem, students build a cube train using exactly the given number of cubes. They explain how they compared the cube train to another object to find which is shorter.

Give each student 10 connecting cubes.

Say: *Marta wants to compare the length of a ribbon to the length of a cube train so she can draw a circle around the object that is shorter. How can she do this? Explain where you place the cube train on the page and why.*

Tell students to think about these Thinking Habits as they solve the problem.
Am I using numbers, units, and symbols correctly? Is my answer clear?

2. Build Understanding
What are you asked to do? [Find a way to compare 2 objects to see which is shorter.]
What tools do you have to solve the problem? [Connecting cubes]

DURING

3. Ask Guiding Questions As Needed
How many cubes should be in your cube train? [3] *Where could you line up the cube train?* [Sample answer: At the left end of the ribbon]

AFTER

4. Share and Discuss Solutions
Start with students' solutions. If needed, project Trevor's work to demonstrate how to compare lengths.

5. Transition to the Visual Learning Bridge
You have made a cube train and explained how to compare its length to the length of another object. Later in this lesson, you will make cube trains of different lengths and compare them to other objects.

6. Extension for Early Finishers
Have students use large paper clips to measure a sheet of paper. Have them link the clips and use them to measure the paper's length. Have them count and write the number. Then have them write a number of paper clips that is shorter than the length of the paper.

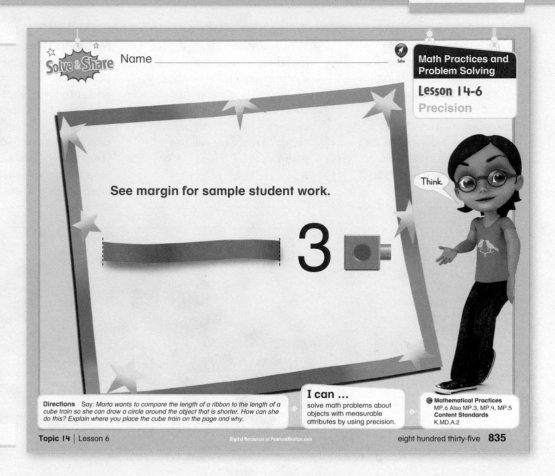

Solve & Share Name _____

Solve

Math Practices and Problem Solving

Lesson 14-6
Precision

See margin for sample student work.

Think.

3

Directions Say: *Marta wants to compare the length of a ribbon to the length of a cube train so she can draw a circle around the object that is shorter. How can she do this? Explain where you place the cube train on the page and why.*

I can …
solve math problems about objects with measurable attributes by using precision.

⊕ **Mathematical Practices**
MP.6 Also MP.3, MP.4, MP.5
Content Standards
K.MD.A.2

Topic 14 | Lesson 6   Digital Resources at PearsonRealize.com   eight hundred thirty-five **835**

Analyze Student Work

Trevor's Work

Holly's Work

Trevor builds a cube train using the correct number of cubes. He explains that if he lines up one end of his cube train with one end of the ribbon, he can look at at the other end to compare. Trevor circles the shorter object.

Holly builds a cube train using the correct number of cubes. She lines up the cubes to compare but circles the longer object.

STEP 2

DEVELOP: VISUAL LEARNING

PEARSON
realize
PearsonRealize.com

Learn   Glossary

The *Visual Learning Bridge* connects students' thinking in Solve & Share to important math ideas in the lesson. Use the *Visual Learning Bridge* to make these ideas explicit. Also available as a *Visual Learning Animation Plus* at PearsonRealize.com

E L L
Visual Learning

What object do you see? [Pencil] *Marta wants to see whether this pencil is longer or shorter than 7 cubes. What attribute is Marta comparing?* [Length] *Do you think the pencil will be longer, or the cubes will be longer?* [Answers will vary.]

What is Marta doing? [Building a cube train] *If Marta uses all the cubes on the table to make her cube train, will she have used the correct number of cubes?* [Yes; She will use seven cubes.]

MP.6 Be Precise *Why does it help to line up the ends of the objects you are comparing?* [If the ends are lined up, I can look at the other end to compare the length.] *Is the cube train longer than the pencil?* [Yes] *How do you know?* [The cube train sticks out farther than the pencil when they are lined up next to each other.]

MP.4 Model with Math *What does the 7 and the picture of the cube represent?* [Marta's cube train of 7 cubes] *Marta is going to circle the picture of the longer object. Should she draw a circle here? Why?* [Yes; This represents the cube train and the cube train is longer than the pencil.]

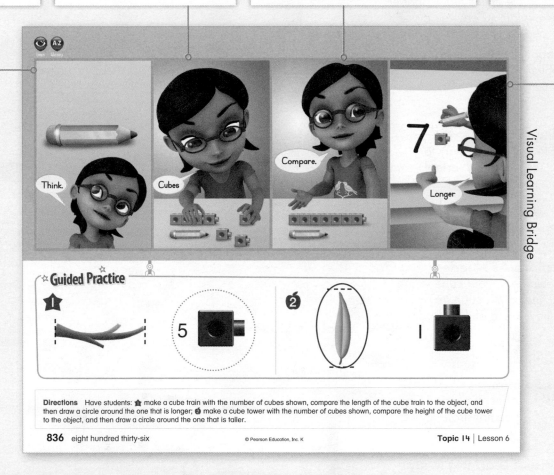

Visual Learning Bridge

Guided Practice

1   5

2 |

Directions Have students: ⭐ make a cube train with the number of cubes shown, compare the length of the cube train to the object, and then draw a circle around the one that is longer; 🍎 make a cube tower with the number of cubes shown, compare the height of the cube tower to the object, and then draw a circle around the one that is taller.

836 eight hundred thirty-six   © Pearson Education, Inc. K   Topic 14 | Lesson 6

Complete the *Do You Understand? Show Me!* problem before starting Guided Practice.

Do You Understand? Show Me! MP.6 Be Precise

Distribute 4 cubes to each student. *Which is longer, your foot or a 4-cube train? What could you use to find out?* [I can use a cube train with 4 cubes. I can put the cube train next to my foot and compare the length.]

Essential
Question

Ask the following Essential Question: *How can you compare the lengths of two objects?* [Sample answer: I can line up the ends of the two objects and look at the other ends. I can see which object sticks out farther to see which is longer and which is shorter.]

Error Intervention: Item 2

If students' comparisons are incorrect,

then help them use the dashed lines as guides to compare the ends of the pictured object.

Reteaching Assign Reteaching Set D, p. 844.

☑ QUICK CHECK

Check mark indicates items for prescribing differentiation on the next page. Items 4 and 5 are each worth 1 point. The Performance Assessment on page 838 is worth up to 3 points.

20–30 min

Tools Assessment

MP.6 Be Precise Listen and look for these behaviors as evidence that students are exhibiting proficiency with MP.6.

- computes accurately
- accurately uses problem-solving strategies
- specifies and uses units of measure appropriately
- decides whether an exact answer or estimate is needed

Items 3–7 MP.4 Model with Math Students can use 2 cube trains to compare. One is given and one is equal to the length of the object. *What does the train with more cubes tell you?* [The longer cube train represents a longer length.]

Item 7 MP.3 Construct Arguments You can extend the task by asking students to consider other lengths in relation to their answer. *Can you tell from your answer whether a cube train with 4 cubes is longer than the twig? Explain.* [Yes; I know a 5-cube train is shorter, and a 4-cube train will be shorter than that.]

Item 8 MP.5 Use Appropriate Tools Strategically Ask students to tell how they would use the tool they have chosen. As appropriate, have students explain why this is the tool they would choose to use.

Item 9 MP.6 Be Precise Look for students who are able to explain their answer clearly. *Would you be able to solve the problem without knowing the number of cubes?* [No; The problem asks how many cubes long the train is.]

Item 10 MP.3 Critique Reasoning Look for students who are able to clearly explain why Carlos is incorrect, focusing on how the train should be lined up with the ribbon. *What might Carlos have done to think he was correct?* [Sample answer: Carlos may not have lined up one end of the cube train with the ribbon.]

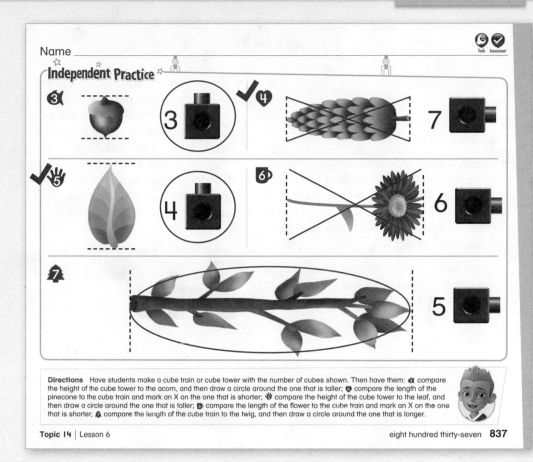

Directions Have students make a cube train or cube tower with the number of cubes shown. Then have them: ❸ compare the height of the cube tower to the acorn, and then draw a circle around the one that is taller; ❹ compare the length of the pinecone to the cube train and mark an X on the one that is shorter; ❺ compare the height of the cube tower to the leaf, and then draw a circle around the one that is taller; ❻ compare the length of the flower to the cube train and mark an X on the one that is shorter; ❼ compare the length of the cube train to the twig, and then draw a circle around the one that is longer.

Topic 14 | Lesson 6   eight hundred thirty-seven **837**

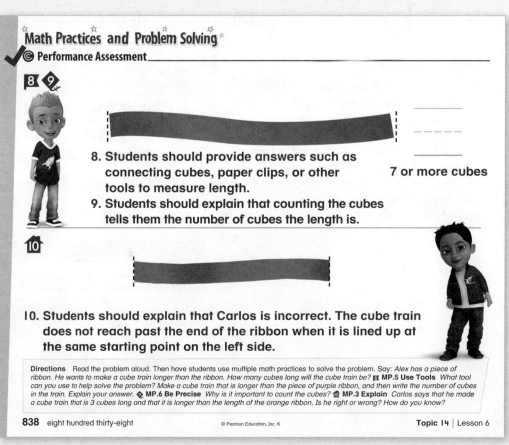

Math Practices and Problem Solving
☑ ⓒ Performance Assessment

8. Students should provide answers such as connecting cubes, paper clips, or other tools to measure length.   **7 or more cubes**
9. Students should explain that counting the cubes tells them the number of cubes the length is.

10. Students should explain that Carlos is incorrect. The cube train does not reach past the end of the ribbon when it is lined up at the same starting point on the left side.

Directions Read the problem aloud. Then have students use multiple math practices to solve the problem. Say: *Alex has a piece of ribbon. He wants to make a cube train longer than the ribbon. How many cubes long will the cube train be?* ❽ **MP.5 Use Tools** *What tool can you use to help solve the problem? Make a cube train that is longer than the piece of purple ribbon, and then write the number of cubes in the train. Explain your answer.* ❾ **MP.6 Be Precise** *Why is it important to count the cubes?* ❿ **MP.3 Explain** *Carlos says that he made a cube train that is 3 cubes long and that it is longer than the length of the orange ribbon. Is he right or wrong? How do you know?*

838 eight hundred thirty-eight   © Pearson Education, Inc. K   Topic 14 | Lesson 6

837–838

STEP 3 ASSESS AND DIFFERENTIATE

Use the **QUICK CHECK** on the previous page to prescribe differentiated instruction.

I Intervention
0–3 points on the Quick Check

O On-Level
4 points on the Quick Check

A Advanced
5 points on the Quick Check

Intervention Activity **I**

Which Train?

Materials

Connecting cubes (or Teaching Tool 8), classroom objects

• Display a classroom object, such as a pencil. Explain that you want to find a cube train that is longer than the pencil. Have students make a cube train that is 3 cubes long. Count to check the cube trains are correct.

• Show how to align the cube train under the pencil. *Is this cube train longer than the pencil?* [No, it is too short.]

• Have students make a new cube train. Ensure the given number of cubes will make the train longer than the pencil. Count to check the cube trains are correct, then compare. *Is this cube train longer or shorter than the pencil?* [Longer] Have students explain how they know that a train of this many cubes is longer than the pencil.

Reteach **I**

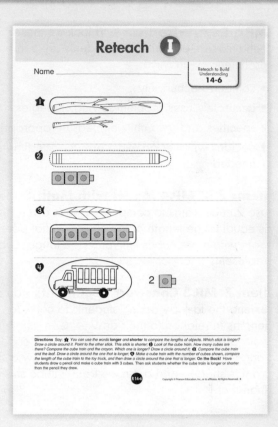

Name _____

Reteach to Build
Understanding
14-6

Directions Say: ★ You can use the words **longer** and **shorter** to compare the lengths of objects. Which stick is longer? Draw a circle around it. Point to the other stick. This stick is shorter; ❷ Look at the cube train. How many cubes are there? Compare the cube train and the crayon. Which one is longer? Draw a circle around it. ❸ Compare the cube train and the leaf. Draw a circle around the one that is longer; ❹ Make a cube train with the number of cubes shown, compare the length of the cube train to the toy truck, and then draw a circle around the one that is longer. **On the Back!** Have students draw a pencil and make a cube train with 3 cubes. Then ask students whether the cube train is longer or shorter than the pencil they drew.

R14-6   Copyright © Pearson Education, Inc., or its affiliates. All Rights Reserved. K

On-Level and Advanced Activity Centers **O** **A**

Center Games

Students work in pairs. In the On-Level activity, students will make a cube train the length of one ribbon and determine whether other ribbons are shorter/longer. In the Advanced activity, students will determine how many ribbons are longer than the ribbon that matches a number tile.

★ On-Level

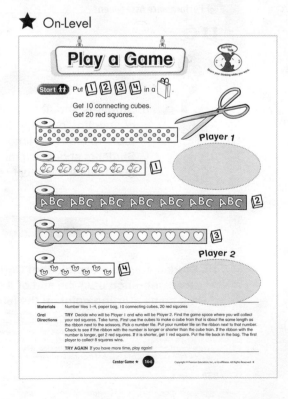

★★ Advanced

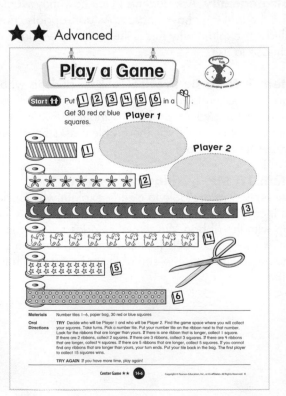

839A   Topic 14

TIMING

The time allocated to Step 3 will depend on the teacher's instructional decisions and differentiation routines.

15–30 min

Help   **Tools**   **Games**

Technology Center ⓘ ⓞ Ⓐ

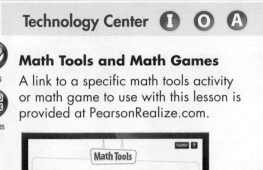

Tools

Games

Math Tools and Math Games

A link to a specific math tools activity or math game to use with this lesson is provided at PearsonRealize.com.

Leveled Assignment

ⓘ Items 1–7 (with help as needed)   ⓞ Items 1–7   Ⓐ Items 1–7

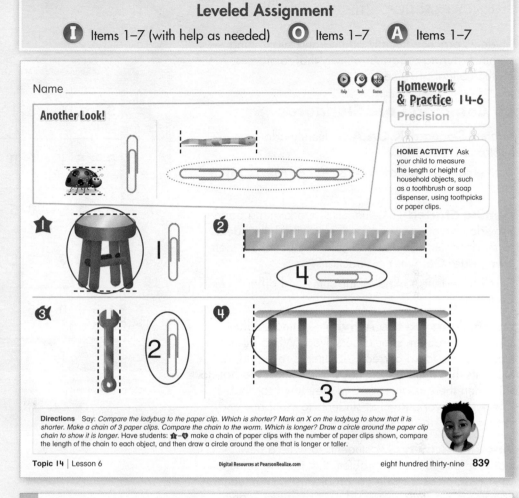

Name _____

Help Tools Games

Homework & Practice 14-6

Precision

Another Look!

HOME ACTIVITY Ask your child to measure the length or height of household objects, such as a toothbrush or soap dispenser, using toothpicks or paper clips.

1 | 1

2 4

3 2

4 3

Directions Say: *Compare the ladybug to the paper clip. Which is shorter? Mark an X on the ladybug to show that it is shorter. Make a chain of 3 paper clips. Compare the chain to the worm. Which is longer? Draw a circle around the paper clip chain to show it is longer.* Have students: ★–♥ *make a chain of paper clips with the number of paper clips shown, compare the length of the chain to each object, and then draw a circle around the one that is longer or taller.*

Topic 14 | Lesson 6   Digital Resources at PearsonRealize.com   eight hundred thirty-nine **839**

© **Performance Assessment** _____

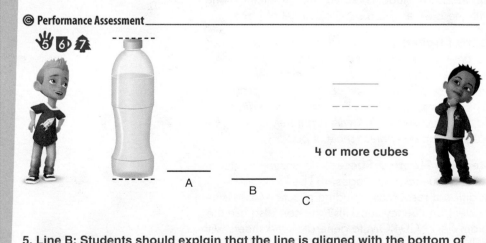

✋5 🌀6 🌲7

4 or more cubes

A   B   C

5. Line B; Students should explain that the line is aligned with the bottom of the water bottle and will provide a direct comparison.

6. Check students' work.

7. Students should explain that Carlos is incorrect. Their explanations should include information such as, Line A is above the bottom of the water bottle or Line B is lined up with the bottom of the water bottle.

Directions Read the problem aloud. Then have students use multiple math practices to solve the problem. Say: *Alex wants to build a cube tower that is taller than his water bottle. How does he know where to place the cube tower to compare the height?* ✋ **MP.6 Be Precise** *Pick a starting line. Which line do you use to compare your cube tower to the water bottle? Explain your answer.* 🌀 **MP.4 Model** *How tall is the cube tower you built? Draw a picture of the cube tower that you built, and then write the number of cubes in the tower.* 🌲 **MP.3 Explain** *Carlos picks Line A to compare. Is he right or wrong? Explain how you know.*

840 eight hundred forty   © Pearson Education, Inc. K   **Topic 14** | Lesson 6

FLUENCY PRACTICE ACTIVITY

Games

FLUENCY PRACTICE ACTIVITY

Students practice fluently adding and subtracting within 5 during a partner activity that reinforces mathematical practices.

© Common Core Standards

Content Standard K.OA.A.5 Fluently add and subtract within 5.

Mathematical Practices MP.3, MP.6, MP.7, MP.8

Getting Started Ask students to work with a partner. Provide crayons needed for the activity. Tell students to record their answers and color the boxes on their own page. Go over the directions.

Remind students to find all the sums and differences on the page.

As Students Do the Activity Remind students that each problem should be solved. When all of the boxes are colored correctly, a letter is revealed. Tell students that if the boxes they have colored do not do this, then there is an error and they need to double check their work. Remind students to compare and discuss their answers.

Another Activity Ask students to write a new addition or subtraction problem that has the same sum or difference as the original problem shown in each square. Have students record their problems along with the answers on a separate sheet of paper.

Extra Challenge *Look at the original problem and the answer you wrote in each square. If the problem is an addition problem, use the same numbers to write a correct subtraction problem. If the problem is a subtraction problem, use the numbers to write a correct addition problem. Work with a partner. Record your problems on a separate sheet of paper.*

Steps to Fluency Success To ensure all students achieve fluency, see pages 431E–431H for additional resources including practice/assessment masters on fluency subskills. You can also use the ExamView® CD-ROM to generate worksheets with multiple-choice or free-response items on fluency subskills.

Online Game The Game Center at PearsonRealize.com provides opportunities for fluency practice.

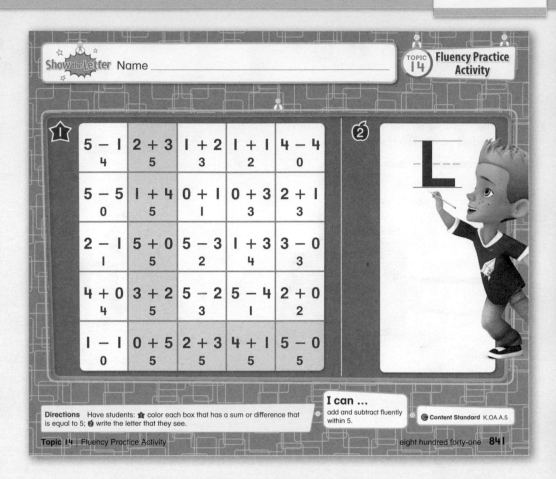

PEARSON
realize.
PearsonRealize.com

A-Z Glossary   **Games**

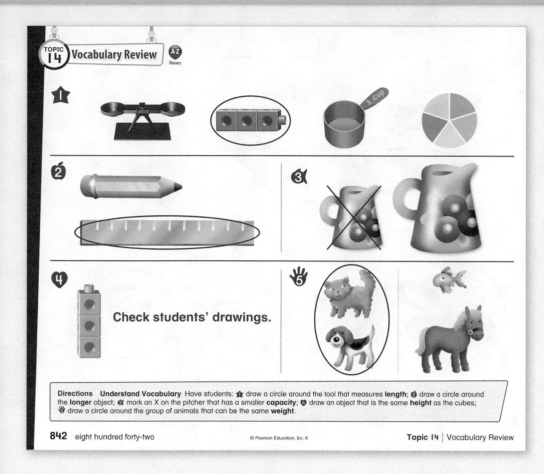

Check students' drawings.

Directions Understand Vocabulary Have students: ✦ draw a circle around the tool that measures **length**; ✿ draw a circle around the **longer** object; ✖ mark an X on the pitcher that has a smaller **capacity**; ❶ draw an object that is the same **height** as the cubes; ✋ draw a circle around the group of animals that can be the same **weight**.

842 eight hundred forty-two   © Pearson Education, Inc. K   **Topic 14** | Vocabulary Review

VOCABULARY REVIEW

Students review vocabulary words used in the topic.

Oral Language Before students do the page, you might reinforce oral language through a class discussion involving one or more of the following activities.

- Have students define the terms in their own words.

- Have students say math sentences or math questions that use the words.

- Play a "What's My Word?" guessing game in which you or a student thinks about one of the words and says a clue that others listen to before they guess the word.

- Play a "Right or Wrong?" game in which you or a student says a sentence that uses one of the words correctly or incorrectly. Then others say "right" or "wrong."

Writing in Math After students do the page, you might further reinforce writing in math by doing one or more of the following activities.

- Tell students to close their books. Then you say the words and have students write them. Students trade papers to check whether the words are spelled correctly.

- Have students work with a partner. Each partner writes a math question that uses one of the words. Then they trade papers and give a written answer that uses the word.

Online Game The Game Center at PearsonRealize.com includes a vocabulary game that students can access any time.

RtI Item Analysis for Diagnosis and Intervention				
Reteaching Sets	**© Standards**	**Student Book Lessons**	**MDIS**	
Set A	K.MD.A.2	14-1	D60	
Set B	K.MD.A.2	14-2	D61	
Set C	K.MD.A.1	14-5	E17	
Set D	MP.6, K.MD.A.2	14-6	E26	

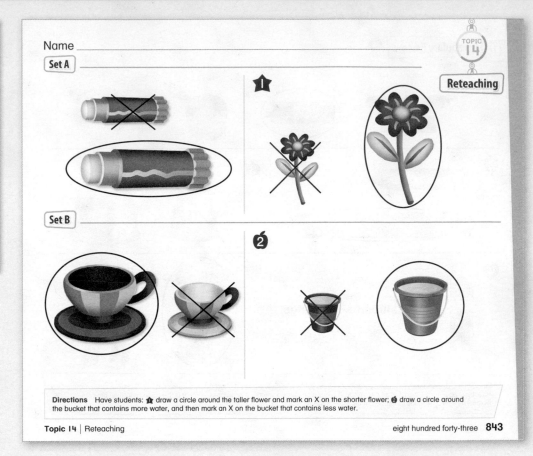

Directions Have students: ⭐ draw a circle around the taller flower and mark an X on the shorter flower; 🍎 draw a circle around the bucket that contains more water, and then mark an X on the bucket that contains less water.

Topic 14 | Reteaching   eight hundred forty-three **843**

Set C

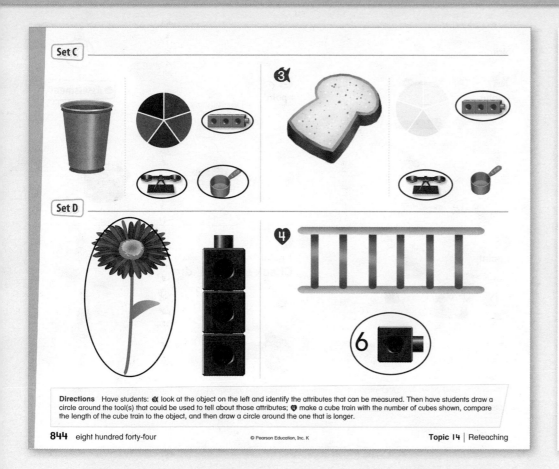

Set D

Directions Have students: ✪ look at the object on the left and identify the attributes that can be measured. Then have students draw a circle around the tool(s) that could be used to tell about those attributes; ✿ make a cube train with the number of cubes shown, compare the length of the cube train to the object, and then draw a circle around the one that is longer.

© Pearson Education, Inc. K

Topic 14 | Reteaching

Response to Intervention

1 RtI

Ongoing Intervention
- Lessons with guiding questions to assess understanding
- Support to prevent misconceptions and to reteach

2 RtI

Strategic Intervention
- Targeted to small groups who need more support
- Easy to implement

3 RtI

Intensive Intervention
- Instruction to accelerate progress
- Instruction focused on foundational skills

TOPIC ASSESSMENT

DESCRIBE AND COMPARE MEASURABLE ATTRIBUTES

ANSWERING THE TOPIC ESSENTIAL QUESTION

How can objects be compared by length, height, capacity, and weight?

Restate the Topic Essential Question from the Topic Opener or project it from the Student's Edition eText.

Ask students to answer the Essential Question (verbally or in writing) and give examples that support their answers. The following are key elements of the answer to the Essential Question. Be sure these are made explicit when discussing students' answers.

- Objects can be compared to see which is longer/shorter, heavier/lighter, or which holds more/less.

  Example: Rayanne has 2 pencils of different lengths. She wants to find out which pencil is longer. Why is it important to line up the ends of objects when comparing by length/height? [Sample answer: You can look at the other end to see which is longer.] Rayanne also has 2 different pencil jars. If one jar has a greater capacity than the other, does it hold more or hold less? [Holds more]

- Objects have measurable attributes.

  Example: Marcus has a number of school supplies: a pencil, a notebook, and a pencil case. What attributes of the pencil could he measure? [Height, weight, length] What attributes of the pencil case could he measure? [Height, weight, capacity, length]

- Different tools can be used to tell about different attributes.

  Example: Paulie is using tools from his classroom to describe the attributes of different objects. He has connecting cubes, string, a balance scale, and a measuring cup. Which tools could he use to tell about length? [Sample answer: Cubes, string] Which tool could he use to tell about capacity? [Sample answer: Cup] Which tool could he use to tell about weight? [Sample answer: Balance scale]

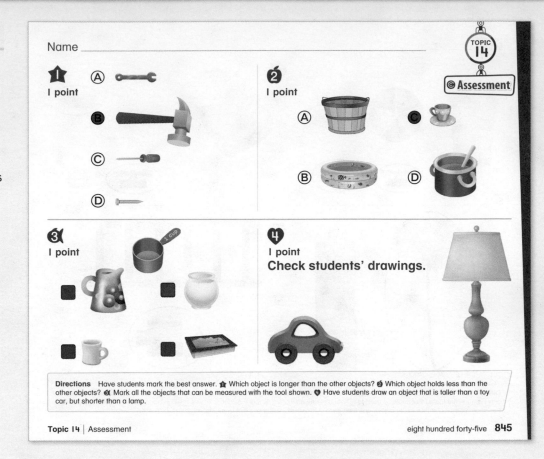

Name _____

1 I point

Ⓐ Ⓑ Ⓒ Ⓓ

2 I point

Ⓐ Ⓑ Ⓒ Ⓓ

3 I point

4 I point

Check students' drawings.

Directions Have students mark the best answer. ⬆ Which object is longer than the other objects? 🍎 Which object holds less than the other objects? ⭐ Mark all the objects that can be measured with the tool shown. 🌸 Have students draw an object that is taller than a toy car, but shorter than a lamp.

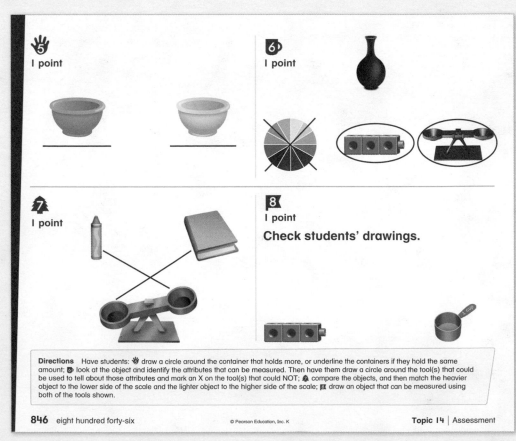

5 I point

6 I point

7 I point

8 I point

Check students' drawings.

Directions Have students: 🖐 draw a circle around the container that holds more, or underline the containers if they hold the same amount; ✋ look at the object and identify the attributes that can be measured. Then have them draw a circle around the tool(s) that could be used to tell about those attributes and mark an X on the tool(s) that could NOT; 🌲 compare the objects, and then match the heavier object to the lower side of the scale and the lighter object to the higher side of the scale; 🚩 draw an object that can be measured using both of the tools shown.

ONLINE TOPIC ASSESSMENT
An auto-scored Topic Assessment is provided at PearsonRealize.com.

EXAMVIEW® TEST GENERATOR
ExamView can be used to create a blackline-master Topic Assessment with multiple-choice and free-response items.

Assessment

Topic Assessment Masters

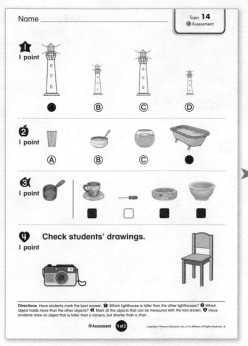

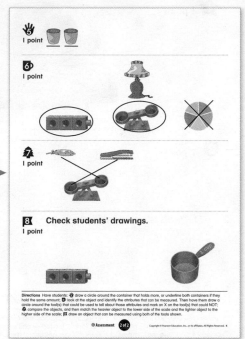

Item Analysis for Diagnosis and Intervention

Item	© Standards	DOK	MDIS
1	K.MD.A.2	1	D60
2	K.MD.A.2	1	D61
3	K.MD.A.1	1	E17
4	K.MD.A.2	3	D60
5	K.MD.A.2	1	D61
6	K.MD.A.1, MP.5	1	E17
7	K.MD.A.2, MP.1	1	D62
8	K.MD.A.1	2	E17

The Topic Assessment Masters assess the same content item for item as the Topic Assessment in the Student's Edition.

Scoring Guide

Item	Points	Topic Assessment Masters
1	1	Correct choice selected.
2	1	Correct choice selected.
3	1	Correct choices selected.
4	1	Correct object drawn.
5	1	Both objects underlined.
6	1	Correct tools of measurement circled.
7	1	Correct objects matched to each side of the balance scale.
8	1	Correct picture drawn.

TOPIC 14

TOPIC PERFORMANCE ASSESSMENT

DESCRIBE AND COMPARE MEASURABLE ATTRIBUTES

Scoring Guide

Item	Points	Topic Performance Assessment in the Student's Edition
1	1	Correct objects circled or marked with an X.
2	2	Correct drawing and both cups underlined.
	1	Correct drawing or both cups underlined.
3	2	Correct drawing and correct object circled.
	1	Correct drawing or correct object circled.
4	1	Correct tools circled and correct tool marked with an X.
5	2	Correct drawing and correct object circled.
	1	Correct drawing or correct object circled.

Item Analysis for Diagnosis and Intervention

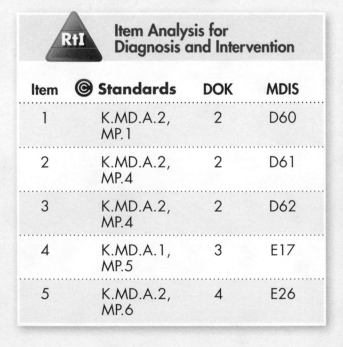

Item	Ⓒ Standards	DOK	MDIS
1	K.MD.A.2, MP.1	2	D60
2	K.MD.A.2, MP.4	2	D61
3	K.MD.A.2, MP.4	2	D62
4	K.MD.A.1, MP.5	3	E17
5	K.MD.A.2, MP.6	4	E26

Name _____

TOPIC 14

Ⓒ Performance Assessment

⭐ 1 point

② 2 points

Check students' drawings.

③ 2 points

Check students' drawings.

Directions Time for Dinner! Say: *Teddy helps his father make dinner. They use different things in the kitchen.* Have students: ⭐ look at the fork and the spoon, and then draw a circle around the longer object and mark an X on the shorter object; ② look at the yellow cup and the red cup, and then mark an X on the cup that holds less or underline the cups if they hold the same amount. Then draw a container that would hold more than the red cup; ③ look at the turkey and the corn, and then draw a circle around the heavier object or underline the objects if they have the same weight. Then draw an object that would weigh less than the corn.

Topic 14 | Performance Assessment   eight hundred forty-seven **847**

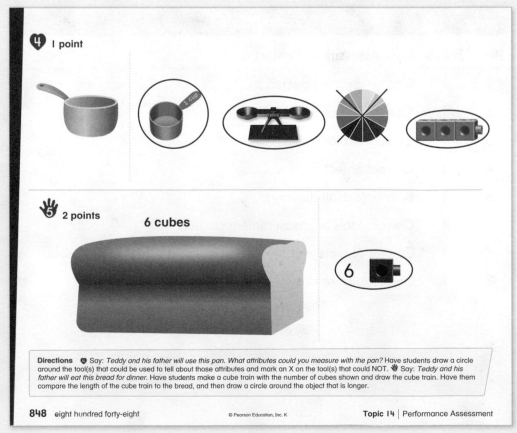

④ 1 point

⑤ 2 points

6 cubes

6 🔲

Directions ④ Say: *Teddy and his father will use this pan. What attributes could you measure with the pan?* Have students draw a circle around the tool(s) that could be used to tell about those attributes and mark an X on the tool(s) that could NOT. ⑤ Say: *Teddy and his father will eat this bread for dinner.* Have students make a cube train with the number of cubes shown and draw the cube train. Have them compare the length of the cube train to the bread, and then draw a circle around the object that is longer.

848 eight hundred forty-eight   © Pearson Education, Inc. K   Topic 14 | Performance Assessment

Topic Performance Assessment Masters

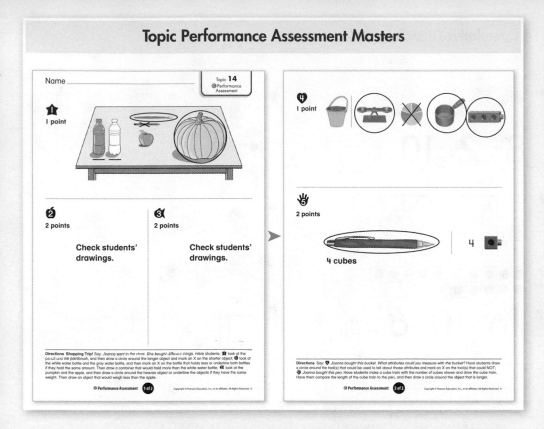

Item Analysis for Diagnosis and Intervention

Item	© Standards	DOK	MDIS
1	K.MD.A.2, MP.1	2	D60
2	K.MD.A.2, MP.4	2	D61
3	K.MD.A.2, MP.4	2	D62
4	K.MD.A.1, MP.5	3	E17
5	K.MD.A.2, MP.6	4	E26

Scoring Guide

Item	Points	Topic Performance Assessment in the Student's Edition
1	1	Correct objects circled or marked with an X.
2	2	Correct drawing and both bottles underlined.
	1	Correct drawing or both bottles underlined.
3	2	Correct drawing and correct object circled.
	1	Correct drawing or correct object circled.
4	1	Correct tools circled and correct tool marked with an X.
5	2	Correct drawing and correct object circled.
	1	Correct drawing or correct object circled.

Topics 1–14 Cumulative/Benchmark Assessment

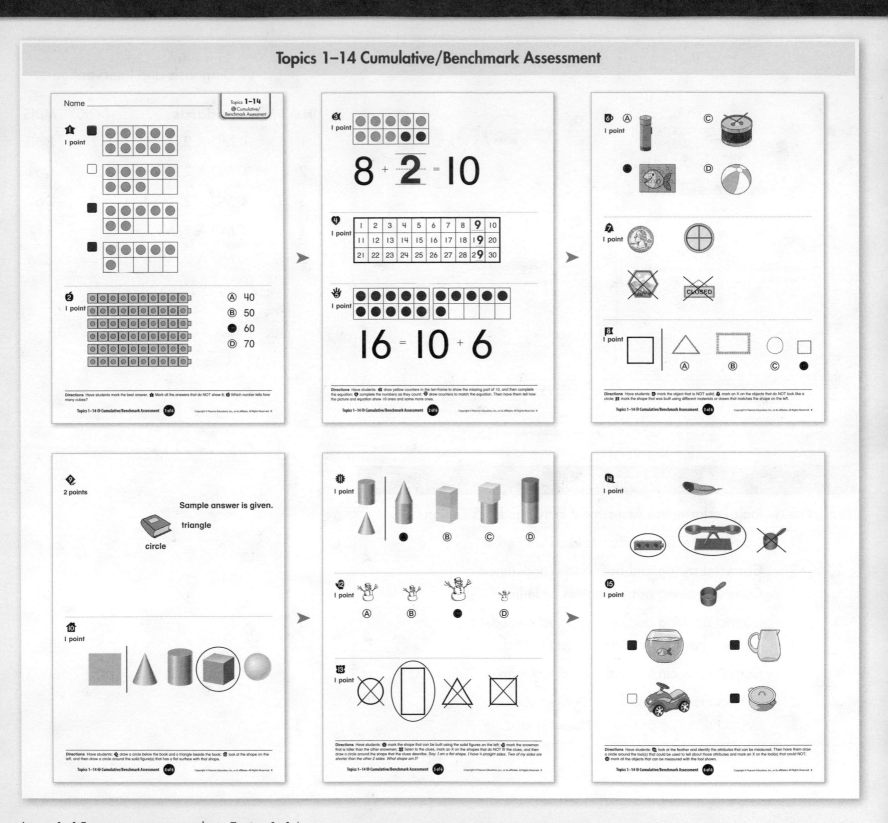

Items 1–15 assess content taught in Topics 1–14.

ONLINE CUMULATIVE/BENCHMARK
ASSESSMENT
An auto-scored Cumulative/Benchmark
Assessment is provided at PearsonRealize.com.

Assessment

RtI Item Analysis for Diagnosis and Intervention

Item	© Standards	DOK	MDIS	Item	© Standards	DOK	MDIS	Item	© Standards	DOK	MDIS
1	K.CC.B.4a	1	A3, A8	6	K.G.A.3	1	D31	11	K.G.B.6	1	D33
2	K.CC.A.1	1	A16	7	K.G.A.2	1	D29, D30	12	K.MD.A.2	1	D9
3	K.OA.A.4, MP.4	2	B11	8	K.G.B.5	1	D29	13	K.G.B.4, MP.1	2	D30
4	K.CC.A.1, MP.7	1	A26	9	K.G.A.1, MP.6	3	D28	14	K.MD.A.1, MP.5	1	E17
5	K.NBT.A.1, MP.3	2	A88	10	K.G.B.4	2	D32	15	K.MD.A.1	1	E17

For items worth 1 point, responses should be completely correct to get a score of 1 point. For other items, use the Scoring Guide below.

Scoring Guide

Item	Points	Topics 1–14 Cumulative/Benchmark Assessment
9	2	Draws a circle and a triangle in the correct position relative to the book.
	1	Draws either a circle or a triangle in the correct position relative to the book.

ENDOF-YEAR ASSESSMENT

Topics 1–14 End-of-Year Assessment

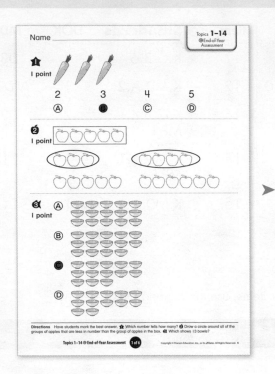

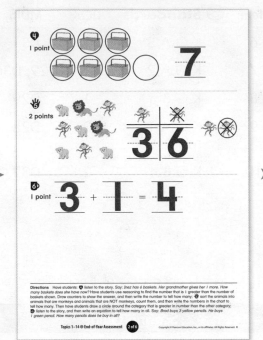

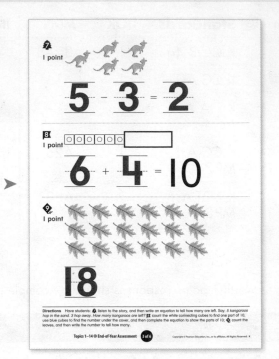

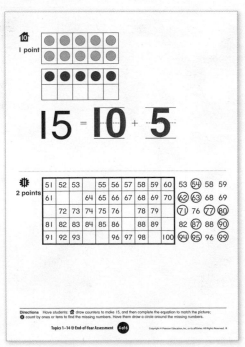

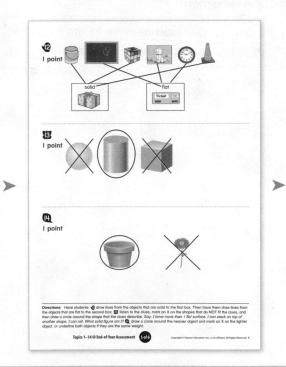

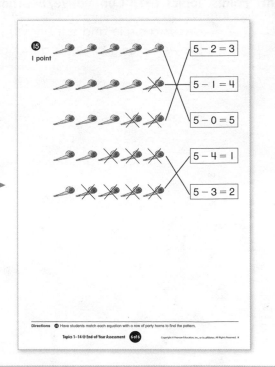

ONLINE END-OF-YEAR ASSESSMENT
An auto-scored End-of-Year Assessment is
provided at PearsonRealize.com.

RtI Item Analysis for Diagnosis and Intervention

Item	Standards	DOK	MDIS	Item	Standards	DOK	MDIS	Item	Standards	DOK	MDIS
1	K.CC.B.4a, K.CC.B.5	1	A1	7	K.OA.A.2, K.OA.A.5, MP.4	2	B6	13	K.G.B.4, MP.1	1	D31
2	K.CC.C.6, MP.2	1	A2, A7	8	K.OA.A.4, MP.2	1	B11, B18	14	K.MD.A.2, MP.6	1	D11
3	K.CC.B.5	1	A3	9	K.CC.A.3, K.CC.B.5	1	A10	15	K.OA.A.5, MP.7	1	B8
4	K.CC.B.4c, K.OA.A.2, K.CC.A.3, MP.1	2	A3	10	K.NBT.A.1, MP.8	2	A88				
5	K.MD.B.3, K.CC.C.6	2	A6, A7	11	K.CC.A.1, K.CC.A.2	1	A13				
6	K.OA.A.2, K.OA.A.5, MP.4	2	B3	12	K.G.A.3	1	D30, D31				

For items worth 1 point, responses should be completely correct to get a score of 1 point. For other items, use the Scoring Guide below.

Scoring Guide

Item	Points	Topics 1–14 End-of-Year Assessment
5	2	Correctly performs all 3 tasks in the item.
	1	Correctly performs 1 or 2 of the 3 tasks in the item.
11	2	All 11 missing numbers are circled.
	1	7–10 missing numbers are circled.

STEP UP TO GRADE 1

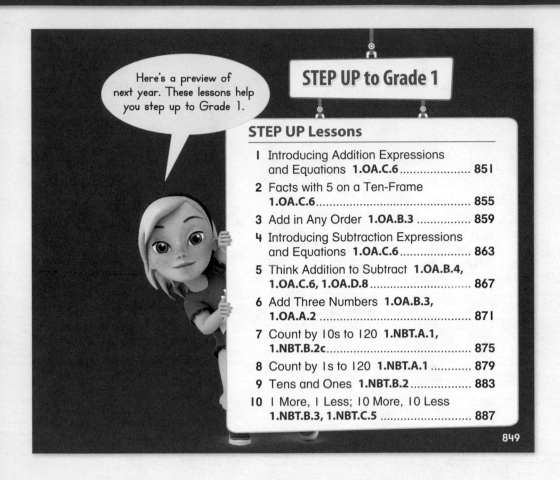

Here's a preview of next year. These lessons help you step up to Grade 1.

STEP UP to Grade 1

STEP UP Lessons

849

These Step-Up Lessons will help prepare students for the next grade. The lessons preview for students some important content from the next grade. These lessons are intended to be used at the end of the school year.

INTRODUCING ADDITION EXPRESSIONS AND EQUATIONS

DIGITAL RESOURCES PearsonRealize.com

 Student and Teacher eTexts
eText

Solve and Share
Solve

Visual Learning Animation Plus
Learn

 A-Z Animated Glossary
Glossary

Math Tools
Tools

LESSON OVERVIEW   **F** **C** **R** FOCUS • COHERENCE • RIGOR

FOCUS

Domain 1.OA Operations and Algebraic Thinking

Cluster 1.OA.C Add and subtract within 20.

Content Standard 1.OA.C.6 Add and subtract within 20, demonstrating fluency for addition and subtraction within 10. Use strategies such as counting on; making ten (e.g., $8 + 6 = 8 + 2 + 4 = 10 + 4 = 14$); decomposing a number leading to a ten (e.g., $13 - 4 = 13 - 3 - 1 = 10 - 1 = 9$); using the relationship between addition and subtraction (e.g., knowing that $8 + 4 = 12$, one knows $12 - 8 = 4$); and creating equivalent but easier or known sums (e.g., adding $6 + 7$ by creating the known equivalent $6 + 6 + 1 = 12 + 1 = 13$).

Mathematical Practices MP.2, MP.4

Objective Write equations to show the parts and the whole.

Essential Understanding Parts of a whole is one interpretation of addition. Addition equations can be used to show parts of a whole.

Vocabulary add, equals, equation, plus, sum

Materials Connecting cubes (or Teaching Tool 8)
Paper bag

COHERENCE

Students in kindergarten have had experience using objects, pictorial models, and equations in addition. This lesson focuses on writing addition equations and understanding the associated vocabulary that students will continue to use with confidence throughout Grade 1.

RIGOR

This lesson emphasizes **conceptual understanding** and **fluency**. Equations can be used as a symbolic representation of the parts of a whole. By using models, students can see more clearly what each term in the equation they write represents. Students work with the equal sign on both the right and left sides of the expression. This allows them to develop their understanding of *equals* with the terms on either side of the equal sign having the same value. Students work toward the goal of achieving fluency with addition to 10 in Grade 1.

ENGLISH LANGUAGE LEARNERS

Reading Use visual and contextual support to develop vocabulary, needed to comprehend increasingly challenging language.

Use with the Visual Learning Bridge on Student's Edition, p. 852.

Help students make a connection between the *plus* and *equal* signs (+ and =) and the vocabulary words *plus* and *equals*. Write an addition equation on the board and say it aloud. Ask students to repeat it after you. *Where is the plus sign? Where is the equal sign?*

Beginning Use connecting cubes to model an addition equation for students. Write the addition equation below the model, such as $5 + 2 = 7$. Say the equation aloud and emphasize the words *plus* and *equals*. Invite students to repeat the equation after you.

Intermediate Have students work in pairs to make an equation together that can be modeled with connecting cubes. Have one student write the addition equation while the other reads it aloud. Then have them trade places and repeat the activity.

Advanced Have students work in pairs to go through the lesson to read each addition equation aloud. Be sure they use the words *plus* and *equals* correctly.

Summarize How can you add parts to find how many there are in all?

COHERENCE: Engage learners by connecting prior knowledge to new ideas.

Students come up with their own way to represent an addition situation with numbers in this problem. This prepares them for the next part of the lesson where they learn how to write an addition equation to represent an addition situation.

10–15 min

Solve

 BEFORE

1. Pose the Solve-and-Share Problem
Provide each student 9 red cubes, 9 blue cubes, and a paper bag.

MP.2 Reasoning In the problem, students check that their answers are reasonable by counting the total number of cubes they picked and making sure that this is the sum of their cubes of each color.

2. Build Understanding
What are you asked to do with the red and blue cubes? [Pull a handful out of a bag.] *What are you asked to show?* [Numbers for how many red and blue cubes I picked in all]

 DURING

3. Ask Guiding Questions As Needed
How many cubes did you pull from the bag? [Sample answer: There are 3 red cubes and 2 blue cubes.] *How can you find the total number of cubes?* [Sample answer: Count all of the red and blue cubes.]

 AFTER

4. Share and Discuss Solutions
Start with students' solutions. Have them share the different ways they showed their cubes. If needed, project Malia's work to discuss how she used numbers to show the cubes she pulled from the bag.

5. Transition to the Visual Learning Bridge
Using various models helps you transition from using models to using symbols to add. Later in the lesson, you will learn how to write equations using symbols.

6. Extension for Early Finishers
If there are no cubes in the bag, how many are there in all? [0]

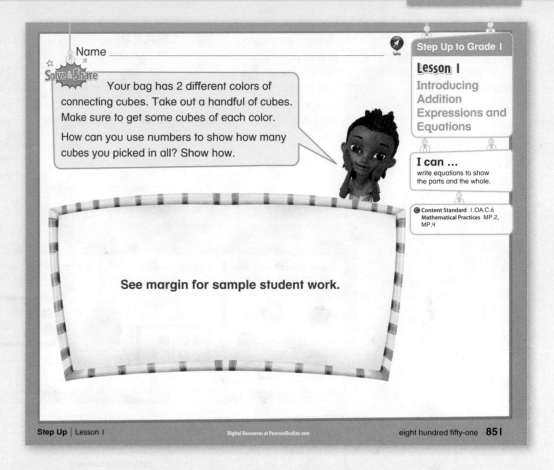

Name _____

Solve & Share
Your bag has 2 different colors of connecting cubes. Take out a handful of cubes. Make sure to get some cubes of each color.

How can you use numbers to show how many cubes you picked in all? Show how.

See margin for sample student work.

Step Up to Grade 1

Lesson 1
Introducing Addition Expressions and Equations

I can ...
write equations to show the parts and the whole.

Content Standard 1.OA.C.6
Mathematical Practices MP.2, MP.4

Step Up | Lesson 1   Digital Resources at PearsonRealize.com   eight hundred fifty-one **851**

Analyze Student Work

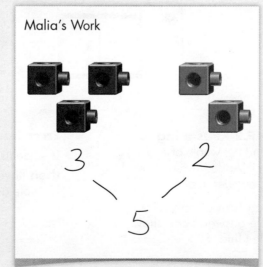

Malia's Work

Malia groups the cubes by color and writes how many of each color and the total number.

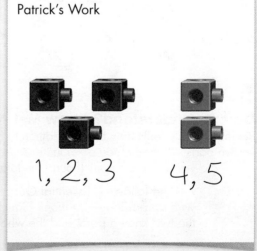

Patrick's Work

Patrick groups the cubes by color and uses numbers to count how many in all. This is fine, but later in the lesson, show Patrick how to use an equation to find a total number of objects.

DEVELOP: VISUAL LEARNING

The *Visual Learning Bridge* connects students' thinking in Solve & Share to important math ideas in the lesson. Use the *Visual Learning Bridge* to make these ideas explicit. Also available as a *Visual Learning Animation Plus* at PearsonRealize.com

Visual Learning

How many red cubes did Kenny pick? [4] *How many blue cubes did he pick?* [2]

What color cubes are in each part? [The cubes in the first part are red; the cubes in the second part are blue.]

MP.2 Reasoning *When you add the numbers, you join the two parts. What is the sum?* [The sum is the number of cubes in all.]

MP.4 Model with Math *What number tells how many are in the red part?* [4] *The blue part?* [2] *How many cubes are there in all?* [6] Have students read the number sentence aloud.

Prevent Misconceptions 1 RtI

Some students may read the words *and* and *is* in an equation. Guide them to use the correct terminology, *plus* and *equals*, when reading equations.

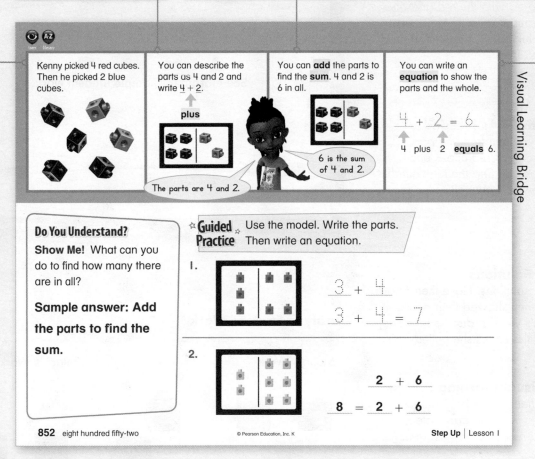

Do You Understand? Show Me! MP.2 Reasoning
Review with students how to use addition to find the whole of two known parts. *What did you do in the exercises?* [Added two numbers.] *What did you do as a result?* [Found the total number in all.]

Essential Question

Ask the following Essential Question: *What can you show with an addition equation?* [Sample answer: I can show the two known parts and the whole I find.]

Error Intervention: Item 2
If students have difficulty writing an equation,

then have them start by describing what they see.
[Sample answer: I see 2 yellow cubes and I see 6 yellow cubes.]

Items 3–5 MP.4 Model with Math If students are still unclear, ask them to look at each picture and say the parts aloud. Then ask them to read the equation aloud.

Item 6 Remind students to gather information from the word problem. *What is the part?* [4] *What is the whole?* [9] *What do you need to do to solve the problem?* [Draw a picture and write an equation.]

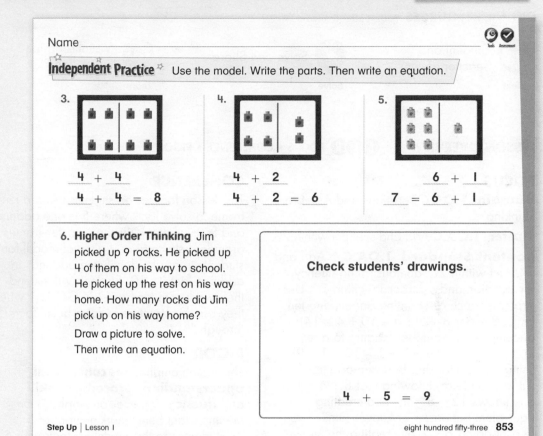

Name _____

Independent Practice Use the model. Write the parts. Then write an equation.

3.
4 + 4
4 + 4 = 8

4.
4 + 2
4 + 2 = 6

5.
6 + 1
7 = 6 + 1

6. **Higher Order Thinking** Jim picked up 9 rocks. He picked up 4 of them on his way to school. He picked up the rest on his way home. How many rocks did Jim pick up on his way home?

Draw a picture to solve. Then write an equation.

Check students' drawings.

4 + 5 = 9

Step Up | Lesson 1

eight hundred fifty-three **853**

Item 7 MP.2 Reasoning *What symbols do you use in an addition equation?* [Plus sign (+) and equal sign (=)] *What two numbers will you use in order to find the sum?* [4 and 3]

Item 8 Remind students that the number of red worms is one part. *What is the other part?* [The number of brown worms] *What is the whole?* [The number of worms in all]

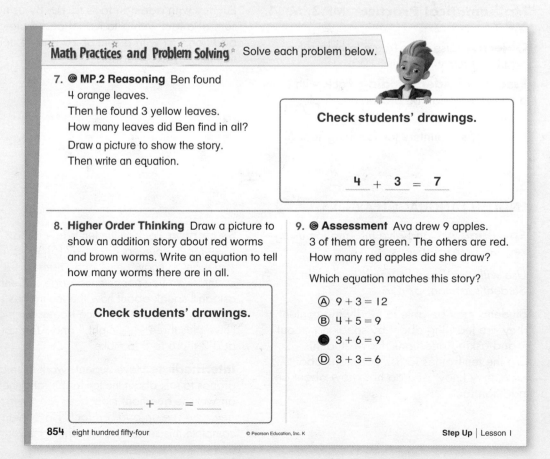

Math Practices and Problem Solving Solve each problem below.

7. ◉ **MP.2 Reasoning** Ben found 4 orange leaves. Then he found 3 yellow leaves. How many leaves did Ben find in all?

Draw a picture to show the story. Then write an equation.

Check students' drawings.

4 + 3 = 7

8. **Higher Order Thinking** Draw a picture to show an addition story about red worms and brown worms. Write an equation to tell how many worms there are in all.

Check students' drawings.

____ + ____ = ____

9. ◉ **Assessment** Ava drew 9 apples. 3 of them are green. The others are red. How many red apples did she draw?

Which equation matches this story?

Ⓐ 9 + 3 = 12
Ⓑ 4 + 5 = 9
● 3 + 6 = 9
Ⓓ 3 + 3 = 6

854 eight hundred fifty-four

© Pearson Education, Inc. K

Step Up | Lesson 1

853–854

FACTS WITH 5 ON A TEN-FRAME

DIGITAL RESOURCES PearsonRealize.com

 Student and Teacher eTexts
eText

 Solve and Share
Solve

 Visual Learning Animation Plus
Learn

Animated Glossary
Glossary

 Math Tools
Tools

LESSON OVERVIEW  FOCUS · COHERENCE · RIGOR

FOCUS

Domain 1.OA Operations and Algebraic Thinking

Cluster 1.OA.C Add and subtract within 20.

Content Standard 1.OA.C.6 Add and subtract within 20, demonstrating fluency for addition and subtraction within 10. Use strategies such as counting on; making ten (e.g., $8 + 6 = 8 + 2 + 4 = 10 + 4 = 14$); decomposing a number leading to a ten (e.g., $13 - 4 = 13 - 3 - 1 = 10 - 1 = 9$); using the relationship between addition and subtraction (e.g., knowing that $8 + 4 = 12$, one knows $12 - 8 = 4$); and creating equivalent but easier or known sums (e.g., adding $6 + 7$ by creating the known equivalent $6 + 6 + 1 = 12 + 1 = 13$).

Mathematical Practices MP.3, MP.4, MP.7

Objective Use a ten-frame to help solve addition facts with 5 and 10.

Essential Understanding Facts with sums 6 through 10 can be broken into 5 plus some more.

Materials Counters (or Teaching Tool 6)

COHERENCE

This lesson focuses on students using a ten-frame to solve facts where 5 is one addend and facts where 10 is the sum. Ten-frames provide a structure and a visual model for students to easily identify the addends in addition facts to 10. Students will extend their work with ten-frames in Grade 1 when they use this structure to solve basic facts through 20.

RIGOR

This lesson emphasizes **conceptual understanding**, **procedural skill**, and **fluency**. It places an emphasis on the important benchmark number of 5. As students use this model for facts with 5 as an addend, they continue to develop their fluency with addition facts to 10. By using the sum of a fact with 5 to model and write an addition fact with a sum of 10, they extend this fluency even further.

ENGLISH LANGUAGE LEARNERS

Speaking Ask and give information using key words/expressions.

Use with the Visual Learning Bridge on Student's Edition, p. 856.

Students may be able to clarify the content they are learning about by speaking about it and asking questions. Have students use the ten-frames to ask questions about what they know and do not know about an addition fact.

Beginning Point to the ten-frame in Box 1. *How many counters are here?* [5] *What do you want to know next? How many more counters do you need?* Encourage students to ask and speak about how the ten-frames show addition facts. Use sentence frames such as "Five plus three ____ eight." and "You can add 2 more to 8 to make ____."

Intermediate Have students work in small groups to talk about the ten-frame, and then answer the question: *How does the ten-frame help you see an addition fact?* Have them complete this sentence stem when answering:

"The ten-frame helps me see an addition fact by ____."

Advanced Ask students to ask each other questions and explain how to use a ten-frame to find an addition fact.

Summarize How can you learn addition facts with a ten-frame?

DEVELOP: PROBLEM-BASED LEARNING

COHERENCE: Engage students by connecting prior knowledge to new ideas.

Students write addition facts for counters shown in ten-frames. This prepares them for the next part of the lesson where they learn how to use a ten-frame to solve facts where 5 is an addend and facts where 10 is the sum.

10–15 min

 Solve

 BEFORE

1. Pose the Solve-and-Share Problem
Provide each student 5 counters.

MP.4 Model with Math In this problem, students model the same mathematical idea by using counters in a ten-frame and by writing an addition equation.

2. Build Understanding
What are you asked to do with the counters? [Put some on the bottom row of the ten-frame.] *What are you asked to write?* [An addition equation for the counters in the ten-frame]

 DURING

3. Ask Guiding Questions As Needed
How many counters are in the top and bottom of the ten-frame? [Sample answer: There are 5 in the top and 3 in the bottom.] *Do you have all of the information that you need to write an addition equation? Explain.* [Yes; Sample answer: I know the parts and the whole.]

 AFTER

4. Share and Discuss Solutions
Start with students' solutions. Have them share their addition equations. If needed, project Dan's work to discuss how his ten-frame matches the addition equation he wrote.

5. Transition to the Visual Learning Bridge
You used counters and a ten-frame to model an addition fact where one of the addends is 5. Then you wrote an equation to match the counters. Later in this lesson, you will use a ten-frame to solve facts where 5 is an addend and then use those sums to write an addition fact for 10.

6. Extension for Early Finishers
Imagine that the ten-frame had only 5 counters. What addition fact with 5 would you write for that ten-frame?
[5 + 0 = 5]

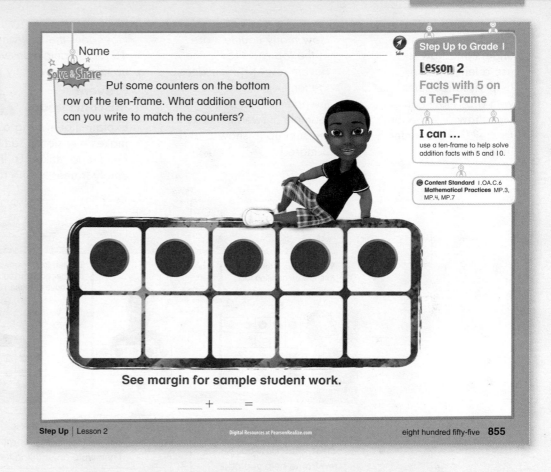

Name _____

Solve & Share

Put some counters on the bottom row of the ten-frame. What addition equation can you write to match the counters?

See margin for sample student work.

___ + ___ = ___

Step Up | Lesson 2   Digital Resources at PearsonRealize.com   eight hundred fifty-five **855**

Step Up to Grade 1

Lesson 2
Facts with 5 on a Ten-Frame

I can ...
use a ten-frame to help solve addition facts with 5 and 10.

Content Standard 1.OA.C.6
Mathematical Practices MP.3, MP.4, MP.7

Analyze Student Work

Dan's Work

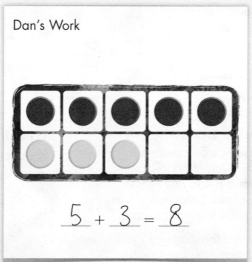

$$5 + 3 = 8$$

Becky's Work

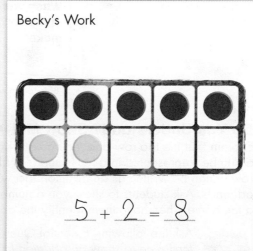

$$5 + 2 = 8$$

Dan explains that although there are 10 spaces in the ten-frame, there are only 8 counters. In this case, 8 is the whole and 5 and 3 are the parts. The addition equation is correct.

Becky explains that there were 5 counters on the ten-frame and then she added 2 more. For her addition equation, she writes $5 + 2 = 8$. The addition equation is incorrect.

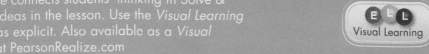

STEP 2 — DEVELOP: VISUAL LEARNING

The *Visual Learning Bridge* connects students' thinking in Solve & Share to important math ideas in the lesson. Use the *Visual Learning Bridge* to make these ideas explicit. Also available as a *Visual Learning Animation Plus* at PearsonRealize.com

Visual Learning

Check that students understand how to use a ten-frame to help visualize sums with a 5. *How can you show 5 in the ten-frame?* [Put 5 counters in the top row.]

How many counters are in the top row? [5] *In the bottom row?* [3] *How does the ten-frame help you see the addition fact 5 + 3 = 8?* [Sample answer: It breaks the sum up to show 5 and 3 more.]

How does the ten-frame help you see the 10 fact? [Sample answer: It breaks the number up to show how many more make 10.]

Prevent Misconceptions — 1 RtI

Explain that making a 5 in the ten-frame makes it easier to see how many more are needed to make 10. It is easier to look for empty frames in one row than in two rows.

MP.3 Construct Arguments

How does the ten-frame show 8 + 2 = 10? [Sample answer: There are 8 red counters and 2 yellow counters, which is 10 in all.]

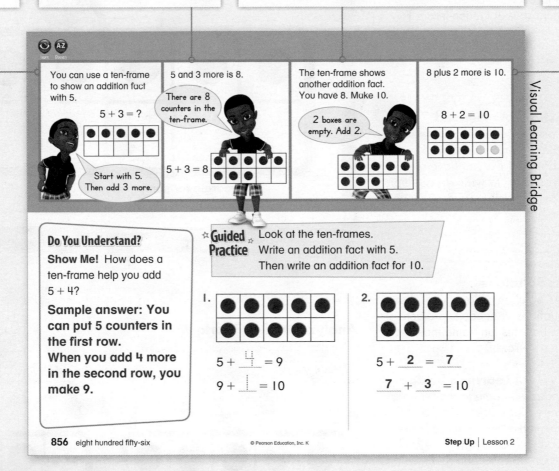

Do You Understand?

Show Me! How does a ten-frame help you add 5 + 4?

Sample answer: You can put 5 counters in the first row. When you add 4 more in the second row, you make 9.

☆**Guided Practice**☆ Look at the ten-frames. Write an addition fact with 5. Then write an addition fact for 10.

1.
$5 + 4 = 9$
$9 + 1 = 10$

2.
$5 + 2 = 7$
$7 + 3 = 10$

856 eight hundred fifty-six   © Pearson Education, Inc. K   **Step Up | Lesson 2**

Do You Understand? Show Me! MP.7 Use Structure

Explain that the top row of a ten-frame always has 5 boxes, so if a number represented in a ten-frame also fills some of the second row, it can be written as an addition fact with 5 being one of the addends. Ask students to show you a number from 6 through 10 on a ten-frame. Then have them identify the addition fact it represents.

 Ask the following Essential Question: *How can you use a ten-frame to show an addition fact that has 5 as one of the addends and an addition fact with a sum of 10?* [Sample answer: For an addition fact with 5 as one of the addends, I know that the top row has 5 counters. I put the number of counters for the other addend in the bottom row. To show an addition fact that has a sum of 10, I know that both rows have a total of 10 boxes. I put counters in the ten-frame for the greater addend. Then I fill the empty boxes in the ten-frame with counters for the other addend.]

Error Intervention: Item 2

If students have trouble finding the fact that adds to 10,

then have them fill the empty spaces with a different color counter.

20–30 min   Tools

Items 3–5 MP.7 Use Structure Remind students that to write an addition fact with 5, look at the number of counters in the second row. To write an addition fact for 10, look at the number of counters missing for the second row.

Item 6 Before students begin drawing, you may wish to have them look at each addition equation and say how far each addend is from 10. Then have students complete the representation to show the complete addition equation.

Name _____

Independent Practice Look at the ten-frames. Write an addition fact with 5. Then write an addition fact for 10.

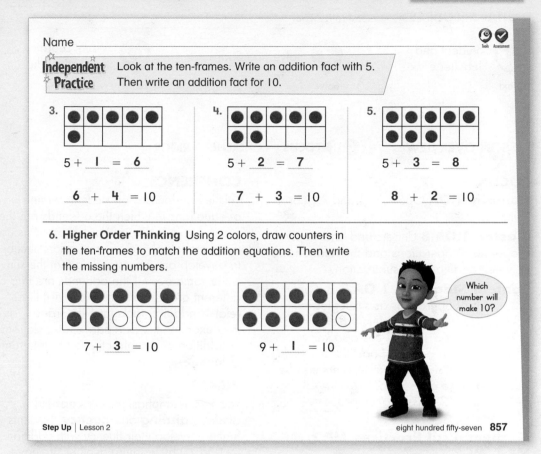

3.
$5 + \underline{1} = \underline{6}$

$\underline{6} + \underline{4} = 10$

4.
$5 + \underline{2} = \underline{7}$

$\underline{7} + \underline{3} = 10$

5.
$5 + \underline{3} = \underline{8}$

$\underline{8} + \underline{2} = 10$

6. **Higher Order Thinking** Using 2 colors, draw counters in the ten-frames to match the addition equations. Then write the missing numbers.

$7 + \underline{3} = 10$

$9 + \underline{1} = 10$

Which number will make 10?

Step Up | Lesson 2

eight hundred fifty-seven **857**

Items 7 and 8 MP.4 Model with Math Each of these problems can be solved with an addition fact with 5. For each problem, ask students: *How do the story, the ten-frame drawing, and the addition equation all show 5 and some more? Explain.* [Answers will vary.]

Item 9 Suggest to students that they write a story about something in their everyday life that could be represented by 7 and 3 more. Have students share their ideas aloud.

Math Practices and Problem Solving Solve each problem below.

7. **MP.4 Model** A team has 5 softballs. The coach brings 3 more. How many softballs does the team have now?

Draw counters in the ten-frame. Then write an addition fact to solve.

$\underline{5} + \underline{3} = \underline{8}$ $\underline{8}$ softballs

8. **MP.4 Model** Marcia reads 5 books. Tanya reads 2 books. How many books did the girls read in all?

Draw counters in the ten-frame. Then write an addition fact to solve.

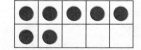

$\underline{5} + \underline{2} = \underline{7}$ $\underline{7}$ books

9. **Higher Order Thinking** Write a new story about adding to 10 in the ten-frame in Item 7. Then write an equation for your story.

Check students' work.

____ + ____ = ____

10. **Assessment** Scott's team has 5 footballs. Scott's coach brings some more. Scott's team now has 10 footballs.

Which addition fact shows how many footballs Scott's coach brought?

Ⓐ $5 + 5 = 10$

Ⓑ $10 + 5 = 15$

Ⓒ $7 + 3 = 10$

Ⓓ $10 + 7 = 17$

858 eight hundred fifty-eight

© Pearson Education, Inc. K

Step Up | Lesson 2

857–858

ADD IN ANY ORDER

DIGITAL RESOURCES PearsonRealize.com

 Student and Teacher eTexts
eText

 Solve and Share
Solve

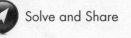 Visual Learning Animation Plus
Learn

 Animated Glossary
Glossary

 Math Tools
Tools

LESSON OVERVIEW 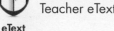 FOCUS • COHERENCE • RIGOR

FOCUS

Domain 1.OA Operations and Algebraic Thinking

Cluster 1.OA.B Understand and apply properties of operations and the relationship between addition and subtraction.

Content Standard 1.OA.B.3 Apply properties of operations as strategies to add and subtract. *Examples: If $8 + 3 = 11$ is known, then $3 + 8 = 11$ is also known. (Commutative property of addition.) To add $2 + 6 + 4$, the second two numbers can be added to make a ten, so $2 + 6 + 4 = 2 + 10 = 12$. (Associative property of addition.)*

Mathematical Practices MP.2, MP.3, MP.4, MP.7

Objective Use the same addends to write two different equations with the same sum.

Essential Understanding Two numbers can be added in any order and the sum will stay the same.

Materials Connecting cubes (or Teaching Tool 8), index cards

COHERENCE

This lesson focuses on students writing pairs of equations in which the addends are the same, but in a different order. Students use visual models of two different colors of cubes to develop an understanding that the sum is the same even if the addends are in a different order. Students will revisit these related addition facts later in Grade 1 as they examine the part-part-whole relationship in addition and subtraction and write families of facts.

RIGOR

This lesson emphasizes **conceptual understanding** and **fluency**. Students further develop their fluency with addition facts to 10 by learning another strategy to use for solving facts. By using the *Commutative Property of Addition*, which states that for whole numbers, $a + b = b + a$, students are able to analyze, solve, and write both vertical and horizontal addition problems that have the same addends in either order.

ENGLISH LANGUAGE LEARNERS

Speaking Speak using content area vocabulary in context.

Use with the Visual Learning Bridge on Student's Edition, p. 860.

Connect 3 red connecting cubes to 1 blue connecting cube and write the addition equation $3 + 1 = 4$ on the board. Point to the 3 and say *addend*. Point to the 1 and say *addend*. Point to the 4 and say *sum*. Ask students to repeat after you either the words *addend* or *sum* as you point to the individual numbers.

Beginning Write three separate addition equations on index cards. Point to the addends in each equation and ask: *What is the number called?* Correct students' pronunciation as needed.

Intermediate Ask students to choose an addition equation from the lesson. Provide them with this sentence frame to talk about the numbers: "The addends are ____ and ____. The sum is ____."

Advanced Pair students with similar proficiency levels. Have each student write several addition equations. Then have them use complete sentences to describe where the addends in the addition equation are located.

Summarize How can you move the addends in an addition equation?

DEVELOP: PROBLEM-BASED LEARNING

COHERENCE: Engage students by connecting prior knowledge to new ideas.

Students analyze addition models and equations that show the same sum but have addends in a different order. This prepares them for the next part of the lesson in which they independently solve and write pairs of equations with the addends in a different order.

10–15 min

Solve

BEFORE

Whole Class

1. Pose the Solve-and-Share Problem
You may wish to provide students with 7 connecting cubes (or Teaching Tool 8) in two different colors.

MP.4 Model with Math In this problem, students use connecting cubes to identify similarities and differences between two equations.

2. Build Understanding
What are you asked to write? [An addition equation to match each cube tower] *What should you discuss with a partner?* [How the two addition equations are the same and different]

DURING

Small Group

3. Ask Guiding Questions As Needed
What is the same about the two cube towers? How is that shown in the addition equations? [The total number of cubes; The sum is the same in both equations] *What is different about the two cube towers? How is that shown in the addition equations?* [The order of the green and yellow cubes; The order of the addends in the two equations is different.]

AFTER

Whole Class

4. Share and Discuss Solutions
Start with students' solutions. If needed, **Solve** project Yao's work to discuss how the order of the addends in the addition equations changes, but the sum does not.

5. Transition to the Visual Learning Bridge
You used connecting cubes to write addition equations for two cube towers and discussed how the addition equations are alike and different. Later in this lesson, you will learn that you can change the order of the addends in any addition equation and that the sum will stay the same.

6. Extension for Early Finishers
Have students use cubes and work together to find other pairs of related addition facts.

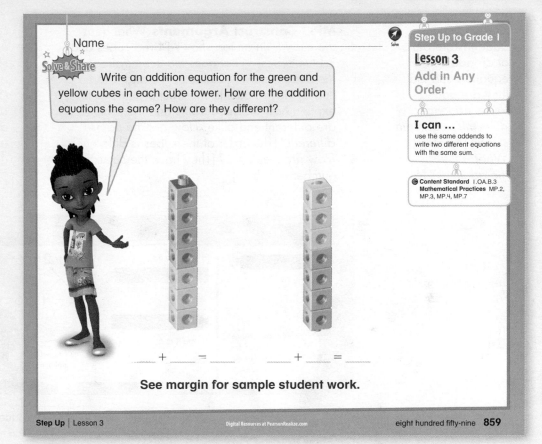

Name _____

Solve & Share
Write an addition equation for the green and yellow cubes in each cube tower. How are the addition equations the same? How are they different?

____ + ____ = ____   ____ + ____ = ____

See margin for sample student work.

Step Up | Lesson 3   Digital Resources at PearsonRealize.com   eight hundred fifty-nine **859**

Step Up to Grade 1

Lesson 3
Add in Any Order

I can ...
use the same addends to write two different equations with the same sum.

Content Standard 1.OA.B.3
Mathematical Practices MP.2, MP.3, MP.4, MP.7

Analyze Student Work

Yao's Work

$4 + 3 = 7$ $3 + 4 = 7$

Ehrin's Work

$4 + 3 = 7$ $3 + 4 = 7$

Yao completes the addition equations correctly. He explains that the addends and the sum are the same, but the order of the addends is different.

Ehrin completes the addition equations correctly. She explains that the addends and the sum are the same, but does not mention the different order of the addends.

DEVELOP: VISUAL LEARNING

The *Visual Learning Bridge* connects students' thinking in Solve & Share to important math ideas in the lesson. Use the *Visual Learning Bridge* to make these ideas explicit. Also available as a *Visual Learning Animation Plus* at PearsonRealize.com

E L L Visual Learning

 Learn   Glossary

Explain that addends are parts of an addition equation and that they are added. *What addends does this cube train show?* [4 and 2] *What is the sum of the addends?* [6]

MP.3 Construct Arguments *What does the cube train on top show?* [4 red cubes and 2 blue cubes] *What does the cube train on the bottom show?* [2 blue cubes and 4 red cubes] Have students construct arguments to explain how the cube trains and the sentences are different and alike. *How are the trains different?* [The order of the cubes is different.] *How are they alike?* [They have the same number of cubes.]

Look at the addition equations. Do they show the same addends and sum? [Yes] *How are the addition equations different?* [The addends are in a different order.]

Look at the sentences and the addition facts. Do they show the same addends and sum? [Yes] Help students generalize that when you change the order of the addends, the sum remains the same.

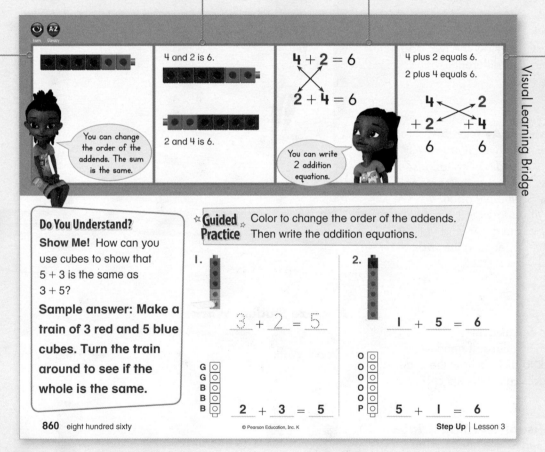

Visual Learning Bridge

4 and 2 is 6.

2 and 4 is 6.

$4 + 2 = 6$
$2 + 4 = 6$

You can change the order of the addends. The sum is the same.

You can write 2 addition equations.

4 plus 2 equals 6.
2 plus 4 equals 6.

$\begin{array}{cc} 4 & 2 \\ +2 & +4 \\ \hline 6 & 6 \end{array}$

Do You Understand?

Show Me! How can you use cubes to show that $5 + 3$ is the same as $3 + 5$?

Sample answer: Make a train of 3 red and 5 blue cubes. Turn the train around to see if the whole is the same.

☆ **Guided Practice** ☆ Color to change the order of the addends. Then write the addition equations.

1.
$3 + 2 = 5$

G
G
B
B
B

$2 + 3 = 5$

2.
$1 + 5 = 6$

O
O
O
O
P

$5 + 1 = 6$

860 eight hundred sixty

© Pearson Education, Inc. K

Step Up | Lesson 3

Do You Understand? Show Me! MP.4 Model with

Math Hold up 2 fingers on your left hand and 3 fingers on your right hand. After students tell you the sum, switch the addends and show 3 fingers on your left hand and 2 fingers on your right hand. Have students write and solve equations for each model. Then have them explain that the sum remains the same, even when the order of the addends is changed.

 Ask the following Essential Question: *If the order of the addends is changed in an addition equation, does the sum change? Explain.* [No; Sample answer: You will still be adding the same two numbers, so the sum does not change.]

Error Intervention: Item 2

If students get a different sum when they change the order of the addends,

then have them use cubes to see how two numbers added in a different order have the same sum.

Item 5 Point out to students that in this problem, the sum for each equation is given first. Make sure students understand that the sums will still be the same in these equations because the addends are the same numbers given in a different order.

Item 9 MP.7 Look for Patterns Make sure students understand what the directions are asking them to do. *The directions are telling you to write two addition equations. Look at the cards. Which two numbers can be added together to equal the number on the other card? [1 and 5] What is one possible addition equation? [1 + 5 = 6 or 5 + 1 = 6] Now write a second addition equation.*

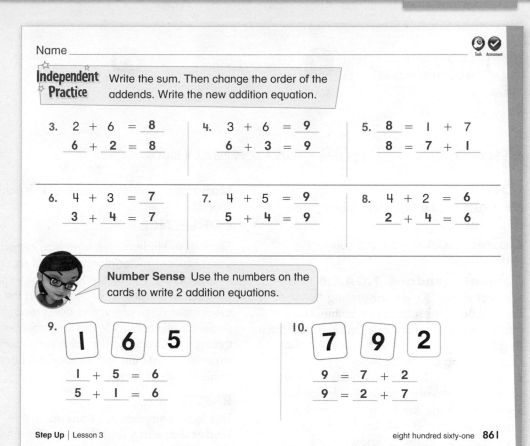

Name _____

Independent Practice Write the sum. Then change the order of the addends. Write the new addition equation.

3. 2 + 6 = **8**
    6 + 2 = **8**

4. 3 + 6 = **9**
    6 + 3 = **9**

5. **8** = 1 + 7
    8 = 7 + **1**

6. 4 + 3 = **7**
    3 + 4 = **7**

7. 4 + 5 = **9**
    5 + 4 = **9**

8. 4 + 2 = **6**
    2 + 4 = **6**

Number Sense Use the numbers on the cards to write 2 addition equations.

9. | 1 | 6 | 5 |

    1 + **5** = **6**
    5 + **1** = **6**

10. | 7 | 9 | 2 |

    9 = **7** + **2**
    9 = **2** + **7**

Step Up | Lesson 3

eight hundred sixty-one **861**

Item 11 MP.4 Model with Math Students need to show that the order in which the cans are collected does not affect the total. Act out placing cubes into a box in reverse order as you restate the problem: 7 cubes, and then 3 cubes. Help students make the connection between the order of how the cubes go into the box and the order of the addends in the addition equations.

Item 13 Encourage students to think about the numerical information provided in the problem. *What number added to 2 equals 8? [6]*

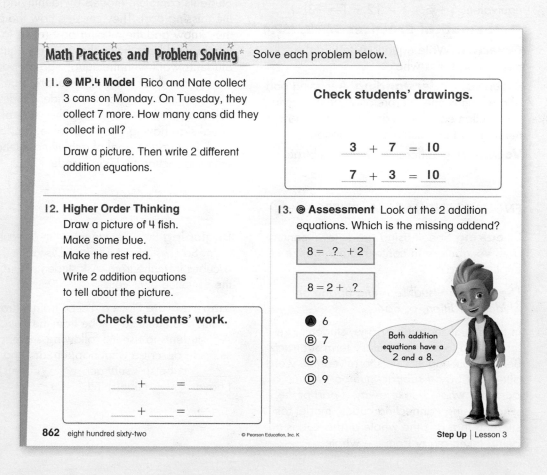

Math Practices and Problem Solving Solve each problem below.

11. **MP.4 Model** Rico and Nate collect 3 cans on Monday. On Tuesday, they collect 7 more. How many cans did they collect in all?

    Draw a picture. Then write 2 different addition equations.

    Check students' drawings.

    3 + **7** = **10**

    7 + **3** = **10**

12. **Higher Order Thinking**
    Draw a picture of 4 fish.
    Make some blue.
    Make the rest red.

    Write 2 addition equations to tell about the picture.

    Check students' work.

    ____ + ____ = ____

    ____ + ____ = ____

13. **Assessment** Look at the 2 addition equations. Which is the missing addend?

    8 = **?** + 2

    8 = 2 + **?**

    Ⓐ 6
    Ⓑ 7
    Ⓒ 8
    Ⓓ 9

    Both addition equations have a 2 and a 8.

862 eight hundred sixty-two

© Pearson Education, Inc. K

Step Up | Lesson 3

INTRODUCING SUBTRACTION EXPRESSIONS AND EQUATIONS

DIGITAL RESOURCES PearsonRealize.com

 Student and Teacher eTexts
eText

 Solve and Share
Solve

 Visual Learning Animation Plus
Learn

 A-Z Animated Glossary
Glossary

 Math Tools
Tools

LESSON OVERVIEW   FOCUS • COHERENCE • RIGOR

FOCUS

Domain 1.OA Operations and Algebraic Thinking

Cluster 1.OA.C Add and subtract within 20.

Content Standard 1.OA.C.6 Add and subtract within 20, demonstrating fluency for addition and subtraction within 10. Use strategies such as counting on; making ten (e.g., $8 + 6 = 8 + 2 + 4 = 10 + 4 = 14$); decomposing a number leading to a ten (e.g., $13 - 4 = 13 - 3 - 1 = 10 - 1 = 9$); using the relationship between addition and subtraction (e.g., knowing that $8 + 4 = 12$, one knows $12 - 8 = 4$); and creating equivalent but easier or known sums (e.g., adding $6 + 7$ by creating the known equivalent $6 + 6 + 1 = 12 + 1 = 13$).

Mathematical Practices MP.2, MP.4

Objective Write equations to find the missing part of a whole.

Essential Understanding A missing part of a whole is one interpretation of subtraction. Subtraction equations can be used to show a missing part of a subtraction situation.

Vocabulary difference, minus, subtract

Materials Connecting cubes (or Teaching Tool 8)

COHERENCE

Students in kindergarten have had experience using objects, pictorial models, and equations in subtraction. This lesson focuses on writing subtraction equations, understanding the associated vocabulary, and using models that students will continue to use with confidence throughout Grade 1. They also gain more experience with the models they will become familiar with in Grade 1.

RIGOR

This lesson emphasizes **conceptual understanding** and **fluency**. Equations are one way to represent subtraction. Students complete models by identifying the missing part. They can see how the part they know and the missing part relate to the whole, and how this is shown in an equation. Students work with the equal sign on both the right and left sides of the expression. This allows them to develop their understanding of *equals* with the terms on either side of the equal sign having the same value. Students work toward the goal of achieving fluency with subtraction to 10 in Grade 1.

ENGLISH LANGUAGE LEARNERS

Speaking Speak using grade-level content area vocabulary in context to internalize new English words.

Use with the Visual Learning Bridge on Student's Edition, p. 864.

In the Visual Learning Bridge, students are introduced to the vocabulary term *subtract*. Begin by asking students to repeat the word after you. Say: *I subtract numbers to find a part of a whole. I take away a part of the whole.* Using connecting cubes, model for students that 8 is the whole and 5 cubes are being taken away from the whole.

Beginning Provide students with a 6-cube train. Say: *I subtract 4 cubes.* Disconnect 4 cubes from the train. Ask students to repeat the sentence after you.

Intermediate Place a 4-cube train in front of students. Remove 1 cube from the train. Ask students to use the following sentence stems to describe what happened: "I have _____ cube(s). I *subtract* _____ cube(s). I have _____ cube(s) left."

Advanced Show students a 5-cube train. Remove 2 cubes from the train. Ask students to describe what you did using the word *subtract*.

Summarize What does it mean to subtract a number from a whole?

DEVELOP: PROBLEM-BASED LEARNING

COHERENCE: Engage learners by connecting prior knowledge to new ideas.

Students use strategies they have learned to find the number of hidden cubes. This prepares them for the next part of the lesson where they learn how to write subtraction equations to find the missing part.

10–15 min

Solve

Whole Class BEFORE

1. Pose the Solve-and-Share Problem
Provide each student 10 connecting cubes to model the problem.

MP.2 Reasoning In the problem, students analyze the mathematical relationship between parts and wholes.

2. Build Understanding
What do you need to find? [The number of hidden cubes] *What tools do you have to help solve the problem?* [Cubes]

Small Group DURING

3. Ask Guiding Questions As Needed
How many cubes does Alex have in all? [5] *How many cubes are on the table?* [3]

Whole Class AFTER

4. Share and Discuss Solutions
Start with students' solutions. Have them share the strategies they used to solve the problem. If needed, project Sandra's work to discuss strategies for finding the missing part.

5. Transition to the Visual Learning Bridge
A missing part of a whole can be found when the whole and the other part are known. Later in the lesson, you will learn how subtraction equations can be used to show a subtraction situation with a missing part.

6. Extension for Early Finishers
Display a train of 8 cubes and identify 8 as the whole. Then hide the train. *What subtraction equation does this show?* [8 − 8 = 0]

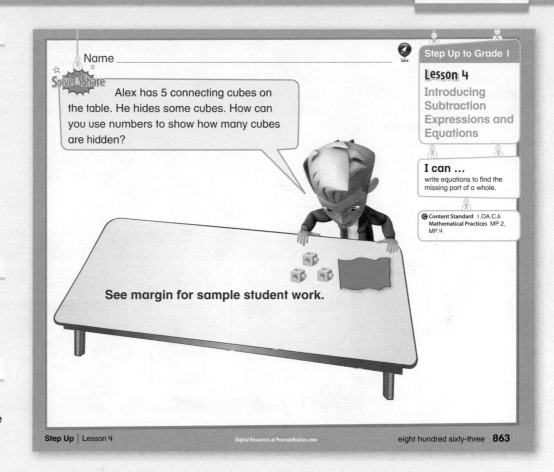

Name _____

Solve & Share

Alex has 5 connecting cubes on the table. He hides some cubes. How can you use numbers to show how many cubes are hidden?

See margin for sample student work.

Step Up to Grade 1

Lesson 4
Introducing Subtraction Expressions and Equations

I can ...
write equations to find the missing part of a whole.

Content Standard 1.OA.C.6
Mathematical Practices MP.2, MP.4

Step Up | Lesson 4   Digital Resources at PearsonRealize.com   eight hundred sixty-three **863**

Analyze Student Work

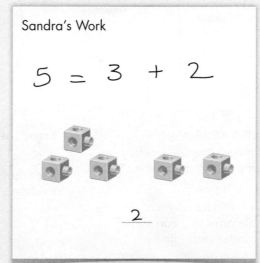

Sandra's Work

$$5 = 3 + 2$$

2

Sandra arranges the cubes in 2 groups and says that 5 is the whole and 3 is one of the parts. There are 2 left over, so that is the missing part. 2 cubes are hidden.

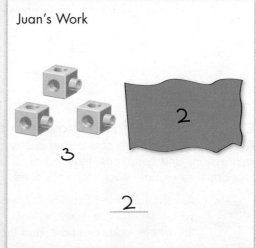

Juan's Work

2

3

2

Juan puts out 3 cubes and uses numbers to count how many in all. Juan says that he counted the 3 cubes on the table and then continued to count to 5 to find how many cubes were hidden.

DEVELOP: VISUAL LEARNING

The *Visual Learning Bridge* connects students' thinking in Solve & Share to important math ideas in the lesson. Use the *Visual Learning Bridge* to make these ideas explicit. Also available as a *Visual Learning Animation Plus* at PearsonRealize.com

E L L
Visual Learning

Learn

Glossary

PEARSON
realize.
PearsonRealize.com

Use the story and the picture to tell what numbers you know. What is the number of cubes in all? What is the known part? [There are 8 cubes in all, and I can see 5.]

What is the whole? [8] *What is one of the parts?* [5] *What can you write to find the hidden part?* [8 – 5]

MP.2 Reasoning *How can you find the difference?* [Subtract] *What is the whole?* [8] *What part do you know?* [5] *What is the hidden part?* [3] *The difference is the part that is left over after you subtract. What is the difference?* [3]

MP.4 Model with Math *What does the subtraction equation show?* [The whole, the known part, and the hidden part] *What is the whole in the subtraction equation?* [8] *What is the known part in the subtraction equation?* [5] *What is the difference?* [3] *How do you read the subtraction equation?* [8 minus 5 equals 3.]

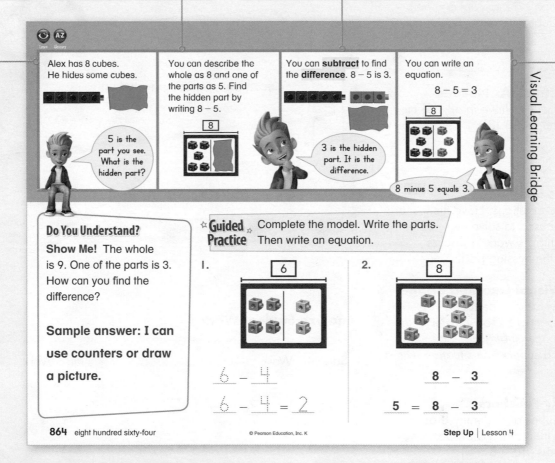

Visual Learning Bridge

Alex has 8 cubes. He hides some cubes.

5 is the part you see. What is the hidden part?

You can describe the whole as 8 and one of the parts as 5. Find the hidden part by writing 8 – 5.

3 is the hidden part. It is the difference.

You can **subtract** to find the **difference**. 8 – 5 is 3.

You can write an equation.
$8 - 5 = 3$

8 minus 5 equals 3.

Do You Understand?

Show Me! The whole is 9. One of the parts is 3. How can you find the difference?

Sample answer: I can use counters or draw a picture.

☆ **Guided Practice** ☆ Complete the model. Write the parts. Then write an equation.

1. [6]
$6 - 4$
$6 - 4 = 2$

2. [8]
$8 - 3$
$5 = 8 - 3$

864 eight hundred sixty-four

© Pearson Education, Inc. K

Step Up | Lesson 4

Do You Understand? Show Me! MP.4 Model with Math Students can use connecting cubes to model their subtraction expressions and equations. Have students use cubes to model their work as they explain each step they used.

Essential Question

Ask the following Essential Question: *What can you show with a subtraction equation?* [Sample answer: I can show the whole, a known part, and the hidden part I find.]

Error Intervention: Item 2

If students have difficulty completing the subtraction equation, **then** have them use connecting cubes to find the missing part by modeling the whole and the part they know.

20–30 min

Tools

Items 3–5 Students may have difficulty understanding that the part-part-whole mat shows the total number of cubes at the top. Have them count all the cubes after they draw the missing part to make sure the total number of cubes equals the number at the top.

Item 6 MP.4 Model with Math Remind students that they can make a model of the subtraction sentence by drawing a picture. *How many kittens are there in all?* [7] *How many will you draw in the basket?* [1] *How many will you draw outside the basket?* [6]

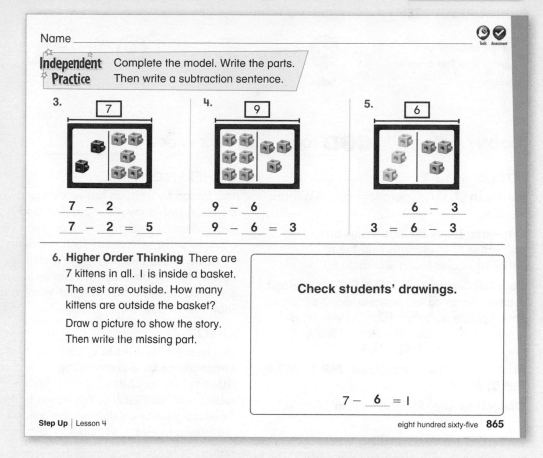

Name _____

Independent Practice   Complete the model. Write the parts. Then write a subtraction sentence.

3.   7

7 – 2
7 – 2 = 5

4.   9

9 – 6
9 – 6 = 3

5.   6

6 – 3
3 = 6 – 3

6. **Higher Order Thinking** There are 7 kittens in all. 1 is inside a basket. The rest are outside. How many kittens are outside the basket?

Draw a picture to show the story. Then write the missing part.

Check students' drawings.

7 – 6 = 1

Step Up | Lesson 4

eight hundred sixty-five **865**

Item 7 MP.2 Reasoning Encourage students to act out the problem with cubes. *How many cubes do you start with?* [8] *How do you show that Lena drops 4 rocks into a pond?* [I can take away 4 cubes.] *What do you need to find?* [How many rocks are left]

Item 9 Encourage students to read the entire story before looking at the answer choices given. *What information is given about the marbles?* [Rob has 9 marbles. He has 2 marbles left after giving some to a friend.]

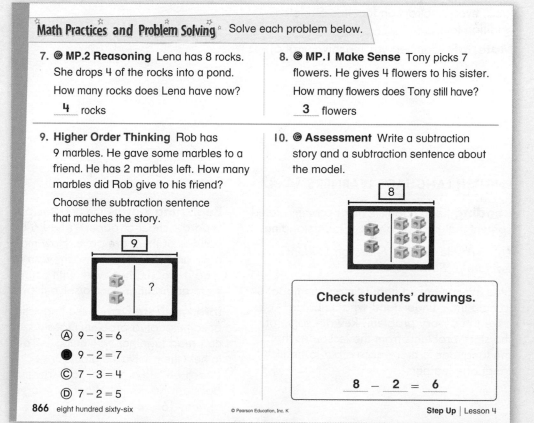

Math Practices and Problem Solving   Solve each problem below.

7. **MP.2 Reasoning** Lena has 8 rocks. She drops 4 of the rocks into a pond. How many rocks does Lena have now?

4 rocks

8. **MP.1 Make Sense** Tony picks 7 flowers. He gives 4 flowers to his sister. How many flowers does Tony still have?

3 flowers

9. **Higher Order Thinking** Rob has 9 marbles. He gave some marbles to a friend. He has 2 marbles left. How many marbles did Rob give to his friend?

Choose the subtraction sentence that matches the story.

9

?

(A) 9 – 3 = 6
● 9 – 2 = 7
(C) 7 – 3 = 4
(D) 7 – 2 = 5

10. **Assessment** Write a subtraction story and a subtraction sentence about the model.

8

Check students' drawings.

8 – 2 = 6

866 eight hundred sixty-six   © Pearson Education, Inc. K   **Step Up** | Lesson 4

THINK ADDITION TO SUBTRACT

DIGITAL RESOURCES PearsonRealize.com

 Student and Teacher eTexts
eText

 Solve and Share
Solve

 Visual Learning Animation Plus
Learn

 Animated Glossary
Glossary

Math Tools
Tools

LESSON OVERVIEW 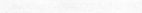 FOCUS • COHERENCE • RIGOR

FOCUS

Domain 1.OA Operations and Algebraic Thinking

Cluster 1.OA.B Understand and apply properties of operations and the relationship between addition and subtraction.

Content Standard 1.OA.B.4 Understand subtraction as an unknown-addend problem. *For example, subtract 10 − 8 by finding the number that makes 10 when added to 8.* Also **1.OA.C.6, 1.OA.D.8**

Mathematical Practices MP.2, MP.4, MP.5, MP.7

Objective Use addition facts to 10 to solve subtraction problems.

Essential Understanding Addition and subtraction have an inverse relationship. This relationship can be used to solve subtraction facts; every subtraction fact has a related addition fact.

Materials Counters (or Teaching Tool 6)

COHERENCE

This lesson focuses on bar models and the relationship between addition and subtraction as students "think addition" in order to solve subtraction facts. Students continue to use this strategy in Grade 1 as they further develop their ability to use a related addition fact in order to solve a subtraction fact.

RIGOR

This lesson continues to emphasize **conceptual understanding** as well as **fluency**. By emphasizing the addition-subtraction relationship, this lesson further develops fluency as students are guided to use previously learned addition facts to solve subtraction facts.

ENGLISH LANGUAGE LEARNERS

Reading Read linguistically accommodated content material to enhance understanding.

Use with the Solve & Share on Student's Edition, p. 867.

Students may need linguistic accommodation to help them understand what is being asked in a story problem. Rewrite some of the story problems from the lesson so that the language is more accessible to English language learners.

Beginning Rewrite the problem on a separate sheet of paper. "I had 6 beach balls. 4 of them are gone. How many beach balls are left?" Point to each word as you read it aloud. Then work with counters to write an addition fact to solve the problem.

Intermediate Provide the linguistically accommodated problem that student pairs can read together with help. Ask questions to help them solve the problem. Ask: *How many beach balls did I have?* [6] *How many beach balls are gone?* [4] *What fact do you want to find?* [6 − 4]

Advanced Read aloud the story problem in the Solve & Share section without changing the text to accommodate English language learners. Have students identify words in the problem that they have trouble understanding.

Summarize How can a subtraction problem be solved by using an addition fact?

DEVELOP: PROBLEM-BASED LEARNING

COHERENCE: Engage students by connecting prior knowledge to new ideas.

Students use counters to show an addition fact. This prepares them for the next part of the lesson where they learn how to use addition facts to help them solve subtraction facts.

10–15 min

Solve

BEFORE

1. Pose the Solve-and-Share Problem
Provide each student with 6 counters.

MP.4 Model with Math In this problem, students use counters to begin developing an understanding of the mathematical relationship between addition and subtraction.

2. Build Understanding
What are you asked to write? [An addition fact to find the answer to 6 − 4] *What tools do you have to help you find the answer?* [Counters]

DURING

3. Ask Guiding Questions As Needed
How many counters do you need to help solve the problem? [6] *Why?* [That is the whole.] *Do you know the parts?* [4 is one part. I have to find the missing part.]

AFTER

4. Share and Discuss Solutions
Start with students' solutions. If needed, project Abby's work to discuss how the addition and subtraction facts are the same and different.

5. Transition to the Visual Learning Bridge
You used counters to show parts and the whole in order to solve a problem that shows how addition and subtraction are related. Later in this lesson, you will solve problems by thinking addition in order to subtract.

6. Extension for Early Finishers
If you know 5 + 2 = 7, what two subtraction facts do you know? [7 − 5 = 2 and 7 − 2 = 5]

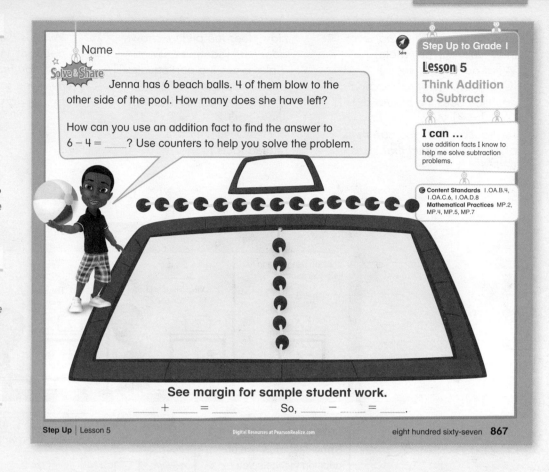

Name _____

Solve & Share

Jenna has 6 beach balls. 4 of them blow to the other side of the pool. How many does she have left?

How can you use an addition fact to find the answer to 6 − 4 = ____? Use counters to help you solve the problem.

Step Up to Grade 1

Lesson 5
Think Addition to Subtract

I can ...
use addition facts I know to help me solve subtraction problems.

Content Standards 1.OA.B.4, 1.OA.C.6, 1.OA.D.8 Mathematical Practices MP.2, MP.4, MP.5, MP.7

See margin for sample student work.

____ + ____ = ____   So, ____ − ____ = ____.

Step Up | Lesson 5   Digital Resources at PearsonRealize.com   eight hundred sixty-seven **867**

Analyze Student Work

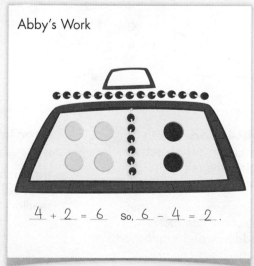

Abby's Work

$4 + 2 = 6$ So, $6 - 4 = 2$.

Abby explains that the parts and the whole are the same in the subtraction and addition facts, but they have different symbols. Knowing that the whole and the parts are the same helped her write an addition fact.

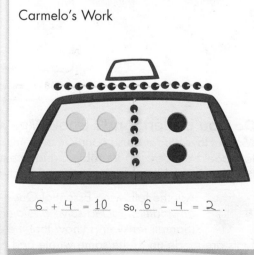

Carmelo's Work

$6 + 4 = 10$ So, $6 - 4 = 2$.

Carmelo writes an addition fact and a subtraction fact, but they do not use the same numbers. This shows that he does not understand how to use the addition fact to help him write the subtraction fact.

DEVELOP: VISUAL LEARNING

The *Visual Learning Bridge* connects students' thinking in Solve & Share to important math ideas in the lesson. Use the *Visual Learning Bridge* to make these ideas explicit. Also available as a *Visual Learning Animation Plus* at PearsonRealize.com

Look at the picture. What does the 7 show? [The whole] What does the 3 show? [One part] What subtraction equation does the picture show? [$7 - 3 = ?$] When you have a subtraction fact, you can think of an addition fact that goes with it.

How does the picture show addition? [Sample answer: 3 plus a missing part equals 7.] Does this picture still show $7 - 3 = ?$ [Yes] How can it show both $7 - 3 = ?$ and $3 + ? = 7$? [They are related facts.]

What is the missing part? [4] What is the addition fact that will help you solve $7 - 3$? [$3 + 4 = 7$]

MP.7 Look for Patterns
What is $7 - 3$? [4] How does $3 + 4 = 7$ help you find $7 - 3 = 4$? [Sample answer: I know that 3 and 4 make 7, and I know from the subtraction problem that one part of 7 is 3; so I know that the other part (the answer) is 4.]

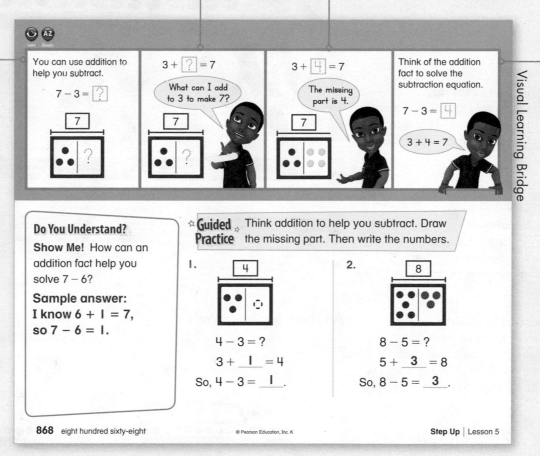

Do You Understand?
Show Me! How can an addition fact help you solve $7 - 6$?
Sample answer: I know $6 + 1 = 7$, so $7 - 6 = 1$.

☆ **Guided Practice** Think addition to help you subtract. Draw the missing part. Then write the numbers.

1.
| 4 |
$4 - 3 = ?$
$3 + \underline{1} = 4$
So, $4 - 3 = \underline{1}$.

2.
| 8 |
$8 - 5 = ?$
$5 + \underline{3} = 8$
So, $8 - 5 = \underline{3}$.

868 eight hundred sixty-eight   © Pearson Education, Inc. K   **Step Up | Lesson 5**

Do You Understand? Show Me! MP.4 Model with Math Have students use counters or familiar classroom objects to model both parts of a problem and to explain the relationship between the addition fact and the subtraction fact.

 Ask the following Essential Question: *How can you use an addition fact to solve a related subtraction fact?*
[Sample answer: I know that the addition and subtraction facts are made up of the same whole and parts. So, I can use one part of the addition fact to find the missing part in the subtraction fact.]

Error Intervention: Item 2
If students have difficulty completing the addition fact,
then remind them to use their drawing of the missing part for help. Tell them that the total number of circles in the drawing should be the same as the whole.

868 Step-Up Lesson 5

Item 3 Students may have difficulty understanding that subtraction facts can help them add. Remind students that the whole is represented by the sum in an addition equation and by the first number in a subtraction equation. For example, in the equations $4 + 5 = 9$ and $9 - 4 = 5$, the whole is 9.

Item 6 MP.2 Reasoning Students may not realize that the idea of an opposite relationship in math can be expressed with shapes as well as with numbers. Point out the inverse relationship between the symbols in the equations. The rectangle represents the whole in both the addition and subtraction equations. The triangle and the star represent the parts in both of the equations.

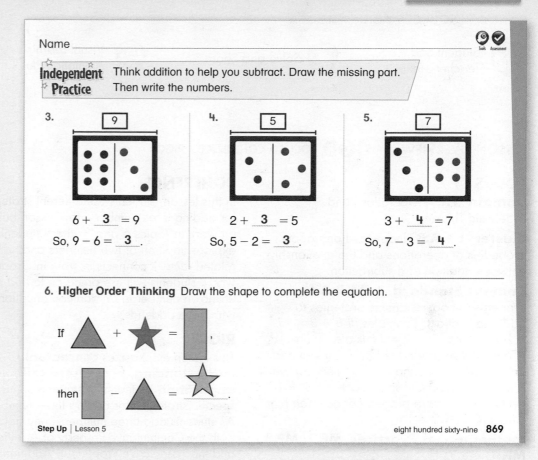

Independent Practice Think addition to help you subtract. Draw the missing part. Then write the numbers.

3. [9]
6 + **3** = 9
So, 9 − 6 = **3** .

4. [5]
2 + **3** = 5
So, 5 − 2 = **3** .

5. [7]
3 + **4** = 7
So, 7 − 3 = **4** .

6. **Higher Order Thinking** Draw the shape to complete the equation.

If ▲ + ★ = ▮,

then ▮ − ▲ = _____ .

Step Up | Lesson 5   eight hundred sixty-nine **869**

Item 7 MP.5 Use Appropriate Tools Strategically If students have difficulty writing the related addition and subtraction equations, have them use a part-part-whole mat to solve the problem. *What is the whole for this problem?* [9, or the number of tickets that Claire needs] *How many counters should you put in one of the parts? Explain.* [Sample answer: I should put 4 counters in one of the parts because Claire has 4 tickets.] *How can you find how many tickets Claire still needs?* [I can put counters in the other part of the mat until I have 9 counters in all. Claire still needs 5 tickets.] *So, what addition and subtraction equations can you write to solve this problem?* [5 + 4 = 9 and 9 − 4 = 5]

Item 9 Remind students to think about the whole, the part they know, and the missing part in the problem. Discuss how parts and wholes relate to an addition equation.

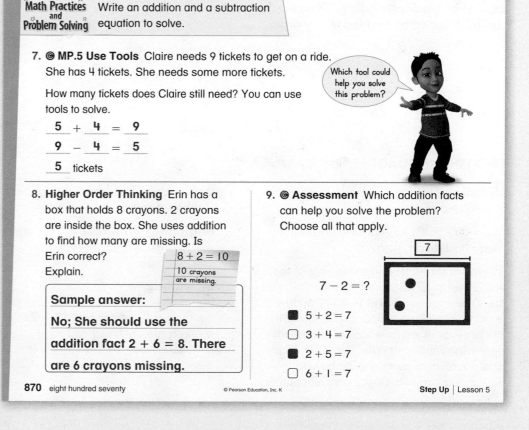

Math Practices and Problem Solving Write an addition and a subtraction equation to solve.

7. ⊚ **MP.5 Use Tools** Claire needs 9 tickets to get on a ride. She has 4 tickets. She needs some more tickets.

How many tickets does Claire still need? You can use tools to solve.

Which tool could help you solve this problem?

5 + **4** = **9**
9 − **4** = **5**
5 tickets

8. **Higher Order Thinking** Erin has a box that holds 8 crayons. 2 crayons are inside the box. She uses addition to find how many are missing. Is Erin correct? Explain.

8 + 2 = 10
10 crayons are missing.

Sample answer:
No; She should use the addition fact 2 + 6 = 8. There are 6 crayons missing.

9. ⊚ **Assessment** Which addition facts can help you solve the problem? Choose all that apply.

[7]
7 − 2 = ?

■ 5 + 2 = 7
☐ 3 + 4 = 7
■ 2 + 5 = 7
☐ 6 + 1 = 7

870 eight hundred seventy   © Pearson Education, Inc. K   Step Up | Lesson 5

ADD THREE NUMBERS

DIGITAL RESOURCES PearsonRealize.com

 Student and Teacher eTexts
eText

 Solve and Share
Solve

 **Visual Learning Animation Plus**
Learn

 Animated Glossary
Glossary

Math Tools
Tools

LESSON OVERVIEW   FOCUS • COHERENCE • RIGOR

FOCUS

Domain 1.OA Operations and Algebraic Thinking

Cluster 1.OA.B Understand and apply properties of operations and the relationship between addition and subtraction.

Content Standard 1.OA.B.3 Apply properties of operations as strategies to add and subtract. *Examples: If 8 + 3 = 11 is known, then 3 + 8 = 11 is also known. (Commutative property of addition.) To add 2 + 6 + 4, the second two numbers can be added to make a ten, so 2 + 6 + 4 = 2 + 10 = 12. (Associative property of addition.)* Also **1.OA.A.2**

Mathematical Practices MP.2, MP.3, MP.4, MP.7

Objective Use different strategies to add three numbers.

Essential Understanding Three numbers can be grouped and added in any order.

COHERENCE

In this lesson, students use different strategies for adding three numbers. This lesson builds on work in Topics 6 and 8 where students explore addition of two numbers and related facts. It connects to work in Grade 1 where students will use precision to find an unknown number in an addition equation with three addends.

RIGOR

This lesson emphasizes **conceptual understanding**, **procedural skill**, and **application** by teaching students some specific strategies for adding three numbers. As students add three numbers, they apply both the Commutative Property of Addition and the Associative Property of Addition. By using these properties, students develop procedural skill as well as their problem-solving skills.

ENGLISH LANGUAGE LEARNERS

Listening Use visual support to confirm understanding.

Use with the Visual Learning Bridge on Student's Edition, p. 872.

To ensure students' understanding of the terms *make 10* and *doubles* that are used in the Visual Learning Bridge, review previous lessons that teach the concepts. Call on students' prior experiences to help them understand the concepts. Use a ten-frame and counters to demonstrate how to make 10 with 8 red counters and 2 yellow counters.

Demonstrate doubles by displaying an equal number of red and yellow counters.

Beginning Write "6 + 4 + 7" on the board. Ask: *Which two numbers make 10?* [6 and 4] *You can make 10 to help you add.*

Intermediate Write "5 + 3 + 2" on the board. Ask: *Can you make a double? Which numbers do you add first?* [3 + 2 makes 5. 5 and 5 are doubles.] *You can make doubles to help you add.*

Advanced Provide students with equations with three addends. Two of the addends should make 10 or doubles. Have pairs work together to make 10 or doubles before they find the sum.

Summarize What strategies can you use for adding three numbers?

STEP
1

DEVELOP: PROBLEM-BASED LEARNING

PEARSON
realize
PearsonRealize.com

COHERENCE: Engage students by connecting prior knowledge to new ideas.

Students explore strategies for adding three numbers. This prepares them for the next part of the lesson where they choose the most appropriate strategy for finding the sum of three addends.

10–15 min

Solve

BEFORE

1. Pose the Solve-and-Share Problem
MP.4 Model with Math Students write equations to model two different ways to solve this addition problem with three addends.

2. Build Understanding
What are you asked to find? [The number of books in all three stacks] *What do you know about the stacks of books?* [There are 3 stacks of books. There are 6 books in each of two stacks and 4 books in the other stack.]

DURING

3. Ask Guiding Questions As Needed
Do you need to add or subtract? [Add.] *What will you add first?* [Sample answer: 6 and 6]

Whole Class
AFTER

4. Share and Discuss Solutions
 Start with students' solutions. Have them share their strategies for adding three numbers. If needed, project and analyze Nick's work to discuss how he made 10 to find the sum.

5. Transition to the Visual Learning Bridge
You wrote two different equations to solve a word problem with three addends. In the next part of the lesson, you will choose a strategy to help you add three numbers.

6. Extension for Early Finishers
How would you add 6 + 4 + 6 + 2? [Sample answer: I can add the 6s first because they are a doubles fact. Then I can add 4 and 2 to make another 6. 12 + 6 = 18]

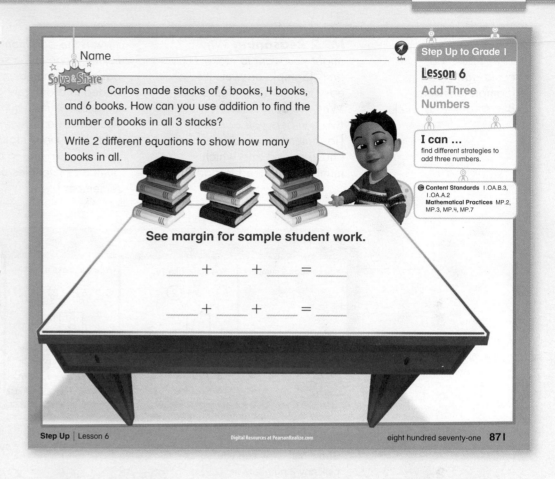

Name _____

Solve & Share

Carlos made stacks of 6 books, 4 books, and 6 books. How can you use addition to find the number of books in all 3 stacks?

Write 2 different equations to show how many books in all.

Step Up to Grade 1
Lesson 6
Add Three Numbers

I can ...
find different strategies to add three numbers.

Content Standards 1.OA.B.3, 1.OA.A.2 Mathematical Practices MP.2, MP.3, MP.4, MP.7

See margin for sample student work.

___ + ___ + ___ = ___

___ + ___ + ___ = ___

Step Up | Lesson 6   Digital Resources at PearsonRealize.com   eight hundred seventy-one **871**

Analyze Student Work

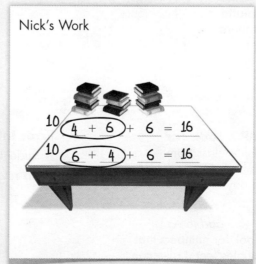
Nick's Work

Nick adds 6 and 4 to make 10 before adding the other 6.

Alexis's Work

Alexis uses the doubles fact 6 + 6 to get 12 before adding the 4. She says that there are two 6s and that she started with one in the first equation and the other in the second equation.

871

DEVELOP: VISUAL LEARNING

The *Visual Learning Bridge* connects students' thinking in Solve & Share to important math ideas in the lesson. Use the *Visual Learning Bridge* to make these ideas explicit. Also available as a *Visual Learning Animation Plus* at PearsonRealize.com

Visual Learning

Learn   Glossary

What are the pairs of numbers that you could add first? [Sample answers: $8 + 6$; $8 + 2$; $6 + 2$]

MP.2 Reasoning *Why might you want to make 10 first?* [Sample answer: It's easy to add a number to 10.] *Why is it helpful to circle the two numbers you add first?* [To remember which numbers I have added and which number I still need to add]

How is this equation different from the one in the second panel? [The numbers are added in a different order.] *Is the sum different when you add in a different order?* [No] *Why does making doubles help you to add three numbers?* [Doubles are easy to remember.]

Can you make 10 with two of these numbers? [No] *Can you make a double?* [No] Explain to students that sometimes they will need to look for any two numbers they know how to add. *Does it matter which two numbers you add first?* [No]

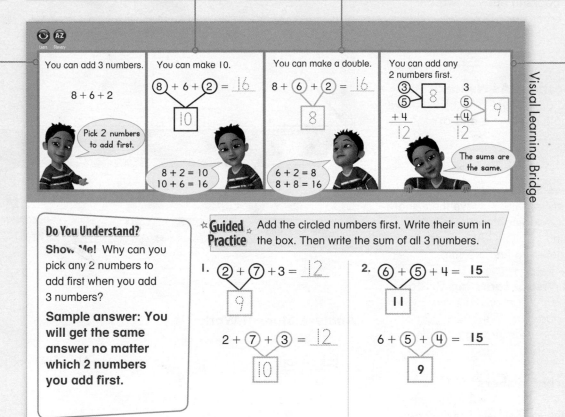

Do You Understand?

Show Me! Why can you pick any 2 numbers to add first when you add 3 numbers?

Sample answer: You will get the same answer no matter which 2 numbers you add first.

☆ **Guided Practice** ☆ Add the circled numbers first. Write their sum in the box. Then write the sum of all 3 numbers.

1. ② + ⑦ + 3 = 12
   [9]

   2 + ⑦ + ③ = 12
   [10]

2. ⑥ + ⑤ + 4 = **15**
   [11]

   6 + ⑤ + ④ = **15**
   [9]

872 eight hundred seventy-two   © Pearson Education, Inc. K   **Step Up | Lesson 6**

Do You Understand? Show Me! MP.7 Look for
Patterns Have students use counters or familiar classroom objects to model finding the sum of three numbers. Guide them to remember that the numbers can be added in any order.

 Ask the following Essential Question: *What are some strategies that you can use to help you add three numbers?* [Sample answer: I can look for numbers that make 10, or add two numbers to make a doubles fact. I also can add any two of the numbers first.]

Error Intervention: Item 2
If students have difficulty finding the correct sums, **then** review addition facts with them.

Items 3–8 MP.3 Construct Arguments Ask a volunteer to explain how he or she solves a given problem. Then ask another volunteer to explain another way to solve the problem. *Is the sum the same, even though the numbers were added in a different way? Explain.* [Yes; Sample answer: You can add the numbers in any order and the sum will be the same.]

Item 9 If students are having difficulty getting started, encourage them to look for doubles facts or ways to make 10 in the puzzle.

Item 10 MP.7 Look for Patterns *What math symbols do you see in the equation?* [Plus sign and equal sign] *What does the number of plus signs tell you about the problem?* [I will be adding three numbers.] *What will you show after the equal sign?* [The sum; the total number of books]

Item 12 Encourage students to think about problem-solving skills and strategies. *How does knowing which numbers Andre added first help you solve the problem?* [Andre made 10 by adding 7 + 3 first. So, I know that Andre should find 10 + 5 next, since 5 is the number of markers in the problem.]

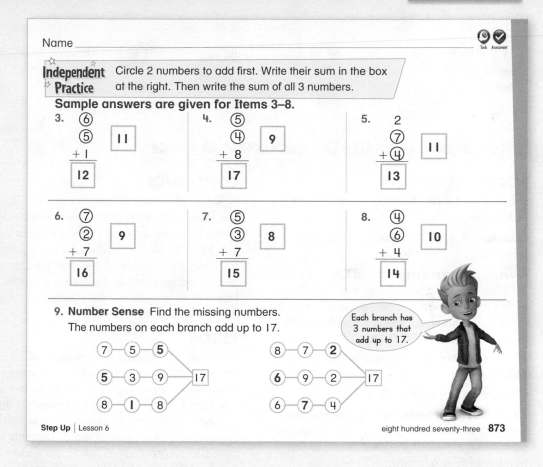

Name _____

Independent Practice Circle 2 numbers to add first. Write their sum in the box at the right. Then write the sum of all 3 numbers.

Sample answers are given for Items 3–8.

3. ⑥
    ⑤   11
    + 1
    12

4. ⑤
    ④   9
    + 8
    17

5. 2
    ⑦   11
    +④
    13

6. ⑦
    ②   9
    + 7
    16

7. ⑤
    ③   8
    + 7
    15

8. ④
    ⑥   10
    + 4
    14

9. **Number Sense** Find the missing numbers. The numbers on each branch add up to 17.

Each branch has 3 numbers that add up to 17.

7 — 5 — **5**
5 — 3 — 9 ⟩ 17
8 — 1 — 8

8 — 7 — **2**
6 — 9 — 2 ⟩ 17
6 — 7 — 4

Step Up | Lesson 6   eight hundred seventy-three **873**

Math Practices and Problem Solving Write an equation to solve each problem below.

10. ◉ **MP.7 Look for Patterns** Oscar puts 9 books on a shelf and 3 books on another shelf. Then he puts 1 book on the last shelf. How many books did Oscar put on all three shelves?

Can you break the problem into simpler parts?

$\underline{9} + \underline{3} + \underline{1} = \underline{13}$

__13__ books

11. **Higher Order Thinking** Explain how to add 9 + 6 + 1. Use pictures, numbers, or words.

Sample answer: First pick two of the numbers and add them, 9 + 1 = 10. Then add the other number to that sum, 10 + 6 = 16.

12. ◉ **Assessment** Andre buys 7 pencils, 5 markers, and 3 pens. He wants to know how many items he bought in all. He added 7 + 3 first. What should Andre add next? Explain.

7 PENCILS   5 MARKERS   3 PENS

10 + 5 = 15; Sample answer:

He made 10 by adding 7 + 3.

Then he adds 10 + 5 to get 15.

COUNT BY 10s TO 120

DIGITAL RESOURCES PearsonRealize.com

 Student and Teacher eTexts
eText

 Solve and Share
Solve

 Visual Learning Animation Plus
Learn

 Animated Glossary
Glossary

Math Tools
Tools

LESSON OVERVIEW **FCR** FOCUS • COHERENCE • RIGOR

FOCUS

Domain 1.NBT Number and Operations in Base Ten

Cluster 1.NBT.A Extend the counting sequence.

Content Standard 1.NBT.A.1 Count to 120, starting at any number less than 120. In this range, read and write numerals and represent a number of objects with a written numeral. Also **1.NBT.B.2c**

Mathematical Practices MP.1, MP.2, MP.7, MP.8

Objective Count by 10s to 120.

Essential Understanding The decade numbers are built on groups of ten. The oral names are similar but not the same as the number of tens counted.

COHERENCE

In Topic 11, students counted to 100. In this lesson, students extend their knowledge of the counting sequence as they count by 10s to 120. Students make the connection between the number of 10s and the tens digit of a two-digit number. This work provides a foundation for place-value concepts that will be explored further in Grade 1.

RIGOR

This lesson emphasizes **conceptual understanding**. Students use pictorial models to compose and decompose decade numbers through 120. By representing these numbers as a number of tens, in standard form, and as the number word, students are consolidating a knowledge of the structure of numbers. The use of a familiar model to show this, a ten-frame, allows students to visualize this structure and understand what digits represent as they count past 100.

ENGLISH LANGUAGE LEARNERS

Listening Learn academic vocabulary heard during classroom instructions and interactions.

Use with the Visual Learning Bridge on Student's Edition, p. 876.

Show a visual of a ten-frame and explain why it is called a ten-frame. *The boxes together look like a frame with 10 dots. When you see a ten-frame with 10 dots, you don't have to count each dot. You know the frame has 10 dots. By using the ten-frames, it is easier to count.*

Beginning Point to the ten-frames in the Visual Learning Bridge. *The ten-frame helps me count.* Then point to each group. *2 ten-frames, 3 ten-frames, 4 ten-frames. What comes next?* [5 ten-frames]

Intermediate Have students work together to draw ten-frames to show the number 40.

Advanced Write the numbers *20, 60, 50,* and *10* on the board. Point to 20 and ask: *How many ten-frames can show this number?* [2] Point to 60 and repeat the question. Continue the activity with 50 and 10. Then ask students to explain how they would use ten-frames to show the number 80.

Summarize How can you use ten-frames to count by 10s?

DEVELOP: PROBLEM-BASED LEARNING

PEARSON
realize.
PearsonRealize.com

COHERENCE: Engage learners by connecting prior knowledge to new ideas.

Students find the easiest way to count a set of counters arranged in ten-frames. This prepares them for the next part of the lesson where they learn how to count groups of 10.

10–15 min

Solve

BEFORE

1. **Pose the Solve-and-Share Problem**
   MP.1 Make Sense and Persevere In this problem, students will formulate a plan to count a large group of counters.

2. **Build Understanding**
   What are you asked to do? [Find the total number of counters.] *How are the counters arranged?* [In ten-frames]

DURING

3. **Ask Guiding Questions As Needed**
   How many groups of 10 are in a ten-frame? [1]
   How many counters are in 1 ten-frame? [10]
   How have you counted 10 quickly before? [I skip counted by tens.]

AFTER

4. **Share and Discuss Solutions**
   Start with students' solutions. If needed, Solve project and analyze Aaron's work to discuss how he counted the counters in the ten-frames.

5. **Transition to the Visual Learning Bridge**
   A filled ten-frame of counters equals one group of ten.

   Later in the lesson, you will learn that skip counting by tens is an easy way to count to large numbers.

6. **Extension for Early Finishers**
   How many groups of 10 are in a hundred chart? [10]

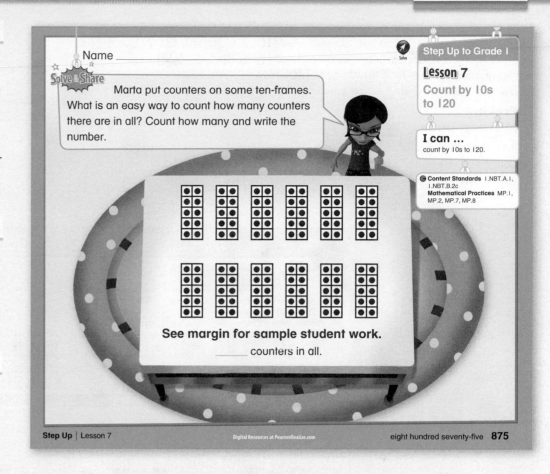

Name _____

Solve

Solve & Share

Marta put counters on some ten-frames. What is an easy way to count how many counters there are in all? Count how many and write the number.

See margin for sample student work.

_____ counters in all.

Step Up | Lesson 7

Digital Resources at PearsonRealize.com

eight hundred seventy-five **875**

Step Up to Grade 1

Lesson 7
Count by 10s to 120

I can ...
count by 10s to 120.

Content Standards 1.NBT.A.1, 1.NBT.B.2c
Mathematical Practices MP.1, MP.2, MP.7, MP.8

Analyze Student Work

Aaron's Work

120 counters in all.

Mary's Work

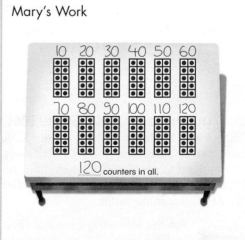

120 counters in all.

Aaron counts the number of counters in one ten-frame. Then he counts the number of ten-frames before skip counting by 10s.

Mary skip counts by 10s to find the total number of counters.

STEP 2

DEVELOP: VISUAL LEARNING

The *Visual Learning Bridge* connects students' thinking in Solve & Share to important math ideas in the lesson. Use the *Visual Learning Bridge* to make these ideas explicit. Also available as a *Visual Learning Animation Plus* at PearsonRealize.com

E L L
Visual Learning

Learn

Glossary

PEARSON
realize.
PearsonRealize.com

Number Sense *What tens do you see?* [10, 20, 30, 40, 50, 60, 70] *How many ten-frames are in each group?* [1, 2, 3, 4, 5, 6, 7] *How many counters are in 7 ten-frames?* [70] *How do you count the counters by 10s, starting with the first ten-frame?* [10, 20, 30, 40, 50, 60, 70]

Prevent Misconceptions

If students have trouble naming the value of tens, have them practice counting the counters by ones on sets of filled ten-frames and name the value. Then have them count the ten-frames by tens.

What tens do you see? [80, 90, 100] *How many ten-frames are in each group?* [8, 9, 10] *How many counters are in 10 ten-frames?* [100] *How many counters would there be if there were one more ten-frame?* [110] *And one more?* [120] *How do you count to 120 by 10s, starting with the first ten-frame?* [10, 20, 30, 40, 50, 60, 70, 80, 90, 100, 110, 120]

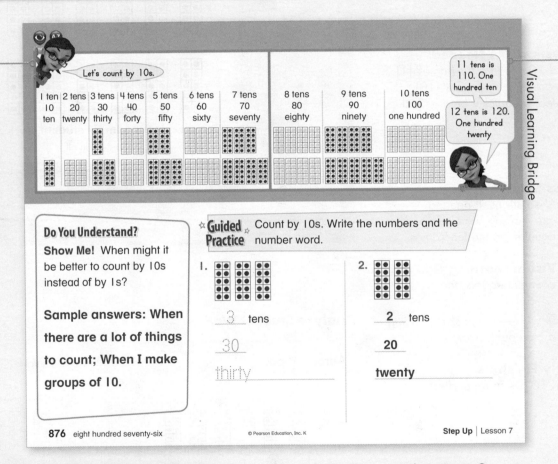

Visual Learning Bridge

Let's count by 10s.

| 1 ten 10 ten | 2 tens 20 twenty | 3 tens 30 thirty | 4 tens 40 forty | 5 tens 50 fifty | 6 tens 60 sixty | 7 tens 70 seventy | 8 tens 80 eighty | 9 tens 90 ninety | 10 tens 100 one hundred |

11 tens is 110. One hundred ten

12 tens is 120. One hundred twenty

Do You Understand?

Show Me! When might it be better to count by 10s instead of by 1s?

Sample answers: When there are a lot of things to count; When I make groups of 10.

☆ **Guided Practice** ☆ Count by 10s. Write the numbers and the number word.

1.

___3___ tens

___30___

thirty

2.

___2___ tens

20

twenty

876 eight hundred seventy-six

© Pearson Education, Inc. K

Step Up | Lesson 7

Do You Understand? Show Me! MP.8 Generalize

Discuss with students why it is faster to count the counters in the exercises by 10s rather than 1s. Ask students to explain why they do not need to count by 1s when they know that each ten-frame has 10 counters. Remind students that counting by 1s and counting by 10s gives the same result.

Essential Question

Ask the following Essential Question: *How can you count to 120 by 10s?* [Sample answer: I can say only the tens: 10, 20, 30, …, 120]

Error Intervention: Item 2

If students have difficulty counting by 10s,

then have them label each ten-frame *1* and *2*, then add *0* after each to show *10* and *20*.

Items 3–5 Students may have difficulty writing the correct number word. Remind students to use the words in the Visual Learning Bridge as a guide to writing number words.

Item 6 MP.7 Look for Patterns Encourage students to develop a plan to find Mike's pattern. *What do you need to find?* [Mike's pattern] *How much is each number increasing by?* [10] *So, what number comes after 30?* [40] *How can you check your work?* [Sample answer: I can skip count by 10s.]

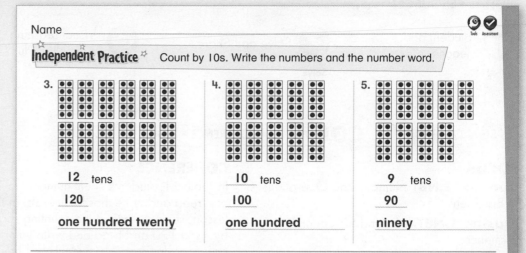

Name _____

☆ **Independent Practice** ☆   Count by 10s. Write the numbers and the number word.

3.
  12 tens
  120
  one hundred twenty

4.
  10 tens
  100
  one hundred

5.
  9 tens
  90
  ninety

Write the missing numbers.

6. **Higher Order Thinking**
   Mike writes a pattern.

   He forgets to write some numbers.
   What numbers did Mike forget to write?

   10, 20, 30, __40__, __50__, 60, 70, __80__, 90, __100__, 110, 120

   What is Mike's pattern?

Step Up | Lesson 7   eight hundred seventy-seven **877**

Item 7 MP.2 Reasoning *How many counters did you draw in each ten-frame?* [10] *How many groups of 10 are in your picture?* [4]

Item 8 MP.1 Make Sense and Persevere Remind students to gather information from the text and illustration. *What do you know?* [There are 6 boxes with 10 books in each box.] *What do you need to find?* [How many books Bo has in all]

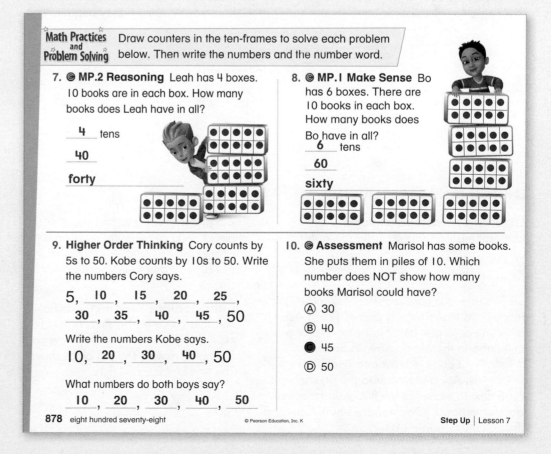

☆ **Math Practices and Problem Solving** ☆   Draw counters in the ten-frames to solve each problem below. Then write the numbers and the number word.

7. ⓒ **MP.2 Reasoning** Leah has 4 boxes. 10 books are in each box. How many books does Leah have in all?

   4 tens
   40
   forty

8. ⓒ **MP.1 Make Sense** Bo has 6 boxes. There are 10 books in each box. How many books does Bo have in all?

   6 tens
   60
   sixty

9. **Higher Order Thinking** Cory counts by 5s to 50. Kobe counts by 10s to 50. Write the numbers Cory says.

   5, __10__, 15, __20__, 25, __30__, 35, __40__, __45__, 50

   Write the numbers Kobe says.

   10, __20__, 30, __40__, 50

   What numbers do both boys say?

   __10__, __20__, __30__, __40__, __50__

10. ⓒ **Assessment** Marisol has some books. She puts them in piles of 10. Which number does NOT show how many books Marisol could have?

    Ⓐ 30
    Ⓑ 40
    ● 45
    Ⓓ 50

878 eight hundred seventy-eight   © Pearson Education, Inc. K   **Step Up** | Lesson 7

COUNT BY 1s TO 120

DIGITAL RESOURCES PearsonRealize.com

 Student and Teacher eTexts
eText

 Solve and Share
Solve

 **Visual Learning Animation Plus**
Learn

 Animated Glossary
Glossary

Math Tools
Tools

LESSON OVERVIEW **F C R** FOCUS • COHERENCE • RIGOR

FOCUS

Domain 1.NBT Number and Operations in Base Ten

Cluster 1.NBT.A Extend the counting sequence.

Content Standard 1.NBT.A.1 Count to 120, starting at any number less than 120. In this range, read and write numerals and represent a number of objects with a written numeral.

Mathematical Practices MP.2, MP.6, MP.7

Objective Count by 1s to 120.

Essential Understanding Counting forward by 1s to 120 follows the same place-value counting rules as counting forward by 1s to two-digit numbers.

COHERENCE

In Topic 11, students count numbers to 100 and read and write those numerals. In this lesson, students extend the counting sequence by 1s to 120 and read and write numbers past 100. In Grade 1, students will have repeated practice at counting to 120 in different ways.

RIGOR

This lesson emphasizes **conceptual understanding**. As students count forward by 1s to 120, they extend their ability to count with two-digit numbers to being able to count with three-digit numbers. Students recognize that the way in which they count the digits in the ones place applies to the way they count digits in the tens and hundreds places, and that these rules apply no matter from which number they begin to count.

ENGLISH LANGUAGE LEARNERS **E L L**

Listening Demonstrate listening comprehension by responding to questions.

Use with the Visual Learning Bridge on Student's Edition, p. 880.

Show students a hundreds flat. Ask: *How many units make up this block?* [100] Ask a volunteer to put 1 unit cube on top of a unit cube in the block. Say: *When I add 1 more unit cube, I have one hundred one unit cubes.* Ask a volunteer to put another unit cube next to the hundreds flat. Ask: *How many do I have now?* [One hundred two] Continue the activity through 110.

Beginning Point to Box 1 and read the text aloud. Ask: *How many blocks are there?* [1] *There are 100 smaller blocks, or unit cubes, in this block. Point to the number that this block shows.* [100]

Intermediate Read the text in Box 2 aloud. Ask: *Do you see 200 small blocks here?* [No] *How many are there?* [101] *How can you tell?* [Sample answer: The big block shows 100. The little block shows 1.]

Advanced After listening to the Visual Learning Bridge being read aloud, ask students: *How can blocks help us count?* [Sample answer: The big block shows 100. The small block shows 1.] Continue counting the number of small blocks. *What do you do to count forward?* Students will explain what counting forward means.

Summarize How can you answer questions about counting to 120?

DEVELOP: PROBLEM-BASED LEARNING

PEARSON
realize.
PearsonRealize.com

COHERENCE: Engage students by connecting prior knowledge to new ideas.
Students count by 1s starting with 100. This prepares them for the next part of the lesson where they learn to count forward to 120.

10–15 min

Solve

Whole Class **BEFORE**

1. Pose the Solve-and-Share Problem
MP.7 Look for Patterns In this problem, students identify a pattern in order to extend the counting sequence to the next 3 numbers after 100. They use the structure of the number system in order to explain their answers.

2. Build Understanding
What numbers were already counted? [98, 99, 100] *What are you asked to do?* [I should count the next 3 numbers after 100. Then I should tell how I know I am right.]

Small Group **DURING**

3. Ask Guiding Questions As Needed
When you count in order, which digit changes first? [The number farthest to the right] *How do you know what number comes next?* [I count 1 more than each number.]

Whole Class **AFTER**

4. Share and Discuss Solutions
Solve Start with students' solutions. Have them explain how they chose the next 3 numbers. If needed, project and analyze Antonia's work to discuss how she counted the next 3 numbers after 100.

5. Transition to the Visual Learning Bridge
You found the next 3 numbers that you would count after 100. Later in the lesson, you will learn how to continue counting after 100 and how to write and say those numbers.

6. Extension for Early Finishers
What are the next 3 numbers after 103? Explain how you know you are right. [104, 105, 106; I know I am right because first I say *one hundred* and then I say the numbers that come after *three* when I count by 1s. I say: *one hundred four, one hundred five, one hundred six.*]

Name _____

Solve & Share

Jada and Alex take turns counting by 1s. Jada counts from 98 up to 100. Now, it's Alex's turn to keep counting. Say the next 3 numbers Alex should count. Tell how you know you're right.

98, 99, 100

___ , ___ , ___

See margin for sample student work.

Step Up to Grade 1

Lesson 8
Count by 1s to 120

I can ...
count by 1s to 120.

Content Standards 1.NBT.A.1
Mathematical Practices MP.2, MP.6, MP.7

Step Up | Lesson 8   Digital Resources at PearsonRealize.com   eight hundred seventy-nine **879**

Analyze Student Work

Antonia's Work

101, 102, 103

Antonia accurately counts the next 3 numbers after 100.

Pedro's Work

110, 120, 130

Pedro confuses larger numbers and does not realize that the counting sequence for the digits after the hundreds is the same as it is for one- and two-digit numbers.

The *Visual Learning Bridge* connects students' thinking in Solve & Share to important math ideas in the lesson. Use the *Visual Learning Bridge* to make these ideas explicit. Also available as a *Visual Learning Animation Plus* at PearsonRealize.com

E L L
Visual Learning

Learn   Glossary

MP.6 Be Precise *How is this number different from numbers such as 97, 98, and 99?* [100 has 3 digits, and 97, 98, and 99 each have 2 digits.] *If we counted all of the little green blocks in this larger block, how many little green blocks do you think there would be?* [One hundred]

Why do you say 101 after 100 when you count forward? [One hundred one is one more than one hundred.]

What does each of these numbers start with when you say it? [One hundred] *Why?* [Each number has one hundred and some ones.] *When you count forward by 1s, which digit changes first?* [The ones digit] *How would you say 101, 102, 103, and 104?* [One hundred one, one hundred two, one hundred three, one hundred four]

Which digit changes when you count by 1s from 116 to 119? [The ones digit] *Which digits change when you continue to count from 119 to 120? Explain.* [The tens digit changes to a 2, and the ones digit goes back to 0 since now there is another ten.]

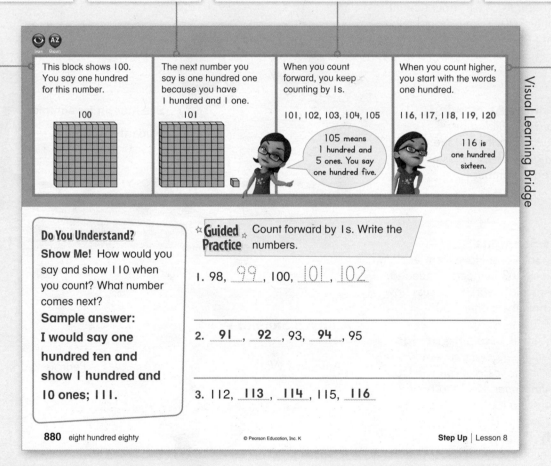

Visual Learning Bridge

This block shows 100. You say one hundred for this number.

100

The next number you say is one hundred one because you have 1 hundred and 1 one.

101

When you count forward, you keep counting by 1s.

101, 102, 103, 104, 105

105 means 1 hundred and 5 ones. You say one hundred five.

When you count higher, you start with the words one hundred.

116, 117, 118, 119, 120

116 is one hundred sixteen.

Do You Understand?

Show Me! How would you say and show 110 when you count? What number comes next?

Sample answer:
I would say one hundred ten and show 1 hundred and 10 ones; 111.

Guided Practice Count forward by 1s. Write the numbers.

1. 98, __99__, 100, __101__, __102__

2. __91__, __92__, 93, __94__, 95

3. 112, __113__, __114__, 115, __116__

880 eight hundred eighty   © Pearson Education, Inc. K   Step Up | Lesson 8

Do You Understand? Show Me! MP.2 Reasoning
Have students use a hundreds flat, a tens-rod, and a ones unit to show and explain their answers. If needed, show how the ten-rod represents a ten.

 Ask the following Essential Question: *How is counting forward from 100 to 120 like counting forward to a two-digit number? How is it different?* [Sample answer: It is the same because you count the numbers after one hundred in the same way. It is different because when you count forward with three-digit numbers, you say the words *one hundred* first.]

Error Intervention: Item 3
If students have difficulty counting by 1s,

then have them use a hundred flat and ones units to model counting the numbers. Emphasize that when counting by 1s from 100, you use the same sequence of numbers as counting by 1s from 12 to 16.

20–30 min   Tools

Items 4–9 MP.7 Look for Patterns Remind students that when counting numbers over 100, the digits that show the tens and ones follow the same sequence as when counting from 0 to 100.

Items 10–11 Students may find it helpful to write the numbers given in the clues before and after the blanks. For example, in Item 10, students could write *112, ___, ___, ___, 116*. This will help guide them to write the possible mystery numbers for the first two clues and identify the mystery number after the third clue.

Item 14 MP.2 Reasoning *What number do you say after 102 when you are counting by 1s?* [103] Have students continue to count the numbers aloud. *How many days do you count on from Monday to Friday?* [4] *What is the fourth number that you count after 102?* [106]

Item 15 Suggest that students check their answers by reading the numbers in order from left to right to determine whether they are counting by 1s.

Name _____

Independent Practice   Count forward by 1s. Write the numbers.

4. 97, __98__, __99__, __100__, 101

5. __103__, 104, __105__, __106__, 107

6. __116__, 117, __118__, 119, __120__

7. __100__, 101, 102, __103__, __104__

8. __109__, __110__, 111, __112__, 113

9. 111, __112__, __113__, 114, __115__

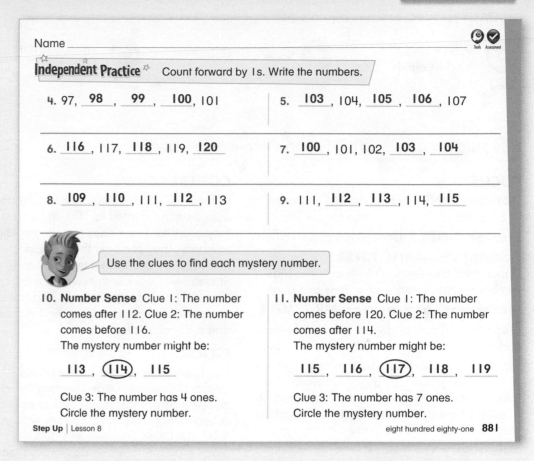

Use the clues to find each mystery number.

10. **Number Sense** Clue 1: The number comes after 112. Clue 2: The number comes before 116.
The mystery number might be:

__113__, (__114__), __115__

Clue 3: The number has 4 ones.
Circle the mystery number.

11. **Number Sense** Clue 1: The number comes before 120. Clue 2: The number comes after 114.
The mystery number might be:

__115__, __116__, (__117__), __118__, __119__

Clue 3: The number has 7 ones.
Circle the mystery number.

Step Up | Lesson 8   eight hundred eighty-one **881**

Math Practices and Problem Solving   Solve each problem below.

12. **Vocabulary** Marta is counting to 120. She says the number that is one **more** than 117. What number does she say?

118

13. In this chart, Manuel writes the numbers 105 to 111 in order. Then he spills water on it. Some numbers rub off. Help Manuel fill in the missing numbers.

| 105 | 106 | 107 | 108 | 109 | 110 | 111 |

14. **MP.2 Reasoning** Savannah hikes 1 mile every day. After hiking on Monday, she has hiked 102 miles. After hiking on Friday, how many miles will she have hiked?

__106__ miles

Think about the days and the numbers you count on.

15. **Higher Order Thinking** Pick a number greater than 100 and less than 116. Write the number in the box.

Then write the three numbers that come before it and the number that comes after it.

_____, _____, _____, [   ], _____

Check students' work.

16. **Assessment** Which shows the correct order for counting forward by 1s? Choose all that apply.

☐ 100, 101, 103, 102

■ 115, 116, 117, 118

■ 104, 105, 106, 107

☐ 115, 116, 119, 120

882 eight hundred eighty-two   © Pearson Education, Inc. K   Step Up | Lesson 8

TENS AND ONES

DIGITAL RESOURCES PearsonRealize.com

 Student and Teacher eTexts
eText

 Solve and Share
Solve

 Visual Learning Animation Plus
Learn

Animated Glossary
Glossary

 Math Tools
Tools

LESSON OVERVIEW   **FCR** FOCUS • COHERENCE • RIGOR

FOCUS

Domain 1.NBT Number and Operations in Base Ten

Cluster 1.NBT.B Understand place value.

Content Standard 1.NBT.B.2 Understand that the two digits of a two-digit number represent amounts of tens and ones.

Mathematical Practices MP.2, MP.4

Objective Count and write numbers by tens and ones.

Essential Understanding When objects are grouped in sets of 10 and leftovers (ones), counting the groups of ten and adding ones tells how many there are in all. Numbers can be used to tell how many.

Vocabulary ones, tens

Materials Connecting cubes (or Teaching Tool 8)
Plastic bags

COHERENCE

In Topic 11, students considered tens and ones as they counted to 100. In this lesson, they count tens and ones to write two-digit numbers. They see how the digits in these numbers represent tens and ones. Students will work with two-digit numbers in Grade 1, including using tens and ones to compare, and adding a two-digit number and a one-digit number.

RIGOR

This lesson emphasizes **conceptual understanding**. Understanding two-digit numbers as groups of tens and ones is a critical concept as students work with greater numbers. Using concrete and pictorial models to compose and decompose tens and ones is vital to a student's number sense. It establishes a foundation for future place-value concepts as well as for addition and subtraction with greater numbers.

ENGLISH LANGUAGE LEARNERS ELL

Listening Learn new language structures heard during classroom instruction and interactions.

Use with the Visual Learning Bridge on Student's Edition, p. 884.

Students may be confused by the language structures "tens digit" and "ones digit." Make it clear to all English language learners that the "ones" and "tens" are place values that will help them understand how large a number is and how to compare numbers of different sizes.

Beginning Point to the 35 in the first box. *There are 3 tens. There are 5 ones. What number do the 3 and 5 make together?*

Intermediate Give students opportunities to learn about tens and ones on their own. Write a two-digit number on the board and ask them to identify the digit in the ones place and the digit in the tens place. Then have them read the number aloud.

Advanced Have partners say two-digit numbers and ask each other which digit is the tens digit and which is the ones digit.

Summarize How can you find the tens digit and the ones digit?

COHERENCE: Engage learners by connecting prior knowledge to new ideas.

In this problem, students will skip count to determine a two-digit number. Later in the lesson, they will be shown specifically that two-digit numbers have a "tens" and a "ones" digit and why these digits have those names.

10–15 min

Solve

BEFORE

1. Pose the Solve-and-Share Problem
Give each student a bag with 10–30 cubes in it.

MP.2 Reasoning In this lesson, students will connect the concepts of 10 ones and 1 ten with two-digit numbers.

2. Build Understanding
What are you asked to find? [The number of cubes that are in the bag] *What should you do first?* [Guess how many cubes there are.]

DURING

3. Ask Guiding Questions As Needed
By what numbers can you count? [2, 5, 10] *Which number is the best to use for this problem?* [Sample answer: 5] *Why?* [Sample answer: If I count by 2s, I might lose track.] *Could you count by 10s?* [Yes] *Why might that be better?* [Sample answer: The larger the number, the harder it will be to miscount.]

AFTER

4. Share and Discuss Solutions
Start with students' solutions. Have them share their strategies for counting larger numbers. If needed, project and analyze Wallace's work to discuss how he counted tens and leftovers and to learn that these leftovers are actually called *ones*.

5. Transition to the Visual Learning Bridge
Large numbers are made up of digits. Later in the lesson, you will learn that the tens digit tells how many groups of 10 can be made from a number, and the ones digit tells how many will be left over.

6. Extension for Early Finishers
What do you think we call the 1 in 100? [1 hundred] *Knowing what you do about tens and ones, how many tens do you think it takes to make 100?* [10]

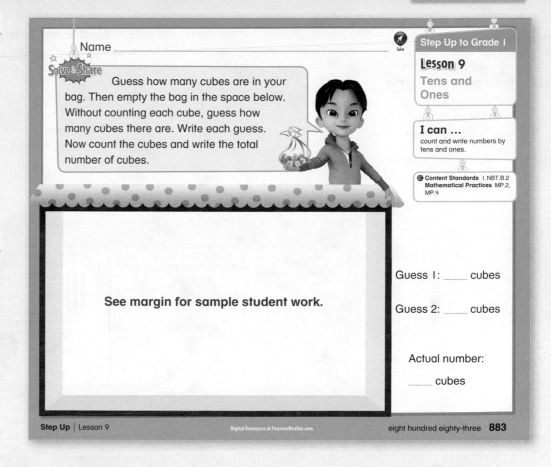

Name _____

Solve & Share

Guess how many cubes are in your bag. Then empty the bag in the space below. Without counting each cube, guess how many cubes there are. Write each guess. Now count the cubes and write the total number of cubes.

See margin for sample student work.

Step Up to Grade 1

Lesson 9
Tens and Ones

I can ...
count and write numbers by tens and ones.

Content Standards 1.NBT.B.2
Mathematical Practices MP.2, MP.4

Guess 1: _____ cubes

Guess 2: _____ cubes

Actual number:
_____ cubes

Step Up | Lesson 9   Digital Resources at PearsonRealize.com   eight hundred eighty-three **883**

Analyze Student Work

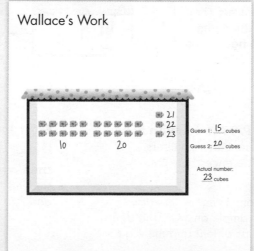

Wallace's Work

Guess 1: 15 cubes
Guess 2: 20 cubes

Actual number: 23 cubes

Veronica's Work

Guess 1: 20 cubes
Guess 2: 30 cubes

Actual number: 29 cubes

Wallace forms as many groups of 10 as he can. Then he counts by tens and counts on by ones.

Veronica counts her cubes by ones. She miscounts and gets the wrong answer.

STEP 2

DEVELOP: VISUAL LEARNING

The *Visual Learning Bridge* connects students' thinking in Solve & Share to important math ideas in the lesson. Use the *Visual Learning Bridge* to make these ideas explicit. Also available as a *Visual Learning Animation Plus* at PearsonRealize.com

Visual Learning

Learn

Glossary

What numbers make up 35? [Sample answer: 30 and 5] How are these numbers like the numbers in 3 tens and 5 ones? [3 tens is 30, and 5 ones is 5.]

A digit is any of the numerals in a number. What are the digits in 35? [3 and 5] Which digit is in the tens place? [3]

MP.4 Model with Math When you use connecting cubes to show a number, you put the groups of ten in the tens place on the place-value mat. The leftover cubes are called ones. Where should you put these cubes? [In the ones place on the place-value mat] How many tens are there in 35? [3] How many ones are there? [5]

MP.4 Model with Math You don't have to put cubes on a place-value mat. You can also write numbers on the mat. The 3 in the tens place means there are 3 tens. What does the 5 in the ones place mean? [There are 5 ones.] Three tens and five ones make 35. You can put the 3 and the 5 together to make the number 35.

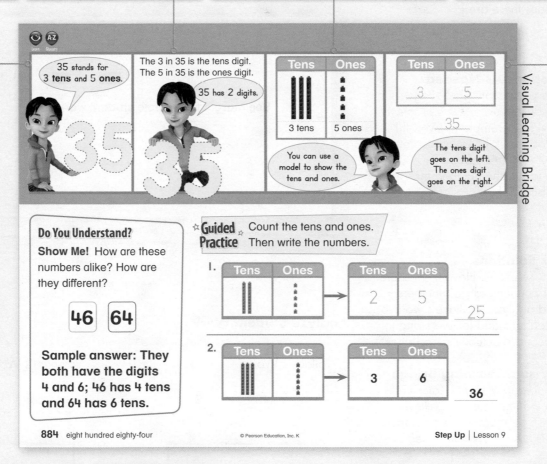

Visual Learning Bridge

Do You Understand?

Show Me! How are these numbers alike? How are they different?

46 64

Sample answer: They both have the digits 4 and 6; 46 has 4 tens and 64 has 6 tens.

☆ **Guided Practice** Count the tens and ones. Then write the numbers.

1. → 2 5   25

2. → 3 6   36

884 eight hundred eighty-four   © Pearson Education, Inc. K   **Step Up** | Lesson 9

Do You Understand? Show Me! MP.4 Model with Math

Have students use connecting cubes to represent their numbers. Ask them to talk about the similarities and differences between the numbers.

Essential Question Ask the following Essential Question: *What do the digits stand for in a two-digit number?* [Sample answer: The digit on the left tells me how many groups of ten, and the digit on the right tells how many ones.]

Error Intervention: Item 2

If students are not sure what the digits in 36 represent,

then refer them to the cubes pictured on the workmat. Remind students that the 3 groups of 10 cubes are shown by the 3 in 36, and that the 6 leftover cubes (1s) is shown by the 6 in 36.

Tools

20–30 min

Items 3–5 MP.2 Reasoning Point out that the ones side of the mat (and the ones digit) will always show a number from 0 to 9. If there were 10 cubes, they would be grouped to show a 10 on the left side of the workmat.

Encourage students to consider the meaning of place value in a number where the tens and ones digits are the same. *Do each of the digits represent the same value?* [No]

Item 6 Ask students to explain the difference between the number of tens and the same number of ones.

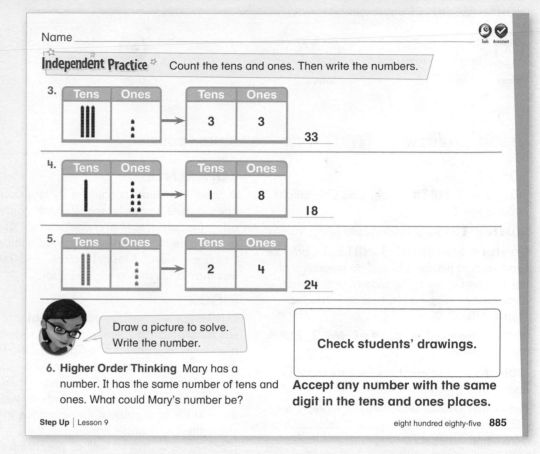

Name _____

Independent Practice   Count the tens and ones. Then write the numbers.

3.

Tens	Ones
|||	⋮

Tens	Ones
3	3

33

4.

Tens	Ones
		⋮

Tens	Ones
1	8

18

5.

Tens	Ones
||	⋮

Tens	Ones
2	4

24

Draw a picture to solve. Write the number.

6. Higher Order Thinking Mary has a number. It has the same number of tens and ones. What could Mary's number be?

Check students' drawings.

Accept any number with the same digit in the tens and ones places.

Step Up | Lesson 9   eight hundred eighty-five   **885**

Item 7 MP.4 Model with Math Students may benefit from showing the problem situation using connecting cubes to represent the number of juice boxes.

Item 8 Suggest that students begin by thinking of a number. The students can use connecting cubes to represent their number in terms of tens and ones.

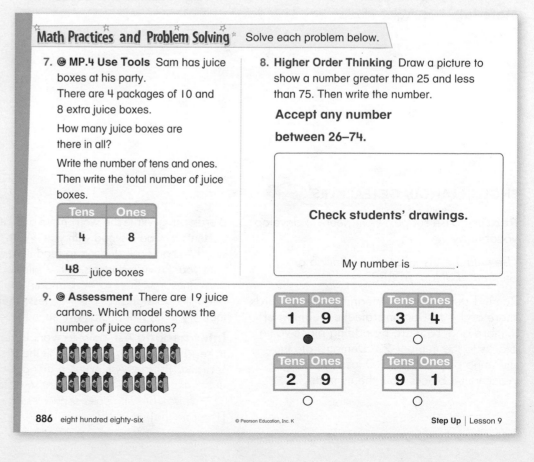

Math Practices and Problem Solving   Solve each problem below.

7. MP.4 Use Tools Sam has juice boxes at his party.
There are 4 packages of 10 and 8 extra juice boxes.

How many juice boxes are there in all?

Write the number of tens and ones. Then write the total number of juice boxes.

Tens	Ones
4	8

48 juice boxes

8. Higher Order Thinking Draw a picture to show a number greater than 25 and less than 75. Then write the number.

Accept any number between 26–74.

Check students' drawings.

My number is _____.

9. Assessment There are 19 juice cartons. Which model shows the number of juice cartons?

Tens	Ones
1	9

●

Tens	Ones
3	4

○

Tens	Ones
2	9

○

Tens	Ones
9	1

○

886 eight hundred eighty-six   © Pearson Education, Inc. K   Step Up | Lesson 9

885–886

1 MORE, 1 LESS; 10 MORE, 10 LESS

DIGITAL RESOURCES PearsonRealize.com

 Student and Teacher eTexts
eText

 Solve and Share
Solve

 Visual Learning Animation Plus
Learn

 Animated Glossary
Glossary

Math Tools
Tools

LESSON OVERVIEW FCR FOCUS • COHERENCE • RIGOR

FOCUS

Domain 1.NBT Number and Operations in Base Ten

Cluster 1.NBT.B Understand place value.

Content Standard 1.NBT.B.3 Compare two two-digit numbers based on meanings of the tens and ones digits, recording the results of comparisons with the symbols >, =, and <. *Also* **1.NBT.C.5**

Mathematical Practices MP.2, MP.5, MP.6, MP.8

Objective Find numbers that are more or less than a given number.

Essential Understanding *1 more, 1 less, 10 more,* and *10 less* express a relationship between 2 numbers.

Vocabulary more, less

Materials Place-Value Blocks

COHERENCE

In Topic 11, students counted by tens and ones to 100. In this lesson, students continue using models of tens and ones as they use place-value models in order to find numbers that are 1 more, 1 less, 10 more, and 10 less than a given two-digit number.

RIGOR

This lesson emphasizes **conceptual understanding**. Students use ten-rods and ones units to model a two-digit number. Then they build upon that model to show a number that is 1 more, 1 less, 10 more, or 10 less than the original number. As students solve these kinds of problems, they continue to strengthen their understanding of the place-value system as well as prepare for two-digit addition and subtraction.

ENGLISH LANGUAGE LEARNERS

Reading Use support from peers to develop vocabulary.

Use with the Visual Learning Bridge on Student's Edition, p. 888.

Remind students of the meanings of the words *more* and *less*. Demonstrate the meaning of 1 more and 10 more by adding place-value blocks to the number 23. Demonstrate the meaning of 1 less and 10 less by taking place-value blocks from the number 32.

Beginning Write the word *more* and ask students to read it aloud with you. Write the word *less* and ask students to read it aloud with you. Provide students with 2 piles of ones units. Ask them to work in pairs to find the pile with *more* and the pile with *less*. Then have them try to find the words written in the lesson.

Intermediate Ask pairs to work together to read the numbers in Box 1 of the Visual Learning Bridge. Ask: *Which box of unit cubes shows more?* [The one that says 26] *Which box of unit cubes shows less?* [The one that says 25]

Advanced Divide students into groups of 2 or 3. Ask them to read Boxes 3 and 4 of the Visual Learning Bridge. Students will discuss how they know which picture shows more and which shows less.

Summarize How did working with a partner help you figure out which group had more or less?

DEVELOP: PROBLEM-BASED LEARNING

PEARSON
realize
PearsonRealize.com

COHERENCE: Engage students by connecting prior knowledge to new ideas.

Students use place-value blocks to find 1 more and 1 less than a given number. This prepares them for the next part of the lesson in which they find 1 more, 1 less, 10 more, and 10 less than given numbers.

10–15 min

Solve

Whole Class BEFORE

1. Pose the Solve-and-Share Problem
Give each student place-value blocks (2 tens rods and 15 ones units).

MP.5 Use Appropriate Tools Strategically
In this problem, students will use place-value blocks in order to determine the number that is 1 more than 12 and the number that is 1 less than 12.

2. Build Understanding
What are you asked to find? [The number that comes before 12 and the number that comes after 12] *What do you know about the numbers?* [One will be greater than 12 and one will be less than 12.]

Small Group DURING

3. Ask Guiding Questions As Needed
What does the word after *mean?* [It means the number is greater than 12.] *What does the word* before *mean?* [It means the number is less than 12.]

Whole Class AFTER

4. Share and Discuss Solutions
Start with students' solutions. Have them share their strategies for finding the number before 12 and the number after 12. If needed, project and analyze Pearl's work to discuss how she used place-value blocks to show 12, the number after 12, and the number before 12.

5. Transition to the Visual Learning Bridge
You used place-value blocks to find the number that comes after 12 and the number that comes before 12. In the next part of the lesson, you will use place-value blocks to show numbers that are 1 more, 1 less, 10 more, and 10 less than a number.

6. Extension for Early Finishers
Have students find the number after 20 and the number before 20. [21; 19]

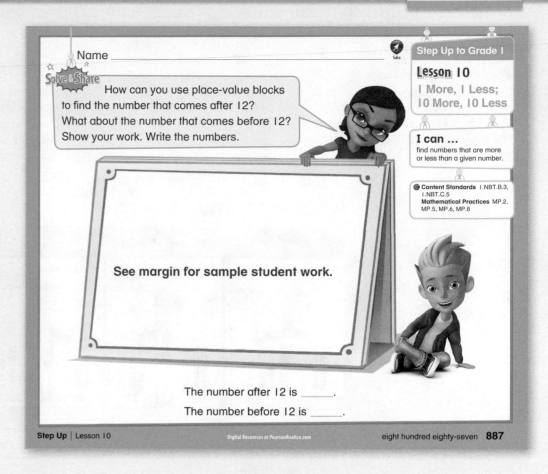

Name _____

Solve & Share

How can you use place-value blocks to find the number that comes after 12? What about the number that comes before 12? Show your work. Write the numbers.

See margin for sample student work.

The number after 12 is _____.
The number before 12 is _____.

Step Up | Lesson 10   Digital Resources at PearsonRealize.com   eight hundred eighty-seven **887**

Step Up to Grade 1

Lesson 10
1 More, 1 Less;
10 More, 10 Less

I can ...
find numbers that are more or less than a given number.

Content Standards I.NBT.B.3, I.NBT.C.5
Mathematical Practices MP.2, MP.5, MP.6, MP.8

Analyze Student Work

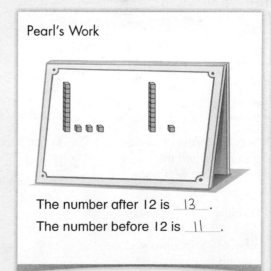

Pearl's Work

The number after 12 is __13__.
The number before 12 is __11__.

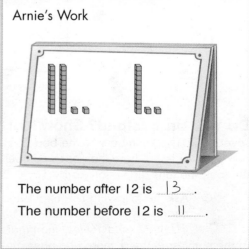

Arnie's Work

The number after 12 is __13__.
The number before 12 is __11__.

Pearl first shows 12 with her blocks. To find the number after 12, she adds 1 ones unit and then counts on from 12: 12, 13. To find the number before 12, she starts with 1 tens rod and 2 ones units and takes away 1 ones unit. As she takes it away, she counts back from 12: 12, 11.

Arnie shows 1 tens rod and 2 ones units. To find the number after 12, he adds 1 tens rod to make 22. To find the number before 12, he takes away 1 tens rod to make 12. Arnie completes the sentences correctly even though the numbers were not modeled correctly.

DEVELOP: VISUAL LEARNING

The *Visual Learning Bridge* connects students' thinking in Solve & Share to important math ideas in the lesson. Use the *Visual Learning Bridge* to make these ideas explicit. Also available as a *Visual Learning Animation Plus* at PearsonRealize.com

Learn   **Glossary**

MP.2 Reasoning
When you add 1 to 25, does the ones or the tens digit change? [The ones digit changes.] *How does it change?* [1 more is added. The ones digit is 1 more than before.]

When you take away 1 from 25, does the ones or the tens digit change? [The ones digit changes.] *How does it change?* [1 is taken away. The ones digit is 1 less than before.]

When you add 10 to 25, does the ones or the tens digit change? [The tens digit changes.] *How does it change?* [1 more ten is added. The tens digit is 1 more than before.]

When you take away 10 from 25, does the ones or the tens digit change? [The tens digit changes.] *How does it change?* [1 ten is taken away. The tens digit is 1 less than before.]

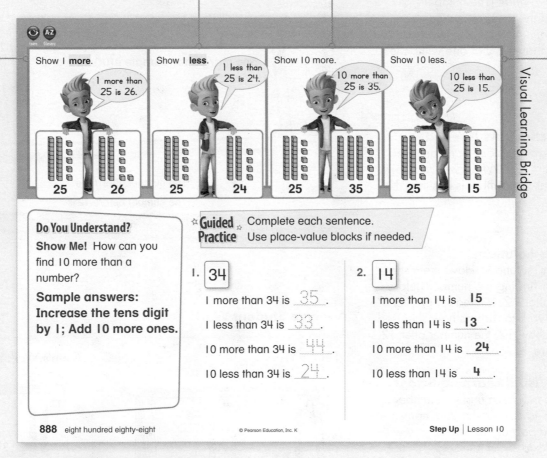

Visual Learning Bridge

Do You Understand?

Show Me! How can you find 10 more than a number?

Sample answers: Increase the tens digit by 1; Add 10 more ones.

★ **Guided Practice** ★   Complete each sentence. Use place-value blocks if needed.

1. **34**

   1 more than 34 is ___35___.

   1 less than 34 is ___33___.

   10 more than 34 is ___44___.

   10 less than 34 is ___24___.

2. **14**

   1 more than 14 is ___15___.

   1 less than 14 is ___13___.

   10 more than 14 is ___24___.

   10 less than 14 is ___4___.

Do You Understand? Show Me! MP.6 Be Precise Write several two-digit numbers on the board. Have students find the number that is 10 more than each number. Point out that with each number, the tens digit changes by 1.

Essential Question Ask the following Essential Question: *How does a number change when you find the number that is 1 more, 1 less, 10 more, and 10 less than that number?* [Sample answer: In the number that is 1 more, the ones digit goes up by 1; in the number that is 1 less, the ones digit goes down by 1; in the number that is 10 more, the tens digit goes up by 10; and in the number that is 10 less, the tens digit goes down by 10.]

Error Intervention: Item 2

If students write *13* to show 1 more than 14,

then remind them that *1 more* indicates a greater number than 14, not a lesser one.

Item 4 MP.5 Use Appropriate Tools
Strategically Remind students that to find 1 less than 50, they can break apart a tens rod into 10 ones units and then take 1 away.

Item 5 Remind students that to find 1 more than 19, they can add 1 ones unit and then join 10 ones units to make a tens rod. After joining the ones units into a tens rod, students should have 2 tens rods.

Name _____

Independent Practice Complete each sentence. Use place-value blocks if needed.

3. **71**
I more than 71 is **72** .
I less than 71 is **70** .
10 more than 71 is **81** .
10 less than 71 is **61** .

4. **50**
I more than 50 is **51** .
I less than 50 is **49** .
10 more than 50 is **60** .
10 less than 50 is **40** .

5. **19**
I more than 19 is **20** .
I less than 19 is **18** .
10 more than 19 is **29** .
10 less than 19 is **9** .

6. **49**
I more than 49 is **50** .
I less than 49 is **48** .
10 more than 49 is **59** .
10 less than 49 is **39** .

7. **85**
I more than 85 is **86** .
I less than 85 is **84** .
10 more than 85 is **95** .
10 less than 85 is **75** .

8. **42**
I more than 42 is **43** .
I less than 42 is **41** .
10 more than 42 is **52** .
10 less than 42 is **32** .

9. **Higher Order Thinking** Circle the picture that shows 10 more than 34. Explain how you know.

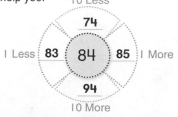

Sample answer: I know because 34 + 10 = 44.

Step Up | Lesson 10   eight hundred eighty-nine **889**

Item 10 MP.8 Generalize Ask: *Which digit will change when you add 10 more to a number?* [The tens digit] *How will it change?* [Sample answer: It will be 1 more than it was before.] *So, what could your instructions say?* [Sample answer: Add 1 to the tens digit.] Point out to students that if the number of tens in a number is 9, then when they find 10 more than that number, the tens digit will become zero and they will write a 1 for 1 hundred.] *What is 10 more than 98?* [108]

Item 13 Ask students to think about how they can use place-value blocks to match each description with a number. *How will you know whether to add or take away place-value blocks to find the number?* [Sample answer: I need to look for key words in the description such as *more* or *less*.]

Math Practices and Problem Solving Solve each problem below.

10. **MP.8 Generalize** Marlon wants to write instructions to tell his friend how to find 10 more than any number. What instructions should Marlon write?
Sample answer: Finding 10 more is the same as adding 10 to any number. You can add 1 to the tens digit.

11. **Number Sense** Fill in the missing numbers. Use place-value blocks to help you.
10 Less
74
I Less **83** **84** **85** I More
94
10 More

12. **Higher Order Thinking** Write and solve a riddle for a number greater than 70 and less than 90. Use "I more than" and "I less than" or "10 more than" and "10 less than" as clues.
Clues: **Sample answer: My number is I more than 75. It is I less than 77.**
My number is **76** .

13. **Assessment** Match each number with its description.

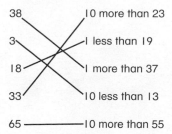

38 — 10 more than 23
3 — I less than 19
18 — I more than 37
33 — 10 less than 13
65 — 10 more than 55

890 eight hundred ninety   © Pearson Education, Inc. K   Step Up | Lesson 10

889–890

Photographs

Every effort has been made to secure permission and provide appropriate credit for photographic material. The publisher deeply regrets any omission and pledges to correct errors called to its attention in subsequent editions.

Unless otherwise acknowledged, all photographs are the property of Pearson Education, Inc.

Photo locators denoted as follows: Top (T), Center (C), Bottom (B), Left (L), Right (R), Background (Bkgd)

001 Jorge Salcedo/Shutterstock;**085L** Evgeny Murtola/Shutterstock;**085R** 2rut/Shutterstock;**135** Michal Kolodziejczyk/Fotolia;**199** James Insogna/Fotolia;**245** Christopher Elwell/Shutterstock;**281** tankist276/Shutterstock;**359** Shutterstock;**431** Winai Tepsuttinun/Shutterstock;**507** Panda3800/Shutterstock;**563** Turbojet/Shutterstock;**621** Andrey Pavlov/Shutterstock;**675** Eugene Sergeev/Shutterstock;**745** Michael Flippo/Fotolia;**799** Singkham/Shutterstock.